COLLEGES OF DISTINCTION

2020

Go beyond the rankings of commercially driven lists.

Discover the college that's right for you.

WWW.COLLEGESOFDISTINCTION.COM

CONTENTS

COLLEGE PROFILE INDEX

WHAT ARE THE COLLEGES OF DISTINCTION?

Since 2000, Colleges of Distinction has been a trusted resource for more than 40,000 guidance counselors across the United States, thousands of parents and students, and hundreds of colleges and universities. Our mission is simple: to help parents and students find not just the "best college," but the right college. We at Colleges of Distinction are trying to do something different—to give you a credible, independent look at schools that may not have the biggest names in higher education, but that consistently do a great job preparing young adults to be lifelong learners. But each school does so in different ways; that's why we don't rank the schools you'll find in this book. Each one commits itself to student success, and we leave it up to you to determine the one that matches your talents and interests, that promises to be the place where you will want to live and learn—the one that's best for *you*.

Every featured college is unique, but they all share key characteristics:

- Their students are bright, motivated, and engaged.
- Their classrooms are interesting, exciting places to explore and learn.
- They offer their students vibrant campuses and communities.
- They turn good students into well-rounded, successful citizens with the capacity to contribute to their communities, their nation, and their world.

If this sounds like what you are looking for in a college, then you are the student (or parent of a prospective student) for whom we wrote this book.

These are schools that get praise from high school guidance counselors across the country, as well as from college admissions officers, professors, students, and satisfied alumni. So why haven't you heard of them?

The truth is, many schools are famous for reasons that have nothing to do with the quality of their education programs. They may have big-time football or basketball programs. They may be known for the path-breaking research

conducted by scientists who never actually teach. Or, they may be recognized for the quality of their PhD programs and medical schools.

The colleges in this book may not receive that kind of publicity, but employers and graduate schools know that Colleges of Distinction produce real winners.

How Do They Do This?

Colleges of Distinction welcome students who demonstrate both academic promise and community involvement. They keep classes small, so professors get to know their students as individuals, not numbers. They encourage athletics and a wide range of cultural, intellectual, and social activities, but they help students keep it all in balance with their studies. They encourage their students to get involved with their own communities while also exposing them to the global community.

Year after year they do a great job, and looking back, their graduates say, "that might not be the right college for everyone, but it was exactly right for me."

In this book, you'll find many small, private, liberal arts colleges; schools of this kind have long been recognized for their focus on personal attention and student engagement. There are public universities in this guide as well, which is a testament to the fact that they can be just as personalized as their private counterparts. There are also single-gender schools, polytechnic institutions, Christian colleges, and more.

As different as these colleges may be from one another, they each have an outstanding reputation among people "in the know." We hope you benefit from finding out more about the hidden gems in higher education today.

How Do Students Choose? And How Can Parents Help?

So, how do high school students select the right college? And, if you are a parent, how do you help your child make the right choice?

Let's be realistic. It's your junior or senior year of high school. You're busy with your school work, concentrating on the SAT or ACT, fitting in school activities, and trying to have a social life—are you likely to devote a huge number of your hours carefully reading every college's marketing materials, pouring over piles of guidebooks, studying the characteristics of hundreds of colleges and universities, and eventually making a deliberate, well-considered decision? Of course not.

According to research by the College Board, the most important source of information for deciding which colleges to apply to is word-of-mouth information. Students listen to advice from teachers and guidance counselors, parents and other family members, and—often most compellingly—from their friends.

College guidebooks are another source of information, and many students and parents make good use of them.

Often, of course, this process will guide you to the right college. Yet there may be excellent schools—maybe the perfect school *for you*—that no one tells you about, that you haven't heard of, and that you won't discover by scanning the top 10 colleges in an annual numerical ranking.

That's where Colleges of Distinctions comes in.

College Guidebooks

It's the "best" college—or the second or third or twentieth best. It ranks at "the top of the list" and it has an "excellent reputation."

Ever wonder what these phrases really mean? Can diverse institutions really be rank-ordered using statistics? How relevant are these measurements to what is going to be the ideal college experience *for you*?

The truth is, it's extremely difficult to quantify and qualify all colleges and universities. For one thing, the very act of measuring colleges is based on the assumption that all students are alike, that they want and need the same things, and that it might be possible to create a single ideal college that would be perfect for everyone. Of course that isn't true.

Unlike high school, college students spend their time studying vastly different subjects. They enter college with a huge variety of expectations, hopes, and dreams. There are no SATs or ACTs to measure achievement, no national "standards of learning" to compare the quality of one college with that of another. There are no published statistical measures on how happy and satisfied students are at over 3,000 colleges in the country.

SO HOW DO WE JUDGE QUALITY?

The Rankings and Ratings Approach

A number of widely read guidebooks make an attempt at comparing schools. *US News and World Report*'s annual "Best Colleges" uses a statistical approach that considers many different factors, all of which they claim contribute to the overall quality of a college. Among the factors *U.S. News* plugs into their statistical formula are:

- The college's overall faculty-to-student ratio
- The number of faculty members with PhDs
- The size of the college's financial endowment
- Faculty salaries
- SAT/ACT scores of incoming students
- Percentage of entering students in the top 10% of their high school class
- Level of alumni giving
- Percentage of applicants rejected
- Student retention and graduation rates

But can you really find the "best" school—especially, the best for you—from statistics alone?

For example, selectivity is fairly easy to measure: divide the number of applicants by the number of applicants rejected. But if a school is hard to get into, does that necessarily mean it is a better place to learn, live, and grow? Would it be the best place for you?

And exactly what does "high selectivity" mean, anyway?

Some schools—in the Northeast, especially—receive so many applications just because of the location. Schools in other parts of the country may have equally as tough entrance requirements, but because fewer students choose to apply to them, they appear—statistically—less selective.

When guidebook editors decide which characteristics to measure, they are making value judgments that greatly affect the results—and they don't necessarily value the same things you do.

For example, if ethnic diversity is important to you, does the guidebook use it as one of its statistical criteria? What about safety on campus? Federal law requires that this information be available in the Campus Safety Office, but it is often not included in the college's marketing materials or in a college guidebook.

When guidebook editors decide what to measure, they shy away from the hard-to-quantify intangibles—quality of life, actual classroom experience, friendliness of the campus—that are vitally important to each student's college experience.

Rankings-based guidebooks provide important information. But, as a smart consumer, you should be aware of their limitations. As you thumb through the rankings, we suggest you ask:

- Is "the best college" really the best college for you? What facts and figures make it "the best"? Are these criteria you value highly?
- Do you value something that can't be measured by statistics? Are spiritual identity, classroom excitement, and active residence life programs important to you?
- As a student at this particular college, will you be able to participate in all the activities in which you have an interest? For example, do you need to be a theatre major in order to audition for a role in a play, or are auditions open to all students? Are all interested athletes welcome to try out for the college's teams?
- How much learning actually goes on at the college you're considering? Who actually does the teaching? Are students excited about what goes on in the classroom and lab?

In addition to college guidebooks based on statistics, there are many kinds of guides, websites, and studies, which may or may not be useful in your college search.

THERE MUST BE A BETTER WAY!

"Rather than wondering, 'What will I do with my college education?' the more important question to ask as you consider college is, 'Who will I be? What kind of person do I want to become? What kind of qualities do I want to nurture? What kind of contribution do I want to make to the world?'"

– Ronald R. Thomas, Former President, University of Puget Sound

Why Do We Call Them Colleges of Distinction?

They may be modest about it, but these schools have just as much history and heritage as the better-known, brand-name colleges. What's more, they have a proven record in four key areas:

1. *Engaged Students:* GPAs and standardized test scores are important, but Colleges of Distinction look for students who will be engaged *outside* the classroom as well as inside it. These students compete in sports, do volunteer work, conduct independent research, and study abroad. They are not just thinkers; they are doers.

2. *Great Teaching:* Professors who teach at Colleges of Distinction know students by name and are committed to seeing them succeed. They're experts in their fields who are dedicated to teaching. Their students learn to analyze problems, think creatively, work in teams, and communicate effectively.

3. *Vibrant Communities:* Colleges of Distinction provide a rich, exciting living-and-learning environment, both on and off campus. They offer a variety of residential options, clubs, and organizations to satisfy every interest; plenty of cultural and social opportunities; and avenues for leadership, character, and spiritual development. Whether they are in rural or urban settings, they provide ways for students to be involved in the life of the surrounding community.

4. *Successful Outcomes:* Colleges of Distinction have a long record of graduating satisfied, productive alumni who go on to make their mark in business, medicine, law, education, public service, and other fields. In terms of the return they offer on investment, these schools are outstanding educational values.

How Did We Choose Them?

First, we asked people "in the know" about higher ed. We polled high school guidance counselors from across the country, asking them to tell us which schools belonged on our list and which ones did not. We also solicited recommendations from heads of admissions at different colleges.

Informally, we sought even more feedback by talking through our list with parents, students, and professors at a variety of institutions around the country.

From this diverse community, common opinions began to emerge; some schools came up again and again.

Having thoroughly polled the available opinions, we then began our own investigation of the institutions that remained on our list. We visited campuses, interviewed a cross-section of the campus community, and sat in on classes. We dug into school records and spoke frankly with admissions directors.

We then sifted through this rather large list looking for characteristics that honor our *"Four Distinctions."*

The result is a book with colleges that we're convinced are terrific places to learn. Measured by both quantitative and qualitative data, these schools come out ahead. While we can't guarantee that you'll have heard of every one of the Colleges of Distinction, chances are you'll find a number that interest and intrigue you.

ENGAGED STUDENTS

Different is good. We like to think of ourselves as unique individuals. When it comes to education, however, we often talk as if one size fits all. Students figure that colleges are pretty much all the same. But educators know that different people learn in different ways.

Who Are You? (And How Do You Learn?)

If you're the kind of person who learns best from talking things through, you're not going to thrive in an environment where you are in a crowd of 500 and listening to talking heads. If you learn by solving problems, then tests or papers emphasizing rote memorization are going to turn you off. One of the best ways to start figuring out how you like to learn is to think about situations where you have learned new information or skills more easily.

When someone gives you directions, do you need to see a map or can you listen to directions by ear? Does it help you to be told what landmarks to look for while driving or do you prefer to think in terms of distance and direction?

How do you prefer to study for tests? Do you like to read material alone, or does it help you to talk it over with a friend? Does it help you to actively write or type material by hand, or is it better to listen to someone repeat it to you?

What activities or hobbies give you pleasure? Are you a physical person who prefers sports or dance? Do you like other performance-based activities, such as singing or acting? Do you enjoy "hands-on" hobbies like carpentry or sculpture? Do you read or write for fun?

It's quite likely that you are unaware of your best learning style. It may be that you've never had the chance to combine your hobbies and passions with your academic interests. Maybe some of your grades have even suffered as a result.

The good news is that college can give you a chance to be a hands-on learner. You can travel abroad to learn a language or take an internship to try out a job. Your campus activities can teach you leadership skills or even academic knowledge while you have fun. The Colleges of Distinction offer you a wide range of ways to get engaged in learning.

Measuring Engagement:

What is it? How can I find it?

The term "engagement" is more than a buzzword. It is a serious part of how good colleges reach their students. Hands-on learning gives you practical skills for the future, all while making learning easier. Important forms of engaged learning include:

1. **Classroom experiences that emphasize reading, writing, and speaking.** Whether it is history, biology, Spanish, or engineering, you should be actively engaged in the skills of analysis and expression. Some lecture-based courses are inevitable at most (though not all!) colleges, but classes that emphasize active learning—learning in which you are truly *involved* in the learning process—help you develop the skills you'll need for success in the workplace and other aspects of your life.

2. **Collaborative learning in and outside the classroom.** Whether through group projects in class or joint research with a professor, collaborative learning reflects the reality that most people do not work alone. Learn to work with others in college, and you'll be ahead in almost any field.

3. **Field Experience.** Learning outside the classroom is especially important in research-based disciplines, but almost any course that involves field experience will give you a leg up on your résumé. Internships, which let you try out a career, and service-learning, which allows students to serve their community as part of a class, are good forms of field experience.

4. **Interacting with other cultures.** Studying abroad or participating in a multicultural experience within the U.S. give students more opportunities than ever to learn about different peoples—and that's great preparation for a job market that is increasingly international and multicultural.

WORD TO THE WISE: ARE YOU ENGAGEABLE?

"College and university admission officers at selective institutions typically have a broad definition of merit as well as a deep commitment to fairness and equity. They know that the ability to contribute and succeed in college goes beyond grades and testing. Typically, selective colleges consider:

- The quality of courses a student has chosen.
- The student's involvement in the school or community.
- The ability of the student to write effectively.
- The student's character and ability to function in a common community (as reflected by recommendations from teachers, employers, and others)."

– *Dean of Admissions, Centre College of Kentucky*

"Standardized exams cannot measure heart (and neither can I, by the way), but we do have ways of getting a read on how much initiative or drive, or whatever you want to call it, plays in the process. Is the student involved outside of class? Is she a leader? Does he write well? How are her interpersonal skills? What do his peers and teachers think of him? All these elements contribute to the equation of whether or not a student is admitted to TCU. Our decisions are holistic in nature as we try to take into account everything we are able to discover about the student."

– *Ray Brown, Dean of Admissions, Texas Christian University*

Before You Visit

Look over any materials you have received from the college. Are there any interesting opportunities that you would like to learn more about?

When making the appointment for your visit, ask if you can meet with someone who knows more about the programs that interest you. For example, is it possible to visit the Study Abroad Office or to meet with a professor who conducts research with students?

Ask School Representatives

Ask an admissions counselor what the school values in an applicant. Does the description sound like a good match for you?

- How many students participate in study abroad, internships, student research, service-learning, and other hands-on opportunities?
- Is there a time when students generally engage in these opportunities (the beginning of junior year, for example)?
- Do you need to qualify for any special programs (like an Honors College) in order to have these opportunities? If so, how well do your qualifications stack up?

Talk with the admissions counselor about your current high school interests and activities. Are there groups on campus in these categories?

Ask Students

What kind of engaging experiences have they had? Study Abroad? Internships? Service? Do they have any planned?

What are their favorite classes? What makes these classes interesting? Do they sound interesting to you?

Have students had any hands-on experiences that they especially enjoyed?

Have they been involved in any research projects, fieldwork, or special trips related to a class? Do these experiences sound interesting to you?

How well does the school work with local resources (businesses, philanthropies, government, museums, and artistic groups) to enrich student education?

A Checklist for Finding...Engaged Students

Doing Your Research

☐ If they do not use NSSE (National Survey of Student Engagement), does the college offer any other measures of how well students are learning?

☐ To what degree does the faculty subscribe to "active learning"? Ask for examples of professors who teach this way.

☐ What percentage of students participate in study abroad, internships and undergraduate research experiences? (More than one-third usually represents a significant part of the campus.)

☐ Does the school have short, one-month terms? (Usually offered in January or May, these can make off-campus experiences easier to integrate into you regular course schedule.)

☐ What summer opportunities are available at the school?

☐ Do scholarships and other financial assistance cover off-campus study?

☐ What opportunities are there for students to build résumés?

☐ Does the school offer research opportunities? (This is especially important for science-oriented students or those considering graduate school in any field.)

☐ Does the school have programs for service learning?

☐ How well does the school work with local resources (businesses, philanthropies, government, museums, and artistic groups) to enrich student education?

GREAT TEACHING

I t's common sense. Better teaching means more learning. But how do you define good teaching? Most prospective college students would like to find a school where they will enjoy the best teaching available. Unfortunately, teaching quality isn't as easy to measure as endowment dollars or the size of dorm rooms.

There are some widely accepted standards defining what "good teaching" is. Once you're familiar with them, it's easier to know which questions to ask.

Most colleges will promise that they have "great faculty," but not every school delivers. Learning about good teaching can help you get beyond the promises to find the quality you're looking for at the colleges you're considering.

According to the American Association of Higher Education, there are seven basic practices in good undergraduate education. Good teaching should:

1. **Encourage contact between students and faculty.** It's easier for faculty to help students when they know each other by name. Likewise, when students feel comfortable approaching professors, they can ask more questions, get involved, and get better help.

2. **Develop reciprocity and cooperation among students.** Good teachers help students learn from each other, not just from the teacher. Not only does this help students learn the subject matter, but it also helps them learn valuable career skills like leadership, creativity, and working in teams.

3. **Use active learning techniques.** Students tend to learn more when they take an active role in their education, rather than just sitting back and waiting for the information to flow in. Active learning techniques include discussion seminars, independent research projects, field work, lab work, internships, and other hands-on opportunities.

4. **Give prompt feedback.** Students need to know what they're doing right, what they're doing wrong, and how to improve. The more opportunities they have for feedback on assignments, the better students can improve and grow.

5. **Emphasize time on task.** Good learning requires time and effort; good teachers help students learn to manage their time by offering concrete guidelines for learning outside the classroom. Unlike high school learning (which emphasizes in-class activities), college learning requires a great deal of commitment outside of the classroom.

6. **Communicate high expectations.** Expect more from students, and they usually deliver. When professors let students know how much they can strive for, students have more incentive to work harder and learn more.

7. **Respect diverse talents and ways of learning.** Different students learn in different ways. Good teaching is more than standing behind a podium; it engages students who learn from visuals, hand-on experience, reading, listening, speaking, and other ways of learning.

As you can imagine, there are different ways to ensure good teaching practices; each of the Colleges of Distinction has its own approach.

Research and Teaching: A Better Relationship

What is a professor's job? Unlike a high school teacher, college professors are not trained teachers in most cases. They are hired as scholars—as experts in their fields. In most schools, that means they are expected to spend time researching and publishing as part of their duties. "Publish or perish" is true whether the field is biochemistry or political science. In addition, most professors are expected to take a hand in running their department or participating on a college committee. Whether that's helping to get books ordered for the library, deciding promotions for fellow faculty, or raising money for the school's annual appeal, service is an important part of the professor's job.

On some campuses, teaching comes far behind research and service in faculty priorities. To put it bluntly, not every school rewards good teaching. Many schools promise personal attention and a great classroom experience; not all of them deliver. At some, most instruction is done by graduate students working as teaching assistants.

Fortunately, many colleges are learning that there's a better way to encourage both research (which helps to keep academics up to date in their fields) and good teaching (which is what brings most undergraduates to the college). At the Colleges of Distinction, you will find classes that are deliberately kept smaller so faculty can give meaningful assignments and get to know their students. Furthermore, they are encouraged to involve students in their research.

Schools that are serious about teaching usually run teaching seminars, institutes, and other serious programs to help professors continue to develop as teachers and academics.

Finally, most teaching-centered schools recruit faculty who genuinely enjoy students. If the faculty at the schools you visit seem happy to speak with their students and are genuinely interested in them—and if professors are happy to speak with you during your visit—chances are you've found a school that really values great teaching.

Profile: The Teaching Scholar at a College of Distinction

Teaching at a College of Distinction is more than lecturing and overseeing work in the laboratory. Among the activities that might fill a professor's typical day are:

- Giving a lecture to first-year students
- Participating in a student-faculty panel about current events
- Attending a departmental meeting on updating class offerings
- Calling prospective students to describe the program
- Moderating a discussion panel in an upper-division class
- Writing graduate school references for former students
- Eating lunch with a student service group in order to plan a weekend project
- Moderating a chat room discussion for an honors class
- Writing feedback for student essay projects
- Working with a student on a paper they are publishing together

Before You Visit

Ask if it is possible to meet with a faculty member in your area of interest. Prepare some questions about the program's requirements, what jobs recent graduates are doing, and what activities and research projects are possible.

If it is not possible to meet with a faculty member, ask if you can email them your questions.

Arrange to visit a class, preferably one for freshmen. Don't worry too much about finding one in your proposed major; just ask for an interesting class that is popular with students. Is this a class you would like to take?

Ask School Representatives

Ask your admissions counselor to clarify any questions you have about class sizes, student-to-faculty ratio, etc. If the schools uses Teaching Assistants (TAs), ask about their role and how often you will encounter them.

Ask your admissions counselor some specifics about student-faculty interaction. Will you have a faculty member as an advisor (helping you pick classes and chart an academic path)? What other opportunities will you have to work closely with faculty?

Ask Students

Ask students about their favorite professors and why they are favorites.

If you eat in the cafeteria or take a campus tour, look at how professors and students interact outside the classroom. Do professors seem accessible?

Do students want to talk to their professors? Does the school use TAs? If so, how? Is it mostly the professors who grade and teach, or mostly the teaching assistants?

A CHECKLIST FOR FINDING...GREAT TEACHING

Doing Your Research

☐ Take a close look at student-to-faculty ratios. 16:1 is about average for any of our *Colleges of Distinction*, and usually indicates plenty of time for faculty to student interaction. The closer this gets to 20:1, the more difficult interaction becomes.

☐ Take a close look at full-time versus part-time faculty. Also look to see how many faculty members are tenured or tenure-track. These faculty members will most likely be at the school from year to year, providing you continuity between your courses.

☐ Does the school use TAs? If so, how? From whom is the most teaching delivered?

☐ Look at average class sizes. What percentage of classes are under 25 students? Under 35?

☐ If some classes are large, what does the school do to promote personal attention? Common ways to promote face-to-face interaction include freshman study groups and small labs in science classes.

☐ Is there a special freshman-year experience that attempts to integrate the major areas of human knowledge as well as writing and speaking skills (rather than on that simply requires freshmen to take unrelated introductory courses in large classes)?

☐ What resources are available to help freshmen adjust academically?

☐ Is there a special office for students with learning disabilities?

☐ Does the school offer majors or programs that will help you achieve your career goals? (Even when a school does not offer the precise major you are looking for, it may offer individualized study options that will make career preparation possible.) Does the college make an effort to relate courses in the humanities, sciences, and social sciences to careers and vocations, perhaps through credit-bearing internships?

☐ If you are undecided about your career goals, how well will the school's curriculum help you find your way? Is there a Career Planning Office that works closely with the faculty?

VIBRANT COMMUNITY

"Just Right:" Where Do You Want to Be?

As with other aspects of choosing a college, finding the right community can be tricky. You'd be surprised how many students transfer, not because of academic difficulty but because they are unhappy with their campus life. The big city that one student finds exciting may be too anonymous and distracting for another student. From athletic opportunities to religious atmosphere, from campus political opinion to cultural opportunities, from community service to residence life, there are a lot of variables to consider when looking at a college campus.

Some Self-Assessments on Campus Life

When you're thinking about campus communities, it's important to be honest with yourself about who you are and what you want. By using these three self-assessments, you can get an idea of what size college you might like, what kind of campus life interests you and in what setting you'd like to study.

SELF-ASSESSMENT #1: COLLEGE SIZE

(Pick A or B)

I like...

(a) my teacher to know my name and understand my problems.

(b) to be somewhat anonymous in class.

When I go to a sporting event as a fan, I like to...

(a) know people in the crowd and on the team as I cheer them on.

(b) be part of a huge crowd in a huge stadium.

If I go to a party where I don't know anybody, I really like it when...

(a) someone introduces themselves and goes out of their way to make me feel welcome.

(b) people leave me alone and let me observe.

When I go to college, I think I would like to...

(a) know everything that's going on, and be able to try many different options.

(b) stick with one or two favorite activities.

ASSESSMENT #2: MY ACTIVITY AND LIVING PRIORITIES

(Check all that apply)

My dream campus would offer...

☐ A particular varsity sport

☐ A particular intramural or club sport

☐ A variety of intramural or club sports

☐ Cheerleading or other sports-booster activities

☐ Political or issue-oriented organizations

☐ Multicultural/-ethnic organizations

☐ Camping or outdoor sports

☐ Greek-letter fraternities/sororities

☐ ROTC or other military opportunities

☐ A particular religious affiliation with college-sponsored spiritual life

☐ No particular religious identity, but many spiritual/religious life groups

☐ Women's-interest organizations

☐ LGBTQ+ organizations

☐ Newspaper, radio, TV, or other media activities

☐ Film or literary clubs

☐ Specific hobby or interest clubs (gun club, anime club, etc.)

☐ A wide array of service-oriented groups

☐ Theatre opportunities for non-majors, both as performers and technicians

☐ Music opportunities for non-majors

☐ Other performance arts, such as dance or mime

☐ Clubs for a particular academic subject or career interest

☐ The chance to live in a "theme" house or residence (all French-speaking, for example, or a service-themed house)

☐ The chance to live in an apartment-style situation

☐ The chance to live in a fraternity or sorority house

☐ Women's-only or men's-only housing

☐ Another residence preference

☐ A wide range of weekend trips and off-campus fun for students

☐ A wide range of touring bands and other visiting performers

ASSESSMENT #3: CAMPUS IDENTITIES

(Check all that apply)

I would be open to exploring campuses that are...

☐ Public (state-supported)

☐ Private

☐ Private, where religion plays a strong role

☐ Single-sex (all women or all men)

☐ Military style

☐ Historically black

☐ Primarily undergraduate

☐ Largely graduate/professional

☐ Engineering focused

☐ Art focused

☐ In a very large city or its suburbs

☐ In a smaller or medium-sized city (such as St. Louis, Cincinnati, or Portland) or its suburbs

☐ In a large "college town"

☐ In a small "college town"

☐ In a rural or wilderness setting

Assessment Outcomes

Assessment #1: College Size

"A" answers are more typical of students at smaller schools; "B" are more typical of students at large universities. If you find you're somewhere in between, then "medium" may be just right for you.

Assessment #2: My Activity and Living Priorities

This exercise should help you sort out what you would like in a campus. You may find it helpful to update this list as you continue your college search and get a better idea about what you like.

Assessment #3: Campus Identities

Don't worry if some of these things are contradictory—the more options you have at first, the better. You can revisit this list as you learn more about various options.

Involvement and Community

Colleges of Distinction offer opportunities inside as well as outside the classroom. Today, campus life is considered to be one of the most important elements in a college education. The Association of College Unions International (ACUI) states that campus life provides a "complement [to] the academic experience through an extensive variety of cultural, educational, social, and recreational programs. These programs provide the opportunity to balance course work and free time as cooperative factors in education."

This also makes you a stronger student. Studies have shown that students who are involved in extracurricular activities graduate at higher rates and do better academically.

In other words, a good campus life not only means doing better academically, but getting more out of your education through more exposure to activities, more chances to apply the ideas you learn in class, more personal growth and discovery, more fun and friends. That "more" also means more opportunities after college, when being well rounded really helps you stand out from the crowd of job applicants.

Some students persuade themselves that campus life really isn't all that important. They figure that college will be a lot like high school: go to class, go to a practice or a meeting, go home. But college is a 24/7 environment: It's your classroom, your social life, and your home all wrapped into one package.

Other students assume that they have to attend a huge campus to have a lot of opportunities. In fact, many discover that small or medium sized schools make it easier to get involved, whereas big schools may be so anonymous that it's difficult to meet people.

You may also want to think about schools with unique identities—church-affiliated colleges, historically black colleges, single-gender colleges, and other special places. What activities are you interested in? Are you a big city or small town person, or somewhere in between? Do you want to be recruited to a professional team, or just compete in the sport you love? The lists in this chapter can give you some places to get started, but don't be afraid to add your own personalized requirements for a college. The choices depend on you and your personality. Finding the right environment is important as you look ahead to a great college experience and a great future.

Ask School Representatives

Drive or walk through the surrounding community/ neighborhood. Is it an area that you like? Ask whether the college has a relationship with the community or whether there are tensions.

If you have a particular activity interest, arrange to visit these programs and their facilities. If possible, ask to speak with faculty or staff who work with the program.

If you are interested in a sport, try to arrange to visit with a member of the coaching staff. If it's not possible to meet, try to get a name and an email address for an inquiry.

Ask Students

Ask students what they do on weekends and for fun. What campus events do they most enjoy?

Visit residence options for freshmen. If possible, ask a resident assistant or hall assistant about the programs available to those living in the residence. Are they programs in which you would like to participate?

Look at signs, posters, and announcements around campus. Are there many activities and events that interest you? Does the political and social atmosphere of the campus seem to fit your personality and values? Reading the student newspaper should give you a sense of what is going on from a student perspective.

Ask a student about his or her favorite campus activities and traditions. Do these sound fun and interesting to you?

WORDS TO THE WISE: ABOUT GETTING INVOLVED

"It was apparent to me early on that though I was new to the university, I was in a place where I could contribute to my school, and affect my community in a way I thought was reserved for older, more seasoned veterans in the college arena."

- Byron Sanders, Alumnus, Southern Methodist University

"Some of the greatest lessons come from campus involvement. Currently, I am the president of the campus chapter of a national economics honor society, chair of elections/secretary for the Student Government Association, and a representative of the Office of Admissions in the Tower Council. Through these associations, I have gotten to really know the women I work closely with day in and day out. This does not just include members of the student body, but various deans, school administrators, and professors. They teach us by listening to us—students have a say in almost all decisions made on campus."

- Mary Frances Callis, Alumna, Agnes Scott College

"We hold our student athletes in high regard as students and as athletes. We respect their contributions on the playing field because we insist that these contributions remain part of a larger undergraduate experience where the classroom comes first and out-of-class activities second… Athletic competition can also be extremely fulfilling at our level. When everyone plays by the same rules, not only is competition spirited and intense, but great athletic traditions can develop."

- Baird Tipson, President of Washington College

A CHECKLIST FOR FINDING…VIBRANT COMMUNITY

Doing Your Research

☐ What activities available on campus match your interests? Are most of the activities you enjoy open to non-majors? For example, if you are interested in theatre but majoring in biology, will you still be able to participate in theatrical productions?

☐ What percentage of students are involved in campus activities?

☐ Are there campus activities that you have never tried but which sound interesting to you?

☐ If you are interested in athletics, does the college offer the sport you play? If you are interested in varsity competition, what are its policies regarding walk-ons? Is there an active intramural program for non-varsity athletes?

☐ What cultural and entertainment opportunities does the campus provide? How does it make use of facilities in the surrounding community?

☐ What special events or speakers were on campus in the last year?

☐ Is the college a suitcase campus? That is, what percentage of the students leave campus on weekends? If there is a vibrant city nearby with a wide range of cultural and social opportunities, students going off campus during the weekend might be a good thing, but it is not a good thing when everyone is going home every weekend!

☐ What kinds of residence options do the college offer? What programs are available to help you make friends, meet people, and settle in? How will your roommate be selected?

☐ Are there health facilities or programs on campus? What kind of counseling and crisis support does the campus offer? Does the college provide resources for students with physical or learning disabilities?

SUCCESSFUL OUTCOMES

One of the problems with *U.S. News and World Report's* annual survey of colleges is that it measures a college's quality largely by SAT scores and high school grades. But if you think about it, these are indicators the college had nothing to do with.

Perhaps a better way of measuring a college's quality would be by studying "outcomes," or what happens after students graduate. Indicators of successful outcomes include the acceptance rate into graduate or professional schools, and the percentage of seniors getting employment in their chosen fields soon after they graduate.

Ultimately, successful outcomes are linked to the alumni who, in a real sense, are the "product" of a college education. What kinds of professions did they enter? Have they distinguished themselves in these professions?

This is how Colleges of Distinction measures successful outcomes.

While entering students are not expected to know right away what their major will be or what they want to become in life—freshman and sophomore years should be largely reserved for experimentation and discovery—it is too often the case that by senior year students still don't know what they want to do.

Colleges of Distinction are especially good at orienting students, right from the beginning, to what they might become in life. They often begin this process by introducing freshmen to the Career Services Office during orientation so that they know what resources are available to them.

Sophomores are then encouraged to consider employment-related internships and externships. Tied closely to these programs are career counseling seminars that help students orient themselves to career possibilities, workshops for resume writing and mock interviews, and career fairs where firms can meet future employees.

By senior year, students enrolled at Colleges of Distinction not only have a fairly good idea of what they will do in their first job, but are well on their way to submitting résumés and having interviews.

For those who plan to go on to a graduate or professional school, the same Career Services Office, working with pre-professional advisors (especially pre-med and pre-law) will give advice about available scholarships and the various exams necessary to get into graduate, medical or law school. College professors, of course, have all gone to graduate school and are an excellent source of advice on master's and doctoral programs.

At most Colleges of Distinction, more than 85% of those seeking employment after graduation will find well-paying jobs with advancement potential within six months of graduating. Similarly, 20% or more of the graduating class will go directly to graduate or professional school. Sixty percent will have gone on for further education within six years of graduation.

Finally, the "product" of Colleges of Distinction—the ultimate outcome—are alumni. Perhaps the major goal of these colleges is to prepare the future leaders of our society—the business leaders who keep our economy strong, the political leaders who govern us, the professional leaders who impact our lives in many ways and on a daily basis. Colleges of Distinction are especially strong in the number of these leaders who attended these institutions. These people not only contribute to society in general, but they also support their institutions in various ways, including helping new graduates get their first job.

In the first place, education should not—indeed cannot—be seen as preparation for only one career. Because of the massive changes we are seeing in society, created in large part by advances in technology, current college graduates will have as many as six or seven entirely different jobs or careers before they retire! Therefore the best preparation for a rapidly changing and utterly unpredictable future is a liberal arts and sciences education. Why? Because liberal arts and sciences provide students with three basic and universal skills that are at the core of any successful career: intellectual flexibility, the ability to communicate effectively, and the skills to engage in lifelong learning.

How is this done? Colleges of Distinction require students to take a wide variety of courses in the social sciences, humanities, and natural and mathematical sciences in addition to majoring in a liberal arts or vocational discipline. The result is a graduate who has the intellectual tools to adapt to the shifts and changes we can expect in the 21st century.

Colleges of Distinction prepare their students not only for the first job, but also for the last job!

Before You Visit

Arrange a visit to the Career Services Office. Make a list of questions to ask about internships and other career exploration opportunities.

Ask if there are recent alumni available in your area with whom you can speak about the school.

Ask School Representatives

Ask your admissions counselor about graduation rates, employment rates, and similar issues.

Ask staff in the Career Services Office or the Alumni Office how alumni help current students.

Ask Students

Ask students about their plans for the future. What is the school doing to help them achieve their goals?

A CHECKLIST FOR FINDING…SUCCESSFUL OUTCOMES

Doing your Research

☐ What information does the school provide about employment-related internships and externships? How many internships can a typical student take?

☐ What professional development does the school offer students? Does the school offer résumé support, mock interviews, career fairs, and other employment support?

☐ What are the employment rates for graduates within 6 months of graduation? Within one year?

☐ If you are considering graduate or law school, does the school provide information about rates of acceptance and give examples of schools to which graduates were accepted?

☐ What is the school's rate of alumni giving? Rates of 30% or more are generally considered fairly strong.

☐ If the school publishes an alumni magazine, ask for a copy with your admissions packet. How important and well-organized does the alumni association seem to be? Are alumni involved in student life? Do they provide a network for students seeking employment?

NAVIGATING ADMISSIONS AND THE COST OF COLLEGE

If you feel that college admissions is a competitive game, you're not alone. College rankings have given the general public the idea that it's no longer enough to be admitted to college. Instead, they imply that to be successful, a student must get accepted to a top-ranked school. Different regions of the country experience this pressure in different ways, but the symptoms are universal.

These days, students and parents spend an enormous amount of time and money on guidebooks, SAT tutors, private admissions counselors, and other tools. In some cases, students may actually be missing out on valuable high school experiences and learning because they focus so much energy on getting into the "right" college.

Many college admissions personnel agree that the climate has become overly competitive, but there is no quick fix. What can you do?

First and foremost, decide which schools are really the best for you—not just a magazine's "best." Where can you be happiest? What schools offer the programs that are right for you? We urge you to worry less about what school is "the best" and instead ask, "Which school is the best for me?"

You are going to spend a lot of valuable time on the college admissions process. Having been through the process ourselves, we at Colleges of Distinction suggest you look past Big Name University. Find the Hidden Gem College that is perfect for you and tailor your strategy to what that school really wants, rather than wasting your resources on a "one-size-fits-all" approach to test prep and applications strategies.

Use the following checklist to prioritize what's important for you as you're looking at schools. You may also want to use our self-assessment in the previous chapters as one of your tools. Good luck!

Narrowing the Field

Once you have finished this section, you should have a fairly complete picture of what you are looking for in a college. Think about the colleges you have visited. Look at the materials colleges have sent you. How many fit the bill? Knock off the ones that just do not match what you're looking for. You'll be left with a list of colleges that approach the ideal college for you.

How well do your SATs, ACTs, and GPA stack up against their average admissions? You can find some of this information in our book; for more up-to-date figures, consult the school's website or other online resources that list this data. Do you score significantly above or below the average? This can give you a very rough estimate of how well you will stack up against other applicants. Don't be discouraged if your scores are lower than the college's average; remember, half of all students admitted to any given college end up having scores and grades below the mid-point, and many of those students have great careers in college and beyond.

Keep in mind that the schools that qualify as Colleges of Distinction consider many other factors when they evaluate student applications.

Do you have any special skills or interests that might appeal to one or more of these schools? Schools with extensive service programs or special service scholarships may take special note of your service activities. Every college needs a flute player in the band, an actor for the drama program, and a reporter for the school newspaper. Schools with competitive swim teams might be especially interested in recruiting a talented swimmer. Be sure to mention these interests and talents.

Are you a member of a group that is under-represented at one of the colleges you are considering? Many schools have far fewer men than women in their student body and, though they won't admit it, are interested in recruiting men to help correct the imbalance. Some campuses have special programs to encourage first-generation students or members of certain ethnic and racial groups to apply. Still other campuses would like to recruit more "legacies," children or grandchildren of alumni.

Do you have life experiences that make you stand out from the crowd? Have you lived abroad or participated in educational travel opportunities? Have you won any special awards or been recognized for your activities? Have you started clubs or programs in your community, at your school, or through your faith group?

Refine your list based on these questions and narrow your choices down to eight or ten colleges: four or five that closely match your interests and to which acceptance is likely; two where the profile might be above yours ("stretches"); and two that have the profiles below yours where admission is almost guaranteed ("safeties"). If you think you'll be unhappy with an acceptance from any of the colleges on your list, cross that school off immediately.

The Facts About Financial Aid: Can You Afford Not to Go to College?

One final issue needs to be discussed: the cost of a college education.

The cost of college is a big public policy issue in America. Parents are usually in shock when they see how expensive college can be, especially private colleges and universities where tuitions have been skyrocketing at rates far beyond inflation.

The truth is, if done the right way, college can be very affordable. If you have financial need, there are federal, state and institutional grants to help pay for a college education. But even students who do not qualify for need-based financial aid can receive merit-based aid if their high school grades and extracurricular activities are noteworthy. So don't look at the so-called sticker price.

After scholarships, campus jobs, and loans are taken into consideration, most colleges are quite affordable.

What About Private Colleges vs. Public Universities?

We all know that tuition at public universities is lower than tuition at private colleges. That's because taxpayers subsidize, or pay to offset the costs of, public tuitions. The fact that the total four-year tuition plus room and board costs at many public universities is $50,000 or less compared to $100,000 or more at private colleges and universities, is discouraging many parents from considering these institutions.

But Things Are Not Always as They Seem!

In many states, large public universities are overcrowded. As a result, students often cannot get their first choice of a major. And since classes are frequently full, it often takes five or six years to graduate! Looking at the situation this way, the student attending a public university will not only pay a total of $65,000 in tuition, room and board for five years, but also forgo a year earning a salary (often another $40,000+) for a total "real" cost of over $100,000. Now the $100,000+ paid to attend a private college that graduates its students in four years or less doesn't look so bad. This fact, together with the scholarship support private colleges can offer, considerably levels the playing field. So you really do have a choice.

Finally, one might ask, "Why take on all these loans? Wouldn't I be better off just getting a job after high school?"

The fact is that college graduates, over a lifetime, earn $2 million more in income than high school graduates. Of course this should not be the major reason you go to college. College-educated people are usually happier in their jobs, healthier, and enjoy all the intangible benefits that a college education provides. Taking on $25,000 or more in college loans (scholarships are free gifts and don't have to be repaid) is insignificant in the long run compared to the earning power of a college degree.

Good luck with your college search. We hope you find the campus that is truly the best for you!

A CHECKLIST FOR...CHOOSING A COLLEGE

Location

I am looking for a school that is:

- ☐ In my hometown
- ☐ Within an easy drive of my hometown
- ☐ Within a one-day drive of my hometown
- ☐ Within a short flight of my hometown
- ☐ Anywhere

Specifically, I am interested in schools in the following states:

Hint: Are you looking for new experiences? Is climate a concern? Do you want to be close to your parents, siblings, or other relatives?

(List the states you are interested in.)

I am interested in a location that is:

Hint: What do you consider a "big" city or a "small" town? People from Los Angeles or New York City may consider cities like St. Louis or Albuquerque very small. If you are from a town of under 10,000, these same cities may seem very large.

- ☐ A really big city
- ☐ A regionally important city
- ☐ A college town
- ☐ A very small town or a rural campus

Academic

Hint: Most students change their majors at least once, so don't feel too concerned if you don't quite know what you want right now. Also, be aware that colleges offer majors that will help you achieve your goals under many different names. And be sure to look for opportunities to design your own curriculum.

Learning experiences that I think I might enjoy include:

- ☐ A unified curriculum in which all students take the same classes
- ☐ A core curriculum through which all students take some of the same classes
- ☐ Special freshman seminars or other freshman-only classes
- ☐ Classes under 10 people before my junior and senior year

- ☐ Classes under 25 people
- ☐ Classes over 100 people
- ☐ Living-and-learning communities where my roommates and neighbors are studying the same major, taking some of the same classes, or have other academic options in common
- ☐ Service-learning programs where my classroom experiences are connected to community service.
- ☐ Studying abroad at a foreign university *(specify institution if you know)*
- ☐ Studying abroad at a program run by my college *(specify country if you know)*
- ☐ Studying off-campus in the United States

Career and Life

I am looking for a college:

- ☐ Where I can explore my career through an internship
- ☐ Where I can explore more than one internship
- ☐ Where there are special resources for undecided majors
- ☐ With a multi-year professional/career development program (begins before senior year)
- ☐ That has specific programs to support my career goals: *(specify)*

I am looking for a college that will:

- ☐ Help me get involved in service opportunities *(specify your interests)*
- ☐ Give me the chance to play a certain sport *(specify)*
- ☐ Help me deepen my spirituality *(specify your interests)*
- ☐ Let me pursue my hobbies and interests through co-curricular activities or groups *(specify your interests)*

Co-curricular programs that interest me are:

(List them)

Other programs that might be interesting to explore include:

(List them)

Help me pursue the following interests: *(List them)*

COLLEGE INSIGHTS: WHAT YOU SHOULD KNOW

BIG PICTURE - PICKING A COLLEGE

WANT YOUR KIDS TO HAVE A SECURE FUTURE? INVEST IN A LIBERAL ARTS EDUCATION

by Christine Henseler, Professor of Spanish and Hispanic Studies, Union College

It's no secret that the dynamics surrounding higher education and postgraduate employment are changing fast these days, and it's no question that our interconnected world is also evolving rapidly. These changes, fueled by technology, politics, and economics, affects the way we learn, work, play, and connect to one another. It's exactly for these reasons that there is no better time to invest in a liberal arts education.

In the world that awaits future graduates, the competitive edge belongs to those with bright, curious, and agile minds. Objective, technological, or scientific knowledge will no longer be enough; the world you or your child will enter after college is already demanding more human-centric solutions to our collective challenges. With this in mind, here are just a few reasons why a liberal arts education is so valuable.

Global Trends

All facets of today's world are bound across borders through digital networks. News can spread in an instant, change is constant, and the future is sure only to become increasingly complex. New technologies, like self-driving cars and 3D printing, are already disrupting the way we work and do business.

The leaders of the future, therefore, will have to apply novel theories and think across disciplines in order to tackle the challenges of the 21st century. They will be individuals who can think differently and challenge the status quo. They will have keen observations, explore new possibilities, and make new and surprising connections.

The goal of liberal arts colleges and universities is to cultivate the kind of innovative thought needed for such new and challenging demands. Though each school's mission is slightly different, most aim to produce leaders who make thoughtful life choices, succeed professionally, and commit themselves to lifelong learning and cultural understanding. With a student-centered focus, these schools engage their students with a wide variety of learning experiences, better preparing them for the challenges of our time.

Employer Trends

"I personally think there's going to be a greater demand in 10 years for liberal arts majors than there were for programming majors and maybe even engineering..."

-Billionaire Investor, Mark Cuban

The needs and demands of employers definitely reflect the global trends of workforce demands. According to the 2016 Job Outlook survey conducted by the National Association of Colleges and Employers, hiring personnel increasingly value and prioritize the skills that are inherently developed in liberal arts institutions. Of those polled:

- 80.1% seek candidates with good leadership skills
- 78.9% want graduates with the ability to work in a team
- 70.2% need employees with good written communication skills
- 70.2% look for workers with good problem-solving skills
- 68.9% prioritize employees' excellent verbal communication skills

Liberal arts graduates have the clear advantage here. Many of their schools implement programs that promote active collaboration between students of different disciplines, and others are challenged with capstone courses and projects to demonstrate their mastery of a subject. They've also been steeped in writing-intensive courses to develop their communication skills, and they have improved their ability to discern context and solve problems through humanities courses like history or philosophy. To students and employers alike, the benefits of learning and thinking across disciplines is invaluable.

Leading businesses are taking notice of these facts. Last year, Forbes published an article explaining why companies like Slack and Ubisoft value their employees' humanities degrees as well as why some American entrepreneurs have chosen to major in philosophy. It is truly apparent that companies need more than technology to gain the competitive edge they seek.

To connect, engage, and to sell to clients, today's employers must build bridges between technology and humanity. Their products must relate their target audiences' histories, cultures, languages, and values. In essence, such an ability to make connections like these is what a liberal arts education is all about.

Academic Trends

Hong Kong, Japan, and other Asian countries are in the process of adopting the United States' liberal arts model. In a recent article in The Atlantic, businessman Po Chung and other education reformers have acknowledge that "it's

past time for (Asian) colleges to introduce a broader range of subjects, to promote greater intellectual curiosity, and to foster creative thinking." Chung and other backers appear to echo the insights of their Silicon Valley counterparts. They, too, are "convinced that these changes will, in turn, build a workforce of rigorous, creative thinkers—just what they think is needed to meet the fast-changing needs of a transforming global economy."

Forward-thinking leaders are recognizing that the future of work and social well-being depend on human-centric solutions. Because of this fact, students who narrowly focus on technical skills are automatically limiting their future options. Unless they make connections, think outside the box, and market themselves more broadly, their professional skills will not withstand the ever-shifting demands of the professional world.

STEM and the Humanities

Tensions are growing around the humanities in western academia. Citing a shortage of scientists and engineers, some have been framing the humanities as an 'unnecessary indulgence' and pressuring students to hone in on STEM (Science, Mathematics, Engineering, and Technology) fields.

Countering this notion is computer science educator Valerie Barr, who adamantly defends the virtues of the arts and humanities and deems them essential to her field. She writes:

"…those who excel in STEM understand that there are non-technical considerations that should guide their work, and those who study humanities understand that there are powerful problem-solving mechanisms and tools that can open up new avenues of application for their knowledge. We need those with strength in the humanities to feel comfortable talking with those who have strength in STEM, and vice versa. This isn't either-or, we have to expose students to both."

While Barr's view is insightful, it hardly begins to settle the debate. More emerging studies have suggested that there is far more to the humanities than its detractors claim. While its benefits may not be immediately obvious, the arts and humanities are far more than a simple "indulgence;" rather, they are a necessity.

Leadership

Leadership, though hard to define, is understandably

at the top of employers' wishlists. The kinds of leaders who are sought by hiring managers are to be empathetic visionaries. They are expected know how to collaborate with a group and guide them through to the end of projects. In contrast, however, the available applicants often end up being the kind of people who look to their superiors to give them the "right answers" without making a real effort to find their own appropriate solutions. These average job-seekers tend to be better trained in rote memorization, not the more subtle, interpersonal, and agile thinking skills that define leaders.

This is where the value of a liberal arts degree becomes clearer. New data suggests that the smaller class sizes and unique programs of liberal arts colleges and universities cultivate the leadership qualities sought by employers. In a recent study, graduates were shown to be 25-45% more likely to become leaders in their localities or professions if they had talked with faculty members about academic and nonacademic subjects outside of the classroom. When their discussions had included peace, justice, and human rights, those numbers jump to 27-52%. In this light, liberal arts degrees become true assets to a job market that favors leaders.

Field of Study	Leadership Skill Gained
English	Writing and Communication
History	Perspective
Philosophy	Logical Thinking
Literature	Critical Thinking
Culture	Understanding Audiences
Arts	Creativity

Earning Potential

There is a common belief that liberal arts graduates earn less than others; however, research finds that this is only true for the first few years after graduation. In fact, a recent study finds a high correlation between a broad undergraduate education and financial success. Those who take the arts and humanities in addition to their main field of study are 31-72% more likely than others to have higher-level positions and earn more than $100,000. This should come as no surprise to us at this point, as the arts and humanities cultivate the kinds of skills that make it easier to rise through positions in business.

Putting the Myth of "Worthless Degrees" to Rest

Tomorrow's challenges call for creative, collaborative workers to reinvigorate and reshape our social and educational structures as well as our business models. To do so, students need rich, diverse educational opportunities to open and expand their minds.

The striking value of a liberal arts education comes from the way it enable students to think through various challenges, contradictions, and tensions. It helps them recognize that the only change worth working for is one that always keeps sight of humanity.

That's why a liberal arts education is a necessity in today's world: our shared humanity requires thoughtful leadership that considers the well-being and progress of all. That's why it's time to put the myth of "worthless degrees" to rest.

4 TIPS FOR CHOOSING A MAJOR

by Chuck Beutel, Vice President for Admission & Enrollment Services, University of St. Francis

Many a high school student looks back on the college planning process only to agonize over the selection of a college major. I have two words of advice on that topic.

First, you probably are closer to a major than you think. Do you have academic subjects that you like or do well in? Do you know of some careers or jobs that appeal to you? Answering one or both of these questions puts you close to finding a major.

Second, over two-thirds of college students change their major—not once, but twice—before graduating. (So did they really know their major anyway?)

You are not alone! About a third of entering college freshman profess that they are either unsure of their major (it could be one of three to five choices) or they are totally undecided and have no idea where to turn.

You don't need to know your major yet.

Remember, you don't need to know your major when you enter college! As much as people will pressure you, don't rush to a decision. You can choose to be undeclared. At most colleges, you will need to complete some general education or liberal education courses before you graduate with any major. That first semester or first year is a great time to get those requirements for graduation completed. You won't be "wasting time" because those courses are needed for the degree—regardless of a major. In completing these courses, you may stumble upon a field or major that excites you. Or a professor may "turn you on" to a discipline that you knew little about. Keep your eyes and ears open.

Here are some tips and sources for additional information on majors and careers.

1. Talk to people who work in careers that interest you.

Spend a day shadowing someone who works in a field you may like. Read about the career. You can find information on many careers by going to the US Bureau of Labor Statistics website. You can read about various careers, their employment outlook and earnings potential, as well as education needed to enter the field.

2. Take an Interest Inventory Assessment.

If you take the ACT exam, you will also complete an Interest Inventory Assessment, which can help you identify possible areas of interest. When registering for the exam, you will go online and complete a series of interest questions (some may seem foolish, but try to answer them honestly). There are no "right" or "wrong" answers—only your answers about how you feel. The report you receive, following the exam, will provide you with very helpful information on majors and careers.

The ACT's "World of Work" Map first identifies your preferences for working with PEOPLE, DATA, IDEAS or THINGS. Looking at the 'pieces of the pie' closest to your preferred map regions, you will see the career areas your answers indicated potential interests. Looking at the LETTER proceeding each interest area, find that letter under the EXAMPLES OF COLLEGE MAJORS to the right, and see some possible college majors from which you might choose.

3. Enroll in an introductory course.

Another strategy would be to enroll in an introductory course for the major during your first or second semester. Let's say you had interests in two majors: accounting and biology. Taking an introductory course in each area helps you learn more about the discipline. But just as important, you can talk to the professor about the discipline. You can network with other students in the class who may have already decided upon this major. All of this can go a long way in helping you make a good decision.

4. Utilize career-finding resources.

Finally, don't forget to utilize the resources of academic advising or the career center. Besides offering information and serving as a sounding board for your thoughts and observations, they can give you access to additional information on majors and careers, or offer you an opportunity to take an Interest Inventory Assessment survey and then go over the results with you, one on one.

Choosing a college major can be an enlightening and enjoyable process if you recognize that it doesn't need to be done today, there are no "right" or "wrong" choices, and the the objective of this process is to find the right "match" for you! Just remember that old saying "if you find something that you LOVE to do, you will never work a day of your life!"

WHAT COLLEGE IS BEST FOR YOU?

by Brad Harsha, Dean of Admissions and Financial Aid, Defiance College

When looking for the school that will become your home for the next four years, and your alma mater afterward, you want to concentrate on what matters most to you.

This can be really difficult to say to a 17-year-old high school student who is depending on his or her parents to help pay for their education. But I encourage you, as you begin this process to look first at the school that is right for you, not anyone else who is part of the college decision process with you. By the end of your college search, although you may have many opinionated supporters it will ultimately be a decision you'll have to live with. So put yourself first in this process and choose for YOU!

My experience searching for a college

I remember my college search more than 20 years ago. I knew what major I wanted to study, but wasn't sure what type of school I wanted to attend.

There are so many different college options that sometimes it can be overwhelming. **However, looking at different factors that are important to you can help to shrink the list of schools that you want to attend.**

I wanted to attend a smaller school as I didn't think I would like a large atmosphere. As I visited many schools I looked at each and tried to visualize myself attending that school and what I thought it would look like. If it didn't seem right, I kept looking.

As a teenager, I had all the answers and I didn't think my parents knew what was best for me. Looking back on my process, my parents gave me the options to look at schools that I was interested in, while at the same time picking recommendations that they thought would be a good fit.

Toward the end of the process, I thought I knew what I wanted, but my father had me look at one more school because he had seen some information on the school that he thought I would enjoy. Because I was very independent I wasn't keen on looking at other schools that my parents suggested, but I said I would check it out.

When I was on campus I discovered that, as much as I tried not to like the school, the perfect "fit" was right in front of me!

What should you look for in a school?

Many factors play into determining whether or not a school is the right fit for you. Since it's such a personal decision, it would be impossible to give you a full list of all the factors to consider.

Still, it helps to have a place to start. Here are some basic considerations to get you started:

- **How big is my ideal school?** A small liberal arts college? Medium sized? Large university? How big of a campus community feels right?

- **How big is my ideal class size?** A lower student-to-teacher ratio tends to foster a productive learning environment, with personalized feedback. Are you okay with 30-person classes? What about a 300-person lecture hall? How important is it to get that extra attention?

- **How involved do I want to be?** Are there expectations that I get involved right away, can I wait a semester, is it required?

- **What is the community like?** Is it safe? Are there things to do? Is it a party-town?

- **Can I see myself being happy here?** This is the most important question of all!

The college search experience is what you make of it

Being a student was such an amazing experience. Finding the right school was a fun and exhilarating milestone, and I was excited to get started! I felt like I had the world at my fingertips.

However, one of the things that I recommend to all students is to enjoy the "whole" experience that college brings, the good and the bad. I describe to families looking for a college that my college experience wasn't perfect, but find me a place that is and I will show you a liar. The college experience is defined by what you make of it, not by what others perceive it to be.

My favorite experiences as a student were the times that I got to hang out with my friends, have pizza, play cards, and watch movies. I remember the many evenings that we stayed up late playing euchre. Sixteen years later, my friends and I still get together to play cards and reminisce about our experiences in college.

What I appreciate most about my experience is how I got there in the first place. My support system knew what I was looking for and supported me throughout my search process. Even when I didn't want their advice, they gave me suggestions based on what I was looking for because in the end, I was the one who was going to college, and I appreciated it every day!

Whether you are the one that is searching for a college, or you are part of the college decision process, make sure your thoughts and advice are being given in a supportive manner and not as directives. By working together in the process, the student has the best chance of success and less likelihood of disappointing someone for not choosing the school that someone else thought they should.

The college search process is both exciting and scary. Make sure that you all find a way to enjoy the process of finding the perfect home for the next four years.

You've Got This

Graduating from high school and the years afterward are a busy time. You might be juggling grades, a job, saving for college, and saying goodbye to your hometown. It's a fun time, too, of course, with new freedom to stay out late, travel, and make your own choices. However, all that adds up to having a lot of other things to do besides deciding on a college, writing essays, and taking all the necessary steps on the road to becoming a college student.

So, just don't forget: you don't have to decide everything at once. Start early by gathering information from sites like Colleges of Distinction, building your lists of Must Haves and Do Not Wants, and making plans for how you will get in, pay for, and finish college. If you give yourself time to plan, you'll have the luxury of blowing off college planning when you're busy and then picking it up again later. After all, this is your plan, your life, and your adventure!

The most important quality you will need to make it through applying to college is persistence. The right college plan will eventually take shape the more you find out about colleges. By the time you know what you want, you'll be ready to go for it and give it everything you've got.

IS COLLEGE PREPARING YOU FOR REAL LIFE?

by Tyson Schritter

Many of today's students report that their undergraduate experience had not prepared them adequately for life after college. Rightly expecting to use their degrees to find jobs in their chosen career path, they are too often dissatisfied with their employment outcomes upon graduation.

According to a survey by McGraw-Hill Education, only 40% of college seniors feel prepared to pursue a career after they receive their degree.

In contrast to the lacking resources and experiences that are most often offered at schools around the nation, McGraw-Hill's research shows that the majority of students across majors recognize the need for internships and other experiential learning, the opportunity to take advantage of career services and training for the job market, and professional networking opportunities while in college. In fact, 71% of students in their survey view the kind of career planning that is commonly overlooked as an "extremely important" aspect of their college education. They reported a need for greater assistance in identifying transferable skills from their majors and promoting themselves to potential employers.

How High-Impact Practices Prepare Students for Life After Graduation

While I'm frustrated by the results of the McGraw-Hill survey, I'm here to tell you that it doesn't have to be this way. In such an increasingly competitive job market, there are things we can do to prepare the next generation to enter the workforce and have successful careers.

The first—and, possibly, the most significant—way we can better help our students is by implementing number of "high-impact practices" into the college curriculum. These practices are a variety of educational opportunities that involve in-depth academic inquiry, collaborative learning, and experiential education.

Many administrators and faculty have already recognized the limitations of lecture-based learning and continually work to create enhanced academic experiences for the undergraduates on their campuses. These programs may include first-year experiences, service-learning, capstone projects, hands-on research, study abroad, and internships. It is with high-impact practices like these that allow students to learn the value of teamwork, develop leadership skills, and apply classroom learning to real-life problems.

The goal is ultimately to create more well-rounded graduates who are better trained to face the challenges of a 21st-century world.

Importance of Internships

When we consider the needs of students who are preparing for new careers, internships have the most noticeable benefit.

Internships (as well as cooperative education, or co-ops) may have been around for decades, but they weren't ever high priorities for many academic institutions that otherwise focused their resources on classroom learning.

Internship programs take students off campus, giving them real-life experience in their chosen career field to contrast their more stagnant lectures within the classroom. To gain temporary, highly useful job experience, students apply for internships at private companies or nonprofit organizations to do part-time work as they continue to take classes. Or, by working in co-ops, students can take a full semester off to work on a full-time basis. Regardless of program, students who participate get practical training and guidance from professional, hands-on mentors.

Interns not only receive practical work experience, but they also gain opportunities to learn more about their intended profession while networking with others who may even be their future employers. As a result of their experiences and new connections, many students can leverage their internships and co-ops into full-time careers.

As the job market tightens up, employers don't want to take chances with untested college graduates. Having at least one internship or co-op experience while in college can dramatically improve a student's chances of getting hired. In fact, as reported by the National Association of Colleges and Employers (NACE) in 2015, 56% of students who had an internship or co-op received job offers upon graduation in contrast to 36% of students without internships.

The Type of Education Matters

There's little question that internships are critical to improve students' chances in the job market. However, graduates' ongoing success also depends on their ability to adapt to changing professions as well as to function within an increasingly global and technological society.

In 2015, the Roosevelt Institute in New York published "Creative Schools for a Thriving Economy," a document in which it is argued that schools should teach creativity instead of "routine cognitive skills."

This research reinforces my own belief that we need to change the fundamental nature of higher education itself. By pursuing an education that incorporates such high-impact practices as writing-intensive classes, research, and capstone projects that incorporate the entirety of a student's academic career, college students can learn how to synthesize a variety of different information. They interact with people from different cultures through service-learning and study abroad, teaching them to consider and appreciate diverse perspectives. And through collaborative courses, first-year experiences, and learning communities, they learn how to work with others in a creative effort to solve problems with an interdisciplinary approach.

How Can College Students Become Better Prepared?

It's no longer enough to attend classes and get good grades. Instead, college students should consider what kinds of extracurricular, interactive, and hands-on experiences their universities offer, taking advantage of programs that promote truly interactive learning. Education beyond the classroom is key, and prospective college students should choose schools with a consideration not just of the campus culture, but also of the out-of-the-box opportunities they provide.

For all college students, it's imperative to communicate effectively and work collaboratively. All should take advantage of communities and initiatives that challenge them to be intellectually and socially successful.

By encouraging students to be active participants in their degrees, as by reimagining college education itself, we can better prepare our students for the demanding world that awaits them beyond their undergraduate careers.

THE TREND TOWARD HOLISTIC EDUCATION IN AMERICAN UNIVERSITIES

by Jamie Odom, Admissions Counselor, John Brown University

When American universities first began, they were structured with an emphasis on holistic education. Recent decades, however, then saw a major shift to a knowledge-based economy, prompting the "college experience" to focus on building more specialized skills for well-paying jobs. However, the pendulum is beginning to swing back to general "horizontal" education rather than specific "vertical" education.

Holistic Education

Students now are not only searching for a university to grow them intellectually, but they are also searching for a university that will develop them holistically: emotionally, spiritually, and intellectually.

Additionally, more and more companies are looking to hire individuals with just as strong EQs (Emotional Quotients, or their ability to recognize and relate to other people's emotions) as they are individuals with high IQs (Intelligence Quotient, the test that supposedly quantifies a person's intelligence based on a series of questions).

The reason for this is simple: graduates who exhibit skills in a diverse grouping of areas are more adaptable in the workplace, making them a strong asset to prospective employers.

For instance, an engineer with a strength in writing and communication who can not only number-crunch, but also deliver an engaging presentation to a board of potential clientele, would make any company proud.

Communication is Key

An area of strong emphasis in the liberal arts education is communication. Whether that be verbal communication or communication using the written word, universities and companies alike are beginning to recognize the importance of such a skill.

Consider the concept of "ethos" when attempting to establish rapport with a future client. Now, imagine these two brief email scenarios:

Client's question: "I'm working on a home electrical issue. Can you give me an estimate on your company's costs?"

Company 1 Reply: "Where's the problem at in the house and I'll tell you how much for the cost."

Company 2 Reply: "We'd love to be of service. What seems to be the problem? That will give us a clearer idea of your cost breakdown."

Both responses technically communicate the same thing, and both companies may be completely competent at their work. In fact, Company 1 may even be better at their work.

However, when presented with both responses, which company do you think the client will choose?

That's right: the company with which they feel is more competent, due to their brief but clear communication style. They instill confidence.

That is one of the goals of the core curriculum: to help students achieve clarity of communication regardless of major.

Everything in Perspective

A growing desire of students in particular is to better understand the world around them from a perspective broader than the one they grew up with. A liberal arts education can help provide that.

For instance, in the honors college at John Brown University, students have the opportunity to take what are known as colloquia courses. In these one-hour courses (designed so that, no matter how heavy the student course load is, they are still able to participate), students can take such classes as International Cinema, Service and Community, the Monastic Life, and Slavery Narratives, to name a few.

In these courses, students from English to Engineering can delve into worlds of study with which they may not otherwise interact.

Students who take these courses not only begin to see layers in which their spheres of study influence others, but it also sparks in them a curiosity to see things from another point of view.

In future careers of teaching or even city design and management, a propensity to see things from multiple points of view can be extremely important.

A common university core, while it may seem frivolous or unimportant to some, are growing a new generation of students into stronger "whole" people, who not only have a strength in their personal field of study (vertical education), but also have the power of a multifaceted education outside their chosen field (horizontal education).

WHOSE OPINION CAN YOU TRUST? AVOIDING BIAS WHEN CHOOSING A COLLEGE

by Tyson Schritter

There are so many outlets from which to gather information about going to college—websites, magazines, books, high school counselors, and even paid advisors—but how can you know who's giving you the best information?

Some magazines may rank colleges while also running advertisements from those same schools. Does that mean the ranking is slanted? Not necessarily; it is common for publications to write about a business while also accepting advertising from it. In fact, there are common rules of practice meant to keep the two sides of the journalism business separate.

That isn't to say that bias never happens, so it's important to approach college rankings with caution. The key to cracking the code of any publication's ranking system is to read all the information provided, not just a number on a list. Each publication will probably reveal some its methods in compiling the rankings, but in reality, it can be easy to pick out decision factors that are not so objective. If you look carefully, you might be able to see some patterns in their choices; they might favor big schools over small ones, small towns over cities, or Ivy League schools over newer ones.

Of course, a little slant doesn't mean that rankings aren't valuable. Any viewpoint or perspective you find about a college can help you piece together your own opinion. Just remember: though these rankings are often based on statistics, the formulas are written by human beings, which means they're neither perfect nor absolute.

Websites are different from print publications in that they often include crowdsourcing, which can provide up-to-the-minute information about a school directly from current students. Look for online reviews, starred rankings, and even comment threads to give you that valuable insider perspective. Of course, any time a site allows reviews and comments, you can naturally expect there to be spam, trolls, and all the hijinks that come with an open door to the general public. You might even find yourself reading paid reviews that are written to be overly positive or super negative prank reviews written by students at rival schools. Even so, it's a good idea to weed through the spam and look around for those "average Joe or Jane" points of view.

High school guidance counselors and paid college advisors—if you can afford them—provide invaluable assistance to help you navigate the maze of college applications, and it can be so helpful to have a professional voice of authority cut through the noise of so many other opinions. One of the best things about working with someone face-to-face is that you get to have a productive dialogue. They can give personally catered recommendations and guidance, and you can ask follow-up questions. Just keep in mind that relying on any one person's opinion on which college to choose is probably not sufficient.

The key to avoiding bias in your college research is to gather as much information as possible from as many sources as you can find. Never let any one source of information make your decision for you; instead, consider multiple perspectives to help construct your conclusion. And finally, choose schools based on the factors that matter most to you. Choosing a college is very personal and highly individual. No matter how many sources you read, the opinion that ultimately matters most is your own.

GET THE MOST OUT OF A COLLEGE VISIT

by Colleges of Distinction Staff

No amount of research can replace the experience of visiting a campus firsthand. By going to a school itself, you can talk directly to current students, take a close look at the residence halls, and make meaningful contact with the admissions office.

Despite the tremendous value that can come from a college visit, some students and parents do not come aptly prepared. In many cases, people don't take the time to plan properly, simply showing up or driving by. Without some foresight, you might risk getting a hasty—and often incorrect—impression of the school.

Get the most out of your college visit! Here are a few tips that will help you:

Pre-Planning

Call to schedule your college visit at least two weeks ahead of time

Many people do not pre-plan their college visit, which can end up leading to an unproductive, spoiled experience. If you call ahead of time, the admissions office will be able to accommodate you and ensure that you get what you need out of your visit.

Make sure to get proper directions to the admissions office

In order to make a good first impression, make sure you know where you're going so that you can arrive on time. Don't only trust your GPS! If you have any questions, ask for help from someone on campus or call the admissions office to help clarify your directions.

If there is anything specific you wish to see, ask ahead of time

Depending upon the time of year, the staff involved in your college visit may not be able to accommodate you with everything you wish to see. For example, it may not be possible to audit a class or stay overnight during a visit in the summer months. Regardless, it can never to ask if there is ever something of specific interest to you.

Be flexible

It may not be possible for the school you're visiting to schedule everything you would like to see, especially during the summer. Be willing to try something else, and always remember that you want to present yourself positively; you still might want to apply to this school later.

If you need to cancel or reschedule, call ASAP

It goes without saying that you can't ever predict emergencies or unforeseen circumstances, but it's nevertheless a common courtesy to contact the admissions office to let them know you can't come. It's important to respect the admissions staff's time, so try not to inconvenience them by failing to show up without any warning.

During the Visit

Ask questions

Take an active role. The college visit is a golden opportunity for you to ask questions about what really matters to you.

Try to do some extra things on your own

Eat in the cafeteria, talk to students, see where people hang out, and tour the neighborhood around the school. If you take a close look on your own, you can get a more complete picture of the school, not just what the admissions office wants to highlight.

Don't discount the school because of bad weather or other uncontrollable circumstances

Some students are quick to cross a school off their list simply because it rained or because they visited during a school break when there weren't many activities going on.

Don't fall into this trap! There are going to be good days and bad days no matter where you go, so try to look past the the inconstant factors and instead focus on the school for what it is and what it can be for you.

Post-Visit

Always write a thank-you note

In order to make a great and lasting impression, write a thank-you note to those you met on campus. This makes it more likely to be remembered when it comes time to review your application.

Make sure you have contact information for any future questions or concerns

Keep business cards and pamphlets in some organized folder so that you can refer to them if necessary.

Make sure to remain in contact with the school

Some schools keep a record of contact information and sometimes use a prospective student's correspondence as a measurement of how interested they are in being admitted.

Talk with your high school counselor about the visit

It's a great idea to bounce your ideas off of parents, relatives, and friends when you weigh the options and experiences from your college visits. You should also make sure, however, to discuss your visit with your counselor, as they can provide a neutral and informative perspective on your experiences.

USING SOCIAL MEDIA IN YOUR COLLEGE SEARCH

Almost every college is building virtual communities through social media. As you conduct your search, there are plenty of opportunities to connect with the school, admissions counselors, prospective and current students, even alumni. You can follow colleges on social media to learn about campus life, take virtual tours and, ultimately, help you decide if the college is a good fit for you. Let's consider some of the most popular social network platforms and how to use each of them:

Facebook

Start by "liking" the college's page, and you'll get a sense of the personality of the school, what conversations

are important, and the hot topics on campus. More importantly, use the information you learn about the college during your interview or in your essay—admissions counselors appreciate that you've taken the time to find out all you can about the school. Beyond the school's official Facebook page, look to see if there are groups that correspond to your special interests or if you can ask questions of admissions counselors.

Twitter

Follow your prospective college on Twitter to discover everything from what lectures and events are happening to what's being served in the dining hall that week. You'll also learn news about what current alumni are doing and what issues are important, whether it's sports, the environment, social change, or new classes.

YouTube

You can watch convocation speeches, take virtual tours, hear guest lectures, and listen to the school's singing group perform. It's a great way to see how active the campus life is and if this seems like a place where you would happily fit in.

Instagram, Flickr, Tumblr, and Pinterest

A picture really is worth a thousand words. Take a look at these image sites, and you'll find everything from ideas for decorating dorm rooms to student life to campus buildings.

Student Bloggers

This can be a great way to learn about and connect with current students. Hear what they are going through, their likes and dislikes, and opportunities they are getting there. Feel free to stop by the comment section and ask a question or two.

Social Media Tips for Students

Just as employers often check a job applicant's online presence, college admissions officers often take a closer look at their candidates. Use common sense, and don't post anything that might give a negative impression in your language, photos, or images. Set up your privacy settings to restrict access; that includes protecting your tweets, and if there are YouTube videos you wouldn't want to be seen, set those to private as well. Make sure your email address is professional (not sexxygurrl96@example. com). Use either firstnamelastname@example.com or create a user name to highlight a special skill (smithkicks@ example.com for a high school football kicker looking to stand out, or smith88keys@example.com for a pianist).

Use your social media presence to highlight your achievements, share your volunteer work, and create your "brand" that will showcase you in your very best light. Create a video of your soccer goals, start a blog of your creative writing, or set up a Pinterest account to "pin" your artwork. The Common Application and the Universal College Application both have places to link to a site. Make the most of social media, both in your search and the application process, to find the college that's your best fit.

APPLYING/GETTING ACCEPTED

MAKE A LIST, CHECK IT TWICE: A COLLEGE APPLICATIONS GUIDE

By Nathan Wilgeroth

There are so many components to a college application that it may be hard to keep track of everything you need. It's never too late to start preparing, even if you haven't yet decided where you're going to apply. Gather what you can, take note of what you still need to do, and keep up with everything you've done. Here's a quick and easy list of all the components you'll want to consider. There are a lot of moving parts involved in this process, so use this as a foundation for a checklist to ensure that you're well on your way to a completed application!

The Basics

Some schools have very specific requirements for their application, but you can be sure that most, if not all, or the schools you apply to will require the following:

High School Transcript

Your transcript is a report of all your grades throughout high school. In most cases, colleges will require that they receive your transcript directly from your high school. Go to your counselor's office and let them know where to send an official document.

Letter(s) of Recommendation

A letter of recommendation is a testament of your hard work and achievement from a trusted teacher, coach, or mentor. Figure out who you'd like to write your letter, and ask far in advance so that they have ample time to help you.

Schools will typically require that the writers of your letters send them directly as well, so make sure your writers know where to submit them.

SAT/ACT Scores

Standardized tests like the SAT and ACT help display your abilities in relation to other students from all across the nation. Because these exams are almost universally considered on college applications, it's important to study hard and test multiple times for the best scores possible.

If you know the schools you're applying to by the time you take the test, you can request where to send your scores while you're still in the testing room! Otherwise, you can find them on the CollegeBoard and ACT websites later on.

Not every school requires SAT/ACT scores as part of their college application, but that doesn't mean you shouldn't take them! Even test-optional schools may award merit scholarships to students with qualifying scores.

Extracurricular Involvement

Colleges like to see that applicants have made valuable use of their free time throughout high school. Compile a list of all your extracurricular activities and take note of how you have served as a leader or a dedicated member. You may also choose to write an activities résumé so that you may expand on your experiences outside of the classroom.

Application Essay

In addition to your activities résumé, your application essay helps admissions officers get a sense of your personality, voice, and perspective. Many schools accept applications through The Common Application, which means that you are often able to focus on *one* prompt as opposed to different prompts for each school. Give yourself plenty of time to write the essay, get it reviewed by a parent/guardian/teacher, and make it the best it can be.

Do Your Research

Every school has its own standards, and it's up to you to know where to fill out your application, what to submit, and when to submit it.

Know Your Deadlines

Some schools have a set deadline for applications, while others accept applications on a rolling basis. Check the website or call/email the admissions office of every school you're applying to so that you know when to have everything finished and submitted.

How to Apply

A vast number of schools accept applications through Common App, though plenty also provide applications on their own website. Again, check with each of your schools to know whether they exclusively accept one form or allow you to submit through either platform.

Extra Considerations

Here are a few extra things to look out for. Always keep your eyes peeled for school-specific requirements!

Supplemental Essays

In addition to the general application essay, some colleges ask for additional, school- or major-specific essays to help better inform their decision. Such supplemental essay prompts may ask you to write about why you're interested in a particular school, why you're pursuing a certain major—anything the school wants to get an idea of you as a prospective student! Keep an eye out for schools with extra essay prompts and plan your writing wisely.

Major-Specific Material

Some majors, especially those related to fine arts, require some sort of material to showcase the work you have done thus far. Check in with the department of your desired major and see whether you're asked to submit an audition or portfolio.

Interview

You might be required to meet face-to-face with an admissions representative from your prospective school. Even if an interview is not required, it can still be enormously helpful. Not only will it allow the school to know your character and personality, but it will also give you the opportunity to learn more about the school and ask questions before you apply and enroll. Check out each school's website to see whether an interview is required as well as how to schedule an appointment.

Other Assessments

The SAT and ACT are not the only standardized tests out there. In fact, some of our very own Colleges of Distinction have begun to accept the Classic Learning Test as part of their considerations. Tests like these take different approaches to the college entrance exam so that they may assess students on alternative criteria.

There are a lot of components to a college application, and if this article taught you anything, it's that each school has its own standards to keep in mind. But there's no need to get overwhelmed! Make a checklist, research all of your potential schools' requirements, and work confidently toward the education of your dreams. Best of luck!

RIGHTS AND RESPONSIBILITIES IN THE ADMISSIONS PROCESS

Those who may be beginning their college search sometimes assume that colleges and universities have complete control over the admissions process. In fact, there are established regulations that almost every college, university, and high school must abide by to be fair and ethical.

The Statement of Principles of Good Practice (SPGP), set forth by the National Association of College Admission Counseling (NACAC), specifies some important rights and responsibilities for every member of the process: students, parents, and counselors.

The Right to Know

One of the most important rights for students and parents is the right to information. College and university professionals (as well as high school college counselors) must provide all of the open, honest information that students need in order to make the best decision about college.

Colleges must be open and consistent about deadlines. The SPGP states that a "College and University member agree that they will include a current and accurate admissions calendar. They will state clearly all deadlines for application, notification, housing, and candidates' reply requirements for both admissions and financial aid." In fully understanding this statement, students have the right to know specific deadlines for submitting their applications without penalty.

Parents and students also have the right to information from their high school guidance counselor. The SPGP says that counselors must "provide a program of counseling which introduces a broad range of postsecondary opportunities to students." That means that parents and students can reasonably expect their high school counselor to make presentations, hold information sessions, and find other ways of making good information about the process available to them.

The Responsibility to Work

Parents and students also have their own obligations in the process. Students might prefer someone else to research for them—after all, it's a big project. But every college-bound student should be responsible for understanding *their* options.

Not only will students learn admission requirements, but also about the institution as a whole. The more informed they are, the more confident they can be in their choices.

Students also have the responsibility to complete their own essays, questions, activity résumé, and all other parts of the application. Parents sometimes feel they should help with the application in order to enhance their son or daughter's chances for admission. In fact, by helping in this way, they will be doing a great deal of harm. Colleges and universities frown on such parental "help"; if it is suspected that Mom or Dad wrote the admissions essay, then the student is much less likely to be admitted.

So what can parents do to help? It is perfectly acceptable for parents to take charge of paying application fees, making sure test scores are sent, and making sure that everything is organized. It is also a great idea for parents to go over admissions materials with students, brainstorm questions to ask during a visit, and even ask questions themselves. Although they should not re-do a student's work, it is acceptable for parents to proofread student essays for spelling and grammar. There are many ways that parents can help their son or daughter with this difficult process.

For More Information

If you are interested in a particular college or university, ask for clear information on what their admissions policies are and what kind of academic programs they offer. The admissions office should be able to provide this information to you.

SAT AND ACT STUDY TIPS

The SAT and ACT are more similar than you might think. There are minor differences between the two tests; the ACT has a science section and the SAT has a math section that doesn't allow the use of a calculator. But with the update of the SAT in 2016, the tests are more similar than ever.

General Study Tips

1. **Take a practice exam.** One of the best ways to understand these two tests, what they'll be like, and which test is best for you is to take a practice test. With subtle differences, you'll find that one test is less stressful or easier for you than the other. The ACT is known for being time rigorous and organized while the SAT is a bit more ponderous, offering

more time to answer each question. Be sure to take an official practice exam that has questions from previous exams.

2. **You only gain points.** If there's a question that you find particularly stressful or difficult, SKIP IT! On both the SAT and the ACT, you gain points for correct answers but are not penalized for incorrect or blank answers. If you're not sure, don't waste time, just guess and move on.

3. **Be aware of difficulty.** In the math section on the SAT and ACT, the questions get more difficult as you work through the section. But remember, the difficult problems are not worth more points. Your time is better spent making sure the majority of the problems are solved correctly than trying to figure out the answer to the last few, most difficult problems.

4. **Don't waste time.** Yes, yes, we know this is obvious advice, but every single second counts on these tests. Every moment is another question answered. Just remember, on the ACT reading section, you get 52 seconds per problem. That minute you were late, yeah, that's one problem not answered and points not gained.

5. **Get rid of obviously incorrect answers.** The more practice questions you read, the more obvious the incorrect answers will become. By eliminating one or more incorrect answers, you improve your chances of choosing or guessing the correct answer.

6. **Read carefully.** Test question writers are not purposefully out to get you, but they do know that time-pressure can make readers hasty and aren't above exploiting that. Make sure to read each word carefully and to fully understand the question being asked.

7. **Practice your weakest area.** Though you should practice test questions from all areas of the test, it's important to not ignore your weakest area. There are likely easy ways to learn a new skill that will significantly improve your score.

8. **Buy a study guide.** Study guides can be extremely useful when preparing for these tests. Before purchasing, be sure that the guide you're buying is reputable. If you're not sure, stick with the official guide.

9. **Understand your mistakes.** Taking a practice test will help you to learn about the test and get a baseline score, but you can take it a step further. If you review the answers you missed, you may notice patterns in area that need more attention. You might also be able to identify certain types of mistakes. Did read the question too quickly? Did you get tripped up by time pressure? Once you understand your mistakes, you can guard against them.

10. **Don't ignore instructions.** As you work to make the most of every second, it can be easy to skip over the instructions. Don't do this—the instructions contain information that you'll need. Be sure to at least skim them, especially in the reading section. The instructions may contain information that sets the scene, introduces the author, or could help you to answer a question.

11. **Underline.** To improve comprehension, don't be afraid to mark on your test. When reading passages and test questions, underline the most important words and phrases.

ACT-specific Study Tips

1. **Monitor your time.** This is important on both the SAT and ACT, but the ACT has more questions packed into the same amount of time as the SAT. On the english section, you get 36 seconds per problem; on the math section, you get 60 seconds per problem; and on the reading section, you get 52 seconds per problem. That's not a lot of time per problem, and it's important to stay on top of answering questions efficiently.

2. **Skip hard questions.** As we've mentioned, time is especially important on the ACT. If you're stuck on a hard question, move on. You can always make a guess as there's no penalty for incorrect answers or unanswered questions, but don't spend too much time.

SAT-specific Study Tips

1. **Use surrounding questions to check answers.** The new SAT includes questions in the reading section that require you to defend your answer. The question asks you to choose the passage that best supports your answer in the previous question. This will help you to check your answers and also to find the correct answer if you're not certain.

2. **Read strategically.** It may not be the most efficient option to read passages in full. Consider a strategy: skim the passage—or even read the questions first.

3. **Answer every question.** There is no penalty for incorrect answers, so it is to your benefit to answer every question. When time is running low, go ahead and fill in the bubbles for unanswered questions.

We hope that these tips are helpful to you as you begin studying for the big test, whether you've chosen the SAT or ACT, or both. Don't forget, you do have the option to take both tests and see which one gives you a more competitive score.

EARLY COLLEGE PREP: WHY YOU SHOULD VISIT YOUR GUIDANCE COUNSELOR

The world beyond high school is full of endless possibilities, and choosing which path you take requires you to think deeply about your individual interests, personality, and goals. As you get closer to graduation, it can be easy to feel isolated and weighed down by every decision you make. It's your future, so that means it's all *your own* responsibility, right?

Not quite. In fact, your high school guidance counselor is there specifically to help you along the way!

A visit to your guidance counselor's office can make a huge impact on how to look for, apply to, and impress your prospective colleges. The earlier you make your way to your counselor's office, the clearer your path will be toward graduation and beyond!

Today's Schedule for Tomorrow's Success

How you spend your time during high school plays a big part in how colleges judge your initiative. Your counselor can help you select which courses and extracurricular activities will best help you meet your graduation requirements, look good on your résumé and, of course, keep you interested and passionate through high school!

Academic advisors are well versed in not only your high school's schedule and graduation requirements, but also the more rigorous courses that certain colleges are looking for—advanced sciences and foreign languages, for example, really shine on an application. Through strategic planning with their advisors, many students are able to exceed requirements and graduate with honors and/or a high class ranking. And with an idea of your interests and the environments in which you thrive, your advisor can help you find clubs you'll like and fit them in your schedule.

Letters of Approval

High school counselors can help you obtain letters of recommendation from your teachers and other faculty members. And if you've been working with them one-on-one, they'd be a perfect reference themselves! Your interaction with them early on will help them note what sets you apart from other college applicants; it will allow them to vouch for your character and the qualities you possess beyond academics, athletics, and extracurriculars. A glowing recommendation from a high school guidance counselor can be just the thing to tip an otherwise borderline application over the edge and into acceptance at some colleges. If a professional in education thinks highly of you, that's sure to carry a lot of weight with admissions officers.

Professional Guidance

Knowing how to apply to college is a brand-new process for you, but for high school guidance counselors, it's literally their job! Your counselor's professional background is one of the most valuable resources you can have—whether you're looking to draft a list of the schools you are interested in, fill out enrollment forms, or get a second opinion on your admissions essays, they are there to help at absolutely no cost to you.

Based on your own personal strengths and weaknesses, they can help you set realistic, attainable goals and make sure you don't over- or underestimate your potential. They can also help you prepare for standardized tests like the ACT and SAT and confirm the range of scores that would get your best chance at admission. And because they've worked with so many students who have had so many different outcomes, they can even introduce you to colleges you may not have considered but are nevertheless perfect for your individual goals.

The Right Price (and the Right Timing!)

With college applications comes a confusing swarm of financial aid options, roadblocks, and forms, so it's always best to get help from someone who can give it. Ask your guidance counselor for help as you fill out and navigate the Free Application for Federal Student Aid (FAFSA)! It's in your best interest to take advantage of the experience and knowledge they have to offer. Beyond answering your questions about financial aid, they can make you aware of any deadlines you need to keep in mind and even review your applications before entry.

Beyond FAFSA, your guidance counselor is fully equipped to show you the kinds of scholarships that would be best for you to pursue. With an understanding of your specific needs, interests, and extracurricular activities, your advisor can direct you to scholarships that you might not have heard of otherwise.

Get Confident

Clear guidance from your counselor can reduce the stress that comes with college applications. And it shows—this boost of confidence will reflect in your application itself, translating into an organized, polished presentation of you as a great candidate.

You can rest a bit more easily when you have a professional on your side. Your high school guidance counselor can encourage you every step of the way and reassure you of any seemingly daunting decisions. They are there to help introduce you to admissions officers and other professionals suited for your goals, keep an eye on deadlines, and make sure all of your transcripts are submitted correctly.

It's more than worthwhile to make the extra effort and utilize your high school guidance counselor as early as you can. You're bound to have questions—where to begin, which direction to take, how to move forward—so always know that you can meet with a professional who is right down the hall. You have nothing to lose and everything to gain by paying your guidance counselor a visit!

WHAT DOES IT MEAN TO BE WAITLISTED OR DEFERRED?

After all the frantic work of putting together an application, waiting for an answer can seem to take forever. Most applicants assume that eventually they will receive a letter with one of two simple outcomes: acceptance or rejection. Yet there are actually other possible outcomes—as if there weren't enough confusion already in the college search process!

You may be informed that your application has been "waitlisted" or "deferred." What does this mean? Should you be concerned? The answer depends on a number of factors.

Waitlists and deferrals are two different things, but they share some similarities. While neither is an outright rejection, they both mean you will have to wait longer to see if you will be admitted.

Being **deferred** can mean a wide variety of things. In most cases, the college has not completed its review of your file and is "deferring" their decision to a later date. Deferrals typically fall into two categories:

- You applied under the Early Action or Early Decision plan and have been pushed back into the regular pool. This may be frustrating, but also has an advantage. If you are accepted into the college/university under regular decision, you are not obligated to attend as you would have been if you were accepted under an Early Decision plan (Early Action is non-binding to begin with). You may feel free to consider offers from other schools.

- You have applied under a regular decision or rolling admission and the college/university would like to have more information in order to make a decision about your application. In almost every case, a college or university would like to see more grades from the senior year or new test scores. If a school receives the information they want, they could admit you earlier.

Being **waitlisted** is unlike being deferred; the college has finished reviewing your file and made a decision to put you on a waiting list for admission.

- Being on a waitlist typically means that you are placed within a "holding pattern" of sorts. The admissions committee may or may not admit students from the waitlist. And unlike a deferral situation, new information does not usually change a waitlist decision.

- If you are placed on a waitlist, you can usually find out if the school has gone to their waitlist in the past and if so, how many students they admitted from the waitlist. In some cases, your chances of eventually getting in are very good; at other colleges, waitlisted applicants are almost never admitted.

It is always wise to apply to another institution and ensure that you have a place somewhere. Do not pin your hopes on a waitlisted college; this is the time to make plans with one of your backup schools.

Whether you are deferred or waitlisted, avoid the temptation to begin a flood of recommendation letters and phone calls to the admissions department. In almost every case, this can have an adverse effect on your chances for admission. Some institutions even state in the letters that they do not take any additional letters of recommendation or phone calls on the student's behalf. If the admissions office does need more materials, they are generally interested in concrete information (test scores, grades, etc.) rather than personal testimony or recommendations.

Remember that if you have been waitlisted or deferred, you have not been denied admission. It's as if you have been asked to stay in the waiting room a little longer, pending an ultimate decision. As with any waiting period, use the time wisely. Improve your grades or test scores, or simply continue your good academic performance. Make sure you have alternate plans with another school, and don't despair. Being waitlisted or deferred is frustrating, but it's not the end of the world, or of your college search.

PAYING FOR COLLEGE

ATTENDING A PRIVATE SCHOOL CAN BE AFFORDABLE

by Tyson Schritter

For most high school students, the cost of college can be daunting. Students have to choose between in-state schools, public universities, religious colleges, and private colleges, all while weighing their options against their budget.

Most students start with the misunderstanding that all private colleges are unaffordable. This is unfortunate, because some of the best higher education in this country is administered in private colleges. If you're looking for a private college that's affordable, look no further—we've created a collection of colleges and tips to help you seek out affordable options for private college.

Why Private Schools Are Affordable

The initial sticker shock that many applicants to private colleges feel is normal. The tuition listed on private college websites can range from $20,000 to $60,000 a year before financial aid, leading many applicants to believe that such schools are not affordable for them.

The truth, however, is that many private colleges offer more financial aid packages, often of a higher value, than public universities. Once you factor in these aid packages, the cost of tuition can many times be equal to or less than that of public schools.

What's the Actual Price of Tuition?

Let's take a moment to define a couple terms to better understand the actual cost of attending a private college.

Posted price: This the price that colleges post on their website, typically considered the maximum price of a full-time student. It's unlikely you'll have to pay that much money.

Net price: This is the price a student will pay after scholarships and grants are deducted from the posted price. This is the price that you should use when comparing the cost of colleges. If one school has offered you a great scholarship, it's net price is likely to be better than that of a comparable school that has not offered any aid.

Knowing the difference between the posted price and the net price can make a big difference in which schools you choose to apply to and attend. Your ultimate decision in which school you choose is deeply impacted by your understanding, calculation, and comparison of your options' net prices.

The Private School Cost Calculation Process

If you're certain that you want to attend a private school, it's time to start looking into which schools will offer you financial aid and how much that aid affects your cost of attendance.

Below are some foolproof steps for you to take in order to calculate the cost of each private school you're interest in. Keep in mind that some factors of the final cost of college won't be included here; special, merit-based scholarships cannot be included in this calculation until you've applied and received the award. If you know how much merit-based scholarship you've been offered, you can get an even more accurate picture of the school's final cost.

FINANCIAL AID TERMS DEFINED

Paying for college can be confusing if you don't understand the terminology. Below are some helpful definitions to common financial aid terms.

Bursar

A college office that handles both the distribution of financial aid and payment of fees and tuition. May also be called financial office, or something similar.

CSS Profile

A secondary financial aid form that the colleges use to help them determine if the student is eligible for their own money. These should be filed early, along with the FAFSA, to receive early information regarding your status for financial aid.

EFC (EXPECTED FAMILY CONTRIBUTION)

This term refers to the results from the FAFSA that shows what your family can contribute financially for educational expenses. In many instances, the EFC is calculated without taking into consideration any unexpected changes in income (not shown by the results from taxes) or other emergencies.

FAFSA

A standard form from the Department of Education that determines eligibility for all state and federal grants. Generally, you must fill this out before a college can begin processing your request for financial aid. They are usually available in November, but most require current tax information to fill out fully.

Federal Stafford Loan Program

Government-subsidized loans that are adjusted by need. No repayment is required while the student is in school.

Financial Aid Package

An offer of money for a student from a college. It usually consists of several kinds of aid, including loans, grants, campus jobs, and may or may not include scholarships. This package fills the gap between parents' contribution and the total cost of college.

Merit Scholarships

Money given to students on the basis of demonstrated ability—academic, performance, service, athletics, etc. It is not based on need, and does not need to be repaid. Most scholarships come from colleges themselves and vary widely from institution to institution. There are also some scholarships available from businesses, alumni organizations, and programs like the National Merit Scholarship.

PLUS Loans

Government-subsidized loans that are limited to the cost of education. Parents do not need to demonstrate need. Interest rates can vary.

Pell Grants

These government grants are awarded to students who need a great deal of financial aid. They do not need to be repaid.

Unsubsidized Stafford Loans

Loans that do not require demonstration of need, and for which interest must be paid while the student is in college. Repayment of the principal begins after graduation.

Work Study

A campus job that may be offered as part of a financial aid package. These usually require 15-20 hours a week on campus and usually allow the student to do some studying while working. Examples might include proctoring a test, or working at a library desk.

Steps to calculate college costs:

- Gather tax documents (ask your parents if you'd like some help).

- Go to a tuition calculator website.

- Plug in your numbers to the tuition calculator.

- Save the results, including the starting cost of tuition, for later comparison.

- Go to the next private college website on your list.

- Continue these steps until you've calculated the cost of each private college you're interested in attending.

Then it's time to make comparisons. Once you've collected all of your data, you can compare the cost of attending each school. This may not be a complete picture if you can't include merit-based scholarships, outside scholarships, or government grants, but it's a good first step in assessing the cost of different private colleges.

The Value of Private Schools

When you consider the actual price you end up paying, private colleges may actually be a better value. Consider that many private schools offer:

- Smaller class sizes

- More interaction between professors and students

- Classes that are more often taught by professors than graduate students

- A smaller, more tightly knit student body

- More opportunities to gain leadership experience

Depending on the experiences and outcomes you want in your college experience, a private school may be an even better value than a public one.

5 Tricks to Make College More Affordable

Public or private, college is a big investment. There's no way to get around this fact in the modern world. Here are five more tips and tricks to help lower your out-of-pocket cost for college.

- **Earn credits elsewhere.** Most colleges allow you to transfer credits from other colleges. There are often limitations to what can transfer and a maximum number of credits that can be completed at other schools, but any transferred credits can help to lower your tuition cost. Look into the credit transfer rules of any school you're interested in attending. Credits can be earned through community college courses either prior to attending college or throughout the summer and winter breaks.

- **Explore all aid options.** You can receive scholarships and grants from many different sources. Your school may offer some, the government has ways of helping out, and there are numerous scholarships out there for special interests, personality traits, and even body characteristics. Don't think that there isn't scholarship money out there for you; aid is available for everyone.

- **FAFSA.** Be sure to fill out your FAFSA application properly and on time. Even if you don't think you're eligible for aid from the government, fill it out and see if you are. Be sure to research other federal aid programs or even aid from your local government.

- **Be creative.** Not only can you earn credits elsewhere, but you can even fulfill requirements in high school by taking AP course, college-level courses online, and through dual-enrollment classes that afford you both high school and college credit at the same time.

- **Reduce materials.** College materials, like textbooks and various supplies, can make up a significant portion of your college costs. Be sure to start your research early and look at many different options before making any purchases. There are many options out there for you to get textbooks for a significantly lower price than at the college bookstore.

Affordable Private Colleges of Distinction

Colleges of Distinction has vetted many of the finest private schools in the country. We hope that this breakdown has helped you realize that an education at a private college is within your financial reach.

HOW TO FIND—AND WIN—SCHOLARSHIPS: YOUR COMPLETE GUIDE

by Jessica Tomer, Editor-In-Chief, CollegeXpress

Even if you ultimately attend a school whose cost truly rivals any other, there's a good chance you could benefit from scholarships. After all, who *wouldn't* benefit from free money? Here's how to find—and win—scholarships.

TIPS FOR FINDING SCHOLARSHIPS

Start ASAP

Believe it or not, you can find scholarships as early as middle school—so it never hurts to start searching early! But if you're past middle school (which many of you are), you should kick your scholarship search into high gear **no later than the end of junior year of high school.** Then keep searching all senior year, and even when you're in college. Basically—search for scholarships until you graduate or all your college costs are paid—whichever comes first.

Make a List of Your Criteria

Having a cheat sheet of your **strengths, interests, and other unique qualities** make searching for scholarships a lot easier. Here are some basic scholarship search criteria to consider:

- Your academic interests/majors
- Your extracurricular activities
- Your hobbies
- Your volunteer experience
- Sports you play
- Performing and/or visual art experience
- Your family's racial/ethnic heritage
- Your hometown and state
- *Anything* you're truly passionate about

And that's just the beginning. There are tons of niche awards out there too. So keep your eyes open—you never know what you might win a scholarship for.

Know Where to Look

You'll probably do most of your research online. These scholarship search engine sites are great places to start:

- CollegeXpress
- Fastweb
- Peterson's
- Scholarships.com
- StudentScholarshipSearch
- Scholly

However, **don't use just one scholarship search engine**. Their databases can vary a lot, so compare what they offer. You should also sign up for notifications from these sites and others, so you get alerts when deadlines are coming up or they add awards matching your criteria.

Besides scholarship search sites, check out all the other places you might find scholarships:

- **Your high school guidance counselor.** Ask for their scholarship recommendations.
- **Google, Bing, etc.** A simple online search can do the trick, especially if you're looking for something super specific, like "scholarships for Irish step dancers."
- **Your family.** See if anyone's employer offers an award.
- **Local organizations.** Groups in your hometown, like a Rotary Club or even places of worship, might offer scholarships to kids from your high school.
- **Library.** Ask if they have a list of local scholarships.
- **Professional organizations.** Find groups related to your interests (for example, the Society of Professional Journalists), and see what scholarships they offer.

Search relentlessly. Cast a wide net, but also remember that the more specific you can get with your scholarship search, the better. For example, you are going to face a lot more competition for a general music scholarship than for an award just for students who play the oboe.

Be Organized

Since you're searching far and wide, you're bound to come up with a pretty big list of scholarships—each one with a unique deadline and application requirements. That's why it's important to stay organized.

A good way to do this is to **keep a running scholarship search spreadsheet.** It's handy for keeping track of awards and all their details. Include fields like deadline, amount, if it's renewable, application requirements (essay, recommendation letter, interview, etc.), and more.

Apply to Every Scholarship You're Eligible for– Seriously

When we say apply to all of the awards you're eligible for, we mean it. All of them. From big, prestigious national awards to teeny-tiny local scholarships, there are literally billions of dollars in awards out there. And every year a lot of them go unclaimed just because no one applied! **So do your best to improve your odds.**

This means conducting a super thorough scholarship search, finding time to write thoughtful essays, and not giving up as you trudge through one…more…application. It also means applying to all those easy "sweepstakes"-style scholarships, because, hey, what have you got to lose? Just keep in mind that your chances of winning those awards are small, since they attract tons of applicants.

TIPS FOR WINNING SCHOLARSHIPS

Make Sure You're Actually Eligible

Even though you should apply for lots of scholarships, make sure you truly qualify for the awards before you start your applications. Try to get eligibility requirements directly from the awarding organization if you can, just in case your scholarship search engine results are outdated.

Write Kick-Butt Essays

We're not going to sugarcoat it: applying for scholarships can mean a lot of writing. But remember: this is your chance to convince the scholarship organization why you deserve this money. Take advantage of the opportunity. Carefully read the essay prompt, and make sure you understand what's being asked. Then tell a unique, thoughtful, specific story. Your story.

Think About Your Story in Advance

You'll probably be asked to write scholarship essays about who you are and what matters to you. It helps to sit down and think about those heavy topics in advance. Ask yourself: What do you care about most and why? How have you made the world a better place? Where do you see yourself in the future? Jotting down your thoughts can help you formulate essay ideas, and may help you come up with additional scholarship search criteria.

Get to Know the Awarding Organization

Who's awarding the scholarship, and what do they care about? Spend some time on their website to get a sense of their goals, mission, and values. Then make sure your scholarship application speaks to those things. Put yourself in the scholarship reader's shoes: Are you the kind of student they're looking for?

Do NOT Miss the Deadline

Missing a scholarship's deadline will ruin your chances. In fact, you should send your applications in a week or two early if you can. This gives you enough time to submit your best work—and you really need to give it your all to be a competitive scholarship applicant. Plus, beating the deadline gives you a buffer in case something goes wrong with your application (not that it will…).

Proofread Your Applications

Be sure to edit your scholarship applications for spelling, grammar, and tone. Also, make sure you answered all the questions and essay prompts correctly. The competition for free money is fierce, and a sloppy application can easily throw you out of the running.

Don't Forget the Little Things

Put effort into small things – like making sure your online presence is respectable, you're polite and mature if/when you interact with scholarship administrators, etc. In short, give your scholarship search your all. It will be worth it in the end.

MONEY MATTERS: THINKING ABOUT FINANCIAL AID

Many families find that applying for financial aid is just as confusing as applying to colleges. Along with the huge number of required forms, they must contend with a new language of terms and abbreviations.

But there is light at the end of the tunnel! Here are some tips to get you going.

Explore All of Your Options Early and Discuss Them with Each Other

The old adage "the early bird catches the worm" is very true when it comes to financial aid. By taking an early look and discovering all possibilities, it can offset a lot of extra work later on and also give the family a head start on reducing the cost.

Check with Your Schools to See What Forms Are Required

All colleges and universities require the FAFSA. Some require the CSS Profile. Others may have their own institutional forms.

Talk to Each Other About Realistic Expectations

Discussing financial matters can be uncomfortable. But the more that your child understands about the family's financial possibilities, the more realistic attitude he or she will take to the college process.

Investigate Every Scholarship Opportunity

Leave no stone unturned! Look everywhere! From guidebooks and websites, the more you search for scholarships, the more possibilities that you uncover. You can begin by asking family members if they belong to any organizations (or their place of employment) that sponsor scholarships for which your child might be eligible. Talk to your counselor—and of course, check with the school to see if there are any special applications necessary for scholarships. (Music scholarships, for example, may require an audition, while others may require interviews, essays, and so forth.)

Establish a Good Working Relationship with the Financial Aid Office

As with the admissions office, you should consider the financial aid office a valuable source of information. By instituting a rapport with your financial aid counselor, your family will have another outlet in which to discuss any special circumstances or ask basic questions.

If You Have Any Special Circumstances, Be Sure to Communicate Them Effectively

Remember: your initial financial aid package is not always the last word. The FAFSA and other forms do not always take into account special circumstances, such as a change in income or a medical emergency that is not reflected in any tax information. Talk to the schools' financial aid office and see if your specific situation can be taken into consideration.

Above all, remember that if you take the time to understand the financial aid process, it will become an easier task than you might have initially imagined. Explore every option, talk to everyone, and make sure to breathe!

PREPARING FOR COLLEGE AND MAKING THE MOST OF YOUR OPPORTUNITIES

HIGH-IMPACT PRACTICES – THE KEYS TO YOUR FUTURE

by Dr. Ross Peterson-Veatch, Interim Vice President of Academic Affairs and Academic Dean, Goshen College

When I was in college, I studied abroad, spending 12 months in South America. The experience completely changed my attitude about why I was in college, what college was for, who I was, and what I wanted to do with my life.

To paraphrase philosopher and educator John Dewey, you don't prepare for the future by drawing a straight line between what you're doing now and what you want, because you don't know what's coming in the future. The real preparation comes in learning to wring the most meaning and knowledge out of the present moment so that you're ready for whatever comes after graduation.

Interestingly, study abroad is a "High-Impact Practice" (HIP), a term coined by the Association of American Colleges and Universities to describe the research-proven top 10 educational practices that are the most beneficial to college students of all backgrounds.

HIPs are the best resource for you to ensure that you're getting the most out of your college education. They provide a platform for synthesizing what you've learned into a coherent narrative, often involving invaluable collaboration and hands-on education.

Research has shown that HIPs are linked with higher grade point averages, and even more importantly, higher student satisfaction with their education.

As you're evaluating college options, look for opportunities like first-year seminars that encourage critical reflection, study abroad programs, internships, and capstone projects. Search the colleges' course catalogs, talk HIPs with your admissions counselor, or set up a meeting with a professor or academic advisor to ask about High-Impact Practices.

One example of an effective High-Impact Practice is Goshen College's Study-Service Term. According to the National Survey of Student Engagement, Goshen students were more likely than their national peers to interact with students of a race or ethnicity other than their own, more likely to complete an internship or field experience, more likely to participate in co-curricular activities, and more likely to acquire a broad general education.

Keep in mind that, just because a school has HIPs available, that doesn't necessarily mean that they're easily accessible to all students. You should also find out what percentage of students at the school have participated in at least one High-Impact Practice.

Remember—your goal for college is to get a great education, and that's exactly what HIPs help ensure. To fully prepare for life after graduation, make sure that High-Impact Practices are a part of your college search process!

COLLABORATIVE AND COMMON LEARNING: LEARN AND GROW WITH YOUR PEERS

by Carol Burton, Associate Provost for Undergraduate Studies, Western Carolina University

Whether you live with a roommate or not, college is all about getting involved and getting to know others.

One of the key elements of any collegiate experience is honing your skills to become a successful member of society upon graduation. Our increasingly diverse world demands that we be interconnected in dynamic and relevant ways, and institutions that prize this aspect of the collegiate experience are setting their graduates up for success. While there are a number of ways to promote and support your personal and professional development, two proven practices that many colleges employ are *collaborative* and *common learning*. Regardless of your chosen career, you will need to work with others to achieve your goals and advance the desired outcomes of your employer. Opportunities for being involved in collaborative and common learning include jointly working on projects and research; sharing learning experiences around broad, integrated themes; enrolling in courses that are team taught by faculty from different disciplines; engaging with campus interdisciplinary themes that link curricular and co-curricular experiences; completing common readings across college levels (e.g. freshman reading); and attending guest speaker series' that are combined with individual reflection and group discussions.

Collaborative Assignments and Projects

Increasingly popular at colleges and universities today, collaborative assignments and projects often mirror the real world of work and life beyond college. Whether you work in healthcare, business, education, the sciences, or some other field, you are sure to find you and your fellow employees frequently organized in teams and expected to work successfully within those teams. Collaborative problem-solving, diverse viewpoints, and different modes of thinking contribute to students' development of:

- richer solutions to problems,
- multi-dimensional and hypothetical thinking,
- consensus-building skills, and
- effective teamwork.

Some universities require students to work on a community-based project that requires multiple angles to solve. For example, at Western Carolina University in North Carolina, this approach to learning has led to a partnership with the local community to respond to the major economic downturn by 1) having students who major in marketing work with the merchants in the town to create and implement a vibrant marketing plan; 2) employing communication student majors to develop public relations jingles for local radio and television broadcast; 3) allowing students majoring in computer information systems to

develop an online application for the town that includes business locations, historic data, and calendar of events; 4) engaging students majoring in business to develop a business sustainability plan for various merchants in the town; and 5) hosting special events for the university community to participate in themed events at a discounted price. Faculty, staff, and administrators provided oversight and support for students in their work with the community.

Common Learning Experiences

Common learning experiences go hand-in-hand with collaborative assignments and projects; however, these experiences often take place university-wide or at the program level rather than in individual courses. An example of common intellectual learning experiences includes campus-wide themes where curricular and co-curricular opportunities are linked by a common topic. For example, at Western Carolina University each year, a committee of students, faculty, and staff propose and vote on a common these around which to entire the entire campus. Topics such as "the decade of the 1960's," "citizenship and civility," "water," "global poverty," "economic inequality," "North Carolina—our state, our time," and "Africa: more than a continent" have been considered and/or adopted at WCU. Students learn by completing common readings across their general studies, attending speaker sessions, engaging in community service, viewing historic and art exhibits, and enrolling in specific courses that focus on the theme.

As a more specific example of a campus theme, WCU most recently selected the theme "Africa—more than a continent" and had a two-year (2015-17) focus on the cultures, diversity, political structures, foods, religions, arts, geography and geology, business, histories, music, hospitality, education, and demographics of the continent. Faculty and students could travel to Africa to study (through courses in anthropology, sociology, and criminal justice), conduct exchanges for professional development (like the partnership between Botswana and WCU's department of Communication Sciences and Disorders), perform musically (in ensembles like the brass quintet), and conduct service-learning projects. The university's dining division even participated in the campus theme by hosting several days' worth of menus to highlight the cuisines of various African countries and cultures. The campus community experimented with Moroccan spiced whitefish, African peanut soup, East African eggplant stew, and West African Jollof rice. Students, staff, and faculty were afforded opportunities to discuss global issues in an African context while learning about the continent and its diverse countries and cultures. See Africa.wcu.edu for additional information on WCU's campus theme.

Common intellectual learning experiences promote learning by A) helping students to see the world as a connected entity; B) providing common language to foster

communication and understanding of various topics; C) fostering student camaraderie and campus engagement; and D) offering faculty and staff new and innovative ways to enhance teaching and learning.

However you define success in college, let a part of that definition be to involve yourself in the unique and innovative ways that universities are helping to shape you for a world beyond your campus.

RELEVANT AND RAW: GLOBAL EDUCATION HELPS REINVENT HIGHER ED

by Jennifer Summerhays, Director of Global Education Programs, Georgian Court University

Is higher education in danger of becoming irrelevant? It has been suggested that colleges and universities are not adapting to the needs and pace of the world. The IBM Institute for Business Value calls upon higher education to be in "pursuit of relevance" by prioritizing practical and applied curricula and improving educational access and experiences. Let's face it, millennials have a sixth sense when it comes to authenticity, transparency, and engagement. They pay attention to advertising that is raw and tells it like it is. They buy products and choose opportunities that are world-connected and engaging. The Yale School of Management suggests that millennials are not easy to please because they challenge brands to be more innovative. Wouldn't they expect the same from their college experience—an education that transcends the classroom and connects them to the world in real ways?

So, how do you know if a college is relevant? How do you know if it is keeping up with our changing world and new population of learners? Here are a few ways to check a college's vital signs:

Global Education: a necessity, not a luxury.

A sure sign of a college's commitment to world relevance can be found in its experiential learning offerings. If the college views the world as an extension of the classroom, and promotes global education programs, you may have a winner.

Once upon a time, "global education" simply meant "semester study abroad"—a privilege reserved for the wealthy, and an unachievable luxury for the majority. But now the world of work requires graduates of all socio-economic backgrounds to possess a certain level of

multicultural competence; to connect and engage with the world in authentic and relevant ways prior to graduation. This real-world demand requires colleges to ensure equal access to international opportunities—to create new, affordable, and impactful ways for all students to encounter the world.

Faculty-Led Study Abroad Programs

While a semester abroad is still a popular choice for students, more are choosing to study abroad in short bursts via Faculty-Led Study Abroad Programs (FLSAPs). These international micro programs pack a punch. They are usually offered over spring, summer, or winter breaks, and can even incorporate a volunteer or internship experience. They can take the shape of a stand-alone course, or an embedded component in an academic course (i.e. Tropical Ecology course with a 10-day lab in Costa Rica). With an eye on world relevance, FLSAPs are old dogs doing new tricks, providing students with career-oriented, discipline-specific international experiences that are led by their trusted faculty. Students have the opportunity to live, study, volunteer, and research abroad side-by-side with their professors.

FLSAPs are in growing demand. For students who have financial and time constraints coupled with limited travel experience, FLSAPs don't require students to leave home for four months; and they are hands-down more affordable than a semester experience. However, these high-impact international programs are not reserved for financially needy or underserved populations. Students from all socio-economic backgrounds are now seeing FLSAPs as financially viable, impactful, and in some cases, preferable ways to receive mentorship, and link academic learning to the world.

The benefits of FLSAPs for students are numerous:

- Generally less expensive than other international program options
- Discipline- and career-specific
- Build community among students and faculty
- Increase students' self-esteem, sense of accomplishment, purpose, academic direction, and interest in leadership
- Increase motivation to graduate in a timely manner
- Gateway experiences to other international study/ volunteer programs

Colleges are starting to understand that FLSAPs are one answer to bridging the gap between academics and the world, and as a result, short-term programs are popping up on campuses around the country – but not all FLSAPs do their due diligence.

How can you recognize a strong short-term international program?

- **Integration with curriculum:** FLSAPs should be thoughtfully linked to academic courses. Teaching and learning is transformative when it marries the experiential with the academic.
- **Affordability:** FLSAPs should be offered at a price-point that allows participation for all students. Payment plans and college micro loans are helpful; and FLSAPs bundled in the cost of a course may allow students to use their financial aid to defer the costs of the program.

- **Pre-Departure Orientation & Preparation:** FLSAPs should require a pre-departure orientation program for students and faculty, along with academic and cultural research that will help prepare them for their experience.
- **The Raw Factor:** It is one thing for colleges to offer "trips," but quite another to provide international educational experiences that are culturally-conscious and locally-integrated. An FLSAP that meets the needs of millennials is raw—it champions minimum impact travel, and maximizes interaction with authentic local culture. Millennials don't want to fill their backpacks with souvenirs; they are in search of stories and unique experiences that they can post on social media or tweet home about. While FLSAPs should be designed with safety in mind, they fall short if students are kept in a bubble abroad.
- **Post-Program Reflection:** A weakness of most international programs is the post-program follow-up. Students come back full of stories, questions, photos, wonder, and even some disappointment. Strong FLSAPs provide students with a forum in which to "unpack" their experiences.

For example, Georgian Court University is using digital storytelling, a way to sit around the virtual campfire with contemporary learners to reflect and share their global experiences. A strong post-program reflection should bring students together, help them create community, and allow them to be candid and even vulnerable about their triumphs and challenges abroad

Millennials and their "brave new world" are challenging higher education to reassess and reinvent. Context is now rivalling content and micro-learning is becoming the accepted avant-garde. To remain relevant, colleges must be humble and brave enough to listen to those they were created to serve. "Experiential," "authentic," "purpose-driven," and "innovative"—these are the words millennials are using to describe the education they want and need. If colleges are too slow to adapt, "Life is short," millennials will say. "We'll just shop around or go somewhere else."

HOW TO PARTICIPATE IN CLASS AND WHY IT'S IMPORTANT

We can all remember a time in class when we hoped the teacher or professor wouldn't call on us. Our fear of saying the wrong thing and sounding silly in front of our classmates is a strong deterrent from raising our hands and volunteering to speak in front of others. In fact, when given the choice most students choose to fly under the radar and avoid the embarrassment of speaking in front of their peers. This is unfortunate because class participation, while sometimes scary, is necessary for getting the most out of an education. Participation actively engages students with the subject matter, pushes them to create concepts, and forces them to show evidence for their claims. Put simply, it makes students work harder. A college education is expensive. Why not get the most out of it?

Students that regularly participate in class are constantly involved with the material and are more likely to remember a greater portion of the information. Active class participation also improves critical and higher level thinking skills. Students who participate in class have studied the material well enough to introduce new concepts to their peers. This level of thinking goes beyond simple comprehension of text, and can also improve memory. Participation can also help students learn from each other, increasing comprehension through cooperation. This can in turn improve relationships between students and between the student and professor.

Avoiding Class Participation

Despite the many benefits of class participation, the vast majority of students do not regularly contribute to their classes. There are several reasons why students choose not to participate in class including class size, time, and course policies. Larger classes, for example, have been shown to increase public speaking fears, as students struggle with the idea of sharing their ideas in front of a large group of people. With that in mind, colleges that encourage their faculty to focus on teaching, rather than research, are more likely to experience higher participation rates, as professors are more engaged with their students.

Encouraging Class Participation

A professor's attitude toward his or her students can dramatically affect class participation in one direction or another. Students are more likely to participate in class if they have a comfortable relationship with their professor. This means that the professor does not write off the student's response or contribution. This also means that the professor is patient with all his or her students, listens to every response with attention, and provides feedback that is both positive and constructive. Professors can increase participation by creating a safe and respectful class environment. They can also improve the situation by learning the names of their students, so that each individual feels that their opinion is valued.

Course policies drastically affect participation. Studies show a greater level of participation when students' contributions were factored into their final grade. In some courses, professors require participation and include it in every student's final grade. Participation can mean anything from asking questions to leading discussions. In other classes, professors simply take mental notes of their students' involvement and contribution to the subject matter.

How to Participate in Class

There are ways to overcome the fear of participation. First, establish a relationship with your professor. It's ok to be honest and explain that you have a fear of public speaking. Second, construct a plan to move forward. Find a participation method that works for you, whether that's asking thought-provoking questions or commenting on the reading. Prepare yourself for success by summarizing the material you would like to share with the class. Next, work your opinion into the discussion so you can demonstrate a higher level of thinking that goes beyond simply reading the assigned material. Finally, provide some evidence as to how you came to your opinion or conclusion. This will show your peers and your professors that you have made an effort to understand the subject. Preparation is key, so practice on your own before class. Saying it once aloud will ease the pain of saying it in front of your peers.

COMMUNITY-BASED LEARNING: YOUR CHANCE TO GROW PERSONALLY AND PROFESSIONALLY

by Abagail Van Vlerah, P.h.D., Dean of Students, LIU Post

Service is an increasingly valuable element of a college education. A university that provides plentiful and meaningful opportunities for service iis an institution that truly creates a rewarding college experience.

Of course, serving those in need has its own intrinsic value, which is why so many young people are focused on tackling the challenges that face their communities and the world. But as an added bonus, the power of service is also clearly visible in the job market, as candidates who can articulate meaningful service experiences are more likely to be hired for sought-after jobs. Several factors that drive this correlation are:

- **Building self-confidence:** Young people who commit themselves to a cause gain self-esteem and experience personal growth. Meaningful public service provides a sense of accomplishment that empowers young people to handle the pressures and challenges of the workplace. Employers know that a job candidate with a track record of successful public service has the potential to be a valuable addition to any team.

- **Learning by doing:** Colleges of Distinction are defined in part by their commitment to providing a wide variety of learning experiences that bring education outside of the classroom. When schools incorporate challenging volunteer projects into coursework, they add a new level of engagement to their students' education; these service-learning projects allow students to hone leadership and decision-making skills in an endeavor with real, impactful results.

- **Working across cultures:** As a result of technological advances and shifts in population, our world is constantly becoming more interconnected. This changing world demands professionals who can work across cultures. Students who engage with problems that take them out of their comfort zones— whether into an underserved community in their region or to an underprivileged community on the other side of the world—become more sophisticated and better suited for cross-cultural work at the professional level.

- **A Spirit Of Community:** Successful service and philanthropy programs are often rallying points for campus communities, bringing together large groups of students, faculty, and staff in support of worthy causes. These programs, which often take the form of extended fundraising events (such as the American Cancer Society's "Relay for Life" or the American Foundation for Suicide Prevention's "Out of the Darkness" walks), do far more than raise money; they provide the setting for many students' fondest memories of their college years, as do programs like "Alternative Spring Break," which engage students in service projects in communities around the country and the world.

A college with a robust tradition of service and philanthropy does more than give you experiences to add to your résumé. It gives you opportunities to join and engage with a community that you will always be able to call your own.

What to Look For

When looking for the college that's right for you, take some time to find out about the service opportunities offered on campus. As you do, keep an eye out for the following hallmarks:

- **Long-running service programs:** Look for opportunities to be part of an ongoing campus tradition or a large-scale community service event. The power of service is even greater and more rewarding when it helps you create a lifelong commitment.

- **International opportunities:** Programs that give you the opportunity to travel abroad to perform service are often powerful experiences. They can also add another dimension to your personal development and career preparation, enabling you to learn to work in a new cultural environment.

- **Integration into coursework:** Look for schools in which you'll have the chance to put the lessons you learn in the classroom into action through service. You'll gain valuable real-world experience while serving a worthy cause, resulting in some of the most memorable days of your college career.

WHAT IS A LIVING-LEARNING COMMUNITY?

Living-Learning Communities (LLCs) are residential programs that allow you to connect with diverse groups of students who share a common focus. Students live together and participate in shared courses, special events, and service projects as a group. LLCs are sponsored by various academic departments, and are designed to foster academic and personal growth. As more colleges and universities introduce LLCs, the possibilities are expanding for these unique housing initiatives, where collaboration and learning extend beyond the classroom.

Why Should I Participate?

Research suggests that participation in a Living-Learning Community leads to increased academic engagement and satisfaction with college experiences. This is even true for students at larger institutions, where Living-Learning Communities can make a campus feel smaller and more accessible. Many LLCs are open to first year students, which can help make the transition from high school to college more comfortable. Students involved in an LLC enjoy a built-in network of friends with shared passions and interests.

What Kinds of Living-Learning Communities Are Available?

Living-Learning Communities vary from campus to campus, but you'll find almost every topic imaginable, including sustainable living, science and engineering, social justice, global studies, and leadership. Languages and shared cultures are also common themes among LLCs. Some communities are devoted to a specific language like Spanish, French, Mandarin, or Japanese. In other cases, an LLC will focus on culture, offering residence opportunities for students who are Native American, African American and Latinx. There are also communities for freshmen, transfers, and honors students. Some schools even allow students to design their own LLCs, which can include everything from electronic music to plant-based eating!

How Is Living in a Living-Learning Community Different from Traditional Student Housing?

The goal of a Living-Learning Community is to help you engage intellectually outside the classroom. Typically, each community gathers weekly for discussions or workshops related to their topic. Dinners, lectures, presentations about off-campus experiences, and social service projects are all part of the living-learning experience. You'll live on the same floor or in the same house as other students in the LLC, so they'll be your neighbors and your classmates.

These communities are a great way to connect with students and faculty who share your passions, broaden your horizons, and act as a member of a vibrant and collaborative living-learning experience.

THE IMPORTANCE OF INTERNSHIPS IN COLLEGE

by Evan Kilgore, Special Projects Coordinator, Grace College

During college, immersive internships are essential to successful outcomes after graduation. Classroom environments may involve you with discussion, debate, and peer interaction, but it's important to seek opportunities for you to apply and develop the academic concepts you're learning in a professional setting as well.

Learning, growing, and most importantly, preparing for life and a career, is what college is all about. Here are a few reasons why college internships are so vital to aid in your career readiness, such as an internship at The Box Tiger Music!

Career Development

Generally, an internship is a task-specific exchange of service for experience between a student and a business. Within internships, classroom concepts suddenly become real tools of the trade as you interact and learn in a professional setting. Internship experiences are formal, formative, and foundational to your career.

Developing your knowledge of workplace collaboration, business etiquette, and strong communication tactics are among the vital "soft skills" that can only be learned on the job. In this way, internships in your area of study will build your résumé and teach you instrumental, career-developing qualities.

Character Growth

Not only do internships help develop your professionalism, but they also encourage character growth. Many employers even value personal qualities over professional knowledge when it comes to employment.

Characteristics like integrity, commitment, and self-motivation are several traits that are learned through an internship. In an article by Chris Myers, a contributing writer for Forbes, he recounts his own experience as an intern as well as the ways it shaped his character. Over the course of his experience, he found a mentor who helped him learn to be humble and indispensable to his employers. These lessons remained with him even as he grew and became a business owner with his own interns. When you leave school, employers will want college graduates with more than just knowledge; they'll want those who possess the individual qualities needed to get the job done well.

Sharpening one's competence is a major benefit of an internship, but building character in the workplace is an equally great advantage. Internships are the perfect place to learn, test your skills, and grow personally, so you can step out and apply what you know to the real world.

A Door to Opportunity

Internships are foundational in preparing students for the workforce and providing opportunities after graduation. Most employers seek career-ready college graduates who have been equipped with prior experiences and skills in a given field.

According to a recent survey by the National Association of Colleges and Employers, the starting annual salary for college graduates who completed a paid internship and were employed in a private, for-profit company was $53,521, while those who did not complete an internship started with an average of $38,572.

The analysis also found that 72.2% percent of college graduates with internship experience received a job offer in contrast to only 36.5% for those who did not complete one

Real-Life Application

At Grace College in Winona Lake, IN, students complete 12 "field" credits as part of their "Applied Learning" requirement. These credits are earned through internships, job-shadowing, research fellowships, student teaching programs, and many more career-developing positions—all of which benefit students as they expand their professional portfolios.

Here are what several Grace students have said about the internship experiences they've been a part of and how those work opportunities validated what they've learned in the classroom.

"I've always heard that internships are incredible learning opportunities, but didn't realize how true that is until mine. The number-one thing I learned is that soft skills and integrity are the most important factors in business."

– *Joel Wesco (B.S. Accounting 2017), Audit and Tax Intern at Crowe Horwath LLP, in Indiana*

"I benefited greatly completing my bachelor's and master's while interning and learned so much about the medical device industry as well as hip and knee replacements. I'm excited to continue in my new role (with the company I interned for) and am thankful for my internship. It helped me get my foot in the door and land my full-time position after graduation, I believe."

– *Cody Sprague (B.S. Biology 2017, M.S. Orthopaedic Regulatory and Clinical Affairs 2017), Paid Intern in Clinical Affairs at Zimmer Biomet in Warsaw, IN*

"I grew not only in my business skills, but also as a young professional, and I am so thankful for the opportunity to learn from such a talented team in the marketing and networking field."

– *Gabrielle Lawrence (B.S. Marketing 2017), Marketing Intern at Hello Events in Nashville, TN*

Deliberative preparation for a rewarding career is a must. Internships are beneficial because they help develop your professional aptitude, strengthen personal character, and provide a greater door to opportunity. By investing in internships, you'll give yourself the broadest spectrum of opportunity when seeking and applying for a job after college.

TRADING SPACES: A PACKING LIST OF ESSENTIAL STUFF FOR YOUR DORM ROOM

Many families know some of the usual items that a college student should bring, but it's hard to think of everything. Of course, personal items from home will aid in the transition, but you'll need more than photos and a teddy bear to get through the year.

Before you buy or pack anything, be sure to check with your school about what items are and are not allowed. Most schools have to be very careful about health and safety regulations, and rules differ from place to place. One school might not allow microwaves; another might have specific regulations about what size of refrigerator is allowed. (See more examples below).

Also, consider talking to a current student about what to pack. They can tell you about the "don't bothers" and "must-haves" for the residences at your new college. They may even know specifics about your building that will be a real help.

In addition, be sure to carefully complete and review your housing contract. By omitting certain information or sending it back incomplete, this could alter your living situation very dramatically. Once you arrive on campus, you could be locked into a living situation you do not care for simply because of a few errors.

In the meantime, here's a list to help you start planning your move. Good luck!

BED AND BEDDING

☐ Sheets. Make sure that you know whether your bed will be regular or extra long. Many college dorms have twin extra-long beds so you will have to buy special sheet sets.

☐ Comforter and/or quilts, blankets, etc. Consider bringing sturdy, easy-to-wash items.

☐ Towels: bath, washcloths and hand towels. Consider marking your name on a tag in permanent marker, especially if you have plain white or other "anonymous" towels.

☐ Alarm clock.

☐ Extra pillow(s) if you will lounge/study on the bed.

HEALTH AND GROOMING

☐ Shower shoes, especially if you will be sharing a shower.

☐ All necessary toiletries (toothbrush, toothpaste, soap, shampoo, and all grooming/cosmetic items). Since space will be cramped, consider buying smaller sizes, at least at first.

☐ Shower bucket/basket/caddy to carry items.

☐ Those who wear makeup might want a portable makeup kit/box, as it may not be feasible to store cosmetics near where the mirror is.

☐ Bathrobe (Especially important if the shower is down the hall!).

☐ Prescription medicines and copies of each prescription.

☐ First-Aid kit, including basic adhesive bandages, disinfectant, aspirin, etc. (This will cut down on trips to the health center!).

CLOTHES AND LAUNDRY

☐ Clothes. Your space will be limited, so only bring what you think you will wear. You can always bring more back to school after your first trip home.

☐ Weather-appropriate outer clothes. You will probably be walking to class; be sure your coat or jacket is right for the climate.

☐ Laundry basket and/or bag.

☐ Laundry detergent, dryer sheets, stain remover stick.

DECOR

☐ Posters. You will probably also be able to buy some of these on campus.

☐ Sticky wall mounts and removable adhesive hooks. Most schools do not allow you to put nails in the walls, so you will need other ways to hang your décor.

☐ Personal pictures, photos, and other favorite items. Avoid heavy frames, since you may not be able to hang them.

☐ Curtains and spring rod, if you like them and your school allows them. Some people like this touch in their room.

☐ Rugs or a piece of carpet if you have vinyl floors, which can be cold and uncomfortable. Check to see if the school allows this.

STUDY STUFF

☐ A sturdy backpack or book bag for everyday use.

☐ Computer and any necessary supplies/accessories. Some schools also offer great discounts on or provide computers, printers, and other electronic necessities.

☐ School supplies, including a calendar or planner as well as basic pens, paper, pencils, and notebooks.

☐ Dry-erase board and marker. You'll want this so people can leave you messages.

FURNISHINGS

☐ Storage for under the bed.

☐ Other storage or organization units. A few stacking plastic crates will come in handy.

☐ Folding chairs for cheap extra seating.

☐ Trashcan and trash bags.

☐ Lamps. Many schools have special fire-safety rules about the size and power of lamps that are allowed, so make sure your lamps are within regulations.

☐ Cleaning supplies. Find out what areas you will be responsible for cleaning. If you have a private or semi-private bathroom, for example, you may be responsible for cleaning the shower and/or toilet.

☐ If you have hard floors, bring a broom. If you have carpet, consider bringing a small, light vacuum. Your floor will get pretty disgusting without it!

☐ Fan (box or floor). Depending on the climate control in the building, you may want this to adjust to your individual needs.

ELECTRONICS AND EQUIPMENT

☐ Multiple outlet surge protectors and extension cords. Check out school safety regulations about allowed cords.

☐ TV, stereo/speakers, DVD player, game systems, tablets, etc.

FOOD AND SNACKS

☐ Small refrigerator. During the first week of school, schools may have refrigerators and microwaves to rent or buy.

☐ Microwave, hot plate, coffeemaker, etc. Check first—many schools have especially strict safety regulations about these items. Also, find out what communal kitchen space may be available.

☐ A few unbreakable dishes: plastic cups, microwave-safe bowl, and small plastic food storage tubs.

☐ A small bottle of dish soap, scrubber, small dishtowel

☐ Snacks: popcorn, chips, sodas, etc. Check about food regulations.

MISC.

☐ A small and inexpensive tool kit.

☐ A large backpack or shoulder bag for possible weekend trips you might take.

COLLEGES OF DISTINCTION BUSINESS FIELD OF STUDY BADGE

We are excited to spotlight already recognized Colleges of Distinction that deliver leading-edge business programs. Economics have always been vital to undergraduate studies, but society is increasingly shaped as much by entrepreneurship and corporate stewardship as it is by public policy, law, education, the humanities, etc.

EARNING A BUSINESS FIELD OF STUDY BADGE

Institutions that earn the Business Field of Study badge exhibit high-impact practices in both their overall undergraduate programs and in their business programs. These institutions also meet criteria specific to their business programs:

Stability: The business program has been active at least 10 years, has shown stability in the number of degrees awarded annually, and is nationally accredited by such organizations as:

- AACSB: Association of Advance Collegiate Schools of Business
- ACBSP: Accreditation Council for Business Schools and Programs
- IACSB: International Accreditation Council for Schools of Business

Multidisciplinary: The program features three or more distinct disciplines, such as marketing, accounting, finance, management, entrepreneurship, IT management, corporate strategy, etc. Students learn to approach business problems with critical thinking rooted in both quantitative and qualitative approaches, and they possess such critical soft skills as leadership, public speaking, information literacy, etc.

Practical experience: The program requires that its students gain experiences working with real-world firms, whether that be through internships, practica, consulting projects, etc.

Collaborative learning: The program emphasizes collaboration among students through methods like case-method teaching, business plan competitions, etc. Students also collaborate with non-business majors, e.g., pre-law, engineering, pre-med, etc.

Business Ethics: These programs graduate students grounded in business ethics. They learn how a firm's obligations extend beyond its shareholders and to a greater ecosystem of customers, employees, investors, communities, suppliers, and the environment.

Dedicated Advising and Counseling: The program has academic advisors/counselors and career counselors dedicated exclusively to Business majors.

High-Impact Practices that are tailored to business majors.

Industry connections: Whether through job placement, internships, co-op opportunities, advisory councils or networking activities, the institution provides students with numerous avenues to build career connections in the field.

ALABAMA
Samford University
Spring Hill College
University of Alabama at Birmingham
University of Montevallo

ARIZONA
Ottawa University-Arizona

ARKANSAS
Arkansas Tech University
Harding University
John Brown University
Lyon College
University of Central Arkansas

CALIFORNIA
Azusa Pacific University
California Polytechnic State University
California State University Long Beach
Chapman University
Concordia University Irvine
Dominican University of California
Holy Names University
La Sierra University
Loyola Marymount University
Mills College
Notre Dame de Namur University
Saint Mary's College of California
Santa Clara University
University of La Verne
University of Redlands
University of San Diego
Whittier College
Woodbury University

COLORADO
Colorado Christian University
Colorado Mesa University
University of Denver
University of Northern Colorado
Western Colorado University

CONNECTICUT
Albertus Magnus College
Eastern Connecticut State University
Fairfield University
Sacred Heart University
University of Hartford
University of New Haven

FLORIDA
Barry University
Flagler College
Florida Institute of Technology
Florida Southern College
Lynn University
Rollins College
Southeastern University
University of Miami
University of South Florida

GEORGIA
Georgia Gwinnett College
Georgia State University
Mercer University
Oglethorpe University
Piedmont College
Reinhardt University
University of West Georgia

IDAHO
Northwest Nazarene University
The College of Idaho

ILLINOIS
Aurora University
Benedictine University
Concordia University Chicago
Elmhurst College
Greenville University
Illinois State University
Illinois Wesleyan University
Judson University
Lewis University
Loyola University Chicago
MacMurray College
McKendree University
North Park University
Olivet Nazarene University
Saint Xavier University
The University of Illinois at Chicago
Trinity Christian College
Trinity International University
University of St. Francis

INDIANA
Anderson University
Ball State University
Bethel University Indiana
Butler University
Hanover College
Taylor University

University of Indianapolis
Taylor University
University of Indianapolis

IOWA
Briar Cliff University
Buena Vista University
Drake University
Mount Mercy University
Northwestern College
University of Dubuque

KANSAS
Baker University
Emporia State University
Friends University
Kansas Wesleyan University
McPherson College
Ottawa University
Southwestern College

KENTUCKY
Lindsey Wilson College
University of Louisville
University of the Cumberlands

LOUISIANA
Centenary College of Louisiana
Louisiana Tech University
Tulane University
University of New Orleans

MAINE
Maine Maritime Academy
University of Maine

MARYLAND
Frostburg State University
Loyola University Maryland
Notre Dame of Maryland University
Salisbury University

MASSACHUSETTS
Assumption College
Curry College
Dean College
Emmanuel College
Lasell University
Nichols College
Northeastern University
Suffolk University
University of Massachusetts Lowell
Western New England University
Worcester Polytechnic Institute

MICHIGAN
Adrian College
Alma College
Concordia University Ann Arbor
Cornerstone University
Siena Heights University
Spring Arbor University

MINNESOTA
Bethel University Minnesota
University of Minnesota Duluth
University of St. Thomas

MISSISSIPPI
Belhaven University
Millsaps College

MISSOURI
Evangel University
Fontbonne University
Missouri State University
Missouri University of Science and Technology
Saint Louis University
Truman State University

MONTANA
Carroll College
Rocky Mountain College

NEBRASKA
Concordia University, Nebraska
Creighton University
Nebraska Wesleyan University
Wayne State College

NEW HAMPSHIRE
Rivier University
University of New Hampshire

NEW JERSEY
Caldwell University
College of Saint Elizabeth
Georgian Court University
Monmouth University
Ramapo College of New Jersey
Rider University
Rutgers University-Newark
Seton Hall University
Stevens Institute of Technology
The College of New Jersey

NEW YORK
Adelphi University
Baruch College
Binghamton University
College of Mount Saint Vincent
Concordia College New York
Daemen College
Dominican College
Elmira College
Fordham University
Hartwick College
Iona College
Keuka College
LIU Brooklyn
LIU Post
Manhattan College
Manhattanville College
New York Institute of Technology
Niagara University
SUNY Geneseo
SUNY New Paltz
SUNY Oswego
St. John Fisher College
St. John's University
St. Joseph's College, New York
St. Thomas Aquinas College
The King's College
The Sage Colleges
University at Albany, SUNY
Utica College

NORTH CAROLINA
Appalachian State University
Belmont Abbey College
Elon University
Gardner-Webb University
High Point University
Lees-McRae College
Lenoir-Rhyne University
Meredith College
Pfeiffer University
University of Mount Olive
University of North Carolina at Greensboro
University of North Carolina–Wilmington
Wake Forest University
Western Carolina University

NORTH DAKOTA
University of Mary

OHIO
Defiance College
Hiram College
Miami University–Oxford
Mount St. Joseph University
Ohio Dominican University
Otterbein University
University of Cincinnati
University of Dayton
Walsh University
Wilmington College
Xavier University

OKLAHOMA
Oklahoma Baptist University
Oklahoma Christian University
Oral Roberts University
University of Science and Arts of Oklahoma
University of Tulsa

OREGON
Corban University
Eastern Oregon University
George Fox University
Pacific University
Portland State University
University of Portland
Warner Pacific University

PENNSYLVANIA
Cabrini University
California University of Pennsylvania
Carlow University
Cedar Crest College
Chatham University
Chestnut Hill College
Drexel University
Elizabethtown College
Geneva College
La Roche University
Lycoming College
Mansfield University of Pennsylvania
Mercyhurst University
Messiah College
Millersville University
Mount Aloysius College
Rosemont College
Saint Francis University
Saint Joseph's University

Seton Hill University
Shippensburg University
Slippery Rock University
Susquehanna University
University of Pittsburgh at Bradford
University of Pittsburgh at Johnstown
University of Scranton
Villanova University
Waynesburg University
West Chester University
Wilson College
York College of Pennsylvania

RHODE ISLAND
Providence College
University of Rhode Island

SOUTH CAROLINA
Coastal Carolina University
College of Charleston
Furman University
Presbyterian College
The Citadel
University of South Carolina Aiken
University of South Carolina Upstate

TENNESSEE
Belmont University
Carson-Newman University
Christian Brothers University
Freed-Hardeman University
King University
Lipscomb University
Maryville College
Middle Tennesee State University
Rhodes College

TEXAS
Abilene Christian University
Angelo State University
Dallas Baptist University
Hardin-Simmons University
Lubbock Christian University
McMurry University
Schreiner University
St. Edward's University
St. Mary's University
Texas Christian University
The University of Texas at Dallas
The University of Texas at San Antonio
Trinity University
University of Houston
University of Mary Hardin-Baylor
University of the Incarnate Word

UTAH
Southern Utah University
Westminster College of Utah

VERMONT
Castleton University
Champlain College
University of Vermont

VIRGINIA
Averett University
College of William & Mary
Emory & Henry College
James Madison University
Mary Baldwin University
Old Dominion University
Radford University
Sweet Briar College
The University of Virginia's College at Wise
University of Mary Washington
University of Richmond
Virginia Wesleyan University

WASHINGTON
Eastern Washington University
Gonzaga University
Northwest University
Seattle Pacific University
Seattle University
Western Washington University

WEST VIRGINIA
Davis & Elkins College

WISCONSIN
Cardinal Stritch University
Concordia University Wisconsin
Marquette University
Northland College
St. Norbert College
University of Wisconsin-La Crosse
University of Wisconsin-Parkside
University of Wisconsin-Stout
University of Wisconsin-Whitewater
Viterbo University
Wisconsin Lutheran College

COLLEGES OF DISTINCTION EDUCATION FIELD OF STUDY BADGE

We are excited to spotlight already recognized Colleges of Distinction that deliver leading-edge education programs. As education transforms alongside the constant changes in technology, public policy, employer demands, and more, the U.S. is in desperate need of educators who are attuned to today's rapid shifts.

EARNING AN EDUCATION FIELD OF STUDY BADGE

Institutions that earn the Education Field of Study badge exhibit high-impact practices in both their overall undergraduate programs as well as their education programs. They further excel in the way they meet criteria specific to their Education programs:

Stability: The program has been in existence over 10 years, has regional accreditation, and has shown stability in the number of degrees awarded annually.

Multidisciplinary: Students specialize or cross-train in distinct education fields, such as early childhood, elementary, secondary, etc.

Practical experience: Preferably as early as the first year, students are exposed to varied real-world teaching experiences: urban and rural, wealthy and economically challenged, large and small, etc.

Non-Education Specialization: The program either requires or strongly encourages students to graduate with a minor, emphasis, specialization, etc., in a subject that they would teach as a professional educator.

Dedicated Advising and Counseling: The program has academic advisors/counselors as well as career counselors who are dedicated exclusively to Education majors.

High-Impact Practices that are tailored to Education majors.

Industry connections: Whether through job placement, internships, co-op opportunities, advisory councils, or networking activities, the institution provides students with a multifaceted approach to build career connections in their field.

ALABAMA
Samford University
University of Alabama at Birmingham
University of Montevallo

ARIZONA
Ottawa University-Arizone
Prescott College

ARKANSAS
Arkansas Tech University
Harding University
John Brown University
Lyon College

CALIFORNIA
Azusa Pacific University
California State University Long Beach
Chapman University
Dominican University of California
Loyola Marymount University
Mills College
Santa Clara University
Simpson University
University of La Verne
University of Redlands

COLORADO
Colorado Christian University
Colorado Mesa University
Naropa University
University of Denver
Western Colorado University

CONNECTICUT
Albertus Magnus College
Eastern Connecticut State University
Sacred Heart University
University of Hartford

FLORIDA
Barry University
Flagler College
Florida Southern College
Lynn University
Rollins College
Southeastern University
University of Miami
University of South Florida

GEORGIA
Brenau University
Georgia Gwinnett College
Mercer University
Piedmont College
Reinhardt University
University of West Georgia

IDAHO
Northwest Nazarene University
The College of Idaho

ILLINOIS
Aurora University
Benedictine University
Concordia University Chicago
Elmhurst College
Greenville University
Illinois State University
Illinois Wesleyan University
Judson University
Lewis University
Loyola University Chicago
McKendree University
North Park University
Olivet Nazarene University
Saint Xavier University
Trinity Christian College
Trinity International University
University of St. Francis

INDIANA
Anderson University
Ball State University
Bethel University Indiana
Butler University
DePauw University
Franklin College
Hanover College
Taylor University
University of Indianapolis

IOWA
Briar Cliff University
Buena Vista University
Drake University
Mount Mercy University
Northwestern College
St. Ambrose University
University of Dubuque

KANSAS
Baker University
Emporia State University
Friends University
Kansas Wesleyan University
McPherson College
Ottawa University
Southwestern College

KENTUCKY
Lindsey Wilson College
University of Louisville
University of the Cumberlands

LOUISIANA
Centenary College of Louisiana
Louisiana Tech University
University of New Orleans

MAINE
Unity College
University of Maine

MARYLAND
Frostburg State University
Loyola University Maryland
Notre Dame of Maryland University
Salisbury University
St. Mary's College of Maryland

MASSACHUSETTS
Assumption College
Curry College
Emmanuel College
Lasell University
Stonehill College
Suffolk University
University of Massachusetts Lowell
Western New England University

MICHIGAN
Albion College
Alma College
Concordia University Ann Arbor
Cornerstone University
Siena Heights University
Spring Arbor University

MINNESOTA
Bethel University Minnesota
University of Minnesota Duluth
University of Minnesota Morris
University of St. Thomas

MISSISSIPPI
Belhaven University
Millsaps College

MISSOURI
Evangel University
Fontbonne University
Missouri State University
Saint Louis University
Stephens College

MONTANA
Rocky Mountain College

NEBRASKA
College of Saint Mary
Concordia University, Nebraska
Creighton University
Nebraska Wesleyan University
Wayne State College

NEW HAMPSHIRE
Rivier University
University of New Hampshire

NEW JERSEY
Caldwell University
College of Saint Elizabeth
Georgian Court University
Ramapo College
Rider University
Seton Hall University
The College of New Jersey

NEW YORK
Adelphi University
Canisius College
College of Mount Saint Vincent
Concordia College New York
Daemen College
Dominican College
Elmira College
Iona College
Keuka College
LIU Post
Long Island University Brooklyn
Manhattan College
Manhattanville College
Niagara University
SUNY Geneseo
SUNY New Paltz

SUNY Oswego
St. John Fisher College
St. John's University
St. Thomas Aquinas College
The Sage Colleges
University at Albany, SUNY
Utica College
Wells College

NORTH CAROLINA
Appalachian State University
Elon University
Gardner-Webb University
High Point University
Lees-McRae College
Lenoir-Rhyne University
Meredith College
Pfeiffer University
University of Mount Olive
University of North Carolina at Greensboro
University of North Carolina–Wilmington
Wake Forest University
Western Carolina University

NORTH DAKOTA
University of Mary

OHIO
Defiance College
Denison University
Hiram College
Miami University–Oxford
Mount St. Joseph University
Ohio Dominican University
Otterbein University
University of Cincinnati
University of Dayton
University of Mount Union
Walsh University
Wilmington College
Wittenberg University
Xavier University

OKLAHOMA
Oklahoma Baptist University
Oklahoma Christian University
Oral Roberts University
University of Science and Arts of Oklahoma
University of Tulsa

OREGON
Corban University
Eastern Oregon University
George Fox University
Pacific University
Portland State University
University of Portland
Warner Pacific University

PENNSYLVANIA
Cabrini University
California University of Pennsylvania
Carlow University
Cedar Crest College
Chatham University
Chestnut Hill College
Drexel University
Elizabethtown College
Geneva College
La Roche University
Lycoming College
Mansfield University of Pennsylvania
Mercyhurst University
Messiah College
Millersville University
Mount Aloysius College
Rosemont College
Saint Francis University
Saint Joseph's University
Seton Hill University
Shippensburg University
Slippery Rock University
Susquehanna University
University of Pittsburgh at Bradford
University of Pittsburgh at Johnstown
University of Scranton
Villanova University
Waynesburg University
West Chester University of Pennsylvania
Wilson College
York College of Pennsylvania

RHODE ISLAND
University of Rhode Island

SOUTH CAROLINA
Coastal Carolina University
College of Charleston
Furman University
Presbyterian College
The Citadel
University of South Carolina Aiken
University of South Carolina Upstate

TENNESSEE
Belmont University
Carson-Newman University
Christian Brothers University
King University
Lipscomb University
Maryville College
Middle Tennessee State University
Rhodes College

TEXAS
Abilene Christian University
Angelo State University
Dallas Baptist University
Hardin-Simmons University
Lubbock Christian University
McMurry University
Schreiner University
Southern Methodist University
St. Edward's University
St. Mary's University
Texas Christian University
University of Mary Hardin-Baylor
University of the Incarnate Word

UTAH
Southern Utah University
Westminster College of Utah

VERMONT
Castleton University
Champlain College
University of Vermont

VIRGINIA
Averett University
College of William & Mary
Emory & Henry College
James Madison University
Mary Baldwin University
Old Dominion University
Radford University
Sweet Briar College
The University of Virginia's College at Wise
Virginia Wesleyan University

WASHINGTON
Eastern Washington University
Gonzaga University
Northwest University
Seattle University
Western Washington University

WEST VIRGINIA
Davis & Elkins College

WISCONSIN
Cardinal Stritch University
Concordia University Wisconsin
Marquette University
Northland College
St. Norbert College
University of Wisconsin-La Crosse
University of Wisconsin-Parkside
University of Wisconsin-Stout
University of Wisconsin-Whitewater
Viterbo University
Wisconsin Lutheran College

COLLEGES OF DISTINCTION ENGINEERING FIELD OF STUDY BADGE

We are excited to spotlight already recognized Colleges of Distinction that deliver leading-edge Engineering programs. The United States' need for graduates trained in Sciences, Technology, Engineering and Math (STEM) continues to escalate with projected employment shortages topping 2.5 million next year.

EARNING AN ENGINEERING FIELD OF STUDY BADGE

Institutions that earn the Engineering Field of Study badge exhibit high-impact practices in both their overall undergraduate programs as well as their Engineering programs. They further excel in the way they meet criteria specific to their Engineering programs:

Stability: The program has been in existence for 10 years or more, has shown stability in the number of degrees awarded annually, and is nationally accredited by ABET (Accreditation Board for Engineering and Technology).

Practical Experience: All students participate in and receive credit for any combination of internships, practica, co-op programs, etc.

Multidisciplinary: The program offers distinct majors in such areas as civil engineering, electrical engineering, industrial engineering, computer engineering, biomedical engineering, mechanical, etc.

Collaborative work: The program hosts a number of team-based experiences, such as hackathons, in which students work together to deliver a technology or product with clear societal benefits.

Soft Skills: The program is invests in graduating engineering leaders, not just engineers, by emphasizing competencies in communication, collaboration and leadership.

Facilities Investment: The program must show sustained, significant investments in facilities and physical assets (such as hardware, software, etc.) to reflect its commitment to enabling skill development in a state-of-the-art environment.

Dedicated Advising and Counseling: The program should have academic advisors/counselors and career counselors who are focused exclusively on this program's majors.

High-Impact Practices that are tailored to Engineering majors.

Industry connections: Whether through job placement, internships, co-op opportunities, advisory councils or networking activities, the institution provides students with a multifaceted approach to build career connections in the field.

ALABAMA
University of Alabama at Birmingham

ARKANSAS
Harding University
John Brown University

CALIFORNIA
California Polytechnic State University
California State University, Long Beach
Santa Clara University
University of California, Santa Barbara
University of California, Santa Cruz
University of San Diego

COLORADO
Colorado School of Mines
University of Denver

CONNECTICUT
Fairfield University
University of Hartford
University of New Haven

FLORIDA
Florida Institute of Technology
University of Miami
University of South Florida

GEORGIA
Mercer University

IDAHO
Northwest Nazarene University

ILLINOIS
Greenville University
North Park University
Olivet Nazarene University
The University of Illinois at Chicago

INDIANA
Hanover College
Rose-Hulman Institute of Technology
University of Indianapolis

IOWA
St. Ambrose University

KENTUCKY
University of Louisville

LOUISIANA
Louisiana Tech University
Tulane University
University of New Orleans

MAINE
Maine Maritime Academy
University of Maine

MARYLAND
Frostburg State University
Loyola University Maryland

MASSACHUSETTS
Northeastern University
University of Massachusetts Lowell
Wentworth Institute of Technology
Western New England University
Worcester Polytechnic Institute

MICHIGAN
Michigan Technological University

MINNESOTA
University of Minnesota Duluth
University of St. Thomas

MISSOURI
Missouri University of Science and Technology
Saint Louis University

MONTANA
Carroll College

NEW HAMPSHIRE
University of New Hampshire

NEW JERSEY
Stevens Institute of Technology
The College of New Jersey

NEW YORK
Binghamton University
Manhattan College
New York Institute of Technology
Rensselaer Polytechnic Institute (RPI)
SUNY New Paltz
Stony Brook University
University at Albany, SUNY

NORTH CAROLINA
Western Carolina University

OHIO
Miami University–Oxford
Otterbein University
University of Cincinnati
University of Dayton
University of Mount Union

OKLAHOMA
Oklahoma Christian University
Oral Roberts University
University of Tulsa

OREGON
George Fox University
Portland State University
University of Portland

PENNSYLVANIA
California University of Pennsylvania
Drexel University
Elizabethtown College
Geneva College
Lafayette College
Messiah College
Saint Francis University
Shippensburg University
University of Pittsburgh at Johnstown
Villanova University
York College of Pennsylvania

RHODE ISLAND
University of Rhode Island

SOUTH CAROLINA
The Citadel

TENNESSEE
Christian Brothers University
Lipscomb University

TEXAS
Abilene Christian University
Southern Methodist University
St. Mary's University
Texas Christian University
The University of Texas at Dallas
The University of Texas at San Antonio
University of Houston

UTAH
Southern Utah University

VERMONT
University of Vermont

VIRGINIA
James Madison University
Old Dominion University
Sweet Briar College

WASHINGTON
Eastern Washington University
Gonzaga University
Seattle Pacific University
Seattle University

WISCONSIN
Marquette University
University of Wisconsin-Stout

COLLEGES OF DISTINCTION NURSING FIELD OF STUDY BADGE

We are excited to spotlight already recognized Colleges of Distinction that deliver leading-edge Nursing programs. According to Bureau of Labor Statistics projections, there will be more than 1 million jobs for registered nurses by 2022. Vanderbilt University researchers report that the shortage in 2025 will be twice the size of any nurse shortage "since the introduction of Medicare and Medicaid in the mid-1960s."

EARNING A NURSING FIELD OF STUDY BADGE

Institutions that earn the Nursing Field of Study badge exhibit high-impact practices in both their overall undergraduate programs as well as their Nursing programs. They further excel in the way they meet criteria specific to their Nursing programs:

Stability: The program program has been active at least 10 years, has shown stability in the number of degrees awarded annually

Excellence: The program's faculty have earned awards and peer recognition for its experience and research, and is nationally accredited by such organizations as:

   ACEN: Accreditation Commission for Education in Nursing

   CCNE: Commission on Collegiate Nursing Education

Practical Experience: The program requires that students engage in residency or clinical work.

High Mastery Rates: A high percentage of the students regularly pass such standardized exams as the NCLEX, HESI A2, etc. Regional leadership in pass rates is also considered.

Dedicated Advising and Counseling: The program has academic advisors/counselors and career counselors who are dedicated exclusively to Nursing majors.

Liberal Arts Exposure: The program is supplemented by a general education curriculum that is multidisciplinary and based in the liberal arts. Such studies help ensure that students develop their problem solving, critical and out-of-the-box thinking skills, practice leadership, and understand a variety of worldviews and perspectives—all crucial factors that set nurses apart as the most compassionate and competent caretakers.

High-Impact Practices that are tailored to Nursing majors.

Industry connections: Whether through job placement, internships, co-op opportunities, advisory councils or networking activities, the institution provides students with a multifaceted approach to build career connections in the field.

ALABAMA
Samford University
Spring Hill College
University of Alabama at Birmingham

ARKANSAS
Harding University
John Brown University
University of Cental Arkansas

CALIFORNIA
Azusa Pacific University
California State University Long Beach
Dominican University of California
Holy Names University
Loyola Marymount University
Simpson University
University of San Diego

COLORADO
Colorado Christian University
Colorado Mesa University

CONNECTICUT
Fairfield University
Goodwin College
Sacred Heart University

FLORIDA
Barry University
Florida Southern College
Southeastern University
University of Miami
University of South Florida

GEORGIA
Brenau University
Georgia Gwinnett College
Mercer University
Piedmont College
University of West Georgia

IDAHO
Northwest Nazarene University

ILLINOIS
Aurora University
Elmhurst College
Greenville University
Illinois State University
Illinois Wesleyan University
Lewis University
Loyola University Chicago
MacMurray College
North Park University
Olivet Nazarene University
Saint Xavier University
The University of Illinois at Chicago
Trinity Christian College
University of St. Francis

INDIANA
Anderson University
Ball State University
Bethel University Indiana
University of Indianapolis

IOWA
Briar Cliff University
Mount Mercy University
Northwestern College
St. Ambrose University
University of Dubuque

KANSAS
Baker University
Emporia State University
Ottawa University

KENTUCKY
Lindsey Wilson College
University of Louisville

MAINE
University of Maine

MARYLAND
Frostburg State University
Notre Dame of Maryland University
Salisbury University

MASSACHUSETTS
Becker College
Curry College
Northeastern University
University of Massachusetts Lowell

MICHIGAN
Alma College
Concordia University Ann Arbor
Spring Arbor University

MINNESOTA
Bethel University Minnesota

MISSISSIPPI
Belhaven University

MISSOURI
Missouri State University
Saint Louis University
Truman State University

MONTANA
Carroll College

NEBRASKA
College of Saint Mary
Creighton University
Nebraska Wesleyan University

NEW HAMPSHIRE
Rivier University
University of New Hampshire

NEW JERSEY
Caldwell University
College of Saint Elizabeth
Georgian Court University
Monmouth University
Ramapo College
Seton Hall University
The College of New Jersey

NEW YORK
Adelphi University
Binghamton University
College of Mount Saint Vincent
Concordia College New York
Daemen College
Dominican College
Elmira College
Hartwick College
Keuka College
LIU Post
Long Island University Brooklyn
New York Institute of Technology
Niagara University
St. John Fisher College
St. Joseph's College, New York
The Sage Colleges
Utica College

NORTH CAROLINA
Appalachian State University
Gardner-Webb University
Lees-McRae College
Lenoir-Rhyne University
Pfeiffer University
University of North Carolina at Greensboro
University of North Carolina–Wilmington
Western Carolina University

NORTH DAKOTA
University of Mary

OHIO
Defiance College
Hiram College
Miami University–Oxford
Mount St. Joseph University
Otterbein University
University of Cincinnati
University of Mount Union
Walsh University
Wittenberg University
Xavier University

OKLAHOMA
Oklahoma Baptist University
Oklahoma Christian University
Oral Roberts University
University of Tulsa

OREGON
George Fox University
University of Portland

PENNSYLVANIA
Carlow University
Cedar Crest College
Drexel University
La Roche University
Mansfield University of Pennsylvania
Mercyhurst University
Messiah College
Millersville University
Mount Aloysius College
Saint Francis University
Slippery Rock University
University of Pittsburgh at Bradford
University of Pittsburgh at Johnstown
Villanova University
Waynesburg University
West Chester University of Pennsylvania
Wilson College
York College of Pennsylvania

RHODE ISLAND
University of Rhode Island

SOUTH CAROLINA
Coastal Carolina University
University of South Carolina Aiken
University of South Carolina Upstate

TENNESSEE
Belmont University
Carson-Newman University
Christian Brothers University
King University
Lipscomb University
Middle Tennessee State University

TEXAS
Abilene Christian University
Angelo State University
Dallas Baptist University
Hardin-Simmons University
Lubbock Christian University
McMurry University
Schreiner University
Texas Christian University
University of Mary Hardin-Baylor
University of the Incarnate Word

UTAH
Southern Utah University
Westminster College of Utah

VERMONT
Castleton University
University of Vermont

VIRGINIA
Averett University
James Madison University
Old Dominion University
Radford University
The University of Virginia's College at Wise

WASHINGTON
Eastern Washington University
Gonzaga University
Northwest University
Seattle Pacific University
Seattle University

WISCONSIN
Cardinal Stritch University
Concordia University Wisconsin
Marquette University
Viterbo University
Wisconsin Lutheran College

COLLEGES OF DISTINCTION CAREER DEVELOPMENT BADGE

What will it take to prepare students to be adaptable in an ever-changing career landscape? We are excited to spotlight already recognized Colleges of Distinction that are exceeding expectations in the area of career development, equipping students with the self-reflection, job market research, and networking skills needed for their lifelong career journey.

EARNING A CAREER DEVELOPMENT BADGE

Institutions with a Career Development badge not only exhibit high-impact practices in their undergraduate programs, but they also meet further criteria specific to career development and services:

Integrated Career Exploration and Preparation: The career services or development office is introduced during new- and transfer-student orientation and then re-introduced during the first semester. The office partners with academic departments to include their resources in the classroom and help guide students toward the services they should be seeking at different points throughout their academic career. Career and major exploration are integrated across all fields of study.

Accessible Programs and Training: The career office's services can be accessed 24/7 and by appointment for one-on-one counseling. These resources include, but are not limited to, self-assessments, résumé and cover letter writing, interviewing, and networking. The office also hosts events and workshops to help students gain feedback and job search skills.

Career-Centered Staff:

- Assessments – The institution offers both career and personal inventories to help students better understand themselves as well as their major and career interests. Whether career services are centralized or decentralized, the institution makes trained career counselors and/or coaches available to review every student's assessment.

- Employer Relations – The school has at least one dedicated staff member for employer relations and corporate partnerships. Furthermore, the university helps connect students and alumni through mentorship and internship programs. Alumni can use some or all services for free.

ALABAMA
Samford University
Spring Hill College
University of Alabama at Birmingham
University of Montevallo

ARKANSAS
Arkansas Tech University
Harding University
John Brown University
Lyon College
University of Central Arkansas

CALIFORNIA
California State University Long Beach
Chapman University
Concordia University Irvine
Dominican University of California
La Sierra University
Loyola Marymount University
Mills College
Notre Dame de Namur University
Saint Mary's College of California
University of California, Santa Barbara
University of California, Santa Cruz
University of La Verne
University of Redlands
University of San Diego
Whittier College
Woodbury University

COLORADO
Colorado Mesa University
Colorado School of Mines
University of Denver
University of Northern Colorado

CONNECTICUT
Albertus Magnus College
Eastern Connecticut State University
Fairfield University
Goodwin College
University of Hartford

FLORIDA
Barry University
Flagler College
Florida Institute of Technology
Lynn University
Southeastern University
University of Miami
University of South Florida

GEORGIA
Georgia Gwinnett College
Georgia State University
Mercer University
University of West Georgia

IDAHO
Northwest Nazarene University
The College of Idaho

ILLINOIS
Benedictine University
Elmhurst College
Greenville University
Illinois State University
Lewis University
Loyola University Chicago
North Park University
Saint Xavier University
The University of Illinois at Chicago
Trinity Christian College
University of St. Francis

INDIANA
Anderson University
Ball State University
Butler University
Franklin College
Hanover College

Rose-Hulman Institute of Technology
Taylor University
University of Indianapolis

IOWA
Drake University
Mount Mercy University
University of Dubuque

KANSAS
Emporia State University
Kansas Wesleyan University

KENTUCKY
Lindsey Wilson College
University of Louisville

LOUISIANA
Louisiana Tech University
Tulane University

MAINE
University of Maine

MARYLAND
Loyola University Maryland
Notre Dame of Maryland University
Salisbury University
St. Mary's College of Maryland

MASSACHUSETTS
Becker College
Curry College
Dean College
Emmanuel College
Lasell University
Nichols College
Northeastern University
Stonehill College
Suffolk University
University of Massachusetts Lowell
Wentworth Institute of Technology
Western New England University
Worcester Polytechnic Institute

MICHIGAN
Hillsdale College

MINNESOTA
Bethel University Minnesota
University of Minnesota Duluth
University of Minnesota Rochester
University of St. Thomas

MISSOURI
Missouri University of Science and Technology
Saint Louis University
Stephens College
Truman State University

NEBRASKA
College of Saint Mary
Creighton University
Nebraska Wesleyan University

NEW HAMPSHIRE
Rivier University

NEW JERSEY
Caldwell University
College of Saint Elizabeth
Georgian Court University
Kean University
Monmouth University
Ramapo College of New Jersey
Rider University
Rutgers University-Newark
Seton Hall University
Stevens Institute of Technology
The College of New Jersey

NEW YORK
Adelphi University
Baruch College
Binghamton University
College of Mount Saint Vincent
Concordia College New York
Elmira College
Fordham University
Hartwick College
Manhattan College
Manhattanville College
Niagara University
Rensselaer Polytechnic Institute (RPI)
SUNY New Paltz
SUNY Oswego
St. Francis College
St. John Fisher College
St. John's University
St. Thomas Aquinas College
Stony Brook University
The King's College
The Sage Colleges
University at Albany, SUNY
Utica College
Wells College

NORTH CAROLINA
Gardner-Webb University
High Point University
Meredith College
Pfeiffer University
University of North Carolina at Greensboro
University of North Carolina–Wilmington
Wake Forest University
Western Carolina University

OHIO
Denison University
Miami University–Oxford
Mount St. Joseph University
Ohio Dominican University
Otterbein University
University of Cincinnati
University of Mount Union
Walsh University
Wilmington College
Xavier University

OKLAHOMA
Oklahoma Baptist University
Oklahoma Christian University
University of Science and Arts of Oklahoma
University of Tulsa

OREGON
Corban University
Eastern Oregon University
George Fox University
Pacific University
University of Portland
Warner Pacific University

PENNSYLVANIA
Cabrini University
California University of Pennsylvania
Cedar Crest College
Chatham University
Drexel University
Duquesne University
Elizabethtown College
La Roche University
Lycoming College
Mercyhurst University
Messiah College
Millersville University
Mount Aloysius College
Saint Francis University
Saint Joseph's University

Seton Hill University
Shippensburg University
Slippery Rock University
University of Pittsburgh at Bradford
University of Pittsburgh at Johnstown
University of Scranton
Villanova University

RHODE ISLAND
University of Rhode Island

SOUTH CAROLINA
Coastal Carolina University
College of Charleston
Presbyterian College
The Citadel
University of South Carolina Aiken

TENNESSEE
Carson-Newman University
Christian Brothers University
Lipscomb University
Maryville College
Middle Tennessee State University
Rhodes College

TEXAS
Hardin-Simmons University
Lubbock Christian University
Schreiner University
Southern Methodist University
St. Mary's University
The University of Texas at Dallas
The University of Texas at San Antonio
Trinity University
University of Houston
University of the Incarnate Word

UTAH
Southern Utah University
Westminster College of Utah

VERMONT
Castleton University
Champlain College
University of Vermont

VIRGINIA
College of William & Mary
James Madison University
Mary Baldwin University
Old Dominion University
Radford University
Sweet Briar College
The University of Virginia's College at Wise
University of Mary Washington
University of Richmond
Virginia Wesleyan University

WASHINGTON
Eastern Washington University
Gonzaga University
Seattle Pacific University
Seattle University
Western Washington University

WISCONSIN
Concordia University Wisconsin
Marquette University
St. Norbert College
University of Wisconsin–Stout
University of Wisconsin–Whitewater

NAVIGATING COLLEGE PROFILES

SAMFORD UNIVERSITY

BIRMINGHAM, ALABAMA

Founded in 1841, Samford University is the largest independently supported university in the state of Alabama. The serene suburban campus, with its rolling hills and stately Georgian Colonial architecture, provides the ideal college environment. On top of that, Samford is only minutes away from Birmingham, a diverse metropolitan area of 1 million people that is rich in culture, history, and spirit.

A FIRE YOU CAN'T PUT OUT: The Reverend Fred Shuttlesworth once described the clamor for justice as "a fire you can't put out." Samford believes that faith challenges us t struggle for a better stat combining scholarship a partnerships, required C weekly opportunities for

GROWTH IN MIND; GR rigorous liberal arts edu students, faculty, and sta challenge and challenge through convocation pro and domestic missions

INTERNATIONAL STUD terms, Samford students China, or a host of other is based out of a renovat West End. This home is v famous cultural attractio

THE MAGIC CITY: Samf the school's serene subu the largest cities in the re biomedical research, hea

www.samford.edu
(800) 888-7218
admissions@samford.edu

STUDENT PROFILE
3,373 undergraduate students
97% of undergrad students are full time
66% female – 34% male
34% of students are from out of state
87% freshman retention rate

FACULTY PROFILE
12 to 1 student/faculty ratio

ADMISSIONS
Selectivity: 83%
SAT Ranges: E 550-650, M 530-630
ACT Ranges: C 23-29, M 22-27, E 24-31

TUITION & COST
Tuition: $29,640
Fees: $850
Room: $5,416
Board: $4,864

Out of State
This percent shows the amount of enrolled undergraduates who come from a different state (or country!) than the one in which the school is located.

Selectivity
Selectivity refers to the percent of applicants who were accepted into the school.

Tuition & Cost
These prices refer to the costs incurred for one year of attendance (before factoring in any financial aid). Listed are the overall tuition, any additional fees that are required, and the cost for living on campus (Room) and signing up for a meal plan (Board).

Undergraduate Students, Full Time, and Gender Breakdown
These numbers show the size of the overall undergraduate student body as well as the percent of all students who attend the school's classes as traditional, full time students (i.e. not online or part-time students). This gives a general idea of the amount and gender breakdown of students who make up the daily campus community.

Freshman Retention Rate
The retention rate indicates the percent of freshmen who enrolled in and returned to the school for their sophomore year.

Student/Faculty Ratio
The student-to-faculty ratio refers to the amount of students there are for every one professor. This can often help indicate how easy it is for professors to interact with their students on an individual level.

SAT & ACT Ranges
These numbers indicate the middle range of accepted students' SAT and ACT scores. Each range shows the 25th and 75th percentile scores of all the students who are enrolled at the school. The lower number means that 25% of admitted students received that score or lower, while the higher number means that 75% of admitted students received that score or lower. Half of the school's admitted students within the ranges, while the other half scored either higher or lower than them.

The 25th/75th percentile range helps show the general scores that were received by other students who applied, got accepted, and enrolled at the school.

E: Evidence-Based Reading & Writing
M: Math
C: ACT Composite Score

Badges
Every school is marked with a badge to indicate in which state it is located. Each Catholic, Christian, and Public school has its own affiliation badge as well (purely Private institutions do not have an extra badge).

Additional badges indicate whether Colleges of Distinction has given our extra seal of approval for the school's Career Development services as well as its Business, Education, Engineering, and/or Nursing programs.

SAMFORD UNIVERSITY

BIRMINGHAM, ALABAMA

Founded in 1841, Samford University is the largest independently supported university in the state of Alabama. The serene suburban campus, with its rolling hills and stately Georgian Colonial architecture, provides the ideal college environment. On top of that, Samford is only minutes away from Birmingham, a diverse metropolitan area of 1 million people that is rich in culture, history, and spirit.

A FIRE YOU CAN'T PUT OUT: The Reverend Fred Shuttlesworth once described the clamor for justice as "a fire you can't put out." Samford believes that faith challenges us to be "on fire" for justice. It provides light in the struggle for a better state, nation, and world. Some of the ways Samford is combining scholarship and faith to change the world include poverty relief partnerships, required Cultural Perspectives, courses, and more than 100 weekly opportunities for community service.

GROWTH IN MIND; GROWTH IN SPIRIT: Few universities offer both a rigorous liberal arts education and support for the spiritual life of their students, faculty, and staff. Samford understands that faith grows with challenge and challenges the faithful to grow. At Samford, faith grows through convocation programs, Christian student interest groups, and foreign and domestic missions

INTERNATIONAL STUDY: In any term, including the January and summer terms, Samford students study in England, Morocco, Spain, Brazil, Costa Rica, China, or a host of other countries. Samford's premiere international program is based out of a renovated Victorian home in the heart of London's famous West End. This home is within walking distance of some of the city's most famous cultural attractions.

THE MAGIC CITY: Samford students enjoy the best of both worlds on the school's serene suburban campus, which is only minutes from one of the largest cities in the region. Birmingham is an international center for biomedical research, healthcare, technology, banking, and communications.

www.samford.edu
(800) 888-7218
admissions@samford.edu

STUDENT PROFILE

3,373 undergraduate students

97% of undergrad students are full time

66% female – 34% male

34% of students are from out of state

87% freshman retention rate

FACULTY PROFILE

12 to 1 student/faculty ratio

ADMISSIONS

Selectivity: 83%

SAT Ranges: E 550-650, M 530-630

ACT Ranges: C 23-29, M 22-27, E 24-31

TUITION & COST

Tuition: $29,640

Fees: $850

Room: $5,416

Board: $4,864

SPRING HILL COLLEGE

MOBILE, ALABAMA

www.shc.edu
(251) 380-3030
admit@shc.edu

Across the liberal arts and sciences, the Spring Hill College's faculty and staff are committed to the Jesuit tradition of *"cura personalis,"* a care for the spiritual, social, and intellectual growth of each person. Spring Hill offers a multidimensional education that provides students from all faiths and backgrounds a foundation for a life of continuous learning and service. It is Alabama's first institution of higher learning, the third-oldest Jesuit college, and the fifth-oldest Catholic college in the United States.

LEAP: The LEAP Program (which stands for Leadership, Engagement and Awareness, and Personal Growth) connects academic learning to the larger world through course-related events and activities. Freshmen sign up for one introductory core course and continue to take LEAP courses that are based around a common theme. With this group of fellow freshmen, faculty, and peer mentors, students experience a sense of community as they learn together and engage with the world outside the classroom.

DONNELLY SCHOLARS: Second-generation college students usually have an advantage over first-generation students in that their parents already know about how to maneuver through the college system. The Donnelly Scholars program, however, aims to close the gap on that advantage so that all graduates may be equipped to become successful alumni.

FOLEY COMMUNITY SERVICE: The Foley Community Service Center partners with multiple elementary, middle, and high schools in the area. It also coordinates with other programs like area nursing homes and hospitals as well as eight environmental programs that tend to Alabama's coastal resources.

Through these partnerships with various organizations, service-learning courses are easily an intrinsic part of SHC's academic curriculum. Accounting students help local residents file their income taxes. Communication arts students develop complete marketing campaigns for local nonprofits. Nursing and teacher education students devote entire semesters to clinical groups or internships. Students explore the work they love, gain practical work experience, and provide a critical service to the community.

STUDENT PROFILE

1,252 undergraduate students

99% of undergrad students are full-time

61% female – 39% male

58% of students are from out of state

72% freshman retention rate

FACULTY PROFILE

13 to 1 student/faculty ratio

ADMISSIONS

Selectivity: 66%

SAT Ranges: E 505-595, M 510-590

ACT Ranges: C 20-25, M 18-24, E 20-27

TUITION & COST

Tuition: $38,190

Fees: $2,458

Room: $7,108

Board: 6,544

THE UNIVERSITY OF ALABAMA AT BIRMINGHAM

BIRMINGHAM, ALABAMA

THE UNIVERSITY OF ALABAMA AT BIRMINGHAM

As a leader among comprehensive public urban research universities with academic medical centers, the University of Alabama at Birmingham inspires and empowers students to change the world. UAB provides a high-quality education with the framework and common language for collaboration and academic success.

SECOND-YEAR EXPERIENCES: UAB acknowledges the stressful responsibilities thrown at second-year students, so its Second-Year Experiences program integrates an engaging, interactive platform to help sophomores stay on track and avoid the "sophomore slump." A few popular features of the SYE program include the SYE Global Learning Initiative, mentoring initiative, and the Outdoor Recreation Excursion Team.

REGIONS INSTITUTE FOR FINANCIAL EDUCATION: The Regions Institute for Financial Education recognizes financial stability as an active, ongoing process that involves awareness of and taking steps toward a more successful life. As a result, the Institute has developed a set of services to help students learn how to resolve their financial issues, including presentations, the Fee Forgiveness Program, peer coaching, financial counseling, and microloans.

BIRMINGHAM: There are so many things to see and do in Birmingham! Whether it's a peaceful hike on Ruffner Mountain, finding a nice picnic spot, or just embracing the wilderness at one of the parks, Birmingham has it all. And as one of the epicenters of Southern jazz, Birmingham is known for its live music tradition that lives in both historic and avant-garde venues.

"I always knew my career path wouldn't be the same as other people. With faculty help, I was networking at conferences and even taking a business class when it interested me." – *Physics alumna Christina Richey, Ph.D.*

www.uab.edu
(205) 934-4011

STUDENT PROFILE

13,134 undergraduate students

74% of undergrad students are full-time

59% female – 41% male

3% of students are from out of state

84% freshman retention rate

FACULTY PROFILE

19 to 1 student/faculty ratio

ADMISSIONS

Selectivity: 92%

SAT Ranges: E 440-630, M 550-740

ACT Ranges: C 21-28, M 21-26, E 22-31

TUITION & COST

Tuition (in-state): $8,328

Tuition (out-of-state): $19,032

Room: $7,532

Board: $4,150

UNIVERSITY OF MONTEVALLO

MONTEVALLO, ALABAMA

UNIVERSITY *of* **MONTEVALLO**

www.montevallo.edu
(205) 665-6030
admissions@
montevallo.edu

With a strong emphasis on undergraduate liberal studies, the University of Montevallo's cumulative experience is designed for students' intellectual and personal growth. Montevallo's vision is to offer academically capable students from all socio-demographic backgrounds an affordable, life-enriching "honors college" experience. Montevallo stresses community service and global awareness within an atmosphere of national, historic beauty and a tradition of innovative cultural expression.

INTERNSHIPS: UM offers a variety of opportunities for students to practice in a professional setting the skills and knowledge they acquire in the classroom. In some majors, applied experiences are central to the curriculum. This is the case for clinical assignments in social work and communication science disorders and for practice teaching in education.

In other majors, such as art, business, and communication studies, students may enroll in an internship for elective credit. Interns may be placed at agencies in the local community or may engage in applied work outside the state through programs such as the Washington Center, a government internship in Washington, D. C.

DIVERSITY: Inspired by the unique history of Montevallo, the University is dedicated to educational, cultural, and social programs designed to combat bias, bigotry, and racism. Montevallo also promotes intercultural dialogue and respect for diversity. There are a variety of opportunities including Korean Culture Club, Minority Student Union, National Association for Multicultural Education, and more Students are also encouraged to participate in various foreign studies courses and study abroad opportunities.

LEARNING COMMUNITIES: Falcon Scholars in Action is an honors program in which UM students serve clients in agencies and programs throughout Shelby County. Students selected are provided with a significant annual stipend in exchange for their service. Examples of services provided include GED/ACT/SAT preparation, tutoring, coordinating physical activities, and providing training in job skills, computer skills, and social skills.

STUDENT PROFILE

2,346 undergraduate students

90% of undergrad students are full-time

67% female – 33% male

78% freshman retention rate

FACULTY PROFILE

14 to 1 student/faculty ratio

ADMISSIONS

Selectivity: 64%

SAT Ranges: E 440-620, M 460-580

ACT Ranges: C 20-26, M 18-25, E 21-28

TUITION & COST

Tuition (in-state): $11,730

Tuition (out-of-state): $24,360

Fees: $670

Room: $6,280

Board: $2,750

OTTAWA UNIVERSITY-ARIZONA

SURPRISE, ARIZONA

Faculty at Ottawa University-Arizona are committed to helping students learn to grow, care for, and balance all aspects of their lives in order to *"prepare for a life of significance"* that is both personally fulfilling and outwardly impactful. OUAZ is blessed to draw upon the rich heritage of its founding institution in Kansas, which is imbued by the spirit of the Ottawa Indian Tribe, in tandem with Baptist missionaries, and has an unquenchable commitment to education. Opened in 2017, Ottawa University-Arizona is student centered, value priced, and technology enabled.

BEYOND THE CLASSROOM: In today's global society, students often hear, "The world is your classroom." At Ottawa University-Arizona, that means traveling abroad, working with inner-city children, and gaining insight from their fellow classmates' diverse backgrounds and experiences.

Other times, it means that the world is brought directly to the students through cultural events, speakers, conferences, and workshops. OUAZ believes that, by exposing students to a broad base of ideas, experiences, and people, they gain a better understanding of who they want to become.

PERSONAL GROWTH: OUAZ is so committed to the notion that students should develop work-ready and practical life skills that it has eliminated standard classes on Wednesdays through each 8-week term. During these "Personal Growth Days," Wednesdays are set aside for advising, tutoring, and private study in the morning. The remainder of the day is split into three parts, which include an impactful speaker presentation, a community dining experience, and "Adulting Workshops" that aim to hone student competencies in such areas as project management, leadership, negotiations, personal finance, research, conflict management, and much more.

PREPARED FOR THE FUTURE: Every student at Ottawa University-Arizona completes a Senior Core capstone course that requires research on social issues. Students must develop possible solutions to address their topics and take action to raise awareness. At OUAZ, students are provided every opportunity to make an impact on the world.

www.ottawa.edu/ouaz
(855) 546-1342
ouazadmiss@ottawa.edu

STUDENT PROFILE
605 undergraduate students

92% of undergrad students are full-time

43% female – 57% male

43% of students are from out of state

FACULTY PROFILE
14 to 1 student/faculty ratio

ADMISSIONS
Selectivity: 55%

TUITION & COST
Tuition: $26,500

Fees: $1,130

Room: $6,400

Board: $5,300

PRESCOTT COLLEGE

PRESCOTT, ARIZONA

Prescott College

At Prescott College, collaboration is emphasized over competition, and interdisciplinary inquiry proceeds alongside professional skill development. Courses are problem-based and solution-oriented; students work together to solve both local and global issues and help shape a more environmentally sustainable and socially just world. Each student can choose to be evaluated through grades and/or a holistic assessment of their competencies as they complete individualized programs of study. Through strong community connections and project-based learning, each student is deeply engaged in direct applications of their knowledge and skills.

PROJECTS ABROAD: At Prescott College's Dopoi Field Station in Kenya, Africa, students work alongside the Maasai people through the Maasai Community Partnership Project. Students participate in activism led by indigenous community members, learn from the perspectives of Maasai people, and become part of grassroots work for social and environmental policy change. Student research has directly contributed to lawsuit successes that have restored land rights for the Maasai.

DREAM COURSES: Rather than prescribing typical sequences of disciplinary courses, Prescott College faculty members expertly design interdisciplinary courses that are based in field- and community-based learning environments in which students develop their skills across multiple disciplines.

One flagship course suite is the Grand Canyon Semester, a field-based interdisciplinary program integrates Wilderness Expeditions & Recreation, Landscape Ecology & Public Lands Issues, and Resource Management & Conservation Leadership. Students spend a semester hiking and rafting the Grand Canyon, learning through research and service with park managers.

"This approach—to save the world one person, one canyon, one Ponderosa Pine at a time—is central to the Prescott College mission." *- Dan Garvey, Former Prescott College President*

www.prescott.edu
(877) 350-2100

STUDENT PROFILE

394 undergraduate students

76% of undergrad students are full-time

65% female – 35% male

67% of students are from out of state

72% freshman retention rate

FACULTY PROFILE

9 to 1 student/faculty ratio

ADMISSIONS

Selectivity: 95%

TUITION & COST

Tuition: $30,888

Fees: $1,665

Room: $6,990

Board: $800

ARKANSAS TECH UNIVERSITY

RUSSELLVILLE, ARKANSAS

www.atu.edu
(800) 582-6953
tech.enroll@atu.edu

Arkansas Tech University is working toward a better tomorrow. With an enrollment of just over 12,000, Arkansas Tech is the third-largest institution of higher learning in the state. One-on-one academic coaching and an academic advising center prove that students are never just a number, but part of a family that helps all students succeed. With leading programs in nursing, STEM, business, and more, Arkansas Tech is a place where students can chart a career path with the the resources to follow it through.

REDESIGNED FOR RESEARCH: Arkansas Tech offers undergraduates resources to apply for grants, connect with faculty, and get started on in-depth research proposals, which they can present at the annual Student Research Symposium. In addition to research outside of the classroom, faculty have started to redesign courses to place a greater emphasis on research and independent inquiry. Whatever students prefer to research, they are able to use direct their passion toward making the world a better place.

ON TRACK: Arkansas Tech's On Track program is a unique opportunity for students to get to know their classmates and supplement their coursework. On Track offers seven tracks: wellness, leadership, citizenship, global cultures, and career building. Within each track are several events—lectures, activities, workshops—through which students become qualified in that field.

Students in the program learn more about their campus and their classmates while giving back to the community around them through service and volunteering. Upon completion of all seven tracks, they are invited to apply for an all-expenses-paid trip with their classmates and faculty. Past sites have included Washington, D.C., and Seattle.

> "I knew engineering would be a challenge, but that hasn't stopped me. Here, I created a new organization and networking opportunities for women in STEM fields."
>
> – *Emily Torrealba*

STUDENT PROFILE

7,896 undergraduate students

81% of undergrad students are full-time

55% female — 45% male

4% of students are from out of state

70% freshman retention rate

FACULTY PROFILE

18 to 1 student/faculty ratio

ADMISSIONS

Selectivity: 90%

SAT Ranges: M 500-620

ACT Ranges: C 18-25, M 18-25, E 17-25

TUITION & COST

Tuition (in-state): $6,780

Tuition (out-of-state): 13,560

Fees: $2,288

Room: $4,542

Board: $3,328

HARDING UNIVERSITY

SEARCY, ARKANSAS

Harding University is a private, Christian, liberal arts university located in Searcy, Arkansas. Committed to the pursuit of academic excellence and the establishment of strong spiritual foundations, the University attracts students representing all 50 states and 54 nations and territories. Harding offers 10 undergraduate degrees in more than 100 majors and 14 pre-professional programs.

DAILY CHAPEL: For 30 minutes every weekday, the entire student body assembles for chapel—a time-honored tradition of worship, community building, and affirmation of Harding's identity as a Christian university. Led by the University president, this shared experience facilitates and strengthens the relationships within the Harding community. Times of joy, sadness, stress, and success are all felt and supported by the University's collective community.

AN ENTIRE MINOR ABROAD: Harding University in Zambia allows students to complete a health missions or medical missions minor in one semester. Students live in a compound that holds the George S. Benson Teachers College as well as an elementary and high school, medical clinic, orphanage, and a "haven" for infants and toddlers who have lost their mothers to AIDS. Classes include Tonga language lessons, African history and African literature, and group trips include safari tours in East Africa as well as Victoria Falls, Lake Victoria, and Kenya.

HU SQUARE 1: HU Square 1 provides student mentoring, learning enhancement seminars, and several other events and programs throughout the year in an effort to connect students to the necessary people, programs, and the essential resources for a successful collegiate career.

As a more personal aspect of the first-year experience, freshmen are matched with student mentors in their first semester. Students are sorted into groups by their Bible class during orientation and then led by peer guides. These upperclassman mentors enroll in freshman-level Bible classes in the fall and support students as they navigate their first semester.

www.harding.edu
(800) 477-4407
admissions@harding.edu

STUDENT PROFILE

4,184 undergraduate students

94% of undergrad students are full-time

55% female – 45% male

83% freshman retention rate

FACULTY PROFILE

14 to 1 student/faculty ratio

ADMISSIONS

Selectivity: 72%

SAT Ranges: E 530-650, M 520-630

ACT Ranges: C 22-28, M 21-27, E 22-31

TUITION & COST

Tuition: $18,690

Fees: $695

Room: $3,592

Board: $3,966

HENDRIX COLLEGE

CONWAY, ARKANSAS

www.hendrix.edu
(501) 450-1362
adm@hendrix.edu

At Hendrix, students work closely with faculty who are devoted to mentoring undergraduate students. Through the "Your Hendrix Odyssey Program," a rare combination of opportunities, resources, and research of a bigger university is achieved while maintaining the small intimate mentoring of a smaller school. Each student is encouraged to pursue their passions and interests not just in the classroom, but far beyond it.

ODYSSEY PROGRAM: *"You learn more when you do more."* That is the educational philosophy behind The Hendrix Odyssey, an exciting component to the curriculum. With six categories and plenty of flexibility, the Odyssey Program encourages all Hendrix students to embark on educational adventures that are personalized to their own interests and abilities. Odysseys come in all shapes and sizes; some students earn Odyssey credit through coursework, while others can benefit from involvement in selected campus activities and organizations.

Other students venture farther afield, engaging in Odysseys that take them off campus and around the world. All approved Odysseys earn transcript recognition. Even better, those who require special funding are eligible for Odyssey grants, which have totaled more than $2.8 million since the program's inception in 2005.

THE ENGAGED CITIZEN: The *"Engaged Citizen"* class is taught as a first-year, team-taught interdisciplinary seminar representing and introducing freshmen to the very heart of a liberal arts education. Courses with such themes as "Art and Spirit" and "Aliens, Robots, and Civilization" all employ unique strategies to explore what it means to be an engaged citizen.

CROSSINGS: *"Crossings"* links courses from different departments while also blending classroom education with hands-on experiences. Each Crossings program is a unique, broad-reading sequence of courses united under such topics as "Food, Language, and Identity" and "The Study of the Mind."

STUDENT PROFILE

1,238 undergraduate students

99% of undergrad students are full-time

52% female – 48% male

38% of students are from out of state

63% freshman retention rate

FACULTY PROFILE

11 to 1 student/faculty ratio

ADMISSIONS

Selectivity: 80%

SAT Ranges: E 560-710, M 540-700

ACT Ranges: C 24-31, M 24-29, E 25-34

TUITION & COST

Tuition: $43,720

Fees: $350

Room: $6,140

Board: $5,786

JOHN BROWN UNIVERSITY

SILOAM SPRINGS, ARKANSAS

Since 1919, John Brown University has educated students from across the globe in a distinctly Christian community, providing an academic, spiritual, and professional foundation for world-impacting careers. JBU enrolls more than 2,400 students from 38 states and 53 countries and is committed to providing quality academics within a distinctly Christian community.

SELF- AND WORLD DISCOVERY: The educational programs at JBU are designed to stimulate curiosity and new discovery. Every day, JBU students are exposed to thought-provoking lectures and interactive projects that prepare them for life after college. Designed to engage the Head, Heart, and Hand, JBU's Core Curriculum seeks to equip students to become lifelong learners, develop a discerning Christian faith, and participate in God's creative and redemptive purposes in the world through their vocation.

More strongly addressing the spiritual, social, and emotional goals of the Core, The Co-Curriculum includes the Chapel program, student organizations, counseling, the Career Development Center, the Academic Assistance Program, intramural sports, the Center for Healthy Relationships, and the student leadership programs.

GATEWAY SEMINAR IN CHRISTIAN SCHOLARSHIP: All freshmen enroll in a gateway course designed to introduce them to the purpose and method of Christian higher education and the distinctive mission of John Brown University. Through the exploration of a particular topic (such as poverty, The Chronicles of Narnia, the Holocaust, or film), students participate in the communal intellectual life and the application of a Christian worldview.

"Law school has always been in the back of my mind, but it didn't become an actual goal until after taking JBU political science classes such as Constitutional Law... As an attorney who is also a Christian, I can focus on my ability to advocate for truth and justice and seek reconciliation." – *Lauren Marsh*

www.jbu.edu
(479) 524-9500

STUDENT PROFILE

1,359 undergraduate students

99% of undergrad students are full-time

59% female – 41% male

57% of students are from out of state

82% freshman retention rate

FACULTY PROFILE

14 to 1 student/faculty ratio

ADMISSIONS

Selectivity: 76%

SAT Ranges: E 550-680, M 530-630

ACT Ranges: C 24-29, M 22-27, E 23-32

TUITION & COST

Tuition: $25,000

Fees: $1,144

Room & Board: $9,040

LYON COLLEGE

BATESVILLE, ARKANSAS

Located in the "Gateway to the Ozarks," Lyon College boasts a rich history and proud Scottish heritage. Top-notch faculty provide hands-on mentoring and research opportunities that undergraduates do not always enjoy at larger universities. With a range of academic majors, numerous pre-professional programs, and an option to develop an individualized course of study, Lyon offers an education suited for a variety of career goals.

ONLY AT LYON: There are so many "Only at Lyon" distinctive experiences to discover that it is difficult to name them all. For example, Lyon has the only pet-friendly campus in the region. It is also the first in the state to hire a professional gamer to head its new esports program. Lyon embraces its Scottish heritage with the Scot as its distinctive athletic mascot, its own crimson and navy blue tartan registered in Scotland, and one of the most significant bagpiping programs in the nation.

INTERNSHIPS AND PRACTICA: Several majors emphasize the importance of internships and practica. For example, journalism students are required to write for an established newspaper; art students work in galleries; religion/philosophy majors assist ministers and chaplains; and science majors work on grant-funded research projects. Those interested in medical careers can participate as "Health Coaches" to make sure their patients understand how to avoid trips to the emergency room or further hospitalization. Some become so involved that they even sign on for extra semesters of work.

"Some of my favorite memories of Lyon College are of my seminar-style history classes... Challenged by our professors to examine evidence, to think for ourselves, and to become more polished writers, my fellow history majors and I were prepared for the wide variety of careers one might expect to result from a rigorous liberal arts education." *– Brad Austin, '94*

www.lyon.edu
(870) 307-7250
admissions@lyon.edu

STUDENT PROFILE

655 undergraduate students

99% of undergrad students are full-time

43% female – 57% male

36% of students are from out of state

71% freshman retention rate

FACULTY PROFILE

11 to 1 student/faculty ratio

ADMISSIONS

Selectivity: 50%

SAT Ranges: E 520-608, M 520-580

ACT Ranges: C 21-28, M 21-26, E 21-30

TUITION & COST

Tuition: $28,550

Fees: $590

Room & Board: $9,810

UNIVERSITY OF CENTRAL ARKANSAS

CONWAY, ARKANSAS

The University of Central Arkansas is one of the most affordable options for higher education in the South. With 156 degrees and certificates, UCA creates an academic community where students can learn and grow both inside and outside of the classroom. Students get the full college experience with UCA's study abroad programs, service-learning initiatives through the Residential Colleges, and small classes taught in a seminar format through the UCA Honors College.

BAUM GALLERY: The Baum Gallery, an educational art museum for the UCA community, presents selected national and international touring exhibitions, sponsors juried student shows, and original exhibits distinctly suited to an academic environment. Many exhibitions, including those presented by UCA students themselves, invite audience interaction and encourage striking dialogue about visual art, ranging from such topics as the creators, studio process, history, criticism, curation, and cultural contexts.

CAREER SERVICES CENTER: The Career Services Center offers educational assistance to all students, such as BOLT (Bears OnLine Training), an online career service resource that helps students develop the skills needed to be successful in their careers. Students can also find business attire in the center's WOW closet. Short for "World of Work," the closet offers business clothes of all sizes for students to rent once per academic year. It's a convenient, affordable way for students to prepare for on-campus interviews, career fairs, and class presentations.

RESIDENTIAL COLLEGES: UCA's Residential College program hosts five living & learning communities as well as one commuter learning community. Those who choose to participate in a Residential College take one class in their residence building, making it more convenient and engaging to study with fellow residents. Each Residential College has a unique theme and character that is further emphasized in its corresponding course.

www.uca.edu
(501) 450-5000

STUDENT PROFILE
9,548 undergraduate students

85% of undergrad students are full-time

59% female – 41% male

9% of students are from out of state

72% freshman retention rate

FACULTY PROFILE
16 to 1 student/faculty ratio

ADMISSIONS
Selectivity: 90%

SAT Ranges: E 470-555, M 500-580

ACT Ranges: C 21-27, M 21-28, E 19-25

TUITION & COST
Tuition (in-state): $6,523

Tuition (out-of-state): $13,046

Fees: $2,001

Room: $3,598

Board: $2,920

AZUSA PACIFIC UNIVERSITY

AZUSA, CALIFORNIA

AZUSA PACIFIC
U N I V E R S I T Y

Azusa Pacific University is an evangelical Christian community of disciples and scholars who seek to advance the work of God through academic excellence in liberal arts and professional programs of higher education—both of which encourage students to develop a Christian perspective of truth and life.

SERVICE AS A CORNERSTONE: Azusa Pacific places a high priority on service learning projects. The Center for Academic Service Learning and Research provides programs for Azusa Pacific students to engage with the surrounding community. The programs vary from teaching local school children to reading with the Azusa Reads program. Students can be involved in the College Headed and Mighty Proud (C.H.A.M.P.) program, where students introduce the idea of college to 600-700 local at-risk fourth graders, and the Azusa Conservatory of Music, which provides free music lessons to area youth.

STUDY AWAY: APU's High Sierra Semester offers students the unique opportunity to step away from the typical college experience by studying in the High Sierras, just south of Yosemite National Park. Each semester, 40 to 50 students embark on the adventure of a lifetime as they enter into a small community. The High Sierra Program holds each student to high academic standards. Classes are taught as part of the university's Great Works Option, which allows students to learn through the integration of all their classes, all while meeting General Studies and Upper Division Elective requirements.

NURSING AND THE COMMUNITY: The Neighborhood Wellness Center is a collaborative project between the city of Azusa and APU's School of Nursing to improve the health and wellbeing of the predominantly underserved families of Azusa and the surrounding area. The center offers several services, including a drop-in center that serves as a community resource. What's more, it also partners with community agencies to develop activities which address the identified health needs of local residents such as stress reduction, exercise, healthy eating, and child safety.

www.apu.edu
(626) 812-3016
admissions@apu.edu

STUDENT PROFILE

5,671 undergraduate students

89% of undergrad students are full-time

66% female – 34% male

20% of students are from out of state

83% freshman retention rate

FACULTY PROFILE

10 to 1 student/faculty ratio

ADMISSIONS

Selectivity: 60%

SAT Ranges: E 480-610, M 510-610

ACT Ranges: C 21-27, M 20-27, E 21-28

TUITION & COST

Tuition: $36,926

Fees: $580

Room: $5,770

Board: $4,024

CALIFORNIA POLYTECHNIC STATE UNIVERSITY

SAN LUIS OBISPO, CALIFORNIA

Cal Poly's Guiding Philosophy, "Learn by Doing," pushes students to take responsibility over their individual academic journeys. Thanks to California Polytechnic State University's rigorous, success-oriented academic environment, the University ensures that students are actively involved in unique educational experiences.

STUDENT COMMUNITY SERVICE: Student Community Service (SCS) mixes student interests with meaningful community service initiatives. SCS promotes leadership among its participants as they work together to enact social change. There are eight different volunteer programs on campus, each of which has its own specific goals and purposes. For example, one group of students may work to support the environment, while others may work to tackle the systematic origins of homelessness.

WRITING-INTENSIVE COURSES: Writing-Intensive Courses are exactly how they sound, structured to develop every student's communication skills in their field of study. The Graduation Writing Requirement must be fulfilled by all Cal Poly students regardless of major. The purpose of such a requirement is to guarantee that students graduate as effective communicators—a commonly overlooked skill that every field requires. Students may opt to take a writing examination to skip the course, but they must pass to receive their diploma.

COLLABORATIVE ASSIGNMENTS AND PROJECTS: It is important that students develop the ability both to work on their own as well as a part of a group. Collaborative assignments involve both individual and group work through which students must hold themselves accountable with individual work while also contributing as a member of a community. This skill is incredibly valuable, as most work environments require a well-rounded work ethic. Collaborating also exposes students to peers with different backgrounds and life experiences.

www.calpoly.edu
(805) 756-2311

STUDENT PROFILE

21,351 undergraduate students

96% of undergrad students are full-time

48% female – 52% male

15% of students are from out of state

95% freshman retention rate

FACULTY PROFILE

22 to 1 student/faculty ratio

ADMISSIONS

Selectivity: 35%

SAT Ranges: E 600-680, M 600-700

ACT Ranges: C 26-31, M 26-32, E 25-33

TUITION & COST

Tuition (in-state): $5,742

Tuition (out-of-state): $17,622

Fees: $3,690

Room: $7,792

Board: $5,323

CALIFORNIA STATE UNIVERSITY LONG BEACH

LONG BEACH, CALIFORNIA

California State University, Long Beach is dedicated to providing a high-quality education founded on the principles of superior teaching, research, and service for the people of California and the world. Motivated by the values of diversity, integrity, and service, CSU Long Beach strives to make its world-class education accessible and inclusive. The university boasts a beautiful campus with state-of-the-art research facilities, performing arts centers, and the Earl Burns Miller Japanese Garden, all of which encourage students to experience the beauty and inspiration the campus has to offer.

MINORITY ACCESS TO RESEARCH CAREERS: The mission of Minority Access to Research Careers (MARC) is to increase diversity in biomedical fields by creating accessible pathways to research opportunities. These opportunities prepare minority students for success in graduate programs and careers in biomedicine. Students who participate in the program receive a monthly stipend, research funds, chances to network with outstanding researchers, and training and preparation for graduate and PhD programs.

COLLEGE OF EDUCATION: The College of Education's Conceptual Framework articulates the intellectual philosophy that drives the mission and vision for the school. CSULB strives to prepare professional educators to promote equity and excellence in the classroom, informing its curriculum with effective pedagogy, an implementation of evidence-based practices, meaningful collaboration, thoughtful leadership, innovation, and scholarship.

INNOVATION CHALLENGE: Students flock to CSULB's Innovation Challenge to prove that their idea, whether it be a product or a service, is worthy of recognition. Senior mechanical engineering students present a design project that is the result of two semesters of work. Students work together to plan, troubleshoot, test, and execute their designs with a meager $400 budget. Groups present their work at the Engineering Innovation Expo in the University Student Union.

www.csulb.edu
(562) 985-5471

STUDENT PROFILE

31,447 undergraduate students

87% of undergrad students are full-time

57% female – 43% male

1% of students are from out of state

87% freshman retention rate

FACULTY PROFILE

26 to 1 student/faculty ratio

ADMISSIONS

Selectivity: 31%

SAT Ranges: E 520-620, M 520-630

ACT Ranges: C 20-26, M 19-26, E 19-26

TUITION & COST

Tuition (in-state): $5,742

Tuition (out-of-state): $16,038

Fees: $1,056

Room: $8,568

Board: $4,590

CHAPMAN UNIVERSITY

ORANGE, CALIFORNIA

Chapman University offers the best of both worlds: a classic liberal arts foundation and pre-professional programs of distinction with strong ties to their industries. The university is known for providing a uniquely personalized education (with a student/faculty ratio of 14:1) and extraordinary learning experiences that begin right at the first day a student arrives on campus. The University's variety of academic opportunities spans everything from performing arts, humanities, and business to economics, film, and the sciences.

ORANGE COUNTY OPPORTUNITIES: Orange County is America's sixth-largest county with more than 3 million people. Chapman's location provides students with valuable connections for internships and job opportunities. Many of America's largest corporations such as Allergan, Disney, Ford Motor Co., and Blizzard Entertainment call Orange County their home or U.S. headquarters. Furthermore, Chapman's location offers much more in the way of education, culture, entertainment, and great weather! A daily sea breeze sweeps over the Chapman campus, the average year-round temperature floating around 72°F.

PERSONALIZED AND COMPREHENSIVE: Chapman's curriculum is designed to turn every student into an inquiring, ethical, and productive member of the global community. As an institution with a liberal arts foundation, Chapman encourages students to explore. Its six shared inquiry areas—artistic, quantitative, natural science, social, written, and values and ethics—truly allow students to pursue interdisciplinary and comprehensive approaches.

A variety of innovative programs give Chapman students interesting options for their education. They can pursue majors in such unique fields as Peace Studies or Kinesiology, or they may enroll in more traditional programs like Business Administration, English, or Chemistry.

www.chapman.edu
(714) 997-6711
admit@chapman.edu

STUDENT PROFILE

7,020 undergraduate students

93% of undergrad students are full-time

60% female – 40% male

34% of students are from out of state

91% freshman retention rate

FACULTY PROFILE

14 to 1 student/faculty ratio

ADMISSIONS

Selectivity: 57%

SAT Ranges: E 600-680, M 590-680

ACT Ranges: C 25-30, M 24-29, E 25-32

TUITION & COST

Tuition: $50,210

Fees: $384

Room: $10,176

Board: $4,734

CONCORDIA UNIVERSITY IRVINE

IRVINE, CALIFORNIA

CONCORDIA
UNIVERSITY **IRVINE**

"Grace Alone. Faith Alone." Concordia University Irvine (CUI) thrives with a spirit of thoughtful insight and compassionate community. Its nationally recognized general education curriculum, "Enduring Questions & Ideas," inspires its students to develop a global mindset that stretches far beyond its Southern Californian walls.

INT 100: CUI recognizes that freshmen need more than a campus tour to feel welcome—it gives all students easy access to support services for academic, emotional, and physical well-being all throughout the first-year transition from high school to college. INT 100: Foundations prepares students for lifelong learning while providing them an extended "orientation" experience. The course sets freshmen up for success, all while strengthening friendships, academic skills, and a reverence for the Christian liberal arts education.

ACADEMIC PROGRAMS: Over 1,500 undergraduate students can choose from over 90 programs and majors—from acting or psychology to youth ministry or business. CUI knows that students have a wide range of interests, so coursework spans across many areas of study to engage students as they reach their educational goals.

PRESIDENT'S ACADEMIC SHOWCASE: CUI's annual President's Academic Showcase for Undergraduate Research is a culminating event that celebrates scholarship in recognition of students' creativity and innovation. With the help of a highly invested faculty mentor, driven students are able to delve into a topic that excites them and construct an interdisciplinary project to be judged by a panel of faculty.

CONCORDIA CARES: Concordia University Irvine's value lies far beyond its outstanding academics; it also stands tall as a beacon of service and community engagement. The Concordia Cares program partners with surrounding community organizations to connect CUI with life-changing volunteer opportunities. This program encourages students to grasp issues of social justice in their own neighborhood while connecting them to other students and people in need.

www.cui.edu
(949) 214-3010
admissions@cui.edu

STUDENT PROFILE
1,821 undergraduate students

90% of undergrad students are full-time

62% female – 38% male

18% of students are from out of state

75% freshman retention rate

FACULTY PROFILE
17 to 1 student/faculty ratio

ADMISSIONS
Selectivity: 58%

SAT Ranges: E 510-610, M 500-590

ACT Ranges: C 20-26, M 18-26, E 20-26

TUITION & COST
Tuition: $34,700

Fees: $700

Room: $6,510

Board: $4,790

DOMINICAN UNIVERSITY OF CALIFORNIA

SAN RAFAEL, CALIFORNIA

Located in a community known for its extraordinary creative and entrepreneurial energy, Dominican's commitment to integrating the liberal arts prepares students for lives of purpose. The University balances academics with extensive practical, hands-on experiences, including service-learning, research, and internships with some of the Bay Area's largest and fastest-growing companies. Upon graduation, students are well prepared to enter professional life or continue their studies in medical or graduate school.

THE DOMINICAN EXPERIENCE: The Dominican Experience supports the personal and academic success of students in all majors. Students engage in four cornerstone experiences: integrative coaching, community engagement, signature work, and digital portfolio development. Together, these practices integrate knowledge with hands-on experiences, the curriculum with the co-curriculum, and the liberal arts with the professions. Students gain and the skills that executives and hiring managers seek in future employees.

AN OUTSTANDING LOCATION: The 80-acre campus is at the center in a historic neighborhood located close to downtown San Rafael's restaurants, sidewalk cafés, movie theaters, live music venues, and a seasonal farmer's market. Though only 30 minutes from San Francisco, Dominican's quiet and safe campus is set at the edge of some of the best hiking and mountain biking trails in the Bay Area. Marin County's popular Stinson Beach is less than an hour from campus, while Lake Tahoe's mountain resorts are a favorite weekend destination for skiers and snowboarders.

BUSINESS: The Barowsky School of Business provides the theoretical knowledge and practical skills needed to launch or advance a business career. It is led by professors who have accumulated years of experience in one of the most vibrant business centers in the world—the San Francisco Bay Area. Students can pursue internships and other activities in San Francisco, Silicon Valley, and Sonoma and Napa ("wine country") counties.

www.dominican.edu
(415) 485-3204

STUDENT PROFILE
1,264 undergraduate students

90% of undergrad students are full-time

76% female – 24% male

8% of students are from out of state

82% freshman retention rate

FACULTY PROFILE
9 to 1 student/faculty ratio

ADMISSIONS
Selectivity: 87%

SAT Ranges: E 515-610, M 520-600

ACT Ranges: C 19.5-25, M 19-25, E 19-26

TUITION & COST
Tuition: $45,350

Fees: $500

Room: $8,280

Board: $6,530

HOLY NAMES UNIVERSITY

OAKLAND, CALIFORNIA

HOLY NAMES UNIVERSITY

www.hnu.edu
(510) 436-1351
admissions@hnu.edu

Nestled in the Oakland Hills with expansive views of the San Francisco Bay, Holy Names University is educating and empowering the next generation of conscientious leaders. HNU prides itself on its atmosphere of openness and inclusion. The University is regularly recognized for the exceptional diversity of its students, be it racial, religious, political, or socioeconomic. Programs in business, criminology, education, nursing, and psychology position Holy Names University students for career advancement and provide new perspectives with a social justice lens.

SERVICE AND ADVOCACY: HNU's students are activists, mentors, and leaders who engage the world at every stage of their education. For instance, students can participate in actions and service projects, like helping out at the Oakland Catholic Worker, walking for breast cancer research, and traveling to Tutwiler, MI, to build houses with Habitat for Humanity. It's the students' own commitment to these projects that makes HNU's vision of service a reality.

FOUNDATION FOR THE FUTURE: Preparation for success is deeply embedded in the HNU Experience. With the foundation of the Connections Project, HNU's first-year experience program, students develop the skills necessary for understanding and action. Goal setting, learning styles, time management, critical reading, and critical thinking are all addressed to facilitate students' understanding of not just how *to* learn, but how *they* learn.

HNU students don't just learn about complex issues and theoretical concepts; they learn how to integrate and apply their knowledge in the community and in the workplace. They learn how to make a difference.

"At HNU, you can be as ambitious as you want. The school allows you to try on any hat you want to, and you take your experience as far as you want to go. If you want to be challenged, the faculty and staff here are willing to push you." *– Nobel H., Kinesiology major*

STUDENT PROFILE
591 undergraduate students

92% of undergrad students are full-time

64% female – 36% male

82% freshman retention rate

FACULTY PROFILE
8 to 1 student/faculty ratio

ADMISSIONS
Selectivity: 53%

SAT Ranges: E 280-330, M 450-540

ACT Ranges: C 17-22, M 16-22, E 16-23

TUITION & COST
Tuition: $37,672

Fees: $516

Room: $6,614

Board: $6,194

LA SIERRA UNIVERSITY

RIVERSIDE, CALIFORNIA

La Sierra University, a Christian institution nationally acclaimed for its diverse campus and service to others, sustains a supportive and nurturing environment for students. It values more than academics, cultivating change in both local and global communities as well as in students' hearts. Student-led organizations and clubs help develop leadership skills and forge lifelong friendships, and ther programs, like Honors or Adventist Colleges Abroad (ACA), provide the chance to travel the world and gain an appreciation for other people, cultures, and faiths.

ACTIVITIES AND EVENTS: Students are always invited to attend Student Association events, the annual Festival of Nations (which celebrates diversity on campus with students from over 40 countries), intramural sports, and TEDx Talks. Other activities include programs hosted by the La Sierra University Church, including film screenings, bowling excursions, and nature hikes. La Sierra also hosts an annual REVO fashion show in which students can serve as designers, models, and more, raising money for such charitable endeavors as an orphanage in Rwanda or outreach efforts in Peru.

GLOBAL LEARNING: La Sierra University students have a chance to take a gap or bridge year, during which they can serve as student missionaries in countries like India, the Philippines, and Papua New Guinea. Many students also choose to take an extra year in order to study abroad in Argentina, Austria, Brazil, England, France, Germany, Italy, Lebanon, or Spain. Through Adventist Colleges Abroad, anyone can completely immerse themselves in another culture, become fluent in another language, and gain an appreciation for the history and communities of others.

UNDERGRADUATE RESEARCH: There are multiple occasions for undergraduate research in each department, but is especially encouraged for students who are members of the Honors program or Sigma Tau Delta. Honors students complete a scholarship project prior to graduation in which they develop an original research and/or creative project to be presented publicly. Students who are part of Sigma Tau Delta are invited to submit research essays for participation in conference presentations each year.

www.lasierra.edu
(951) 785-2176
admissions@lasierra.edu

STUDENT PROFILE

2,029 undergraduate students

90% of undergrad students are full-time

60% female – 40% male

75% freshman retention rate

FACULTY PROFILE

13 to 1 student/faculty ratio

ADMISSIONS

Selectivity: 48%

SAT Ranges: E 440-601, M 430-520

ACT Ranges: C 16-22, M 16-21, E 15-22

TUITION & COST

Tuition: $31,140

Fees: $990

Room & Board: $8,250

LOYOLA MARYMOUNT UNIVERSITY

LOS ANGELES, CALIFORNIA

Loyola Marymount University is rooted in its Roman Catholic tradition—a relationship that is directly connected to the school's personal and academic goals and success. LMU promotes both the intellectual and personal growth of each student, instilling in them a socially conscious mindset in the interest of a healthy, happy global community.

SERVICE AT LMU: Every month, LMU takes on a new service initiative with a local non-profit agency. and communicates it to the entire campus community. Details of the project,are shared with the student body in order to rally volunteers and keep students aware. Projects change every month, allowing LMU to touch several different parts of the community.

One ongoing LMU service initiative is *El Espejo*. Spanish for "mirror," this project emphasizes a theme of reflection by encouraging volunteers to find a common connection between themselves and those they are helping. *El Espejo* connects LMU students with at-risk middle school students in the community to educate and mentor them on the importance intellectual and personal growth.

FIRST-YEAR EXPERIENCE: LMU's first-year experience takes a holistic approach to preparing students for successful college careers. Students explore themselves while also engaging with their peers as they utilize different resources and explore the foundations of critical thinking.

Every incoming freshman is also required to finish a common reading assignment prior to arriving on campus. After introducing themselves to the theme of the book, they then attend a presentation by the author herself within the first two weeks of school. The common reader is a shared experience among students that sets the tone for their first semester.

LMU|LA
Loyola Marymount University

www.lmu.edu
(310) 338-2750
admission@lmu.edu

STUDENT PROFILE
6,391 undergraduate students

96% of undergrad students are full-time

56% female – 44% male

31% of students are from out of state

91% freshman retention rate

FACULTY PROFILE
10 to 1 student/faculty ratio

ADMISSIONS
Selectivity: 52%

SAT Ranges: E 600-680, M 580-680

ACT Ranges: C 26-31, M 25-29, E 27-33

TUITION & COST
Tuition: $45,460

Fees: $926

Room & Board: $14,066

MILLS COLLEGE

OAKLAND, CALIFORNIA

Historically a college for women only, Mills continues its proud tradition at the undergraduate level as a community of women and gender nonbinary students. Mills offers a transformative educational experience to talented students in a highly individualistic yet intensely inclusive environment. Immersed in a community committed to fighting for gender and racial justice, Mills students graduate empowered to make a statement in their careers and the world around them.

A DIVERSE CORE: The Mills Core Curriculum advances the college's mission by providing a diverse intellectual experience for all students. With three facets—Foundational Skills, Modes of Inquiry, and Contributions to Knowledge & Community—the Mills Core allows students the freedom to choose courses that match their interests while meeting academic goals. Every Mills student learns about international cultures, race and gender power dynamics, effective communication skills, and more. The Mills Core and equips students to engage and lead in a diverse world.

BE IN THE BAY: Mills College is located in the San Francisco Bay Area, one of the most diverse areas in the United States. Work at industry leaders and innovative startups in Silicon Valley, explore the art and history of San Francisco, and celebrate the diversity of Mills' hometown, Oakland. The San Francisco Bay Area extends from picturesque Napa Valley and Sonoma in the North Bay to world-famous Silicon Valley in the South Bay. In between are the historic Haight-Ashbury district, the LGBTQ-friendly Castro district, and the iconic Golden Gate Bridge.

GET MPOWERED: With the *M*Power signature academic experience, Mills students are granted access to a strong community of support with an academic success network of faculty and staff who follow them throughout their college careers. *M*Power provides the opportunity for students to engage in their community through service projects, internships, and international trips. Mills' Bay Area location offers students an especially exciting chance to connect with cutting-edge companies to engage with their interests and help guide their career search.

MILLS

www.mills.edu
(510) 430-2135
admission@mills.edu

STUDENT PROFILE

753 undergraduate students

96% of undergrad students are full-time

100% female — 0% male

20% of students are from out of state

74% freshman retention rate

FACULTY PROFILE

11 to 1 student/faculty ratio

ADMISSIONS

Selectivity: 86%

SAT Ranges: E 513-640, M 495-600

ACT Ranges: C 21-29, M 19-26, E 21-31

TUITION & COST

Tuition: $29,340

Fees: $1,537

Room & Board: $13,883

NOTRE DAME DE NAMUR UNIVERSITY

BELMONT, CALIFORNIA

Notre Dame de Namur (NDNU) features personal attention, quality courses and instructors, and a range of majors. Professors at NDNU are not only gifted instructors, but they are also committed to advising and mentoring students through the college journey. The university strives to give students the tools, knowledge, and inspiration to successfully engage and expand their talents. NDNU's location also presents learning opportunities through community engagement and internships that can't be found elsewhere.

COMMUNITY ENGAGEMENT: Named in honor of Sister Dorothy Stang, who advocated for land rights of poor farmers in the Amazon rainforest in Brazil, the Stang Center seeks to build on her legacy for positive social change. Students work through the center and alongside community organizations involved in tutoring, housing and homelessness, family and women's shelters, food banks, restorative justice, environmental preservation, and other issues.

STUDENT GROUPS: NDNU features a variety of clubs and activities that bring together students with common interests in careers, shared identity, social action, and sports. Profession-related clubs include groups interested in accounting, art therapy, business, pre-medicine, and political science.

The campus also offers student groups such as the Black Student Union, The *Bohemian* literary and arts magazine, Debate League, Gender and Sexuality Awareness (PLUS+ Club), the International Students Association, Latinos Unidos, 'Nesian Love (Polynesian students' group), and the W.A.Y. (We Accept You), which encourages interfaith dialogue.

"I would say you should come to NDNU because we're social justice oriented. There are small class sizes. Your teachers know you; you build a relationship with them so they can help you further your career." *- Bette, NDNU Student*

www.ndnu.edu
(650) 508-3600
admiss@ndnu.edu

STUDENT PROFILE
871 undergraduate students

77% of undergrad students are full-time

66% female – 34% male

18% of students are from out of state

62% freshman retention rate

FACULTY PROFILE
12 to 1 student/faculty ratio

ADMISSIONS
Selectivity: 82%

SAT Ranges: E 440-530, M 430-550

ACT Ranges: C 17-21

TUITION & COST
Tuition: $34,910

Fees: $440

Room: $9,312

Board: $4,932

SAINT MARY'S COLLEGE OF CALIFORNIA

MORAGA, CALIFORNIA

Since its founding in 1863, Saint Mary's College of California has been dedicated to exceptional academics that engage the intellect and the spirit. The Lasallian tradition of John Baptist de La Salle inform the core tenets of Saint Mary's mission to inspire students to lead lives of transformative service. SMC's Bay Area location, excellent athletic program, and Lasallian approach to education are just a few distinctions that set it apart. At SMC, students choose from over 30 programs within the School of Liberal Arts, the School of Economics and Business Administration, and the School of Science.

INTERNSHIPS: Saint Mary's proximity to the Bay Area has provided students access to various internship opportunities. And in 2016, the college established the Accelerated Career Entry Students (ACES) program, which develops partnerships with non- and for-profit organizations to develop programs that focus students' personal and professional development through college. The "stairway of success" program helps move students from mentored internships in their first year and graduation and straight to entry-level employment.

THE CORE CURRICULUM: Serving as the foundation for student learning at Saint Mary's is the Core Curriculum. Students explore in depth three intellectual areas: Habits of Mind, Pathways to Knowledge, and Engaging the World. Through student-centered classes that bulk up their academic skills and global perspectives, students learn the skills, knowledge, and values that will continue to develop throughout their time at SMC.

"[The Career and Professional Development Services] helped me present my best self by developing a career 'plan of attack,' a high-quality LinkedIn page, role-playing job interviews, and a personal branding campaign."

– *Jordan Trafton, Philosophy Major and Investment Analyst, '18*

---

www.stmarys-ca.edu
(925) 631-4224
smcadmit@stmarys-ca.edu

STUDENT PROFILE

2,675 undergraduate students

98% of undergrad students are full-time

57% female — 43% male

12% of students are from out of state

85% freshman retention rate

FACULTY PROFILE

11 to 1 student/faculty ratio

ADMISSIONS

Selectivity: 77%

SAT Ranges: E 540-630, M 520-620

ACT Ranges: C 22-27, M 20-26, E 21-28

TUITION & COST

Tuition: $48,988

Fees: $200

Room & Board: $15,524

SANTA CLARA UNIVERSITY

SANTA CLARA, CALIFORNIA

Santa Clara University, a comprehensive Jesuit, Catholic university, offers its students rigorous undergraduate curricula in arts and sciences, business, and engineering. It was founded 1851 by the Society of Jesus on the site of Mission Santa Clara de Asis, the eighth of 21 California missions. Today, the University is committed to promoting academic excellence, enriching its educational experience through the Jesuit philosophy of educating the whole person, fostering an engaged community, and realizing opportunities available through its location in the San Francisco Bay Area and Silicon Valley.

INTEGRATED STUDIES: Three interdisciplinary Centers of Distinction engage faculty and students with society in the areas of Jesuit values and community-based learning; applied ethics; and science, technology, and social entrepreneurship.

As part of the core curriculum, all students select and complete a "Pathway," which is a cluster of 3-4 courses that center around a common theme. Topics like health, humanities, justice, and social issues promote integrative, intentional learning.

LIVING & LEARNING: One unique aspect of Santa Clara life is the Residential Learning Communities. Upon entering Santa Clara, all students select a Residential Learning Community (RLC) in which to live and share classes with peers who have many common interests. Students select an RLC based on their interest in topics such as natural history, diversity, sustainability or social justice, excited to combine their academic, residential, and social components of campus life.

COMMUNITY-BASED LEARNING: Santa Clara students work with and learn from marginalized groups both in the region and farther afield. They earn course credit through partnerships for community-based learning, choosing opportunities like tutoring elementary-school students in San Jose or assisting at an immigration law clinic. Through these partnerships, students work at more than 50 sites in and around Silicon Valley—in schools, clinics, health-care centers, church parishes, and homeless shelters.

www.scu.edu
(408) 554-4700
admission@scu.edu

STUDENT PROFILE
5,499 undergraduate students

98% of undergrad students are full-time

50% female – 50% male

42% of students are from out of state

94% freshman retention rate

FACULTY PROFILE
11 to 1 student/faculty ratio

ADMISSIONS
Selectivity: 60%

SAT Ranges: E 630-710, M 640-730

ACT Ranges: C 28-32

TUITION & COST
Tuition: $49,233

Fees: $625

Room & Board: $14,487

SIMPSON UNIVERSITY

REDDING, CALIFORNIA

Simpson University, California's only Christian university north of Sacramento, has been educating and shaping world-influencers for nearly 100 years. And as one of only four schools of higher education of The Christian and Missionary Alliance denomination, Simpson's students come from all over the world. More than 30 percent of traditional undergraduates are first-generation college students, and ethnic diversity characterizes almost one-third of the population.

WORLDSERVE: With the long-standing motto of "Gateway to World Service" Simpson relaunched student-led mission teams in 1994. And since then, more than 1,700 students have served on spring and summer teams throughout nearly 30 percent of the world. One outlet for service, the WorldSERVE program, is a yearlong discipleship journey that invests in and challenges students as they prepare for short-term mission service. A number of those students have gone on to full-time missionary service as a result of their experience while at Simpson.

OUTDOOR LEADERSHIP: One of Simpson's most distinctive majors is Outdoor Leadership, designed to prepare students for leadership careers in adventure-based programs. The university's location makes it ideal for the program, as students are able to practice multiple outdoor skills in beautiful nearby settings. The major includes an Immersion Semester, where students take several trips to such locations as Yosemite National Park, Joshua Tree National Park, Lassen Volcanic National Park, and Crater Lake National Park.

"My education at Simpson was a well-rounded one that forced me to grow and challenged me in ways I never thought would be possible. I was given a way to approach the secular world from a Christian viewpoint which will be beneficial for my future teaching career and as a Christian scientist." - *Leanne Davis, biology major, class of 2015*

www.simpsonu.edu
1 (888) 9-SIMPSON
admissions@simpsonu.edu

STUDENT PROFILE
788 undergraduate students

94% of undergrad students are full-time

66% female — 34% male

12% of students are from out of state

82% freshman retention rate

FACULTY PROFILE
11 to 1 student/faculty ratio

ADMISSIONS
Selectivity: 52%

SAT Ranges: E 440-555, M 420-550

ACT Ranges: C 18-24

TUITION & COST
Tuition: $27,250

Fees: $100

Room: $4,570

Board: $3,780

UNIVERSITY OF CALIFORNIA, SANTA BARBARA

SANTA BARBARA, CALIFORNIA

U C Santa Barbara is a noted institution located on the edge of the Pacific, a perfect natural environment for research. The serene atmosphere is conducive not only to academic success, but also many outdoor and recreational activities.

RESIDENTIAL EXPERIENCES: The First-Year Residential Experience acts as a comfortable introduction to university life. UCSB strongly encourages first-year students to join one of these communities so that they are more easily taught how to access university resources, receive counseling from academic advisors, and bond with their classmates.

The Second-Year Residential Experience, an extension of the first-year experience, further engages students through leadership- and citizenship-building activities. Many who participate in the SYRE work as mentors to guide students living on the first-year residential floor, sharing all they themselves have come to love about UCSB.

UCDC: The UCDC program is a partnership between schools in California and Washington D.C. Though this program, students from UCSB and other California institutions are able to work, study, and intern in the nation's capital. UCDC is open to junior and senior students looking to expand their educational and hands-on experience. Some elect to do an internship, which requires 32 hours of work a week, while others choose to complete a research seminar and take elective courses for credit.

EUREKA!: EUREKA! is a one-of-a-kind, hands-on program that introduces first-year STEM students to the greater science community. Students involved in EUREKA! have the opportunity to explore career options and network with faculty and peers within the program. EUREKA! also offers opportunities for undergraduate research, a privilege most often awarded to upperclassmen.

www.ucsb.edu
(805) 893-2881

STUDENT PROFILE
22,186 undergraduate students

98% of undergrad students are full-time

54% female – 46% male

6% of students are from out of state

93% freshman retention rate

FACULTY PROFILE
18 to 1 student/faculty ratio

ADMISSIONS
Selectivity: 33%

SAT Ranges: E 600-680, M 590-720

ACT Ranges: C 28-33, M 26-32, E 26-34

TUITION & COST
Tuition (in-state): $11,502

Tuition (out-of-state): $39,516

Fees: $2,949

Room & Board: $15,169

UNIVERSITY OF CALIFORNIA, SANTA CRUZ

SANTA CRUZ, CALIFORNIA

UNIVERSITY OF CALIFORNIA
SANTA CRUZ

UC Santa Cruz has a steadfast commitment to the intellectual growth of its students. The University promotes active engagement with the community as well as environmental stewardship. Faculty work closely with students providing individualistic attention that drives real results.

ENVIRONMENTAL STUDIES INTERNSHIP: The Environmental Studies Internship is an important component of the environmental studies major. That said, the internship is not limited to that specific area of study; any UCSC student can apply. The program places students in group and individual internship positions at domestic and international agencies. With both part- and full-time options available, any student looking to apply themselves to the betterment of the environment has the chance to make a difference.

UCEAP: The University of California Education Abroad Program (UCEAP) provides UC students a range of global education and internship opportunities. Students can receive UC credit for their work abroad, and some can even petition to have their classes count toward their major or minor.

There are nearly 400 program options available in more than 40 countries for all time lengths and majors. All students are welcome to participate as soon as their sophomore year. Some of the most popular destinations include Australia, France, Hong Kong, Mexico, Morocco, Russia, Singapore, and Spain.

CUIP: The Chancellor's Undergraduate Internship Program allows undergraduates to build important job skills like leadership and time management while working on a project that also counts toward their degree. Under the direction of a mentor, students take an active leadership role that allows them to step out of their comfort zone and test their boundaries. The program, which requires students to work 15 hours a week, even provides a scholarship to pay for a large portion of registration fees.

---

www.ucsc.edu
(831) 459-2131
admissions@ucsc.edu

STUDENT PROFILE

17,577 undergraduate students

97% of undergrad students are full-time

50% female – 50% male

4% of students are from out of state

91% freshman retention rate

FACULTY PROFILE

19 to 1 student/faculty ratio

ADMISSIONS

Selectivity: 51%

SAT Ranges: E 580-660, M 580-680

ACT Ranges: C 26-31, M 25-30, E 24-31

TUITION & COST

Tuition (in-state): $11,502

Tuition (out-of-state): $39,516

Fees: $2,518

Room & Board: $16,055

UNIVERSITY OF LA VERNE

LA VERNE, CALIFORNIA

University of La Verne

Located outside Los Angeles, California, the University of La Verne is one of the oldest colleges in the state. Founded in 1891, the campus is home to 2,800 undergraduate students who study a variety of academic majors. The university's liberal arts, education, business, and science programs prepare graduates for lifelong learning.

A PROGRAM FOR EVERYONE: La Verne offers over 70 undergraduate majors that empower students to combine their academic interests with potential career choices. Many majors like criminology, Kinesiology, child development, movement and sports science, or e-commerce are uncommon at other universities. The flexibility to double major, minor, or establish a concentration allows La Verne students to choose from all of the academic offerings at the University. No matter what, they are certain to be prepared for successful and productive lives after college.

FORWARD-THINKING: The University of La Verne is located in beautiful Southern California. While it enjoys a rich 120-year history, it is vibrant, spirited, and forward-thinking, creating an atmosphere that feels brand new. Excitement is in the air, and history is being made at the University of La Verne. In 2011, Dr. Devorah Lieberman was installed as the first female President of the University.

MENTORSHIPS: La Verne students have the opportunity to not only pursue their academic interests, but also to gain tangible and valuable experiences in their future careers. Faculty renowned in their respective fields work closely with students to guide and mentor them through their professional endeavors. For example, Mike Bennett, an internationally known percussionist credits much of his success to his time spent with his La Verne music professor.

Examples like this abound in various programs at the University of La Verne. The strong one-on-one and small-group interactions between faculty and students are the backbone of what makes any University of La Verne student successful.

www.laverne.edu
(909) 448-4026
admission@laverne.edu

STUDENT PROFILE
5,168 undergraduate students

73% of undergrad students are full-time

59% female – 41% male

79% freshman retention rate

FACULTY PROFILE
15 to 1 student/faculty ratio

ADMISSIONS
Selectivity: 48%

SAT Ranges: E 510-600, M 510-593

ACT Ranges: C 19-25, M 18-25, E 18-24

TUITION & COST
Tuition: $39,915

Fees: $1,535

Room: $6,950

Board: $6,230

UNIVERSITY OF REDLANDS

REDLANDS, CALIFORNIA

A private liberal arts and sciences institution in the heart of Southern California, University of Redlands is committed to educating the hearts and minds of its students through an emphasis on personalized education, service, and experiential learning. In addition to more than 50 programs of study in the arts and sciences, University of Redlands also offers impressive pre-professional opportunities in pre-health, pre-law, and education as well as more than 100 study abroad opportunities.

LIBERAL ARTS INQUIRY: Liberal Arts Inquiry requirements (LAIs) ensure all students obtain a breadth and depth of knowledge during their time at University of Redlands. LAI categories range from Community Engagement and Reflection to Inquiries into Self and Society. Students can fulfill each requirement with a variety of courses, allowing them to pursue coursework that's always of interest.

REDLANDS, CA: University of Redlands is located in the heart of Southern California, just between Los Angeles and Palm Springs. At the base of the snow-capped Mount San Gorgonio, the University provides easy access to the beaches of Orange County, winter adventures in Big Bear, and places to go rock climbing within Joshua Tree National Park.

The award-winning, 160-acre residential campus features orange groves, architectural landmarks, a palm tree-lined main street, and Outdoor Programs trips nearly every weekend. Redlands maintains its small-town charm with many coffee shops, eateries, and a weekly farmer's market.

"Redlands allowed me to truly pursue what I love to do— to learn and to explore. I received an incredible education and traveled throughout the United States and the world to seven different countries. I attribute all of this to the University, to which I will always owe my gratitude."

– Casey McGrath '14

www.redlands.edu
(909) 748-8074
admissions@redlands.edu

STUDENT PROFILE

3,130 undergraduate students

80% of undergrad students are full-time

57% female – 43% male

82% freshman retention rate

FACULTY PROFILE

12 to 1 student/faculty ratio

ADMISSIONS

Selectivity: 75%

SAT Ranges: E 540-630, M 530-620

ACT Ranges: C 23-28, M 21-27, E 23-28

TUITION & COST

Tuition: $47,722

Fees: $350

Room & Board: $13,862

UNIVERSITY OF SAN DIEGO

SAN DIEGO, CALIFORNIA

USD's community of scholars are committed to educating the whole person—intellectually, physically, spiritually, emotionally, socially and culturally. The university provides a character-building education that fosters independent thought and an open-minded and collaborative world view. It proudly welcomes and respects those whose lives are formed by different traditions, recognizing their important contributions to a pluralistic society and to an atmosphere of open discussion and discovery, which is essential to a liberal arts education.

THE FRESHMAN PRECEPTORIAL PROGRAM: The Freshman Preceptorial program begins each USD student's academic career with a combination of advising, orientation, and an introduction to college-level scholarship. The preceptor, a faculty member in the student's intended area of study, has frequent contact with each advisee and continues advising throughout the student's general education program.

RESEARCH CONFERENCES: The "Creative Collaborations" conference showcases the vibrant student-faculty interactions that are a hallmark of a USD education. This conference celebrates the intellectual life at USD and provides all undergraduate students an opportunity to present their preliminary and completed research and creative projects in an environment with other students and faculty. Working side-by-side and engaged in intellectual pursuits with their faculty mentors, USD students gain lifelong experiences that extend well beyond the classroom.

SCHOOL LOCATION: The University of San Diego's 180-acre space rests atop a mesa overlooking San Diego, Mission Bay and the Pacific Ocean. The distinctive Spanish Renaissance architecture and breathtaking views provide an idyllic environment that's endlessly conducive to learning. With the sun shining an average of 300 days per year and an average temperature of 70.5 degrees, recreational options abound. Google virtually any San Diego destination, and it will likely be within 20 minutes of USD.

www.sandiego.edu
(800) 248-4873
admissions@sandiego.edu

STUDENT PROFILE

5,677 undergraduate students

98% of undergrad students are full-time

54% female – 46% male

38% of students are from out of state

90% freshman retention rate

FACULTY PROFILE

14 to 1 student/faculty ratio

ADMISSIONS

Selectivity: 50%

SAT Ranges: E 590-670, M 590-680

ACT Ranges: C 26-30, M 25-29, E 25-33

TUITION & COST

Tuition: $50,450

Fees: $736

Room: $9,622

Board: $3,752

WESTMONT COLLEGE

SANTA BARBARA, CALIFORNIA

Westmont College students receive a rigorous liberal arts education and grow spiritually on a campus filled with natural beauty. After four years, they graduate as men and women with intellect and character who have reaped the rewards of an outstanding faculty and first-rate experiential learning opportunities.

ENTREPRENEURS FOR THE FUTURE: Westmont is proud of the entrepreneurial focus of its programs. Recently, professor David Newton, chairman of the economics and business department, took part in a discussion on CNN that featured colleges with strong entrepreneurial programs. Westmont students take part in the Spirit of Entrepreneurship and Enterprise Development (SEED) Venture Forum, which requires students to create business plans and offers the opportunity for students to receive advice from local businesspeople.

A BEAUTIFUL CAMPUS: Set on 133 acres in the foothills of the Santa Ynez Mountains outside Santa Barbara, Westmont's wooded and scenic campus provide an ideal environment for a residential college. The campus includes buildings and land from two former estates and the historic Deane School for Boys. The grounds feature the pathways, stone bridges, and garden atmosphere typical of Montecito, a suburb of Santa Barbara. The campus is located three miles uphill from the ocean, which can be seen from certain spots on campus.

UNITED IN SERVICE: Serving others is an important part of the Westmont experience. Students have countless service opportunities on campus, in the community, and in other countries. Every year, around four hundred students travel to Ensenada, Mexico, to work with twenty churches on hundreds of projects. They work with faculty and staff on construction projects, in orphanages, vacation Bible school programs, and ministry through theatre and athletics. Other international ministries have traveled to Costa Rica, India, and Israel.

www.westmont.edu
(805) 565-6200
admissions@
westmont.edu

STUDENT PROFILE

1,300 undergraduate students

100% of undergrad students are full-time

61% female – 39% male

29% of students are from out of state

83% freshman retention rate

FACULTY PROFILE

10 to 1 student/faculty ratio

ADMISSIONS

Selectivity: 85%

SAT Ranges: E 580-700, M 550-680

ACT Ranges: C 23-30, M 23-28, E 23-33

TUITION & COST

Tuition: $42,890

Fees: $1,154

Room: $8,610

Board: $5,276

WHITTIER COLLEGE

WHITTIER, CALIFORNIA

The essential heart of Whittier College was formed at its founding by Quakers in 1887. Those roots are distinct among California colleges, even though Whittier hasn't been religiously affiliated since the 1930s. What hasn't changed, however, is a mission based on the core belief that no one is inherently superior to anyone else; that everyone has unique gifts that should be respected, developed, and shared. One illustration of this is that Whittier has always welcomed students irrespective of gender, race, religion, or social status. Few Whittier students fit stereotypes; even fewer want to.

OUT-OF-THE-BOX LEARNING: Whittier's innovative curriculum is undeniably rooted in the liberal arts tradition and fit for real-world application. Its interdisciplinary approach fosters amazing collaboration among professors from disparate disciplines. And, of course, more and more fields are themselves interdisciplinary, such as Global Studies and Environmental Studies. Each can straddle several disciplines, ranging from biochemistry and economics to sociology and politics.

RESEARCH AND FIELDWORK: Whittier students work in close collaboration with world-class thinkers and doers. Their professors have the powerful credentials that are found at mega-universities, but they are uniquely dedicated teachers who actually enjoy working with undergraduates. They regularly act as advisors and assist students who may be breaking new ground on their own research.

"Because I was so involved on campus while I was at Whittier, I learned how to be very resourceful. I loved putting on events, so connecting with organizations and people all over campus helped me learn how to collaborate and make things happen." – *Cassey Ho '09 (Named by "Time" magazine one of the 25 most influential people on the Internet)*

www.whittier.edu
(562) 907-4238
admission@whittier.edu

STUDENT PROFILE
1,681 undergraduate students

98% of undergrad students are full-time

57% female – 43% male

18% of students are from out of state

78% freshman retention rate

FACULTY PROFILE
11 to 1 student/faculty ratio

ADMISSIONS
Selectivity: 74%

SAT Ranges: E 510-620, M 500-600

ACT Ranges: C 21-27

TUITION & COST
Tuition: $45,720

Fees: $590

Room: $7,414

Board: $6,096

WOODBURY UNIVERSITY

BURBANK, CALIFORNIA

Established in 1884, Woodbury University is a small, private, fully accredited, non-profit institution. Its undergraduate and graduate degree programs transform students into innovative professionals who also learn the value of social responsibility as both local and global citizens. Students who choose Woodbury reflect the cultural diversity of Southern California and, through the University's transformative educational programs, are empowered to put their talents to work and do extraordinary things.

REAL-WORLD EXPERIENCE: The School of Architecture's various centers and institutes truly underscore the holistic nature of its field, taking students out of the studio and into the real world through a dedicated program of fieldwork.

The Arid Lands Institute enables students to strategize and demonstrate to cities how to rethink certain policies, introducing ways that architects can utilize dry-land designs to assess the climate change. And through its Urban Policy Center, the University continues to support the infiltration of architects into civic positions where they can affect legislative decisions.

FINAL PROJECTS: Before graduation, each student undertakes a significant project to demonstrate what they have learned. Whether they work alone or in a group, they are sure to challenge themselves with a strong understanding of their field. Typical assignments might be creating a new app, designing a new solar building, or serving as CEO of a simulated business.

ONE CAMPUS–ONE COMMUNITY: Woodbury is a diverse community of students from more than 40 countries and dozens of regional and national ethnicities. From the outset, the school comes together as a community through the "One Book, One Campus" program, which engages students and faculty in campus-wide discussions around a single book. What's more, the campus community expands further through a project hosted by student group La Voz Unida, who invites parents to shadow their students on campus for a day.

WOODBURY UNIVERSITY

www.woodbury.edu
(818) 252-5221
information@
woodbury.edu

STUDENT PROFILE

1,023 undergraduate students

90% of undergrad students are full-time

51% female – 49% male

15% of students are from out of state

73% freshman retention rate

FACULTY PROFILE

9 to 1 student/faculty ratio

ADMISSIONS

Selectivity: 62%

SAT Ranges: E 500-600, M 455-588

ACT Ranges: C 19-24, M 17-24, E 16-25

TUITION & COST

Tuition: $38,370

Fees: $1,485

Room: $7,150

Board: $4,770

COLORADO CHRISTIAN UNIVERSITY

LAKEWOOD, COLORADO

COLORADO CHRISTIAN
UNIVERSITY

www.ccu.edu
(303) 963-3200
admissions@ccu.edu

Founded in 1914, Colorado Christian University delivers a world-class education to thousands of students around the globe. The University's primary goal is to produce graduates who think critically, live faithfully, and impact their spheres of influence. With a steadfast commitment by dedicated faculty, hardworking administration, and students who hunger for academic and Biblical learning, Colorado Christian University is in a class of its own.

CENTENNIAL INSTITUTE: CCU's Centennial Institute is a public-policy think tank whose mission is to "sponsor research, events, and publications to enhance public understanding of the most important issues facing our state and nation." Through the Centennial Institute, select CCU students may apply for the 1776 Scholars program, which exists to mentor America's next generation of leaders—patriots who have the intellectual curiosity, moral compass, and youthful energy to make positive differences in this great nation. The Institute's scholars benefit from political training from prominent politicians and thought-leaders.

STUDENT DISCIPLESHIP: Discipleship groups (D-Groups) at CCU offer freshmen the chance to get to know other students on a deep spiritual level. D-Groups offer consistent communities for encouragement, accountability, and support. They are also safe places to ask questions in small group settings, share prayer requests, and become actively engaged in their peers' spiritual lives. Ultimately, each group's focus is to grow closer to Jesus while also growing closer to one another in authentic relationships.

ANNUAL SYMPOSIUM: Each year, CCU students break from their traditional class schedules for a two-day symposium on topics that impact CCU's core values: faith, family, and freedom. During the event, nationally known experts challenge the CCU community to help restore values in topics ranging from civil liberties, compassion for the poor, the free-market system, apologetics, and religious freedom.

STUDENT PROFILE

6,537 undergraduate students

28% of undergrad students are full-time

66% female – 34% male

77% freshman retention rate

FACULTY PROFILE

16 to 1 student/faculty ratio

TUITION & COST

Tuition: $29,870

Fees: $500

Room: $5,830

Board: $5,252

COLORADO MESA UNIVERSITY

GRAND JUNCTION, COLORADO

Colorado Mesa University, in Grand Junction, Colorado has always been an institution dedicated to providing an exceptional education at an affordable price. Founded in 1925, CMU has a long history of evolution, growing from a junior college to a vibrant university that offers more than 100 programs, including short-terms certificates, associate degrees, bachelor's degrees, master's degrees, and a doctoral program. To accommodate a growing student body of about 11,000, the campus has undergone numerous expansions resulting in state-of-the-art learning facilities across 90 acres in the heart of Grand Junction.

OUTDOOR RECREATION CENTER: Surrounded by mountains and mesas, deserts and rivers, Colorado Mesa's backyard is filled with unparalleled opportunities for year-round recreation. With organizations like the CMU Outdoor Program, students can explore their own backyard throughout the year or trek around the world during winter and summer breaks. Trips and activities include ice climbing, visits to natural hot springs, cross-country skiing and snowshoeing, whitewater rafting, kayaking, and rock climbing.

INTERNSHIPS: Colorado Mesa University lies in the heart of a growing business community. With a vibrant downtown area of small businesses, a dynamic industrial workforce and headquarters of several large companies, opportunities abound for students to gain real-world experience in their fields before graduation.

"In the nursing program we had the opportunity to have over 1,000 clinical hours in multiple specialties. The small class sizes at CMU made it easy to get one-on-one help with my instructors, be able to ask questions, and make lifelong friendship with my classmates."

– Emilia Ludwig, '16, St. Mary's Hospital Medical Center Registered Nurse

www.coloradomesa.edu
(970) 248-1875
admissions@
coloradomesa.edu

STUDENT PROFILE

8,384 undergraduate students

84% of undergrad students are full-time

53% female – 47% male

14% of students are from out of state

74% freshman retention rate

FACULTY PROFILE

20 to 1 student/faculty ratio

ADMISSIONS

Selectivity: 81%

SAT Ranges: E 470-590, M 470-570

ACT Ranges: C 17-24, M 17-24, E 17.25-24

TUITION & COST

Tuition (in-state): $8,343

Tuition (out-of-state): $22,200

Fees: $963

Room: $6,100

Board: $5,068

COLORADO SCHOOL OF MINES

GOLDEN, COLORADO

Colorado School of Mines is a leading institution in the science and engineering fields with a focus on energy and the environment. Students have the opportunity to engage in undergraduate research, develop leadership skills inside and outside of the classroom, and explore their interests through a variety of social and professional experiences. Established in 1874, Colorado School of Mines offers nearly 70 degree programs and additional minors, all of which adhere to the institution's mission to foster a responsibility to help develop a better world.

MINES WITHOUT BORDERS: Mines Without Borders (MWB) strives to improve the quality of life in marginalized communities by engaging students in sustainable projects. Students have practiced humanitarian engineering through such sustainability-promoting projects as designing a well-water distribution system in Los Gomez, Nicaragua, and implementing a foot bridge in San Juan to protect the town from floods during the rainy season.

UNIQUE MINORS: Undergraduate students have the opportunity to pursue a minor in such areas as Aerospace Studies, Biomechanical Engineering, Computer Sciences, Energy, Leadership in Social Responsibility, and more. The benefits of a minor are plentiful, whether a student wants to stand out in the job market or prepare for graduate study.

RESEARCH AT MINES: There are many opportunities to explore research through Mines' world-class facilities, faculty, and partnerships with national laboratories and international institutions. Students have the option to conduct research at one of Mines' departmental or institutional centers, the Colorado Center for Renewable Energy Economic Development, and more.

Recruiting at CSM is always a rewarding experience. Mines continues to turn out good intern and full-time candidates, and the services of the Career Center are always very much appreciated." - *ConocoPhillips*

www.mines.edu
(888) 446-9489
admissions@mines.edu

STUDENT PROFILE
4,788 undergraduate students

96% of undergrad students are full-time

29% female – 71% male

43% of students are from out of state

93% freshman retention rate

FACULTY PROFILE
16 to 1 student/faculty ratio

ADMISSIONS
Selectivity: 56%

SAT Ranges: E 640-710, M 670-740

ACT Ranges: C 28-32, M 28-33, E 27-33

TUITION & COST
Tuition (in-state): $16,170

Tuition (out-of-state): $35,220

Fees: $2,216

Room: $6,673

Board: $5,224

NAROPA UNIVERSITY

BOULDER, COLORADO

Naropa purposefully creates an environment rich in self-discovery by combining traditional academics with experiential education and mindfulness practice. Known as contemplative education, Naropa's one-of-a-kind way of educating builds intellectual acuity, a strong sense of self-awareness, and practical skills. These skills combine to inspire students to create meaningful careers that contribute to the greater good.

CELEBRATION, ECO-STYLE: Naropa hosts a number of events that celebrate the environment, green solutions, and sustainable practices. Each year, the university celebrates Sustainability Day in the fall, and Earth Day in the spring. Additionally, the Naropa community participates in the annual RecycleMania, a national competition for universities to divert waste from landfills.

NAROPA-PRENEURS: Equipped with self awareness, outstanding analytical and communication skills, and the courage to take chances, Naropa graduates go on to make meaningful lives for themselves as writers, social entrepreneurs, teachers, lawyers, artists, therapists, doctoral students, community recyclers, world travelers, and lifelong learners.

PERSONALIZED STUDIES: Naropa's Interdisciplinary Studies program offers students the opportunity to design their own custom major by integrating two to three disciplines taught at the school. Students receive support in designing their course of study and work with faculty mentors throughout their academic journey.

"The contemplative approach, in my opinion, is more effective to the learning process... What I experience here is permanently imprinted in my being, because I do it with enthusiasm and use the integrity of my being to present myself for classes—I always show up with my body, mind, and spirit." *– Marina B., BA Contemplative Psychology Class of 2020*

www.naropa.edu
(303) 546-3572
admissions@naropa.edu

STUDENT PROFILE

419 undergraduate students

92% of undergrad students are full-time

66% female – 34% male

61% of students are from out of state

73% freshman retention rate

FACULTY PROFILE

9 to 1 student/faculty ratio

ADMISSIONS

Selectivity: 98%

TUITION & COST

Tuition: $32,900

Fees: $170

Room & Board: $10,058

UNIVERSITY OF DENVER

DENVER, COLORADO

The only campus in the country to require a face-to-face interview for every admission candidate, University of Denver is focused on admitting students who are most likely to succeed at DU. Offering exceptional preparation for the professional world, lively and energetic students from across the globe, and the opportunity to make lifelong connections with faculty and fellow students, the University of Denver is the perfect choice for students looking to join a community of adventurous learners.

DIGITAL MEDIA STUDIES: DU offers an extraordinary digital media studies program, combining communications, computer science, and art. A graduate of this program was hired to do graphics for *The Matrix Reloaded*. Another similar program, animation and game development, is offered through the division of engineering and computer science.

A TEAM EFFORT: DU encourages active learning as opposed to the lecture-test format. Group dialogue is encouraged, and professors bring technology into the classroom. All students are required to have a laptop. DU students complete foundational courses, core curriculum requirements, and courses from their chosen major and minor, equipping them with sophisticated thinking skills and cross-disciplinary knowledge.

SERVICE LEARNING: Each year, about 1,500 DU students participate in service-learning courses. From courses on philosophy and social justice to intensive Spanish language and Mexican/Mayan cultural immersion, students can choose from a broad range of topics.

IF THE SCHOOL FITS...: DU strongly encourages all applicants to complete a Hyde Interview, an interview program in which students have a conversation with one to three members of DU's community (including faculty, staff and alumni) in more than thirty cities each year. Though grades and test scores play the largest role in admission decisions, the interview helps DU admit students who are motivated, honest, and open to new ideas. The interviews also serve to show prospective students that personal attention is more than a catchphrase at DU—it is a practice.

www.du.edu
(303) 871-2036
admission@du.edu

STUDENT PROFILE

5,765 undergraduate students

95% of undergrad students are full-time

53% female – 47% male

58% of students are from out of state

87% freshman retention rate

FACULTY PROFILE

11 to 1 student/faculty ratio

ADMISSIONS

Selectivity: 58%

SAT Ranges: E 590-680, M 570-670

ACT Ranges: C 25-30, M 24-28, E 24-31

TUITION & COST

Tuition: $47,520

Fees: $1,149

Room: $7,806

Board: $4,806

UNIVERSITY OF NORTHERN COLORADO

GREELEY, COLORADO

UNIVERSITY OF NORTHERN COLORADO

www.unco.edu
(970) 351-2881
admissions@unco.edu

The University of Northern Colorado is a public, doctoral/professional university located an hour north of Denver between the towering Rocky Mountains and blue-skied plains of eastern Colorado. UNC offers over 100 undergraduate and graduate degrees in areas of education and counseling, business, health and exercise sciences, the arts, and social sciences.

SUCCESS LOOKS LIKE YOU: The key to succeeding *after* college can be the right guidance *during* college. UNC's Career Services office provides the Success Looks Like You program, where alumni and local professionals come to campus for advising, mentorship, and panels for students in every major.

GAIN PROFESSIONAL EXPERIENCE: UNC students across disciplines participate in co-curricular and professional experiences in addition to their coursework. Business majors participate in a Professional Experience before graduating, ensuring that they're prepared for the demands of a modern workplace. Education and nursing students participate in student teaching and clinical rotations, respectively. Many programs offer job shadowing, tours of local organizations, and more. UNC students understand what it takes to succeed in the professional world, whatever the field.

COMMUNITY ENGAGEMENT: One example of students engaging on campus and in the community while also furthering their careers happens at the UNC Cancer Rehabilitation Institute, where students implement research on the effects of exercise on cancer survivors to improve their quality of life.

"The way that my classes were structured, the support I had from my professors who were actively practicing what they were teaching ... I was able to able to create a new field that I really wanted to work in and that helped push me to evaluate the world in a different way." - *Mackey Saturday '07*

STUDENT PROFILE

8,900 undergraduate students

90% of undergrad students are full-time

65% female – 35% male

14% of students are from out of state

72% freshman retention rate

FACULTY PROFILE

17 to 1 student/faculty ratio

ADMISSIONS

Selectivity: 91%

SAT Ranges: E 500-610, M 490-580

ACT Ranges: C 19-25, M 18-25, E 19-25

TUITION & COST

Tuition (in-state): $7,830

Tuition (out-of-state): $19,518

Fees: $2,358

Room: $5,304

Board: $5,900

WESTERN COLORADO UNIVERSITY

GUNNISON, COLORADO

www.western.edu
(970) 943-2119
admission@western.edu

Deep in the heart of the Rocky Mountains, Western Colorado University delivers computer science, engineering, a full liberal arts curriculum, and career preparation to 3,000 undergraduate and graduate students at an affordable cost. The university's tight-knit community ensures students receive personalized attention and gain real-world experience before graduation. Set in the unique Gunnison Valley, Western offers students endless opportunities for adventure and hands-on learning, both in and outside of the classrooms.

ACTIVITIES IN GUNNISON: The spectacular Gunnison Valley offers Western students a tight-knit community of passionate mountain dwellers. A free shuttle to the Crested Butte Mountain Resort makes it easy for Mountaineers to take full advantage of Colorado's best natural resources. And with more than 50 student-run clubs and organizations on campus, Western is an exciting place to live and learn.

Whether they work at campus radio station KWSB, join the Western Theatre Company, attend diverse programming at the university's vibrant Multicultural Center, or adventure with Wilderness Pursuits, Mountaineers find that there's always something going on in Gunnison.

HANDS-ON LEARNING: From their first year on campus, Western Mountaineers are immersed in academic adventure. It's easy to see that Western emphasizes hands-on learning: students strap on waders to study stream ecology, research the effects of elevation on athletes in the High-Altitude Performance Lab, and build business plans for local ski areas.

STUDY ABROAD: Whether they're journeying to Egypt to study emerging democracies in conflict zones or taking advantage of Western's relationship with Harlaxton University in England, Mountaineers take their travels seriously. Western's Master in Environmental Management program has also partnered with the Peace Corps Prep Program to help Western students earn their master's degrees while serving overseas.

STUDENT PROFILE

2,429 undergraduate students

75% of undergrad students are full-time

43% female – 57% male

30% of students are from out of state

69% freshman retention rate

FACULTY PROFILE

18 to 1 student/faculty ratio

ADMISSIONS

Selectivity: 86%

SAT Ranges: E 500-590, M 500-590

ACT Ranges: C 20-25, M 18-25, E 19-25

TUITION & COST

Tuition (in-state): $6,624

Tuition (out-of-state): $18,096

Fees: $3,490

Room: $5,030

Board: $4,605

ALBERTUS MAGNUS COLLEGE

NEW HAVEN, CONNECTICUT

The Dominican tradition is the driving force of all that makes Albertus Magnus College an excellent academic community in which to grow. Not only is the pursuit of Veritas, or truth, shown in the well-rounded, exploratory liberal arts curriculum that supports every major, but it is also noticeable in the everyday interactions between students and faculty alike. Students at Albertus Magnus College are curious, and they are always seeking new ways to approach scholarly challenges and social issues alike in an attempt to grow as lifelong learners and successful members of their community.

ALBERTUS SERVES: Every day, students involved in Campus Ministries and other student-run clubs and organizations are tackling issues in the greater New Haven area, providing help wherever it is needed. The College also provides opportunities for students to serve through internships, providing them practical work experience while helping others. Academics, professional experience, and the fight for the common good are all intertwined.

In May of 2018, the Fearless Falcons participated in a Day of Service as part of the four days of festivities for the inauguration of Albertus' 14th President Marc M. Camille, Ed.D. More than 2,300 volunteers cleaned up local parks and community gardens, walked in support of various charities, prepared food for soup kitchens, and moved books in the library.

INNOVATIVE: Albertus embraces technology's ability to enhance human creativity as well as human creativity's ability to enhance technology. aims to enhance the capacity for technological innovation and human creativity. The College is constantly developing a multi-use Digital Media and Creative Arts Education Center to provide academic programs that leverage advances in digital technologies.

"A liberal arts education introduces us to what we have to offer. When we have the power of analysis we won't conform to prevailing ideas and practices." *– Meteka Joseph '18*

www.albertus.edu
admissions@albertus.edu

STUDENT PROFILE
1,113 undergraduate students

86% of undergrad students are full-time

67% female – 33% male

5% of students are from out of state

FACULTY PROFILE
13 to 1 student/faculty ratio

ADMISSIONS
Selectivity: 58%

SAT Ranges: E 410-540, M 400-510

TUITION & COST
Tuition: $31,570

Fees: $490

Room & Board: $13,400

EASTERN CONNECTICUT STATE UNIVERSITY

WILLIMANTIC, CONNECTICUT

Eastern Connecticut State University is the state's designated public liberal arts university. A predominantly undergraduate institution, Eastern attracts and welcomes a diverse community of learners who are supported by a teaching faculty, staff, administrators, and a residential campus that promotes intellectual curiosity, integrity, and social responsibility.

UNDERGRADUATE RESEARCH: At Eastern, students of all majors and class levels conduct research. As undergraduates, their high-quality work is published in academic journals and presented at local and national conferences—from Eastern's own CREATE conference to the respected Posters on the Hill and National Conference on Undergraduate Research.

NEW MAJORS AND MINORS: Recent new majors include Criminology, Health Sciences, Finance, New Media Studies, Liberal Studies, and Philosophy. Recent minors include Bioinformatics, Environmental Health Science, Insurance, and Fashion and Costume Design.

CENTER FOR COMMUNITY ENGAGEMENT: Eastern and the town of Willimantic maintain a mutually beneficial relationship that continues to strengthen due to the Center for Community Engagement (CCE). The CCE organizes numerous special events, such as the annual Day of Giving holiday meal, as well as semester-long service programs that affect long-term change, such as tutor programs with Willimantic Public Schools. In the 2018-19 academic year, more than 2,500 students volunteered 27,500 hours.

> "I was walking in the Student Center one day and the assistant dean came up to me and congratulated me. He knew my name and my accomplishments. That doesn't happen at larger schools."
>
> – Stefanie Dominguez '18, Early Childhood Education major

www.easternct.edu
(860) 465-5286
admissions@easternct.edu

STUDENT PROFILE

4,818 undergraduate students

89% of undergrad students are full-time

56% female – 44% male

6% of students are from out of state

76% freshman retention rate

FACULTY PROFILE

16 to 1 student/faculty ratio

ADMISSIONS

Selectivity: 60%

SAT Ranges: E 520-610, M 500-580

ACT Ranges: C 19-24, M 18-24, E 19-25

TUITION & COST

Tuition (in-state): $5,424

Tuition (out-of-state): $16,882

Fees: $5,495

Room: $7,500

Board: $5,550

FAIRFIELD UNIVERSITY

FAIRFIELD, CONNECTICUT

Fairfield

www.fairfield.edu
(203) 254-4100
admis@fairfield.edu

Established in 1942 with roots in one of the modern world's oldest intellectual and spiritual traditions, Fairfield University is a leading Catholic, Jesuit University. The University offers a comprehensive core curriculum, more than 40 undergraduate majors,16 interdisciplinary minors, and a wide range of opportunities for service and civic engagement. Committed to the Jesuit ideals of broad intellectual inquiry, Fairfield University fosters a strong sense of community among its students and offers an educational experience that encourages the pursuit of social justice and the cultivation of the whole person: body, mind, and spirit.

ART FACILITIES: The new Bellarmine Art Museum serves as a learning laboratory for students and members of the regional community with a rich and varied collection of paintings, sculptures, and decorative arts objects. Through an ongoing series of lively and informative lectures, these 'public conversations' present eminent opinion-makers, artists, authors, and contributors to the humanities and sciences. The Open VISIONS Forum, for example, is a popular lecture series that engages the 'life of the mind' with students and the Connecticut community.

UNDERGRADUATE RESEARCH: Fairfield students gain valuable research, scholarship, publication, and presentation experiences through a wide array of student-faculty, group, and independent opportunities. Through such resources as the Office of Prestigious Scholarships and Fellowships and the Office of Service-Learning, the university provides challenging opportunities for students to participate in research and scholarly endeavors.

WELL-ROUNDED CURRICULUM: The core curriculum requires students to take 60 credits in five areas including mathematics and natural sciences; history and social/behavioral sciences; philosophy, religious studies, and ethics; English and the arts; and modern or classical languages and literature. Fairfield doesn't view the core as a checklist to get through, but rather as an important, integrated, and interdisciplinary component of well-rounded education.

STUDENT PROFILE
4,113 undergraduate students

94% of undergrad students are full-time

60% female — 40% male

73% of students are from out of state

90% freshman retention rate

FACULTY PROFILE
12 to 1 student/faculty ratio

ADMISSIONS
Selectivity: 61%

TUITION & COST
Tuition: $46,490

Fees: $675

Room: $8,750

Board: $5,530

GOODWIN COLLEGE

EAST HARTFORD, CONNECTICUT

Goodwin College is a place where students can learn, grow, and succeed in a community of hard-working, motivated students, faculty, and staff. The College aims to give students a career-focused education, tailoring the experience in the classroom to the upcoming demands of their future employers. Such a future-driven educational environment embodies the way that Goodwin strives to make the college experience fruitful, worthwhile, and altogether fulfilling.

EXPLORING DIVERSITY: Goodwin College provides students with many opportunities to explore cultures and embrace in both their campus community and the world around. One of the ways in which the Goodwin community celebrates multiculturalism is through the popular African Heritage Club. In this organization, students explore and teach one another of the many traditions and cultures of different African communities.

STUDENT-LED ACTIVITIES: Just a few clubs and organizations available include such groups as the environmental science club, a number of dance crews, intramural sports, and more.

ACADEMIC SUCCESS CENTER: Goodwin College's Academic Success Center (ASC) promotes and fosters student learning and development by providing free tutoring to all Goodwin College students. Tutoring is available by appointment or on a walk-in basis by both professional and peer tutors who happily help students work through difficult assignments and ideas. And for busy students, online tutoring is available to 24 hours a day to save an extra trip to campus.

"If it had not been for the ASC, I wouldn't have the drive and confidence that I have today, and for that, I am thankful. The resources and help I was given made me the student that I am and will someday make me the nurse that I aspire to become." *- Olivia Stacey, student*

www.goodwin.edu
(800) 889-3282

STUDENT PROFILE

3,394 undergraduate students

12% of undergrad students are full-time

82% female — 18% male

4% of students are from out of state

59% freshman retention rate

FACULTY PROFILE

11 to 1 student/faculty ratio

TUITION & COST

Tuition: $19,988

Fees: $900

SACRED HEART UNIVERSITY

FAIRFIELD, CONNECTICUT

Distinguished by the personal attention it provides its students, Sacred Heart University is recognized for its commitment to academic excellence, award-winning advisement program, cutting-edge technology, championship Division I athletic teams, and nationally recognized community service programs. Situated in Fairfield, Connecticut, the main campus is ideally located one hour north of New York City and two and a half hours south of Boston. The surrounding neighborhood of Fairfield has its own charm as well; students enjoy the city's five miles of shoreline, marinas, parks, open space, and plenty of shopping and fine dining.

WELCH EXPERIENCE: Just one hallmark example of SHU's focus on active learning is the Welch Experience program for students in the Jack Welch College of Business & Technology. The program includes faculty-led courses abroad, research, mentoring, and co-curricular activities designed to develop career awareness, business acumen, and leadership capabilities.

MAJOR IN SUCCESS: The University offers students the opportunity to participate in its innovative "Major in Success (MIS)" program to understand how their unique talents and skills can be used to set and achieve their goals. This highly effective, structured program is open to all undergraduates, particularly catering to the needs of first-and second-year students. MIS is implemented over the course of several weeks through individual and group career counseling, which also includes the use of popular career and personality assessment inventories.

"From building new facilities to hiring professors with real-world work experience, students are set up to succeed from day one. Sacred Heart is truly an amazing living and learning community and in just my first year alone, I have learned so much and had many positive experiences with great friends!" *– Abigail K. '21; Milford, CT*

www.sacredheart.edu
(203) 371-7880
enroll@sacredheart.edu

STUDENT PROFILE

5,907 undergraduate students

87% of undergrad students are full-time

65% female – 35% male

62% of students are from out of state

83% freshman retention rate

FACULTY PROFILE

13 to 1 student/faculty ratio

ADMISSIONS

Selectivity: 60%

SAT Ranges: E 550-620, M 550-620

ACT Ranges: C 23-27

TUITION & COST

Tuition: $42,800

Fees: $270

Room: $10,900

Board: $5,060

UNIVERSITY OF HARTFORD

WEST HARTFORD, CONNECTICUT

The University of Hartford recognizes that students are just as complex as the world around them. As a dynamic liberal arts institution, UHart encourages exploration across disciplines and beyond the norm. Sitting just outside of Hartford, Connecticut, the University of Hartford has spent over 60 years nurturing a diverse student body with strengths across academics, athletics, and the arts. And while UHart's population may be small, it makes a big impact across 100+ fields of study. University of Hartford prides itself as "a university for the world," graduating scholars who spread their talents to every corner of the professional sphere.

UHART HONORS: The honors program at the University of Hartford provides students with an excellent opportunity to further challenge themselves and enhance their education. With exclusive honors courses, close faculty mentorship, and interdisciplinary seminars, these tenacious students push themselves to their full potential. And it certainly doesn't go unnoticed; an annual colloquium gives students the chance to showcase their excellent work and share their passions with others.

CAREER SERVICES: Each student at the University of Hartford has the opportunity to participate as an intern not only to gain professional experience but also earn academic credit toward their degree.

Students are encouraged to meet with their academic advisors and visit the on-campus career services department. With the helpful staff by their side, they prepare for the future with résumé assistance and career exploration.

"I learned a lot about myself. Who I am, who I want to be. Sometimes, you go long periods without experiencing any significant personal growth, and sometimes it happens all at once." – *Liel A., International Studies & Economics*

UNIVERSITY OF HARTFORD

www.hartford.edu
(800) 947-4303
admission@hartford.edu

STUDENT PROFILE

5,069 undergraduate students

88% of undergrad students are full-time

51% female – 49% male

52% of students are from out of state

73% freshman retention rate

FACULTY PROFILE

10 to 1 student/faculty ratio

ADMISSIONS

Selectivity: 81%

SAT Ranges: E 520-620, M 510-610

ACT Ranges: C 21-27

TUITION & COST

Tuition: $36,088

Fees: $2,822

Room: $8,008

Board: $4,338

UNIVERSITY OF NEW HAVEN

WEST HAVEN, CONNECTICUT

University of New Haven

www.newhaven.edu
(203) 932-7000
admissions@
newhaven.edu

University of New Haven is a private, comprehensive, student-focused institution that is a recognized leader in experiential education with an emphasis on career preparation. Here, the experience of learning is both personal and pragmatic, guided by distinguished faculty who care deeply about individual student success. As leaders in their fields, faculty provide the inspiration and recognition needed for students to fulfill their potential and succeed at whatever they choose to do.

CORPORATE CHALLENGE: Through the Corporate Challenge, student groups competitively perform field work on a case study prepared for them by the College of Business and a local business organization. The case study, relevant to emerging issues in business, engages participants in an ongoing project that produces real results within the local business. Finalists receive awards, scholarships, and cash prizes.

BUSINESS FOR THE REAL WORLD: Through an innovative combination of faculty-led research, work-integrated learning internships and co-op programs, academic service-learning, and numerous study abroad programs, students at the University of New Haven are not just given an education; they are prepared to be successful after graduation.

The College of Business, for instance, sponsors a three-tiered mentoring program that includes Business Leader to Student, Student-to-Student, and E-mentoring programs. Additionally, graduating seniors get an added benefit as they accompany an industry professional throughout the day to get firsthand experience of their workplace and career.

HIGH-TECH UNIVERSITY: The University keeps up with the latest in high-tech educational innovations to fully engage students and faculty in the learning and teaching process. The Tegrity learning system allows faculty members to record class lectures and post them online so students can download actual audio and video of the class to review. Numerous computer labs and wireless technology help ensure that students can stay connected across campus, enabling them to study on their own time and in their own way.

STUDENT PROFILE

5,147 undergraduate students

94% of undergrad students are full-time

53% female – 47% male

59% of students are from out of state

79% freshman retention rate

FACULTY PROFILE

16 to 1 student/faculty ratio

ADMISSIONS

Selectivity: 88%

SAT Ranges: E 510-610, M 500-600

ACT Ranges: C 21-27, M 19-26, E 20-25

TUITION & COST

Tuition: $36,770

Fees: $1,400

Room: $9,860

Board: $5,750

AVE MARIA UNIVERSITY

AVE MARIA, FLORIDA

Ave Maria University provides a unique and engaging liberal arts education in the Catholic tradition. Students at Ave Maria learn the skills necessary to succeed in the workforce and make an impact in the community. While at Ave Maria, students travel the world, serve their communities, and learn more about God and their relationship with Him as Catholics. Located in beautiful Southwest Florida, Ave Maria is a place for students to learn, live, and grow into the next generation of leaders and faithful servants.

UNDERGRADUATE RESEARCH: Across disciplines, undergrads have a number of opportunities to conduct research and take an independent look into their coursework. This can take many forms—history students complete theses and help construct museum exhibits, theatre students get to understand and perform the works of Shakespeare, and science students investigate Alzheimer's and other diseases.

FAITH HOUSEHOLDS: In groups of up to 17 students each, those who participate in Faith Households study, live, and pray together throughout their time at Ave Maria. These groups are designed to help students grow academically, spiritually, socially, and morally with the independence to shape their experience however they see fit. They even discover their individual purpose through the creation of their own covenants, agreements on spiritual, academic, personal, and physical standards that the Household will uphold. Students can find a community all while developing their leadership and team-building skills.

THE MOTHER TERESA PROJECT: In the spirit of Mother Teresa, Ave Maria's unique Mother Teresa Project is dedicated to serving and educating the global community. Students who participate study the life and work of Mother Teresa, all while designing service projects in Florida, across the United States, and even internationally.

Groups work together to grow in their faith as they help others understand Mother Teresa's teachings, meeting once a month to see lectures, go on retreats, and plan outreach for community service.

AVE MARIA
UNIVERSITY

www.avemaria.edu
(239) 280-2500

STUDENT PROFILE

1,072 undergraduate students

97% of undergrad students are full-time

51% female – 49% male

68% freshman retention rate

FACULTY PROFILE

14 to 1 student/faculty ratio

ADMISSIONS

Selectivity: 42%

SAT Ranges: E 500-630, M 480-600

ACT Ranges: C 21-27, M 18-26, E 20-26

TUITION & COST

Tuition: $19,135

Fees: $835

Room: $6,240

Board: $4,715

BARRY UNIVERSITY

MIAMI SHORES, FLORIDA

Barry University

Barry University provides a higher education experience that applies what is learned in the classroom to a constantly changing and diverse world, promoting civic engagement for the betterment of humanity. Barry is focused on inspiring and training the next generation of change agents and leaders.

CENTER FOR COMMUNITY SERVICE INITIATIVES: Barry University's Center for Community Service Initiatives is the university's clearinghouse for community engagement. It functions as a catalyst for the pursuit of social justice among students, faculty, and staff. Past community service projects include farm-workers' rights advocacy, human trafficking awareness initiatives, business development in low-income areas, and photography projects for at-risk teens.

INNOVATIVE ANSWERS: Barry's service learning programs integrate coursework with community needs, facilitating engagement at the local, national, and global levels. Barry University students collaborate with community partners to pursue systematic, self-sustaining solutions to human, social, economic, and environmental problems. This is accomplished through community service, service-learning, community-based research, internships, practicum and field placements, and advocacy projects.

PERSONAL GROWTH: At Barry, students enjoy a full range of extracurricular activities, including intramural sports, student government, and more than 60 clubs and organizations. And from its "GLO party" and "Founders' Week" in the fall to Homecoming and the "Festival of Nations" in the spring, it is clear to see that tradition and involvement thrive at Barry.

THE NEXT GENERATION OF CHANGE AGENTS: Faithful to its traditions, the Barry University experience fosters individual and communal transformation. In this way, student learning leads to knowledge and truth, reflection leads to informed action, and a commitment to social justice leads to collaborative service. Barry graduates apply their learning and service to their constantly changing and diverse world, promoting civic engagement for the betterment of humanity.

www.barry.edu
(800) 695-2279
admissions@barry.edu

STUDENT PROFILE

3,505 undergraduate students

85% of undergrad students are full-time

60% female — 40% male

61% freshman retention rate

FACULTY PROFILE

13 to 1 student/faculty ratio

ADMISSIONS

Selectivity: 85%

SAT Ranges: E 470-560, M 410-500

ACT Ranges: C 17-20, M 16-20, E 16-21

TUITION & COST

Tuition: $29,700

Fees: $150

Room & Board: $10,800

FLAGLER COLLEGE

ST. AUGUSTINE, FLORIDA

Located within the beautiful, historic city of St. Augustine, Flagler College exudes all the charm and wonder that has attracted generations of explorers and entrepreneurs to the Florida coast. Its forward-thinking curriculum is inspired by Henry M. Flagler himself, a remarkable innovator known for the many hotels he built to make the Florida coast the vacation destination it is today. Flagler College is full of culture, and its students and faculty are bursting with curiosity. Its curriculum challenges critical-thinking skills and prepares students to take on the world as confident leaders.

PASSPORT CO-CURRICULAR PROGRAM: As an incentive to encourage students to cultivate their curiosities outside of the classroom, the Passport Co-Curricular Program requires students to attend a variety of events that exhibit all the great perspectives of a liberal arts education. Typical Passport-credited events include concerts, plays, and debates, all of which support and deepen students' academics across all disciplines.

SCHOOL LOCATION: Flagler College is located in the tropical paradise of St. Augustine, Florida. This bustling tourist town is vibrant with art, eateries, and shopping centers that always give adventurous minds something to do. It is surrounded by more than 40 miles of pristine beaches, standing at the center of everything that make Florida beautiful.

UNDERGRADUATE RESEARCH: Research at Flagler has been recognized both nationally and around the world, and with the help of Flagler's Internal Funding Awards, students are able to travel to conferences and access materials without needing to worry about expenses.

Recent student research has covered the sociological issues of female sportscasters in the athletics industry, biological processes among a community of phytoplankton in California, and the economic complexities of China's rivalry with America as a global superpower. Students are guaranteed the opportunity to sink their teeth into any topic within any discipline.

www.flagler.edu
(904) 819-6220
admissions@flagler.edu

STUDENT PROFILE

2,675 undergraduate students

52% of undergrad students are full-time

65% female – 35% male

43% of students are from out of state

72% freshman retention rate

FACULTY PROFILE

16 to 1 student/faculty ratio

ADMISSIONS

Selectivity: 57%

SAT Ranges: E 520-610, M 430-550

ACT Ranges: C 21-26, M 18-24, E 21-26

TUITION & COST

Tuition: $18,850

Fees: $100

Room: $5,800

Board: $5,540

FLORIDA INSTITUTE OF TECHNOLOGY

MELBOURNE, FLORIDA

www.fit.edu
(321) 674-8030
admission@fit.edu

Founded in 1958—the same year as NASA and in the same county as Kennedy Space Center—Florida Tech has always been a university for students who shoot for the stars. In fact, Florida Tech started as a night school for early space program workers, providing the advanced education they needed in order to win the space race. Today, with its dive-in, buckle-up, hands-on approach to education, Florida Tech is a top choice for students interested in innovation, hard work, and lofty goals.

DIVING IN FROM THE START: A key part of every Florida Tech student's education is engaging in hands-on activities on day one. From laboratory experience to outside-the-classroom fieldwork and collaborative projects, learning is an active, immersive endeavor. In their first year, students may write a new business plan, engineer a solution to a common problem, or even fly a plane.

THE FLORIDA FACTOR: Being in Melbourne on the "Space Coast" of Florida, students find themselves a short drive from the Atlantic Ocean and just 45 minutes from NASA-Kennedy Space Center. As a result, opportunities to study the ocean, marine life, and extreme weather abound—not to mention all the inside looks at the future of astronomy and space exploration. Students can research the effects of hurricanes, the depletion of fish populations, meteorology, astrobiology, rocket science, and more.

RESEARCH FUELS EXPERIENCE: Research is the backbone of a Florida Tech education, complementing students' in-class learning and connecting them to experienced professors who care about their success.

Undergraduates can assist faculty on advanced research; past projects have investigated blackholes, autism, drone usage, the atmosphere of Mars, and more. Students in their first year can also assist upperclassmen on their Senior Design projects with research, giving them a glimpse of the academic requirements to come while connecting them with a peer mentor.

STUDENT PROFILE

3,411 undergraduate students

96% of undergrad students are full-time

29% female – 71% male

52% of students are from out of state

89% freshman retention rate

FACULTY PROFILE

14 to 1 student/faculty ratio

ADMISSIONS

Selectivity: 65%

SAT Ranges: E 570-660, M 580-680

ACT Ranges: C 25-30, M 25-30, E 24-32

TUITION & COST

Tuition: $41,720

Room: $7,000

Board: $5,880

FLORIDA SOUTHERN COLLEGE

LAKELAND, FLORIDA

Florida Southern is nationally recognized for excellence in experiential education and the opportunity for students to study abroad, participate in professional internships, and graduate in four years. Offering more than 70 undergraduate and graduate degree programs, the College enrolls 3,000 students from 50 states and 50 countries. Florida Southern's 113-acre, lakeside campus is ideally located directly between Tampa and Orlando in Lakeland, Florida—one of the fastest growing metropolitan areas.

STUDY ABROAD : Through an innovative Junior Journey program, all incoming first-year students are guaranteed a travel experience in their junior or senior year, which is included in their tuition. Florida Southern students pursue their interests around the world in exciting locations such as Australia, China, Costa Rica, Ireland, Italy, New Zealand, Spain, and the United Kingdom.

ACADEMIC PROGRAMS: FSC 's 70+ programs of study, including business, computer science, nursing, communication, psychology, biology, art, education, marine biology, music, and theatre performance. Pre-professional programs include pre-medicine, -pharmacy, -dentistry, -law, and -engineering.

ADVISORS: All first-year students adjust quickly to academic life through a unique program pairing each student with a faculty advisor for regular meetings during the first semester. In addition, Florida Southern is one of the few colleges in the country with a dedicated Dean of Student Success who helps students make the most of the College's many academic resources.

"Even in the best environment, college students go through difficult times. It's the support from RAs, faculty, and resources like the Counseling and Wellness Centers that help you through. EVERYONE here wants to see you excel; they are always there—pushing you to be your best."

– Colby Firestone '21

www.flsouthern.edu
(863) 680-4111
fscadm@flsouthern.edu

STUDENT PROFILE
2,496 undergraduate students

99% of undergrad students are full-time

64% female – 36% male

37% of students are from out of state

82% freshman retention rate

FACULTY PROFILE
12 to 1 student/faculty ratio

ADMISSIONS
Selectivity: 50%

SAT Ranges: E 580-660, M 550-640

ACT Ranges: C 23-29, M 21-27, E 23-30

TUITION & COST
Tuition: $35,600

Fees: $748

Room: $7,070

Board: $4,600

LYNN UNIVERSITY

BOCA RATON, FLORIDA

Lynn is agile, dedicated, forward-looking, and well placed. It embraces new ideas and technologies that empower its faculty to deliver creatively its nationally praised core curriculum. The Lynn community believes in providing an open and supportive environment in which professors, academic advisors, and mentors are readily available. Lynn University concentrates on the art of teaching, making good students great and great students remarkable.

ACCELERATED BACHELOR'S DEGREE: Lynn's accelerated bachelor's degree is an incredibly unique program that offers students the chance to complete a 4-year degree in just 3 years. Students who participate work closely with academic advisors to create a degree program that is unique to their individual needs. There are countless benefits to participation in this program. Students in the accelerated bachelor's degree can take extra courses at no cost. They also enjoy the advantage of an early graduation, decreased tuition, the opportunity to design their own path of study, and the ability to jumpstart their careers to get ahead in the workplace.

THE CONSERVATORY OF MUSIC: In addition to practicing daily with renowned faculty-artists, students admitted to the Conservatory of Music enjoy a full-tuition scholarship and the opportunity to be featured in more than 10 live performances each year.

JANUARY (J)-TERM: The January Term is a unique learning experience in which students can apply academic theories to projects, social initiatives, and internships. The goal of a J-Term is to allow students to more deeply explore their disciplines through real-life application. Students are expected to complete one course each January Term that explores specialized and application-based subjects.

iEXPLORE: Lynn's iExplore program helps undecided majors explore career options that may lead to a declared major of interest. An iExplore Advisor builds a personal profile to see what strengths and interests a student has. A tailored program is then created to help the student explore career options and a coordinating major.

www.lynn.edu
(561) 237-7900
admission@lynn.edu

STUDENT PROFILE

2,204 undergraduate students

83% of undergrad students are full-time

48% female – 52% male

50% freshman retention rate

FACULTY PROFILE

17 to 1 student/faculty ratio

ADMISSIONS

Selectivity: 85%

TUITION & COST

Tuition: $35,260

Fees: $2,250

Room & Board: $11,970

ROLLINS COLLEGE

WINTER PARK, FLORIDA

Rollins
EST. 1885

Rollins' extraordinary undergraduate and graduate degree programs feature small classes taught by renowned faculty. The academic experience is enhanced by study abroad and internship opportunities as well as ways to participate in student organizations and the local community. Bordering Lake Virginia, Rollins has a lush, 70-acre campus located in Winter Park in the heart of Central Florida.

AREAS OF STUDY: The College offers a wide range of majors and minors in a variety of areas, including expressive arts, humanities, interdisciplinary study, sciences and mathematics, social sciences, as well as pre-professional programs. The 3/2 Accelerated Management Program allows students to graduate with a bachelor's degree and an MBA from Rollins in five years. Additionally, a variety of Rollins-approved, off-campus programs offer the opportunity to extend education beyond the borders of the campus.

ACHIEVED SCHOLARS: Rollins has a long history of producing students who are awarded a wide variety of prestigious scholarships. Since receiving its first Fulbright award in 1951, Rollins has produced a total of 49 Fulbright scholars, 24 of whom have been awarded since 2006.

BEAUTIFUL CAMPUS IN A BEAUTIFUL CITY: The Rollins College campus is awe inspiring. The tree-lined, 70-acre lakefront campus is located two blocks from historic downtown Winter Park and just minutes from downtown Orlando and Central Florida. The cities allow students to enjoy Florida's natural beauty and take courses in buildings known for their magnificent Spanish-Mediterranean style.

SUSTAINABILITY: Rollins has been a leader in environmental education and sustainable business practices for more than 20 years. Sustainability-focused academics, initiatives, and student-led programs have become ingrained in nearly every facet of life at Rollins. Its overall dedication to environmental stewardship has given it the recognition as one of the most environmentally responsible colleges in the U.S. and Canada.

www.rollins.edu
(407) 646-2161
admission@rollins.edu

STUDENT PROFILE

2,612 undergraduate students

94% of undergrad students are full-time

60% female – 40% male

34% of students are from out of state

83% freshman retention rate

FACULTY PROFILE

11 to 1 student/faculty ratio

ADMISSIONS

Selectivity: 64%

TUITION & COST

Tuition: $48,335

Room: $8,715

Board: $6,015

SOUTHEASTERN UNIVERSITY

LAKELAND, FLORIDA

Choosing the right college is about finding a place that provides the support for a lifetime of service to others. And SEU gives students the foundation they need to succeed in *life*, not just at work. SEU has more than 80 degree programs to choose from as well as a thriving community that inspires deep, personal, and meaningful relationships. And SEU's campus is growing! The University recently opened its 125,000-square-foot living-and-learning facility, which includes new residence halls, a visual and performing arts space, a Bloomberg financial lab, and a food court.

SEU WORSHIP: The student-led music ministry of Southeastern University, SEU Worship, writes, performs, and professionally produces original worship songs every year. As of summer 2018, SEU Worship reached more than 13 million streams on Spotify.

ACCELERATION TO SUCCESS: The 4+1 Degree Programs enable students to earn both a bachelor's and master's degree in just a total of five years. These accelerated programs for Business, Education, and Social Work not only to save money, but also time in pursuit of a dream profession.

Beyond these three fields, SEU equips students in every field with the tools and paths they need for a bright future. For instance, students can enjoy guaranteed acceptance to medical school in the University's cooperation with Lake Erie College of Osteopathic Medicine.

SPIRITUAL LIFE: The spiritual development of each student is the very core of SEU's mission. Through chapel services, mission trips, community outreach, faith integration in the classroom, and so much more, faith is fostered, nurtured, and strengthened on a daily basis.

"If you could look at the DNA of my heart and soul, you'd see influencers from SEU all over it. I am who I am because of SEU." – *Kendall Altmyer, '13 & '15*

www.seu.edu
(863) 667-5018
admission@seu.edu

STUDENT PROFILE
4,788 undergraduate students

89% of undergrad students are full-time

56% female – 44% male

47% of students are from out of state

68% freshman retention rate

FACULTY PROFILE
20 to 1 student/faculty ratio

ADMISSIONS
Selectivity: 46%

SAT Ranges: E 500-610, M 470-570

ACT Ranges: C 19-24, M 17-24, E 17-25

TUITION & COST
Tuition: $24,360

Fees: $1,000

Room & Board: $9,550

UNIVERSITY OF MIAMI

MIAMI, FLORIDA

University of Miami is known for its major research initiatives. The University is involved in nearly $330 million in research a year—a vast majority of which is put to good use at the Miller School of Medicine. UM grooms its students to become strong individuals with excellent leadership skills. Students are taught to recognize their duty to both the local community as well as the global society.

THE COLLEGE OF ENGINEERING RESIDENCE: The College of Engineering has an established residence in University Village. Students living in the apartment are involved in a residential research experience in collaboration with the National Science Foundation. The focus of the project is develop habits of sustainability in conjunction with new technology.

CIVIC ENGAGEMENT: University of Miami regards service as an integral part of the undergraduate experience and pushes students to recognize their duty to the community.

One UM initiative allows UM students to serve underprivileged and underrepresented high school students in Miami-Dade County, working directly with high school teachers to fine tune their curriculum and approach to teaching. Another initiative utilizes the creative minds of UM students to work with community partners to promote affordable housing. Through these and more, students have the amazing opportunity to shape the city around them and enact positive change.

UNDERGRADUATE RESEARCH: The College of Arts and Sciences is the #1 authority on undergraduate research at UM. Research is an amazing opportunity for students to demonstrate both their knowledge and curiosity within a specific area of study. Research can vary from collaborating with a professor to creating original work abroad. And with such beneficial initiatives as the "Beyond the Book" scholarship, students can conduct fieldwork or summer lab research while receiving a $2,500 stipend.

www.miami.edu
(305) 284-6000
admission@miami.edu

STUDENT PROFILE
10,832 undergraduate students

94% of undergrad students are full-time

52% female – 48% male

55% of students are from out of state

91% freshman retention rate

FACULTY PROFILE
12 to 1 student/faculty ratio

ADMISSIONS
Selectivity: 36%

SAT Ranges: E 620-700, M 610-720

ACT Ranges: C 28-32, M 26-32, E 28-34

TUITION & COST
Tuition: $47,040

Fees: $1,444

Room: $7,880

Board: $5,786

UNIVERSITY OF SOUTH FLORIDA

TAMPA, FLORIDA

Founded in 1956, the University of South Florida is a major metropolitan research university located in the heart of Tampa Bay. Bright, talented students hailing from over 128 countries come to the University of South Florida to experience everything the institution has to offer: student access, innovative research opportunities, and a rigorous, interdisciplinary academic environment. USF graduates enter the workforce as thoughtful, dedicated, innovative citizens ready to change the world.

EMERGING LEADERS INSTITUTE: The inspiring Emerging Leaders weekend retreat prepares 50-60 first-year students to take on leadership roles at USF. Students learn to enhance their understanding of leadership, explore their personal values and interests, and meet other aspiring students to make lasting friendships. The retreat is led by a team of successful student leaders who routinely make a major impact on campus themselves.

FKL CORE: The Foundation of Knowledge and Learning (FKL) Core Curriculum is designed to provide students with a diversity of ideas, concepts, and ways of acquiring new knowledge. The FKL Core emphasizes the importance of inquiry as a means of developing complex intellectual skills. Students who are undecided are encouraged to use the core as an opportunity to explore various disciplines.

UNDERGRADUATE RESEARCH: Students are encouraged to seek out research opportunities as early as their freshman year. As one of the top research institutions in Florida, USF offers students rich, challenging opportunities to further their studies.

"At USF, a fundamental principle of our student success initiative is the belief that all students, regardless of race, ethnicity, and socioeconomic status, can and will succeed if given the opportunity to do so." *- Paul Dosal, Vice President for Student Success and Student Affairs*

www.usf.edu
(813) 974-2011

STUDENT PROFILE
31,772 undergraduate students

78% of undergrad students are full-time

54% female – 46% male

8% of students are from out of state

90% freshman retention rate

FACULTY PROFILE
22 to 1 student/faculty ratio

ADMISSIONS
Selectivity: 45%

SAT Ranges: E 580-650, M 570-660

ACT Ranges: C 24-29, M 23-27, E 23-30

TUITION & COST
Tuition (in-state): $4,559

Tuition (out-of-state): $15,473

Fees: $1,851

Room: $5,750

Board: $3,950

BRENAU UNIVERSITY

GAINESVILLE, GEORGIA

COLLEGE PROFILES: GEORGIA

www.brenau.edu
(770) 534-6100
admissions@brenau.edu

Founded in 1878 as a single-gender undergraduate institution, Brenau University now comprises a wide range of undergraduate and graduate degree programs with a mission to prepare students for extraordinary lives. Brenau's name is as unique as the institution itself. It comprises the first four letters of *"brennen,"* a German word related to refining precious metals, and first two letters of the Latin word for gold, *"aurum."* The translated meaning became the motto for Brenau College women: *"as gold refined by fire."*

FOUR PORTALS OF LEARNING: Brenau's Four Portals of Learning is a liberal arts-based curriculum that transcends traditional academic disciplines and touches on all learning platforms. The Four Portals through which Brenau students pass expand students' world views; improve communication and skills; excite intellectual curiosity through research; and stimulate creative expression through exposure to the arts.

In its ambitious plan to reform liberal arts education by blending it with professional preparation, Brenau creates an environment for improving students' critical thinking—"the ultimate transferable job skill."

REAL-WORLD SCIENCE: Undergraduate health science and doctoral physical therapy students have the rare opportunity to work together with Dr. Heather Ross, associate professor of physical therapy, and Dr. Jessi Shrout, cytotechnologist and assistant professor of biology, on groundbreaking laboratory research. Studying stem cells in rat brains, these students play a crucial part in the pursuit of finding new treatments for stroke victims.

ART AT BRENAU: As a traditional showplace for fine arts, Brenau boasts one of the most impressive permanent art collections of painting, sculpture, and other art works of any institution of its size. The university is the first—and only—academic partner of the world-class High Museum of Art in Atlanta. Among the roughly 6,500-piece Permanent Art Collection is an impressive selection of pop art and mid-20th century modern works by such artists as Andy Warhol, Robert Rauschenberg, Roy Lichtenstein, and James Rosenquist.

STUDENT PROFILE

1,736 undergraduate students

62% of undergrad students are full-time

91% female — 9% male

15% of students are from out of state

65% freshman retention rate

FACULTY PROFILE

11 to 1 student/faculty ratio

ADMISSIONS

SAT Ranges: E 440-560, M 420-530

ACT Ranges: C 17-23, M 16-22, E 16-23

TUITION & COST

Tuition: $28,650

Fees: $400

Room & Board: $12,418

GEORGIA GWINNETT COLLEGE

LAWRENCEVILLE, GEORGIA

Georgia Gwinnett
COLLEGE

Georgia Gwinnett College doesn't believe in preserving the status quo. It believes that every student should have every opportunity to succeed. No other college is blazing trails, raising standards, and revolutionizing the college experience like Georgia Gwinnett, where education is a journey that challenges, supports, and connects students.

HOLDING ITS OWN: GGC's innovative approach to higher education is working. Its first-year retention rates greatly surpass other Georgia state colleges and are comparable to state universities. Such rates are unusually high for minority students. Nothing affirms Georgia Gwinnett more than its dramatic growth. Having opened its doors to 118 students in 2006, it now serves nearly 13,000 students only 12 years later.

EVER EVOLVING: From the exciting new Student Center and dramatic Library and Learning Center to the spacious residence halls, all of GGC's facilities are comfortable, modern, and functional. And, with a successful athletics program, another academic building in the works, and ever-expanding programs, students are part of the college's exciting growth.

A STEP ABOVE THE REST: At GGC, students and faculty engage in collaborative group activities and active, hands-on learning experiences. Every classroom is wired with "smart" capabilities, providing modern instructional technologies to and keep students connected. Whether by laptop or tablet, students can study organic chemistry, text questions or quiz answers to their professors, or even download a lecture the same day they heard it in person. GGC's style is not all about lectures and tests; rather, it's about giving students the tools to succeed in the real world.

ACADEMIC SUPPORT: Georgia Gwinnett arms students with an unstoppable support system. While no college can guarantee student success, GGC is specifically designed to help students succeed. Personal faculty mentorship keeps students on track, and professors contact students who miss class to find out if they need help. Many programs, including free tutoring, have been developed to support students regardless of their academic level.

www.ggc.edu
(678) 407-5313
ggcadmissions@ggc.edu

STUDENT PROFILE

12,287 undergraduate students

77% of undergrad students are full-time

1% of students are from out of state

67% freshman retention rate

FACULTY PROFILE

18 to 1 student/faculty ratio

ADMISSIONS

SAT Ranges: E 460-560, M 450-550

ACT Ranges: C 17-22, M 16-22, E 15-21

TUITION & COST

Tuition (in-state): $3,920

Tuition (out-of-state): $14,634

Fees: $852

Room: $4,855

Board: $1,624

GEORGIA STATE UNIVERSITY

ATLANTA, GEORGIA

www.gsu.edu
(404) 413-2000

Founded in 1913, Georgia State University is a leading public research institution in the heart of downtown Atlanta. Georgia State is proud to provide a rich experience with award-winning faculty, hundreds of student organizations, myriad research opportunities, and one of the most diverse student bodies in the country. Students, faculty, and staff are all committed to cultivating a campus culture founded on mutual respect, ambition, hard work, and perseverance.

FRESHMAN LEARNING COMMUNITIES: Freshman learning communities (FLC) are designed to help students acclimate to their new environment and experience the expectations of the academic and personal journey they are about to embark on. During their first semester, students participate in an FLC based on their academic interests and enjoy a support team, built-in study buddies, and the peace of mind that all the courses they take can apply to any major they choose.

FLC's are built around specific fields of interest—STEM, business, arts and humanities, policy studies, health, education, social sciences, and undeclared.

ATLANTA, GA: Georgia State's campus is nestled in bustling downtown Atlanta. Students have uninhibited access to the arts, culture, business, and sports events the big city has to offer. As the leading economic center of the Southeast, Atlanta has rich opportunities in business, government, healthcare, and non-profit sectors.

UNDERGRADUATE RESEARCH: The Georgia State University Honors College Undergraduate Research Program provides undergraduate students opportunities to conduct research across campus, nationally, and internationally. Students from all disciplines and levels are encouraged to seek interesting and challenging opportunities.

Every year, the Georgia State Undergraduate Research Conference highlights and recognizes the groundbreaking research taking place across Georgia State's campus.

STUDENT PROFILE

25,770 undergraduate students

77% of undergrad students are full-time

59% female – 41% male

12% of students are from out of state

83% freshman retention rate

FACULTY PROFILE

23 to 1 student/faculty ratio

ADMISSIONS

Selectivity: 70%

SAT Ranges: E 530-620, M 510-600

ACT Ranges: C 19-26, M 20-26, E 20-26

TUITION & COST

Tuition (in-state): $6,984

Tuition (out-of-state): $21,843

Fees: $2,128

Room: $10,560

Board: $3,832

MERCER UNIVERSITY

MACON, GEORGIA

Mercer University, one of America's oldest and most distinctive universities, is located right in the heart of Georgia. Founded in 1833, Mercer offers liberal arts, law, medicine, engineering, and pharmacy all at the same institution. In addition, Mercer also offers business, teacher education, nursing, music, and theology. With over 60 undergraduate programs to choose from, students are sure to find the degree that fits their interests.

MERCER SERVICE SCHOLARS: Mercer Service Scholars (MSS). MSS is a dynamic program that engages diverse students in substantive service in both the local community and internationally. Mercer Service Scholars are leaders on campus and develop to become leaders in their careers and lifelong contributors to their communities.

A recent project of MSS is LEAP—Local Engagement Against Poverty. This is a student-led service initiative that is focused on addressing the needs of those living below the poverty line in the local community. To date, students have logged more than 7,000 hours of service.

CENTER FOR COLLABORATIVE JOURNALISM: Mercer is committed to meeting the demands of today's workforce through the creation of new and innovative academic programs, such as the Center for Collaborative Journalism. This program is the first of its kind in the nation to adopt a medical-school model for journalism education, engaging the Mercer community with news staffs of *The Telegraph* and Georgia Public Broadcasting to advance journalistic excellence in the digital age.

OUTSTANDING ALUMNI: Mercer's alumni network encompasses more than 60,000 alumni who live throughout the U.S. and in more than 70 countries around the world. By sponsoring numerous events each year, including "Mercer Mingles" in cities where alumni live, the Alumni Association helps graduates further strengthen the legacy of their University. Among Mercer's alumni ranks are 12 governors, four United States senators, an attorney general of the United States, and numerous other professionals.

www.mercer.edu
(478) 301-2650
admissions@mercer.edu

STUDENT PROFILE

4,747 undergraduate students

87% of undergrad students are full-time

62% female – 38% male

86% freshman retention rate

FACULTY PROFILE

13 to 1 student/faculty ratio

ADMISSIONS

Selectivity: 73%

SAT Ranges: E 590-670, M 580-670

ACT Ranges: C 25-30, M 24-31, E 24-28

TUITION & COST

Tuition: $35,700

Fees: $300

Room: $6,174

Board: $5,979

OGLETHORPE UNIVERSITY

ATLANTA, GEORGIA

OGLETHORPE
UNIVERSITY

An Education Designed to be Different: Founded in 1835, Oglethorpe is Atlanta's leading liberal arts and sciences university, renowned for its groundbreaking Core program. Oglethorpe holds a unique position as a traditional liberal arts college in a vibrant international city, and offers an academically rigorous undergraduate education combined with opportunities to apply that knowledge through unparalleled experiences.

ALIVE WITH POSSIBILITIES: At Oglethorpe, the promise of a great education is matched by a dedicated and passionate faculty. Whether they are teaching courses in their discipline or a section of Oglethorpe's unique Core curriculum, faculty members bring a wealth of knowledge to classroom discussions as they push students to delve deeper into the subject at hand.

Included in the faculty are textbook authors, National Endowment for the Humanities fellows, a Guggenheim fellow, a French knight, a political columnist, scholars of Shakespeare and the Civil War, community activists, and academic organization leaders.

SPECIALTY PROGRAMS: The Rich Foundation Urban Leadership Program exposes students to civic life while exploring the history and philosophy of citizen leadership through the ages. The Urban Ecology program, led by one of the first urban ecology PhDs in the nation, combines ecology, environmental science, economics, psychology, and public policy to produce scientists and urban planners focused on sustainable urban growth.

GLOBAL EDUCATION: Students engage on an international level through the Center for Global Education, which offers study through partner institutions in twelve countries. There are also short-term, for-credit trips throughout the year and unique associate programs with Oxford University (England) and the Umbria Institute (Italy). In 2012, Oglethorpe launched a strategic partnership with study abroad provider Global LEAD. Within this partnership, Oglethorpe introduced GO: Rome, a study abroad center in Italy, part of the "Global Oglethorpe" program, in the summer of 2014.

www.oglethorpe.edu
(404) 364-8307
admission@
oglethorpe.edu

STUDENT PROFILE

1,250 undergraduate students

93% of undergrad students are full time

59% female – 41% male

31% of students are from out of state

77% freshman retention rate

FACULTY PROFILE

16 to 1 student/faculty ratio

ADMISSIONS

Selectivity: 58%

SAT Ranges: E 570-670, M 540-640

ACT Ranges: C 22-28, M 20-27, E 22-30

TUITION & COST

Tuition: $36,400

Fees: $280

Room & Board: $12,960

PIEDMONT COLLEGE

DEMOREST, GEORGIA

PIEDMONT COLLEGE

www.piedmont.edu
(706) 778-8500 ext.1529
ugrad@piedmont.edu

Piedmont College was founded in 1897 to do one thing: provide a rock-solid academic experience for students who want to enrich their lives with the best foundation in the liberal arts. Today, students who come to Piedmont from across Georgia and from around the world continue to find an educational opportunity that is second to none in the Arts & Sciences, Business, Education, and Nursing & Health Sciences.

EXPERIENTIAL LEARNING: As part of their undergraduate curriculum, students are to design their own projects around six "Compass Points:" Social Ethics, Creativity & Innovation, Leadership, Vocation, Cultural Awareness, and Service-Learning. The experiences gained through Compass projects are included in each student's official transcripts, making it easier for future employers to judge the value of their co-curricular efforts.

UP TO DATE: Students love to learn at Piedmont because professors love to *teach* at Piedmont. Faculty are always working to develop innovative programs to meet the needs of such growing fields as Forensic Science; Athletic Training; Exercise and Sport Science; Healthcare Administration; and Cardiovascular Technology, the first of its kind in Georgia.

ACCELERATING TO THE FUTURE: The traditional path to earning a juris doctor degree requires four years of undergraduate education and three years of law school, but Piedmont's 3 + 3 accelerated JD program helps qualified students reduce education costs and launch their legal career in only six years total.

"Piedmont College is a challenging school, but in a good way... The professors here are really amazing, and there are so many opportunities at Piedmont to get involved. Now, I have a job in the medical field and am making a great path for myself." - *Katie Woodward '18, Toccoa, Georgia*

STUDENT PROFILE

1,281 undergraduate students

91% of undergrad students are full-time

66% female – 34% male

67% freshman retention rate

FACULTY PROFILE

10 to 1 student/faculty ratio

ADMISSIONS

Selectivity: 60%

SAT Ranges: E 490-580, M 460-550

ACT Ranges: C 19-24, M 17-24, E 18-24

TUITION & COST

Tuition: $24,264

Fees: $200

Room: $5,502

Board: $4,368

REINHARDT UNIVERSITY

WALESKA, GEORGIA

Reinhardt University

www.reinhardt.edu
(770) 720-5526
admissions@reinhardt.edu

Students find Reinhardt's academic programs engaging, challenging, and rewarding—an investment that yields positive returns to their personal and professional lives. Graduates take full advantage of Reinhardt's opportunities and enter their professions with the richness of a broad liberal arts education. They are well prepared, having gained specific professional skills through their participation in engaged classroom experiences, co-curricular enrichments, challenging research projects, rewarding service initiatives, exciting internships, and life-transforming studies abroad.

LEARNING WHILE SERVING: Reinhardt professors value the experience of learning while serving others and therefore help students apply the skills they learn in class to help others. For instance, Digital Art students produced videos for local non-profit organizations. Business technology students partnered with SERV International, raising money for children living in an orphanage in Kenya. Marketing majors led a campus-wide awareness and fund-raising campaign for "Imagine No Malaria." And students in Sociology spent their spring break in Ixmiquilpan, Mexico, to provide education, food, and clean water to underserved families of the region.

CONVOCATION OF ARTISTS AND SCHOLARS: The Robert L. Driscoll Convocation of Artists and Scholars is an annual student performance, exhibition, and research conference. Students from all across campus read research papers, share internship experiences, show artwork, and perform music and theatrical productions. For nearly a week in the beauty of a North Georgia spring, Reinhardt celebrates student learning among the blooms.

FIRST-YEAR EXPERIENCE: From the beginning of students' college careers, Reinhardt plugs them into courses that set them on paths for success at college, in careers, and for life. First-year students enroll in a Critical Thinking Seminar that is individually themed by the professor who teaches the course. Past courses have been centered on exciting topics like The Curiosity Cabinet; Film and Environmental Studies; and Blazing the Trails: The Role College Students Played in the Civil Rights Movement.

STUDENT PROFILE

1,425 undergraduate students

89% of undergrad students are full-time

48% female – 52% male

7% of students are from out of state

60% freshman retention rate

FACULTY PROFILE

13 to 1 student/faculty ratio

ADMISSIONS

Selectivity: 90%

SAT Ranges: E 510-600, M 490-590

ACT Ranges: C 18-23, M 17-24, E 18-24

TUITION & COST

Tuition: $23,300

Fees: $1,000

Room & Board: $10,500

UNIVERSITY OF WEST GEORGIA

CARROLTON, GEORGIA

UNIVERSITY *of*
West Georgia

At the University of West Georgia, students and faculty alike transform lives and change perceptions, constantly challenging themselves to ask "what if" and refusing to accept that possibilities are limited. The University embraces diversity. It values community. It drives growth. The entire community engages and works collectively to be the best comprehensive university it can be. Amazing things happen to students who *Go West.*

UWG LEAP: As a part of the Liberal Education and America's Promise (LEAP) educational initiative from the Association of American Colleges and Universities, UWG's LEAP West! has a goal of creating professionally versatile and successful students who are capable of navigating real-world problems.

LEAP West! encourages and supports collaboration among colleges and departments to develop university-wide initiatives, including new and revised learning communities, strengthened participation within major and minor programs, up-to-date capstone seminars, and an ever-increasing number of experiential learning opportunities for students.

PROFESSIONAL EDUCATOR DEVELOPMENT: UWG Career Services works cooperatively with campus partners, employers, and community members to expose students to their own professional potential. One example of these cooperative efforts includes a collaboration to present a day of professional development for education majors. The program has included motivational speeches about the importance of teaching, connecting with students and their parents, and the pros and cons of using technology in the classroom. Students also learned about the hiring process for their individual school systems as well as what helps candidates stand out.

CAREERS IN SCIENCE: Career Services sponsors three industry nights for students in science-focused fields: Healthcare, Logistics/Management, and STEM. Each event includes an industry panel of experts that engages students in discussions about the state of each industry, the kinds of skills and education needed, career paths, and opportunities available. This is also a great chance to network with the industry guests.

---

www.westga.edu
(678) 839-5600
admiss@westga.edu

STUDENT PROFILE

11,135 undergraduate students

78% of undergrad students are full-time

63% female – 37% male

7% of students are from out of state

69% freshman retention rate

FACULTY PROFILE

19 to 1 student/faculty ratio

ADMISSIONS

Selectivity: 59%

ACT Ranges: C 18-22, M 17-22, E 18-22

TUITION & COST

Tuition (in-state): $5,330

Tuition (out-of-state): $18,812

Fees: $2,024

Room: $5,600

Board: $4,888

NORTHWEST NAZARENE UNIVERSITY

NAMPA, IDAHO

NORTHWEST NAZARENE UNIVERSITY

Northwest Nazarene University believes that education should be about the transformation of the whole person—intellectually, socially, physically, and spiritually. An accredited Christian liberal arts university, NNU offers over 80 areas of study, 18 master's degrees, and 2 doctoral degrees. In addition to its campus in Nampa, Idaho, the University also offers programs online as well as in Boise, Idaho Falls, and in cooperation with programs in 35 countries.

SUCCESSFUL GRADUATES: Doctors? Yes. Lawyers? Of course. Professors, ministers, and teachers? Plenty. NNU graduates leave prepared to embark on any and every career path and to pursue advanced degrees at some of the best graduate schools in the country. Most importantly, NNU graduates leave prepared to make the world a better place. They are creative, socially responsive adults who are ready to represent Christ in a changing world.

FRESHMAN AND SENIOR EXPERIENCES: Students begin their freshman year at NNU in Freshman Seminar, a class designed to build a foundation of skills that encourage success. After three years, students are prepared to take on the challenge of their senior capstone class, internship, and/or research project. NNU seniors are discovering exciting methods with which to put their education into practice, producing professional, Hollywood-style films; crafting franchise-winning business plans; designing Idaho's first satellite; testing new computer software with million-dollar companies; and more!

"In my four years at NNU, I was deeply impacted by a loving community that was not afraid to share; share in life, share in joy, share in struggle, and share in relationship. It is a community that prepared me for a career in which teaching and modeling this same attitude of sharing is vitally important." – *Sheldon Field, NNU Alum*

---

www.nnu.edu
1 (877) NNU-4-YOU
admissions@nnu.edu

STUDENT PROFILE
1,248 undergraduate students

87% of undergrad students are full-time

59% female – 41% male

43% of students are from out of state

79% freshman retention rate

FACULTY PROFILE
16 to 1 student/faculty ratio

ADMISSIONS
Selectivity: 96%

SAT Ranges: E 520-640, M 500-610

ACT Ranges: C 20-27, M 18-26, E 20-28

TUITION & COST
Tuition: $30,550

Fees: $500

Room: $3,400

Board: $4,590

THE COLLEGE OF IDAHO

CALDWELL, IDAHO

Being part of a small community means more opportunity at The College of Idaho. More opportunity to work one-on-one with professors, more opportunity to be a leader, and more opportunity to pursue one's individual passions. With alumni who include three governors, seven Rhodes Scholars, and two Pulitzer and Academy Award winners, the C of I has demonstrated its success preparing graduates who succeed. A College of Idaho education empowers students to gain transformational, relevant experiences that prepare them to lead productive and fulfilling lives.

PEAK CURRICULUM: The C of I's innovative PEAK Curriculum—inspired by the independent spirit of its unique Idaho setting—is designed to provide an education that is both broad and deep. Through PEAK, every student earns a major and three minors spread across the four knowledge peaks of the fine arts and humanities, natural sciences, social sciences, and professional studies. Each student designs an individualized academic path based on his or her own passions and goals, rather than taking a checklist of courses.

PERFORMING WITH PROFESSORS: Music students benefit from the C of I's relationship with the renowned Boise Philharmonic Orchestra. Members of The College of Idaho Langroise Trio—comprised of the Boise Philharmonic's principal violinist, violist and cellist—offer coaching sessions and weekly master classes for C of I students. Boise Philharmonic internships also are available, giving students an opportunity to perform with a professional metropolitan-level orchestra.

ENACTUS: Students of all majors can participate in the College's chapter of ENACTUS, which connects students and local business leaders committed to using the power of entrepreneurial action to transform lives and shape a more sustainable world. With support from the C of I's business faculty, students in ENACTUS have collaborated with businesses on a variety of economic development projects.

www.collegeofidaho.edu
(208) 459-5305
admission@
collegeofidaho.edu

STUDENT PROFILE

936 undergraduate students

96% of undergrad students are full-time

50% female – 50% male

78% freshman retention rate

FACULTY PROFILE

9 to 1 student/faculty ratio

ADMISSIONS

Selectivity: 76%

TUITION & COST

Tuition: $28,000

Fees: $755

Room: $4,460

Board: $4,732

AURORA UNIVERSITY

AURORA, ILLINOIS

Aurora University is one of the premier Illinois universities. Its mission statement, *"an inclusive community dedicated to the transformative power of learning"* is experienced each day in the lives of AU students. Aurora University believes in taking students from where they are to where they want to be by following its core values of integrity, citizenship, continuous learning, and excellence.

HANDS-ON LEARNING: In class, AU students from various majors take advantage of special hands-on learning opportunities. Students in the Dunham School of Business, for example gain practical knowledge as well as engage with the local community through the VITA (Volunteer Income Tax Assistance) program. Aurora University is one of the few universities in Illinois to be licensed by the IRS to be a VITA partner. Through this program, accounting students prepare tax returns free of charge for taxpayers, including persons who are elderly, low income, individuals with disabilities, and those who are non-English speaking.

PRACTICAL EXPERIENCE: Athletic training students apply their burgeoning skills by working with student-athletes, seeing real results as they prepare their peers to head back onto the field. AU additionally offers students interested in a career in athletic training a Bachelor of Science in Exercise Science and a Master of Science in Athletic training in five years via a 3+2 dual degree option. Through this initiatives and many others available in all programs at AU, students gain real-world experience to complement and deepen what they learn in the classroom.

"AU inspired me to crave knowledge and to look for a career that will teach me something new every day. After graduation, I didn't feel like I was done learning. I felt like I had just scratched the surface and for that, I'm beyond grateful." *– Alyssa, Communication graduate*

www.aurora.edu
(630) 844-5533
admission@aurora.edu

STUDENT PROFILE

3,944 undergraduate students

90% of undergrad students are full-time

65% female — 35% male

11% of students are from out of state

75% freshman retention rate

FACULTY PROFILE

19 to 1 student/faculty ratio

ADMISSIONS

Selectivity: 81%

SAT Ranges: E 490-580, M 480-570

ACT Ranges: C 19-24, M 17-24, E 17-24

TUITION & COST

Tuition: $24,800

Fees: $260

Room: $6,500

Board: $5,200

BENEDICTINE UNIVERSITY

LISLE, ILLINOIS

Benedictine University

Benedictine University is a Catholic university located just outside of Chicago, Illinois. In the Benedictine tradition, students get an engaging education that emphasizes learning outside of the classroom as much as inside. With an emphasis on group learning and community involvement, Benedictine students become close with one another and build a network for success in college and beyond.

EXPLORE SEVERAL DISCIPLINES: Benedictine University is committed to providing a well-rounded, interdisciplinary education. Through a series of Interdisciplinary Seminars, students learn to analyze differing perspectives, make their own conclusions, and understand both historical and current issues. The Benedictine curriculum first exposes students to Catholicism and the Benedictine educational tradition, followed by lessons of the "Common Good," with courses on climate change, healthcare, and more.

GIVING BACK, ONE S.T.E.P. AT A TIME: Throughout their time at Benedictine, students commit not only to growing as individuals, but to helping the community grow as well. The Serving Together Engaging Our Purpose (S.T.E.P.) program connects Benedictine with local, national, and international service-learning projects. Weekly opportunities to serve meals in the local community, partnerships with organizations across the Midwest, and the chance to teach and in the Philippines or Bolivia are just a few ways in which Benedictine students learn by doing good for others.

LEARN AS A COMMUNITY: One of the best ways for students to learn is through collaboration, which is intrinsic to a Benedictine University education.

The school's Learning Communities requirement provides students the chance to learn and work as a group, fostering good relationships and interpersonal skills along the way. Groups of students take course concepts outside of the classroom through music ensembles, mission trips, Model UN, and more. Each cohort works closely with a faculty member, allowing them to create a dialogue that leads to both academic and personal growth.

www.ben.edu
(630) 829-6300
admissions@ben.edu

STUDENT PROFILE

2,692 undergraduate students

88% of undergrad students are full-time

54% female — 46% male

10% of students are from out of state

72% freshman retention rate

FACULTY PROFILE

15 to 1 student/faculty ratio

ADMISSIONS

Selectivity: 65%

SAT Ranges: E 490-600, M 490-590

ACT Ranges: C 19-25, M 18-25, E 18-24

TUITION & COST

Tuition: $32,700

Fees: $1,590

Room: $7,800

Board: $1,680

CONCORDIA UNIVERSITY CHICAGO

RIVER FOREST, ILLINOIS

CONCORDIA UNIVERSITY CHICAGO

Through its College of Arts and Sciences, College of Business, College of Education, College of Graduate Studies, and College of Innovation and Professional Programs, Concordia University Chicago offers more than 140 areas of undergraduate and graduate study in small classes taught by professors who are passionate about teaching and student success. Students choose CUC to open up their world and be inspired throughout their collegiate career and beyond.

FAITH THAT ENGAGES: Concordia University Chicago's faith community reflects the Lutheran tradition with a welcoming of other Christian denominations as well. Within a Christian framework, students seek greater meaning in their spiritual and work lives. They grow in faith as they participate in a variety of service activities as well as daily chapel services, spiritual life campus ministries, and mission trips.

INTERNSHIPS: The Chicago area is home to more than 30 Fortune 500 company headquarters that connect students' education to real-world opportunities. Internships for unique hands-on learning are highlights of many programs in business, education, healthcare, and much more. Recent internship sites include Allstate Insurance, CBS-2 News Chicago, the Chicago Symphony Orchestra, Loyola University Medical Center, and Chicago's world-renowned Shedd Aquarium—just to name a few.

"For me, CUC's location in suburban River Forest, Illinois, could not have been any better. It was far enough from the city to feel like home to me yet close enough to visit downtown Chicago any day. I loved the big city feel, even though it was quite foreign to me, and I liked being able to get out and attend concerts and other events." *- Caleb Akers '17*

www.cuchicago.edu
(877) 282-4422
admission@cuchicago.edu

STUDENT PROFILE

1,462 undergraduate students

93% of undergrad students are full-time

59% female – 41% male

27% of students are from out of state

73% freshman retention rate

FACULTY PROFILE

10 to 1 student/faculty ratio

ADMISSIONS

Selectivity: 7600%

SAT Ranges: E 490-590, M 500-580

ACT Ranges: C 20-25, M 17-25, E 20-25

TUITION & COST

Tuition: $31,926

Fees: $954

Room: $6,280

Board: $3,716

ELMHURST COLLEGE

ELMHURST, ILLINOIS

www.elmhurst.edu
(630) 617-3400
admit@elmhurst.edu

A private, four-year college, Elmhurst College provides a great education at an excellent value, consistently ranking among the top colleges and best values in the Midwest. In small classes throughout the liberal arts and sciences, Elmhurst students work with faculty whose top priority is teaching and mentoring. The College is located in the heart of the Chicago metropolitan area, 13 miles west of the Loop.

CITY OF ELMHURST: Elmhurst College is located in the quiet suburb of Elmhurst, a community of over 46,000 that has been called "the quintessential Chicago suburb." Downtown Elmhurst is just two blocks north of the campus. Several museums, a library, an eight-screen movie theater, a variety of restaurants, a rail line to downtown Chicago, and much more are all within walking distance.

GAINING THE RIGHT TOOLS: The academic programs at Elmhurst are characterized by their real-world connections and responsiveness to student needs. Students conduct research and defend their results, analyze data, think critically, solve problems collaboratively, study and write across disciplines, and learn to formulate new ideas. Each year, students of all majors share their original research at the Undergraduate Research and Performance Showcase.

PROFESSIONAL DEVELOPMENT: The Russell G. Weigand Center for Professional Excellence aims to support and propel the professional aspirations of all students. Here, students can develop their résumé, take career-guidance courses, and receive mentoring and advising.

Off campus, students can participate in a wealth of internship and job-shadowing experiences, both in the Chicago area and beyond. One student recently shadowed a renowned neurosurgeon in San Francisco; another worked on staff at the Mayo Clinic in Rochester, Minnesota.

"I like the one-on-one interaction, the intimacy you get in class. We're spoiled." – *Jennifer Pierce '19*

STUDENT PROFILE

2,796 undergraduate students

97% of undergrad students are full-time

61% female – 39% male

9% of students are from out of state

78% freshman retention rate

FACULTY PROFILE

14 to 1 student/faculty ratio

ADMISSIONS

Selectivity: 67%

SAT Ranges: E 500-600, M 493-590

ACT Ranges: C 20-26, M 18-26, E 20-26

TUITION & COST

Tuition: $37,454

Fees: $500

Room: $6,244

Board: $4,266

GREENVILLE UNIVERSITY

GREENVILLE, ILLINOIS

GREENVILLE
UNIVERSITY

Greenville University has served Christ, creation, and community for over 126 years. Along with its rich history and prestigious academics, Greenville strives to empower students by providing several opportunities to create a valuable and lasting university experience. Greenville University students are motivated and equipped to make real change in the world.

www.greenville.edu
(800) 345-4440
admissions@
greenville.edu

EXPERIENCE FIRST: Greenville's focus on the student experience offers opportunities to learn both inside and outside of the classroom. Undergraduate research and field experience are core components of its curriculum. Toward the end of their studies, students are asked to use the knowledge they've gained to solve real issues in the community, nation, or world. With Experience First, students can work with industry leaders and gain hands-on experience, solve challenges, and provide fresh innovations for the companies and organizations for whom they work.

STUDENT PROFILE

994 undergraduate students

93% of undergrad students are full-time

50% female – 50% male

41% of students are from out of state

73% freshman retention rate

NURTURED PASSION: Each of GU's departments and offices is involved in nurturing the holistic development of students by including them in the campus community. This means celebrating solidarity and unity through the traditional Ivy Planting Ceremony during New Student Orientation. It also means challenging students' minds by hosting high-profile guest speakers and thought-provoking colloquia. The University's vision states that each student is created with a unique capability to shape the world.

FACULTY PROFILE

11 to 1 student/faculty ratio

ADMISSIONS

Selectivity: 58%

SAT Ranges: E 400-540, M 440-540

ACT Ranges: C 18-25, M 16-25, E 16-24

"Studying at Greenville University gave me the opportunity to have an intimate and personalized education in which to cultivate my base knowledge in the liberal arts and sciences. I was able to know my professors personally, which allowed them to learn of my interests and my passions."

– David Brooks '14, Engineering

TUITION & COST

Tuition: $25,488

Fees: $232

Room: $4,152

Board: $4,428

ILLINOIS STATE UNIVERSITY

NORMAL, ILLINOIS

Illinois State University serves a diverse student body through immersive, career-minded programming across a range of subjects. The university prides itself in its core values: Pursuit of Learning and Scholarship, Individualized Attention, Diversity, Integrity, and Civic Engagement. And thanks to these pillars, the university motto, *"gladly we learn and teach,"* truly speaks for itself. Regardless of a student's goals for the future, extra projects like independent research prove to be excellent additions to a résumé. It's no wonder why Illinois State graduates are not only highly accepted in the workforce, but highly sought after.

CENTER FOR COMMUNITY ENGAGEMENT: Illinois State offers students a variety of opportunities to integrate civic engagement into their academic experience through such programs as the Minor in Civic Engagement and Responsibility, Ethnic Studies Minor, and Urban Studies Minor. Students can also apply to the Undergraduate Fellow Program to research social issues affecting different communities.

FESTIVAL ISU: Illinois State thrives with over 400 student organizations, including the Student Government Association. Every fall, Illinois State holds a showcase to spotlight these student organizations along with 100 local businesses. The event takes place at the Quad to welcome students back to campus and introduce the community to all the great things happening on and around campus. The festival is a great way for incoming students to explore their interests, join clubs, and make new friends.

FUTURE EDUCATORS. CURRENT DIFFERENCE-MAKERS: The Chicago Teacher Education Pipeline and Stevenson Center for Community and Economic Development prepares students to be be active educators in both the local and global community. Such incredible programs and resources give education majors the chance to student teach as lower-income schools and any other student with a drive to serve to apply their knowledge to effecting tangible change.

www.illinoisstate.edu
(309) 438-2181
admissions@
illinoisstate.edu

STUDENT PROFILE

18,330 undergraduate students

94% of undergrad students are full-time

55% female – 45% male

3% of students are from out of state

81% freshman retention rate

FACULTY PROFILE

18 to 1 student/faculty ratio

ADMISSIONS

Selectivity: 89%

ACT Ranges: C 21-26, M 19-26, E 20-26

TUITION & COST

Tuition (in-state): $11,108

Tuition (out-of-state): $22,215

Fees: $2,953

Room: $5,334

Board: $4,614

ILLINOIS WESLEYAN UNIVERSITY

BLOOMINGTON, ILLINOIS

www.iwu.edu
(309) 556-3031
iwuadmit@iwu.edu

Where the multitalented go to learn. IWU is a true renaissance university at which students are encouraged to explore all of their interests. Double majors in diverse subjects like physics and music are common. Students have a host of compelling opportunities to enrich their education with off-campus experiences that might involve spending a year at Pembroke College/Oxford University or perhaps a semester in Washington D.C. through American University.

OFF-CAMPUS STUDY: The community surrounding Illinois Wesleyan offers distinctive opportunities for students who look to supplement their classroom experiences with off-campus learning experiences. The best example of this is the Action Research Center, which coordinates research projects undertaken by Illinois Wesleyan University students, faculty, and staff in partnership with groups in the larger central Illinois community.

Current projects include work on McLean County's ten-year plan to end homelessness, a tutoring and mentoring program, and work with the Ecology Action Center to reduce pesticide use.

GATEWAY COLLOQUIUM COURSE: Relationships with professors are developed early with the help of the distinctive Gateway colloquium course, a small, discussion-oriented course designed to develop first-year students' proficiency in writing academic and public discourse. This course is capped at 15 students. In fact, class sizes across the university are a small average of 17, making one-on-one interaction with achieved professors part of the IWU experience.

All of Illinois Wesleyan's courses are taught by professors, and 92 percent of the faculty members hold terminal degrees in their fields. Every professor holds at least five office hours each week, and it is not uncommon for faculty members to seek out students for participation in independent studies and research projects.

STUDENT PROFILE

1,649 undergraduate students

100% of undergrad students are full-time

55% female – 45% male

17% of students are from out of state

89% freshman retention rate

FACULTY PROFILE

10 to 1 student/faculty ratio

ADMISSIONS

Selectivity: 61%

SAT Ranges: E 590-690, M 605-705

ACT Ranges: C 24-29, M 24-28, E 23-30

TUITION & COST

Tuition: $45,654

Fees: $202

Room: $6,622

Board: $3,952

JUDSON UNIVERSITY

ELGIN, ILLINOIS

At Judson University, students thrive within an active campus community, creating friendships and experiences that go on to last a lifetime. Incredible facilities provide abundant resources for research, internships, and exploration among the many avenues of each student's desired path.

THE CHICAGO SEMESTER: Judson offers its students the opportunity to engage in prolonged off-campus study in the city of Chicago. Participants of the Chicago Semester program take part in an intensive internship experience, learning the ins and outs of an industry by delving into the processes within this major city center. Aside from professional development, students have the chance to test their independence and grow through an exploration of all the cultural attractions that Chicago has to offer.

THE RISE PROGRAM: Judson's "Road to Independent living, Spiritual formation, and Employment" (RISE) Program is a unique opportunity to provide a post-secondary education for individuals with an intellectual disability. The RISE Program gives students with intellectual disabilities the college life experience as well as the chance to build upon their strengths, growing for independent living and customized employment within a caring Christian community.

SHARK TANK: Judson University has long stood as a haven for creative minds within the Christian worship and architecture arenas. It continues to foster such a reputation for creativity with its entrepreneurial idea competition, Shark Tank.

Inspired by the ABC Network's reality business pitch series *"Shark Tank,"* Judson's annual event serves as a platform for students to foster creative ideas and deliver them in a presentation before a panel of judges. This competition is part of an ongoing effort to implement projects in the Business department, partnering students and faculty for experiential learning opportunities.

www.judsonu.edu
(847) 628-2510
admissions@judsonu.edu

STUDENT PROFILE

1,081 undergraduate students

70% of undergrad students are full-time

55% female – 45% male

33% of students are from out of state

72% freshman retention rate

FACULTY PROFILE

9 to 1 student/faculty ratio

ADMISSIONS

Selectivity: 71%

SAT Ranges: E 435-590, M 435-580

ACT Ranges: C 19-25, M 18-26, E 18-25

TUITION & COST

Tuition: $28,408

Fees: $1,026

Room & Board: $9,840

LEWIS UNIVERSITY

ROMEOVILLE, ILLINOIS

Lewis University, guided by its Catholic and Lasallian heritage, provides students a liberal and professional education, grounded in the interaction of knowledge and fidelity in the search for truth. Lewis promotes the development of the complete person through the pursuit of wisdom and justice. Fundamental to its Mission is a spirit of association, which fosters community in all teaching, learning, and service.

DISTINCT PROGRAMS WITH DISTINCT OUTCOMES: As the largest undergraduate nursing program in Illinois among private, nonprofit schools, Lewis University's College of Nursing and Health Professions has a nearly 100 percent pass rate on nursing licensure (NCLEX) exams. And, as the only air traffic control program in Illinois, the Aviation Program at Lewis consistently boasts an above average pass rate on the Federal Aviation Administration (FAA) Maintenance Technician (AMT) Exam.

No matter their field, graduates leave Lewis prepared to lead in their careers and make a difference in their communities.

LASALLIAN TEACHING: Lewis University is a Catholic University in the Lasallian tradition. Following the teachings of St. John Baptist de La Salle, the patron saint of educators and founder of the De La Salle Christian Brothers, Lewis faculty are devoted to great teaching.

Every Lewis professor is driven to their students toward academic and personal growth. They regard the University Mission as a guiding principle to promote the development of the complete person through the pursuit of wisdom and justice. Fundamental to the Mission is a spirit of association, which fosters community in all teaching, learning, and service.

BUSINESS PLAN COMPETITION: To encourage entrepreneurship, the University hosts the Business Plan Competition, which is open to all undergraduate and graduate students. Students formulate an idea, develop a business plan, and pitch their idea to a panel of judges. The winner(s) of the competition earn $5,000 to be used towards their business venture.

www.lewis.edu
(815) 836-5250
admission@lewisu.edu

STUDENT PROFILE

4,217 undergraduate students

85% of undergrad students are full-time

52% female – 48% male

7% of students are from out of state

82% freshman retention rate

FACULTY PROFILE

13 to 1 student/faculty ratio

ADMISSIONS

Selectivity: 58%

SAT Ranges: E 520-600, M 520-600

ACT Ranges: C 21-26, M 19-26, E 21-26

TUITION & COST

Tuition: $33,270

Fees: $150

Room & Board: $10,820

LOYOLA UNIVERSITY CHICAGO

CHICAGO, ILLINOIS

Superior education in a world-class city. An outstanding, nationally lauded institution, Loyola University Chicago continues to advance the 450-year-old Jesuit tradition of rigorous academic study grounded in the liberal arts. Loyola helps students prepare for meaningful careers with top programs in business, the sciences, and other disciplines, along with opportunities for internships in Chicago and beyond. Loyola's well-rounded, transformative education will help each student develop as a whole person—intellectually, physically, socially, and spiritually.

ENGAGING PROFESSORS: Based on the Jesuit principle of holistic education, Loyola's Core Curriculum teaches students to examine, compare, and integrate learning across disciplines. Students learn from professors who are experts in their fields, 93% of whom have the highest degree in their field. With Loyola's student/faculty ratio of 14:1, students have ample opportunity to interact personally with their instructors both in and out of the classroom.

CHICAGO: Loyola combines the best of campus and city life with diverse living and learning opportunities in Chicago. Loyola's picturesque Lake Shore Campus is situated on the shores of Lake Michigan and provides a campus oasis just eight miles north of downtown Chicago.

Located on Chicago's Magnificent Mile in the heart of the city, Loyola's Water Tower Campus connects students to myriad internship, job, and service opportunities. The Water Tower Campus is also home to Baumhart Hall, a twenty-five-story residence hall that features a student center, fitness center, study lounge, food court, and more.

Loyola students have immediate access to concerts, museums, plays, vibrant nightlife, and other cultural and recreational activities. Getting around town is easy—both campuses have stops on the local CTA transit line, and the student U-Pass provides unlimited rides throughout Chicago's public transportation system.

www.luc.edu
(800) 262-2373
admission@luc.edu

STUDENT PROFILE

11,420 undergraduate students

94% of undergrad students are full-time

66% female – 34% male

41% of students are from out of state

83% freshman retention rate

FACULTY PROFILE

14 to 1 student/faculty ratio

ADMISSIONS

Selectivity: 71%

SAT Ranges: E 570-660, M 550-650

ACT Ranges: C 24-29, M 23-28, E 24-31

TUITION & COST

Tuition: $41,720

Fees: $1,358

Room: $8,800

Board: $5,280

MACMURRAY COLLEGE

JACKSONVILLE, ILLINOIS

MacMurray College is a private, four-year, coeducational college with a focus on career-directed, comprehensive education. It prides itself on providing an accessible and affordable education to students of all ages in the form of both online and blended courses. The College also offers financial aid through grants and scholarships to 98% of students. With 33 majors and pre-professional programs, three online programs, 10 athletic teams, and an active and involved student body of more than 550 coeds, MacMurray is sure to have something for anyone!

SCHOOL LOCATION: The MacMurray campus is located in west-central Illinois in the city of Jacksonville, about 30 miles west of the state capital of Springfield. Jacksonville is a community rich in historical treasures, thriving with arts, education, and culture, and wrapped in Midwest hospitality.

From its historical connections to the Civil War and Abraham Lincoln to its platform of modern businesses today, the area is loaded with culture. There is a small-town friendliness mixed with vibrancy from a richness of natural sites, intellectual institutions, and businesses.

INTERNSHIPS: Whether through curriculum-based practica or the Career Experience Program, the internship opportunities offered at MacMurray College are "custom designed" for the individual student.

DESIGNED TO PREPARE: MacMurray College believes that experience is the best teacher. MacMurray's curriculum is designed to offer experiential education opportunities and internships in order to better prepare students for their chosen career field. It is because of this that the MacMurray degree opens a world of opportunity, enabling graduates to be successful throughout their professional and personal lives.

Mac alumni know that their school has equipped them with a love for lifelong learning, and they know that attaining a job requires more than a quick-fix résumé. Their promising futures are enabled by the way they had been nurtured to think creatively and communicate effectively.

MacMurray COLLEGE
Founded 1846

www.mac.edu
(217) 479-7056
admissions@mac.edu

STUDENT PROFILE
521 undergraduate students

96% of undergrad students are full-time

55% female – 45% male

63% freshman retention rate

FACULTY PROFILE
14 to 1 student/faculty ratio

ADMISSIONS
Selectivity: 60%

SAT Ranges: E 480-578, M 500-550

ACT Ranges: C 18-22, M 17-23, E 16-22

TUITION & COST
Tuition: $25,340

Fees: $760

Room & Board: $8,925

MCKENDREE UNIVERSITY

LEBANON, ILLINOIS

www.mckendree.edu
(618) 537-6831
inquiry@mckendree.edu

A*Personalized and Balanced Education.* The McKendree experience enlightens, empowers, excites, and educates inquisitive minds. The balanced educational equation at McKendree allows for success in the classroom as well as intellectual development outside the classroom. With small class sizes that facilitate close relationships between professors and students, McKendree offers a truly personal approach to education.

PERSONALIZED EDUCATIONAL EQUATION: In addition to the internship opportunities that are offered to McKendree students, there are a number of opportunities for students to learn outside the classroom, including credit-bearing independent study.

A large majority of McKendree professors are published scholars who are well known and respected for their writing and research, and many of them often receive assistance from their students in exchange for college credit—a valuable opportunity for the entire McKendree community.

BLENDED FOR BALANCED LIVES: McKendree's unique location is a blend of a small-town environment with a pleasant suburban feel. The 236-acre main campus is within twenty-five minutes west of downtown St. Louis, with the popular Carlyle Lake at an equal distance to the east.

McKendree students truly get the best of both worlds, experiencing the serenity and security of a small town while having all the advantages of a large metropolitan area. Its proximity to the city gives access to career opportunities, cultural events, shopping, professional sports, and entertainment.

FACULTY ADVISORS: Faculty are involved even further through their role as academic advisors. Every student is assigned a faculty advisor to help them develop course plans that meet curriculum requirements while also making room for their personal interests. Advisors may or may not be associated with first-year students' declared interests, but as each student becomes more developed in their major, they are placed with an advisor within their academic department.

STUDENT PROFILE

2,104 undergraduate students

80% of undergrad students are full-time

54% female — 46% male

30% of students are from out of state

75% freshman retention rate

FACULTY PROFILE

14 to 1 student/faculty ratio

ADMISSIONS

Selectivity: 62%

SAT Ranges: E 483-590, M 483-568

ACT Ranges: C 19-25, M 18-26, E 19-24

TUITION & COST

Tuition: $28,560

Fees: $1,080

Room: $5,020

Board: $4,760

NORTH PARK UNIVERSITY

CHICAGO, ILLINOIS

NORTH PARK UNIVERSITY CHICAGO

Founded in 1891, North Park University prides itself on its deep Christian roots and its commitment to providing a world-class education in the liberal arts, professional studies, and theology. North Park's location in Chicago offers students a unique opportunity to learn, serve, and develop their faith in an increasingly diverse community.

www.northpark.edu
(800) 888-6728
admissions@
northpark.edu

CRUX: Crux is a living-learning cohort in which first-year students are inspired to develop their identity in Christ while experiencing the city. Coursework, experiential learning, mentorship, and discipleship training comprise the Crux experience, earning students college credit while living and learning within an on-campus cohort. They also complete multiple service projects to further develop a life of community engagement.

FIRST-GENERATION COHORT: The Lighthouse Cohort Program is an annual scholarship program for first-generation college students that invites a cohort of ten first-year, first-generation students to take part in academic, social, and service events alongside each other and their dedicated faculty. This program is a four-year commitment that supports students in the cohort through regular meetings and events throughout their college career.

CATALYST 606: Through Catalyst 606, North Park University provides unique outlets through which to promote hands-on learning, community engagement, and real-world engagement. Those who participate can take afternoon courses that require them to use the city of Chicago as their classroom, applying the theory they learn in the classroom to real problems affecting the Chicago community. From the arts to business, every student has a Catalyst 606 opportunity.

KEYSTONE COURSES: As part of their Core Curriculum, Junior and Senior North Park students enroll in Keystone Courses, which are designed to help them direct what they have studied to their future goals. Whether they plan to pursue a job or graduate studies, the Keystone Courses connect their intellect, passion, and service in pursuit of a meaningful and inspired future.

STUDENT PROFILE
2,029 undergraduate students

89% of undergrad students are full-time

63% female – 37% male

23% of students are from out of state

71% freshman retention rate

FACULTY PROFILE
10 to 1 student/faculty ratio

ADMISSIONS
Selectivity: 54%

SAT Ranges: E 490-600, M 510-590

ACT Ranges: C 19-24, M 17-24, E 18-24

TUITION & COST
Tuition: $27,990

Fees: $630

Room: $4,890

Board: $4,830

OLIVET NAZARENE UNIVERSITY

BOURBONNAIS, ILLINOIS

www.olivet.edu
(800) 648-1463
admissions@olivet.edu

Faith is at the heart of superior academics, nationally competitive athletics, thriving social atmosphere, and countless ministry opportunities. Olivet's main campus is located 50 miles south of Chicago in the historic village of Bourbonnais, Illinois. The area offers shopping, restaurants, entertainment, and outdoor recreation through the Kankakee River State Park system. Students benefit from ONU's proximity to Chicago's cultural, sports, and entertainment attractions. Plentiful professional internships and employment opportunities are additional advantages.

SERVICE: Service to the local and global community is a central theme in many Olivet academic programs.

Social work students organize an annual Christmas party and toy drive for children of jail inmates, while business students have created integrated marketing plans for small businesses in Swaziland and Haiti.

Senior engineering students have traveled to South America to install water purification systems for impoverished villages, and physical science students conduct interactive astronomy shows in Olivet's all-digital planetarium for hundreds of elementary students every year.

4+1 PROGRAMS: Students have the opportunity to accelerate their work toward a graduate degree with Olivet's 4+1 programs. In just five years, students can earn a bachelor's degree and a master's in either business administration or organizational leadership. An accelerated program in engineering offers a bachelor's degree and a master's in engineering management.

CAMPUS MINISTRY: Weekly chapel services, student-led Party with Jesus, and local churches offer students, faculty and staff the opportunity to worship and grow together. Chapel services, held in the 3,046-seat Centennial Chapel, regularly feature renowned spiritual, business, political, and other leaders who offer instruction and inspiration for the ONU community.

STUDENT PROFILE

3,358 undergraduate students

93% of undergrad students are full-time

59% female — 41% male

44% of students are from out of state

75% freshman retention rate

FACULTY PROFILE

17 to 1 student/faculty ratio

ADMISSIONS

Selectivity: 73%

SAT Ranges: E 510-620, M 510-610

ACT Ranges: C 20-26, M 19-26, E 20-27

TUITION & COST

Tuition: $33,950

Fees: $990

Room & Board: $7,900

SAINT XAVIER UNIVERSITY

CHICAGO, ILLINOIS

Saint Xavier University is a distinguished four-year private institution founded by the Sisters of Mercy in 1846. Chicago's oldest Catholic university and the first Mercy college in the United States, Saint Xavier provides a transformative educational experience to 4,000 students at its Chicago campus with more than 40 undergraduate programs in the College of Arts and Sciences, Graham School of Management (GSM), and School of Nursing.

SUPPORT SERVICES: The Career Services team prepares, educates, and empowers students and alumni to explore opportunities, develop skills, and make the connections necessary for lifelong career success.

From freshman year through graduate school and beyond, Career Services offers individual career advising, workshops, internship and job fairs, networking events, and alumni career panels, all of which are designed to assist in every step of the journey. With Career Services, students cross the bridge from academic to professional life, equipped with the tools needed to use their SXU degrees to their fullest potential.

DIVERSITY: SXU students come from diverse backgrounds and have a wide range of interests and goals. Approximately 60 percent are first-generation college students. Saint Xavier University has been ranked highly in diverse student population, with more than one-third of SXU undergraduates coming from underrepresented ethnic backgrounds.

DISCOVER CHICAGO: Saint Xavier lies only 20-30 minutes from downtown Chicago, which is full of world-class museums, shopping, restaurants, theaters, and more. The city is an inexhaustible source of cultural enrichment, recreation, and inspiration.

Through the "Discover Chicago" program, SXU makes it easy for students to take advantage of the city's treasures. The program offers free access to a wide range of attractions and events, including visits to the Chicago Art Institute and trips to Chicago Bulls home games.

www.sxu.edu
(773) 298-3050
admission@sxu.edu

STUDENT PROFILE

2,927 undergraduate students

90% of undergrad students are full-time

64% female – 36% male

4% of students are from out of state

72% freshman retention rate

FACULTY PROFILE

14 to 1 student/faculty ratio

ADMISSIONS

Selectivity: 75%

SAT Ranges: E 520-598, M 470-590

ACT Ranges: C 19-23

TUITION & COST

Tuition: $32,800

Fees: $1,080

Room: $6,746

Board: $4,594

TRINITY CHRISTIAN COLLEGE

PALOS HEIGHTS, ILLINOIS

Trinity Christian College has been changing students' lives since 1959, having been begun by a group of entrepreneurs who wanted to develop Chicago-area Christians who would put their faith into action. As a smaller college, Trinity provides students with individualized attention, harnessing an extensive network throughout Chicago in order to make a difference in the world. Through a Biblically informed liberal arts education, the College community endeavors to provide an environment of Christian integrity and love, enhancing and supporting the entire learning experience.

TRINITY BUSINESS NETWORK: The Trinity Business Network (TBN) is committed to providing Christ-centered business learning opportunities for Trinity Christian College students, alumni, and friends. To fulfill this mission, TBN hosts regular speaking engagements with local and nationally known business people, small group discussions, educational workshops, and seminars.

NEW PROGRAMS: As the world changes and new needs arise, Trinity is committed to providing new and innovative programs that meet the demands of today's market.

Trinity recently introduced new programs in Art Therapy, Health Communication, HR Management, Writing and Web Design, Music and Worship, Recreation and Sport Management, Youth Ministry, Cross-Cultural Ministries, and Christian Ministry. Each program will continue to provide hands-on internship or field experience for every student to ensure that they are fully trained for life after graduation.

OFFICE OF CAREER AND VOCATION: Trinity is intentional to bring the necessary skills and knowledge to students as soon as they begin their orientation experience. Students are each mentored on how to develop productive résumés as early as their freshman year, and faculty regularly partner with the Office of Career and Vocation to best develop insight on the various career paths and outcomes of their students' majors.

---

www.trnty.edu
(708) 239-4708

STUDENT PROFILE
1,107 undergraduate students

82% of undergrad students are full-time

67% female – 33% male

86% freshman retention rate

FACULTY PROFILE
10 to 1 student/faculty ratio

ADMISSIONS
Selectivity: 83%

SAT Ranges: E 545-595, M 510-600

ACT Ranges: C 19-26, M 18-25, E 19-27

TUITION & COST
Tuition: $28,200

Fees: $475

Room & Board: $9,680

TRINITY INTERNATIONAL UNIVERSITY

DEERFIELD, ILLINOIS

Many Stories, One Mission." Trinity International University educates men and women to engage in God's redemptive work in the world by cultivating academic excellence, Christian faithfulness, and lifelong learning. At the heart of Trinity's mission lies its commitment to its four core values— Christ Centeredness, Community Focused, Church Connectedness, and Cultural Engagement.

EMERGE AS A LEADER: Trinity International University has the resources for every student to become an effective leader. The Emerging Leaders program connects incoming freshmen with upperclassmen and university representatives who guide them toward success. Participants also have exclusive access to an informative course and a variety of events that allow them to shine as servant-leaders on campus and in their community.

Other opportunities, open to all students, include student government, major-specific clubs, religious organizations, and multicultural Affinity Groups. Whatever the interest, TIU provides an outlet for students to learn about their passions and grow as leaders in the process.

PROGRAMS AND GENERAL EDUCATION: TIU offers over 70 programs of study. Dual degree programs are also available in Bioethics, Intercultural Studies, and Non-Profit Leadership. Students are exposed to learning opportunities across disciplines through the general education requirements. Using the Bible as a guiding document, students learn about the arts, humanities, science, economics, and more.

LEARNING THROUGH EXPERIENCE: Trinity International University students are expected to gain knowledge both in and out of the classroom. Every degree program requires students complete an experiential learning course— an internship, service-learning, student teaching, or field work. Through experience, students learn how each piece of their education works together to prepare them for the future.

www.tiu.edu
(847) 317-7000
admissions@tiu.edu

STUDENT PROFILE
448 undergraduate students

93% of undergrad students are full-time

44% female – 56% male

53% of students are from out of state

57% freshman retention rate

FACULTY PROFILE
14 to 1 student/faculty ratio

TUITION & COST
Tuition: $32,398

Fees: $630

Room: $5,800

Board: $5,000

UNIVERSITY OF ILLINOIS AT CHICAGO

CHICAGO, ILLINOIS

www.uic.edu
(312) 996-7000

Located in one of the most vibrant cities in the world, UIC helps students unleash their potential. Students enjoy 87 bachelor's programs, a low student-to-faculty ratio, and award-winning professors who are regarded as experts in their field. The University of Illinois at Chicago is proud to support one of the most ethnically and culturally diverse campuses in the nation, so every member of the community has a place in which to learn and thrive.

LIVING-LEARNING COMMUNITIES: UIC is proud to offer students unique ways to live and learn on campus. Living-learning communities comprise of committed students who share a common interest. Students can choose from 15 different communities with topics ranging from Pre-Health to Women in Science and Engineering.

Students also enjoy the benefits of making deeper connections with peers, having built-in study buddies, and gaining easy access to experiential learning opportunities that are relevant to their field of study.

UNDERGRADUATE RESEARCH: As Chicago's only public research university, UIC presents students unique opportunities for innovation and discovery. Some notable initiatives include re-shaping educational policy; developing cleaner, more sustainable energy; driving economic development; and more. Undergraduate students are encouraged to participate in as many research opportunities as possible. The Office of Undergraduate Research is ready and happy to help students with every step of the process from finding a faculty mentor to securing funding for travel to research conferences.

ACADEMIC CENTER FOR EXCELLENCE: The Academic Center for Excellence provides learning support services to enable all UIC students to accomplish their academic goals. Students can make appointments with success coaches to create an individualized approach to personal success, allowing themselves to understand their best study skills and learning strategies.

STUDENT PROFILE

19,448 undergraduate students

92% of undergrad students are full-time

50% female — 50% male

80% freshman retention rate

FACULTY PROFILE

19 to 1 student/faculty ratio

ADMISSIONS

SAT Ranges: E 530-650, M 550-680

ACT Ranges: C 20-26, M 20-26, E 20-26

TUITION & COST

Tuition (in-state): $10,584

Tuition (out-of-state): $23,440

Fees: $3,120

Room: $7,930

Board: $4,000

UNIVERSITY OF ST. FRANCIS

JOLIET, ILLINOIS

The University of St. Francis in Joliet, IL, is a Catholic university rooted in the liberal arts. As a welcoming community of learners who are challenged by Franciscan values, everyone at USF is mindful of the compassionate, peacemaking tradition that encourages the pursuit of knowledge, faith, wisdom, and justice. USF strives for excellence in all programs, preparing women and men to contribute to the world through service and leadership.

STUDENT RESOURCES: The College of Business' "Small Business Incubator," located at USF's downtown St. Bonaventure Campus, allows Entrepreneurship students to work with businesses to help develop their own startup.

College of Nursing students utilize the SIM Lab and Skills Lab, getting hands-on experience in simulated hospital environments before working with real patients. USF even offers a cadaver lab to give biology and pre-health sciences students the opportunity to expand their understanding of anatomy through hands-on dissection.

For College of Education students, the annual Chrysalis Retreat gives students time to reflect on themselves and their passions to become teachers.

PRIMED FOR SUCCESS: USF Saints have multiple opportunities to enroll in supportive programs that set them up for success throughout and beyond college. The USF Summer Academy, for example, is designed to help students adjust to college life and the challenge of college-level coursework.

The university also offers the Success Scholars program to first-generation college students as a way to help them navigate an unfamiliar environment and grow as leaders.

"USF students become very close. Everyone gets to know each other. Being at USF has enabled me to understand my purpose in life." – *Jessica Nayder, nursing student*

www.stfrancis.edu
(800) 735-7500
admissions@stfrancis.edu

STUDENT PROFILE

1,599 undergraduate students

81% of undergrad students are full-time

65% female – 35% male

7% of students are from out of state

80% freshman retention rate

FACULTY PROFILE

13 to 1 student/faculty ratio

ADMISSIONS

Selectivity: 52%

SAT Ranges: E 490-630, M 540-610

ACT Ranges: C 20-25, M 19-25, E 20-25

TUITION & COST

Tuition (in-state): $31,150

Tuition (out-of-state): $31,150

Fees: $320

Room & Board: $9,358

WHEATON COLLEGE

WHEATON, ILLINOIS

www.wheaton.edu
(800) 222-2419
admissions@wheaton.edu

A Wheaton College education prepares students for lives that are wholly dedicated to serving Christ and His kingdom. The College is largely tied to the Christian church, the values of which are implemented in every facet of the College experience. Wheaton is concerned with the success of its students—success that can be used to perpetuate and best live out those Christian values.

GLOBAL LEARNING: Even as students change location and gain new perspectives, they carry with them their commitment to the service of God. Wheaton offers its students several opportunities to travel abroad, the trips of which can take the form of international internships, semester-long study, and research initiatives that incorporate cross-cultural perspectives.

Students can benefit directly from school funds through such grants as the International Internship Travel Grant and the Global Scholar award. These allow students to venture out into the world without worrying as much about finances, enabling them to focus on life-changing work experience or research in a different country.

WHEATON IN NETWORK: The Career Development Center and online Wheaton in Network (WiN) tool connects members of the Wheaton network to one another through various postgraduate inquiries and career interests.

THE IMPORTANCE OF THE CHRISTIAN CHURCH: The values of the Christian Church are prioritized at Wheaton. Serving the needs of the Church is paramount regardless of profession. And, with a heart for progression, faculty and staff work to advance the Kingdom of God through education and practice.

Students are encouraged to come together through love and commitment to Christ, as both the educational and personal aspects of Wheaton College come together to make an inclusive community, bound together by service and perpetuation of Christian ideals.

STUDENT PROFILE

1,688 undergraduate students

99% of undergrad students are full-time

61% female – 39% male

52% of students are from out of state

88% freshman retention rate

FACULTY PROFILE

11 to 1 student/faculty ratio

ADMISSIONS

Selectivity: 48%

SAT Ranges: E 590-680, M 560-670

ACT Ranges: C 26-30

TUITION & COST

Tuition: $50,520

Fees: $330

Room: $6,918

Board: $6,050

ANDERSON UNIVERSITY

ANDERSON, INDIANA

Anderson University offers more than 50 majors with experiential and service-learning experiences. Notably unique majors include engineering, national security studies, and sport marketing. Campus Ministries connects students to the local community through volunteer work at such places as local shelters, prison ministry, and nursing homes.

FACILITIES ON CAMPUS: AU's new Cybersecurity Engineering Laboratory allows for state-of-the-art learning opportunities with blade chassis, a set of enterprise access switches, core routers, and more. Students and faculty can run complex code or work on research using the high-capacity servers.

The Situation Room, modeled after the same room in the White House, gives security studies students classroom space to respond to mock crises and a video conferencing setup to allow more opportunities to hear from National Security experts.

The School of Nursing and Kinesiology features a Swim Ex rehabilitation pool, a sports medicine center, and a human performance center. And the Falls School of Business features its own financial stock trading room, which serves as a real-time, high-tech laboratory classroom that simulates a realistic Wall Street environment.

TRI-S: Founded in 1964, the Tri-S program (Study, Serve, Share) is designed to let students learn from other cultures while serving in communities around the world. Through Tri-S, students explore other cultures while participating in work camps, service, or ministry projects.

"My time at AU helped me to grow into the person I am today, through faculty, Tri-S trips, and deep friendships. AU gave me space to learn about public relations *and* Christian ministries in an environment where I never felt like the two were in conflict." – *Christina Nesslage BA '18*

ANDERSON UNIVERSITY

www.anderson.edu
(800) 428-6414
info@anderson.edu

STUDENT PROFILE
1,506 undergraduate students

95% of undergrad students are full-time

59% female – 41% male

24% of students are from out of state

65% freshman retention rate

FACULTY PROFILE
10 to 1 student/faculty ratio

ADMISSIONS
Selectivity: 73%

SAT Ranges: E 450-550, M 460-560

ACT Ranges: C 19-25, M 19-25, E 17-25

TUITION & COST
Tuition: $29,950

Fees: $500

Room: $6,180

Board: $3,710

BALL STATE UNIVERSITY

MUNCIE, INDIANA

BALL STATE UNIVERSITY

www.cms.bsu.edu
(765) 285-8300
askus@bsu.edu

Ball State is committed to education with an innovative approach. Students are given a wide range of opportunities to explore their passions through immersive and experiential learning methods. Ball State's unique entrepreneurship program, as well as its many impact and service initiatives, make the University an ideal environment in which to learn and grow.

COMMUTER AMBASSADORS: Ball State recognizes that the first year of college is a big transition—one that may prove extra difficult for students who commute to school. To rectify this, Ball State established Commuter Ambassadors to bridge the gap between on- and off-campus first-year students. Commuter Ambassadors are available to answer any questions about Ball State and help commuters get used to the campus community.

CHRISTY WOODS: Christy Woods serves as classroom for the students and members of the Ball State community. This outdoor teaching laboratory features a lush forest filled with several plant communities. Ball State has two greenhouses, an indoor classroom, and an outdoor interpretation area within the Woods.

SUPPLEMENTAL INSTRUCTION: Ball State founded a Supplemental Instruction initiative in order to provide extra support to students taking large lecture-based classes that historically turn out high fail/withdrawal rates. This Supplemental Instruction is run by peer mentors who themselves have already taken and passed the course. Students struggling with coursework are helped through study sessions, tutoring, note-taking tips, and additional lectures.

DAVID OWSLEY MUSEUM OF ART: Grandson of one of the University founders, David Owsley has contributed a great deal to the campus museum of art. The museum features a wide array of pieces from around the world with an emphasis on European and American artworks. Students and community members alike are invited to stop in and observe all that the museum has to offer.

STUDENT PROFILE

17,004 undergraduate students

89% of undergrad students are full-time

60% female – 40% male

19% of students are from out of state

78% freshman retention rate

FACULTY PROFILE

17 to 1 student/faculty ratio

ADMISSIONS

Selectivity: 62%

SAT Ranges: E 550-630, M 530-610

ACT Ranges: C 20-24, M 18-24, E 19-24

TUITION & COST

Tuition (in-state): $9,112

Tuition (out-of-state): $25,280

Fees: $662

Room & Board: $10,034

BETHEL UNIVERSITY INDIANA

MISHAKAWA, INDIANA

The mission of Bethel University, affiliated with the Missionary Church, is to transform communities through Christ-centered graduates. Bethel's liberating academic programs challenge the mind, enlarge the vision, and equip the whole person for lifelong service. Students are challenged to explore multiple perspectives in a wide variety of topics, all from a Christian worldview. Offering over 50 areas of study, Bethel University has made an impact in many ways on many lives.

TASK FORCE: Every Bethel College student has the opportunity to venture out into the world and take part in Task Force Teams, charitable missions that serve areas of need across the globe. Some of the most recent Task Force Teams have gone on to Kenya to nurture orphaned children, France to contribute to the marketing of a tourist activism ministry, and Indonesia to provide healthcare and resources to underprivileged neighborhoods.

SPIRITUAL LIFE: At the core of all that Bethel does is a committed focus on each student's spiritual development. The university is dedicated to building lives of commitment for leadership in the church and the world. Spiritual growth is nurtured at chapel (the heartbeat of Bethel) twice per week as well as in small group gatherings that plunge students deeper into their walk with God. Beyond the opportunities to grow in community through residence hall and small group Bible studies, students can also be the hands and feet of Christ through events like Bethel's annual Service day.

NURSING SIMULATION: Nursing students have the incredible advantage of a brand-new simulation lab. This lab features two critical care hospital rooms and high-tech patient simulators that function and respond to students' care in a realistic way. Through these simulations, students are able to practice urgent procedures in a low-risk environment.

Nursing students who study at Bethel learn to remain calm and make calculated decisions in dire situations, skills that cannot be obtained simply by sitting in a lecture hall. They graduate a step ahead of the curve, level headed and ready to provide compassionate and effective care.

---

betheluniversity.edu
(574) 807-7600
admissions@
betheluniversity.edu

STUDENT PROFILE

1,388 undergraduate students

81% of undergrad students are full-time

64% female – 36% male

27% of students are from out of state

76% freshman retention rate

FACULTY PROFILE

12 to 1 student/faculty ratio

ADMISSIONS

Selectivity: 98%

SAT Ranges: E 440-560, M 470-590

ACT Ranges: C 20-25, M 20-25, E 19-26

TUITION & COST

Tuition: $27,580

Fees: $450

Room: $4,160

Board: $4,260

BUTLER UNIVERSITY

INDIANAPOLIS, INDIANA

Butler's liberal arts courses exercise students' ability to nurture and employ the skills that are essential for a job in any field. The University graduates lifelong learners who are able not only to make a living, but to make a life of purpose. At Butler, students receive a well-rounded education that incorporates a liberal arts perspective into professional fields of study. Students have several options to choose from, with 60 academic programs that span over 6 colleges as well as pre-professional programs in the areas of engineering, law, medicine, and veterinary medicine.

INTERNSHIP & CAREER SERVICES (ICS): Internship & Career Services in an incredibly useful tool for students, providing the resources and guidance they need to reach their individual postgraduate goals. Through frequent academic advising and occasional counseling, students are guided through the rigorous process of selecting an area of study and, ultimately, a career path. ICS also offers self-assessments to help students better understand their own talents and professional potential.

ENRICHED OFFERINGS: Butler has been lauded for such beneficial academic and campus resources as the first-year experience, study abroad, internships, service-learning, and research projects. These resources ensure that every student digs deeply into their education with hands-on approaches to learning.

Professors are researchers and scholars, practicing and exercising their talents through truly creative inquiry. They create a solid foundation that is grounded in the liberal arts and tied to more focused professional studies.

PULSE: The Programs for Leadership and Service Education (PULSE) is a resource available to assist any club or group, supporting students with the means to carry out the goals of their organizations. It is also the place to go to seek information regarding upcoming events and activities, serving as a great tool for getting involved.

www.butler.edu
(317) 940-8100
admission@butler.edu

STUDENT PROFILE

4,293 undergraduate students

97% of undergrad students are full-time

60% female – 40% male

55% of students are from out of state

89% freshman retention rate

FACULTY PROFILE

11 to 1 student/faculty ratio

ADMISSIONS

Selectivity: 65%

SAT Ranges: E 580-660, M 570-660

ACT Ranges: C 25-30, M 24-29, E 24-31

TUITION & COST

Tuition: $38,900

Fees: $960

Room: $6,513

Board: $6,830

DEPAUW UNIVERSITY

GREENCASTLE, INDIANA

When it comes down to it, an education has to be about more than rote memorization and textbooks. In order for students to be truly successful, they need hands-on experience. DePauw University has met these needs as a premier institution of higher education at which students have endless opportunities to succeed both academically and personally.

SERVICIO EN LAS AMÈRICAS: Servicio en Las Amèricas is an immersion program focused on service and global citizenship. Participants begin the program by taking three weeks of Spanish at DePauw and then spend two weeks performing various acts of service in Latin America. All participants are asked to sign a contract, promising only to speak Spanish for the duration of the trip.

MANAGEMENT ACCELERATOR PROGRAM: The Management Accelerator Program is considered an Extended Studies credit and is open to sophomores, juniors, and seniors. The program, which takes place during Winter Term, explores the foundations of business and what it takes to make an organization run smoothly.

HONORS PROGRAMS: Self-motivated students who love a good challenge are encouraged to explore the honors options at DePauw. Currently, the university has four Fellows programs, as well as an Honors Scholars program. In each of the tracks, students have the benefit of an intimate learning environment that fosters both personal and academic growth.

The programs available include the Honors Scholars Program, Environmental Fellows Program, Management Fellows Program, Media Fellows Program, and Science Research Fellows.

FACULTY-LED EXTENDED STUDIES PROGRAMS: Faculty-led study abroad takes place during Winter Term and May Term, during which experienced faculty lead expeditions in foreign locations. Students benefit greatly from the experience and enjoy the mixture of exploration and lecture.

COLLEGE PROFILES: INDIANA

DEPAUW UNIVERSITY
Est. 1837

www.depauw.edu
(765) 658-4006
admission@depauw.edu

STUDENT PROFILE
2,158 undergraduate students

99% of undergrad students are full-time

52% female – 48% male

46% of students are from out of state

89% freshman retention rate

FACULTY PROFILE
9 to 1 student/faculty ratio

ADMISSIONS
Selectivity: 67%

SAT Ranges: E 560-650, M 550-680

ACT Ranges: C 24-29, M 23-30, E 23-28

TUITION & COST
Tuition: $47,026

Fees: $812

Room & Board: $12,529

FRANKLIN COLLEGE

FRANKLIN, INDIANA

Franklin College uses an interdisciplinary approach to craft students into the next generation of diverse thinkers and leaders. With innovative practices such as the Immersive Term, robust research opportunities, and a professional development program that spans all four years, students leave with the academic and professional foundations to succeed in any field. Franklin sits on the cutting edge of colleges integrating the demands of modern employers with engaging and interesting course content.

THE IMMERSIVE TERM: Franklin College learning isn't limited to the traditional fall and spring semesters. The innovative Immersive Term sits in between these two—the entire month of January is reserved for a non-traditional experience of some kind. Immersive Terms include everything from comparing Harry Potter films to those of Alfred Hitchcock with tenured faculty to volunteering in Uganda.

This unique practice allows students to explore and expand their interests. Internships, studying abroad, or taking a non-traditional course helps students make connections between their regular coursework and other aspects of society and education. Franklin College's commitment to the Immersive Term fulfills their promise of creating well-rounded citizens who are equipped to take on the world.

PDP: As soon as a student sets foot on campus, Franklin College sets their sights on what's to come after graduation. The four-year Professional Development Program (PDP) encapsulates every step of that process—goal setting, résumé building, networking and, finally, landing the perfect job.

The PDP also gives students essential life skills, such as understanding healthcare benefits and building a personal finance plan. The program isn't exclusively about helping students find an internship or job; it places an emphasis on giving them what they need to make informed personal decisions for the rest of their lives. Every student also completes an internship before graduation, because experiential learning is an important way to both cement their skills and explore their interests.

www.franklincollege.edu
(317) 738-8075
admissions@ franklincollege.edu

STUDENT PROFILE

1,016 undergraduate students

95% of undergrad students are full-time

52% female – 48% male

9% of students are from out of state

75% freshman retention rate

FACULTY PROFILE

11 to 1 student/faculty ratio

ADMISSIONS

Selectivity: 78%

SAT Ranges: E 500-610, M 510-590

ACT Ranges: C 19-25, M 18-25, E 18-26

TUITION & COST

Tuition: $30,735

Fees: $185

Room: $5,490

Board: $3,725

HANOVER COLLEGE

HANOVER, INDIANA

Situated on 650 acres of woods on the banks of the Ohio River, Hanover College is a private liberal arts institution dedicated to the livelihood of its distinctive intellectual community. Hanover encourages students to take charge of their education and future as committed, curious learners. Hanover offers 33 majors in the liberal arts as well as a design-your-own-major option for students to individualize their education.

MEET THE POLICY-MAKERS: Political science students are able to take courses that send them directly to the source of the most important policies impacting the U.S and the world. Through the Field Study of Washington, D.C., students can conduct independent research and complete interviews with policy-makers across the legislative, judicial, and executive branches of government. The Field Study of the United Nations introduces students to the inner workings of essential U.N. functions, allowing them to interact with diplomatic officials from around the world.

BUSINESS SCHOLARS PROGRAM: The practical and experiential Business Scholars Program allows students to experience what it is like to solve real, pressing business problems. Those who participate in the Program complete a course alongside an internship in which they analyze cases and work on an actual consulting project. Scholars also get the opportunity to meet with prominent business leaders and participate in workshops that perfect their résumé writing and interview skills.

SUMMER RESEARCH: Designed to emphasize experiential learning in a biological sub discipline, the Summer Research Fellows program encourages students to work closely with a professor on an active research project over the summer. Students even receive a monetary award and stipend to cover room and board.

Hanover students are consistently recognized for their academic excellence through opportunities to present their findings at regional and national conferences. They also have the opportunity to publish their work in peer-reviewed scientific journals, including the *Journal of Freshwater Ecology and Ethology, Ecology, and Evolution*.

www.hanover.edu
(800) 213-2178
admissionvisit@
hanover.edu

STUDENT PROFILE
1,089 undergraduate students

99% of undergrad students are full-time

54% female – 46% male

79% freshman retention rate

FACULTY PROFILE
13 to 1 student/faculty ratio

ADMISSIONS
Selectivity: 84%

SAT Ranges: E 540-640, M 530-620

ACT Ranges: C 22-27, M 20-27, E 21-28

TUITION & COST
Tuition: $35,750

Fees: $770

Room: $5,600

Board: $5,630

ROSE-HULMAN INSTITUTE OF TECHNOLOGY

TERRE HAUTE, INDIANA

One of the early institutions to focus primarily on STEM education, Rose-Hulman Institute of Technology was founded in 1874 as an all-male engineering college. Now, Rose-Hulman has transformed its once lesser-known presence into a dominating, coeducational force in engineering, math, and science. Rather than employing a one-size-fits-all approach to STEM, the Rose-Hulman experience is highly personalized and flexible enough to support an immense range of professional goals.

EXCLUSIVE FACILITIES: Rose-Hulman's one-of-a-kind curriculum is complemented by its one-of-a-kind facilities. Its high-tech MiNDs Lab, for example, enables Rose-Hulman to be one of the only undergraduate institutions to offer hands-on study with micro- and nanoscale technology, and the Oakley Observatory gives students direct access to in-demand, professional equipment.

Undergraduates are also able to collaborate with researchers and medical surgeons at the JRSI Laboratory, which focuses on improving the long-term efficacy of hip- and knee- replacement surgeries. Here, students and clinical research interns shadow world-renowned surgeons as they work on real patients in need of joint replacement.

ENGINEERS WITHOUT BORDERS: Through international travel with some of the top professionals in engineering, students discover new ways to use technology in the interest of nurturing a sustainable environment. The program brings new technology to communities across the globe, teaching how to live in a way that supports both the state of the environment and the health of those living in it.

This meaningful experience challenges participants to manage projects with an awareness not only of practical, scientific complexities, but also of the cultural, political, and ethical factors that influence the integration of new technology.

www.rose-hulman.edu
(800) 248-7448
admissions@
rose-hulman.edu

STUDENT PROFILE

2,168 undergraduate students

99% of undergrad students are full-time

25% female — 75% male

55% of students are from out of state

91% freshman retention rate

FACULTY PROFILE

11 to 1 student/faculty ratio

ADMISSIONS

Selectivity: 61%

SAT Ranges: E 610-690, M 650-760

ACT Ranges: C 27-32, M 28-34, E 25-33

TUITION & COST

Tuition: $44,847

Fees: $3,165

Room: $8,559

Board: $5,502

TAYLOR UNIVERSITY

UPLAND, INDIANA

The intellect and the spirit coexist harmoniously at Taylor University. Here, students find a high-quality learning experience based on Christian ideals of truth and life. Students have the chance to take advantage of a unique leadership development initiative, a nationally recognized study abroad program, and cutting-edge scientific research opportunities, all while concurrently advancing their spiritual development in a caring Christian community.

FELLOWSHIP, FRIENDSHIP, AND FAITH: Student life at Taylor provides the chance to learn outside the classroom. The biblical concept of the Body of Christ is evident as students live, serve, and learn together.

Whether competing with their residence floor in the intramural flag football championship, working with Project Mercy alongside a team of fellow students in Ethiopia, or creating an award-winning film for the Heartland Film Festival, Taylor students are engaged in a variety of events that contribute to their growth and to the campus community.

Chapel services, during which the entire student body gathers in worship, are held three times a week on Monday, Wednesday, and Friday mornings. Attendance is not taken at chapel, yet students nevertheless consistently fill the pews.

ACTIVE FAITH: Faculty and students work collaboratively, both in class and out, to achieve learning outcomes appropriate to each student's vocational calling.

Members of the Taylor faculty are noted for their ability to reconcile intellectual pursuits and faith. Taylor's Honors Guild emphasizes the integration of faith and learning, ideas and values, and discussion and student initiative. Each January, freshmen in the Honors Guild are part of a unique overseas learning experience in which their faith and intellect meet real world experiences. Past trips have included Jordan, Northern Ireland, and South Africa.

www.taylor.edu
(765) 998-5134
admissions@taylor.edu

STUDENT PROFILE

2,110 undergraduate students

87% of undergrad students are full-time

56% female – 44% male

53% of students are from out of state

90% freshman retention rate

FACULTY PROFILE

13 to 1 student/faculty ratio

ADMISSIONS

Selectivity: 87%

SAT Ranges: E 530-650, M 515-640

ACT Ranges: C 22-29, M 22-28, E 22-31

TUITION & COST

Tuition: $32,640

Fees: $245

Room: $4,860

Board: $4,385

UNIVERSITY OF INDIANAPOLIS

INDIANAPOLIS, INDIANA

UIndy

The University of Indianapolis, founded in 1902, is a private liberal arts institution offering 100+ undergraduate degree programs, 40+ master's degree programs, five doctoral programs, and a variety of certificate programs. The University's motto, "Education for Service," is central to its identity and purpose. This philosophy is integrated into the curriculum of every academic program, engaging students and faculty in international and domestic service-learning trips, volunteer opportunities, and community involvement projects, often in the context of their own careers.

INTERNSHIPS & CAREER PLACEMENTS: The University's Professional Edge Center guides ongoing exposure to working professionals, connecting students to internships, employment opportunities, and mentorships.

From day one, the Professional Edge Center helps students—even those who haven't decided on a major—identify career pathways and develop professional skills. The Professional Edge Center team is organized into sector experts, giving students the opportunity to work one-on-one with a career advisor dedicated to their field. According to a student survey, 94 percent of grads said that the Center gave them an advantage in their careers.

DIVERSITY & GLOBAL LEARNING: University of Indianapolis serves an inclusive student body and promotes cross-cultural understanding across campus. The University's dedication to cultural diversity and international exchange has made the campus a welcoming environment for students from more than 60 nations.

"You don't just come in, learn and leave. It's more of a family atmosphere; we all help each other. The University of Indianapolis brought me out of my comfort zone and helped me define my future and career."

– DeAndre Grayson, pre-athletic training, Class of 2017

---

www.uindy.edu
(317) 788-3216
admissions@uindy.edu

STUDENT PROFILE

4,384 undergraduate students

87% of undergrad students are full-time

64% female – 36% male

11% of students are from out of state

75% freshman retention rate

FACULTY PROFILE

13 to 1 student/faculty ratio

ADMISSIONS

Selectivity: 82%

SAT Ranges: E 500-590, M 490-590

ACT Ranges: C 19-25, M 18-25, E 18-24

TUITION & COST

Tuition: $28,836

Fees: $852

Room & Board: $9,150

BRIAR CLIFF UNIVERSITY

SIOUX CITY, IOWA

Briar•Cliff
UNIVERSITY

With a University-wide orientation toward service and outreach, Briar Cliff was founded in 1930 by the Sisters of Saint Francis of Dubuque, with a mission to educate students in the Franciscan tradition of service, caring, and openness to all. Briar Cliff University provides an outstanding education, offering more than 30 majors for undergraduates as well as an array of graduate and online degree-completion programs.

UNDERGRADUATE RESEARCH : Briar Cliff students have the distinct and rare honor to conduct undergraduate research alongside their professors. Through their collaborative work, students get to bulk up their résumés and form close relationships with valuable professionals to add to their networks.

In addition to one of the region's only educational cadaver labs, Briar Cliff is home to fully equipped laboratories that complement students' nursing, kinesiology, chemistry, and biology studies.

The University is also surrounded by 150 acres of the nation's largest urban tallgrass prairie, an outdoor classroom that is just as beautiful as it is educational. BCU also maintains the Siouxland Research Center in order to help non-profit organizations in the area perform research.

THE BRIAR CLIFF REVIEW: Founded in 1989, the Briar Cliff Review is a nationally renowned literary and art magazine that showcases emerging writers and artists. Its annual publication has played a significant part in developing several authors' careers, including New York Times and #1 international best-selling author Jenna Blum.

PROFESSIONAL DEVELOPMENT SCHOOL: The Professional Development School not only gives education majors fulfilling hands-on experience, but it also enriches the education of students from local elementary and high schools. This collaboration between BCU and the broader community provides students with the extraordinarily rare opportunity to gain hundreds of hours of experience in the classroom before they even begin student teaching.

www.briarcliff.edu
(712) 279-5200
admissions@briarcliff.edu

STUDENT PROFILE
945 undergraduate students

76% of undergrad students are full-time

59% female – 41% male

50% of students are from out of state

55% freshman retention rate

FACULTY PROFILE
11 to 1 student/faculty ratio

TUITION & COST
Tuition: $28,650

Fees: $1,136

Room: $4,196

Board: $4,786

BUENA VISTA UNIVERSITY

STORM LAKE, IOWA

BUENA VISTA UNIVERSITY

www.bvu.edu
(800) 383-9600
admissions@bvu.edu

Buena Vista University is dedicated to transforming students to succeed in both the academic and professional worlds through a groundbreaking, interdisciplinary liberal arts education. Students can study education, business, biological sciences, and more. BVU also offers degree-completion (at 16 locations throughout Iowa), online, and graduate programs to fit the busy schedule of working adults. A variety of scheduling options and class formats makes it easy to get a degree. BVU students earn an average scholarship of more than 50 percent off of tuition.

STORM LAKE, IOWA: Located along the shores of the gorgeous Storm Lake, Buena Vista University welcomes its students into a safe, comfortable campus environment that is full of outlets for fun, adventure, and inspiration. Storm Lake can double as a spot for peaceful reflection as well as a site for incredibly fun outdoor recreation. BVU provides students with paddleboards, canoes, bikes, and more for all the adventure they crave.

In addition to the beautiful natural atmosphere of Storm Lake, students can get their fill of recreation through the small yet bustling town right next to campus. Places to shop, eat, and hang out are certainly not limited.

CORE CURRICULUM: Structured around the University's three "Signature Skills"—problem solving, integrative learning, and effective communication—BVU's general education program gives its students a well-rounded education that covers a whole range of disciplines.

The general education's "Foundations" and "Explorations" requirements encourages students to stretch out of their comfort zones, taking courses in mathematics, communication, the humanities, fine arts, science, business, and social sciences so that they may be prepared for any challenge that life may bring them.

All academic careers conclude with a general education capstone, a final course that assesses students' abilities to approach a subject from interdisciplinary perspectives.

STUDENT PROFILE

1,982 undergraduate students

84% of undergrad students are full-time

66% female – 34% male

15% of students are from out of state

77% freshman retention rate

FACULTY PROFILE

9 to 1 student/faculty ratio

TUITION & COST

Tuition: $35,194

Room & Board: $9,872

DRAKE UNIVERSITY

DES MOINES, IOWA

Drake University is committed to providing an exceptional learning environment that prepares students for meaningful personal lives, professional accomplishments, and responsible global citizenship. The University is distinguished by collaborative learning among students and staff alike.

THE DRAKE CURRICULUM: The Drake Curriculum gives students a solid foundation from which they can individually build both their educational and personal journeys. This curriculum trains students to become critical thinkers who engage in higher-level conceptualization.

There are three components to the Drake Curriculum, which include the first-year seminar, areas of inquiry, and a senior capstone.

FIRST-YEAR SEMINAR: First-year seminar classes are designed to engage students with exciting and unique subject matters right at the start of their educational experience. Seminar courses have 19 or fewer students, all of whom will live in the same building as one another. This structure is designed to encourage comfortable participation in class as well as meaningful relationships outside of it.

AREAS OF INQUIRY: As students progress through college, they are to choose classes that suit and support their majors. No matter the concentration, however, they must also take 1-2 courses within each of Drake's 10 "Areas of Inquiry." These designations, which range from Quantitative Literacy to Critical Thinking, ensure that all students of all majors have the same foundational skill set for high-level thinking and success.

THE SENIOR CAPSTONE: The Senior Capstone is a chance for each student to demonstrate all they have learned over their first three years in college. This culminating capstone requirement is structured differently for every major, playing out in the format of field experience to an individual research project.

Drake UNIVERSITY

www.drake.edu
(515) 271-3181
admission@drake.edu

STUDENT PROFILE
3,098 undergraduate students

95% of undergrad students are full-time

57% female – 43% male

70% of students are from out of state

87% freshman retention rate

FACULTY PROFILE
11 to 1 student/faculty ratio

ADMISSIONS
Selectivity: 69%

SAT Ranges: E 540-660, M 560-690

ACT Ranges: C 24-30, M 24-32, E 24-29

TUITION & COST
Tuition: $38,916

Fees: $146

Room: $5,486

Board: $4,672

MOUNT MERCY UNIVERSITY

CEDAR RAPIDS, IOWA

www.mtmercy.edu
(319) 368-6460
admission@mtmercy.edu

Mount Mercy was founded on academic excellence, offering students a values-based curriculum. Established on five critical concerns—earth, immigration, nonviolence, racism, and women—MMU's curriculum guides students in exploring and working towards a more just, equal, and peaceful world. Hands-on work often accompanies classroom learning, giving students the experience needed to start their careers with confidence.

STUDY ABROAD: Since 2009, Mount Mercy education students have had the opportunity to study abroad in Canterbury, England, as part of an exchange partnership with Christ Church University. Students participate in CCU education courses and visit rural and urban schools in Canterbury. Partner schools also include Carlow College in Ireland and University of Stirling in Scotland. MMU students have the opportunity to study abroad at hundreds of other institutions as well through the University's collaboration with AIFS.

DEGREE IN THREE: Mount Mercy University makes it possible to earn a bachelor's degree in three years. This helps students save time and money while getting a jumpstart on their careers.

MMU PLUS: Students interested in furthering their education with Mount Mercy also have a fast-track option with the MMU Plus program. Through the plan, undergraduate students begin taking graduate courses during their junior and senior years and are thus enabled to complete both bachelor's and master's degrees in under five years.

"My foundations class helped me realize the things I'm already doing in my day-to-day work. I now have definitions behind behaviors—almost like a dictionary for my professional life. I'm beginning to understand how I lead, but also how I respond to leaders as a follower."

– Sauvik Goswami | '20 MSL

STUDENT PROFILE

1,488 undergraduate students

72% of undergrad students are full-time

69% female – 31% male

13% of students are from out of state

72% freshman retention rate

FACULTY PROFILE

15 to 1 student/faculty ratio

ADMISSIONS

Selectivity: 63%

ACT Ranges: C 19-25, M 18-24, E 18-24

TUITION & COST

Tuition: $32,862

Fees: $1,000

Room & Board: $9,915

NORTHWESTERN COLLEGE

ORANGE CITY, IOWA

At Northwestern College, standout academics and a firm Christian faith mean big opportunities to learn and grow. More than 80 academic programs lead to a bachelor's degree, and a growing online program leads to seven options for a Master's of Education. Highly ranked study abroad programs, extensive internship opportunities, and impactful research experiences with professors help prepare them for their careers. Faith is integrated into the whole Northwestern experience, so students are empowered to follow Christ and pursue God's redeeming work in the world.

CHAPEL AND CHRISTIAN FORMATION: Chapel services, held twice a week, bring the campus community together to learn about God, the world, and how to make a difference in it. Nationally known speakers such as Hugh Halter, Jerry Sittser, and Sarah Thebarge challenge students, as do area Christian leaders, faculty and staff, and other students.

The student-led Sunday Night Praise & Worship service is a popular way to start a new week. In the dorms and apartments, nearly 500 students meet in small discipleship groups on a weekly basis to pray, study the Bible, and talk about how their faith integrates with what they're learning.

OUTSTANDING LEARNING FACILITIES: More than $45 million has been spent on construction and renovation projects at Northwestern since 2003. Among those are the DeWitt Theatre Arts Center, which has been called the best college theatre facility in Iowa, and the new DeWitt Family Science Center, which was completed in the fall of 2018. The eco-friendly facility houses classrooms, laboratories, and faculty offices for the departments of biology, chemistry, and nursing.

"If you're looking for authentic Christian community, I can guarantee that NWC is the place to be. For me and many others, Northwestern College is home."

– Caley Vink '19, political science major, Zeeland, Michigan

www.nwciowa.edu
(800) 747-4757
admissions@nwciowa.edu

STUDENT PROFILE

1,006 undergraduate students

94% of undergrad students are full-time

56% female – 44% male

43% of students are from out of state

75% freshman retention rate

FACULTY PROFILE

11 to 1 student/faculty ratio

ADMISSIONS

Selectivity: 71%

SAT Ranges: E 540-620, M 530-640

ACT Ranges: C 21-27, M 20-27, E 20-27

TUITION & COST

Tuition: $32,100

Fees: $350

Room & Board: $9,600

ST. AMBROSE UNIVERSITY

DAVENPORT, IOWA

A private, Roman Catholic institution located in Davenport, Iowa, St. Ambrose University strives to inspire students with a stimulating academic environment, all while providing a multitude of opportunities to develop leadership skills that will support them throughout the professional world. St. Ambrose offers more than 60 majors that integrate a strong Catholic intellectual tradition into both academics and extracurriculars.

PERSONAL ATTENTION: Every St. Ambrose student is valued as an individual. With the help of their academic advisor, each student seamlessly navigates their way through college in pursuit of their personal goals.

Their advisors, who are professors in their own field of study, equip them with more than a four-year plan that gets them to graduation—they equip them with a four-year plan that makes the most of their major and ensures that they take the courses that truly interest them. In this way, students fulfill their degree requirements with courses that cater specifically to their goals.

INTERNSHIPS: More than 75% of St. Ambrose students participate in an internship before graduation. Their connections for full- or part-time internships can simultaneously earn them both professional experience and course credit. What's more, St. Ambrose shows its strong belief in the value of internships by offering a free elective course to those who want to intern.

ST. AMBROSE ABROAD: St. Ambrose hosts a diverse range of international programs for its students. In partnership with other universities all around the globe, students can travel to such places as the United Kingdom, Spain, Ecuador, Italy, Korea, Japan, Germany, Cyprus, Croatia, and many more.

"Curiosity means never being satisfied with what you know; it's about knowing there's always more to learn. St. Ambrose has elevated my expectations for myself and the skills I want to develop." *– Perla Hernandez '20*

www.sau.edu
(563) 333-6300
admit@sau.edu

STUDENT PROFILE

2,311 undergraduate students

93% of undergrad students are full-time

55% female – 44% male

63% of students are from out of state

80% freshman retention rate

FACULTY PROFILE

11 to 1 student/faculty ratio

ADMISSIONS

Selectivity: 63%

SAT Ranges: E 510-600, M 510-590

ACT Ranges: C 20-26, M 19-26, E 20-26

TUITION & COST

Tuition: $31,532

Fees: $280

Room: $6,816

Board: $4,208

UNIVERSITY OF DUBUQUE

DUBUQUE, IOWA

UNIVERSITY *of* **DUBUQUE**
THE DIAMOND UNIVERSITY

The University of Dubuque is a private University affiliated with the Presbyterian Church (U.S.A.). It was founded in 1852 by Dutch immigrant Adrian Van Vliet to educate German-speaking ministers who could communicate with incoming immigrants. In 1902, new programs emerged to form what is now the University of Dubuque. The University is continually expanding in order to adapt to the world's ever-changing social, economic, and academic challenges.

STUDENT SERVICES: The University of Dubuque commits to helping each student, regardless of need, feel comfortable and at home. For example, Disability Services provides the necessary accommodations to differently abled students so that they may live comfortably throughout UD's campus.

Additionally, the TRIO/Student Support Services facility brings students from disadvantaged backgrounds in touch with federal programs that provide multiple services and opportunities to help them thrive.

STUDENT HOUSING AND FACILITIES: Comfortable living is a given at the University of Dubuque. Three modern, ecologically sustainable dorms cater specifically to first-year students, providing an extra platform for new friendships to form twenty-four hours a day. These dorms, among other residence halls, apartments, and townhomes, become bedrocks for community. Each on-campus residence hall acts as a base for close-knit relationships and activities.

THE DIAMOND EDUCATION MODEL.: The University of Dubuque developed Diamond—an education model that focuses all classroom learning around four key principles: Academics, Stewardship, Vocation, and Community and Character.

Diamond helps students reach their full potential by promoting an environment that is student centered and individually focused. Students are prepared to manage change by building confidence, developing flexibility, and encouraging critical thinking.

www.dbq.edu
(563) 589-3000

STUDENT PROFILE

1,964 undergraduate students

85% of undergrad students are full-time

44% female – 56% male

58% of students are from out of state

66% freshman retention rate

FACULTY PROFILE

10 to 1 student/faculty ratio

ADMISSIONS

Selectivity: 73%

SAT Ranges: E 420-570, M 430-530

ACT Ranges: C 16-22, M 16-23, E 15-21

TUITION & COST

Tuition: $34,070

Fees: $1,500

Room: $5,150

Board: $5,060

BAKER UNIVERSITY

BALDWIN CITY, KANSAS

Baker University's academic reputation is built on its liberal arts tradition. Its professors challenge students while giving them the tools to rise to new heights. Baker offers more than 40 areas of study and encourages students to explore unique educational experiences through hands-on learning.

HANDS-ON PR EXPERIENCE: Some business students got the opportunity to travel to Atlanta through an interterm course known as Bowl Game Extravaganza: Sport Public Relations in Action. This course showed them the ins and outs of the event operations and strategies connected to the Chick-fil-A Bowl and other organizations.

UNIQUE SOCIOLOGY COURSE: Alongside an associate professor, sociology students can make weekly trips to an area correctional facility as part of the Inside-Out Prison Exchange Program. During this course, students interact with inmates to learn more about the criminal justice system.

The lessons that come from these often-stifled voices inspire students to take their knowledge far beyond their experience. For example, through her Senior Sociology Semester after completing the Inside-Out Prison Exchange Program, a Baker student developed and facilitated a poetry-writing workshop for 11 incarcerated writers at the Topeka Correctional Facility.

DEVELOPING LEADERS: Members of Mungano, Baker's student-run diversity organization, regularly attend the Big XII Conference on Black Student Government, where participants gain the tools and knowledge to become successful leaders for their organizations and communities.

"I feel my experience at Baker has fully equipped me to take on the adventure of medical school. The factual knowledge I've learned is obviously important, but it's also been a place where I've experienced a lot of emotional and spiritual growth, which is equally vital for success." *- Brandon, student*

---

www.bakeru.edu
(785) 594-8325
admission@bakeru.edu

STUDENT PROFILE

1,771 undergraduate students

60% of undergrad students are full-time

57% female – 43% male

24% of students are from out of state

68% freshman retention rate

FACULTY PROFILE

7 to 1 student/faculty ratio

ADMISSIONS

Selectivity: 86%

SAT Ranges: E 460-540, M 490-570

ACT Ranges: C 21-25, M 21-26, E 20-26

TUITION & COST

Tuition: $28,430

Fees: $530

Room: $3,910

Board: $4,400

EMPORIA STATE UNIVERSITY

EMPORIA, KANSAS

Emporia State offers over 200 academic programs—many are nationally recognized—across liberal arts and sciences, business, education and library and information management. Focused on the mission of "preparing students for lifelong learning, rewarding careers, and adaptive leadership," Emporia State provides high-impact, real-world learning opportunities, internships, and research projects for students with faculty mentors.

ART FORUM: During the fall and spring semesters, the Department of Art hosts a visiting artist every two weeks. Artists showcase their work, work with students and share their career paths and experiences.

One example of these visits is the annual weeklong Glass Blowout (ESU offers the only bachelor's in Glass Blowing in the state of Kansas) in which the visiting artist shows students different techniques throughout the week. The week culminates in a public event, which includes hot glass demonstrations, live music, and a glass auction.

STUDENT-PROFESSOR RESEARCH PROJECTS: From day one at Emporia State, students have the opportunity to work alongside professors in research.

Every other year, students also dip their toes in the water of the Bahamas while conducting research in the Tropical Field Ecology Course and learning about 200 marine life species, corals, and sea turtles. And, during spring break 2017, students experienced the Santa Fe Trail firsthand through a high-impact class called "Footpaths Through Mexico—Immigration Then and Now." The course took students on a six-day road trip from Council Grove, Kansas, to Santa Fe, New Mexico, giving them a look at living history.

RESEARCH & CREATIVITY DAY: Emporia State understands the hard work students put into their research, which is why each year both undergraduate and graduate students have the opportunity to showcase their research during Research & Creativity Day. Students present research orally, through poster presentations, or through 3-minute thesis presentations.

www.emporia.edu
(620) 341-5465
go2esu@emporia.edu

STUDENT PROFILE

3,497 undergraduate students

94% of undergrad students are full-time

63% female – 37% male

9% of students are from out of state

75% freshman retention rate

FACULTY PROFILE

17 to 1 student/faculty ratio

ADMISSIONS

Selectivity: 85%

ACT Ranges: C 19-25, M 18-25, E 18-25

TUITION & COST

Tuition (in-state): $5,154

Tuition (out-of-state): $19,071

Fees: $1,604

Room: $5,280

Board: $3,632

FRIENDS UNIVERSITY

WICHITA, KANSAS

FRIENDS
UNIVERSITY

www.friends.edu
(316) 295-5000
admissions@friends.edu

Friends University, a Christian university of Quaker heritage, equips students to honor God and serve others by integrating their intellectual, spiritual, and professional lives. Friends University believes learning happens everywhere throughout life. No matter which of the more than 70 areas of study a student chooses, the classroom is only the beginning. From competing in athletic competitions to performing in fine arts productions, Friends' students engage in a wide variety of campus activities.

FRIENDS EXPERIENCE: The "Friends Experience" seminar course helps first-year and new transfer students learn how to be successful in their new lives on campus, both socially and academically. It connects students with campus resources and provides them with information on topics such as academic success skills, four-year graduation plans, managing financial matters, and developing positive relationships.

UNIQUE PROGRAMS: Not only does Friends University offer traditional liberal arts fields of study, but it also has several unique academic niches. The University's Zoo Science degree program, for example, is one of the only of its kind in the country. Students in this program benefit from a 20-plus-year relationship with the Sedgwick County Zoo that allows them to obtain practical experience working with zoo animals and personnel.

On the other end of the liberal-arts spectrum, Friends University's dance program is among the top in the region. Additionally, dancers from New York, Chicago, and Dallas have graced the stage in Sebits Auditorium with their extraordinary talents and expertise.

> "The positive Christian environment and role models at Friends University make for a great education experience and exhibit a family and caring atmosphere that have helped me throughout my career."
>
> *– Ardith Rooney Dunn, health and physical education and math graduate*

STUDENT PROFILE

1,110 undergraduate students

81% of undergrad students are full-time

56% female — 44% male

20% of students are from out of state

73% freshman retention rate

FACULTY PROFILE

10 to 1 student/faculty ratio

ADMISSIONS

Selectivity: 48%

SAT Ranges: E 480-550, M 470-600

ACT Ranges: C 19-25, M 17-25, E 18-24

TUITION & COST

Tuition: $27,965

Fees: $450

Room: $3,800

Board: $4,180

KANSAS WESLEYAN UNIVERSITY

SALINA, KANSAS

At Kansas Wesleyan University, students learn in a small, vibrant, and caring environment that nurtures academic, spiritual, moral, and social growth. Students can pursue their academic AND personal interests. It's called the Power of AND, and it accentuates the importance of learning outside the classroom. Leadership, character development, relationship management, and communication are just a few life skills that are learned on the performance stages and on the fields of competition.

THE WESLEYAN JOURNEY: It is critical for today's college students to have a global perspective, and KWU understands that studying abroad for a full semester is not an option for all students. Because of this, every academically qualifying student who has been at KWU for four semesters can take get academic credit in a service-learning course for free or at a low cost.

These Wesleyan Journeys, often life-changing experiences, take place during breaks in places like Costa Rica, Germany, Florida, and New York City.

RESEARCH EXPERIENCES: An increasing number of the University's students are attaining competitive placements in National Science Foundation-funded Research Experiences for Undergraduates (REU).

Just a few trailblazing projects include developing a new methodology for searching encrypted data, building a molecule to selectively target cancer cells, and creating a simulated reality controlled by hand motions.

SCHOOL LOCATION: Salina, with a population of 50,000, is the sixth largest city in Kansas. It has a robust theatre and arts community and a regional health care center. More than 83 restaurants and a mall provide students with dining, entertainment, and employment options. They also enjoy the bowling alley, water park, zoo, disc golf courses, health clubs, and theaters.

Salina is just over an hour from Wichita, one hour from Manhattan, and less than three hours from Kansas City.

www.kwu.edu
(785) 833-4305
admissions@kwu.edu

STUDENT PROFILE
693 undergraduate students

91% of undergrad students are full-time

41% female – 59% male

58% of students are from out of state

55% freshman retention rate

FACULTY PROFILE
12 to 1 student/faculty ratio

ADMISSIONS
Selectivity: 54%

SAT Ranges: E 460-550, M 470-540

ACT Ranges: C 19-24, M 17-24, E 16-22

TUITION & COST
Tuition: $28,980

Room & Board: $8,950

MCPHERSON COLLEGE

MCPHERSON, KANSAS

At McPherson College, students learn by doing. McPherson College applies an entrepreneurial mindset to education through initiatives like its entrepreneurial minor; design your own major; and its Horizon Fund Grants, micro-grants that support student ideas to solve problems in the world around them. Partnerships across campus, across the community, and across the country also make it possible for 90 percent of all McPherson College graduates to participate in at least one internship before graduation.

ENTREPRENEURSHIP: McPherson College believes that the classic concept of liberal arts is intimately tied to the modern idea of entrepreneurship, as concepts of entrepreneurship appear across the curriculum, faculty practices, and student life. Students can choose the entrepreneurship minor to accompany any major or apply for the Horizon Fund grants to help them explore or carry out an original entrepreneurial idea.

HANDS-ON EXPERIENCES: Entrepreneurial Faculty provide opportunities for real, hands-on participation and career-oriented experiences in and outside of the classroom. For example, investment classes get the chance to manage $300,000 of the college's endowment. Students research trends and make decisions on how to invest these funds and then compare their results to those of the professional fund managers.

The unique automotive restoration program also delivers engaging curriculum to its students by expert craftsmen with an aim to compete at Pebble Beach.

CLUBS & ORGANIZATIONS: Student clubs and organizations add a wide variety of events and activities on campus.

From awareness campaigns like the annual color run to a car show organized by CARS Club, a student-organized annual car show held each year in May, the event attracts hundreds of classic automobiles and motorcycles to the quad from around the country.

www.mcpherson.edu
(620) 242-0400
admiss@mcpherson.edu

STUDENT PROFILE
725 undergraduate students

93% of undergrad students are full-time

36% female – 64% male

64% freshman retention rate

FACULTY PROFILE
13 to 1 student/faculty ratio

ADMISSIONS
Selectivity: 48%

SAT Ranges: E 550-630, M 480-550

ACT Ranges: C 20-24, M 19-25, E 18-24

TUITION & COST
Tuition: $27,077

Fees: $746

Room: $3,528

Board: $4,782

OTTAWA UNIVERSITY

OTTAWA, KANSAS

Preparing diverse student populations for lives of enlightened faith and inspired leadership is the vision of Ottawa University. Why? Because the administration and faculty at Ottawa University know that education doesn't happen in a vacuum. Instead, students must learn to grow, care for, and balance all aspects of their lives in order to *prepare for a life of significance."* That's why every student who enrolls at Ottawa University generates a "LifePlan" during their academic tenure to help guide them as they enter life beyond college.

NOT WHAT TO THINK, BUT HOW TO THINK: From embracing spiritual values to executing business practices, students are pushed to explore, research, and evaluate questions for themselves, arriving at answers rather than spoon-feeding long lists of facts and information. At Ottawa University, mastery is as much about the discovery of knowledge as it is the knowledge itself.

ADAWE (SAY WHAT?): In 2008, Ottawa University established the Adawe LifePlan Center to serve as the epicenter for academic advising, counseling, and career services. Adawe (pronounced "a-dah-way") is an Ottawa word that means "to trade."

Tutoring services, experiential learning opportunities, workshops, personal counseling, spiritual exploration, academic advising, and career services are all available to students through the Adawe Center, letting students know that someone has their back—someone who will help them navigate through college and beyond, both academically and personally.

FROM TEXTBOOK TO TANGIBLE: When an F5 tornado destroyed the town of Greensburg, KS, Ottawa University students were on hand to assist with recovery and rebuilding efforts. Students have also traveled to Israel, Kenya, Australia, and the Amazon for cross-disciplinary trips. They have performed in Carnegie Hall, participated in national forensics tournaments, and traveled to the Sundance Film Festival to work as movie critics.

www.ottawa.edu
1 (800) 755-5200
admiss@ottawa.edu

STUDENT PROFILE
706 undergraduate students

97% of undergrad students are full-time

42% female – 58% male

56% of students are from out of state

66% freshman retention rate

FACULTY PROFILE
16 to 1 student/faculty ratio

ADMISSIONS
Selectivity: 28%

TUITION & COST
Tuition: $28,980

Fees: $1,635

Room: $8,615

Board: $5,890

SOUTHWESTERN COLLEGE

WINFIELD, KANSAS

Southwestern focuses on life, not just the life of the mind. SC upholds a perennial promise to educate students in the liberal arts tradition to think, analyze, solve, communicate, and create. This gives Moundbuilders the broad foundations required to excel not just as professionals, but also as people. Moundbuilders learn to be nimble thinkers who can adapt and solve problems—who can invent new solutions. Ultimately, the college emphasizes leadership and service in a world without boundaries.

FOCUSED ON VALUES: Founded by the Methodists, the college maintains strong connections with the United Methodist Church and is therefore able to create unique opportunities for students and faculty alike.

Even students who don't identify as Christian nevertheless find great value in attending a college with a history like Southwestern's. Embracing respect, care, and curiosity, the Southwestern College community is interested in asking big questions and opening discussion up to a challenging range of differing perspectives.

SERVICE AND SCHOLARSHIP: Southwestern College's commitment to community outreach is apparent in its mission: "Leadership through service in a world without boundaries." Groups like the Discipleship Team, Leadership Team, and Green Team are all spreading the love to the surrounding community with active, intelligent, and compassionate SC scholars.

PREP 499: It's a given: students who choose Southwestern College are guaranteed personal attention as they sort out their career path and goals for the future. Beginning their freshman year, new Moundbuilders take the PREP 499 seminar, which sets time aside specifically for them to prepare for their job or graduate school search, application, and interview processes.

The course gives each student a consistent schedule with which to meet with their faculty advisor as well as the resources they need to get involved in a skill-building internship. And throughout the rest of college, students continue to meet with these advisors and work further toward their futures.

www.sckans.edu/campus
(800) 846-1543
scadmit@sckans.edu

STUDENT PROFILE
1,096 undergraduate students

53% of undergrad students are full-time

37% female – 63% male

63% of students are from out of state

62% freshman retention rate

FACULTY PROFILE
10 to 1 student/faculty ratio

ADMISSIONS
Selectivity: 51%

SAT Ranges: E 420-520, M 420-510

ACT Ranges: C 18-23, M 17-23, E 16-22

TUITION & COST
Tuition: $30,000

Room: $3,620

Board: $4,140

CENTRE COLLEGE

DANVILLE, KENTUCKY

www.centre.edu
(859) 238-5350
admission@centre.edu

Students are bound to enjoy a personalized education that's second to none while engaging themselves in an active, vibrant community. Centre College's "Southern twist" creates a warm and pleasant atmosphere conducive to new friendships and make meaningful connections. In such a welcoming environment, students thrive as they are challenged both in and out of the classroom with rigorous academics and extracurricular opportunities

CENTRE COMMITMENT: As part of the Centre Commitment, all Centre students are guaranteed an internship, study abroad, and graduation within four years, or Centre will provide up to a year of additional study, tuition-free.

Semester-long study is offered at campuses in England, France, and Mexico, with exchange programs in Japan, Northern Ireland, and England. A variety of three-week study opportunities are available at other locations around the world, including Italy, Vietnam, Barbados, Spain, and Turkey.

TAKE CHARGE: Centre offers twenty-seven majors and thirty minors. In addition to traditional majors, Centre opens up the opportunity and encourages students to self-design majors that are right for them. Double majors are common, and Centre offers dual-degree engineering programs with four major universities.

A WELCOME ENVIRONMENT: Centre College is located in historic Danville, Kentucky, on a 115-acre campus with sixty buildings, thirteen of which are included in the National Register of Historic Places. The College features amazing athletic, academic, and library facilities.

Nationally recognized for its high quality of life, Danville is progressive, safe, friendly, and perfectly placed as a gateway to the region and the world. It's called the City of Firsts for its many historical milestones, including the first courthouse in Kentucky as well as the first post office west of the Alleghenies. In 2000, the city helped Centre host the year's only vice presidential debate.

STUDENT PROFILE

1,450 undergraduate students

100% of undergrad students are full-time

51% female – 49% male

44% of students are from out of state

91% freshman retention rate

FACULTY PROFILE

11 to 1 student/faculty ratio

ADMISSIONS

Selectivity: 76%

SAT Ranges: E 590-580, M 580-730

ACT Ranges: C 26-31, M 25-31, E 26-34

TUITION & COST

Tuition: $39,300

Room: $4,975

Board: $4,975

LINDSEY WILSON COLLEGE

COLUMBIA, KENTUCKY

One of the fastest growing private colleges in Kentucky, Lindsey Wilson College has strived to provide students with a living-learning experience truly enriched with welcoming Methodist values. LWC first opened in 1904 as Lindsey Wilson Training School, then transitioned into an exclusively junior college, and finally developed into today's four-year, baccalaureate degree-granting institution in 1985. Over the past thirty years, the student population has blossomed alongside the College's facilities, budget, and impact on the surrounding community.

CENTER FOR ENTREPRENEURSHIP: LWC's Center for Entrepreneurship serves as an incubator hub for students to implement their business ideas on a practical level. The facility is loaded with the resources and tools necessary for business planning and organization.

STUDY ABROAD: Lindsey Wilson offers a variety of study and internship experiences abroad. In alliance with the Cooperative Undergraduate Programs Abroad (COUPA), LWC works with other colleges and universities to organize credit-bearing, short-term programs.

Some of the most popular COUPA trips take students to London and Northern Ireland, but opportunities additionally span all across the world. With the help of their involved advisors, students can make informed choices as they search for the perfect program for their field of study and cultural interests alike.

"My educational experience at Lindsey Wilson College prepared me for the real world job market... LWC always expected my best effort and provided me with the opportunities to fulfill my goals and dreams."

– Taylor Smith Morrison, Bachelor of Arts, Elementary Education Class of 2012, Master of Education, Teacher as Leader, Class of 2017

www.lindsey.edu
(270) 384-8100
admissions@lindsey.edu

STUDENT PROFILE

2,047 undergraduate students

93% of undergrad students are full-time

61% female – 39% male

20% of students are from out of state

61% freshman retention rate

FACULTY PROFILE

12 to 1 student/faculty ratio

ADMISSIONS

Selectivity: 61%

ACT Ranges: C 18-23, M 17-23, E 17-24

TUITION & COST

Tuition: $25,080

Fees: $270

Room: $3,420

Board: $6,005

UNIVERSITY OF LOUISVILLE

LOUISVILLE, KENTUCKY

University of Louisville is a premier research institution with a strong focus on the liberal arts and sciences. Students are actively involved in their individual educational experiences and have plenty of opportunities to succeed, both in the classroom and as a member of the campus community.

BOOK IN COMMON: All incoming freshmen are to complete a reading assignment prior to arriving on campus to create a shared, academic experience among all first-year students. The reading, known as Book in Common, eases students into college-level academics while encouraging the development of critical thinking skills.

Through a series of related events and programs, students engage in conversation about the book's topic throughout the span of their freshman year. Faculty work closely with students to explore ideas and themes present within the text.

LIVING-LEARNING COMMUNITIES: Living-learning and themed communities are unique housing options that connect students through academics and common interests. Louisville offers several different community options that help students explore their passions and build a foundation for academic and personal success.

Louisville offers six different living learning communities that range in structure and subject matter. Engineering, Pre-Dental, Honors Service, Honors Science, Honors 2nd-Year Science, and Public Health LLCs all immerse students in their area of focus, extending their academic prowess to their social lives as well.

There are four themed communities available at University of Louisville, including the Social Justice-Themed Community, All-Male Themed Community, Metropolitan College Themed Community (to create an environment that emphasizes time management and work-life balance), and Green Room (to connect students to opportunities for sustainability-focused initiatives).

UNIVERSITY OF LOUISVILLE

www.louisville.edu
(502) 852-6531
admitme@louisville.edu

STUDENT PROFILE

15,546 undergraduate students

77% of undergrad students are full-time

51% female — 49% male

20% of students are from out of state

81% freshman retention rate

FACULTY PROFILE

15 to 1 student/faculty ratio

ADMISSIONS

Selectivity: 75%

SAT Ranges: E 540-640, M 530-650

ACT Ranges: C 22-28, M 21-28, E 22-30

TUITION & COST

Tuition (in-state): $11,068

Tuition (out-of-state): $26,090

Fees: $196

Room: $5,180

Board: $3,194

UNIVERSITY OF THE CUMBERLANDS

WILLIAMSBURG, KENTUCKY

The University of the Cumberlands is dedicated to helping students build a "life more abundant." The campus maintains a small, tightly knit community that encourages a connection of research with practice. Located in Williamsburg, Kentucky, UC propels its graduates out into a world of possibility. With a University of Cumberlands education, students are equipped to lead and serve in a global community.

PREPARING FOR THE REAL WORLD: Students' futures as postgraduates are always on the mind of UC faculty and staff. Specific courses within UC's general education incorporate career-readiness assessment and guidance, providing every student with a career counselor who can set them in a clear direction.

And of course, what better way to prepare for the professional world than by working in it firsthand? All Cumberlands students have the opportunity to complete skill- and network-building internships, most of which can even qualify for course credit.

SERVICE AND MOUNTAIN OUTREACH: At UC, servant leadership is unmistakably at the center of learning and campus activities. In fact, community service is a degree requirement!

The school's community culture, however, makes it natural for all everyone to contribute far more than what's asked of them. A majority of student-led groups make community engagement an inherent part of their activities.

One noted organization founded entirely by Cumberlands students is the Mountain Outreach program. In a heartfelt effort to improve the lives of struggling local families, Mountain Outreach has dedicated over thirty years to renovating households, making significant repairs, and even building nearly 150 homes from the ground up.

www.ucumberlands.edu
(606) 539-4240
admiss@
ucumberlands.edu

STUDENT PROFILE

3,315 undergraduate students

55% of undergrad students are full-time

57% female – 43% male

62% freshman retention rate

FACULTY PROFILE

17 to 1 student/faculty ratio

ADMISSIONS

Selectivity: 74%

SAT Ranges: E 450-570, M 460-560

ACT Ranges: C 19-25, M 17-24, E 19-25

TUITION & COST

Tuition: $22,640

Fees: $360

Room & Board: $9,000

CENTENARY COLLEGE OF LOUISIANA

SHREVEPORT, LOUISIANA

Centenary is a selective, private, residential liberal arts college affiliated with the United Methodist Church. The College offers 22 majors in the arts and sciences along with more than 30 minors, academic concentrations, and pre-professional programs in allied health fields, business, education, engineering, law, and museum management.

CENTENARY IN PARIS: An engaging Centenary education begins with a unique and unforgettable common global-learning experience: Centenary in Paris. All first-year students at Centenary have the opportunity to complete their first college course during this intensive learning experience.

Students travel to Paris for 8-10 days, live in an international student hostel, and take rigorous courses such as "Daily Bread—Sustainability in Paris," "Paris Noir—Black American in the City of Light," or "Writing Paris/Writing Home."

MEETING NEW NEEDS: The College has recently added new minors in both Engineering Sciences and Legal Studies and has expanded concentrations in the Business Administration degree to include fields such as Leadership, Investments, International Business, and Energy Business.

An articulation agreement with Baylor's Louise Herrington School of Nursing provides admission preference to Centenary students interested in pursuing an accelerated nursing degree through the FastBacc program.

CREDO AND CHALLENGE: Credo and Challenge, the first two courses in Centenary's TREK program, are designed to introduce students to a practical application of the liberal arts. Credo, Latin for "I believe," allows students to explore their values and beliefs in the context of their academic ambitions.

In the second-semester Challenge courses, students choose from innovative, research-driven seminars examining some of the global challenges of the 21st century, including rapid technological developments, economic expansion, globalization, conflict, and environmental change.

www.centenary.edu
(318) 869-5131
admission@centenary.edu

STUDENT PROFILE

533 undergraduate students

98% of undergrad students are full-time

56% female — 44% male

78% freshman retention rate

FACULTY PROFILE

9 to 1 student/faculty ratio

ADMISSIONS

Selectivity: 62%

SAT Ranges: E 520-600, M 510-610

ACT Ranges: C 22-28, M 20-27, E 21-30

TUITION & COST

Tuition: $35,900

Room: $7,090

Board: $6,200

LOUISIANA TECH UNIVERSITY

RUSTON, LOUISIANA

LOUISIANA TECH
—— UNIVERSITY ——

www.latech.edu
(318) 257-2000

Louisiana Tech University offers an innovative academic experience that prepares students for the next step in their careers. Students at Louisiana Tech forge their own unique paths, with research, community service, internships, and entrepreneurship supplementing a strong foundation in the classroom. Tech partners with industry leaders in every field to offer an up-to-date view of the world students are preparing to enter.

INNOVATION & ENTREPRENEURSHIP: Louisiana Tech students are innovators, and the Center for Entrepreneurship and Information Technology provides a home for those who want to get a head-start on their big ideas before graduation. The Center helps groups enter in competitions and develop creative products alongside academic and industry professionals.

SERVICE-LEARNING: The Center for Academic and Professional Development makes it easy for any professor to incorporate service in their courses. Some examples of how service has supplemented classwork include community clean-up in Ruston, construction in Honduras, and more. Many majors, including nursing, even offer major-specific service-learning opportunities that allow students to do good while practicing their skills. Students have the opportunity to teach aspiring photographers, keep Ruston informed of important community news, and more.

RUSTON: Louisiana Tech is located in Ruston, Louisiana, a college town with the atmosphere to prove it. There are plenty of places to eat and shop in the historic downtown district, beautiful scenery to experience in a hike across Lincoln Parish Park, and incredible performances for the biggest local and national musicians. Ruston may be a small town, but its possibility for adventure is enormous.

SENIOR CAPSTONE: Many areas of study require a senior capstone project or practicum. Students of every concentration take a semester to see a project from start to finish with their group, understanding project management and the requirements of a modern workplace. Students learn from historic examples and form their own final presentations as they prepare for life beyond college.

STUDENT PROFILE

11,328 undergraduate students

71% of undergrad students are full-time

49% female – 51% male

80% freshman retention rate

FACULTY PROFILE

25 to 1 student/faculty ratio

ADMISSIONS

Selectivity: 65%

SAT Ranges: E 440-540, M 430-560

ACT Ranges: C 22-27, M 20-26, E 22-29

TUITION & COST

Tuition (in-state): $6,400

Tuition (out-of-state): $15,313

Fees: $3,245

Room: $2,910

Board: $3,450

TULANE UNIVERSITY

NEW ORLEANS, LOUISIANA

Tulane University is located in the picturesque city of New Orleans. The University is hailed for its research initiatives, as well as its commitment to developing students into leaders. Tulane's motto, 'Not for one's self, but for one's own,' is an educational philosophy that drives academic and personal growth in a collegiate setting.

FIRST-YEAR EXPERIENCE: Tulane's first-year program is known as TIDES, which stands for Tulane Interdisciplinary Experience Seminar. TIDES gathers students in small groups and promotes the exchange of ideas and bonding among peers.

TIDES is offered in 70 different seminar courses, meaning students have countless options when it comes to selecting a class that speaks to their interests. In small groups, students learn by interacting, while faculty promote engagement with coursework and further encourage students to work with one another.

PUCLIC SERVICE: The Public Service requirement is a unique element of Tulane's curriculum. The University believes that service to the community is an integral part of the undergraduate experience. Students need to come to a place of understanding, where academics are utilized in order to make a positive change in the community.

In order to satisfy this requirement, students must complete a service learning course and participate in a program approved by the Center for Public Service. Some examples of programs include an academic service-learning internship, faculty-sponsored public service research, and a capstone experience with a focus on public service.

FELLOWS PROGRAM: The Public Service Fellows Program trains students to act as leaders for both on- and off-campus service initiatives. Public Service Fellows gain experience while leading initiatives and developing solutions to community issues.

www.tulane.edu
(504) 865-5731
undergrad.admission@
tulane.edu

STUDENT PROFILE

7,871 undergraduate students

85% of undergrad students are full-time

59% female – 41% male

83% of students are from out of state

93% freshman retention rate

FACULTY PROFILE

8 to 1 student/faculty ratio

ADMISSIONS

Selectivity: 21%

SAT Ranges: E 670-740, M 660-750

ACT Ranges: C 30-33, M 27-32, E 31-35

TUITION & COST

Tuition: $48,920

Fees: $4,040

Room: $8,342

Board: $6,194

UNIVERSITY OF NEW ORLEANS

NEW ORLEANS, LOUISIANA

THE UNIVERSITY of NEW ORLEANS

www.uno.edu
(504) 280-6595
admission@uno.edu

The University of New Orleans is the only public research university in greater New Orleans. It has educated students from all 50 states and more than 140 countries and grants bachelor's, master's, and doctoral degrees within four academic colleges and interdisciplinary studies. UNO is located along the shores of Lake Pontchartrain in a quiet, residential section of New Orleans. It is a 15-minute drive from the French Quarter and downtown New Orleans.

UNDERGRADUATE RESEARCH: The UNO Center for Undergraduate Research facilitates collaboration between undergraduate students and faculty while promoting undergraduate research to both internal and external audiences.

PURSUE (the Privateer Undergraduate Research and Scholarly UNO Experience) provides students with a mechanism to find faculty research mentors. Selected students are even awarded with paid student work positions to work on their research projects.

JAZZ AT THE SANDBAR: Now in its 29th season, Jazz at the Sandbar is one of the University's most well known and beloved traditions. Established in 1990 by faculty member Ellis Marsalis, this live music performance series pairs UNO jazz studies students with professional musicians in front of an audience at a first-class on-campus venue.

ACADEMIC PROGRAMS: Many of UNO's most well-known programs are those that are tied to its location, including hotel, restaurant, and tourism administration; film; music; planning and urban studies; civil engineering; earth and environmental sciences; educational leadership; and one of the few naval architecture and marine engineering programs in the nation.

Naval architecture and marine engineering students take advantage of the region's only tow tank, a 125-foot-long tank that allows for in-water testing of model boats and marine structures.

STUDENT PROFILE

5,909 undergraduate students

81% of undergrad students are full-time

49% female – 51% male

6% of students are from out of state

71% freshman retention rate

FACULTY PROFILE

19 to 1 student/faculty ratio

ADMISSIONS

Selectivity: 57%

SAT Ranges: E 540-640, M 510-620

ACT Ranges: C 20-25, M 19-25, E 21-27

TUITION & COST

Tuition (in-state): $9,354

Tuition (out-of-state): $14,190

Room: $5,545

Board: $3,700

MAINE MARITIME ACADEMY

CASTINE, MAINE

Founded by an act of the 90th Maine Legislature in March of 1941, Maine Maritime Academy is a public, co-educational college with courses of study in engineering, management, science, and transportation. Rigorous courses and experiential learning prepare students for success as mariners, engineers, supply chain managers, logistics professionals, and scientists.

TRAINING CRUISES: MMA is the only college in the United States with a dedicated sail training program that leads to a U.S. Coast Guard license as mate on an auxiliary sail vessel. At the end of their freshman and junior years, students pursuing an unlimited U.S. Coast Guard license to be an engineer or deck officer participate in training voyages aboard a former Navy oceanographic research vessel.

First-year students (4/C Midshipmen) complete a summer training voyage on the training ship during which they will learn the basics of life at sea, introductory seamanship, operation of ship's machinery, and shipboard safety regulations and procedures. Third-year students (2/C Midshipmen) will complete a second training cruise on the training ship, taking an active role in the daily operation of the training ship and supervising 4/C Midshipmen.

CADET SHIPPING: Students pursuing a U.S. Coast License to be an engineer or deck officer are assigned as cadets on merchant vessels to further familiarize themselves with shipboard procedures while acquiring days at sea.

EXPERIENTIAL LEARNING: As a career-oriented college, MMA is focused on preparing students for their future positions well before graduation. Its curriculum is supported by a wealth of specialized laboratories, state-of-the-art simulators, research vessels, marine science labs, power plant and navigation simulators, a wet lab, and much more.

Experiential learning is at the core of an MMA education; in fact, most majors include a field experience or internship as part of the standard curriculum. Notable opportunities include at-sea engineering experience, marine biology cruises aboard research vessels, and operations training in operating plants that generate electrical power.

MAINE MARITIME ACADEMY

www.mma.edu
(800) 464-6565
admissions@mma.edu

STUDENT PROFILE

1,018 undergraduate students

97% of undergrad students are full-time

15% female – 85% male

77% freshman retention rate

FACULTY PROFILE

13 to 1 student/faculty ratio

ADMISSIONS

Selectivity: 80%

SAT Ranges: E 490-590, M 500-590

ACT Ranges: C 18-24, M 19-24, E 16-23

TUITION & COST

Tuition (in-state): $10,250

Tuition (out-of-state): $23,600

Fees: $3,028

Room: $4,040

Board: $6,070

UNITY COLLEGE

UNITY, MAINE

America's Environmental College

Unity College is a leader in the environmental movement, focused on sustainability in the classroom and in the real world. The friendly campus community is full of active learners who collaborate on various academic and research opportunities. Rigorous coursework and experiential learning opportunities prepare students for 21st-century environmental jobs and graduate school degree programs in a number of fields. Unity's alumni are environmental stewards, effective leaders, and responsible citizens.

TAKE ROOT: Students at Unity engage in a variety of exciting experiences including a four-day wilderness trip through the Nova orientation program, numerous internship and study abroad opportunities around the world, and several professional certificate programs.

CERTIFICATES: Students can earn several professional certifications, including Wilderness First Responder, Open Water SCUBA through the Professional Association of Diving Instructors, Forest Protection Officer with the U.S. Forest Service, Interpretive Guide through the National Association for Interpretive Standards, Teacher Certification for science (grades 7-12), and a Type-II law enforcement commission.

GET OUTDOORS, GET REAL: The Unity College campus comprises of 225 acres of fields and woodlands overlooking Lake Winnecook.

On the main campus, students can find the first and only Passive House-Certified student residence hall in the U.S., an organic garden that supplies food to dining services; a student-run recycling program; a Sugar Shack for sap boiling and maple syrup production; and an Adirondack shelter used as an outdoor classroom.

DEAN'S CUP: Every year, students can participate in the Dean's Cup, a year-long competition among residence halls celebrating diversity and strong community involvement. Events include home-run derbies, chili cook-offs, karaoke contests, laser tag tournaments, and the final event: a Big Wheels race through campus!

www.unity.edu
(833) 864-8946
admissions@unity.edu

STUDENT PROFILE
704 undergraduate students

99% of undergrad students are full-time

51% female – 49% male

64% freshman retention rate

FACULTY PROFILE
15 to 1 student/faculty ratio

ADMISSIONS
Selectivity: 89%

TUITION & COST
Tuition: $27,150

Fees: $1,200

Room: $6,240

Board: $4,160

UNIVERSITY OF MAINE

ORONO, MAINE

University of Maine is the flagship institution of the University Maine system. The University is focused on student success—an initiative achieved through world-class faculty members, state-of-the-art facilities, and a strong commitment to research.

MAINE MENTOR PROGRAM: The Maine Mentor program is an awesome networking resource available to students and alumni. The program allows participants to search for and contact working alumni across many different careers. This is especially beneficial for students, who can get a firsthand look at different industries and career paths.

THEMED COMMUNITIES: Living-Learning Communities (LLCs) break down the larger campus community into smaller, themed groups. There are many benefits to participation in an LLC, including greater academic performance, support from peers and faculty, and a sense of belonging. UMaine offers 7 different community options, each of which has its own unique focus.

Some LLCs, like the *Engineering and Tech* and *S-Cubed* (Support for Science Students) groups, cater to scientifically minded students looking to surround themselves with their academic passions.

LLCs like *FirstGen*, *The Well*, and *Choice Housing* are available for first-generation college students, those interested in healthy lifestyle practices, and those committed to substance-free lifestyles, respectively.

In addition, *Green Living* promotes conservation and the pursuit of sustainable initiatives, and *Leave Your Print* trains students in team building and professional development.

TRAVEL COURSES: Travel courses are faculty-led programs that involve both traditional classroom instruction and site visits. Travel courses take place during winter break, spring break, and May term. Even though the excursions are short, students have the chance to experience another culture and learn from a UMaine professor.

www.umaine.edu
(207) 581-1561
umaineadmissions@
maine.edu

STUDENT PROFILE

9,323 undergraduate students

87% of undergrad students are full-time

47% female – 53% male

42% of students are from out of state

76% freshman retention rate

FACULTY PROFILE

16 to 1 student/faculty ratio

ADMISSIONS

Selectivity: 90%

SAT Ranges: E 470-590, M 480-600

ACT Ranges: C 21-26, M 20-26, E 20-25

TUITION & COST

Tuition (in-state): $8,370

Tuition (out-of-state): $27,240

Fees: $2,258

Room: $5,154

Board: $5,010

FROSTBURG STATE UNIVERSITY

FROSTBURG, MARYLAND

Frostburg State University is a student-centered institution dedicated to providing transformative experiences as part of students' educational journey. This foundation launches its graduates to professional success, achieved through not only strong academics and experiential education, but also personal attention from knowledgeable faculty and staff. From small classes led by excellent professors to prestigious internships, exciting research, and abundant study abroad opportunities, Frostburg offers a quality, affordable education.

CAMPUS RESOURCES: Students of the natural sciences—from geography to ethnobotany—make use of the vast resources found in the Appalachian Mountains that surround Frostburg. The campus' close proximity to several state parks, forests, and wildlife management areas also means that there are plenty of opportunities to volunteer or intern.

PROGRAMS: In addition to strong traditional programs, FSU features a number of unique and distinctive academic majors, including Ethnobotany and such environmental programs as Wildlife and Fisheries, Sustainability Studies, Forestry, and Environmental Analysis & Planning.

Students may also enroll in Recreation and Parks Management with concentrations in Adventure Sports and Therapeutic Recreation as well as Adventure Sports Management.

CAREER & PROFESSIONAL DEVELOPMENT CENTER: The staff at the Career & Professional Development Center are raring to help FSU's diverse students develop the intellectual and experiential tools they need to excel as professionals.

The Center helps create campus culture that actively supports, educates, and empowers students to make career decisions and gain skills relevant to their future in a rapidly changing workplace. Students can partner with the Center to take on internships, connect with employers, or just learn more to improve their prospects as graduates.

www.frostburg.edu
(301) 687-4201
fsuadmissions@
frostburg.edu

STUDENT PROFILE

4,358 undergraduate students

84% of undergrad students are full-time

52% female – 48% male

9% of students are from out of state

77% freshman retention rate

FACULTY PROFILE

16 to 1 student/faculty ratio

ADMISSIONS

Selectivity: 78%

SAT Ranges: E 470-570, M 460-550

ACT Ranges: C 17-23, M 16-23, E 15-22

TUITION & COST

Tuition (in-state): $6,600

Tuition (out-of-state): $20,320

Fees: $2,572

Room: $4,882

Board: $4,516

LOYOLA UNIVERSITY MARYLAND

BALTIMORE, MARYLAND

LOYOLA
UNIVERSITY MARYLAND

Loyola University Maryland is a Roman Catholic, Jesuit private university dedicated to the education of the whole person. The ninth oldest Jesuit college in the country, LUM instills in its students a broad base of knowledge that is supported by a strong liberal arts core.

BALTIMORE: The city of Baltimore is just a stone's throw away, and its vibrant lifestyle is open to the Loyola community. Students are encouraged to explore the city and take advantage of the many different cuisines and cultural attractions that line its streets. They can also reach out to the community and offer up their service to organizations and people in need.

THE JESUIT PHILOSOPHY: Loyola offers more than 30 undergraduate majors as well as 40 minors and several graduate programs. The low student-to-faculty ratio of 12:1 affords personalized learning experience, emphasizing the individual spirit and pushing each student to discover their passions and talents.

The University is proud to embrace the Jesuit philosophy in collaboration with its educational ideals. The Jesuit philosophy concerns the development and of the whole person and the progression of the body, mind, and spirit. No part can be left behind, because each part complements the others.

SPIRITUAL LIFE: As a Catholic institution, Loyola offers daily mass, prayer and worship services, and several other spiritual outlets to anyone on campus. Students of all faiths are welcomes to express their spiritual and religious belief, as the University aims to be a welcoming and supportive campus for its entire community.

THE STUDY: The Study is a school-wide program that provides students with academic assistance, offering such amenities as tutoring and advising. The Study aims to maximize students' educational experiences and help them reach their full potential. Such a resource makes sure that students leave no stone unturned, exposing them to all of their options and encouraging them to pursue what interests and excites them.

www.loyola.edu
(410) 617-5012
admission@loyola.edu

STUDENT PROFILE
3,924 undergraduate students

99% of undergrad students are full-time

58% female – 42% male

84% of students are from out of state

85% freshman retention rate

FACULTY PROFILE
11 to 1 student/faculty ratio

ADMISSIONS
Selectivity: 75%

TUITION & COST
Tuition: $46,160

Fees: $1,400

Room: $10,705

Board: $4,080

NOTRE DAME OF MARYLAND UNIVERSITY

BALTIMORE, MARYLAND

Notre Dame of Maryland University's approach to education has prepared thousands of high-level performers and creators of social change. The University is consistently responsive to the needs of a student body that's hungry to learn and a world that's hungry for compassionate leaders. NDMU embodies the pioneering educational tradition and social justice mission that, more than a century ago, spurred the College of Notre Dame to welcome the first class of women pursuing four-year baccalaureate degrees.

GLOBAL LEARNING: NDMU is the first university in Maryland to be granted United Nations Non-Governmental Organization (NGO) Status. This classification offers NDMU students regular trips to the U.N. to participate in a range of international learning experiences. U.N. ambassadors are also brought to campus as part of NDMU's Visiting Ambassador Program.

WOW FESTIVAL: NDMU brings local, national, and international contributors to the stage during the WOW Festival to celebrate and discuss the issues most important to women, such as equal pay, race, gender equality, politics, activism, education, health, and more.

TRAILBLAZERS: NDMU's Trailblazer Scholars program provides academic enrichment and student support to first-generation college students. It provides high-impact experiences that collectively ensure first-generations years of postgraduate fulfillment, steeping them in a comfortable environment of friends and mentors.

"NDMU has prepared me for the next step by offering clinical experience in amazing hospitals… It's given me real-life experience caring for patients."

– *Madalyn Dewling, Alum, NDMU Class of 2018, Nursing*

NOTRE DAME OF MARYLAND UNIVERSITY

www.ndm.edu
(410) 532-5330
admiss@ndm.edu

STUDENT PROFILE

816 undergraduate students

65% of undergrad students are full-time

95% female – 5% male

16% of students are from out of state

82% freshman retention rate

FACULTY PROFILE

7 to 1 student/faculty ratio

ADMISSIONS

Selectivity: 71%

SAT Ranges: E 440-580, M 430-530

ACT Ranges: C 17-22

TUITION & COST

Tuition: $34,800

Fees: $1,270

Room: $8,500

Board: $3,000

SALISBURY UNIVERSITY

SALISBURY, MARYLAND

Salisbury University (SU) is nationally recognized for academic excellence. Its creative curriculum emphasizes undergraduate research, study abroad, professional internships, and civic engagement. Located on Maryland's historic Eastern Shore, SU offers 43 undergraduate majors and 17 graduate programs, including doctorate programs in Nursing Practice and Education.

PACE: SU's 8,700 students are active citizens locally, nationally, and internationally. Through the Institute for Public Affairs and Civic Engagement (PACE), students engage in the political process, intern for state and local governments, and attend national political conventions.

Many PACE students are involved in intensive, multi-faceted, year-long civic experiences through the Presidential Citizen Scholars Program.

INTERNSHIPS: SU's Career Services Office calls internships "the single most important thing you can do to gain career-related experience." Internships are mandatory for some majors and strongly recommended for all. Business students, for example, are required to have an Applied Business Learning Experience (ABLE) that includes both a faculty-guided class and a work-site internship.

Conflict analysis and dispute resolution majors have interned around the world, while environmental studies students have interned through fellowships at the U.S. Environmental Protection Agency. This is just a sampling of the many internship opportunities available to SU students.

> "In addition to wonderful professors, Salisbury University has tons of resources… I took a history class and was able to go to SU's Nabb Research Center for Delmarva History and Culture and have my hands on primary sources that are hundreds of years old."
>
> *– Alexis Larson, SU Conflict Analysis and Dispute Resolution Major*

www.salisbury.edu
(410) 543-6161
admissions@salisbury.edu

STUDENT PROFILE

7,444 undergraduate students

95% of undergrad students are full-time

56% female – 44% male

13% of students are from out of state

83% freshman retention rate

FACULTY PROFILE

15 to 1 student/faculty ratio

ADMISSIONS

Selectivity: 62%

SAT Ranges: E 575-640, M 570-640

ACT Ranges: C 20-25, M 18-25, E 20-25

TUITION & COST

Tuition (in-state): $7,122

Tuition (out-of-state): $16,824

Fees: $2,702

Room: $6,950

Board: $5,000

ST. MARY'S COLLEGE OF MARYLAND

ST. MARY'S CITY, MARYLAND

As Maryland's public honors college, St. Mary's College offers the kind of undergraduate, liberal arts education and small-college experience found at exceptional private colleges, all while remaining committed to its ideals of affordability, accessibility, and diversity. By combining the virtues of public and private education, St. Mary's College provides a unique alternative for students and their families. This special identity underpins the College's success along with its reputation for excellence.

INTERDISCIPLINARY STUDY: St. Mary's College is a leader in interdisciplinary study. Students can engage in multiple fields of study like African and African Diaspora Studies; Asian Studies; Democracy Studies; Environmental Studies; Materials Science; Museum Studies; Neurosciences; and Women, Gender, and Sexuality Studies. Recent course offerings have been as unique as The Neuroscience of Sex and Gender.

THE ST. MARY'S PROJECT: The St. Mary's Project is a year-long, independently designed and executed course of study that serves as a capstone experience. Working in close conjunction with one or more professors, the St. Mary's Project provides the opportunity to explore any idea or question that a student finds especially intriguing and highly personal.

Past projects include "Geospecific 3-dimensional Databases for Real-Time Visual Simulation;" "Economic Aid for Women-Centered Cultures;" and "The Economics of Essential Medicines in Poor Countries."

"St. Mary's challenged and expanded my narrow worldview and sparked a desire to better understand the contours of the world order. This spark inspired my career path as an international development and humanitarian worker and, in all honesty, changed my life." *– Dave Elseroad '01, political science*

StMARY'S
COLLEGE *of* MARYLAND

www.smcm.edu
(240) 895-5000
admissions@smcm.edu

STUDENT PROFILE
1,572 undergraduate students

97% of undergrad students are full-time

58% female – 42% male

6% of students are from out of state

82% freshman retention rate

FACULTY PROFILE
9 to 1 student/faculty ratio

ADMISSIONS
Selectivity: 80%

SAT Ranges: E 540-650, M 530-640

ACT Ranges: C 23-28, M 21-28, E 21-27

TUITION & COST
Tuition (in-state): $11,878

Tuition (out-of-state): $27,640

Fees: $2,928

Room: $7,622

Board: $5,580

ASSUMPTION COLLEGE

WORCESTER, MASSACHUSETTS

ASSUMPTION
COLLEGE

Students—whether on AMC's Worcester, Massachusetts, campus or on its campus in Rome, Italy—are engaged participants in Assumption's classic liberal arts education, exploring new ideas and making connections across disciplines. To prepare for the workforce, students learn cutting-edge theory and best practices, conduct innovative research, and develop excellent communication and critical-analysis skills.

STUDY ABROAD: Assumption students may choose to spend either a semester or year abroad. There also are shorter international experiences available. In recent years, Assumption College students have studied throughout the world in locations like Australia, Brazil, England, France, Italy, Japan, and the Netherlands.

The College opened its own campus in Rome, Italy, in 2013. Students studying in Rome are immersed in the very best of the classic liberal arts tradition, which is woven into the fabric of the campus's home city. From art to history to politics, students gain a deeper understanding of the world in which they live as well as its ancient and modern origins.

SOPHIA: The SOPHIA (SOPHomore Initiative at Assumption College) program is specially designed to help students discover a deeper connection between their spiritual, personal, and professional lives.

By combining residential, academic, and travel opportunities under the guidance of four dedicated faculty mentors, SOPHIA strives to foster a culture of vocational exploration at Assumption College that will help students pursue productive lives of meaning.

LIVELY INVOLVEMENT: The Venerable Father Emmanuel d'Alzon, founder of the Augustinians of the Assumption, envisioned a Catholic college that would embrace the "pursuit of truth." Today, Assumption furthers that mission through its 35 majors and 47 minors in the liberal arts, sciences, business, and professional studies programs.

www.assumption.edu
(866) 477-7776
admiss@assumption.edu

STUDENT PROFILE

2,084 undergraduate students

93% of undergrad students are full-time

59% female — 41% male

82% freshman retention rate

FACULTY PROFILE

11 to 1 student/faculty ratio

ADMISSIONS

Selectivity: 79%

TUITION & COST

Tuition: $38,848

Fees: $750

Room: $7,720

Board: $4,476

BECKER COLLEGE

WORCESTER, MASSACHUSETTS

With nationally recognized programs in nursing, video game design, and animal studies, Becker College prepares graduates for the challenges and opportunities of the 21st century. The College offers a wide range of quality undergraduate, graduate, and adult evening programs, offered online and on-campus. On-site clinics (animal care and mental health counseling) and labs (nursing SIMs and crime lab) all provide students with hands-on training.

AGILE MINDSET: Becker prepares students for the future by encouraging adaptive learners with entrepreneurial skills. Students will cultivate skills in empathy, divergent thinking, and social and emotional intelligence.

All of this is part of the "Agile Mindset" academic model to future-proof students. Therefore, the Core curriculum is infused with components of the Agile Mindset that include developing competency in critical thinking and analysis, sensitivity to ethical and moral issues in society, and appreciation of artistic endeavors.

YUNUS: Yunus Social Business Centre @ Becker allows students to gain experience and knowledge in social business practices. It is the first-of-its-kind at a U.S. institution of higher education.

SEMESTER IN THE CITY: Semester in the City is a semester-long internship through the College for Social Innovation that gives students a chance to make an impact in the community while earning college credit.

Social Innovation Fellows spend a rigorous 30+ hours per week with a leading Boston-area non-profit, business, or public sector agency focused on such social issues as health, education, social justice, and the environment.

GLOBAL INNOVATION: The Colleen C. Barrett Center for Global Innovation and Entrepreneurship serves as the hub for innovation, business, gaming, entrepreneurship, and interactive media. It houses Becker's popular game design program, Augmented Reality and Virtual Reality lab, and esports team.

---

www.becker.edu
(508) 373-9400
admissions@becker.edu

STUDENT PROFILE

1,797 undergraduate students

85% of undergrad students are full-time

57% female – 43% male

46% of students are from out of state

73% freshman retention rate

FACULTY PROFILE

14 to 1 student/faculty ratio

ADMISSIONS

Selectivity: 69%

SAT Ranges: E 490-590, M 480-580

ACT Ranges: C 20-26, M 18-25, E 19-25

TUITION & COST

Tuition: $35,600

Fees: $3,600

Room & Board: $13,800

CURRY COLLEGE

MILTON, MASSACHUSETTS

Curry College provides rigorous and relevant academic programs to undergraduate and graduate students. Its rich blend of liberal arts and career-directed programs is enhanced by practical field experiences and co-curricular activities. Students are attracted to Curry's friendly and caring academic community.

DIVERSITY: At Curry College, diversity is central to excellence in education, not a separate goal. The College believes that training students to become inclusive, empathetic citizens requires consistent learning throughout all four years of study. Regardless of their program of study, students are encouraged to develop a deep respect for diversity in all its forms.

PAL: The internationally acclaimed Program for Advancement of Learning (PAL) at Curry College was established in 1970 as the nation's first college-level program for students with language-based learning differences.

PAL is the longest-standing comprehensive support program designed to help intelligent and motivated students with language-based learning differences achieve at the college level. PAL faculty at the master's and doctoral level work directly to provide individual or small-group instruction.

EPORTFOLIO: Students at Curry College maintain an ePortfolio that tracks their beginning first-year inquiry course all the way up to their junior-year inquiry. This digital portfolio demonstrates the reflection and integration of learning within the entire Gen Ed curriculum. The ePortfolio also supports a responsibility for learning, providing both evidence and direction for career choices and longer-term career advancement.

MILTON, MA: Only seven miles from downtown Boston, Curry's proximity to the city gives students access to a wide variety of internships and clinical placements. Curry's location is also less than two miles from the scenic Blue Hills, a natural reservation which offers skiing, hiking, horseback riding, and resources for environmental education and recreation.

www.curry.edu
(617) 333-2210
adm@curry.edu

STUDENT PROFILE

2,565 undergraduate students

80% of undergrad students are full-time

60% female — 40% male

68% freshman retention rate

FACULTY PROFILE

13 to 1 student/faculty ratio

ADMISSIONS

Selectivity: 90%

SAT Ranges: E 470-560, M 460-540

ACT Ranges: C 18-23, M 17-24, E 17-22

TUITION & COST

Tuition: $36,780

Fees: $2,156

Room: $8,275

Board: $7,140

DEAN COLLEGE

FRANKLIN, MASSACHUSETTS

Dean College is a private, residential New England College grounded in a culture and tradition that all students deserve the opportunity for academic and personal success. A uniquely supportive community for more than 150 years, Dean has woven together extensive student support and engagement with exceptional teaching and innovative campus activities. Graduates are lifelong learners who thrive in their careers, embrace social responsibility, and demonstrate leadership.

THE DEAN DIFFERENCE: Dean College prides itself in "The Dean Difference." This College-wide commitment to success is a holistic effort that integrates academics with faculty support and community involvement.

Built into each class is a strong network of support, and supplemented by academic growth are a variety of meaningful community engagement activities. Through The Dean Difference, students find an interwoven sense of meaning behind everything they do as a Dean College scholar.

SPORTS MANAGEMENT: Through Dean's one-of-a-kind Center for Business, Entertainment, and Sports Management (The Center), students are given exclusive internship opportunities and job-shadowing days with multi-billion dollar companies such as Kraft Sports & Entertainment, The Pawtucket Red Sox, and The Providence Bruins.

DEAN CAREERLINK: 100% of Dean students are guaranteed access to internships that bulk their résumés and provide them with employable skills. Every student completes an internship at some point throughout the academic career, working with such companies as The Boston Ballet, New England Patriots, Ralph Lauren, and UMass Medical Center.

"Dean allows all students to be unique. The Dean Difference is having the ability to use all of the resources that Dean offers and shape yourself for the future." - *Courtney, Student*

www.dean.edu
(877) TRY-DEAN
admissions@dean.edu

STUDENT PROFILE

1,260 undergraduate students

87% of undergrad students are full-time

53% female – 47% male

62% freshman retention rate

FACULTY PROFILE

17 to 1 student/faculty ratio

ADMISSIONS

SAT Ranges: E 370-490, M 370-490

ACT Ranges: C 16-21

TUITION & COST

Tuition: $39,234

Fees: $500

Room: $10,634

Board: $6,202

EMMANUEL COLLEGE

BOSTON, MASSACHUSETTS

EMMANUEL COLLEGE

www.emmanuel.edu
(617) 735-9715
enroll@emmanuel.edu

Emmanuel College's 17-acre campus is located within the bustling Fenway neighborhood of Boston, Massachusetts. Today it thrives as a co-educational, residential institution in the city's scientific, cultural, and medical center. Emmanuel's more than 70 undergraduate programs promote investigation across a breadth of disciplines. Whether they pursue science, business, nursing, education, or the humanities, students enthusiastically embrace the College's mission to foster effective and ethical leaders for the 21st-century workplace.

GUARANTEED INTERNSHIPS: At Emmanuel, 100% of undergraduate students participate in an internship or other real-world learning experience as a standard component of the curriculum.

Within walking distance or a short ride on public transportation, students reach dozens of industry-leading organizations in medicine, finance, media, and many other fields. In addition, Emmanuel is part of the Longwood Medical and Academic Area, one of the world's premier centers of education, culture, and biomedical research.

COLLEGES OF THE FENWAY: Emmanuel is a founding member of the Colleges of the Fenway (COF) consortium—along with Massachusetts College of Art and Design, MCPHS University, Simmons University, and Wentworth Institute of Technology—which offers an enhanced student life experience that allows for academic and social collaboration.

Together, COF students can cross-register for courses at each other's colleges, eat in each other's dining halls, and get involved in joint activities ranging from performing arts and jazz bands to intramural sports.

THE CAPSTONE EXPERIENCE: Emmanuel seniors culminate their academic journey through the Capstone Experience, which challenges them to complete a project that ties together their coursework and knowledge. Through the Capstone, every student in every major gains significant experience in consolidating and presenting advanced scholarly material.

STUDENT PROFILE

1,976 undergraduate students

98% of undergrad students are full-time

75% female – 25% male

78% freshman retention rate

FACULTY PROFILE

13 to 1 student/faculty ratio

ADMISSIONS

SAT Ranges: E 560-650, M 540-630

ACT Ranges: C 24-27

TUITION & COST

Tuition: $41,028

Fees: $420

Room & Board: $15,444

LASELL UNIVERSITY

NEWTON, MASSACHUSETTS

www.lasell.edu
(617) 243-2225
info@lasell.edu

An innovator in education for over 160 years, Lasell is a comprehensive, coeducational university that enrolls more than 1,800 undergraduate students. Lasell complements traditional approaches with active learning experiences—a teaching method the University calls Connected Learning. Lasell University is committed to the idea of learning by doing through internships, service-learning, and challenging projects both in and out of the classroom.

CONNECTED LEARNING: Classes at Lasell are capped at 25, which means that there is no crowd to get lost in. In fact, students may even receive personal calls from faculty throughout their freshman year to help keep them on track.

Lasell University complements traditional teaching approaches with active learning experiences. The community is committed to learning by doing through internships, service-learning, and challenging projects that link theory with practice.

RESEARCH ACROSS THE CURRICULUM: The Research across the Curriculum (RAC) program offers a range of research grant and credit opportunities at every level and in every field of study at Lasell—from the arts and sciences to business and allied health. Through RAC work, students are challenged to demonstrate investigative skills, apply information literacy, and communicate empirical information effectively.

PROXIMITY: At Lasell, students can go from college town to Beantown in 8 minutes. Students can intern with top companies such as Bank of America, Northwestern Mutual, Boston Globe Media Partners, Wayfair, New Balance, and Marriott Hotels.

Through internships, students can connect what they learn in class with what's expected of them on the job. They can travel from the laid-back comfort of campus to the roaring atmosphere of Fenway Park, the cobblestone streets of Beacon Hill, or the seemingly endless storefronts of Back Bay.

STUDENT PROFILE

1,731 undergraduate students

96% of undergrad students are full-time

64% female – 36% male

41% of students are from out of state

73% freshman retention rate

FACULTY PROFILE

13 to 1 student/faculty ratio

ADMISSIONS

Selectivity: 81%

SAT Ranges: E 500-580, M 480-580

ACT Ranges: C 19-23

TUITION & COST

Tuition: $33,300

Fees: $1,300

Room & Board: $14,800

NICHOLS COLLEGE

DUDLEY, MASSACHUSETTS

Nichols College is a college of choice for business and leadership education due to its distinctive career-focused and leadership-based approaches to learning both in and out of the classroom. Founded in 1815, Nichols transforms today's students into tomorrow's leaders through dynamic, career-focused business and professional education. Nichols serves students who are interested primarily in a comprehensive business education that is supported by a strong liberal arts curriculum.

EMERGING LEADERS PROGRAM: Nichols believes that leadership is a quality that everyone can learn and possess. The Emerging Leaders Program (ELP) is a four-year initiative that helps students develop their own leadership style, cultivating the leader within through structured study and practice.

PROFESSIONAL DEVELOPMENT: The four-year, award-winning Professional Development Seminar is a required course at Nichols. It is custom designed to help each student stand out in the professional world.

Each year, students are guided through levels of professionalism as they learn stand-out skills. Topics of the seminar include Making the Transition, Developing Your Brand, Refining Your Skills, and Launching Your Career.

WOMEN'S LEADERSHIP: The Institute for Women's Leadership focuses on the issues and challenges that uniquely impact women's roles in business. Students conduct research, participate in gatherings, and attend speaking events while developing their leadership potential and serving as a helpful resource for women in the community at large.

FISCHER INSTITUTE: At Nichols, students can always find opportunities to expand their intellectual and cultural values beyond what they currently know. The school's Fischer Institute provides such community-building experiences as guest lectures from national and international speakers, campus community events, performing arts events, and faculty-led outings. These experiences bring context to the social, political, and cultural events and ideas they are bound to encounter throughout their lives.

Nichols College
Learn. Lead. Succeed.

www.nichols.edu
(800) 470-3379
admissions@nichols.edu

STUDENT PROFILE

1,321 undergraduate students

93% of undergrad students are full-time

38% female – 62% male

40% of students are from out of state

75% freshman retention rate

FACULTY PROFILE

17 to 1 student/faculty ratio

ADMISSIONS

SAT Ranges: E 470-570, M 470-570

ACT Ranges: C 19-24

TUITION & COST

Tuition: $34,615

Fees: $1,100

Room & Board: $14,250

NORTHEASTERN UNIVERSITY

BOSTON, MASSACHUSETTS

Northeastern University's approach to education contains research, experiential learning, and active engagement. Northeastern gives its students the tools they need to succeed, both in the classroom and beyond. Students are developed into hard-working leaders who recognize their duties to the global community.

CO-OPS: Co-Ops allow students to gain real-world experience through the application of academic theories and concepts. Recently, nearly 10,000 students participated in a co-op in a single year, many for the second or third time.

This is directly associated with post-graduate placement rates; 90% of students are enrolled in grad school or employed full time within 9 months of graduation. Northeastern believes that preparation is the root of success, and co-ops position students to accomplish great things once they have graduated.

SERVICE-LEARNING: There are two components to service-learning: coursework and community service. By coupling these two elements, students have the chance to apply what they have learned in the classroom to the needs of the community.

More than 41,000 hours of service are completed every year, and over 1,100 students get involved. Northeastern has developed over 80 partnerships in 3 countries. On top of this, Northeastern offers 73 different service-learning courses, affording students plenty of opportunity to get involved.

STUDENT RESEARCH: Undergraduate research is alive and well at Northeastern, with over 100 students receiving awards each year and 500 pursuing research-style co-ops.

Northeastern allows students to showcase their work at its annual Research, Innovation, and Scholarship Expo. Most importantly, research demonstrates ingenuity and resourcefulness to employers, making Northeastern grads highly marketable.

www.northeastern.edu
(617) 373-2200
admissions@
northeastern.edu

STUDENT PROFILE

13,825 undergraduate students

100% of undergrad students are full-time

51% female – 49% male

61% of students are from out of state

97% freshman retention rate

FACULTY PROFILE

14 to 1 student/faculty ratio

ADMISSIONS

Selectivity: 27%

SAT Ranges: E 680-750, M 690-770

ACT Ranges: C 32-34, M 30-34, E 32-35

TUITION & COST

Tuition: $48,560

Fees: $937

Room: $8,680

Board: $7,560

STONEHILL COLLEGE

EASTON, MASSACHUSETTS

STONEHILL COLLEGE

Located just outside Boston, Stonehill College is a selective Catholic college on a beautiful campus with 80+ majors in the liberal arts, sciences, and business. Nearly 91% of students participate in internships, study abroad, research, practicum, and field work.

SURE: The Stonehill Undergraduate Research Experience (SURE) is an incredible research opportunity for undergraduates. It involves 8 to 10 weeks of intense research during the summer with a professor, a stipend of up to $3,500, and the opportunity to co-publish and present at professional conferences and is a significant addition on graduate school applications.

CORNERSTONE PROGRAM: The core of Stonehill's liberal arts curriculum is the Cornerstone Program, which leads students to examine the self, society, culture, and the natural world through courses in ethics, sciences, language, and more. Students take an interdisciplinary Learning Community, which explores an interrelated topic from two academic perspectives, and a major Capstone course for seniors.

BREADTH: Stonehill offers more than 80 academic majors and minor areas of study in the liberal arts, sciences, business, and pre-professional advising programs. Stonehill's most popular programs are biology, biochemistry, English, political science, criminology, psychology, accounting, prelaw, and education.

EASTON, MASSACHUSETTS: Stonehill is located in Easton, Massachusetts; a friendly residential community nestled between New England's largest capital cities. Ideally located just 22 miles from Boston and 37 miles from Providence, Stonehill College is perfectly situated for internships, service opportunities, job prospects, museums, professional sports games, cultural events, and more.

The beautiful, 384-acre campus features traditional landscaping, ponds, wooded trails, Georgian-style architecture, and award-winning student housing.

---

www.stonehill.edu
(508) 565-1373
admission@stonehill.edu

STUDENT PROFILE

2,498 undergraduate students

99% of undergrad students are full-time

59% female – 41% male

39% of students are from out of state

86% freshman retention rate

FACULTY PROFILE

12 to 1 student/faculty ratio

ADMISSIONS

Selectivity: 72%

TUITION & COST

Tuition: $41,300

Room: $9,657

Board: $6,103

SUFFOLK UNIVERSITY

BOSTON, MASSACHUSETTS

Founded in 1906, Suffolk University is a four-year, private university in the heart of Boston. Suffolk offers more than 60 undergraduate programs through the College of Arts & Sciences and Sawyer Business School. Suffolk's location in downtown Boston gives students unparalleled access to many opportunities in the Boston metro area, including prestigious internships and job placements.

REFLECTING A DIVERSE WORLD: Suffolk has convened a task force on diversity both to foster an inclusive, welcoming community and to serve as an example for other institutions in Greater Boston. The Office of Diversity Services is a dedicated resource for Suffolk's AHANA and LGBTQ+ communities, and cultural associations and their programming extend the welcoming environment to all of campus.

A PLACE TO LEARN: Suffolk students don't just pursue academic majors; they live them. Entrepreneur students develop original ideas and make them a reality. Government majors gain real-world experience in politics at the State House and in Suffolk's Campaign Lab Summer Institute.

History students visit the sites that helped inspire the American Revolution. Environmental studies and science majors conduct fieldwork at the R.S. Friedman Field Station, a living laboratory for observing and studying marine life on the coast of Maine.

AN EXCITING, URBAN UNIVERSITY: Boston is the quintessential college town, home to about 300,000 students from all over the globe. Its dynamic intellectual energy is unmatched by any other city. There are no real borders to the University's campus—Boston and Suffolk simply blend together to create a vibrant urban dynamic that students enjoy every day.

At Suffolk, students study just steps away from City Hall and the Massachusetts State House, a few blocks from Boston Common and Faneuil Hall, and a short T ride from pretty much everything else Boston has to offer.

www.suffolk.edu
(617) 573-8460
admission@suffolk.edu

STUDENT PROFILE

5,030 undergraduate students

95% of undergrad students are full-time

54% female – 46% male

28% of students are from out of state

77% freshman retention rate

FACULTY PROFILE

13 to 1 student/faculty ratio

ADMISSIONS

Selectivity: 84%

SAT Ranges: E 500-600, M 500-580

ACT Ranges: C 21-26

TUITION & COST

Tuition: $37,128

Fees: $142

Room: $12,398

Board: $3,312

UNIVERSITY OF MASSACHUSETTS LOWELL

LOWELL, MASSACHUSETTS

www.uml.edu
(978) 934-3931
admissions@uml.edu

Whether or not students enter college with a dedicated career plan, UMass Lowell can propel them into the professional world with a clear and a sturdy purpose that is altogether backed by an immense range of experiences. The University offers programs in an endless array of fields, ensuring that its students can delve into their interests and discover new ones.

UMASS INNOVATION: The Office of Entrepreneurship and Economic Development oversees several programs to encourage and nurture their entrepreneurial spirit.

Through outlets for innovation and collaboration, the Difference Maker program, Idea Challenge, and three College Competitions maintain the drive for real-world change. It's at UMass Lowell that society, the economy, and the environment are not just things to study, but things to assess and improve.

GLOBAL ENTREPRENEURS EXCHANGE (GE2): Students can explore their creativity and entrepreneurship beyond the UMass Lowell campus and community through the Global Entrepreneurs Exchange (GE2) program.

Through GE2, students participate in a two-week immersion abroad in such countries as India, China, Guyana, and Thailand, attending class in the morning and working on their business projects in the afternoon.

"Through my experience I have really grown to be a more motivated and confident character. I have had the opportunity to meet a variety of different people around the world and immerse myself in their culture first hand... I really can't imagine my life without it." – *Gregory Ensom '17*

STUDENT PROFILE

14,012 undergraduate students

75% of undergrad students are full-time

38% female – 62% male

8% of students are from out of state

86% freshman retention rate

FACULTY PROFILE

17 to 1 student/faculty ratio

ADMISSIONS

Selectivity: 69%

SAT Ranges: E 560-650, M 570-660

ACT Ranges: C 24-29, M 24-28, E 22-29

TUITION & COST

Tuition (in-state): $14,350

Tuition (out-of-state): $31,415

Fees: $450

Room: $8,254

Board: $4,242

WENTWORTH INSTITUTE OF TECHNOLOGY

BOSTON, MASSACHUSETTS

WENTWORTH
INSTITUTE OF TECHNOLOGY

www.wit.edu
(800) 556-0610
admissions@wit.edu

Wentworth Institute of Technology is an independent, nationally ranked institution offering career-focused education through 19 bachelor's degree programs. Areas of concentration include applied mathematics, applied science, architecture, business management, computer science, cybersecurity, computer networking, construction management, design, engineering, and engineering technology.

INNOVATION & ENTREPRENEURSHIP: Exceptional academics provide the raw materials for new discoveries, and students are encouraged to leverage what they learn to identify and serve unmet needs. Students learn to design more efficient and effective solutions for existing problems, building new products, systems, and businesses that will benefit society.

The world faces a diversity of challenges—technical, medical, economic, environmental, structural, sustainable—that have a profound impact on our daily lives. Wentworth provides opportunities for students to identify and engage with these issues, generating innovative ideas and solutions that make the world a better place.

Because such solutions are inherently complex and multifaceted, the very effort to innovate inspires students to collaborate with peers and faculty from other majors and disciplines.

EPIC LEARNING: Most people who work in engineering, technology, and related disciplines work with people outside their own organization: funders, investors, clients, customers, contractors, sub-contractors, regulators, or fans. Professionals need to listen to others-—grasping their needs, desires, and concerns—and respond appropriately.

Wentworth is open to external collaborators of all sorts and interested in engaging learning opportunities wherever they arise. For instance, Wentworth's mechanical engineering students have refined the design of stoves produced by Aid Africa, a non-governmental organization (NGO) active in northern Uganda.

STUDENT PROFILE
4,341 undergraduate students

91% of undergrad students are full-time

22% female – 78% male

33% of students are from out of state

83% freshman retention rate

FACULTY PROFILE
18 to 1 student/faculty ratio

ADMISSIONS
Selectivity: 76%

SAT Ranges: E 530-630, M 550-650

ACT Ranges: C 22-27, M 23-27, E 21-25

TUITION & COST
Tuition: $33,950

Room: $11,090

Board: $3,100

WESTERN NEW ENGLAND UNIVERSITY

SPRINGFIELD, MASSACHUSETTS

WNE
WESTERN NEW ENGLAND
U N I V E R S I T Y

www1.wne.edu
(800) 325-1122
learn@wne.edu

With four Colleges—Arts and Sciences, Business, Engineering, and Pharmacy and Health Sciences, as well as a School of Law—Western New England University offers wide-ranging the academic opportunities. Its emphasis on collaboration, leadership, entrepreneurship, and experiential learning all challenge students to do more, be more, and achieve more than they ever imagined.

COMBINED DEGREE PROGRAMS: Western New England University offers several combined degree programs. The school's 3+3 law and Six-year Engineering/Law programs is a six-year course of study that leads to both an undergraduate and a law degree. Similarly, students can complete a five-year program to earn both an undergraduate degree and a master's degree in business or engineering

In the Health Sciences major, students can pursue concentrations in Pre-physician Assistant or Pre-Optometry programs leading to programs with partner institutions.

WORK SMARTER, DREAM BIGGER: The University offers nearly 50 undergraduate programs, including criminal justice, sport management, communication, psychology, mechanical engineering, and Pre-Pharmacy.

"The support that I received from my professors was tremendous. My education at Western New England prepared me to dive into the research environment, and my advisors helped me to find out what I wanted to pursue and achieve my goals." *– Kwasi Amofa, Biomedical Engineering, Fulbright and Whitaker Scholar, MERLN Institute for Technology—Inspired Regenerative Medicine*

STUDENT PROFILE

2,736 undergraduate students

96% of undergrad students are full-time

37% female – 63% male

49% of students are from out of state

78% freshman retention rate

FACULTY PROFILE

12 to 1 student/faculty ratio

ADMISSIONS

Selectivity: 81%

SAT Ranges: E 480-570, M 500-610

ACT Ranges: C 21-27

TUITION & COST

Tuition: $33,338

Fees: $2,402

Room & Board: $13,442

WORCESTER POLYTECHNIC INSTITUTE

WORCESTER, MASSACHUSETTS

From the moment first-year students step foot on the WPI campus, they are introduced to the foundational tools they need to succeed in their college careers and the rest of their lives. The one-of-a-kind WPI Plan puts knowledge to action, engaging teams of students through projects that address real-world issues. While most WPI students are STEM or business majors, their curriculum is enriched with courses in the liberal arts and humanities so that they develop as well-rounded, insightful leaders.

THE WPI PLAN: An inherent component of the WPI curriculum, project-based learning challenges students to apply what they learn in the classroom to practical, real-world contexts. The engaging WPI Plan prepares students for lifelong inquiry and success, immersing them in first-year and capstone projects, service-learning initiatives, and even global research abroad.

WOMEN IN STEM: WPI makes conscious efforts to increase parity in the STEM fields by encouraging more women to study mathematics and science. Through various women's programs—networking, workshops, health/fitness classes and seminars, and women's empowerment organizations—WPI women are bolstered to become active leaders and scholars in an otherwise male-dominated field.

UNDERGRADUATE CO-OP: The Undergraduate Co-Op Program at WPI provides students with full-time, professional employment at a real company for 4-8 weeks. Such an immersive program helps participants grow accustomed to the working world and all the skills they need to navigate the professional sphere.

Not only do they learn how to conduct themselves at work, how to negotiate salary, and more, but they are also often recruited to continue working for their company after graduation.

www.wpi.edu
(508) 831-5286
admissions@wpi.edu

STUDENT PROFILE
4,435 undergraduate students

97% of undergrad students are full-time

36% female – 64% male

52% of students are from out of state

95% freshman retention rate

FACULTY PROFILE
13 to 1 student/faculty ratio

ADMISSIONS
Selectivity: 48%

TUITION & COST
Tuition: $47,988

Fees: $640

Room: $8,122

Board: $6,096

ADRIAN COLLEGE

ADRIAN, MICHIGAN

With over 40 majors and pre-professional programs to choose from, more than 80 student organizations, and 22 varsity sports, the opportunities to achieve and excel are limitless at Adrian College. Whether students are applying their liberal arts education in AC's innovative Institutes, directing a play in historic Downs Hall Studio Theatre, or scoring in new athletic facilities like the Arrington Ice Arena, Adrian College students are a part of a 151-year history as it surges into the future.

CROSSING BOUNDARIES: Adrian College's "Model Arab League" course has offered students an opportunity to study international politics, hone their research and speaking skills, and travel to Washington D.C. to compete with other nationally recognized schools in a simulation experience.

Model Arab League is a student leadership development program administered by the National Council on U.S.–Arab Relations. Participants learn about the politics and history of the Arab world and the arts of diplomacy and public speech.

QUALITY EDUCATION: Adrian faculty do not complacently reuse old lectures; they attend conferences in order to stay up to date on the latest ideas in teaching. Additionally, they can also be found winning awards and giving presentations about their own teaching, research, and successes.

For example, Art professor Garin Horner was recently the featured speaker at the Great Lakes Conference on Teaching and Learning, and Biology professor Marti Morales-Ensign participated in a teaching and research symposium held by the National Science Foundation.

RIBBONS OF EXCELLENCE: Adrian students learn in an environment rooted in a philosophy called the "Ribbons of Excellence." These ribbons support the College's mission, which is rooted in high standards of living.

The Ribbons of Excellence are Caring for Humanity and the World; Crossing Boundaries and Disciplines; Thinking Critically; Developing Creativity; and Learning throughout a Lifetime.

www.adrian.edu
(800) 877-2246
admissions@adrian.edu

STUDENT PROFILE

1,653 undergraduate students

97% of undergrad students are full-time

48% female – 52% male

21% of students are from out of state

69% freshman retention rate

FACULTY PROFILE

12 to 1 student/faculty ratio

ADMISSIONS

Selectivity: 58%

SAT Ranges: E 420-505, M 420-510

ACT Ranges: C 19-24, M 17-25, E 17-24

TUITION & COST

Tuition: $34,040

Fees: $850

Room: $5,160

Board: $5,660

ALBION COLLEGE

ALBION, MICHIGAN

Students at Albion gain more than just a strong liberal arts education that will guide them in their career fields of choice. They develop their innate curiosity, their focus, and their sense of personal accomplishment, both in and outside the classroom and on and off campus. They emerge with the tools they need not just for success, but for a fulfilling life.

FURSCA: Through the Foundation for Undergraduate Research, Scholarship, and Creative Activity (FURSCA), students build on their studies to discover or create something entirely new. As early as freshman year, students work with a faculty member to choose a subject, develop a methodology, pursue an interest, interpret findings, and present results.

About 50 students each year are chosen for competitive grants to fund their research. Recent funded projects have explored crustaceans in river systems in Suriname, personality differences in investment choices, art and autism, and time-of-day effects on problem solving, among a host of others.

ALBION ADVANTAGE: An Albion graduate becomes a part of a powerful network of more than 23,000 fellow Britons who work in nearly every career imaginable, stay involved, keep in touch, and support one another.

In addition to this network, career readiness at Albion is enhanced by the Albion Advantage, a four-year program of academic and career exploration for students in any major. Beginning with the first semester on campus, students integrate their liberal arts-focused academic work with career preparation. They apply what they learn in the classroom through work with expert faculty; through internships in business, government, and nonprofit settings; and through involvement in campus organizations.

The program culminates in the Albion Advantage Pledge, the College's assurance that students will have post-graduate support, such as an additional research experience, an internship, or extended career services, if desired, as they pursue their life's work.

www.albion.edu
(517) 629-0321
admission@albion.edu

STUDENT PROFILE

1,512 undergraduate students

100% of undergrad students are full-time

54% female – 46% male

26% of students are from out of state

75% freshman retention rate

FACULTY PROFILE

11 to 1 student/faculty ratio

ADMISSIONS

Selectivity: 68%

SAT Ranges: E 510-630, M 500-610

ACT Ranges: C 20-26, M 18-26, E 20-26

TUITION & COST

Tuition: $45,070

Fees: $520

Room: $6,080

Board: $6,300

ALMA COLLEGE

ALMA, MICHIGAN

www.alma.edu
(800) 321-2562
admissions@alma.edu

Alma College is at its best when it's working with students who don't have all the answers, but love to ask the questions. A beautiful residential college located in the middle of Michigan's Lower Peninsula, Alma College offers an individualized education through which each student is encouraged to identify personal and professional goals as they chart a path for the future. Alma does not prescribe a formula for success; rather, it helps students discover their options and open the right doors.

PROGRAMS OF EMPHASIS: Alma students have the ability to design their own area of concentration to meet specific educational or career goals.

In recent years, students have graduated with Programs of Emphasis majors in such fields as arts management; archaeology and anthropology; environmental policy and community advocacy; foreign service and international law; and music technology and digital media.

ADVENTURE RECREATION: Alma College is located in the middle of Michigan, which offers excellent outdoor recreational areas and the longest freshwater coastline in the United States.

Alma's Adventure Recreation program sponsors student weekend programming experiences that include camping, kayaking, snowboarding, and skiing to such locations as Sleeping Bear Dunes, Mackinac Island, the Pictured Rocks, and Boyne and Caberfae mountains.

STUDENT PROFILE

1,396 undergraduate students

99% of undergrad students are full-time

58% female – 42% male

9% of students are from out of state

79% freshman retention rate

FACULTY PROFILE

12 to 1 student/faculty ratio

ADMISSIONS

Selectivity: 64%

SAT Ranges: E 520-620, M 520-600

ACT Ranges: C 20-27, M 19-26, E 19-27

TUITION & COST

Tuition: $41,138

Fees: $260

Room & Board: $11,384

"I received a solid foundation at Alma, both scientifically and personally. Alma's liberal arts background helped foster a solid knowledge of many areas, not just one track, and I think that propelled me to excel in graduate work and as a professional at CDC." *– Emily Weston Parker '01, an epidemiologist with the Centers for Disease Control and Prevention (CDC)*

CONCORDIA UNIVERSITY ANN ARBOR

ANN ARBOR, MICHIGAN

Concordia University Ann Arbor's beautiful campus on the banks of the Huron River fosters a collegial environment for students to intersect their learning and faith. Realizing that today's academic landscape is ever changing, the university's administration has committed itself to preparing students to stand apart from the crowd, share their God-given talents and gifts in service to others, and *Live A Life That Is Uncommon*. Undergraduates can choose from 60 majors in one of five schools, the most recent of which is the state-of-the-art School of Nursing.

GENERAL EDUCATION: CUAA's core curriculum runs for the first three semesters and includes a freshman seminar that focuses on community engagement, faith, global citizenship, and being a neighborly human being. While coursework within disciplines might differ in focus, all students are exposed to writing-intensive courses, research-focused courses, service-learning, and experiential learning components.

CEIR: The Office of Career Engagement and Industry Relations offers a number of resources online and in-person for students, alumni, and employers. Students can visit the Career Engagement Studio on campus to access career coaching, internship preparation, or opportunities for post-grad employment.

The "Take 20 program offers students easy access to quick, 20-minute engagements on skills" that help boost career readiness. Students can use this opportunity to interact with the Career Engagement Studio staff as well as peers and alumni.

ADVISING: Advisors work individually with every undergraduate to register for the classes best suited for them as well as navigate the plan for their academic career. They also introduce students to campus tools and resources., ensuring that academic and student life offices work together to make sure students know where to get the support they need.

www.cuaa.edu
(734) 995-7300
admission@cuaa.edu

STUDENT PROFILE

940 undergraduate students

95% of undergrad students are full-time

54% female – 46% male

17% of students are from out of state

FACULTY PROFILE

10 to 1 student/faculty ratio

ADMISSIONS

Selectivity: 50%

ACT Ranges: C 18-25, M 18-25, E 19-25

TUITION & COST

Tuition: $29,180

Fees: $270

Room: $5,870

Board: $6,750

CORNERSTONE UNIVERSITY

GRAND RAPIDS, MICHIGAN

Cornerstone
UNIVERSITY®
BUILD A LIFE THAT MATTERS

www.cornerstone.edu
(616) 222-1426
admissions@
cornerstone.edu

At Cornerstone University, students are more. More than a major. More than a degree. Each student is a story. At Cornerstone, students are encouraged to discover their unique gifts and abilities, they are pushed to think outside their comfort zones, and they are equipped to graduate with the skills needed to make an impact on the world for Christ.

TERRA FIRMA: Meaning "firm foundation" in Latin, Cornerstone's yearlong Terra Firma orientation program provides new students a strong foundation for both academic and spiritual growth. Together, they enjoy off-campus outings, take part in a service-learning project in the Grand Rapids community, and learn about what it means to thrive in college.

CALLING MATTERS: Cornerstone believes in helping students discover their callings. CU's LIFEPATH program provides purpose-guided academic and career planning to help students discover how God has gifted and equipped each of them with unique skills, abilities, and passions.

Staff members help students make meaning of their talents, interests, and values, providing such additional services as networking, résumé development, graduate school preparation, and internship and job search strategies.

Academic advisors also assist students in planning their schedules and accessing any academic support services they may need.

"Being a student at Cornerstone was an extremely influential time due to the Christian role models I met there… I wouldn't change a thing… I felt I received a top-notch education paired with valuable relationships with professors, staff, and other students who influenced me to be more Christ-like." *- Rex Pickar CU '16*

STUDENT PROFILE

1,550 undergraduate students

83% of undergrad students are full-time

59% female – 41% male

18% of students are from out of state

80% freshman retention rate

FACULTY PROFILE

12 to 1 student/faculty ratio

ADMISSIONS

Selectivity: 73%

SAT Ranges: E 480-600, M 470-580

ACT Ranges: C 19-26, M 18-26, E 18-25

TUITION & COST

Tuition: $25,360

Room & Board: $9,630

HILLSDALE COLLEGE

HILLSDALE, MICHIGAN

Hillsdale College was founded in 1844 by men and women who described themselves as *"grateful to God for the inestimable blessings"* of civil and religious liberty, *"believing that the diffusion of sound learning is essential to the perpetuity of those blessings."* The College has maintained institutional independence to continue its trusteeship of the intellectual and spiritual inheritance derived from the Judeo-Christian faith and Greco-Roman culture.

THE HONOR CODE: All students at Hillsdale College are to sign an Honor Code that animates their lives throughout their four years: *"A Hillsdale College student is honorable in conduct, honest in word and deed, dutiful in study and service, and respectful of the rights of others. Through education the student rises to self-government."* Self-government is a challenge with the promise of a rich reward: liberty of the soul.

Virtus tentamine gaudet. Strength rejoices in the challenge. This truth, the motto of Hillsdale College, means that to be strong in virtue, one must welcome a challenge.

OFF-CAMPUS OPPORTUNITIES: Hillsdale students have a number of off-campus opportunities available to them. For example, those in the natural sciences can utilize the College's G.H. Gordon Biological Station, a 685-acre field research laboratory located in the northern part of Michigan's Lower Peninsula. Such is just a one of the many offerings across many disciplines.

"I really liked the fact that we were all immersed in a wide variety of disciplines, that we all came together as a unified community of scholars. And I've found a strong foundation in writing, history, and philosophy has practical value, especially for scientists." *– Heidi Hendrickson '09, is pursuing postdoctoral research in chemistry at Yale University.*

www.hillsdale.edu
(517) 437-7341
admissions@hillsdale.edu

STUDENT PROFILE

1,446 undergraduate students

99% of undergrad students are full-time

48% female – 52% male

67% of students are from out of state

91% freshman retention rate

FACULTY PROFILE

9 to 1 student/faculty ratio

ADMISSIONS

Selectivity: 36%

SAT Ranges: E 655-740, M 620-725

ACT Ranges: C 29-32, M 26-31, E 30-35

TUITION & COST

Tuition: $27,090

Fees: $1,278

Room: $5,640

Board: $5,750

KALAMAZOO COLLEGE

KALAMAZOO, MICHIGAN

As one of the oldest institutions in America, Kalamazoo College prepares its students for success. Collaboration with faculty and experiential learning opportunities groom students into intelligent and mindful leaders of tomorrow.

K-PLAN: Kalamazoo's K-Plan is a structure for liberal arts education made up of four parts: Depth and Breadth in the Liberal Arts; Learning Through Experience; International and Intercultural Experience; and Independent Scholarship.

The K-Plan is specific to each student and tailored to their individual needs and interests. There is plenty of academic and personal support available to students. Kalamazoo is concerned with graduating strong, intellectual leaders. With this goal in mind, K-Plan works to meet the needs and expose the talents of each student.

SOCIAL JUSTICE LEADERSHIP: Kalamazoo values social justice and expects every student to observe tolerance and equality of all groups.

Students and faculty can propose specific efforts to the Arcus Center for Social Justice and see that they are followed through. Kalamazoo's commitment to social justice is outlined in a set of values, which are to inspire unity, spark intellectual growth, nurture leadership, build community, and embrace change.

THE GUILDS: Recently, Kalamazoo implemented the Guilds, an ever-growing network of promising students and alumni. The Guilds are separated into different interests and careers to help students and alumni find those who can help them navigate their career pursuits.

In addition to the Guilds, Kalamazoo's Discovery Externship Program links students with alumni all over the world to live and work with them—a priceless experience whereby students gain industry knowledge and build their professional network.

www.kzoo.edu
(269) 337-7166
admission@kzoo.edu

STUDENT PROFILE

1,436 undergraduate students

99% of undergrad students are full-time

57% female — 43% male

31% of students are from out of state

90% freshman retention rate

FACULTY PROFILE

13 to 1 student/faculty ratio

ADMISSIONS

Selectivity: 73%

SAT Ranges: E 600-690, M 580-690

ACT Ranges: C 26-30, M 25-30, E 25-33

TUITION & COST

Tuition: $46,350

Fees: $490

Room: $4,569

Board: $4,821

MICHIGAN TECHNOLOGICAL UNIVERSITY

HOUGHTON, MICHIGAN

Michigan Technological University

Michigan Technological University is a leading research institution in technological advancement and innovation. The student-to-faculty ratio of 12:1 gives way to a collaborative environment in which student research leads to amazing discovery.

THE ENTERPRISE PROGRAM: The Enterprise Program brings together students of varying disciplines to work on real-world client projects. Each team functions like a company in which every individual brings something valuable to the table.

There are awesome opportunities available through Enterprise—some students get to create and test their own prototypes, while other teams get to work abroad. During the business process, participants have the chance to work with industry leaders, government organizations, members of the community, and faculty advisors.

In the past, students have worked with companies like General Motors, Kimberly Clark, and The Department of Energy.

UNIVERSITY STUDENT LEARNING GOALS: Michigan Tech approaches undergraduate education from 8 different University Student Learning Goals (USLG). Each goal outlines a specific skill or purpose within the core curriculum, altogether contributing to the educational experience.

Disciplinary Knowledge; Knowledge of the Physical and Natural World; Global Literacy; Critical and Creative Thinking; Communication; Information Literacy; Technology; and Social Responsibility and Ethical Reasoning altogether form the bedrock for everything the Michigan Tech successfully instills in its students.

www.mtu.edu
(888) 688-1885
mtu4u@mtu.edu

STUDENT PROFILE

5,890 undergraduate students

93% of undergrad students are full-time

27% female – 73% male

25% of students are from out of state

83% freshman retention rate

FACULTY PROFILE

13 to 1 student/faculty ratio

ADMISSIONS

Selectivity: 74%

SAT Ranges: E 570-660, M 590-680

ACT Ranges: C 25-30, M 25-30, E 23-30

TUITION & COST

Tuition (in-state): $14,774

Tuition (out-of-state): $32,018

Fees: $300

Room: $5,827

Board: $4,650

SIENA HEIGHTS UNIVERSITY

ADRIAN, MICHIGAN

SIENA HEIGHTS UNIVERSITY

www.sienaheights.edu
(517) 264-7180
admissions@
sienaheights.edu

At Siena Heights, students do so much more than earn degrees. They develop interests that transform into passions. They discover talents they never knew they had. They make friendships that last forever. Siena Heights University has dedicated almost a century to creating an educational environment in which students feel both instantly comfortable and infinitely challenged. That's the Siena Effect.

STUDENT SUCCESS: Siena's professors would be intimidating if they weren't some of the the most personable people one could meet. Faculty put student success first, getting to know each student's personal strengths and struggles.

Additionally, faculty even work closely with one another so that they may foster interdisciplinary experiences. If a political science professor recognizes a student's love for writing, for example, he may recommend a literature course on Orwell. Or a sculpture professor could spark a student's interest in theatre set design. When learning is based on real relationships, there's no limit to where it can lead.

GENDER AND ETHNIC STUDIES INSTITUTE: The new Gender and Ethnic Studies Institute is expected to be a leader in exploring race, ethnicity, gender, and sexuality. This institute, a one-of-a-kind addition to the University's Ethnic and Gender Studies minor, is aimed not only to enhance learning in the classroom, but also to support the lives of underserved populations on and around campus.

And, with the support of SHU's Office of Diversity and Inclusion, the institute is constantly thinking up ways to educate the community about the ways that race, ethnicity, gender, and sexuality are constructed and treated in society.

STUDENT PROFILE

2,035 undergraduate students

61% of undergrad students are full-time

58% female — 42% male

11% of students are from out of state

70% freshman retention rate

FACULTY PROFILE

12 to 1 student/faculty ratio

ADMISSIONS

Selectivity: 67%

SAT Ranges: E 440-550, M 430-540

ACT Ranges: C 17-22, M 16-23, E 15-21

TUITION & COST

Tuition: $26,558

Fees: $594

Room & Board: $10,990

> "I have the best job in the universe, being mayor of the best city in the state of Michigan. ... I would not be here if not for Siena Heights. I recognize that."
>
> *– Bobby Hopewell '96, Mayor of Kalamazoo, MI, and health care executive*

SPRING ARBOR UNIVERSITY

SPRING ARBOR, MICHIGAN

At Spring Arbor University's core is a dedication to help students pursue a life of wisdom, grounded in a Christian liberal arts education and the cultivation of academic and spiritual growth. Since its founding in 1873, Spring Arbor University (SAU) has developed this culture. That commitment continues today. "The Concept" guides the university, serving as the cornerstone of academic and spiritual life both on campus and beyond.

TOTAL COMMITMENT: Spiritual life is a priority across campus. Outside of the classroom, the entire student body gathers on Mondays and Wednesdays for chapel services, participating in worship and listening to engaging messages from a variety of speakers from across campus and the nation. Other worship opportunities include Worship Arts Vespers Experience (WAVE), which is led by worship arts majors. Students also take advantage of local ministry opportunities, small groups, and annual retreats in pursuit of deepening and strengthening their relationship with Christ.

COMMUNITY OF LEARNERS: Every month, SAU holds a Community of Learners seminar in which faculty members present extracurricular lectures on topics they have been researching. These lectures give students opportunities to explore topics outside of their majors and engage with their professors as fellow learners and academics.

NATURAL SCIENCE SEMINARS: Similar to Community of Learners events, the department of chemistry and biology hosts regular natural science seminars. Faculty, current students, and alumni often participate in these events, giving science and non-science students alike a glimpse into both on- and off-campus research projects.

POLING CENTER: Dedicated in 2008, the 38,000-square-foot Poling Center for Global Learning and Leadership houses the Gainey School of Business, offices for the social sciences, classrooms, meeting areas, and a CP Federal Credit Union Trading Center. The facility is equipped with some of the same technology that is used daily on Wall Street and trains students for Series 7 certification, Bloomberg equities, and Bloomberg fixed income products.

www.arbor.edu
(517) 750-6468
admissions@arbor.edu

STUDENT PROFILE
1,957 undergraduate students

71% of undergrad students are full-time

66% female – 34% male

79% of students are from out of state

56% freshman retention rate

FACULTY PROFILE
11 to 1 student/faculty ratio

ADMISSIONS
Selectivity: 67%

SAT Ranges: E 510-615, M 490-590

ACT Ranges: C 20-27, M 18-25, E 20-28

TUITION & COST
Tuition: $27,150

Fees: $600

Room: $4,490

Board: $5,150

BETHEL UNIVERSITY MINNESOTA

SAINT PAUL, MINNESOTA

BETHEL
UNIVERSITY

www.bethel.edu
(651)638-6242
undergrad-admissions@
bethel.edu

Bethel University is a comprehensive liberal arts university that offers more than 100 different undergraduate degree programs. As a leader in Christian higher education since its establishment in 1871, Bethel creates graduates who are prepared to face obstacles and opportunities with the skills, experience, and faith needed to succeed.

R.E.A.L. EXPERIENCE: Students are not just taught how to find the first job after graduation. They are prepared for successful, meaningful lives—something best obtained through a strong foundation in the liberal arts. The R.E.A.L. Experience (Relevant. Experiential. Applied. Learning.) exposes students to a variety of hands-on learning activities, giving applicable meaning to what they are taught in the classroom. It's no wonder why Bethel students graduate with the knowledge and experience needed to succeed in this rapidly changing world.

THE ARTS: Bethel is proud to offer some of the most respected arts communities among Christian colleges. The university hosts 13 vocal and instrumental performance groups as well as theatrical ensembles that cater to all artistic interest. Patrons of the arts can enjoy numerous performances in the Benson Great Hall or catch one of five annual stage productions in the intimate Black Box Theatre. Bethel is also home to two art galleries that exhibit the works of both nationally and internationally recognized artists.

COMMUNITY PARTNERSHIPS: Bethel University forges relationships with the surrounding Minnesotan community, encouraging students to embrace the power of service to gain perspective while changing lives. One example, *Act Six*, is a collaborative program that awards scholarships to students from historically underrepresented populations. Recipients extend the gift by engaging in philanthropic community development opportunities. Through this initiative, students are empowered to take charge and learn to lead as they bring change to their neighborhoods.

Other students routinely engage with the surrounding Frogtown community through service and other kinds of civic, social, and spiritual engagement.

STUDENT PROFILE

2,901 undergraduate students

83% of undergrad students are full-time

62% female – 38% male

19% of students are from out of state

85% freshman retention rate

FACULTY PROFILE

11 to 1 student/faculty ratio

ADMISSIONS

Selectivity: 83%

SAT Ranges: E 530-690, M 500-670

ACT Ranges: C 21-27, M 21-27, E 21-27

TUITION & COST

Tuition: $36,060

Fees: $150

Room: $5,830

Board: $4,510

UNIVERSITY OF MINNESOTA DULUTH

DULUTH, MINNESOTA

The University of Minnesota Duluth is a medium-sized regional university that nurtures students through a rigorous, robust undergraduate experience. Its community of learners and scholars promotes student success, provides an enriching experience, and commits to core values that shape every aspect of the university and its purpose. Founded on the pillars of discovery, engagement, inclusivity, and excellence, UMD continues to prepare successful leaders of society.

STUDENT ASSOCIATION: As the official voice of the student body, the University of Maryland Duluth Student Association (UMDSA) is tasked with representing and lobbying for student interests in policy-making procedures. Students interested in having their voice be heard should take advantage of this wonderful leadership opportunity.

UNDERGRADUATE RESEARCH: The Undergraduate Research Opportunity Program (UROP) allows students to utilize a range of resources as they work alongside a faculty mentor in engaging research. Students may even be eligible to receive financial support. Upon completion, students present their findings at the annual UMD Undergraduate Research/Artistic Showcase.

STUDY ABROAD: Studying abroad is a great way to begin a lifetime of exploration. UMD encourages all students to explore new horizons, make new memories, and become seasoned global citizens. The Study Abroad office offers a full range of advising and support services to students on such issues as program selection; academic, financial, and travel planning; registration; culture shock; and re-entry.

FIRST-YEAR EXPERIENCE: The first year on campus is full of discovery, new experiences and, of course, a little bit of stress. UMD's first-year experience is therefore designed to alleviate some of that stress through comprehensive support and guidance. In-classroom freshman seminars enhance the first-year experience, giving students an immediate sense of support and a great start to their university career.

www.d.umn.edu
(218) 726-7171
umdadmis@d.umn.edu

STUDENT PROFILE

10,118 undergraduate students

88% of undergrad students are full-time

47% female – 53% male

13% of students are from out of state

77% freshman retention rate

FACULTY PROFILE

18 to 1 student/faculty ratio

ADMISSIONS

Selectivity: 77%

SAT Ranges: E 520-640, M 530-640

ACT Ranges: C 22-26, M 21-27, E 20-26

TUITION & COST

Tuition (in-state): $12,016

Tuition (out-of-state): $17,134

Fees: $1,628

Room & Board: $7,608

UNIVERSITY OF MINNESOTA MORRIS

MORRIS, MINNESOTA

UNIVERSITY OF MINNESOTA
MORRIS

www.morris.umn.edu
(320) 589-6035
admissions@
morris.umn.edu

A University of Minnesota Morris degree garners respect; it's known that the campus attracts students who are serious about learning. Young people come to Morris with an exceptional amount of innate curiosity.

GLOBAL STUDENT TEACHING: Morris offers select education students the incredible opportunity to gain teaching experience abroad. Student teachers learn how instruction styles differ in foreign locations, as well as the challenges that face students across the world.

The program is a great way for education students to explore the culture and history of a new place, while also gaining practice in their chosen field. The countries associated with the program include Austria, Ghana, Ireland, Italy, New Zealand, Poland, and Spain.

UNDERGRADUATE RESEARCH: Undergraduate research is one of the most challenging and rewarding experiences a student can have. Research involves many skills including creative inquiry, methodology, interpretation, proper citation, editing, discovery, and in some cases, presentation. In other words, students WHO engage in research benefit from the experience and get to develop these skills on an advanced level. Morris provides undergraduates with the opportunity to engage in research, whether that's as part of a group or an individual pursuit.

COMMUNITY ENGAGEMENT: Service to others continues to be an engaging and positive experience for UMM students and faculty alike.

There are several different ways to get involved, including Tutoring, Reading, and Enabling Children (TREC), an awesome initiative that allows UMM students to work directly with local pre-K through 6th grade students. They work both in the classroom and at after-school programs. This kind of continued support is a way to make a stronger impression on the students, thus encouraging their good performance in school.

STUDENT PROFILE

1,771 undergraduate students

93% of undergrad students are full-time

56% female – 44% male

12% of students are from out of state

78% freshman retention rate

FACULTY PROFILE

12 to 1 student/faculty ratio

ADMISSIONS

Selectivity: 58%

SAT Ranges: E 490-580, M 530-690

ACT Ranges: C 22-28, M 22-27, E 21-28

TUITION & COST

Tuition (in-state): $11,896

Tuition (out-of-state): $13,896

Fees: $950

Room: $3,752

Board: $4,162

UNIVERSITY OF MINNESOTA ROCHESTER

ROCHESTER, MINNESOTA

ROCHESTER

www.r.umn.edu
(507) 258-8686
applyumr@r.umn.edu

The University of Minnesota Rochester is a specialized institution designed with healthcare careers in mind. Adjacent to the Mayo Clinic, UMR takes advantage of its considerable professional and academic resources to offer a personalized education for each and every student. Students work in teams, research with world-class medical professionals, and learn about the demands of modern healthcare. Whatever their motivation, students looking to become the next generation of leaders in medicine have a home at UMR.

HANDS-ON HEALTHCARE: UMR is located right next door to the leading medical center in the U.S., the Mayo Clinic, giving students a direct connection to cutting-edge medical practices and research. Mayo staff, in addition to UMR's world-class faculty, open up a world of opportunities for students to take part in in-depth, hands-on research.

In Directed Study and Research courses, students can either take on an independent project or support faculty in their existing research. Directed research offers students a close relationship with their professors, which can lead to further employment opportunities or the development of a valuable professional network.

THREE R'S: At the University of Minnesota Rochester, every student is engaged in an in-depth healthcare education. But the real world is about more than just medicine—UMR's diverse liberal arts core connects the pursuit of a cutting-edge healthcare education to the literature and skills needed to be a well-rounded citizen.

To make sure students are engaged and interested in the material, every single course at UMR follows Three R's—*Relevance, Relationships*, and *Rigor*. Every course is *relevant* with a connection between their future career and their classwork; helpful in building *relationships* between classmates, faculty, and medical professionals; and *rigorous* with a high-quality pre-healthcare curriculum.

STUDENT PROFILE

472 undergraduate students

93% of undergrad students are full-time

75% female – 25% male

13% of students are from out of state

69% freshman retention rate

FACULTY PROFILE

13 to 1 student/faculty ratio

ADMISSIONS

Selectivity: 51%

SAT Ranges: E 620-720, M 610-690

ACT Ranges: C 22-26, M 22-26, E 21-26

TUITION & COST

Tuition: $12,944

Room & Board: $10,914

UNIVERSITY OF ST. THOMAS

ST. PAUL, MINNESOTA

UNIVERSITY OF St.Thomas

Inspired by the Catholic intellectual tradition, the University of St. Thomas educated students to be morally responsible leaders who think critically, act wisely, and work skillfully to advance the common good.

CIVIC ENGAGEMENT: Civic engagement allows students to give back to the community through thoughtful integration of coursework and academic theory. In a service-learning course, students split their time between lecture, service, and reflection. The reflection component of the course is especially important, as it allows students and faculty to re-adjust their approach in order to provide the best service.

Currently, UST offers service-learning opportunities during the year, J-Term, and summer. Just a few examples of the offered courses include Communication in the Workplace; Conservation Geography; Global Health in Uganda; Veteran's Affairs; and Multi-Cultural Communication in Diverse Organizations (Hawai'i).

TALKING CIRCLES: Named after the Native American tradition of the talking circle, in which members would gather to discuss issues and possible solutions, the Talking Circles retreat for first-year students is a community-building opportunity for UST members to enact change. The retreat takes place at the end of January Term and lasts for three days.

FALL LEADERSHIP INSTITUTE: The Fall Leadership Institute (FLI) is an annual event for undergraduate students. The conference explores the foundations of successful leadership and examines ways that students can develop their own skills.

FLI is highly collaborative, with students and experienced faculty working together to find solutions and break new ground. Some of the concepts covered at the conference include marketing, time management, and fiscal management.

www.stthomas.edu
(651) 962-6150
admissions@stthomas.edu

STUDENT PROFILE

6,199 undergraduate students

96% of undergrad students are full-time

46% female – 54% male

21% of students are from out of state

88% freshman retention rate

FACULTY PROFILE

14 to 1 student/faculty ratio

ADMISSIONS

Selectivity: 84%

SAT Ranges: E 540-650, M 550-680

ACT Ranges: C 24-29, M 24-28, E 23-29

TUITION & COST

Tuition: $40,224

Fees: $909

Room: $6,304

Board: $3,750

BELHAVEN UNIVERSITY

JACKSON, MISSISSIPPI

Belhaven University is a place where top-rated faculty and a nurturing environment converge to bring students to their best, then propel them beyond what is believed to be achievable. Belhaven leads its students to capture career and personal success and encourages the development of spiritual maturity that will withstand the trials of life. With nationally recognized academics, a Christ-centered worldview, and the faith-affirming support to become more, Belhaven's charming and warm-weather campus is home to fabulous events and intensely fun activities.

ARTS: Belhaven is steeped in arts heritage, having contributed to the intellectual, cultural, and spiritual growth of the state since 1883. Belhaven is 1 of 30 institutions in the nation that is accredited in Music, Dance, Theatre, and Visual Arts. Belhaven is the only Christian university that has obtained this accreditation and also offers a Bachelor of Fine Arts in creative writing.

INTERNSHIPS: Internships are available throughout many of the academic programs that Belhaven offers to its students. Ranging from Social Work to Sports Medicine: Exercise Science, there are many opportunities for students to get real-world experiences which prepares them for future careers.

A SOLID EDUCATION: At Belhaven, academic excellence is met with passion. Its unending pursuit of academic excellence is supported with personal mentoring in every degree. Belhaven provides a solid foundation in the comprehensive liberal arts to develop well-educated individuals.

Belhaven students experience one-of-a-kind academic programs, including the WorldView Curriculum, which chronologically intertwines the critical core disciplines of literature, history, art, religion, and music in a comprehensive rigorous format.

SERVICE: With the motto *"To Serve, Not to Be Served,"* Belhaven's reach extends locally, nationally, and internationally. From the annual Martin Luther King Clean-Up day to ministering students in places like Africa or Haiti, the common bond is service.

BELHAVEN UNIVERSITY

www.belhaven.edu
(800) 960-5940
admission@belhaven.edu

STUDENT PROFILE

2,482 undergraduate students

50% of undergrad students are full-time

66% female — 34% male

63% freshman retention rate

FACULTY PROFILE

10 to 1 student/faculty ratio

ADMISSIONS

Selectivity: 59%

TUITION & COST

Tuition: $23,900

Fees: $350

Room & Board: $8,000

MILLSAPS COLLEGE

JACKSON, MISSISSIPPI

MILLSAPS COLLEGE

www.millsaps.edu
(601) 974-1050
admissions@millsaps.edu

Aclose-knit community of leaders with vision: founded in 1890, Millsaps College offers an open and exciting environment for eager minds. The dynamic and enthusiastic faculty work hand-in-hand with an engaged student body to open new doors in liberal arts education.

FUTURE PROFESSIONALS: Millsaps has a long tradition of offering one of the best and strongest pre-med programs in the state. Every year, graduates claim a significant number of the one hundred open slots at University of Mississippi Medical School. About 15 percent of each year's graduates major in biology or chemistry. Millsaps also offers a strong pre-law program with its political science and history majors.

Beyond the sciences, Millsaps' business program is fully accredited by AACSB and accounts for 15 to 20 percent of total graduate and undergraduate enrollment every year. Accounting, economics, and business administration are the main focuses in the business division.

FAITH & WORK INITIATIVE: The Millsaps College Faith & Work Initiative, funded by the Lilly Endowment, provides an array of seminars, courses, and internships that allow students to explore their personal and professional futures as they relate to issues of ethics, values, faith, and the common good.

EFFECTIVE WRITERS: Unlike many colleges, Millsaps has developed a writing program that is independent of its English department. The program teaches students how to develop the art of communication, which is essential for any career. Millsaps embraces the philosophy that writing cannot be taught in just one semester of freshman composition. Instead, it is taught continuously and within the context of every discipline.

The college's required writing portfolio allows students to gather and reflect on a variety of their academic writings. Millsaps is working to expand experiential education, internships, and study abroad, seeking to internationalize students through semester-long programs.

STUDENT PROFILE

807 undergraduate students

99% of undergrad students are full-time

49% female – 51% male

54% of students are from out of state

78% freshman retention rate

FACULTY PROFILE

9 to 1 student/faculty ratio

ADMISSIONS

Selectivity: 49%

SAT Ranges: E 560-660, M 550-660

ACT Ranges: C 22-28, M 20-26, E 23-30

TUITION & COST

Tuition: $36,380

Fees: $2,550

Room: $7,500

Board: $5,900

EVANGEL UNIVERSITY

SPRINGFIELD, MISSOURI

Offering more than 70 academic programs, Evangel University is on the cutting edge of today's professional fields and vocational ministry training. Its commitment to the integration of faith, learning, and life attracts students from a wide variety of Christian backgrounds. These students have a strong commitment to academics and an even stronger desire to combine their Christian faith with every aspect of their lives.

REAL-WORLD EXPOSURE: At Evangel, education is not limited to the classroom. Faculty and university leadership are dedicated to providing numerous opportunities for students to learn more about their discipline outside of classroom hours.

In 2018, Evangel held its first Cybersecurity and Ethics Symposium for those entering the field of information technology. Participants were able to listen to and engage in the discussion between top leaders at such companies as O'Reilly Auto Parts and Dell Technologies.

UNDERGRADUATE RESEARCH: Evangel hosts a research symposium every April as a joint effort of three departments—Behavioral and Social Sciences, Kinesiology, and Natural and Applied Sciences—to celebrate research.

Psychology students present on personality theory, chemistry students speak on applied sustainability, and kinesiology students research the impact of texting and walking—regardless of what they look into, Evangel's students immerse themselves fully in their research and understand how they can make a positive impact on the world around them.

SPRINGFIELD: Springfield offers multiple employment opportunities, access to amazing churches, and service opportunities at Evangel's partner, Convoy of Hope.

Foodies and coffee connoisseurs keep busy sampling dining options, and fine art buffs can explore area museums and art galleries. Hands down, Springfield's affordability and amenities make Evangel a perfect place to attend college.

www.evangel.edu
(800) 382-6435

STUDENT PROFILE

1,627 undergraduate students

90% of undergrad students are full-time

55% female – 45% male

79% freshman retention rate

FACULTY PROFILE

14 to 1 student/faculty ratio

ADMISSIONS

Selectivity: 94%

SAT Ranges: E 500-610, M 470-570

ACT Ranges: C 19-25, M 17-25, E 18-25

TUITION & COST

Tuition: $22,146

Fees: $1,275

Room: $4,304

Board: $4,218

FONTBONNE UNIVERSITY

ST. LOUIS, MISSOURI

Fontbonne University in St. Louis, MO, is home to a compact campus, strong values, big hearts, and passionate people. Students can choose from 43 rigorous, relevant undergraduate majors and 14 graduate programs—as well as numerous minors, certificates, and concentrations—that range from highly lauded programs like deaf education, dietetics, and fine arts, to new, innovative disciplines like cyber security, bioinformatics, and One Health.

DEDICATED SEMESTER: The university's annual Dedicated Semester takes place each fall and serves as a community learning experience. The entire campus focuses on a single topic of discussion like Disability; Happiness; the Immigrant Experience; and Security, Privacy, & Freedom. Specialized courses, guest speakers, experiential learning opportunities, and book clubs make the Dedicated Semester a chance for everyone to come together to learn.

GLOBAL LEARNING: Diversity and inclusion have been a hallmark at Fontbonne University since its inception. With nearly 300 international students and the highest diversity percentage of private schools in St. Louis, Fontbonne's campus represents the real world, preparing students to lead inclusively upon graduation.

UNDERGRADUATE RESEARCH: Because faculty members lead small classes, they easily act as valuable mentors throughout the research process. Some of Fontbonne's undergraduate research projects have earned patents in cybersecurity and created new "best practice" developments in communication disorders and speech pathology.

> "Being a transfer student, I thought it would be difficult connecting with my classmates because most of them have been together for 2 years already. I was very wrong... The environment and sense of community is what drew me towards Fontbonne and is what I will continue to rave about to others." – *Nina, elementary education major*

---

www.fontbonne.edu
(800) 205-5862
fbyou@fontbonne.edu

STUDENT PROFILE

893 undergraduate students

86% of undergrad students are full-time

62% female – 38% male

24% of students are from out of state

80% freshman retention rate

FACULTY PROFILE

10 to 1 student/faculty ratio

ADMISSIONS

Selectivity: 92%

ACT Ranges: C 20-26, M 19-25, E 20-27

TUITION & COST

Tuition: $25,980

Fees: $360

Room & Board: $9,989

MISSOURI STATE UNIVERSITY

SPRINGFIELD, MISSOURI

Missouri State University is a public university system founded in 1905. Even with an enrollment of 26,000+ students, the university provides a close-knit community of passionate and steadfast learners committed to ethical leadership, cultural competence, and community engagement. These are the pillars of the university's unique public affairs mission, granted by the Missouri General Assembly. Students learn to emphasize a continued understanding of the world and how to make it a better place.

COMMUNITY ENGAGEMENT: Missouri State University's Center for Community Engagement (CCE) serves as an interdisciplinary hub for publicly engaged service, education, and research.

The Center promotes community engagement by encouraging faculty to utilize research and teaching activities that are associated with public interest, providing students with articulated public engagement experiences tied to their academics. And, by obtaining community input and feedback, MSU fosters a more collective community impact and capacity.

ETHICAL LEADERSHIP: Missouri State prepares students for the future by helping them understand the ethical dimensions of leadership. Learning how to lead allows them to be better able to employ what they learn in the classroom and help bring about change in their community.

BEAR CLAW: The Bear CLAW (Center for Learning and Writing) offers free academic support for MSU's education community, linking students, faculty, and staff alike to resources that help them succeed. Not only does the Bear CLAW provide formal tutoring, but it also cultivates a space for collaboration and workshopping among knowledgeable consultants, coaches, and leaders.

"I have mentors and friends that are administrators and professors. They're all here for me if I need anything. That's not just because I am a student governor; I think it's like that for any student." – *Tyree Davis IV, administrative management and interpersonal communication major from Raytown, Missouri*

Missouri State UNIVERSITY

www.missouristate.edu
(800) 492-7900
info@missouristate.edu

STUDENT PROFILE

16,965 undergraduate students

88% of undergrad students are full-time

58% female – 42% male

9% of students are from out of state

78% freshman retention rate

FACULTY PROFILE

21 to 1 student/faculty ratio

ADMISSIONS

Selectivity: 85%

SAT Ranges: E 500-630, M 518-590

ACT Ranges: C 21-26, M 20-26, E 21-27

TUITION & COST

Tuition (in-state): $6,540

Tuition (out-of-state): $14,850

Fees: $1,048

Room: $6,486

Board: $2,642

MISSOURI UNIVERSITY OF SCIENCE AND TECHNOLOGY

ROLLA, MISSOURI

www.mst.edu
(573) 341-4165
admissions@mst.edu

Missouri S&T is a leading research institution that brings together the collaborative efforts of both faculty and students. The University's commitment to technological and scientific discovery has led to amazing achievements, both in the realms of academia as well as return on investment.

HIT THE GROUND RUNNING: Hit the Ground Running (HGR) is a summer program that allows incoming freshmen to get a sneak peek of college life. Participants come to campus for a three-week program to explore areas of math, chemistry, and English. Students are also introduced to the campus, helpful research tips, and leadership opportunities. As an added bonus, participants earn credit for their work.

LEARNING COMMUNITIES: Living-Learning Communities (LLCs) connect students through an integration academics into residence life. In an LLC, students benefit from academic and personal support form their peers and professors alike.

Connections Communities are residential experiences that focus~ on a specific theme or interest, structured to make it easy to organize events and activities. In the *Holistic LLC*, students learn how to maintain a healthy balance in their academic and social endeavors.

The *Voyager LLC*, exclusive to first-year students, has participants live with one another and take classes structured in block scheduling. Through their shared experiences and lifestyle, freshmen are able to thrive in a safe and supportive environment in which they can explore their passions get comfortable at the University.

CO-OPS: S&T students are eligible for Co-Op experiences when they enter their second year. A Co-Op is a great way to get a leg up on the competition, immersing them in projects that grant them industry knowledge as well as hands-on experience in their field of interest.

STUDENT PROFILE

6,919 undergraduate students

89% of undergrad students are full-time

24% female – 76% male

15% of students are from out of state

81% freshman retention rate

FACULTY PROFILE

19 to 1 student/faculty ratio

ADMISSIONS

Selectivity: 84%

SAT Ranges: E 520-640, M 580-700

ACT Ranges: C 25-31, M 26-30, E 24-31

TUITION & COST

Tuition (in-state): $7,896

Tuition (out-of-state): $24,568

Fees: $1,350

Room: $6,640

Board: $3,600

SAINT LOUIS UNIVERSITY

ST. LOUIS, MISSOURI

SAINT LOUIS UNIVERSITY.

www.slu.edu
(314) 977-2500
admission@slu.edu

Saint Louis University is a Catholic, Jesuit University ranked among the top research institutions in the nation. The University fosters the intellectual and character development of more than 13,000 students. Founded in 1818, it is the oldest university west of the Mississippi and the second oldest Jesuit university in the United States. Through teaching, research, health care, and community service, SLU has provided a one-of-a-kind education for nearly two centuries.

MAJOR EXPLORATION: The Student Success Center understands the difficulty that comes with choosing a major and establishing goals for the four-year collegiate journey. Through Major Exploration Advising, faculty members open up a space for students to express their interests, fears, and goals and collaborate with them to help the make decisions for their education and beyond.

Major Exploration not only helps students decide what to study, but also how to transition in and out of college with a firm foundation.

SCHOLARS PROGRAMS: The Scholars Programs at SLU exist to get students on the path to their master's degrees as efficiently as possible. Throughout their undergraduate careers, students in a Scholars Program make early efforts to assure themselves success in graduate school.

For example, Pre-Law Scholars are guaranteed admission to the SLU Graduate School of Law, while Medical Scholars can apply to the SLU School of Medicine as early as their sophomore year. Some Scholars Programs even set the course for students to get their master's degrees in just five years.

THEMED HOUSING: Themed houses feature French, German, and Spanish language floors with resident faculty members. Other themed housing includes several floors for Micah Program participants and Learning Community options for students who prefer to live among peers who share the same major.

STUDENT PROFILE

9,910 undergraduate students

67% of undergrad students are full-time

61% female — 39% male

61% of students are from out of state

90% freshman retention rate

FACULTY PROFILE

9 to 1 student/faculty ratio

ADMISSIONS

Selectivity: 64%

SAT Ranges: E 590-690, M 580-700

ACT Ranges: C 25-31, M 24-29, E 25-33

TUITION & COST

Tuition: $41,540

Fees: $626

Room: $6,124

Board: $4,872

STEPHENS COLLEGE

COLUMBIA, MISSOURI

Founded in 1833 with the goal to educate and inspire young women, Stephens College has evolved into an innovative, independent, and spirited institution with a women's education that is truly unparalleled. What sets the College apart from other schools is what's known as the "Stephens difference." Characterized by a blend of hands-on learning with a broad liberal arts education, the difference helps students identify their passions and grow into confident leaders.

WOMEN'S ADVANTAGE: Research demonstrates the impressive benefits of attending an all-female college. On average, graduates from women's colleges see more success than those who from co-ed colleges, taking on more leadership roles and excelling far into senior-level positions. Students are heard, valued, and challenged as they grow to be the best they can be.

A HOME, A FAMILY: The incredible comfort of the Stephens campus is an obvious reason as to why students embrace it as their home away from home. The beautiful grounds, tight-knit community, and a pet-friendly policy are all easy to fall in love with. To say that Stephens students thrive is an understatement; both on and off campus, there is always the opportunity to meet new people, have fun, and feel supported.

The Office of Institutional Advancement and Initiatives goes further to connect current and former students alike to productive work opportunities. Students and alumnae are involved in a network that opens the door to professional journeys beyond the classroom, fostering meaningful connections that benefit them in both their careers and personal lives.

"I have been able to confidently accomplish all projects and tasks assigned to me. My first week, I was asked to pack a styling kit to send abroad to Amsterdam. I felt incredibly prepared and even contacted my teacher thanking her for her excellent advice." *- Emily Csengody*

STEPHENS COLLEGE

www.stephens.edu
(573) 876-7207 Ext. 4207
inquiry@stephens.edu

STUDENT PROFILE
653 undergraduate students

83% of undergrad students are full-time

99% female – 1% male

61% freshman retention rate

FACULTY PROFILE
9 to 1 student/faculty ratio

ADMISSIONS
Selectivity: 53%

SAT Ranges: E 510-595, M 450-555

ACT Ranges: C 19-25, M 17-23, E 19-26

TUITION & COST
Tuition: $22,500

Fees: $200

Room: $4,600-$8,770

Board: $3,742

TRUMAN STATE UNIVERSITY

KIRKSVILLE, MISSOURI

Truman State University believes in the joy of learning. The college experience is about more than memorizing facts. At Truman State, small classes, participation in discussions, and real-world opportunities, are intrinsic to student life. Students who come to Truman State University join campus groups and make friendships that last a lifetime. Most of all, they receive an education that prepares them to excel in any field.

THE PORTFOLIO PROJECT: The portfolio project at Truman is a great way for students to keep track of their achievements. Students keep an evolving record of projects in several areas, including critical thinking, interdisciplinary thinking, historical analysis, scientific analysis, aesthetic analysis, and creative work and reflection. Students can track how they have grown and developed over the course of their college experience.

ACTIVE STUDENTS: The Kirksville community has several unique recreational opportunities for active students to enjoy. The Kirksville Aquatic Center, an indoor/outdoor pool complex, offers a variety of activities, classes, and programs designed to appeal to people of all ages, including a six-lane indoor pool perfect for swimming and relaxing.

Thousand Hills State Park includes 3,080 acres of beautiful rolling hills and a 573-acre lake. Located ten minutes from the Truman campus, Thousand Hills provides the perfect setting for hiking, camping, fishing, and waterskiing.

A WORLD OF OPPORTUNITY: At Truman, the ties that are created truly last a lifetime. Truman alumni can be found all over the world, in every field, and will serve as a powerful network for students in the future.

Truman graduates demonstrate courageous, visionary, and service-oriented leadership as responsible citizens who make significant contributions to their families and their communities. They carry with them the desire to learn for the sake of knowledge, the sensitivity and insight to appreciate cultural diversity, and the ability to think freely and communicate effectively.

www.truman.edu
(660) 785-4114
admissions@truman.edu

STUDENT PROFILE

5,898 undergraduate students

87% of undergrad students are full-time

59% female – 41% male

15% of students are from out of state

86% freshman retention rate

FACULTY PROFILE

16 to 1 student/faculty ratio

ADMISSIONS

Selectivity: 67%

SAT Ranges: E 605-705, M 580-715

ACT Ranges: C 24-30, M 24-28, E 24-32

TUITION & COST

Tuition (in-state): $7,352

Tuition (out-of-state): $14,136

Fees: $304

Room: $5,730

Board: $2,908

CARROLL COLLEGE

HELENA, MONTANA

Located in Montana's state capital, Helena, Carroll College is a private, four-year, Catholic diocesan college that provides a first-rate undergraduate education to nearly 1,500 students. Founded in 1909, Carroll has distinguished itself as a preeminent and award-winning leader in its academic programs, including pre-medical, natural sciences, nursing, engineering, mathematics, the social sciences, and the liberal arts. Scientific research, service-learning, education abroad, and an energetic, campus-wide sense of faith form cornerstones of the Carroll educational experience.

AN EDUCATION IN BALANCE: At Carroll College, it is believed that a supportive community is a crucially valuable factor in academic success. Carroll students and faculty don't just occupy classrooms together; they engage in all sorts of ways and in all sorts of contexts, like in professors' offices for one-on-one instruction, in the Cube for a bite to eat, in meetings with peer ministers to plan retreats, and even along the trail up Mount Helena for a friendly jog.

The college experience is a great lesson in work-life balance. At Carroll, students find it easy to work hard at school while also competing on Saints teams, enjoying dinner with friends, hanging out with hall mates, and participating in annual activities.

SCHOLARS FOR LIFE: Carroll's motto is *Non Scholae sed Vitae*—Not for School but for Life. The College's alumni proudly testify that the Carroll experience develops each student as an individual and prepares them for the constantly changing challenges that arise in their respective profession. As Carroll graduates, they enter society with a deep sense of commitment to humankind and a thriving passion to live a full, well-rounded life.

GLOBAL OUTREACH: The College's Engineers Without Borders chapter, Carroll Outreach Team, and Campus Ministry all offer regular trips to Latin America, South America, Europe, and Africa. All around the world, Carroll students work alongside their professional mentors to help mitigate local problems, improving public health and building infrastructure.

www.carroll.edu
(406) 447-4384
admission@carroll.edu

STUDENT PROFILE

1,362 undergraduate students

94% of undergrad students are full-time

60% female – 40% male

61% of students are from out of state

84% freshman retention rate

FACULTY PROFILE

11 to 1 student/faculty ratio

ADMISSIONS

Selectivity: 78%

SAT Ranges: E 540-640, M 540-630

ACT Ranges: C 22-28, M 21-27, E 21-27

TUITION & COST

Tuition: $33,500

Fees: $980

Room: $4,972

Board: $4,636

ROCKY MOUNTAIN COLLEGE

BILLINGS, MONTANA

ROCKY MOUNTAIN
C O L L E G E

www.rocky.edu
(406) 657-1026
admissions@rocky.edu

Rocky Mountain College is Montana's oldest college, founded in 1878. As a comprehensive four-year liberal arts college, RMC takes pride in its commitment to excellence and consideration of all points of view. The College joins the traditions of liberal arts with the heritage of practical training for specific careers.

CHARLES MORLEDGE SCIENCE BUILDING: With the completion of Phase I of its "ImpACT Today, Transform Tomorrow" capital campaign, Rocky Mountain College now boasts the most advanced dedicated laboratory facility in the region. The Dr. Charles Morledge Science Building provides Rocky Mountain College students and faculty with state-of-the-art research and teaching spaces in every discipline of the natural arts, meeting the needs of a growing student body and accelerating lab-based science instruction.

WHEATLEY LECTURE SERIES: RMC and the United Methodist Church revived the Wheatley Lectures after a ten-year hiatus on March 8, 2018. This popular lecture series honors the ideals of Bishop Melvin E. Wheatley, focusing on social justice, the promotion of an inclusive church, academic inquiry, pastoral care, and ethics.

With the theme *cultivating community in fracturing times, returning civility to civil dialogue*, the lecture series has had a worthwhile and timely revival. The Wheatley Lectures emphasize the importance of strengthening community through constructive dialogue within modern discourse.

"I always wanted to have a career in space technology. When I was in high school, I didn't think it was possible for me, a small town girl from Laurel, Montana. Thanks to the support of Rocky's faculty and staff, I have been able to do some amazing things and to show young girls in Montana that anything is possible." *– Ayla Grandpre, Class of 2018*

STUDENT PROFILE

879 undergraduate students

98% of undergrad students are full-time

49% female – 51% male

47% of students are from out of state

67% freshman retention rate

FACULTY PROFILE

11 to 1 student/faculty ratio

ADMISSIONS

Selectivity: 58%

SAT Ranges: E 490-590, M 500-585

ACT Ranges: C 20-25, M 19-25, E 19-24

TUITION & COST

Tuition: $28,962

Fees: $590

Room: $4,140

Board: $4,312

COLLEGE OF SAINT MARY

OMAHA, NEBRASKA

Founded in 1923, College of Saint Mary (CSM) is a thriving Catholic university located in the heart of Omaha, Nebraska. College of Saint Mary is committed to providing access and affordable education to women while fostering potential and leadership through academic excellence, scholarship, and lifelong learning. With an enrollment over 1,100, College of Saint Mary offers undergraduate and graduate degrees in many of today's high-paying, in-demand fields, including physician assistant studies, occupational therapy, nursing, science, education, business, and legal studies.

WOMEN LEADERS: CSM believes that the world benefits from strong women leaders. Each of its degree programs provide an engaging depth of knowledge coupled with opportunities to apply learning to the real world.

CSM graduates are happuly welcomed into businesses, classrooms, clinics, hospitals, courtrooms, studios, and stages—both locally and across the nation. In fact, 92 percent of graduates are employed or pursuing continuing education within six months of commencement.

OMAHA, NEBRASKA: Located in the heart of Omaha, home of four Fortune 500 companies, CSM's 40-acre campus is adjacent to Aksarben Village's vibrant and bustling retail and entertainment space, as well as Baxter Arena. CSM is minutes from such world-class attractions as the Henry Doorly Zoo and Aquarium, Joslyn Art Museum, Lauritzen Gardens, and CenturyLink Center Omaha.

"I've been truly blessed to be surrounded by such intelligent, strong women here at CSM. As I continue to grow and venture onto the next journey life holds for me, I remember the laughter, knowledge and relationships this place has brought me and just revel in thought at how quickly, but beautifully, time has passed by." *– Shabnam Waheed '18*

www.csm.edu
(402) 399-2400
admissions@csm.edu

STUDENT PROFILE

810 undergraduate students

98% of undergrad students are full-time

100% female – 0% male

21% of students are from out of state

84% freshman retention rate

FACULTY PROFILE

11 to 1 student/faculty ratio

ADMISSIONS

Selectivity: 60%

TUITION & COST

Tuition: $20,750

Room & Board: $7,850

CONCORDIA UNIVERSITY, NEBRASKA

SEWARD, NEBRASKA

CONCORDIA UNIVERSITY NEBRASKA

Concordia University, Nebraska, a Lutheran, Christ-centered institution, is a fully accredited, coeducational university. 98% of recent Concordia graduates are in graduate school or employed within six months of graduation. Concordia offers more than 70 undergraduate, graduate, and professional programs in an excellent academic and Christ-centered community that equips men and women for lives of learning, service, and leadership in the church and world.

A STUDENT-CENTERED EDUCATION: Concordia University, Nebraska is a place where students can find their heart's calling and be equipped to answer it. At Concordia, the culture is about students. It's about serving others, being part of a vibrant, Christian community, and maximizing gifts and talents.

At Concordia, the foundation of a Christ-centered, Lutheran university is evident in the community who gathers to worship together, the classmates who genuinely support each other, and the professor who cares about every aspect of students' well-being.

The variety of programs and quality of the academics at Concordia allow students to explore their passions and choose a course of study that they are confident about pursuing. Christ is an integral part of Concordia's classroom environment. Professors tie Christ, service to others, and practical skill-building opportunities to academic content.

SEWARD: Concordia's hometown of Seward, Nebraska, population just over 7,000, makes it easy to adjust to college life by providing everything students need. Seward has the #1 lowest crime rate of 31 Nebraska cities with 5,000+ people.

In Seward, students are part of the community, and they are safe and welcome. Students can also experience the entertainment and city life of Lincoln, less than half an hour away.

---

www.cune.edu
(402) 643-7233
admiss@cune.edu

STUDENT PROFILE

1,684 undergraduate students

73% of undergrad students are full-time

54% female – 46% male

75% freshman retention rate

FACULTY PROFILE

14 to 1 student/faculty ratio

ADMISSIONS

Selectivity: 75%

SAT Ranges: E 480-550, M 440-550

ACT Ranges: C 21-26, M 19-26, E 20-26

TUITION & COST

Tuition: $30,400

Fees: $600

Room: $3,400

Board: $4,700

CREIGHTON UNIVERSITY

OMAHA, NEBRASKA

Creighton University is the only university in the country to offer education in seven health professions—medicine, dentistry, pharmacy, nursing, occupational therapy, physical therapy and public health—as well as outstanding programs in arts and sciences, business, and law, all on one walkable campus. One of 28 Jesuit colleges and universities in the country, Creighton offers a purposeful education established on academic excellence, social justice, and personal growth.

SCSJ:: The Schlegel Center for Service and Justice (SCSJ) is committed to building a community of faith in service for justice. SCSJ members participate in the school's justice and peace studies program. SCSJ also sponsors ongoing disaster relief for such organizations as the International Federation of Red Cross and Red Crescent Societies, the American Red Cross, Catholic Charities USA, and Catholic Relief Services.

CHI HEALTH: In 2012, Creighton expanded its academic affiliation with the largest health care system in the region, which is now called CHI Health. CHI Health's network of health care facilities are the primary clinical teaching sites for the School of Medicine and Creighton's other health sciences schools.

Other programs of note include Creighton's respected Center for Health Policy and Ethics as well as internationally renowned centers of excellence in cardiac care, hard-tissue research, osteoporosis, hereditary cancer, and patient outcomes research.

RESEARCH: More than 100 faculty research projects are under way at Creighton on any given day, and the vast majority of them involve undergraduate students. University-wide, research grants are awarded in undergraduate, graduate, and professional programs.

Creighton is a leader in cancer research and treatment through the Creighton Cancer Center and the Hereditary Cancer Institute. Headed by world-renowned researcher Henry T. Lynch, M.D., the Hereditary Cancer Institute is the nation's only cancer registry to track all forms of hereditary cancer.

www.creighton.edu
(402) 280-2703
admissions@creighton.edu

STUDENT PROFILE

4,255 undergraduate students

94% of undergrad students are full-time

56% female – 44% male

79% of students are from out of state

89% freshman retention rate

FACULTY PROFILE

11 to 1 student/faculty ratio

ADMISSIONS

Selectivity: 72%

SAT Ranges: E 520-640, M 550-650

ACT Ranges: C 25-30, M 24-28, E 24-31

TUITION & COST

Tuition: $37,086

Fees: $1,664

Room: $6,024

Board: $4,678

NEBRASKA WESLEYAN UNIVERSITY

LINCOLN, NEBRASKA

NEBRASKA WESLEYAN UNIVERSITY

Nebraska Wesleyan University is an independent Methodist liberal arts college of roughly 2,000. The university's steadfast commitment to putting learning into action through internships, study abroad, service-learning, and collaborative research has yielded tremendous outcomes for students and alumni. NWU is among the nation's leaders in Fulbright scholars, Academic All-Americans, and NCAA Postgraduate Scholarship winners.

INNOVATIVE STUDY: Nebraska Wesleyan University adopted an innovative general education curriculum in 2013. Moving away from a "cafeteria approach" in which students build their class schedules by choosing "a little of this" and "a little of that," Nebraska Wesleyan now offers a format in which students select an interdisciplinary "thread."

Here, they explore universal topics from the perspectives of multiple academic disciplines. This approach to a liberal arts education helps students see more explicitly the connections between different fields.

INTENSELY INVOLVED: A strong community makes it possible for Nebraska Wesleyan students to put what they learn into action. BFA students in theatre, for example, participate in an average of six shows per year. Their shows are consistently embraced and well attended by the community.

Additionally, 100 percent of NWU business students conduct internships due to their strong reputation with local, regional, and even national businesses. These businesses are eager to place—and hire—NWU students.

"The faculty are here because they like to do that. If they didn't want teaching to be their first responsibility, they wouldn't be teaching at a school like ours." - *Kathy Wolfe*

www.nebrwesleyan.edu
(402) 465-2218
admissions@
nebrwesleyan.edu

STUDENT PROFILE

1,779 undergraduate students

88% of undergrad students are full-time

60% female – 40% male

15% of students are from out of state

75% freshman retention rate

FACULTY PROFILE

11 to 1 student/faculty ratio

ADMISSIONS

Selectivity: 71%

SAT Ranges: E 530-670, M 510-630

ACT Ranges: C 22-28, M 21-27, E 20-27

TUITION & COST

Tuition: $31,974

Fees: $920

Room: $5,200

Board: $4,052

WAYNE STATE COLLEGE

WAYNE, NEBRASKA

Wayne State College, long recognized for providing educational excellence in a small, friendly setting, has been the educational and cultural anchor of northeast Nebraska for more than 100 years. What began as an institution devoted to teacher education has transformed into the region's most affordable leading comprehensive college. Wayne State College offers more than 90 undergraduate degrees and four graduate programs. True to its beginning roots as a teacher's college, education continues to be one of the most popular majors on campus.

EDUCATION: NENTA (Northeast Nebraska Teacher Academy) places highly qualified Wayne State College teaching majors as substitute teachers in participating school districts. Wayne State College students gain real-world teaching experience while the 14 participating school districts gain insight from students who are learning the latest in curriculum and instruction. This kind of real-world experience makes Wayne State College teaching majors some of the most sought after and employable students after graduation.

PRE-HEALTH: Students wishing to explore a career in medicine, pharmacy, dentistry, dental hygiene, or clinical laboratory science are prepared for post-graduate study thanks to the RHOP (Rural Health Opportunities Program) program. Students accepted into the program receive a tuition waiver for their undergraduate study at Wayne State and are automatically accepted into programs at the University of Nebraska Medical Center (UNMC).

ALUMNI SUCCESS: A Wayne State degree puts graduates in good company.. Wayne State graduates include young scientists honored for their work by Nobel laureates, Fulbright winners, a former governor, many state senators, doctors, business executives, lawyers, actors, reporters, and even an Elvis impersonator.

A Wayne State degree places graduates among the 98 percent of WSC alumni either employed or attending graduate school within six months of graduation. Many WSC graduates join a state education workforce in which one out of every 10 teachers holds a degree from Wayne State.

www.wsc.edu
(866) 972-2287
admissions@wsc.edu

STUDENT PROFILE

2,757 undergraduate students

87% of undergrad students are full-time

58% female – 42% male

17% of students are from out of state

69% freshman retention rate

FACULTY PROFILE

18 to 1 student/faculty ratio

TUITION & COST

Tuition (in-state): $5,138

Tuition (out-of-state): $10,276

Fees: $1,710

Room: $3,640

Board: $3,790

SIERRA NEVADA COLLEGE

INCLINE VILLAGE, NEVADA

Sierra Nevada College incorporates the unique environmental qualities and characteristics of the Lake Tahoe region into its academic mission and core curriculum, which altogether emphasize the importance of environmental, social, economic, and educational sustainability. At SNC Tahoe, professors employ a "learn by doing" approach to education in its three areas of educational excellence: Creativity, Leadership, and Sustainability.

RESEARCH IN EVERY FIELD: Undergraduate research isn't limited to one major at Sierra Nevada College. From Psychology to English, students work with their faculty and apply their coursework to projects that can have real impact on the world. Whether supporting local non-for-profit organizations or researching the environmental impact of ski resorts on local animal life, students make a difference in their local and academic communities.

NATURAL BEAUTY: National forests, the Sierra Mountains, and the shores of Lake Tahoe are right around the corner of SNC, giving students more than enough to explore throughout their undergraduate career. Sierra Nevada College utilizes its surroundings with many unique outdoor adventure trips for both first-timers and long-time outdoors aficionados.

FUN AND FRIENDLY COMPETITION: The culture of competition and performance at SNC goes far beyond the classroom. Students across the disciplines actively participate in both official and unofficial competitions and performances, including open mic nights and rail jams in the backcountry.

Through the robust student activity program, students can engage in paddleboard/beach clean-up days, trips to San Francisco for the "Poetry Crawl," and excursions to Yosemite for the annual spring waterfall trip.

"The professors at SNC have really shown me how much I can accomplish. Through their support, I have become a better student than I ever thought I could be."

– Deidre Wolff '18, Biology

www.sierranevada.edu
(866) 412-4636
admissions@
sierranevada.edu

STUDENT PROFILE

448 undergraduate students

92% of undergrad students are full-time

45% female – 55% male

68% freshman retention rate

FACULTY PROFILE

10 to 1 student/faculty ratio

ADMISSIONS

Selectivity: 69%

SAT Ranges: E 460-560, M 450-580

ACT Ranges: C 19-24, M 17-24, E 19-23

TUITION & COST

Tuition: $31,685

Fees: $954

Room & Board: $12,764

RIVIER UNIVERSITY

NASHUA, NEW HAMPSHIRE

One of the most affordable universities in the region, Rivier University offers more than 50 distinctive degree programs. The University prides itself on its small classes led by accomplished faculty who create an active, experiential learning environment. At the heart of the Rivier experience are Catholic values. Founded in 1933 by the Sisters of the Presentation of Mary, Rivier University is a Catholic institution committed to its mission of transforming hearts and minds to serve the world.

FIRST-YEAR SEMINAR & EXPERIENCES: In Rivier's core curriculum, *Journeys of Transformation*, students explore challenging questions: Who am I? Who is my neighbor? What is the world? How shall I live? What shall I do? Opportunities for service-learning, servant leadership, civic engagement, or community service are incorporated throughout the core to support the intellectual growth of students and enhance student leadership.

FACILITIES: The facilities on Rivier's campus benefit students of all majors. Housed in the Education Center, the Landry Early Childhood Center offers on-campus day care, preschool, and kindergarten programs. Rivier students can use the facility to observe children in their early stages of development.

The University's Nursing Center offers a complete Simulation Lab and teaching facilities. Also on campus are laboratories for other disciplines, including the sciences, computer technology, psychology, and writing. Additionally, business students can track real-time global financial data in the McLean Center for Finance and Economics.

EMPLOYMENT PROMISE: Students graduate from Rivier University, ready to think critically, act ethically, and communicate precisely in visual, oral, and quantitative formats.

Confident in the quality of its educational experience, Rivier offers students an Employment Promise Program. The University promises invested students that they will secure a full-time job within nine months of graduation. If they do not, they will receive additional financial or educational support.

www.rivier.edu
admissions@rivier.edu

STUDENT PROFILE

1,426 undergraduate students

64% of undergrad students are full-time

81% female – 19% male

81% of students are from out of state

73% freshman retention rate

FACULTY PROFILE

13 to 1 student/faculty ratio

ADMISSIONS

Selectivity: 68%

TUITION & COST

Tuition: $29,990

Fees: $1,100

Room: $6,490

Board: $5,678

UNIVERSITY OF NEW HAMPSHIRE

DURHAM, NEW HAMPSHIRE

University of New Hampshire

www.unh.edu
(603) 862-1360
admissions@unh.edu

The University of New Hampshire brings together the benefits of a smaller school educational experience with bigger school perks like research and fieldwork. Students are encouraged to give back to the community through shared and applied interdisciplinary knowledge.

THE WASHINGTON CENTER INTERNSHIP: University of New Hampshire has for a long time sustained a relationship with the Washington Center. Through this affiliation, students have the opportunity to intern with one of the many businesses in Washington D.C. There are internships available across most disciplines, and participants work in government agencies, think tanks, major corporations, and more!

DAILY WALK-IN WORKSHOPS: The Advising and Career Center is an awesome resource available to all students. The center hosts daily walk-in workshops that focus on a specific skill or topic related to career-building. No appointment is necessary, and UNH encourages all students to drop by and see what the center has to offer. Some of the topics include: Starting Your Résumé, Internships and Job Shadowing, LinkedIn 101, and Career Fair Prep.

DISCOVERY: *Discovery*, the core curriculum at University of New Hampshire, exposes students to a range of disciplines and topics. By the time students graduate, they will have studied everything from humanities to physical and biological sciences.

Discovery also equips students with valuable skills like problem solving, critical thinking, effective inquiry, polished writing skills, and higher-level conceptualization. Within the core curriculum, there are certain requirements that each student must satisfy before they can receive their degree, one of which includes Inquiry 444.

Inquiry 444 is the study of one topic from many different perspectives. No matter the topic, Inquiry pushs students to expand their horizons and consider more than one interpretation of a subject or issue.

STUDENT PROFILE

13,005 undergraduate students

97% of undergrad students are full-time

55% female – 45% male

58% of students are from out of state

86% freshman retention rate

FACULTY PROFILE

18 to 1 student/faculty ratio

ADMISSIONS

Selectivity: 77%

SAT Ranges: E 540-630, M 530-630

ACT Ranges: C 23-28, M 22-27, E 22-28

TUITION & COST

Tuition (in-state): $14,770

Tuition (out-of-state): $29,340

Fees: $3,297

Room: $7,024

Board: $4,860

CALDWELL UNIVERSITY

CALDWELL, NEW JERSEY

Beautiful, affordable, and equipped with nationally accredited programs, Caldwell University is the only Dominican college in New Jersey and one of only 19 Catholic colleges in the U.S. that are guided in the tradition of St. Dominic. With one of the lowest private college tuitions in New Jersey, and significant financial assistance offered to 90% of students, a Caldwell University education is a great value!

HEALTH EDUCATION: Caldwell's Inter-Professional Health Education collaborative provides new programs in the health professions, including B.S. degrees in Public Health Education, Health Science, and Healthcare Administration. These programs, as well as the B.S. in Nursing, offer students exciting new career opportunities in one of the fastest growing job markets.

Many unique combined programs in medicine, veterinary medicine, dentistry, occupational or physical therapy, and athletic training are also offered.

HIGH-QUALITY FACILITIES: Recent campus improvements continue to enhance all aspects of student life. Additional dorm space accommodates recent growth; a new CARES center acts as a one-stop for student needs; and a Learning Commons offers students a technology-oriented collaboration center in which to excel throughout their course work.

A campus-wide technology transformation is in full force with new tools for 3D printing, engaging 360-video, technology-infused learning environments, and a quadrupled Wi-Fi footprint.

"Caldwell University has quickly become a haven for my growth as a student as well as an adult. The faculty, staff, and student body fosters an environment of development and acceptance. I am excited to be able to call Caldwell my home today and for years to come!"

– Christopher Lepore, Class of 2020, Communications and Media Studies

www.caldwell.edu
(973) 618-3500
admissions@caldwell.edu

STUDENT PROFILE

1,603 undergraduate students

90% of undergrad students are full-time

68% female – 32% male

7% of students are from out of state

84% freshman retention rate

FACULTY PROFILE

12 to 1 student/faculty ratio

ADMISSIONS

Selectivity: 64%

SAT Ranges: E 470-570, M 460-580

ACT Ranges: C 17-22, M 17-24, E 15-22

TUITION & COST

Tuition: $32,250

Fees: $1,700

Room & Board: $12,300

COLLEGE OF SAINT ELIZABETH

MORRISTOWN, NEW JERSEY

COLLEGE OF
Saint Elizabeth
MORRISTOWN, NJ

The College of Saint Elizabeth (CSE) is a community of learning in the Catholic liberal arts tradition for students of diverse ages, backgrounds, and cultures focused on engaged learning for leadership in service to others. CSE was established almost 120 years ago as the state's first four-year Catholic college for women. The College became fully co-educational at the undergraduate level in 2016. CSE is devoted to preparing responsible leaders for meaningful lives in a changing world and is committed to providing a superior educational experience that is also affordable.

ENCOURAGING THE ARTS: The Annunciation Center is home to the Dolan Performance Hall and the Therese A. Maloney Art Gallery, both of which host numerous art exhibitions, concerts, dance performances, and other events throughout the year.

The outdoor Greek Theatre, built in 1932 as a recreation of the Theater of Dionysius in Athens, hosts performances every summer in collaboration with the Shakespeare Theatre of New Jersey.

SERVICE-LEARNING: Service is a vital aspect of CSE's culture. Through a grant from the Campus Kitchens Project, CSE helps develop innovative solutions to local food insecurity. Students collect unused food from the dining hall, as well as augmented donations by community organizations, and create frozen meals for local organizations that serve the hungry.

The College's mentoring program pairs undergraduates with seasoned professionals to support their transition from student to employee. Managed through CSE's Experiential Learning Center, mentors and mentees communicate monthly for at least two semesters.

SCHOOL LOCATION: Located on 200 beautiful acres that overlook the Watchung Mountains in Morris County, CSE is a suburban campus located just 35 miles from New York City, which can be accessed by a convenient train station at the edge of the campus.

www.cse.edu
(800) 210-7900
apply@cse.edu

STUDENT PROFILE

497 undergraduate students

99% of undergrad students are full-time

75% female – 25% male

7% of students are from out of state

68% freshman retention rate

FACULTY PROFILE

9 to 1 student/faculty ratio

ADMISSIONS

Selectivity: 65%

SAT Ranges: E 400-500, M 390-480

TUITION & COST

Tuition: $31,620

Fees: $1,698

Room & Board: $12,744

GEORGIAN COURT UNIVERSITY

LAKEWOOD, NEW JERSEY

GEORGIAN COURT UNIVERSITY
THE MERCY UNIVERSITY OF NEW JERSEY

Located in Lakewood, NJ, GCU advances a curriculum that is broad enough to be truly liberal, yet specialized enough to provide in-depth preparation for careers or further study. As part of its mission, GCU devotes significant academic and financial resources to serving high-need, underserved students, many of whom are the first in their family to attend college. GCU offers a nurturing campus environment with individualized attention and guidance, centered on the core Mercy values of respect, integrity, justice, compassion, and service.

MERCY COLLEGIATE SOCIETY (MCS): The Mercy Collegiate Society, the sponoring organization of GCU, engages college students in the charism and work of Catherine McAuley, the foundress of the Sisters of Mercy. This group is based on four pillars: social networking, service to the local and global community, the deepening of the spiritual dimension of the person, and engaging in the purest form of leadership: servitude.

COIL PROGRAM: Through the Collaborative Online International Learning (COIL) program, an extension of the Office of Global Education, faculty members integrate a globally networked learning component into existing courses, connecting with other parts of the world (and with students abroad) for such international online components as global peer reflections on shared readings, debates and/or discussions, collaborative project work, etc.

CHART THE COURSE: GCU's unique Chart the Course program assists at-risk students who need to fulfill general education credits by offering them free courses during the winter and summer terms.

"At GCU, I flourished and gained the competence and confidence to chase and catch my dreams—all while finding my true north. That is the impact that Georgian Court University has had on my life." *– Floyd Barnett III, M.B.A. '08, Director, Global Pricing and Business Transformation*

www.georgian.edu
(732) 987-2700
admissions@georgian.edu

STUDENT PROFILE

1,447 undergraduate students

93% of undergrad students are full-time

74% female – 26% male

6% of students are from out of state

72% freshman retention rate

FACULTY PROFILE

12 to 1 student/faculty ratio

ADMISSIONS

Selectivity: 69%

SAT Ranges: E 460-570, M 450-550

ACT Ranges: C 17-22, M 16-18, E 15-24

TUITION & COST

Tuition: $30,800

Fees: $1,460

Room: $5,404

Board: $5,404

KEAN UNIVERSITY

UNION, NEW JERSEY

Global learning, active faculty, and a welcoming environment make Kean University a fantastic place for students to expand their worldview as leaders. A national leader in diversity and the only public American university with a campus in China, Kean is uniquely suited to help students of all backgrounds succeed while exploring the world. Career planning, advising, and even coursework are done with input from experts from across campus, ensuring the most up-to-date and effective programs possible.

CHINA AND BEYOND: The cornerstone of international study at Kean is Wenzhou-Kean University, the only China campus of any public American university. Wenzhou-Kean offers students the opportunity to study in this full-fledged university environment at the same price of the Kean home campus in New Jersey. Other study abroad options include semester, summer, and year-round travel as well as short faculty-led 'Travelearn' trips that supplement traditional courses with global exploration.

CAREER SERVICES: Kean's Career Services is a campus-wide, coordinated effort to ensure students are planning for the future from the moment they set foot on campus. Each college has its own assistant director of Career Services, which ensures that every student has a career counselor who truly understands the ins and outs of their academic and career path.

Career planning is integrated into the curriculum, with the first-year seminar content designed to keep students looking to the future. Career activities are spread out throughout the four years on campus, with events, coursework, and personalized advising available to every student.

LEADERSHIP AND SERVICE: Through the Leadership Institute, students can develop their leadership skills through a stream of service that culminates in a special certification. At each level—Bronze, Silver, Gold, and Platinum—students grow close to their cohort, learn what it means to be service oriented, and focus on all aspects of modern leadership. They can even track their service ion a co-curricular transcript, which reflects everything they've done outside the classroom for employers and graduate programs to see.

www.kean.edu
(908) 737-7100
admitme@kean.edu

STUDENT PROFILE

11,984 undergraduate students

79% of undergrad students are full-time

60% female — 40% male

3% of students are from out of state

76% freshman retention rate

FACULTY PROFILE

17 to 1 student/faculty ratio

ADMISSIONS

Selectivity: 82%

SAT Ranges: E 440-540, M 440-530

ACT Ranges: C 16-22

TUITION & COST

Tuition (in-state): $7,909

Tuition (out-of-state): $14,811

Fees: $4,198

Room: $10,227

Board: $3,286

MONMOUTH UNIVERSITY

WEST LONG BRANCH, NEW JERSEY

Monmouth University is just one mile from the beach, which means that, when the wind blows west, the smell of the ocean air washes over campus. The Hawk family is a tight-knit community that offers students guidance and support. A phrase that sums up this closeness is often heard around campus and at the Division I athletic games: *"Hawks fly together."*

TRANSFORMATIVE TEN: Designed to help students connect their major to prospective career options, the Transformative Ten (T10) is a series of ten events that prepare students for life after Monmouth. This initiative is a direct response to student demand for exploring majors and career opportunities, including activities to develop student leadership, communication, problem-solving, teamwork, digital literacy, and networking.

Students who attend at least three T10 events during the academic year are invited to a capstone luncheon that features a keynote speaker with incredible insight on employment and industry trends.

GLOBAL LEARNING: Monmouth faculty integrate a variety of service-learning experiences into the on-campus curriculum to highlight such global issues as food security, migration, community health, and education access. Whether they study abroad or take unique courses designed by Monmouth professors, students are sure to hone their intercultural competencies through service and scholarship.

"Monmouth provided me with the opportunity to do field research not only in the US, but in the Bahamas as well. We snorkeled almost on a daily basis and got to experience sustainable living. Monmouth helped me to establish friendships and professional connections with both students and professors that are imperative to my future."

– Arturo Romua, 2013

MONMOUTH UNIVERSITY

www.monmouth.edu
(732) 571-3456
admission@
monmouth.edu

STUDENT PROFILE

4,704 undergraduate students

96% of undergrad students are full-time

58% female – 42% male

17% of students are from out of state

79% freshman retention rate

FACULTY PROFILE

13 to 1 student/faculty ratio

ADMISSIONS

Selectivity: 74%

SAT Ranges: E 490-600, M 480-590

ACT Ranges: C 19-26

TUITION & COST

Tuition: $37,438

Fees: $700

Room: $7,986

Board: $5,995

RAMAPO COLLEGE

MAHWAH, NEW JERSEY

www.ramapo.edu
(201) 684-7300
admissions@ramapo.edu

Ramapo College of New Jersey is sometimes mistaken for a private college. This is, in part, due to its unique interdisciplinary academic structure, its size of approximately 6,000 students, and its pastoral setting in the foothills of the Ramapo Mountains on the New Jersey/New York border. The College's mission is focused on the four "pillars" of a Ramapo education—international, intercultural, interdisciplinary, and experiential—all of which are incorporated throughout the curricula and extracurriculars.

STUDENT ENGAGEMENT PROJECT: Ramapo College offers a comprehensive Student Engagement Project, which lasts the duration of a student's undergraduate studies at RCNJ.

One of the "Key Points of Engagement," as they are known at Ramapo College, is a structured opportunity for first-year students to have substantive out of class interaction with peers, faculty, staff; a common experience that deepens understanding of self or others; or an opportunity to connect in- and out-of-class learning.

INTERNSHIPS: Ramapo College students participate in a wide variety of internships and co-op programs to gain valuable career experience during their academic career at RCNJ. Area corporations that provide opportunities for Ramapo College students to pursue internships include TD Bank, Sharp Electronics Corporation, Pearson Education Corporation, WNET-TV, BMW North America, Mercedes-Benz North America, Stryker, and area hospitals.

Due to the College's proximity to New York City, internships abound. In fact, 250 companies in New York City alone offer internships to Ramapo College students in addition to opportunities in NJ and NY State.

SCHOOL LOCATION: Ramapo College is located in Mahwah, NJ, just a bus ride from Manhattan. The Palisades Center Mall is located just 20 minutes away in West Nyack, while outdoor lovers will enjoy the Ramapo Mountain Reservation in Mahwah and Harriman State Park in Harriman, NY. There truly is something for everyone near Ramapo College.

STUDENT PROFILE

5,262 undergraduate students

91% of undergrad students are full-time

55% female – 45% male

4% of students are from out of state

88% freshman retention rate

FACULTY PROFILE

16 to 1 student/faculty ratio

ADMISSIONS

Selectivity: 63%

SAT Ranges: E 530-610, M 520-620

ACT Ranges: C 21-26, M 18-26, E 21-26.5

TUITION & COST

Tuition (in-state): $11,902

Tuition (out-of-state): $21,243

Fees: $2,472

Room: $8,650

Board: $3,800

RIDER UNIVERSITY

LAWRENCEVILLE, NEW JERSEY

www.rider.edu
(609) 896-5042
admissions@rider.edu

For more than 150 years, students have chosen Rider to develop the knowledge, skills and confidence needed for career success or to pursue advanced study. Rider students are connected by a desire to make a difference as members of a global community that begins on campus and extends around the world.

MULTICULTURAL LEADERSHIP INSTITUTE: Rider is a welcoming community. The Multicultural Student Leadership Institute (MSLI) celebrates student diversity in all forms—from nationality, ethnicity, and age, to gender and sexual orientation, religious beliefs, marital status, and disabilities. MSLI's semester-long program helps students transition to Rider and develop essential leadership skills so their voice and perspective can be heard.

REBOVICH INSTITUTE FOR NEW JERSEY POLITICS: Every year, the Rebovich Institute hosts a series of campus events that bring leading state and national political figures to campus. Dedicated to public service and the scholarly analysis of government, public policy, and elections in New Jersey, the Institute also coordinates political internships through which students can network and gain experience.

SHADOW EXPERIENCE: Through a special partnership with Rider alumni and area community business leaders, students majoring in the liberal arts and sciences can spend 25 hours in a professional setting related to their career interest while developing valuable networking connections with a mentor and others in the field.

"A Rider education is unique; it might be a small school, but the opportunities are huge. The focus is on learning and hands-on experiences. From day one I was involved...Rider doesn't waste your time."

– *Mary-Lyn Buckley '18, Summer Intern, WABC-TV Eyewitness News, NYC*

STUDENT PROFILE

3,830 undergraduate students

92% of undergrad students are full-time

58% female – 42% male

23% of students are from out of state

78% freshman retention rate

FACULTY PROFILE

10 to 1 student/faculty ratio

ADMISSIONS

Selectivity: 10%

SAT Ranges: E 500-600, M 500-590

ACT Ranges: C 20-25, M 18-24, E 20-25

TUITION & COST

Tuition: $42,120

Fees: $740

Room: $10,020

Board: $5,260

RUTGERS UNIVERSITY-NEWARK

NEWARK, NEW JERSEY

Rutgers University-Newark is a leading urban research university in Newark, New Jersey. Rutgers-Newark's diverse student body uses their time on campus for community and self-improvement. With more than 40 majors, premier faculty and staff, and a location both within a major urban center and near several more, Rutgers-Newark gives students the tools to become successful professionals and engaged citizens.

GLOBAL LEARNING: Rutgers-Newark offers more than 180 programs on six continents for students interested in expanding their worldview beyond Newark. Students can go for a few weeks or an entire semester, and some programs include service-learning elements through which participants can learn by doing in communities across the globe.

IN AND OF NEWARK: Rutgers University-Newark is an anchor for the entire Newark area, allowing students the chance to learn and live in the cultural center of New Jersey. Newark is a home for the arts, sports, and cultural and historical centers.

INTERNSHIPS: Rutgers-Newark offers students several opportunities to take their learning beyond the classroom through experiential learning. The Career Development Center will help students in their job search, giving them the resources to land a high-quality internship. More service-oriented students can work with the Office of University-Community Partnerships to find a nonprofit or community service opportunity that provides the chance to learn, grow, and give back.

"I am very grateful to be spending my college years at an institution that fosters success in its students. As a scholarship recipient, I am humbled to be given the opportunity to excel in such a rich environment. If I had not come to Rutgers University-Newark I would not be where I am now." – *Ahmed Bendary, Biology '15*

www.newark.rutgers.edu
(973) 353-5205
newark@
admissions.rutgers.edu

STUDENT PROFILE

8,551 undergraduate students

84% of undergrad students are full-time

55% female – 45% male

2% of students are from out of state

84% freshman retention rate

FACULTY PROFILE

15 to 1 student/faculty ratio

ADMISSIONS

Selectivity: 64%

SAT Ranges: E 500-580, M 510-590

TUITION & COST

Tuition (in-state): $11,619

Tuition (out-of-state): $27,560

Fees: $2,466

Room: $8,216

Board: $5,050

SETON HALL UNIVERSITY

SOUTH ORANGE, NEW JERSEY

Seton Hall offers superior opportunities for career development before and after graduation. More than 75 percent of students participate in an internship, practicum, or clinical program to gain professional experience, and the university boasts an international alumni network more than 70,000 strong. The university combines the resources of a large university with the personal attention of a small liberal arts college. Its attractive suburban campus is only 14 miles by train, bus, or car to New York City.

AWARD-WINNING MOBILE COMPUTING PROGRAM: Offering a completely wireless campus, Seton Hall's award-winning Mobile Computing Program provides all incoming, full-time freshmen with a brand-new, fully loaded laptop.

Incoming freshmen receive their laptops the summer before they enter Seton Hall, giving them the opportunity to become part of the Seton Hall community as early as freshman orientation. The laptops also allow faculty to integrate technology and cutting-edge learning into the classroom.

STATE-OF-THE-ART TECHNOLOGY AND FACILITIES: Seton Hall places a major emphasis on the use of state-of-the-art technology and facilities, such as the trading room at the Stillman School of Business and Sim Man, a portable and advanced patient simulator for College of Nursing students.

Students can also get involved in the award-winning radio station WSOU, produce their own programming on Pirate TV, or get hands-on experience conducting focus groups in the new Market Research Center.

SERVICE AND EXPERIENTIAL LEARNING: Every Seton Hall undergraduate student participates in at least one community service/volunteer project, and many students also participate in a career-based experiential education program prior to graduation.

Career-based experiences include student teaching, clinicals, practica, field placements, and internship experiences.

www.shu.edu
(973) 313-6146
thehall@shu.edu

STUDENT PROFILE

5,969 undergraduate students

93% of undergrad students are full-time

54% female – 46% male

29% of students are from out of state

85% freshman retention rate

FACULTY PROFILE

14 to 1 student/faculty ratio

ADMISSIONS

Selectivity: 73%

SAT Ranges: E 570-640, M 570-640

ACT Ranges: C 24-28, M 23-27, E 23-29

TUITION & COST

Tuition: $38,400

Fees: $2,188

Room: $9,560

Board: $5,614

STEVENS INSTITUTE OF TECHNOLOGY

HOBOKEN, NEW JERSEY

www.stevens.edu
(201) 216-5194
admissions@stevens.edu

Since its founding in 1870, Stevens Institute of Technology has made a steadfast commitment to innovation and research. A community of practice, and an institution of action, Stevens Institute of Technology continues to defend its reputation as a leader of research in the fields of technology, engineering, financial systems, healthcare, and environmental sustainability.

REAL-WORLD READINESS: From the beginning, new students are afforded a first-year course in entrepreneurial thinking that gives them an early introduction to the complexities of innovation. Through the course, students conceive of new ideas and services, interact with experienced marketing professionals, learn strategy and finance, and finally present their projects to their professor and fellow students.

The entrepreneurial mindset continues throughout all four years of college; a majority of students conclude their senior year with a Senior Design Project, a collaborative effort to plan and present new initiatives to a panel of professionals. Some projects have the potential to get picked up and created as real startups.

CAREER CENTER: The Stevens Career Center helps make success a reality for students and alumni. Staff members provide personalized guidance to each student upon their arrival as a freshman and all the way through to graduation.

These Career Advisors help students decide what classes to take for their professional goals and map out a personalized course of action for their future. And thanks to its strong and proud network of alumni, Stevens runs an Externship Program that enables freshmen to spend their winter break shadowing an alum.

STUDENT PROFILE

3,123 undergraduate students

100% of undergrad students are full-time

30% female – 70% male

34% of students are from out of state

94% freshman retention rate

FACULTY PROFILE

10 to 1 student/faculty ratio

ADMISSIONS

Selectivity: 44%

SAT Ranges: E 640-710, M 680-760

ACT Ranges: C 29-33, M 28-33, E 27-34

TUITION & COST

Tuition: $48,784

Fees: $1,770

Room: $8,000

Board: $6,400

THE COLLEGE OF NEW JERSEY

EWING TOWNSHIP, NEW JERSEY

The College of New Jersey is on a mission to keep the most talented students from NJ within their home state for their college education. The College of New Jersey combines the best practices of the finest private institutions with a public mission.

WINTER AND SUMMER PROGRAMS: Throughout the winter and summer sessions, faculty lead TCNJ students on intensive study abroad experiences to extend their fields of study beyond the home campus and into various destinations around the world. These short-term programs allow faculty to have their students focus intensely on one topic, all while guiding them along the journey of a lifetime.

BONNER INSTITUTE: TCNJ's Bonner Institute for Civic and Community Engagement is responsible for connecting students, faculty, and staff to service opportunities both in and outside of the campus. The Institute addresses a wide array of social issues, ranging from poverty to environmental needs.

One component of the program is the Bonner Community Scholars Corps, a small group of highly committed students who receive academic scholarship for their engagement. Scholars are also responsible for motivating the campus community to get involved.

THE HONORS PROGRAM: The TCNJ Honors program is specially designed to challenge academically gifted students. Participants enjoy an intimate community of intellectual leaders and peers, engaging in exciting, advanced coursework in small-class settings. They also benefit from graduate school preparation, access to exclusive fellowship opportunities, and an incredible advantage in the development of their leadership skills.

SCHOOL LOCATION: TCNJ is located in the suburb of Ewing. Students can see shows, hear performances, observe an art gallery, or get involved in the local television and radio stations in the area.

www.tcnj.edu
(609) 771-2131

STUDENT PROFILE

6,955 undergraduate students

97% of undergrad students are full-time

58% female – 42% male

6% of students are from out of state

94% freshman retention rate

FACULTY PROFILE

13 to 1 student/faculty ratio

ADMISSIONS

Selectivity: 48%

SAT Ranges: E 590-660, M 580-670

TUITION & COST

Tuition (in-state): $12,632

Tuition (out-of-state): $24,061

Fees: $3,517

Room: $8,970

Board: $4,231

ADELPHI UNIVERSITY

GARDEN CITY, NEW YORK

Adelphi University provides students with a personalized education that fully prepares them for successful, fulfilling careers. Internships, many of them paid, are central to an Adelphi education and help students refine their career objectives, make connections, and gain work experience.Welcoming one of its most diverse classes ever in the fall of 2019, Adelphi has students from 41 states and 58 countries, providing an environment that encourages cultural and personal growth.

GLOBAL LEARNING: Levermore Global Scholars (LGS) is a program of distinction designed to enrich both the social and international dimensions of a college education. Adelphi's nongovernmental organization status allows students to attend special briefings at the United Nations; three-quarters of these students participate in special activities with the U.N. each year.

LGS students have studied globalization while traveling in China, immersed themselves in sustainability in Costa Rica, visited schools to better understand education's role in Cuba, and explored issues of conflict transformation and the arts in Kosovo.

SENIOR CAPSTONE: Adelphi is relentlessly dedicated to fostering the success of its students in college and beyond. All Adelphi undergraduates complete a capstone course or project as part of their major.

Depending on the major, these may include portfolios of creative projects, senior seminars, and significant research papers and projects. The goal is to give students the opportunity to demonstrate their learning in a comprehensive and meaningful way.

> "I have the latitude to be as inventive and creative as I want to be in the classroom."
>
> – *Salvatore Primeggia '64, M.A. '66, Ph.D., professor of sociology*

www.adelphi.edu
(516) 877-3039
admissions@adelphi.edu

STUDENT PROFILE
5,307 undergraduate students

95% of undergrad students are full-time

69% female – 31% male

7% of students are from out of state

81% freshman retention rate

FACULTY PROFILE
12 to 1 student/faculty ratio

ADMISSIONS
Selectivity: 74%

SAT Ranges: E 540-630, M 540-640

ACT Ranges: C 22-27, M 20-27, E 21-27

TUITION & COST
Tuition: $36,920

Fees: $1,740

Room: $10,510

Board: $5,520

BARUCH COLLEGE - CITY UNIVERSITY OF NEW YORK

NEW YORK, NEW YORK

Baruch College is a diverse and inclusive campus in the heart of New York City. With three colleges, 29 majors, and a student body representing 160 countries, Baruch offers a space for people of all interests and backgrounds. Baruch leverages its Big Apple location and incredible diversity to offer students an experience that broadens their worldview and prepares them for any and all career paths. Students can explore their academic interests, travel the world, and plan their next step.

THE BARUCH PATHWAY: A modern core curriculum requires flexibility, and Baruch College students enjoy the option to chart their own course through Pathways at Baruch. After getting the basics in math, science, and English, students complete the flexible core, which works to expand each student's worldview by offering courses in several areas. Students are exposed to courses on Creative Expression, U.S. and global cultures, the sciences, and philosophy and ethics.

LEADERSHIP TRAINING: At Baruch, students are welcomed to improve their leadership skills in a variety of ways. Every active member of a school-affiliated club participates in a series of leadership activities based on the "Social Change Model," which explores what it means to be a leader and how anyone can enact social change. Students looking to go deeper into their development as leaders can participate in T.E.A.M. Baruch, which qualifies participants to work as paid peer mentors who guide and support new students.

DIVERSITY AND GLOBAL LEARNING: Baruch College is one of the most ethnically diverse campuses in the nation, which Baruch celebrates and expands upon through study abroad and other cultural enrichment programs. Interested students can expand their worldview through the Global Student Certificate, a year-long co-curricular program that teaches Baruch students how to work in multicultural settings, improve their communication skills, and access cultural events across New York City.

www.baruch.cuny.edu
(646) 312-1000

STUDENT PROFILE

15,253 undergraduate students

76% of undergrad students are full-time

49% female – 51% male

3% of students are from out of state

90% freshman retention rate

FACULTY PROFILE

19 to 1 student/faculty ratio

ADMISSIONS

Selectivity: 29%

SAT Ranges: E 580-660, M 610-690

TUITION & COST

Tuition (in-state): $6,530

Tuition (out-of-state): $13,920

Fees: $532

Room & Board: $14,594

BINGHAMTON UNIVERSITY

BINGHAMTON, NEW YORK

Binghamton offers a wide array of personal and academic opportunities that range from international education to research initiatives. The University's commitment to student success is of paramount importance, and students are given the tools they need to excel and make a difference.

OUTDOOR PURSUITS: Outdoor Pursuits is all about getting students outside and excited about physical activity. Students partake in outdoor adventures and learn about the importance of conservation and environmental education. Students are involved in service-learning efforts, team-building exercises, and physical activity.

EMERGING LEADERS PROGRAM: The Emerging Leaders Program (ELP) is a program dedicated to enriching students' drive for leadership development. This certificate program spans over the course of a semester and connects students with the University and community as a whole, opening up the possibilities for them to take action and take charge.

All students who participate in ELP will be part of a knowledge community (KC) comprised of approximately 13 students. KCs are led by a faculty advisor, a professional staff program advisor, and peer mentors. ELP students are involved in a series of activities that promote success. They gain experience with networking and bolster their skills in interactive leadership workshops.

INVOLVEMENT TRANSCRIPT: Binghamton's Involvement Transcript keeps a record of each one of a student's extracurricular activities during college. By the time they graduate, students already have a comprehensive summary of their involvement, helping them show employers how they spent their free time.

Being active outside of the classroom is a great way to show potential as a hard-working employee. Every student can keep a record of their activities on B-engaged, a student portal for tracking events, to show off their participation as a leader, volunteer, of member of an organization.

BINGHAMTON UNIVERSITY
STATE UNIVERSITY OF NEW YORK

www.binghamton.edu
(607) 777-2171
admit@binghamton.edu

STUDENT PROFILE

13,737 undergraduate students

97% of undergrad students are full-time

49% female – 51% male

5% of students are from out of state

91% freshman retention rate

FACULTY PROFILE

19 to 1 student/faculty ratio

ADMISSIONS

Selectivity: 40%

SAT Ranges: E 640-711, M 650-720

ACT Ranges: C 28-31

TUITION & COST

Tuition (in-state): $6,670

Tuition (out-of-state): $21,550

Fees: $2,853

Room: $9,567

Board: $5,010

CANISIUS COLLEGE

BUFFALO, NEW YORK

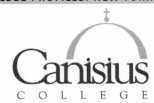

Canisius students receive a transformational education. They work with professors on world-changing research projects, participate in a rigorous academic curriculum, and actively create a better community on both a local and global scale. The College is not just a place from which to earn a degree, but rather a haven for success and true education. Students who are fascinated by the world and curious about their place in it are bound to thrive at Canisius.

UNLIMITED POSSIBILITIES: At Canisius, students can choose from more than 125 majors, minors, and special programs, enjoying a flexible curriculum that can be catered to their overall goals. Dual and even triple majors are encouraged, the combinations of which range from mainstream to ingenious.

Inspired students have mixed digital media arts with psychology, music with political science, biology with studio art, and English with European studies and international business.

LIFE-CHANGING COURSES: Canisius professors are remarkably visionary, inventing exceptionally innovative courses that the College supports with special funding.

Just a few examples that typical of the extraordinary Peter Canisius Distinguished Professorships include "The Holocaust in History, Literature, and Film;" "The Native American Experience in Their Own Words and in Their Own Ways;" and "Christianity on the Road Less Traveled."

CANISIUS ABROAD: Sure, most colleges offer study in foreign countries, but at Canisius the experiences are both varied and exceptional.

A couple of examples include interning with Parliament in London and teaching English to school kids in Poland, France, or China. Some students can even extend their stay in Europe through their participation in EuroSim, an international competition that simulates the European Union.

www.canisius.edu
(716) 888-2200
admissions@canisius.edu

STUDENT PROFILE

2,398 undergraduate students

96% of undergrad students are full-time

50% female – 50% male

13% of students are from out of state

83% freshman retention rate

FACULTY PROFILE

11 to 1 student/faculty ratio

ADMISSIONS

Selectivity: 78%

SAT Ranges: E 520-630, M 520-630

ACT Ranges: C 22-28, M 23-28, E 22-28

TUITION & COST

Tuition: $34,966

Fees: $1,488

Room: $7,764

Board: $5,454

COLLEGE OF MOUNT SAINT VINCENT

RIVERDALE, NEW YORK

COLLEGE OF MOUNT SAINT VINCENT

The College of Mount Saint Vincent seeks to engage the development of the whole person. Every field of study emphasizes analytical skills; critical thinking; clear communication; and moral and religious thought. The Mount offers over 70 nationally recognized degree programs and course offerings, including majors and minors in the sciences and mathematics, humanities and the arts, social sciences, accounting, business, communication, education, and nursing, among others.

PUBLIC POLICY RESEARCH: The Fishlinger Center for Public Policy Research allows students, faculty, and other members of the academic community to conduct comprehensive studies and analyze public opinion on key policy concerns. Through independent and objective research, scholars in the Fishlinger Center enhance the relationship between the work of the College and the common good.

OUTSIDE THE CLASSROOM: From its academic, cultural, and professional institutions to its history and the dynamics of its diverse population, New York offers countless and unparalleled ways to enrich an education.

For example, accounting, business, and economics students visit the floor of the New York Stock Exchange; visual arts students complete outdoor photography tours throughout Manhattan and Brooklyn; and biology students conduct ecological studies in the Hudson River and Van Cortlandt Park in the Bronx.

"The Mount offers a lot of opportunities for students to unleash their energies and skills. I like to think that Mount students don't wait for things to happen—they make things happen." *- Teresita Ramirez, Associate Professor of Business and Economics*

mountsaintvincent.edu
(718) 405-3267
admissions@
mountsaintvincent.edu

STUDENT PROFILE

1,695 undergraduate students

95% of undergrad students are full-time

69% female – 31% male

72% freshman retention rate

FACULTY PROFILE

13 to 1 student/faculty ratio

ADMISSIONS

Selectivity: 91%

SAT Ranges: E 450-540, M 430-520

ACT Ranges: C 18-22, M 16-21, E 16-21

TUITION & COST

Tuition: $35,620

Fees: $1,480

Room & Board: $9,500

CONCORDIA COLLEGE NEW YORK

BRONXVILLE, NEW YORK

Founded in 1881, Concordia College New York is a 4-year, private, liberal arts, Christian-based college located in suburban Westchester County, New York. Concordia aspires to enhance the lives of students by weaving together academics, vibrant student life, experiential learning opportunities, co-curricular programs, and campus spiritual life into a tapestry of lifelong learning.

BRONXVILLE: Concordia's beautiful, residential campus is set in the tranquil village of Bronxville. The century-old campus features nearly 30 buildings, including original "College Gothic" structures designed by the architect who designed Ellis Island, a world-class worship and performance hall, a state-of-the-art academic center and library, on-and-off campus residence halls, and awesome athletic facilities, all set in immaculately landscaped grounds.

Bronxville is one square mile in size and is home to 7,000 inhabitants including diplomats, corporate executives, bankers, lawyers, and a wide range of other professionals. From the Bronxville train station, it is 30 minutes to Grand Central Station in the heart of New York City.

FACULTY WHO CARE: Students can expect nothing but the best from professors. Faculty are accomplished scholars and researchers dedicated to the student's experience rather than their own. 75% of faculty holds the highest possible degree.

ACROSS DSICIPLINES: The curriculum at Concordia College New York is ideal for students interested in interdisciplinary or cross-disciplinary education. Concordia students encounter a community where questions are as important as answers.

With a curriculum where all fields of knowledge intersect, they gain real-world experiences that alter the course of their lives. The school's liberal arts philosophy is built on the history of human experience, supporting a Christian community in which the multicolored fabric of diversity thrives.

www.concordia-ny.edu
(800) 937-2655
admission@
concordia-ny.edu

STUDENT PROFILE

1,129 undergraduate students

91% of undergrad students are full-time

74% female – 26% male

16% of students are from out of state

76% freshman retention rate

FACULTY PROFILE

11 to 1 student/faculty ratio

ADMISSIONS

Selectivity: 76%

SAT Ranges: E 480-560, M 450-580

ACT Ranges: C 18-24, M 17-23, E 17-23

TUITION & COST

Tuition: $30,250

Fees: $1,350

Room: $6,600

Board: $5,276

DAEMEN COLLEGE

AMHERST, NEW YORK

Distinctively Daemen. Daemen is a student-centered College with dedicated, highly qualified faculty who value personalized teaching and intellectual excellence. The college prepares students for successful careers by offering rigorous academic programs that develop the liberal arts-based skills necessary for lifelong learning and intellectual growth.

STUDENT CENTERED: Daemen's innovative Professional Pathway Program enhances the liberal arts degree with academic and experiential learning opportunities that are fully integrated into the individual curriculum with no additional time or cost.

Through the Pathways, students focus on Core and free electives in an interdisciplinary series of courses that are all designed to prepare them for their future careers. They learn to apply their critical thinking, writing, and communication skills to real-world experiences.

RESEARCH THINK TANK: The Student/Faculty Interdisciplinary Think Tank offers students the opportunity to work with faculty members on significant research projects. Students receive research scholarships and get acknowledged for their work through publications, showings, presentations, or other forms of public recognition.

Many students who participate in research go on to present at national conferences, gaining valuable presentation skills and networking opportunities that provide preparation for graduate school and careers.

"Reaching the achievements on my list has proved to me that Daemen makes things happen. No goal, no dream, is too far out of reach. There are endless amounts of opportunities at your feet; all you have to do is pick them up." – *Emily Buzzard, Social Work BASW/MSW*

www.daemen.edu
(800) 462-7652
admissions@daemen.edu

STUDENT PROFILE

1,712 undergraduate students

87% of undergrad students are full-time

70% female – 30% male

5% of students are from out of state

78% freshman retention rate

FACULTY PROFILE

11 to 1 student/faculty ratio

ADMISSIONS

Selectivity: 54%

SAT Ranges: E 520-610, M 520-620

ACT Ranges: C 21-26

TUITION & COST

Tuition: $28,830

Fees: $600

Room: $9,850

Board: $3,550

DOMINICAN COLLEGE

ORANGEBURG, NEW YORK

Since 1952, Dominican College has provided students with an environment that cultivates unique bonds and life-long relationships. In surveys, students rave about their personal connections to their professors and the family feel of the campus, enjoying their small classes taught by highly regarded faculty. The Dominican College community focuses entirely on students' engagement, success, connections to the community, and preparation to live full and significant lives.

YEAR-ROUND ACTIVITIES: There are many opportunities to become involved in the Dominican College community both on campus and off. Dominican College students participate in Alternate Spring Break in Mississippi to help rebuild damaged communities. They also engage in twice-yearly service trips to the Dominican Republic in which they live with rural families, teach school, and assist in building infrastructure.

"Founders Week" and "Fire in the Sky" in the fall, as well as "Earth Week" in the spring, are traditions that bring the whole College community together. Faculty and staff vs. student softball games, Iron Chef Dominican, poetry slams, dances, and socials are a few other examples of campus activities found in this vibrant living and learning community.

ALUMNI NETWORK: The College's alumni give back to the College community by making themselves available to current students through mentoring, lectures, career round tables, and life-after-college events.

Alumni have gone on to rewarding careers in nursing, physical therapy, occupational therapy, education, government, law, law enforcement, athletic training, management, real estate, culinary arts, banking, advocacy, social work, business, and professional sports (to name just a few).

The Dominican Difference is apparent in the kind of people who come through the College's programs; they are not just good at what they do, but they also contribute to their communities and their world in meaningful ways through their commitment and service.

www.dc.edu
(866) 432-4636
admissions@dc.edu

STUDENT PROFILE
1,425 undergraduate students

89% of undergrad students are full-time

67% female – 33% male

29% of students are from out of state

74% freshman retention rate

FACULTY PROFILE
15 to 1 student/faculty ratio

ADMISSIONS
Selectivity: 69%

SAT Ranges: E 450-540, M 430-540

ACT Ranges: C 17-22

TUITION & COST
Tuition: $27,588

Fees: $860

Room & Board: $12,670

ELMIRA COLLEGE

ELMIRA, NEW YORK

ELMIRA COLLEGE

A national, top-tier liberal arts college founded in 1855, Elmira College is proud of its 160-year reputation for academic distinction. From the very beginning, Elmira has placed its focus on academic rigor. It was, in fact, the first college for women with a course of study equal in rigor to the best men's colleges of the time. Today, as a co-educational institution, Elmira continues that same focus on academic rigor and student opportunities.

TERM III: One of Elmira's unique features is its 6-week Term III in April and May. The College offers many experiential learning opportunities in Term III, allowing students to do immersive and intensive work in a number of different fields (and countries!). This can include student teaching, clinical work, and research.

JULIA REINSTEIN '28 SYMPOSIUM: Each year, the Women's and Gender Studies Program organizes the weeklong Julia Reinstein '28 Symposium, made possible by a bequest from college alumna Julia Reinstein '28, a feminist, early lesbian activist, and strong supporter of women's issues. In cooperation with Students Against Sexism and Stereotypes (SASS), the Symposium annually features a different theme and keynote speaker.

MAJOR ELMIRA LANDMARKS: The City of Elmira was the summer home of American author Mark Twain. The Mark Twain Study, now located on the Elmira College campus, is the study in which the famous author penned Tom Sawyer, Huck Finn, and other iconic works. Quarry Farm, where Twain and his family spent more than 20 summers, now serves as a research center for faculty and international scholars studying Mark Twain's life and works.

www.elmira.edu
(800) 935-6472

STUDENT PROFILE
938 undergraduate students

89% of undergrad students are full-time

71% female – 29% male

65% freshman retention rate

FACULTY PROFILE
10 to 1 student/faculty ratio

ADMISSIONS
Selectivity: 85%

TUITION & COST
Tuition: $41,900

Room: $6,400

Board: $5,600

"There is something about Elmira that is quite unique... Nursing school is difficult...beyond difficult...but to walk into a classroom day after day and have a professor know your name, your story, and what you need to succeed? That makes all the difference." *– Allii Fontaine '15*

FORDHAM UNIVERSITY

BRONX, NEW YORK

Fordham is a laboratory in which to explore deep meaning and true measures of success. It is a place in which to acquire the knowledge, skills, confidence, and experience needed to succeed, regardless of field. Fordham offers the kind of firm foundation and competitive edge that creates successful leaders in the workplace. Its faculty members are scholars who challenge students to reach beyond their perceived limitations and mentors who lend their support and expertise. The Fordham faculty and curriculum educate the whole person.

UNIQUE ACADEMIC OFFERINGS: Special academic offerings include honors programs; study abroad; dual-degree programs with Fordham's graduate schools; and pre-professional programs in law, medicine, and other health professions. Fordham's G.L.O.B.E. international business program combines liberal arts and business courses, ultimately preparing students for multinational careers.

Undergraduate students often collaborate with faculty on original research, and they also work with faculty and staff to prepare to compete for Rhodes and Fulbright scholarships as well as other prestigious fellowships and scholarships.

ENERGETIC STUDENT BODY: More than 143 student organizations offer a remarkable range of programming that capitalizes on the cultural resources of New York City.

Each year, the community-service program gives hundreds of students an opportunity to work together on volunteer projects at dozens of sites in New York City, including soup kitchens, nursing homes, transitional shelters, hospitals, and community parks.

JESUIT EDUCATION: Fordham has a proud history of approaching education in a distinctly Jesuit way, one that emphasizes cura personalis, a commitment to nurturing the whole person—mind, body, and spirit—and challenging students to surpass their perceived limitations.

www.fordham.edu
(800) 367-3426
enroll@fordham.edu

STUDENT PROFILE
9,599 undergraduate students

95% of undergrad students are full-time

58% female — 42% male

55% of students are from out of state

91% freshman retention rate

FACULTY PROFILE
15 to 1 student/faculty ratio

ADMISSIONS
Selectivity: 46%

SAT Ranges: E 620-700, M 610-710

ACT Ranges: C 27-31, M 26-30, E 27-34

TUITION & COST
Tuition: $49,645

Fees: $1,341

Room & Board: $17,445

HARTWICK COLLEGE

ONEONTA, NEW YORK

HARTWICK COLLEGE

At Hartwick, lots of personal attention, growth, and discovery are the norm, not the exception. Hartwick's student/faculty ratio of 10:1 means that professors know students by name, as the average class size is only 15 students. Professors and staff get to know their 1,200 students well, challenging and encouraging them to pursue opportunities they might not have considered on their own. Hartwick's 35 majors include business and nursing as well as six new majors in sustainability, public health, criminal justice, creative writing, global studies, and actuarial mathematics.

PEACE CORPS PREPARATORY PROGRAM: Hartwick is one of only three colleges in New York State—and one of only a few dozen nationwide—to offer a Peace Corps Preparatory Program. In this program, Hartwick students gain meaningful experiences and build the kinds of skills that are sure to make them more competitive when applying as volunteers.

Students in this amazing program are at a competitive advantage when applying to serve in the Peace Corps and other international development organizations.

CENTER FOR CRAFT FOOD & BEVERAGE: Just one other way in which Hartwick provides students with hands-on, real-world experience is through its internships at its very own Center for Craft Food & Beverage. The first and only of its kind in New York State, this Center is designed to be Hartwick's brewing industry resource for quality testing, research, and education. In fact, the Center currently provides support to over 400 breweries, malthouses, distilleries, and farms.

"As a member of Student Senate, I was able to serve on committees with members of the College's Board of Trustees. Through networking and with help from David H. Long '83, CEO of Liberty Mutual, I actually secured a job after graduation!" *- Rachel Griffing '18, Business and Political Science*

www.hartwick.edu
(607) 431-4150
admissions@hartwick.edu

STUDENT PROFILE

1,194 undergraduate students

98% of undergrad students are full-time

59% female – 41% male

20% of students are from out of state

70% freshman retention rate

FACULTY PROFILE

11 to 1 student/faculty ratio

ADMISSIONS

SAT Ranges: E 460-540, M 460-560

ACT Ranges: C 21-26

TUITION & COST

Tuition: $44,650

Fees: $860

Room: $6,460

Board: $6,000

IONA COLLEGE

NEW ROCHELLE, NEW YORK

In the tradition of the Christian Brothers and American Catholic higher education, Iona College is a diverse community of learners and scholars dedicated to academic excellence. Iona's students, faculty, staff, and administrators embody the values of justice, peace, and service. Together, the Iona College community shares a mission to make a positive impact on the lives of others and to move the world.

CHALLENGED TO MOVE THE WORLD: Iona College is one of the most highly accredited institutions in New York with 10 college and program accreditations. Iona has a commitment to combining a career-focused education with a liberal arts curriculum, challenging and preparing students for success.

Throughout students' academic careers, service-learning projects, and internships, they always have someone to encourage and challenge them to move the world.

LAPENTA-LYNCH TRADING FLOOR: The LaPenta-Lynch Trading Floor in the School of Business offers students a simulated trading environment featuring 20 high-end networked trading desks and a continuous live data feed from Bloomberg.

Students learn firsthand using the same technology and analytic tools used on Wall Street and are able to build and track investment portfolios as if they were on an actual trading floor or in a corporate finance office.

NEW CORE CURRICULUM: Iona introduced a new core curriculum that provides a common learning experience to prepares its students for ethical, engaged citizenship and lifelong learning through the lenses of diversity, sustainability, and a global perspective.

Framed by the values of peace, justice, civic engagement, and service, the content-rich, interdisciplinary liberal arts curriculum is cohesively structured and characterized by an emphasis on critical thinking and literacy in its many forms.

---

www.iona.edu
(914) 633-2502
admissions@iona.edu

STUDENT PROFILE

3,287 undergraduate students

90% of undergrad students are full-time

53% female – 47% male

20% of students are from out of state

FACULTY PROFILE

16 to 1 student/faculty ratio

ADMISSIONS

Selectivity: 88%

TUITION & COST

Tuition: $40,172

Fees: $2,200

Room & Board: $15,736

KEUKA COLLEGE

KEUKA PARK, NEW YORK

KEUKA COLLEGE

Believe in What We Can Do Together

www.keuka.edu
(315) 279-5254
admissions@keuka.edu

Many students agree that attending Keuka College is like joining a new family. The growing campus community supports personal experiences in all facets of student life. Keuka professors, accomplished contributors to their respective fields of scholarship, consider teaching their calling and guide every student in the work of educating her or himself.

TEAMWORKS!: Keuka College has a ropes course right on campus for those who love the outdoors, adventure, and physical challenges. Since 1989, Keuka College's TeamWorks! adventure staff has been developing customized programs for school and college groups, nonprofits, church groups, and corporations to build teamwork and success strategies.

Those who join TeamWorks! can participate in such off-campus adventures as whitewater rafting, rock climbing, cave diving, and more.

STUDENT EMPLOYMENT: On a small campus of fewer than 1,000 students, there are plenty of work-study positions available. Without the College's student employment workforce, Keuka would have to hire more than 100 full-time employees. Part-time jobs on campus allow students to explore their interests, build résumés, and earn extra spending money. Work-study jobs range from serving as referees at intramural games to working at the circulation desk in the library.

THE KEUKA COLLEGE WAY FORWARD: No matter what major a student chooses, Keuka College offers the opportunity to design customized, real-world experiences to let them explore their interests and possibilities every year. This Field Period® can be an internship, a cultural experience (either stateside or abroad!), a community service project, an artistic endeavor, or a spiritual-based exploration.

Just a few of the companies with which students have conducted a Field Period® study include The San Francisco 49ers, the U.S. District Attorney's Office, Scholastic Publishing, and the American Cancer Society.

STUDENT PROFILE

1,671 undergraduate students

82% of undergrad students are full-time

74% female – 26% male

8% of students are from out of state

70% freshman retention rate

FACULTY PROFILE

9 to 1 student/faculty ratio

ADMISSIONS

Selectivity: 86%

TUITION & COST

Tuition: $31,748

Fees: $1,300

Room: $5,912

Board: $6,232

LIU BROOKLYN

BROOKLYN, NEW YORK

As the original campus of the Long Island University system, LIU Brooklyn is overflowing with a history of academic excellence and social justice. Its private liberal arts education prepares its students for lifelong success. The University's downtown location offers students a place to cultivate continual growth and broaden their intercultural and education experience. LIU Brooklyn offers many opportunities for students to learn both in the classroom and out in the world.

www.liu.edu/brooklyn
(718) 780-6110
bkln-admissions@liu.edu

LIU HONORS: LIU Brooklyn's honors college allows students to elevate their learning with challenging coursework in an enriched liberal arts environment.

Through the honors program, students have the ability not only to work alongside motivated peers and network with professionals, but they can also take on exciting, active learning experiences like a wilderness seminar co-sponsored by the National Collegiate Honors Council and the U.S. Park Service. What's more, honors students have exclusive access to globetrotting travel seminars, venturing off to such cultural centers as Venice, Madrid, Paris, London, and Dublin.

PROFESSIONAL CONNECTIONS: LIU Brooklyn offers over 35 different degree programs, each of which is run by faculty who are excited to make personal connections with their students.

As a student at the University, one can be confident that there is always a professor or advisor who can get them in touch with professionals, internships, and hands-on experience related to their field of interest. And with the bustling city right outside campus, students are never far from an industry professional who can help them find their niche in the real world.

"LIU Brooklyn continues to enable students to realize their full potential as ethically grounded, intellectually vigorous, and socially responsible global citizens."

STUDENT PROFILE

3,945 undergraduate students

86% of undergrad students are full-time

70% female – 30% male

19% of students are from out of state

64% freshman retention rate

FACULTY PROFILE

13 to 1 student/faculty ratio

ADMISSIONS

Selectivity: 84%

SAT Ranges: E 500-610, M 500-630

ACT Ranges: C 19-27, M 20-27, E 18-28

TUITION & COST

Tuition: $35,038

Fees: $1,940

Room: $8,532

Board: $5,188

LIU POST

BROOKVILLE, NEW YORK

LIU Post is a scenic, historic, and scholarly campus that offers a small-school environment with the access and resources of a major metropolitan university. LIU Post offers more than 250 undergraduate, graduate, doctoral, and certificate programs. Its 307-acre campus is home to both the world-renowned Tilles Center for the Performing Arts and the Bethpage Federal Credit Union Stadium, where students, alumni, family, and friends gather to cheer on the Pioneers' top-ranked NCAA Division II athletics programs.

EXPERIENTIAL EMPLOYMENT: LIU Post is a national leader in student-powered entrepreneurship and engaged learning opportunities. In 2014, the Student-Run Business Committee worked with the campus community to launch four on-campus businesses that employ students into all levels of operation.

LIU Post now has eight student-run businesses, all of which are shining examples of LIU's dedication to fostering entrepreneurship in its community as well as its commitment to provide students with real-world experiences.

THE LIU PROMISE: The LIU Promise is a commitment to providing the right tools, guidance, and support for student achievement. LIU students are immediately assigned an LIU Promise Success Coach who follows them all the way through graduation. Coaches are the point of contact for everything students need, from academic and career counseling to campus activities and financial aid.

SOMETHING FOR EVERYONE: At LIU Post, students find a vibrant community of passionate and driven people. Its broad and comprehensive catalog of majors and degree programs across nine academic units offers the flexibility to explore interests, discover intellectual passions, and embark on academic paths that lead students to careers of their dreams.

Outside the classroom, many students choose to participate in any of 12 Greek organizations and more than 70 student organizations, including student government, jazz ensembles, the "Pioneer" newspaper, and more.

FIND OUT HOW GOOD YOU REALLY ARE.

www.liu.edu/post
(516) 299-2900
post-enroll@liu.edu

STUDENT PROFILE
6,316 undergraduate students

45% of undergrad students are full-time

59% female – 41% male

14% of students are from out of state

78% freshman retention rate

FACULTY PROFILE
14 to 1 student/faculty ratio

ADMISSIONS
Selectivity: 83%

SAT Ranges: E 530-620, M 525-620

ACT Ranges: C 21-26, M 20-26, E 21-26

TUITION & COST
Tuition: $35,038

Fees: $1,940

Room: $8,532

Board: $5,188

MANHATTAN COLLEGE

RIVERDALE, NEW YORK

MANHATTAN COLLEGE

With over 160 years of history, Manhattan College is at the forefront of outstanding, comprehensive colleges. Through the years, one constant has guided the College: the Lasallian Catholic heritage upon which it was built. Christian Brothers and lay teachers alike have educated generations of leaders with five programs in the arts, business, education, engineering, the sciences, and over 40 major fields of study for virtually any chosen profession.

INSPIRING FACULTY: In the future as in the past, it is the faculty who are the torchbearers of Manhattan's educational mission. The Christian Brothers, through their scholarship and compassion, paved the way for the lay faculty who followed.

Today, a scholarly body of men and women does credit to the institution, pursuing research activities and offering qualified students the opportunity to work alongside them outside the normal classroom environment.

DIVERSITY: Manhattan believes that educators have a responsibility not only to prepare students for careers, but to make them more knowledgeable, sensitive, and tolerant of other cultures. A Manhattan College student is sure to be an informed citizen of an increasingly interdependent world.

ETHICAL GROWTH, NOT JUST INTELLECTUAL: Over and above their professional accomplishments, graduates have demonstrated that they learned well the ethical lessons that were part of their Manhattan education. Nowhere is this more poignantly apparent than in their contributions at the World Trade Center site. From the earliest days, Jaspers have always proven their ability and ethical standards as citizens of the world.

"Being Lasallian means being part of a thought-provoking community that exposes you to diverse perspectives and the importance of taking action on social issues."

– Julia Galdiz '17, Allied Health Major

www.manhattan.edu
(718) 862-7200
admit@manhattan.edu

STUDENT PROFILE

3,664 undergraduate students

99% of undergrad students are full-time

45% female – 55% male

31% of students are from out of state

85% freshman retention rate

FACULTY PROFILE

13 to 1 student/faculty ratio

ADMISSIONS

SAT Ranges: E 530-623, M 520-620

ACT Ranges: C 23-28

TUITION & COST

Tuition: $39,300

Fees: $3,887

Room & Board: $16,220

MANHATTANVILLE COLLEGE

PURCHASE, NEW YORK

www.mville.edu
(914) 323-5464
admissions@mville.edu

Manhattanville College, founded in 1841, is a private, coeducational college. Located on 100 acres in Purchase, New York, it is approximately 30 minutes from New York City, 5 minutes from the business district of White Plains, New York, and 15 minutes from Greenwich, Connecticut. With a wide variety of academic programs, a diverse student population, and a wealth of community service found at Manhattanville College, it is fulfilling its mission to educate ethical and socially responsible future leaders in a global community.

ACADEMIC VARIETY: In the interest of making the college experience as worthwhile as possible, Manhattanville College offers a variety of dual, student-designed, and interdisciplinary majors. What's more, students may cross-register with SUNY Purchase so that they can make use of both schools' resources.

Manhattanville's standalone academic programs are just as exciting. For example, the Political Science department and the Sociology department work with the Connie Hogarth Center for Social Action to organize rallies and host an educational film and lecture series. This is an excellent way to make education tangible and dynamic.

SERVICE AND SCHOLARSHIP: Many of Manhattanville College's service programs are coordinated by The Sister Mary T. Clark Center for Religion and Social Justice, which hosts weekly service opportunities and spiritual events. Activities include volunteering in a soup kitchen, mentoring teenagers in a homeless shelter, working on theatrical projects alongside young adults with disabilities, and teaching literary skills to children at a local library.

Along with the The Sister Mary T. Clark Center for Religion and Social Justice, Manhattanville College offers the unique "4th Credit Option," which awards experiential learning credit to students who take academic courses that include community service and civic engagement projects.

STUDENT PROFILE

1,544 undergraduate students

98% of undergrad students are full-time

60% female – 40% male

27% of students are from out of state

70% freshman retention rate

FACULTY PROFILE

10 to 1 student/faculty ratio

ADMISSIONS

Selectivity: 90%

SAT Ranges: E 510-580, M 520-600

ACT Ranges: C 21-25, M 20-25, E 21-26

TUITION & COST

Tuition: $38,120

Fees: $1,450

Room: $8,680

Board: $5,840

NEW YORK INSTITUTE OF TECHNOLOGY

NEW YORK & OLD WESTBURY, NEW YORK

New York Institute of Technology

Students today aren't content with status-quo lectures and classes. They want an active, hands-on education that will propel them into the real world. NYIT (New York Institute of Technology) responds to its students' passion for discovery, creativity, and collaboration by providing them with a modern education that leads to rewarding careers. The moment a student enrolls at NYIT, their potential to succeed expands thanks to an educational approach that is equally strong in up-to-the-minute academics and hands-on career preparation.

AN INTERDISCIPLINARY APPROACH: As a polytechnic university that is home to many diverse academic programs, NYIT is always pursuing interdisciplinary projects that allow students to understand how different disciplines and ways of thinking mesh to create superior solutions. NYIT students are constantly exposed to learning environments within and outside their major to ensure they receive an education that is responsive to needs and challenges close to home and around the world.

OPENING DOORS TO OPPORTUNITY: Whether NYIT students are winning the world championships in robotics competitions like VEX or revitalizing urban sites in New York while collaborating with architecture students in Italy, they are making names for themselves long before they graduate. NYIT's annual Symposium of University Research and Creative Expression (SOURCE) gives undergraduate and graduate students an opportunity to present independent, semester-long research projects.

"I don't think I would ever be motivated if not for the opportunities I've gotten at NYIT. You always have a chance to prove yourself, show yourself, learn more, and it's just all up to you." – *Denisolt Shakhbulatov*

www.nyit.edu
(800) 345-NYIT
admissions@nyit.edu

STUDENT PROFILE
3,619 undergraduate students

90% of undergrad students are full-time

36% female – 64% male

15% of students are from out of state

77% freshman retention rate

FACULTY PROFILE
13 to 1 student/faculty ratio

ADMISSIONS
Selectivity: 77%

SAT Ranges: E 510-610, M 530-620

ACT Ranges: C 21-27, M 20-27, E 20-27

TUITION & COST
Tuition: $35,585

Fees: $1,305

Room & Board: $9,320

NIAGARA UNIVERSITY

NIAGARA COUNTY, NEW YORK

NIAGARA UNIVERSITY

Niagara University is a comprehensive institution that blends the best of a liberal arts and professional education while remaining grounded in a values-based, Catholic tradition. With more than 80 majors, nearly 60 minors, six pre-professional options, and 4+1 combined master's programs, NU students are immersed in meaningful real-world learning opportunities from the moment they step foot on the university's beautiful campus.

PRACTICAL EXPERIENCE = JOBS: It's no fluke that NU graduates are so highly sought after by graduate schools and employers. Niagara graduates are ready for the real world because they've *experienced* the real world.

Those types of real-world learning opportunities help Niagara alumni translate their practical education into top jobs within their career fields. According to a recent survey, 97 percent of NU graduates reported being employed or enrolled in graduate school within one year of graduation.

IMPACT: IMPACT is a measured approach to instilling in NU students a model of collective impact that creates systemic change through project-based learning. It is a comprehensive and individualized service program that places more emphasis on professional and personal growth as opposed to one that highlights hours of service. Students are involved in projects ranging from the county's domestic violence program to doing historical research for non-profit agencies.

NU students can take advantage of other practical work experiences, too. College of Education students begin working in classrooms in their freshman year, while College of Business Administration students can pursue a five-year MBA with an undergraduate degree.

And, as part of a cruise management course aboard a major cruise line, students in the College of Hospitality and Tourism Management have the opportunity to work alongside management in a variety of jobs, including food service and guest relations.

www.niagara.edu
(716) 286-8700
admissions@niagara.edu

STUDENT PROFILE

2,902 undergraduate students

96% of undergrad students are full-time

62% female — 38% male

8% of students are from out of state

83% freshman retention rate

FACULTY PROFILE

11 to 1 student/faculty ratio

ADMISSIONS

Selectivity: 84%

SAT Ranges: E 510-600, M 510-600

ACT Ranges: C 21-26, M 19-26, E 19-24

TUITION & COST

Tuition: $31,700

Fees: $1,480

Room & Board: $13,200

PURCHASE COLLEGE

PURCHASE, NEW YORK

Just 35 miles north of bustling New York City, Purchase College is nestled among 500 acres of fields and forests. It offers rigorous programs in both the liberal arts and sciences as well as professional conservatory training programs in the visual, performing, and theatre arts—the quality of which is guaranteed by the College's association within the State University of New York (SUNY) System. This range of opportunity makes Purchase College a fantastic choice for the student who has a variety of interests.

THINK WIDE OPEN: Purchase Students are encouraged to seek answers "outside the box" of academics. Commonly referred to as the "quirky" SUNY, Purchase College is an inclusive, diverse, and sustainable community. The motto "Think Wide Open" is a phrase that speaks to Purchase's focus on the creative process and intellectual curiosity.

GUEST SPEAKERS: Purchase welcomes artists, thought leaders, authors, and scholars throughout the year to teach master classes, host workshops, perform, and lecture.

The popular Durst Distinguished Lecture Series has welcomed such authors as Neil Gaiman, Claudia Rankine, and Michael Chabon. Creative minds and innovative thinkers revel in the opportunity to inspire Purchase's future leaders.

STUDY ABROAD: The Office of International Programs and Services (OIPS) provides students options in over 600 programs across 50 countries. Purchase students have trained in Beijing, explored Indian food and art, and even studied in Honduras.

STUDENT SUPPORT: From orientation to beyond graduation, Purchase has support in place for all students and alumni. The Advising Center can help with a number of future-forming processes, whether that be planning a course load for the semester or setting up a plan for a future career. Even after graduation, alumni can use the center to network, find job postings, or even seek out interns and extras.

Purchase College
STATE UNIVERSITY OF NEW YORK

www.purchase.edu
(914) 251-6000

STUDENT PROFILE

4,164 undergraduate students

92% of undergrad students are full-time

58% female – 42% male

17% of students are from out of state

81% freshman retention rate

FACULTY PROFILE

14 to 1 student/faculty ratio

ADMISSIONS

Selectivity: 44%

SAT Ranges: E 575-620, M 530-610

ACT Ranges: C 22-27, M 21-26, E 22-29

TUITION & COST

Tuition (in-state): $7,070

Tuition (out-of-state): $16,980

Fees: $1,853

Room: $9,098

Board: $5,450

RENSSELAER POLYTECHNIC INSTITUTE (RPI)

TROY, NEW YORK

Rensselaer Polytechnic Institute aims to provide transformative solutions to such contemporary challenges as climate change; humanity's food, water, and energy supplies; the need for sustainable infrastructure; and national and global security. It is an institution for innovative thinkers who strive to make impactful change. Every day, RPI innovators are pursuing multidisciplinary feats with specializations in Energy, Environment, and Smart Systems; Biotechnology and the Life Sciences; Media, Arts, Science, and Technology; Computational Science and Engineering; and Nanotechnology and Advanced Materials.

ART_X: Students can explore the connections between art, science, and technology through Art_x.

Here, student artists, scientists, engineers, architects, and business experts challenge each other to think innovatively and create new ideas. Art_x efforts on campus include interdisciplinary workshops, lectures, concerts, pop-up classes, team-taught courses, and collaborative projects.

THE ARCH, SUMMER HERE: The Arch is an enrichment initiative that allows students to participate in a co-op or internship for a full semester.

Prior to their semester away, rising juniors enroll in a summer semester with access to faculty and staff in specialized classes; workshops; and on-campus programs and guest speakers. This immersive experience prepares students for their next academic and professional endeavors.

"The Arch is quite different from the regular semesters and the teacher interaction is much better. I also enjoy having some online assignments, which give me more flexibility."

– Haotong Shen'19, Business Management

www.rpi.edu
(518) 276-6216
admissions@rpi.edu

STUDENT PROFILE
6,366 undergraduate students

100% of undergrad students are full-time

32% female – 68% male

57% of students are from out of state

93% freshman retention rate

FACULTY PROFILE
13 to 1 student/faculty ratio

ADMISSIONS
Selectivity: 43%

SAT Ranges: E 640-730, M 680-770

ACT Ranges: C 28-32

TUITION & COST
Tuition: $51,000

Fees: $1,305

Room: $8,480

Board: $6,480

ST. FRANCIS COLLEGE

BROOKLYN, NEW YORK

St. Francis College is a private Franciscan school that provides an innovative and affordable education to students in Brooklyn, NY. Support resources are a point of pride for St. Francis, which connects students with academic and faculty advisors on day one for a wide network that can help them succeed. With 72 fields of study, partnerships with local industry leaders, and a welcoming, vibrant community, St. Francis College supports students academically while preparing them for the professional world.

INTERNSHIPS: St. Francis College is located in New York City, a hotbed of innovation. With a wide array of industries represented both in Brooklyn and around the city, students are encouraged—and, in some cases, required— to complete an internship experience. Around 70% of students complete an internship before graduating, an experience that gives them an edge in finding and landing prestigious, fulfilling full-time jobs after college.

SFC Innovate is a program that focuses on matching students to internships at New York startups. Through partnerships with local developers, venture capitalists, and companies, students can get a firsthand look at the most innovative firms in the city by working alongside them.

COMMON CORE: At St. Francis, the core curriculum is more than just checking boxes on the way to graduation; it is about both academic and self-improvement. All students go outside of their major and build a foundation that teaches them how to use technology, understand the world's religions, communicate effectively, and live in a healthy way. They then investigate five distinct Bodies of Knowledge that help them understand the cultural, scientific, creative, social, and historical foundations of the world.

> "I look up to my professors tremendously, especially my accounting professors. They have given me so much guidance already in helping me understand what I need to do to achieve my goals." *- Melissa Jagdharry, Accounting '18*

www.sfc.edu
(718) 522-2300

STUDENT PROFILE

2,288 undergraduate students

92% of undergrad students are full-time

59% female — 41% male

5% of students are from out of state

74% freshman retention rate

FACULTY PROFILE

14 to 1 student/faculty ratio

ADMISSIONS

Selectivity: 63%

SAT Ranges: E 480-570, M 470-550

ACT Ranges: C 20-24

TUITION & COST

Tuition: $25,188

Fees: $1,000

Room & Board: $15,300

ST. JOHN FISHER COLLEGE

ROCHESTER, NEW YORK

St. John Fisher College has experienced significant enrollment and program growth, igniting fast-moving change to an already beautiful campus. It's a place where tradition and innovation continue to be joined hand-in-hand. Fisher students find everything they need to shape their future: a lively, inspiring, and welcoming campus community; the foundation of a liberal arts education that touches every part of their life; and the guidance of faculty whose expertise sheds light on students' chosen fields.

PROGRAMS OF STUDY FOR GUARANTEED SUCCESS: With 37 majors and minors and 11 pre-professional programs, Fisher caters to a diverse range of undergraduate student interests.

Not only are all of Fisher's programs rich with material that make students masters in their fields, but the College's pre-health, pre-engineering, and pre-law programs also provide easy-to-follow course plans that make their educational careers go as smoothly as possible.

THE TEDDI DANCE FOR LOVE: Fisher's longest-running student tradition, the Teddi Dance for Love, is a fun, inspiring event that exemplifies the College's commitment to service. It calls upon hundreds of students every year to raise money for Camp Good Days and Special Times, an organization that brings life-changing experiences to children diagnosed with cancer.

A 24-hour dance marathon that features live performances and nonstop dancing, the Teddi Dance for Love helps children and families affected by cancer, all while creating memories that Fisher students will value for the rest of their lives. To date, the event has raised over $1 million.

"I had opportunities to walk alongside members of the community to raise money for cancer research, experience two internships in different fields, and accept a full-time position with a Fisher alumnus immediately after I graduated." - *Molly Zies '19*

www.sjfc.edu
(585) 385-8000
admissions@sjfc.edu

STUDENT PROFILE
2,737 undergraduate students

96% of undergrad students are full-time

59% female — 41% male

4% of students are from out of state

87% freshman retention rate

FACULTY PROFILE
12 to 1 student/faculty ratio

ADMISSIONS
Selectivity: 64%

SAT Ranges: E 540-620, M 540-630

ACT Ranges: C 22-26, M 21-27, E 20-26

TUITION & COST
Tuition: $33,500

Fees: $810

Room: $7,940

Board: $4,460

ST. JOHN'S UNIVERSITY

QUEENS, NEW YORK

ST. JOHN'S UNIVERSITY

www.stjohns.edu
(718) 990-2000
admhelp@stjohns.edu

Those who become a part of St. John's University discover a world of opportunity available at New York City's largest Catholic university. For 150 years, St. John's has prepared students to become real leaders in both their careers and communities. Today, St. John's offers more than 100 academic programs, dynamic study abroad opportunities, and a focus on service, altogether supplying the knowledge and tools needed for success in a constantly changing world.

CAMPUS OF OPPORTUNITY: St. John's has three residential New York City campuses: a park-like, 96.5-acre campus in Queens; a wooded, 16.5-acre campus on Staten Island; and an award-winning "vertical" campus in Manhattan's financial district. Like the city itself, St. John's is a cosmopolitan community, drawing students from 46 states and 115 foreign countries.

St. John's students are not just metropolitan, but they are also global, studying at the University's Rome and Paris locations as well as dozens of other cities throughout the world.

GLOBAL PASSPORT: Global Studies is a vital part of the educational experience at St. John's. Through the Global Passport Program, students can study abroad as early as their very first year at St. John's, traveling to locations throughout Europe, Asia, Africa, and Latin America at virtually any time throughout the calendar year.

What's more, St. John's unique Discover the World program lets students earn 15 credits living, learning, and serving in three cities all within a single semester.

OUTSTANDING PROFESSORS: Students at St. John's learn from professors who are internationally acclaimed scholar-teachers. More than 90 percent of professors at St. John's hold the Ph.D. or other terminal degree in their fields, having received prestigious awards like Guggenheim, Fulbright, and more.

STUDENT PROFILE

16,761 undergraduate students

69% of undergrad students are full-time

58% female – 42% male

83% freshman retention rate

FACULTY PROFILE

17 to 1 student/faculty ratio

ADMISSIONS

Selectivity: 68%

SAT Ranges: E 540-620, M 520-630

ACT Ranges: C 22-29

TUITION & COST

Tuition: $39,690

Fees: $830

Room: $10,670

Board: $6,350

ST. JOSEPH'S COLLEGE

BROOKLYN, NEW YORK

Established in 1916, St. Joseph's College provides an affordable liberal arts education to a diverse group of students at its three campuses: SJC Brooklyn, SJC Long Island, and SJC Online. Independent and coeducational, St. Joseph's prepares students for lives of integrity, intellectual and spiritual values, social responsibility, and service. These are lives that are worthy of the College's motto, *Esse non videri*, "To be and not to seem."

COMPLETE EDUCATION: There are some things that just can't be learned in a classroom. At St. Joseph's College, students are encouraged to take part in fieldwork, research, internships, and study abroad trips prior to graduation.

For instance, child study majors don't wait until senior year to become student teachers; they start logging teaching hours in freshman year and graduate with four solid years of classroom experience. Recreation majors complete internships at local health or recreation facilities; art students learn to analyze and appreciate art by visiting world-famous museums; history students explore the architecture of hidden NYC neighborhoods; and biology students conduct research with their professors.

COMMON HOUR: Every day, St. Joseph's students take a break for Common Hour from 12:30-1:30 p.m., gathering for both planned activities and spontaneous fun. This is their time to listen to guest lecturers, debate contemporary issues, enjoy live music and dance performances, and mingle with fellow students over lunch.

MULTICULTURAL STUDENT LIFE: The Office of Multicultural Student Life provides students with an opportunity to celebrate and embrace the diversity of the world through a variety of educational programs, including off-campus trips, interactive workshops, and events.

The Office has sponsored trips to diversity-related conferences, Broadway plays, and even the monumental inauguration of President Barack Obama. In addition, students are encouraged to discuss current events and other hot topics that educate and empower them to express, question, learn, and transform.

www.sjcny.edu
(718) 9405800

STUDENT PROFILE

929 undergraduate students

86% of undergrad students are full-time

68% female – 32% male

9% of students are from out of state

82% freshman retention rate

FACULTY PROFILE

11 to 1 student/faculty ratio

ADMISSIONS

Selectivity: 68%

SAT Ranges: E 440-530, M 428-530

ACT Ranges: C 18-22, M 18-23, E 15-23

TUITION & COST

Tuition: $28,590

Fees: $750

ST. THOMAS AQUINAS COLLEGE

SPARKILL, NEW YORK

From the day students first arrive, St. Thomas Aquinas College celebrates their strengths, talents, and individuality. The College encourages students to push past their limits and strive for great things, providingthe opportunities for students to learn and grow in mind, body, and soul. With a choice of leading-edge academic programs, exciting field experiences, NCAA Division II athletics, and an array of student clubs, students can expand their world and grow intellectually and creatively.

EXPERIENTIAL TRAINING: Combining academic rigor with experiential training, STAC prepares students to excel in high-profile fields, from business to education, and in specialized subfields, such as accounting, forensic science, graphic design, sports management, and social media.

STAC is continually evolving its programs of study and recruiting new scholars to its faculty so that it can best prepare students to think outside the box. Those pursuing careers in media can learn in the College's television studio, which is part of their Media Lab. Students in scientific fields have access to the latest technical equipment, such as a DNA sequencer. Future teachers gain hands-on knowledge of lesson planning with SMART technology.

IN THE COMMUNITY: The largest organization on campus, the Spartan Volunteers, hosts fundraisers for local nonprofits, collects books for underprivileged inner-city schools, and gives food and clothing to New York City's homeless during the popular monthly Midnight Run. These are just a few examples of how STAC students are reaching out as responsible citizens.

"STAC has a reputation for being a great school for education. The faculty prepared me, and my peers were collaborative and helpful... I believe I am a better educator today because of that." *– Anne Marie Gwizdak '07/'08, Elementary and Special Education, MSEd - Literacy*

www.stac.edu
(845) 398-4100
admissions@stac.edu

STUDENT PROFILE
1,180 undergraduate students

97% of undergrad students are full-time

48% female – 52% male

18% of students are from out of state

81% freshman retention rate

FACULTY PROFILE
14 to 1 student/faculty ratio

ADMISSIONS
Selectivity: 76%

SAT Ranges: E 460-560, M 450-560

ACT Ranges: C 18-25

TUITION & COST
Tuition: $32,250

Fees: $800

Room & Board: $13,650

STONY BROOK UNIVERSITY

STONY BROOK, NEW YORK

Stony Brook University is a leading research university with a diverse student body. Its students personalize their college experience through a wide variety of course offerings, numerous avenues for learning outside the classroom, and an emphasis on experiential learning. Stony Brook University takes an innovative approach to teaching that celebrates a student's individuality, recognizing that there is no one-size-fits-all path.

UNDERGRADUATE RESEARCH: Stony Brook University was one of the first schools to emphasize undergraduate research through the formation of the Undergraduate Research and Creative Activities program in 1987. All undergraduate students are eligible to participate in research, whether it be for credit, as a paid research assistant, or simply as a complement to regular coursework.

All students need to do is reach out to a faculty member in their field and work alongside them throughout the project. URECA helps connect students with summer research opportunities at both Stony Brook and other universities, providing the tools to request grants, get published, and present at national conferences.

CAREER COMMUNITIES: In addition to a robust offering of Career Center services, Stony Brook allows students across disciplines to join Career Communities of faculty, staff, employers, and students of similar interests and goals. Communities give students access to personalized career coaching, curated newsletters featuring job opportunities, and connections with Stony Brook alumni and community members to build a personal network. Stony Brook understands that students' career interests and major may not align, so Career Communities are open to students across majors.

LEARNING COMMUNITIES: Students are placed in on-campus housing based on their chosen Stony Brook college, keeping classmates with similar interests and courses together. This goes beyond the typical living experience by offering neighbors and roommates the opportunity to grow, study, and learn alongside one another.

www.stonybrook.edu
(631) 632-6868

STUDENT PROFILE

17,364 undergraduate students

93% of undergrad students are full-time

47% female — 53% male

7% of students are from out of state

90% freshman retention rate

FACULTY PROFILE

18 to 1 student/faculty ratio

ADMISSIONS

Selectivity: 42%

SAT Ranges: E 590-680, M 620-730

ACT Ranges: C 26-31, M 26-32, E 24-32

TUITION & COST

Tuition (in-state): $6,670

Tuition (out-of-state): $24,180

Fees: $2,587

Room: $8,402

Board: $5,044

SUNY GENESEO

GENESEO, NEW YORK

SUNY Geneseo takes intellectual minds, transforms them to see their abilities, and then shows them how to be socially responsible citizens. Students enrolled at Geneseo are part of a collaborative environment in which academics meet civic engagement.

WASHINGTON INTERNSHIP PROGRAM: The Washington Internship Program is a study away option that offers countless benefits and leadership opportunities. Participants of the program experience a near full-time internship, an academic course, and a Leadership Forum. Students build professional networks through interaction with industry leaders.

HUMANITIES I IN NEW YORK CITY: Humanities I is a faculty-led program that takes place for four weeks during the summer. Participants have the chance to study in NYC—the heart of art, culture, and architecture.

Students begin their coursework at Manhattan College, where they can enjoy the peaceful campus and safe environment. After studying various texts, art, and ideas, students travel into the city to visit museums and monuments that pair with their coursework.

STUDY ABROAD MENTOR PROGRAM: The Study Abroad Mentor Program is a new addition to Geneseo's global education effort. Students who have studied abroad through one of SUNY's sponsored programs are called to share their experiences with the campus community. These mentors assist underclassmen with decisions regarding their own program selection, ensuring that they have the best global experience possible.

FIRST-YEAR ADIRONDACK ADVENTURE: The First-Year Adirondack Adventure is an awesome excursion during which participants travel to Lake Placid and stay at a youth hostel for five days.

This trip is a great transition into college; many times, students are anxious to leave home, but the Adirondack Adventure eases this transition through team-building activities and close interaction with faculty and peers.

www.geneseo.edu
(585) 245-5571
admissions@geneseo.edu

STUDENT PROFILE
5,556 undergraduate students

98% of undergrad students are full-time

60% female — 40% male

2% of students are from out of state

86% freshman retention rate

FACULTY PROFILE
19 to 1 student/faculty ratio

ADMISSIONS
Selectivity: 72%

SAT Ranges: E 570-650, M 550-650

ACT Ranges: C 24-29

TUITION & COST
Tuition (in-state): $6,670

Tuition (out-of-state): $16,320

Fees: $1,738

Room: $7,890

Board: $5,324

SUNY NEW PALTZ

NEW PALTZ, NEW YORK

SUNY New Paltz is an academically rigorous public university in the heart of New York State's scenic Hudson Valley, just north of New York City. People from around the world can "come as they are" and collaborate in a friendly, tolerant, and supportive environment. At New Paltz, artists work with entrepreneurs to add smart design to business plans, engineers partner with future teachers to bring technology into the k-12 classroom, and the liberal arts provide a core set of adaptable skills that truly make NP alumni stand out.

PUBLIC POLICY: The Benjamin Center for Public Policy Research is a one-of-a-kind organization in which students can work on policy issues that move the news cycle. It serves the New York community with evaluative studies, giving students unique opportunities to work with lawmakers, businesses, and media outlets on projects that truly affect people's lives.

The Benjamin Center also supports *The Legislative Gazette*, New York's premier public affairs-reporting internship program. Students can earn both class credit and a twice-monthly stipend while reporting on state government.

HVAMC: SUNY New Paltz is home to the Hudson Valley Advanced Manufacturing Center, where digital fabrication experts work with one of the largest and most advanced collections of 3D printers anywhere in the U.S.

HVAMC offers classes in Computer-Aided Design (CAD) software and helps New Paltz students of all majors integrate 3D printing technologies into their education.

SUSTAINABILITY: The College maintains a sense of responsibility to the environment as it works with the campus community to protect the Earth and reduce energy costs through sustainable practices.

New Paltz is also a great place for students interested in green careers, with degree programs and concentrations that focus on sustainability in science and engineering, business, social sciences, and other disciplines.

---

www.newpaltz.edu
(845) 257-3200
admissions@newpaltz.edu

STUDENT PROFILE

6,586 undergraduate students

94% of undergrad students are full-time

61% female – 39% male

3% of students are from out of state

83% freshman retention rate

FACULTY PROFILE

15 to 1 student/faculty ratio

ADMISSIONS

Selectivity: 41%

SAT Ranges: E 550-640, M 540-630

ACT Ranges: C 24-29, M 22-27, E 23-30

TUITION & COST

Tuition (in-state): $6,870

Tuition (out-of-state): $16,650

Fees: $1,384

Room: $8,862

Board: $4,600

SUNY OSWEGO

OSWEGO, NEW YORK

www.oswego.edu
(315) 312-2250
admiss@oswego.edu

Dream, Discover, Do… *The Oswego Way*. SUNY Oswego offers engaging student life activities and programming alongside an exceptionally diverse curriculum with academic programs in four distinct schools: Business; Education; Liberal Arts & Sciences; and Communication, Media & the Arts. The possibilities are endless with an extensive choice of academic options and majors, an outstanding faculty, internships, co-ops, service-learning, and study abroad opportunities that foster learning and encourage the exchange of ideas.

PRACTICED AND PREPARED: SUNY Oswego students are gritty, nimble, and hard working. They prepare for future careers through minds-on, hands-on engagement with faculty and staff on the college's Oswego and Syracuse campuses, the surrounding communities, and around the globe. Oswego students enrich the communities they touch by sharing their knowledge and talent and leading with kindness and compassion for all.

STUDENT ACTIVITIES: Students always have exciting ways to engage themselves in campus and cultural activities. Throughout the year, Oswego students are invited and encouraged to explore opportunities to join clubs and organizations, find their fit, and make new friends.

In addition, each of SUNY Oswego's 13 residential communities is designed to provide students with memorable and inclusive home-away-from-home experiences. The campus is rich in traditions that unify students, faculty, staff, and alumni. And, what's more, Oswego's famous chicken patty is renowned on and off campus, proudly boasting its own social media following.

"Some of our highest-performing people that we have here at SRC are SUNY Oswego grads. As we bring in more and more grads from Oswego, we see them make an impact from day one and rise to higher levels in the organization."

– Joseph Lauko, senior vice president, SRC, Inc.

STUDENT PROFILE

7,038 undergraduate students

96% of undergrad students are full-time

50% female – 50% male

76% freshman retention rate

FACULTY PROFILE

17 to 1 student/faculty ratio

ADMISSIONS

Selectivity: 54%

SAT Ranges: E 540-620, M 530-620

ACT Ranges: C 21-26

TUITION & COST

Tuition (in-state): $7,070

Tuition (out-of-state): $16,650

Fees: $1,570

Room: $8,790

Board: $5,350

THE KING'S COLLEGE

NEW YORK, NEW YORK

The King's College, the only Christian liberal arts college in New York City, seeks students who desire to transform society through principled leadership grounded in biblical truth. Within this close-knit community, each student is placed in one of ten Houses, which altogether make up the heart of student life and the foundation of the greater community. King's students graduate well prepared for rewarding, significant work.

HOUSE CUP: Each year, the Houses compete against one another for the coveted House Cup. House Cup competitions include The Great Race (a massive scavenger hunt through New York City), a drama competition, a basketball tournament, and Interregnum in April.

MEANINGFUL NETWORK: Students work with faculty to develop a plan that suits their individual, long-term career goals and integrates their faith with their work. With a strong alumni network in the City and an extended network of friends of the College, students can connect with people in the industries that interest them to learn more about careers and find job opportunities.

COLLABORATION: King's uses group projects to prepare students for real-world engagement and success. For example, students in Business Strategy participate in the annual international Capsim Foundation competition in which participants create a business simulation and navigate real-time market effects in the areas of finance, product development, and human resources.

In seven out of the past eight years, King's students have risen to the final round, and in 2018 and 2019, they took first place against hundreds.

"There is no better preparation for law than the kind of philosophy we got at King's: following the rules of logic, defining terms carefully, and seeking agreement on sources of authority." – *Lucas Croslow (Politics, Philosophy, and Economics '10), J.D. Yale Law School, Clerk on the U.S. Court of Appeals for the D.C. Circuit*

www.tkc.edu
(570) 208-5858
admissionsoffice@tkc.edu

STUDENT PROFILE
529 undergraduate students

98% of undergrad students are full-time

65% female – 35% male

91% of students are from out of state

79% freshman retention rate

FACULTY PROFILE
15 to 1 student/faculty ratio

ADMISSIONS
Selectivity: 54%

SAT Ranges: E 590-670, M 530-640

ACT Ranges: C 24-29, M 23-26, E 25-33

TUITION & COST
Tuition: $37,000

Fees: $690

Room: $14,400

Board: $2,784

THE SAGE COLLEGES

TROY & ALBANY, NEW YORK

Russell Sage College and Sage College of Albany collaborate to make up The Sage Colleges. Russell Sage College offers programs in the liberal arts and sciences, professional programs focusing on leadership, and a performing arts program. Sage College of Albany, awarding bachelor's degrees since 2002, offers respected programs in visual arts, business, legal studies, computer science, and more. Frequent shuttles between Russell Sage College and Sage College of Albany make the resources on each campus accessible to all Sage students.

STUDENT-CENTERED: Sage faculty are active scholars for whom teaching is the priority, and Sage classes are small, which supports individualized learning opportunities.

Oxford Style Tutorials, limited to an intimate five students per section, zero-in on specialized topics, including some entertaining subjects, like the Broadway theatre season, and hard-to-fathom ones, like black holes.

CROSS-PROFESSIONAL TRAINING: Sage fosters interdisciplinary education, which in turn improves teamwork among professions that work together. Students learn to form partnerships during the academic journey, which ultimately prepares them to build productive working relationships when they graduate.

In particular, the Health Sciences programs stress interprofessional education and create opportunities for future occupational and physical therapists, nurses, dieticians, mental health professionals, and others to learn together.

"We have to become comfortable collaborating with each other as students... I will definitely stay involved as an advocate for interprofessional collaboration. I've accepted its importance as a student and will put it in practice as a professional." – *Gina Gerlach, Occupational Therapy*

www.sage.edu
(518) 244-2217
admissions@sage.edu

STUDENT PROFILE
1,305 undergraduate students

89% of undergrad students are full-time

79% female – 21% male

12% of students are from out of state

79% freshman retention rate

FACULTY PROFILE
10 to 1 student/faculty ratio

ADMISSIONS
Selectivity: 56%

TUITION & COST
Tuition: $28,364

Fees: $1,500

Room: $6,430

Board: $5,978

UNIVERSITY AT ALBANY, SUNY

ALBANY, NEW YORK

UNIVERSITY AT ALBANY
State University of New York

www.albany.edu
(518) 442-3300
ugadmissions@albany.edu

The University at Albany, founded in 1844, is an agent of positive change in terms of academic success, professional development, and global good. With nine schools and colleges, the university offers innovative programs paired with hands-on learning, enabling students to gain impressive skills for their careers.

INNOVATIVE PROGRAMS: UAlbany is paving the way to the careers of tomorrow. With the first-in-the-nation College of Emergency Preparedness, Homeland Security, and Cybersecurity, students are equipped for careers in critical security fields.

The Atmospheric Science program utilizes some of the nation's most advanced facilities and resources, and programs like Criminal Justice, Social Welfare, Psychology, Biology, Public Policy, and Political Science gain the University national attention.

TOP FACILITIES: UAlbany's on-campus facilities enable the highest levels of learning by utilizing the most advanced technology. Students enjoy art exhibitions at the Art Museum, and they themselves can dabble in the arts in the Boor Sculpture Studio. Those interested in science can get involved in throughout the Life Science Research Building or Cancer Research Center.

The Massry Center for Business, a state-of-the-art facility for UAlbany's renowned School of Business, is LEED Gold certified and home to several smart-technology classrooms.

PRE-PROFESSIONAL ORGANIZATIONS: Students are committed to advancing their careers through 86 pre-professional student groups.

With organizations like the Forensic Science club, the Middle Earth Peer Assistance Program, the Pre-Medical Club, the UAlbany Stock Exchange, and Women in Positions of Power, students drive their future forward by surrounding themselves with motivated individuals and meaningful networking opportunities.

STUDENT PROFILE

13,508 undergraduate students

94% of undergrad students are full-time

51% female – 49% male

5% of students are from out of state

83% freshman retention rate

FACULTY PROFILE

19 to 1 student/faculty ratio

ADMISSIONS

Selectivity: 54%

SAT Ranges: E 550-650, M 530-610

ACT Ranges: C 22-26

TUITION & COST

Tuition (in-state): $6,670

Tuition (out-of-state): $21,550

Fees: $2,820

Room: $8,364

Board: $5,500

UTICA COLLEGE

UTICA, NEW YORK

UTICA COLLEGE

Utica College is an innovative, private university with the resources to personalize education for each and every student. Students leave Utica College with the tools needed to change the world in their workplaces and in their communities. With an 11:1 student-to-faculty ratio, a comprehensive student support network, and cutting-edge facilities, a Utica College education prepares students for rewarding careers, responsible citizenship, enlightened leadership, and fulfilling lives.

A TEAM THAT CARES: Starting in their freshman year, Utica College students are introduced to their CARE Team, which brings together an academic advisor, a student success coach, a career coach, and a financial aid counselor to provide a single point-of-contact for every area of concern. The CARE Teams ensure students are planning for their collegiate and career futures from the beginning of their time at Utica. By taking an active role in each student's life, CARE Teams offer the personalized resources and relationships needed to excel at Utica and in the workforce.

AFFORDABLE EXCELLENCE: In 2016, UC made headlines when it reset tuition, reducing its price by 42% with a commitment to affordability. Scholarships, grants, loans, and part-time employment reduce the out-of-pocket costs for most families, often by more than half the cost of tuition. A quality, private education at UC is more affordable than one might think.

HANDS ON: UC offers students ample opportunity to get hands-on experience beyond the classroom. Students present at national conferences, utilize cutting-edge facilities, and get to know faculty who are leaders in their fields. In the past, students have investigated light pollution, produced NPR reports, and even discovered a new species of bacteria.

"Everyone here believes in me. When a college professor tells you, one-on-one, that you can do it, it's meaningful. They saw more in me than I saw in myself."

– Alfonzo Whitehurst, Education '17

www.utica.edu
(315) 792-3006
admiss@utica.edu

STUDENT PROFILE

3,602 undergraduate students

81% of undergrad students are full-time

59% female – 41% male

12% of students are from out of state

70% freshman retention rate

FACULTY PROFILE

12 to 1 student/faculty ratio

ADMISSIONS

Selectivity: 84%

SAT Ranges: E 510-600, M 520-620

ACT Ranges: C 20-26

TUITION & COST

Tuition: $21,560

Fees: $550

Room & Board: $11,670

WELLS COLLEGE

AURORA, NEW YORK

Wells College

www.wells.edu
(315) 364-3264
admissions@wells.edu

A world of possibilities lie within Wells College's lakeside campus, including DIII athletics, graduate-level research, and transferable financial aid that continues in semesters abroad. Wells offers a well-rounded, rigorous liberal arts degree that inspires students to embrace new ways of knowing and to respond ethically to the interdependent worlds to which they belong.

COMMUNITY PROFESSIONAL EXPERIENCE: Only 10% of healthcare providers choose to practice in a rural area, which often means that there is an urgent need with few resources to address it. During the summer, Wells students travel to a rural community in New York for the Rural Health Immersion Program, through which they can shadow health professionals to observe the unique health needs and challenges that face the area.

CAYUGA LAKE: Situated on more than 300 scenic acres overlooking Cayuga Lake in central New York, Wells offers the simplicity and safety of the Finger Lakes' village living with easy access to metropolitan and educational centers: a half hour from Ithaca, 1 hour from Rochester and Syracuse, and approximately 5 hours from New York City, Philadelphia, and Boston.

IN THE REAL WORLD: The small faculty-to-student ratio gives Wellsians valuable flexibility when it comes to professional experience. Students receive one-on-one guidance to secure off-campus internships, and they can conduct real research and co-author articles with their professors. Student work may even be selected for the National Conference on Undergraduate Research (Wells students have been invited to present for over 30 years)!

STUDENT PROFILE

461 undergraduate students

99% of undergrad students are full-time

64% female – 36% male

23% of students are from out of state

72% freshman retention rate

FACULTY PROFILE

9 to 1 student/faculty ratio

ADMISSIONS

Selectivity: 79%

ACT Ranges: C 21-28, M 19-26, E 21-30

TUITION & COST

Tuition: $29,400

Fees: $1,500

Room: $11,000

Board: $3,000

"Much of the learning process at Wells occurs outside of the classroom and in small groups. This...gives me the opportunity to get to know most of my students as individuals. It is enjoyable to watch them grow as scientists over their four years here, and then beyond."

– Dr. Christopher Bailey, Professor of Chemistry

APPALACHIAN STATE UNIVERSITY

BOONE, NORTH CAROLINA

Appalachian State University's picturesque location and lively academic environment make it the perfect place to learn and grow. The University combines the intimacy of a smaller school with the research opportunities of a larger institution to provide students with the ultimate learning experience.

RESIDENTIAL LEARNING COMMUNITIES: Appalachian State embraces residential learning communities (RLCs) for the many benefits they offer in student development, including better grades, deeper involvement, and increased academic and social support.

Most RLCs involve a set of courses that link the residence component of the community to academics. Students engage in an educational experience in which their peers and faculty become part of the journey.

Just a few RLC examples include the "Art Haus," which caters to aspiring artists; "Brain Matters," which spends all year exploring the psychology of emotion and the human condition; and "New State of Mind" for out-of-state students who want to explore more of their new home in North Carolina.

SYE: The Sophomore-Year Experience (SYE) RLC is especially tailored to second-year students who are still contemplating their majors. SYE aims to help sophomores narrow down a career path through various resources and supportive advising.

STUDY ABROAD 101: Leaving the country can be intimidating, but Study Abroad 101 gives students the tools they need to prepare for life-changing travel. This workshop covers all the abroad opportunities available at Appalachian State and gives students an idea of what to expect.

Topics covered in the workshop include program types, tips on how to find a program, costs, coursework and approval, scholarships, financial aid, and the application process. After students have completed Study Abroad 101, they are then invited to take Study Abroad 102, which aids in the application process itself.

www.appstate.edu
(828) 262-2120
admissions@appstate.edu

STUDENT PROFILE

17,017 undergraduate students

94% of undergrad students are full-time

55% female – 45% male

10% of students are from out of state

89% freshman retention rate

FACULTY PROFILE

16 to 1 student/faculty ratio

ADMISSIONS

Selectivity: 70%

SAT Ranges: E 560-640, M 540-630

ACT Ranges: C 23-27, M 23-27, E 23-28

TUITION & COST

Tuition (in-state): $4,242

Tuition (out-of-state): $19,049

Fees: $3,060

Room: $4,339

Board: $3,834

BELMONT ABBEY COLLEGE

BELMONT, NORTH CAROLINA

belmontabbeycollege.edu
1 (888) 222-0110
admissions@bac.edu

Founded in 1876 by Benedictine monks, Belmont Abbey continues to celebrate the 1,500-year-old Benedictine monastic tradition of prayer and learning while welcoming a diverse body of students regardless of religious affiliation. Belmont Abbey's education exposes the mind, body, and spirit to the value of the higher things. Such a pursuit of excellence is matched only by the college's quest to lead lives of virtue.

CAMPUS MINISTRY: Belmont Abbey's campus ministry lives by *"Ora et Labora,"* prayer and work. Students involved can pray with one another as well as learn from the monks on campus. They may also put their faith to meaningful action; in collaboration with local organizations—such as the Boys and Girls Club, Catherine's House, and Habitat for Humanity—campus ministry students give back to their community through service.

THE CORE OF AN ABBEY EDUCATION: The Belmont Abbey Core is an essential part of the curriculum that explores Western history and culture, the humanities, the Catholic tradition, and more. The foundations of the institution's culture are rooted in the works of Western history's great minds, introducing James Joyce, St. Thomas Aquinas, Homer, Shakespeare, and others to understand how historic texts have shaped our modern world.

COMMON GROUND: With the help of a common summer reading and discussion, students automatically find solidarity and connection with their faculty and classmates. There are plenty of chances to bond outside of the classroom, too. Students regularly go on field trips and campus tours with faculty, and the annual "Love the Abbey Day" gets students up and moving to give back to their campus and the wider Belmont community.

"There's something about the education at Belmont Abbey College that gets so far down into the soul, they end up hitting something so human in us that we discover who we are." *- Elisa Torres '17*

STUDENT PROFILE

1,505 undergraduate students

96% of undergrad students are full-time

50% female – 50% male

40% of students are from out of state

64% freshman retention rate

FACULTY PROFILE

16 to 1 student/faculty ratio

ADMISSIONS

Selectivity: 79%

SAT Ranges: E 480-600, M 470-580

ACT Ranges: C 19-24, M 18-24, E 20-25

TUITION & COST

Tuition: $18,500

Fees: $300

Room: $6,700

Board: $4,466

ELON UNIVERSITY

ELON, NORTH CAROLINA

Elon students are fully involved. This is a university of boundless opportunity in which students have a passion to fulfill their roles as global citizens. Elon's four-year core curriculum has a strong global focus and is organized around the themes of inquiry, knowledge, and communication, putting students' knowledge into action on campus and around the world.

THE ELON EXPERIENCES: Elon students connect their education to the real world through hands-on learning. The university's signature program, The Elon Experiences, provides a natural extension of the work done in the classroom.

The Elon Experiences can be completed individually or combined to suit students' specific goals. For example, students can seek out service opportunities while they're abroad. They can also find internships that correlate with their multi-year research project and establish leadership development programs in local schools.

STRONG CORE: Elon's four-year core curriculum has a strong global focus and is organized around the themes of inquiry, knowledge, and communication. Students learn to see the world through many different perspectives and understand the complex relationships among the world's people, cultures, beliefs, and environments.

The curriculum complements everyone's major, focusing on the liberal arts and sciences that are so important to Elon's mission and so vital for globally engaged citizenship in a democratic society. Students explore ideas and expand their worldview.

The learning goals of the Core Curriculum reflect the same skills expected in the workplace, including critical thinking, writing, and problem-solving skills. Elon has undertaken an extensive Writing Excellence Initiative to help students in all majors develop written communication skills that they will use throughout their lives.

www.elon.edu
(336) 278-3566
admissions@elon.edu

STUDENT PROFILE

6,045 undergraduate students

97% of undergrad students are full-time

60% female – 40% male

81% of students are from out of state

89% freshman retention rate

FACULTY PROFILE

12 to 1 student/faculty ratio

ADMISSIONS

Selectivity: 67%

SAT Ranges: E 580-670, M 560-660

ACT Ranges: C 25-29, M 24-28, E 25-31

TUITION & COST

Tuition: $33,829

Fees: $444

Room: $5,900

Board: $5,969

GARDNER-WEBB UNIVERSITY

BOILING SPRINGS, NORTH CAROLINA

Gardner-Webb University, located just outside of Charlotte, North Carolina, fosters an all-inclusive campus community that values its Christian roots, diversity, and academic excellence. From the on-campus bell tower that overlooks Lake Hollifield to the surrounding community of Boiling Springs, Gardner-Webb surrounds students with a rich and abundant culture. And because GWU is concerned about the needs of others in order to grow in knowledge and wisdom, the University enthusiastically affirms active participation in influential and impactful initiatives.

DIMENSIONS: Each Tuesday morning within the walls of the University's Student Center, guest speakers invite students to listen to their proclamations of faith and their commitment to strong ethics.

These weekly speeches allow a range of thought leaders to emphasize the importance and relevance of the Baptist values that are upheld within the campus community. Referred to as "Dimensions," the lectures promote religious growth and a strong intent of service to God.

PREPARED FOT EVERYTHING: The world-class academic programs at Gardner-Webb University are rooted in the liberal arts and purposed to help students achieve their post-graduation goals.

Whether through leadership experience in ROTC, a national Honors conference presentation, or a trip to Costa Rica to earn a Spanish minor, Gardner-Webb emphasizes the tangible experiences that enhance one's academic, professional, and personal pursuits.

"I do not know of any other University that prepares students so broadly and deeply. At Gardner-Webb, everyone is invested in making your experience the best it can be... I'd choose Gardner Webb every time if I had to do it over again." *– Chelsea Sydnor, '18*

GARDNER-WEBB UNIVERSITY

www.gardner-webb.edu
(800) 253-6472
admissions@
gardner-webb.edu

STUDENT PROFILE

2,215 undergraduate students

80% of undergrad students are full-time

65% female – 35% male

71% freshman retention rate

FACULTY PROFILE

11 to 1 student/faculty ratio

ADMISSIONS

Selectivity: 53%

SAT Ranges: E 500-610, M 500-590

ACT Ranges: C 19-25, M 18-25, E 18-24

TUITION & COST

Tuition: $30,310

Fees: $390

Room: $5,100

Board: $4,980

HIGH POINT UNIVERSITY

HIGH POINT, NORTH CAROLINA

HIGH POINT UNIVERSITY
Premier Life Skills University

www.highpoint.edu
(800) 345-6993
admiss@highpoint.edu

High Point University is the Premier Life Skills University working to transform the lives of students through a broad spectrum of academic coursework that are complemented by experiential learning programs like internships, research, and service-learning. Innovative educational initiatives like the President's Seminar on Life Skills ensure students not only grow in specific academic areas of expertise, but also develop competencies in communication, networking, coachability, fiscal literacy, and service. These are among the traits HPU refers to as *"life skills,"* which employers rank as the most critical skills necessary to succeed in the workplace.

EXPERIENTIAL LEARNING: At HPU, 25% of everything taught has an experiential component, as professors want their students to stretch themselves, work in the community, and find out firsthand what "real" means. Students then discover that experience is the best teacher. And with the university's opportunities for internships, study abroad, and research, they graduate prepared.

A CARING CULTURE: As HPU President Nido Qubein reminds faculty and staff, *"You can't teach values; you must model them."* This sets the tone for HPU's entire campus. Faculty and staff understand that they serve as heroes, models, and mentors to students. Every member of HPU's campus is willing to provide one-on-one guidance and support.

STUDENT PROFILE

4,407 undergraduate students

99% of undergrad students are full-time

59% female – 41% male

78% of students are from out of state

79% freshman retention rate

FACULTY PROFILE

14 to 1 student/faculty ratio

ADMISSIONS

Selectivity: 81%

SAT Ranges: E 530-620, M 520-620

ACT Ranges: C 21-27, M 20-26, E 21-27

TUITION & COST

Tuition: $30,748

Fees: $4,370

Room & Board: $14,130

> "When I interned with organizations like USA Track and Field, Under Armour, and IMG College, I was up against a field of qualified candidates from large universities. What set me apart was the real-world experience I received at HPU and the attitude they instilled within me to never be afraid of a challenge."

– Mikaela Campbell, Class of 2018, Associate at the NBA in New York City

LEES-MCRAE COLLEGE

BANNER ELK, NORTH CAROLINA

Lees-McRae College, founded in 1900, is a private, four-year institution that provides a well-rounded experiential education within the Blue Ridge Mountains of western North Carolina. Offering a diverse array of undergraduate and graduate degrees, Lees-McRae College fosters personal growth and exploration while providing a platform for environmental and community stewardship. Its core mission is to develop strong candidates for marketplace demands through creative, collaborative, and critical thinking with a focus on experiential learning.

COLLABORATIVE ASSIGNMENTS AND PROJECTS: Lees-McRae students work together to achieve larger goals. For example, students work alongside expert faculty at the May Wildlife Rehabilitation Center to nurture and rehabilitate injured wildlife, while those in the May School of Nursing and Health Sciences participate in team-diagnostic practices as well as mock emergency simulations.

SERVICE AND SOCIAL JUSTICE: Over the course of April, students across campus participate in events for Sexual Assault Awareness Month, working in coordination with the Lees-McRae Campus Life; Delta Zeta Nu, a community service-based sorority; and OASIS, a local nonprofit that serves survivors of sexual and domestic violence.

Students also participate in such projects as the Clothesline Project, including Tea Week, a week-long event filled with presentations, films, and games in order to learn about a variety of topics related to sex, sexuality, and gender.

DIVERSITY/GLOBAL LEARNING: From Wildlife Rehabilitation to Nursing, students can travel the world helping those in need all while exercising their acquired skills.

Recently, a group of Wildlife Rehabilitation students traveled to New Zealand to learn about indigenous wildlife and volunteer in a rehabilitation center. Similarly, nursing students traveled to Haiti to serve in one of several area hospitals.

www.lmc.edu
(828) 898-5241
admissions@lmc.edu

STUDENT PROFILE
921 undergraduate students

97% of undergrad students are full-time

67% female – 33% male

64% freshman retention rate

FACULTY PROFILE
12 to 1 student/faculty ratio

ADMISSIONS
Selectivity: 71%

TUITION & COST
Tuition: $24,878

Fees: $1,000

Room: $5,142

Board: $5,616

LENOIR-RHYNE UNIVERSITY

HICKORY, NORTH CAROLINA

Founded in 1891, Lenoir-Rhyne University is a co-educational, private liberal arts institution with more than 50 undergraduate degree programs and more than 30 graduate degree programs. With a 13:1 student-to-faculty ratio, LR enrolls more than 2,700 undergraduate and graduate students and has had eleven consecutive years of enrollment growth. At its core, LR also encourages lifelong learning, service, and faith in its students as they navigate the world around them.

TEACHING SCHOLARS PROGRAM: Lenoir-Rhyne University is proud to serve aspiring teachers through the highly competitive Teaching Scholars Program. Applicants should have a record of academic excellence and portray a deep desire to serve students through a career in teaching. Scholars will connect early and often with Hickory-area school districts throughout their programs of study where they will serve as tutors, small group leaders, and instructional assistants.

BRIDGES TO DREAMS: LR's Bridges to Dreams program assists undergraduate students toward completion of a graduate degree. Through dual enrollment, qualified LR undergraduates may begin graduate courses while still completing an undergraduate degree. These graduate courses may meet both undergraduate and graduate degree requirements.

NURSING SCHOLARS PROGRAM: LR's Nursing Scholars Program enhances the undergraduate experience of LR's high-performing students with an interest in earning a Bachelor of Science in Nursing. Throughout the program, students receive personalized academic support, enrichment opportunities, and a learning community with other top academic pre-nursing students.

"When I came to Lenoir-Rhyne, I wanted to know everyone by name. I chose LR because it was the best overall fit. The recommendations and reputation of the nursing program were unmatched." *- Jake Pierce '20, Nursing*

LENOIR~RHYNE UNIVERSITY

www.lr.edu
(828) 328-7300
admission@lr.edu

STUDENT PROFILE

1,699 undergraduate students

91% of undergrad students are full-time

60% female – 40% male

16% of students are from out of state

68% freshman retention rate

FACULTY PROFILE

13 to 1 student/faculty ratio

ADMISSIONS

Selectivity: 77%

SAT Ranges: E 480-590, M 480-590

ACT Ranges: M 18-24, E 18-25

TUITION & COST

Tuition: $37,400

Room & Board: $12,510

MEREDITH COLLEGE

RALEIGH, NORTH CAROLINA

Meredith College has been educating strong, confident women for more than a century. Students at Meredith are seen as the unique individuals they are while they identify and learn how to use their innate strengths. And most importantly, Meredith's personal approach to education means that each student is prepared for a successful career and a satisfying life after she graduates.

IN-DEPTH, COLLABORATIVE LEARNING: Each program of study at Meredith incorporates interdisciplinary study, experiential learning, and global awareness. The Fashion Merchandising and Design program sponsors trips to Paris, New York's Garment District, and the Atlanta Merchandise Mart. Students in the education program select a major of their choice and earn education licensure alongside their degree. And humanities students learn from Raleigh's archives, museums, and historic sites.

UNIQUE ON-CAMPUS FACILITIES: Meredith is home to the Meredith Autism Program, an early intervention program for children diagnosed on the autism spectrum. It is one of the only programs of its kind in the U.S. to offer hands-on clinical course experience to undergraduates.

Also available are the Ellen Brewer House, a child care program that gives child development majors real-world experience, and the Human Performance Lab, where exercise and sports science students conduct research and learn to conduct fitness assessments.

"A women's college education can make anyone feel like their voice will be heard and appreciated. I am more articulate in my thoughts, more articulate in my opinions—I am not one to shy away from a question or change my beliefs for others anymore."

– Maria Fernanda Diaz Jimenez, '18

---

www.meredith.edu
(919) 760-8581
admissions@meredith.edu

STUDENT PROFILE

1,563 undergraduate students

98% of undergrad students are full-time

100% female — 0% male

15% of students are from out of state

80% freshman retention rate

FACULTY PROFILE

11 to 1 student/faculty ratio

ADMISSIONS

Selectivity: 63%

SAT Ranges: E 510-610, M 490-590

ACT Ranges: C 19-26, M 17-24, E 18-25

TUITION & COST

Tuition: $38,520

Fees: $100

Room & Board: $11,360

PFEIFFER UNIVERSITY

MISENHEIMER, NORTH CAROLINA

Pfeiffer University is a private liberal arts university affiliated with the United Methodist Church. Its mission is to prepare leaders for lifelong learning and service. Pfeiffer's traditional undergraduate campus is in Misenheimer, N.C.—approximately 40 miles northeast of Charlotte. Since its founding in 1885, Pfeiffer has continually grown in academic excellence, developing new programs to meet the needs of its students and emphasizing the ideals of Christian service.

THE PFEIFFER JOURNEY: Pfeiffer strives to provide a holistic education to each and every student. Sending students on the Pfeiffer Journey, the University dedicates each year to different levels of progression toward their postgraduate careers.

In the first year, students get grounded with a foundational exposure to campus resources. Sophomores are then encouraged to explore their academic options, and juniors integrate their experiences with leadership and volunteer work. The senior year rounds off the Journey with culminating capstone projects and portfolios.

ENGAGED AND INSPIRED: Pfeiffer University is a tremendous place to learn, filled with multi-talented students, dedicated faculty, and supportive administrators. Students learn to be effective group members and leaders as they plan and implement their own programs for their fellow Pfeiffer University students and staff.

CAREER SERVICES: Pfeiffer offers excellent guidance for its students' future careers in the global marketplace. Programs are continually updated to partner students with the best of the community's employers, including the Michelin tire manufacturer, which has supported students in all aspects of the company like data analysis and injury prevention.

With an educational model that blends ideology, research, and practical application, students learn to collaborate through group work and discover the value of civic engagement in a changing society.

www.pfeiffer.edu
(800) 338-2060

STUDENT PROFILE

813 undergraduate students

90% of undergrad students are full-time

52% female – 48% male

61% freshman retention rate

FACULTY PROFILE

10 to 1 student/faculty ratio

ADMISSIONS

Selectivity: 66%

SAT Ranges: E 460-560, M 450-540

ACT Ranges: C 16-22, M 16-22, E 14-21

TUITION & COST

Tuition: $28,560

Fees: $1,014

Room: $5,836

Board: $5,122

UNIVERSITY OF MOUNT OLIVE

MOUNT OLIVE, NORTH CAROLINA

University *of*
MOUNT OLIVE

The University of Mount Olive has become one of the most unique and fastest-growing universities in North Carolina. The University offers rigorous academic programs, over 60 majors and minors, experienced faculty, small class sizes, and Division II athletics with a winning tradition. Grounded in the liberal arts, the University of Mount Olive helps individuals realize their creative potential while preparing graduates for professional careers.

NOBLE GOAL: The University of Mount Olive began with a simple yet meaningful goal: to change the lives of students. Not just to teach them, but also to help every student grow as an individual while preparing them for a lifetime of meaningful and productive work, personal growth, and community leadership.

The University of Mount Olive has awarded more than 20,000 degrees since its founding in 1951. Students arrive on campus to learn, listen, and explore the possibilities and opportunities of faith and education.

INTEGRATED LEARNING: Through the liberal arts programs at the University of Mount Olive, opportunities abound for students to explore their potential Rather than just allowing the academic, spiritual, and social parts of students' lives to coexist, the University of Mount Olive strives to teach students how to combine them, helping their lives take on a new dimension.

"UMO prepared me for my career by providing me with not only an academic education, but also a professional education, ensuring that I have the knowledge and confidence I need in order to succeed. I am currently conducting surgical research and plan to continue my education and pursue a career in the medical field. "

– *Casey Fiechter from Louisville, KY*

www.umo.edu
1(844) 866-4625
admissions@umo.edu

STUDENT PROFILE

2,854 undergraduate students

48% of undergrad students are full-time

64% female — 36% male

15% of students are from out of state

68% freshman retention rate

FACULTY PROFILE

12 to 1 student/faculty ratio

ADMISSIONS

Selectivity: 53%

SAT Ranges: E 430-538, M 440-528

ACT Ranges: C 17-22, M 16-21, E 15-21

TUITION & COST

Tuition: $21,194

Room & Board: $8,800

UNIVERSITY OF NORTH CAROLINA AT GREENSBORO

GREENSBORO, NORTH CAROLINA

UNCG

www.uncg.edu
(336) 334-5243
admissions@uncg.edu

Every day, UNC Greensboro creates a remarkable real-world impact. It can be seen every day. In the hard work, inventive ideas, and powerful collaborations that define communities. In schools, hospitals, and businesses. In the everyday and extraordinary achievements that add up to the remarkable impact of UNC Greensboro. It's in the students—those who have excelled their entire lives and those bursting with potential that needs to be cultivated. It's in the faculty who create and share the knowledge that makes the region and the world healthier, more vibrant, and more prosperous. It is as true today as it has been for 125 years: UNC Greensboro is relentlessly focused on helping each student unleash their potential.

FIRST-CLASS FACULTY, FIRST-CLASS FACILITIES: UNC Greensboro faculty embody what it means to be a teacher-scholar. They're mentors who are tenaciously devoted to the success of their students, and they're nationally and internationally recognized researchers in their respective fields.

Excellent teaching is combined with the university's state-of-the-art facilities— the SELF Design Studio in the School of Education, the newly renovated studios in the School of Dance, the nursing simulation labs with SimMom technology, and more—to prepare students for their future endeavors.

EXPERIENCE FOR ACHIEVEMENT: UNCG offers a rich array of opportunities outside of the classroom to prepare for success beyond the university.

The Bryan School of Business and Economics maintains relationships with local corporations to facilitate internships. And students in the Department of Consumer, Apparel, and Retail Studies present their work in an annual fashion show in downtown Greensboro.

Furthermore, School of Theatre seniors participate in the annual Industry Showcase in New York City, performing for top producers, agents, and casting directors.

STUDENT PROFILE

16,238 undergraduate students

87% of undergrad students are full-time

67% female — 33% male

5% of students are from out of state

77% freshman retention rate

FACULTY PROFILE

17 to 1 student/faculty ratio

ADMISSIONS

Selectivity: 84%

SAT Ranges: E 500-590, M 490-570

ACT Ranges: C 20-25, M 18-24, E 19-24

TUITION & COST

Tuition (in-state): $7,331

Tuition (out-of-state): $22,490

Room: $5,381

Board: $3,657

UNIVERSITY OF NORTH CAROLINA – WILMINGTON

WILMINGTON, NORTH CAROLINA

UNIVERSITY of NORTH CAROLINA WILMINGTON

Education should very obviously be the focus of any college experience. While this might seem like a clear point, many schools fail to articulate why that idea is so important. UNCW recognizes that an educational journey is about constant academic discovery. Students need to take ownership of their educations—pushing boundaries and posing creative inquiry that drives intellectual innovation.

CORNERSTONE LEARNING COMMUNITIES: Students involved in Cornerstone Learning Communities take courses that are linked to one another, and professors in the program collaborate with one another to enhance this unique, educational experience. As an added benefit, those students who participate enjoy smaller classroom dynamics, which leads to an increased sense of worth and individualized attention.

Participation in this program means the completion of three University requirements as well as the experience of practicing academic theories outside of the classroom.

UNCW CAREER CENTER: The UNCW Career Center is a resource available to all facets of the UNCW community, from alumni to undergrads. The purpose of the center is to provide guidance to participants looking to develop their career or career goals.

UNCW students are encouraged to join the alumni association for the many benefits it affords its members upon graduation. Alumni have access to career services even after graduating, allowing them to seek guidance whenever they are looking to expand their career goals.

The association is also helpful for networking, bringing members of the UNCW community in touch with one another, including the many successful alumni who are working at top-level positions and businesses.

www.uncw.edu
(910) 962-3243
admissions@uncw.edu

STUDENT PROFILE
14,502 undergraduate students

85% of undergrad students are full-time

62% female – 38% male

16% of students are from out of state

87% freshman retention rate

FACULTY PROFILE
18 to 1 student/faculty ratio

ADMISSIONS
Selectivity: 67%

SAT Ranges: E 600-660, M 585-650

ACT Ranges: C 23-27, M 21-26, E 22-27

TUITION & COST
Tuition (in-state): $4,443

Tuition (out-of-state): $18,508

Fees: $2,557

Room: $6,660

Board: $3,830

WAKE FOREST UNIVERSITY

WINSTON-SALEM, NORTH CAROLINA

WAKE FOREST
U N I V E R S I T Y

www.wfu.edu
(336) 758-5201
admissions@wfu.edu

A Wake Forest education is concerned with the development of the entire individual. Students need to push themselves to find out what is comfortable and what is not. They need to be willing to fail and be ready to succeed. Students must grab their educational experience and run with it, testing the boundaries of their own potential and learning about the talents they possess. Wake Forest reminds students that while their college experience is about discovering themselves, it is also about understanding their duty to the global community.

A DIVERSE COMMUNITY: A Wake Forest education is about diversity—an amalgam of ideas, talents, ethnicity, socioeconomic backgrounds, geographical differences, and all aspects of the human condition that differ from one individual to the next.

Such a mindful mixture makes for an ideal learning experience whereby students can expand their wealth of knowledge to reach beyond what is easy and comfortable.

THRIVE: Balancing the many aspects of college life can be incredibly hard. Aside from academic stress, students can struggle with unhealthy eating habits and new social demands. Wake Forest has established a program to combat those difficulties.

Known as "*Thrive,*" this initiative is available to all students and consists of eight components, each of which is concerned with the overall well-being of the individual. Areas of focus span from emotional to financial well-being.

RETHINKING SUCCESS: *"Rethinking Success"* is an initiative that challenges all higher education faculty and staff to assess their positions as teachers and mentors. The focus of the movement is to be in a constant state of learning and reinventing so as to better prepare students to meet the demands of a global society.

STUDENT PROFILE

5,102 undergraduate students

99% of undergrad students are full-time

54% female – 46% male

70% of students are from out of state

94% freshman retention rate

FACULTY PROFILE

11 to 1 student/faculty ratio

ADMISSIONS

Selectivity: 28%

TUITION & COST

Tuition: $50,524

Fees: $876

Room: $9,012

Board: $6,342

WESTERN CAROLINA UNIVERSITY

CULLOWHEE, NORTH CAROLINA

Western Carolina University is nestled in a beautiful mountain valley in proximity to Great Smoky Mountain National Park and the Blue Ridge Parkway. The university's rich, 129-year history is rooted in providing quality and rigorous academic programs that serve the students of the region and beyond. The natural scenic beauty of the campus in Cullowhee, North Carolina, provides an ideal study environment that also affords students the opportunity to apply their learning in real settings through community engagement and rich campus programs.

LIBERAL STUDIES: Every WCU bachelor's degree is a symbol not only of a student's mastery of his or her major, but also of a student's deep understanding of a wide range of disciplines. All undergraduate students supplement their education with a core curriculum of foundational courses that strengthen their communication and critical-thinking skills through a variety of contexts.

In addition to the Liberal Studies core requirements is a set of Perspectives courses, which challenge students to think outside of their selected academic majors. More than simple introductory courses, the Perspectives courses push students to grasp unfamiliar topics in varied disciplines.

INTERNSHIPS: While there are countless internship opportunities in the surrounding cities of Western North Carolina, WCU gives students access to internship programs both nationally and in countries all across the world.

FINISH IN FOUR: WCU's Finish in Four initiative is the university's pledge to provide every resource necessary for students to complete their degrees within four years.

Students who pledge to Finish in Four commit to meeting with their advisers who then, in turn, may direct them toward extraordinarily helpful tutors and counselors or programs to ensure their success. No matter how much help a student may need, WCU guarantees a successful route to graduation to all who pledge to Finish in Four.

www.wcu.edu
(828) 227-7317

STUDENT PROFILE

9,835 undergraduate students

87% of undergrad students are full-time

54% female — 46% male

9% of students are from out of state

79% freshman retention rate

FACULTY PROFILE

17 to 1 student/faculty ratio

ADMISSIONS

Selectivity: 39%

SAT Ranges: E 520-620, M 510-600

ACT Ranges: C 20-25, M 19-25, E 20-25

TUITION & COST

Tuition (in-state): $3,926

Tuition (out-of-state): $7,926

Room & Board: $10,103

UNIVERSITY OF MARY

BISMARCK, NORTH DAKOTA

The University of Mary in Bismarck, North Dakota, was founded in 1959 by the Benedictine Sisters of Annunciation Monastery. Beginning as a four-year undergraduate college of education and nursing, it has since expanded to offer 55 undergraduate majors, 14 master's programs, and four doctoral programs. The hallmarks of the University of Mary are in its innovation and distinctiveness.

YEAR-ROUND CAMPUS PROGRAM: Mary has launched a groundbreaking 'Year-Round Campus' program that allows students the option to complete a bachelor's degree in 2.6 years and a master's degree in four! This program allows students to realize an estimated lifetime financial benefit of more than $600,000 by graduating with two degrees in just four years.

SUCCESS: With a job or graduate school placement rate of 96 percent, Mary graduates succeed in obtaining employment or continuing their studies at the next level. Mary offers professional preparation programs, including such fields as business, education, nursing, physical therapy, other health science specializations (like respiratory therapy), and specializations in engineering (civil, electrical, mechanical).

ELA: Offered as an optional community, students in the Emerging Leaders Academy (ELA) receive personal mentorships by leaders in their chosen professions. The program is designed for those who want to make a profound impact through their career, going beyond Mary's already robust internships and experiential learning programs.

"...every graduate who walks across the Commencement stage is a better person than when they first arrived on campus. Hearts and minds are transformed through the curriculum, the sense of community, the people, and the many opportunities offered." *– Katelyn, Class of 2018*

www.umary.edu
(701) 355-8030
enroll@umary.edu

STUDENT PROFILE

2,237 undergraduate students

80% of undergrad students are full-time

63% female – 37% male

75% freshman retention rate

FACULTY PROFILE

14 to 1 student/faculty ratio

ADMISSIONS

Selectivity: 76%

SAT Ranges: E 465-580, M 470-580

ACT Ranges: C 21-26, M 20-26, E 20-26

TUITION & COST

Tuition: $16,470

Fees: $1,754

Room: $3,100

Board: $4,160

DEFIANCE COLLEGE

DEFIANCE, OHIO

Defiance College emphasizes learning based on the four pillars of its institutional mission, *"to know, to understand, to lead, to serve."* The liberal arts-based institution offers 40+ majors and pre-professional programs designed to prepare students to live in the world and change it for the better. Founded in 1850, the 150-acre campus is located in Northwest Ohio, an area of picturesque farmland at the confluence of the Auglaize and Maumee rivers. Defiance offers bachelor's, master's, and associate degrees for different learners at different stages of their educational journey.

PROJECT 701: DC hosts a student-run nonprofit that is believed to be the only one of its kind at any college. Project 701 gives students opportunities to progress from hands-on service to learning about leadership, creating their own service projects, and implementing them as a true, functioning nonprofit.

Projects include student-run businesses that provide computer repair and graphic design services, a program that provides food on weekends for children in need, and a reading and writing center for local children.

SERVICE-LEARNING AND LEADERSHIP: DC is home to the McMaster School for Advancing Humanity, an innovative research program devoted to teaching, service, scholarship, and action to improve the human condition.

Through its program, students and faculty make a lasting impact as they apply their academic expertise to real-world contexts. In recent years, participants have developed projects and established partnerships in Belize, Cambodia, Tanzania, and Panama.

> "Not only am I in the field of study that I enjoy, I've been given many opportunities to expand my leadership skills, volunteer in the community, and even apply the knowledge I've gained at an international scale."

– *Ely King, Mathematics and Business Administration major*

www.defiance.edu
(419) 783-2359
admissions@defiance.edu

STUDENT PROFILE
584 undergraduate students

90% of undergrad students are full-time

44% female – 56% male

60% freshman retention rate

FACULTY PROFILE
11 to 1 student/faculty ratio

ADMISSIONS
Selectivity: 56%

SAT Ranges: E 360-490, M 340-470

ACT Ranges: C 18-22, M 17-23, E 15-22

TUITION & COST
Tuition: $31,480

Fees: $710

Room: $5,500

Board: $4,550

DENISON UNIVERSITY

GRANVILLE, OHIO

Denison's academic mission is to educate students to become independent thinkers and active citizens of a democratic society. At Denison, each student is recognized for their individual value. A Denison education means that no students hide in the back of the class, as they are all encouraged to make themselves known and take advantage of their educational experience. While each student does choose a specific major to study, Denison provides a liberal arts framework on which they can build a solid foundation on which to grow as well-rounded thinkers.

STUDENT RESEARCH: Undergraduate Denison students are afforded countless opportunities to involve themselves in research initiatives, no matter their field of study. And, with the additional offering of the Gilpatrick House, student researchers can enhance and support their efforts with unique residential resources.

Both summer-term and senior researchers are able to live in this House so that their groundbreaking work is given all the attention it deserves.

GREEN CAMPUS: Denison embraces sustainability, aiming to protect and maintain economic, social, and environmental resources throughout the University and beyond. Through research initiatives, investments, and a campus-wide commitment, Denison's conscious efforts are met with the utmost respect.

CAREER DEVELOPMENT: Within six months of graduation, over 85% of Denison graduates are employed, pursuing graduate school, or engaging in postgraduate service. The Office of Career Exploration & Development and The Gilpatrick Center for Student Research & Fellowships are incredibly important resources for students' future pursuits.

Students can discover and achieve their career aspirations through such services as career advising, on-campus recruiting, internships, externships, résumé and cover letter development, mock interviews, networking, graduate school preparation, and various workshops.

DENISON UNIVERSITY

www.denison.edu
(740) 587-6276
admission@denison.edu

STUDENT PROFILE

2,341 undergraduate students

99% of undergrad students are full-time

55% female – 45% male

67% of students are from out of state

91% freshman retention rate

FACULTY PROFILE

9 to 1 student/faculty ratio

ADMISSIONS

Selectivity: 37%

SAT Ranges: E 600-690, M 600-690

ACT Ranges: C 28-31, M 26-30, E 28-34

TUITION & COST

Tuition: $49,310

Fees: $1,130

Room: $6,790

Board: $5,540

HIRAM COLLEGE

HIRAM, OHIO

Hiram College prepares students to answer tough questions, solve complex problems, and communicate their ideas through a broad, interdisciplinary curriculum rooted in liberal arts. Recognizing that learning doesn't just take place in the classroom, 100 percent of Hiram students complete an internship, research, or study-away experience as they connect classroom learning with the "real world."

TECH AND TREK: Introduced in fall 2017, Hiram's Tech and Trek program puts an iPad Pro, Apple pencil, and keyboard bundle in the hands of every full-time traditional student. This is all part of Hiram's New Liberal Arts: integrated study, high-impact experiences, and mindful technology.

THE HIRAM PLAN: Often referred to as the 12+3 plan, The Hiram Plan structures the College's academic semester to include twelve weeks of traditional classes, a one-week break, and three weeks of a single-course intensive period.

After a typical semester of multiple classes, students dive deeply into a particular topic of study. The three-week intensive period is often used for focused research, service-learning, internship experience, or a trip abroad.

ETHICS THEME: Every year, Hiram College focuses on an ethics-related theme. For example, this last year's theme, which explored the idea of "citizen," brought students together both on campus and within the larger community to learn how to better engage in difficult conversations about challenging topics.

HIRAM CONNECT: The Hiram Connect program gives students the opportunity to develop both personally and professionally through internships, study-away trips, and and other ways to apply their education to real-world contexts.

Together, each of Hiram Connect's hands-on programs challenge students to discover what they want to do, who they are now, and who they want to become.

www.hiram.edu
(330) 569-5169
admission@hiram.edu

STUDENT PROFILE

967 undergraduate students

87% of undergrad students are full-time

53% female – 47% male

18% of students are from out of state

70% freshman retention rate

FACULTY PROFILE

10 to 1 student/faculty ratio

ADMISSIONS

Selectivity: 64%

SAT Ranges: E 480-610, M 460-590

ACT Ranges: C 18-24, M 17-24, E 17-24

TUITION & COST

Tuition: $32,700

Fees: $1,600

Room: $5,150

Board: $5,040

MIAMI UNIVERSITY – OXFORD

OXFORD, OHIO

www.miamioh.edu
(513) 529-2531

Miami University provides a rigorous collegiate curriculum. Students are given the opportunities of a large university while experiencing the personalized teaching and attention found at small colleges. It functions through the observance of five "Guiding Principles:" Mutuality, Integrity, Equity, Preparedness, and Inclusion.

COMBINED BACHELOR'S-MASTER'S PROGRAM: Miami hosts more than 20 programs that offer a combined bachelors-masters degree. Students wishing to pursue a combined degree option may declare their interest at any point during their undergraduate experience. Of course, the earlier the better, as the programs take planning and academic advising.

In a combined degree program, students complete their undergraduate courses first and then spend extra time on campus to complete their master's through a shortened graduate-level curriculum.

THREE-YEAR PATHWAYS: Select first-year students who enter Miami with previously completed credits are given the opportunity to earn their degree in just three years. The Three-Year Pathways track is open to students who have completed college-level courses while in high school.

Beginning their academic journey at an advanced level, three-year degree candidates hit the ground running with a cost-efficient plan that sends them straight to their future careers.

MIAMI'S REACH: Miami has several different abroad options that range in duration and destination, but one of the more popular programs is Miami's own Dolibois European Center in Luxembourg. Directly learning from Miami staff, participating students are continually exposed to the same top-tier academics and community service that is so highly valued by the University.

Not only do students gain skills in cross-cultural communication, but they also naturally develop a greater sense of respect, tolerance, and appreciation for unfamiliar cultures and perspectives.

STUDENT PROFILE

17,147 undergraduate students

97% of undergrad students are full-time

50% female – 50% male

35% of students are from out of state

91% freshman retention rate

FACULTY PROFILE

14 to 1 student/faculty ratio

ADMISSIONS

Selectivity: 68%

SAT Ranges: E 580-670, M 610-710

ACT Ranges: C 26-31, M 25-30, E 25-32

TUITION & COST

Tuition (in-state): $12,168

Tuition (out-of-state): $31,421

Fees: $2,790

Room: $7,945

Board: $4,893

MOUNT ST. JOSEPH UNIVERSITY

CINCINNATI, OHIO

MOUNT ST. JOSEPH UNIVERSITY

One of the most important things about going to college is being open. Open to possibilities and creativity. Open to opportunity and experiences. Mount St. Joseph University is the ideal environment for such a receptive frame of mind because it offers an atmosphere of guided and unguided discovery; students are encouraged to explore and encounter by design and by chance. What's the result? Each student's own personal definition of success along with the skills to achieve it.

NEW PROGRAMS: Mount St. Joseph University has received provisional approval to begin a Physician Assistant (PA) program. The Mount is the only university in the Greater Cincinnati area to offer a PA program, with its first class of students having started coursework in January 2018.

TALENT OPPORTUNITY PROGRAM: The Talent Opportunity Program, known as TOP, incentivizes students to engage in specific learning experiences that prepare them for the global marketplace. For example, the bronze level of the program has students take the Foundations of Professionalism Course, participate in a leadership development opportunity, and attend such events as the Etiquette and Networking Dinner.

At the end of the 2016 academic year, 100 percent of gold-level TOP students had secured full-time employment or graduate school admission upon earning their undergraduate degree at Mount St. Joseph University.

WORLDWIDE ENGAGEMENT: Study abroad programs and cultural trips transport students near and far in their learning, including immersion with the Cherokee people of North Carolina as well as formalized course work through Richmond—the American International University—in London, England.

Students at the Mount can go on faculty-led trips. Each August, a group of students join Dr. Jim Bodle and Dr. Elizabeth Barkley on a trip to New York City to learn about non-government organizations' role in helping the United Nations achieve its Sustainable Development Goals by the year 2030.

www.msj.edu
(513) 244-4531
admission@msj.edu

STUDENT PROFILE

1,177 undergraduate students

85% of undergrad students are full-time

57% female – 43% male

19% of students are from out of state

72% freshman retention rate

FACULTY PROFILE

11 to 1 student/faculty ratio

ADMISSIONS

Selectivity: 73%

SAT Ranges: E 490-578, M 490-578

ACT Ranges: C 20-24, M 18-24, E 19-24

TUITION & COST

Tuition: $29,000

Fees: $1,000

Room: $9,442

OHIO DOMINICAN UNIVERSITY

COLUMBUS, OHIO

Connect Passion with a Purpose at Ohio Dominican University. Founded in 1911 in the Catholic Dominican tradition, ODU is committed to developing the whole person. At Ohio Dominican, students can choose to study one of 40 majors (or of nine master's programs)—each of which is designed to prepare them for a career in a rapidly expanding field—including education, science, government, business, technology, and healthcare. Ohio Dominican has a degree that matches any student's passion.

4+1 OFFERINGS: At Ohio Dominican, students have the opportunity to earn both their bachelor's and master's degrees in just five academic years thanks to its 4+1 program. ODU 4+1 grants participants a Master of Arts in English, Master of Business Administration, Master of Science in Healthcare Administration, and Master of Science in Sport Management.

Students can apply a program during their junior year and, come senior year, they take graduate-level courses. By the end of the fourth year, the students receive their bachelor's degree and immediately enroll as full-time graduate students to complete their master's in one year.

HANDS-ON LEARNING AT OHIO DOMINICAN: At Ohio Dominican, students participate in a wide range of hands-on labs and activities to support and enliven the material they learn in the classroom.

These activities could include participating in student teaching at a local school; walking to the Alum Creek to study fish, birds, and other creatures; breaking a sweat as a participant in a Wingate test for an Exercise Science class; or presenting research at ODU's annual Research Symposium.

REWARDING CAREERS: Ohio Dominican's Career Development Center offers comprehensive resources as a student-centered hub for access to meaningful internships and rewarding careers.

Approximately 92 percent of students surveyed in 2017 were either employed full time or attending graduate school within six months of graduating.

www.ohiodominican.edu
(800) 955-6446
admissions@
ohiodominican.edu

STUDENT PROFILE

1,076 undergraduate students

86% of undergrad students are full-time

53% female — 47% male

6% of students are from out of state

65% freshman retention rate

FACULTY PROFILE

14 to 1 student/faculty ratio

ADMISSIONS

Selectivity: 75%

SAT Ranges: E 450-560, M 470-540

ACT Ranges: C 19-24, M 17-25, E 17-23

TUITION & COST

Tuition: $31,100

Fees: $580

Room & Board: $11,220

OTTERBEIN UNIVERSITY

WESTERVILLE, OHIO

OTTERBEIN
UNIVERSITY

www.otterbein.edu
(614) 823-1500
uotterb@otterbein.edu

Since its founding in 1847, Otterbein has been recognized for its pace-setting ideals: its nationally groundbreaking integrative studies curriculum; its standing among the country's first coeducational institutions; its commitment to experiential learning; and its long-standing values in serving and advancing a greater good. Today, Otterbein continues to boldly anticipate its responsibilities to advancing the public good.

CUTTING-EDGE OPPORTUNITIES: The Point, Otterbein's STEAM innovation Center, gives students the chance to work side-by-side with active researchers and startup companies in a space equipped with sophisticated tools, labs, and special manufacturing and engineering equipment.

FIVE CARDS: To ensure that all students may apply the knowledge they gain in the classroom to real-world settings, the University developed a signature initiative known as The Five Cardinal Experiences.

These "Cards" are earned through authentic experiences that challenge students to analyze out-of-classroom contexts through Community Engagement; Internships and Professional Experience; Global and Intercultural Engagement; Leadership and Citizenship; and Undergraduate Research and Creative Work.

SOCIAL JUSTICE: The Office of Social Justice & Activism oversees a group of students called the Social Justice Ambassadors. These student ambassadors serve as an extension of OSJA by facilitating monthly programs, gauging campus climate, and connecting Otterbein to community partners.

"I feel prepared to learn new things, and I have an interconnected foundational knowledge to ground me. Otterbein makes learning fluid and overlapping so that you don't graduate wondering why you took the classes you took." – *Sean Kirk '18, Biochemistry & Molecular Biology and Psychology*

STUDENT PROFILE

2,367 undergraduate students

95% of undergrad students are full-time

62% female – 38% male

15% of students are from out of state

81% freshman retention rate

FACULTY PROFILE

11 to 1 student/faculty ratio

ADMISSIONS

Selectivity: 76%

SAT Ranges: E 520-655, M 520-650

ACT Ranges: C 21-27, M 21-27, E 21-27

TUITION & COST

Tuition: $31,424

Fees: $450

Room: $5,958

Board: $5,300

UNIVERSITY OF CINCINNATI

CINCINNATI, OHIO

University of
CINCINNATI

Located in the bustling city of Cincinnati, UC offers students an unparalleled academic experience, the difference of which lies in the community, people, and ideas it fosters. Committed to serving the people of Ohio and beyond, UC equips students with the tools and experience to think critically about the world around them. The University of Cincinnati prides itself on its commitment to diversity and inclusion of students, faculty, and staff to create an environment where innovation and freedom of intellectual inquiry flourish.

COOPERATIVE EDUCATION: UC boasts one of the oldest and largest cooperative education programs in the nation. This comprehensive, rigorous program is a unique opportunity for students to gain valuable experience in their field. UC is committed to making paid, supervised, major-related work experience and self-reflection available to all students.

Over the past 100 years, UC has cultivated impactful partnerships with organizations from a variety of fields. Students can work for anything from a community-based nonprofit to a Fortune 500 company. Each year, more than 3,500 students participate in this program and graduate with a robust, diverse résumé.

UNDERGRADUATE RESEARCH: The University of Cincinnati is proud to be one of the most renowned research universities in the nation. Its Office of Undergraduate Research supports students as they conduct and present groundbreaking research. ReCON, the Research and Creative Opportunities Network, is an undergraduate student organization where student researchers develop connections with each other, graduate students, faculty, and other research professionals.

CENTER FOR COMMUNITY ENGAGEMENT: Students, faculty, and staff work with community partners to make a positive impact on their communities through meaningful voluntary service. Opportunities range from semester- and year-long opportunities like Bearcat Buddies to short-term opportunities like Days of Service. No matter how big or small, these opportunities reflect UC's commitment to making the world a better place.

www.uc.edu
(513) 556-0000

STUDENT PROFILE

26,559 undergraduate students

85% of undergrad students are full-time

49% female – 51% male

16% of students are from out of state

86% freshman retention rate

FACULTY PROFILE

16 to 1 student/faculty ratio

ADMISSIONS

Selectivity: 76%

SAT Ranges: E 560-660, M 560-680

ACT Ranges: C 23-28, M 23-28, E 22-29

TUITION & COST

Tuition (in-state): $9,322

Tuition (out-of-state): $25,656

Fees: $1,678

Room: $6,624

Board: $4,494

UNIVERSITY OF DAYTON

DAYTON, OHIO

University of Dayton

At the University of Dayton, learning doesn't happen just for the sake of learning. It's about making a difference right now, as an undergraduate. Recently, UD students have created solar-powered equipment to sterilize medical devices, designed cost-effective cargo planes using new composites, developed fitness programs for grade-schoolers, explored the complexities of urban education, and managed and invested nearly $11 million of the University's endowment. Making the world a better place begins one student at a time. That's why the University of Dayton's more than 800 faculty members create interactive learning environments.

HIRE-A-FLYER: Hire-a-Flyer is an invaluable online network that allows students to search job openings, post résumés, schedule interviews with employers, and register for career-related events. Within this network, students can also find the Alumni Career Network, which connects them with skilled, knowledgeable UD alumni.

FIRST-RATE OPPORTUNITIES: University of Dayton graduates consistently take jobs with the nation's best firms and are accepted into top graduate programs. Many seniors receive multiple job offers months before graduation.

UD helps students prepare for their careers beginning on their first day on campus. From cooperative education and internships to on-campus recruiting, career advising, and job-search strategies, Career Services assists students in exploring career interests, experiencing real work environments, and evolving in their chosen field.

DAYTON: With a recording studio, radio station, café, and numerous creative spaces, ArtStreet is ready whenever creativity strikes.

There's also plenty to do in the city of Dayton itself. Located on the edge of campus, Brown Street offers a variety of shops and restaurants, and downtown offers a lively nightlife with coffeehouses, galleries, theater, music, minor league baseball and a laser-lit riverfront park.

www.udayton.edu
(800) 837-7433
admission@udayton.edu

STUDENT PROFILE

8,499 undergraduate students

95% of undergrad students are full-time

48% female – 52% male

51% of students are from out of state

90% freshman retention rate

FACULTY PROFILE

15 to 1 student/faculty ratio

ADMISSIONS

Selectivity: 72%

SAT Ranges: E 550-650, M 550-660

ACT Ranges: C 24-29, M 24-28, E 23-30

TUITION & COST

Tuition: $41,750

Room: $7,900

Board: $5,280

UNIVERSITY OF MOUNT UNION

ALLIANCE, OHIO

At the heart of a Mount Union education is a drive to foster an exceptional experience that enhances students' personal growth and wellbeing. Opportunities for leadership development, social responsibility, and spiritual growth guide them as they seek and solidify a sense of self in preparation for their roles in a global society. Mount Union's nearly 2,300 students can select from 56 undergraduate degrees, both broad-based and career-specific, as well as a number of graduate degrees.

IN-DEMAND PROGRAMS: Over the course of the past decade, Mount Union has added a number of high-demand and academically rigorous undergraduate majors to its curriculum.

Recent additions include criminal justice, biomedical engineering, civil engineering, computer engineering, electrical engineering, mechanical engineering, national security and foreign intelligence analysis, nursing, and risk management and insurance.

INTERCULTURAL COMPETENCE: Mount Union is committed to creating an inclusive culture that values diversity and fosters an environment in which all students can learn.

The University offers diversity-specific academic programs, including minors in African American studies and gender studies. In addition, diversity-related student organizations and annual events altogether contribute to the effort to foster a global mindset and develop intercultural competence.

> "My strong point has always been in the science field, but taking classes such as economics and art have helped me develop skills outside of my major. Now I feel more comfortable writing and researching about subjects that I didn't know much about before coming to Mount."
>
> *- Alyssa Adams '20; Neuroscience Major; Mentor, Ohio*

www.mountunion.edu
(800) 334-6682
**admission@
mountunion.edu**

STUDENT PROFILE

2,155 undergraduate students

100% of undergrad students are full-time

45% female – 55% male

19% of students are from out of state

77% freshman retention rate

FACULTY PROFILE

13 to 1 student/faculty ratio

ADMISSIONS

SAT Ranges: E 480-600, M 488-600

ACT Ranges: C 20-26, M 18-25, E 18-26

TUITION & COST

Tuition: $30,460

Fees: $400

Room & Board: $10,200

WALSH UNIVERSITY

NORTH CANTON, OHIO

Walsh University believes in a small university setting that promotes academic excellence, a diverse exchange of ideas, and close student-teacher interactions. It provides its students a an education that fosters critical thinking, effective communication, spiritual growth, and personal, professional, and cultural development. Ultimately, it encourages individuals to act in accordance with reason, guided by the example and teachings of Jesus Christ.

STUDENT RETREATS: Student retreats, such as the Discover Retreat for freshmen and the Shape Retreat for sophomores, challenge students to make new friends, reflect on changes within their lives, and enhance their leadership potential. These non-denominational retreats offer students some time away from the daily grind to focus on their personal enrichment.

CULTURAL EVENTS: Walsh hosts several cultural events, including the International Dinner, World Week, theatre performances by the Walsh Genesius Players, and music by the Walsh University Chorale.

STUDENT COLLABORATION: At Walsh, students' own personal values and interests help shape their educational experiences. Walsh in turn supports their passions by providing the framework and resources to help them excel. For instance, "The Garage" is a student-directed business incubator in which students can develop enterprising skills and collaborate on business ideas.

"I had so many opportunities in the DeVille School of Business. In addition to being a co-founder of The Garage, I was in the student investment club where we actually invested real money in the stock market. All of this helped me land a consulting position at Ernst & Young right after graduation, and I owe it all to Walsh." – *Iagos Lucca '17*

www.walsh.edu
(800) 362-9846
admissions@walsh.edu

STUDENT PROFILE

2,009 undergraduate students

87% of undergrad students are full-time

59% female – 41% male

10% of students are from out of state

74% freshman retention rate

FACULTY PROFILE

13 to 1 student/faculty ratio

ADMISSIONS

Selectivity: 79%

SAT Ranges: E 540-630, M 480-580

ACT Ranges: C 20-26, M 18-26, E 19-25

TUITION & COST

Tuition: $27,650

Fees: $1,500

Room: $5,770

Board: $4,960

WILMINGTON COLLEGE

WILMINGTON, OHIO

www.wilmington.edu
(937) 481-2260
admission@
wilmington.edu

Wilmington College knows that within each of its students is a remarkable ability to change the world. WC is a community of action—one that graduates students with hundreds of hours of practical application under their belt. It provides the launching pad for promising futures through more than 25 majors, the most popular of which are agriculture, athletic training, business, sport management, and education.

FEED THE MIND, FEED THE WORLD: Agriculture, WC's largest major, plunges students into the field—literally—through hands-on work in the campus' own greenhouses and crop and animal production farm. Whether they conduct research in the new Center for the Sciences & Agriculture, tend to the land on WC's campus farm, or travel to learn about sustainable farming methods in Costa Rica, students are equipped with the tools and knowledge to steer food production toward a sustainable, fruitful future.

HOME FOR ALL: Founded by the Religious Society of Friends (Quakers), WC has always been a community dedicated to inclusivity, peacemaking, and an embrace of difference. As such, WC supports active initiatives to educate the campus community about social justice and diversity.

Just a few of the organizations that help WC's multicultural spirit thrive are the Native American Student Association, the Latino Student Association, the Black Student Initiative, the Jewish Culture Club, and SPECTRA, which celebrates the LGBTQ+ community.

"Wilmington's agriculture program prepared me to succeed not only in the agriculture field, but also in the larger business community by focusing on the applied side of a degree. My Wilmington experience and connections opened doors that I didn't even know existed."

– Linda S. '92; Senior Scientist, Procter & Gamble

STUDENT PROFILE

1,169 undergraduate students

94% of undergrad students are full-time

53% female – 47% male

11% of students are from out of state

68% freshman retention rate

FACULTY PROFILE

14 to 1 student/faculty ratio

ADMISSIONS

Selectivity: 84%

SAT Ranges: E 490-640, M 480-620

ACT Ranges: C 19-24, M 18-25, E 17-23

TUITION & COST

Tuition: $24,300

Fees: $700

Room: $4,590

Board: $5,010

WITTENBERG UNIVERSITY

SPRINGFIELD, OHIO

For more than 160 years, Wittenberg University has developed students' individual gifts and talents by using an active, engaged learning environment that provides an outstanding foundation for successful careers and meaningful lives. Wittenberg embraces its mission in every corner of campus to ensure that students' personal paths to understanding, achievement, and purpose remain at the center of the university's attention. Reflecting its Lutheran heritage, Wittenberg challenges students to become responsible global citizens, to discover their callings, and to lead lives of compassion and integrity.

ENGAGED LEARNING: At Wittenberg, learning extends beyond the walls of the traditional classroom, from local archaeological digs to theatre performances at international festivals.

Through the WittEntrepreneurs Program, students from any discipline can launch, operate, and manage an enterprise on campus. At the Springfield Center for the Arts at Wittenberg University, students can learn about arts management and education. The possibilities are endless.

THE WITTENBERG COMMITMENT: The Wittenberg Commitment is a four-year personal and professional development plan that promises students a seamless transition into college.

The commitment includes comprehensive academic and vocational advising, the creation of a "WittFolio" to share with graduate schools and potential employers, access to the Wittenberg alumni network for mentoring and career resources, and a Four-Year Graduation Guarantee.

CITIZENS AND LEADERS: From collaborative research to helping orphans in an African nation, Wittenberg students grow understand that there never is just one point of view, one answer, or one truth. The choices they make and the issues they face are best understood within multiple contexts. The broader the vision, the more confident and successful they are.

www.wittenberg.edu
(877) 206-0332
admission@
wittenberg.edu

STUDENT PROFILE

1,701 undergraduate students

98% of undergrad students are full-time

54% female – 46% male

23% of students are from out of state

70% freshman retention rate

FACULTY PROFILE

12 to 1 student/faculty ratio

ADMISSIONS

Selectivity: 74%

SAT Ranges: E 540-650, M 530-620

ACT Ranges: C 22-28, M 20-26, E 21-27

TUITION & COST

Tuition: $39,450

Fees: $890

Room: $5,394

Board: $5,170

XAVIER UNIVERSITY

CINCINNATI, OHIO

Rich history and traditions, great opportunities for academic and social growth, and the promise of a rewarding future come with a Xavier degree. Xavier University provides a holistic education with over 145 academic clubs, student organizations, campus activities, international study opportunities in six continents, a small student-to-faculty ratio, and an excellent reputation with employers. With a better education for a better world, Xavier students unlock their unlimited potential.

A CAMPUS OF SUPPORT AND OPPORTUNITY: From the moment freshmen arrive on campus, Xavier's support services provide the guidance and support they need to stay on track. These services encourage students to get involved in on-campus activities, inform students of the University's services and resources, monitor and encourage academic progress, and help resolve any personal problems.

Through the Manresa orientation program, upperclassmen help incoming freshmen learn everything they need to know about the University, including where to eat and how to find their first classes.

INTERNSHIPS: Xavier's location in Cincinnati provides the resources to help students gain meaningful experience through local internships. 13 Fortune 1000 companies operate in Cincinnati. In the past, students have interned with Procter and Gamble, Cincinnati Reds, and the Cincinnati Bengals.

THE WORLD BEYOND: The surrounding Cincinnati area offers many cultural resources and leisure activities, including the Cincinnati Ballet, Newport Aquarium, and the nation's largest Oktoberfest. Professional sports include the Cincinnati Reds baseball team, the Cincinnati Bengals football team, and the Cyclones hockey team.

For students who prefer to spend time on campus, Xavier's student clubs and organizations promote a constant stream of events that include performances by well known comedians, late-night movies, improv, and student plays.

www.xavier.edu
(877) 982-3648
xuadmit@xavier.edu

STUDENT PROFILE

4,634 undergraduate students

94% of undergrad students are full-time

54% female – 46% male

59% of students are from out of state

84% freshman retention rate

FACULTY PROFILE

11 to 1 student/faculty ratio

ADMISSIONS

Selectivity: 74%

SAT Ranges: E 540-620, M 520-620

ACT Ranges: C 22-28, M 21-27, E 22-29

TUITION & COST

Tuition: $37,000

Fees: $230

Room: $6,750

Board: $5,710

OKLAHOMA BAPTIST UNIVERSITY

SHAWNEE, OKLAHOMA

Oklahoma Baptist University is a highly ranked Christian liberal arts university in Shawnee, Oklahoma. Founded in 1910, OBU seeks to transform lives by equipping students to pursue academic excellence, integrate faith with all areas of knowledge, engage a diverse world, and live worthy of the high calling of God in Christ.

THE MILBURN CENTER: The Milburn Center for Student Success and Academic Advising is committed to the success of every student. Staff and resources are available to assist students of all majors, classifications, and academic needs.

Staff assist students with comprehension of course material, as well as in the development of study, research, analytical, reading, writing, and critical thinking skills.

SENIOR EXPERIENCE: OBU students have the opportunity to demonstrate expertise within their disciplines through capstone projects and courses. These experiences push students to apply all the knowledge they have gained and demonstrate preparedness for applying their degree in a professional capacity.

OBU's student experience culminates in not only the knowledge needed to succeed after college, but also in the development of character, faith, and integrity—all that sets OBU graduates apart from those from other institutions.

"Not only did I gain the foundational skills I needed to succeed as a nurse, but I also received a Christ-centered education that incorporated faith into every aspect of our studies. I am thankful that faith was a large part of my education, as I believe it makes me better equipped to care for and serve the patients that walk through the doors of our clinic every day." *- Worthy Walker, Class of 2010*

www.okbu.edu
(405) 585-5000
admissions@okbu.edu

STUDENT PROFILE

1,902 undergraduate students

100% of undergrad students are full-time

59% female — 41% male

32% of students are from out of state

68% freshman retention rate

FACULTY PROFILE

15 to 1 student/faculty ratio

ADMISSIONS

Selectivity: 60%

SAT Ranges: E 460-600, M 460-565

ACT Ranges: C 20-26, M 18-25, E 20-27

TUITION & COST

Tuition: $22,710

Fees: $2,600

Room: $3,250

Board: $3,760

OKLAHOMA CHRISTIAN UNIVERSITY

EDMOND, OKLAHOMA

Oklahoma Christian University opens its doors to faith-infused learning both at home and abroad. Featuring a close-knit community where students, faculty, and staff go the extra mile for each other, the OC community is fiercely dedicated to high standards of scholarship. Its professors' commitment to students goes beyond the classroom—their office doors are open, and they spend time side-by-side with students in the cafeteria, at games against the University's NCAA rivals, and in real-world ministry as part of the Ethos spiritual life program.

ETHOS: Spiritual life is at the core of the Oklahoma Christian University experience. Through the Ethos program, students use their gifts and talents to practice spiritual disciplines in five dimensions: Community, Discipleship, Discovery, Servanthood, and Worship.

Students take charge of their spiritual growth and earn "kudos" (spiritual life credits) by attending Big Chapel, small group Bible studies, community service projects, speaker events, and more. Engaging in endless combinations of activities, students can track their participation and document their journey via a University-developed phone application.

PRACTICAL EXPERIENCE: Academic departments regularly partner with the Office of Career Services to place students in internships for practical experiences within their curricula.

Engineering students take Toastmasters classes to improve their oral communication skills, while health science and nursing students join the student-led Eagles Health Initiative to educate community members about important issues like mental health.

Additionally, education students can serve as reading buddies to inner-city elementary schoolers. OC students are constantly practicing their crafts while pursuing their vocation.

www.oc.edu
(405) 425-5050
admissions@oc.edu

STUDENT PROFILE

1,817 undergraduate students

97% of undergrad students are full-time

51% female – 49% male

54% of students are from out of state

75% freshman retention rate

FACULTY PROFILE

13 to 1 student/faculty ratio

ADMISSIONS

Selectivity: 65%

SAT Ranges: E 510-640, M 510-640

ACT Ranges: C 20-27, M 20-28, E 18-26

TUITION & COST

Tuition: $22,760

Fees: $300

Room: $4,455

Board: $3,735

ORAL ROBERTS UNIVERSITY

TULSA, OKLAHOMA

ORAL ROBERTS UNIVERSITY

ORU is a liberal arts university founded on a vision of educating the Whole Person—mind, body, and spirit. Faculty and staff believe their students are called to use this Whole Person education and the power of the Holy Spirit to bring God's healing to the uttermost bounds of the earth. ORU offers over 70 undergraduate majors, all strengthened by a well-rounded liberal arts curriculum and a forward-thinking, globally-focused faculty and administration, that set up graduates to thrive in whatever sphere God has called them to.

HOLISTIC GROWTH: No matter their area of study, each student is evaluated based on the Whole Person Assessment (WPA). These standards reflect the outcomes that are ingrained in the University's mission, ensuring that everyone who receives an ORU education has been fulfilled holistically to become spiritually alive, intellectually alert, physically disciplined, socially adept, and professionally competent.

FACULTY OF FAITH AND SCHOLARSHIP: ORU faculty, who are leaders themselves, inspire their students with the knowledge they gained from such institutions as Yale and Harvard as well as such companies as Microsoft and NASA. ORU students enjoy close relationships with their teachers, hands-on internships with their professors' peers, and the chance to discover new things as assistants in faculty-led research.

Additionally, ORU students and faculty take full advantage of the University's new Global Learning Center, a state-of-the-art educational facility that utilizes Augmented and Virtual Reality (AVR) to deepen the learning experience while simultaneously making it more fun!

SPIRITUAL LEADERS: A radiating sense of spirituality is palpable the moment one steps on campus. Through the Chaplain Program, every wing of ORU housing is appointed a student chaplain who helps foster a compassionate, supportive environment among their residents. As guiding faith leaders, these chaplains are committed to forming close relationships with their floormates, all while nurturing the community's passion for God.

www.oru.edu
(918) 495-6518
admissions@oru.edu

STUDENT PROFILE

3,098 undergraduate students

93% of undergrad students are full-time

60% female – 40% male

52% of students are from out of state

84% freshman retention rate

FACULTY PROFILE

14 to 1 student/faculty ratio

ADMISSIONS

Selectivity: 93%

SAT Ranges: E 500-623, M 490-590

ACT Ranges: C 20-26, M 18-25, E 20-27

TUITION & COST

Tuition: $26,700

Fees: $1,028

Room: $4,390

Board: $5,060

UNIVERSITY OF SCIENCE AND ARTS OF OKLAHOMA

CHICKASHA, OKLAHOMA

The University of Science and Arts of Oklahoma is the state's only public liberal arts college. Its mission is to provide the public with a distinctive and accessible liberal arts and sciences education. In combining an interdisciplinary core curriculum with superior instruction in major fields of study, USAO aims to provide a thorough education that prepares students for meaningful, purposeful lives.

IDS: The world is complex, and so many complex challenges face this generation. USAO's Interdisciplinary Studies (IDS) program is a carefully designed sequence of courses that incorporates many academic traditions while building connections between them.

These classes are generally team-taught by two or more professors from different disciplines. The IDS program is the spine that has held USAO's liberal arts mission upright for 50 years.

LIVING PROOF: USAO graduates are living proof that the liberal arts model will enable students to learn, exercise critical thinking, and communicate. Regardless of a student's path, the skills gained at USAO are time-tested and designed to last.

This is why USAO is recognized by the American Council of Trustees and Alumni as one of only 23 universities nationwide to meet the highest standards in requiring every student to have a solid foundation in core subjects.

CHICKASHA: Chickasha, a small town of 17,000, is 35 miles from Oklahoma City's metro area, which features a variety shopping and arts events.

The town is the proud home of the internationally recognized Festival of Light, a holiday extravaganza that features displays of more than 3.5 million Christmas lights.

www.usao.edu
(405) 574-1357
usao-admissions@
usao.edu

STUDENT PROFILE
882 undergraduate students

82% of undergrad students are full-time

65% female – 35% male

7% of students are from out of state

72% freshman retention rate

FACULTY PROFILE
13 to 1 student/faculty ratio

ADMISSIONS
Selectivity: 52%

SAT Ranges: E 395-500, M 420-510

ACT Ranges: C 19-24, M 18-25, E 16-22

TUITION & COST
Tuition (in-state): $6,030

Tuition (out-of-state): $16,380

Fees: $1,170

Room: $3,020

Board: $3,010

UNIVERSITY OF TULSA

TULSA, OKLAHOMA

A Better Fit for a Better Tomorrow. The University of Tulsa is a private, doctoral-degree granting, accredited, coeducational institution founded in 1894. It offers students a rare combination—the resources and opportunities of a large university with the personal attention and mentoring typically found at a much smaller college. A warm classroom environment and state-of-the-art facilities give students an engaging college experience.

EVOLVING PROGRAMS FOR CONTEMPORARY INTEREST: Student interest in the burgeoning energy management field factored into the creation of the School of Energy Economics, Policy, & Commerce. This program prepares undergraduates for careers in upstream and midstream sectors of the global energy industry.

EXPERIENTIAL LEARNING: TU students learn by doing. For example, Third Floor Design, the student-run graphic design agency, provides award-winning promotional materials to Tulsa-area nonprofits.

The College of Arts and Sciences is home to several major scholarly journals (e.g., the James Joyce Quarterly, Tulsa Studies in Women's Literature and Nimrod), all of which afford undergraduates opportunities to learn about the business of publishing.

INFORMATION SECURITY: TU's reputation as a leader in information security education and research is well established, unique in its breadth and depth. The university trains federally certified computer security experts. Since 1996, its Institute for Information Security (iSec) has produced some of the country's leading professionals in information security, digital forensics, Internet security, and telecommunications security.

GREENHOUSE FOR CREATIVITY: The Collins College of Business is home to Studio Blue, a self-described greenhouse for creativity. Students from every discipline use this campus resource to exercise their right brains in innovative problem solving.

www.utulsa.edu
(918) 631-2307
admission@utulsa.edu

STUDENT PROFILE

3,343 undergraduate students

96% of undergrad students are full-time

44% female – 56% male

39% of students are from out of state

88% freshman retention rate

FACULTY PROFILE

11 to 1 student/faculty ratio

ADMISSIONS

Selectivity: 39%

SAT Ranges: E 590-720, M 560-720

ACT Ranges: C 25-32, M 24-30, E 25-34

TUITION & COST

Tuition: $40,484

Fees: $1,025

Room: $6,394

Board: $6,412

CORBAN UNIVERSITY

SALEM, OREGON

Corban University is committed to preparing students to be Christian thought leaders in today's culture, thriving as part of society in a wide variety of careers while living for Christ. Students are challenged to ask questions, search for answers, and build a biblically-based worldview so that they can lead with conviction, integrity, and intelligence. Expert faculty with professional career experience remain active in their fields while building mentoring relationships with students.

FACULTY ADVISORS: Corban faculty take an active role in each student's college experience, serving as advisors to students from the moment they enroll at Corban. Through the Freshman Seminar program, all incoming freshmen are assigned to a small, faculty-led group of students who share their academic interests.

During Warrior Welcome, as well as throughout the fall semester, students meet with their seminar group, getting to know one another, discussing strategies to transition successfully to college life, and developing a growing understanding of their chosen discipline.

BE INSPIRED: Corban is a place of authentic Christianity. Students and faculty alike love Jesus, and it shows. Residence hall Bible studies and chapel, which meets three times a week, encourage students to grow in their faith. Regular guest speakers and events like the Christian Thought Leader Conference and Women of Grit challenge students to live authentically and wrestle intentionally with current cultural issues.

MAKING A DIFFERENCE: Students who attend Corban have the opportunity to serve in the community with churches and non-profit organizations through Corban's REACH program.

This program emphasizes Corban's mission "to educate Christians who will make a difference in the world for Jesus Christ," as students serve in organizations that focus on education and literacy, hunger and housing, dignity and justice, conservation, or mentoring and coaching.

www.corban.edu
(503) 581-8600
admissions@corban.edu

STUDENT PROFILE

913 undergraduate students

95% of undergrad students are full-time

60% female – 40% male

42% of students are from out of state

77% freshman retention rate

FACULTY PROFILE

12 to 1 student/faculty ratio

ADMISSIONS

Selectivity: 59%

SAT Ranges: E 568-620, M 500-580

ACT Ranges: C 20-26, M 18-25, E 18-25

TUITION & COST

Tuition: $32,380

Fees: $997

Room & Board: $10,316

EASTERN OREGON UNIVERSITY

LA GRANDE, OREGON

EASTERN OREGON
UNIVERSITY

www.eou.edu
(800) 452-8639
admissions@eou.edu

Officially designated Oregon's Rural University in 2018, EOU cultivates innovative partnerships with communities across the region to expand economic and educational opportunities for all. About 1,300 students attend EOU on campus in La Grande, OR, a small college town nestled in the Grande Ronde Valley. On-campus programs include art, theatre, and music, as well as chemistry, nursing, and agricultural sciences.

ASTEO SCHOLARS: EOU students majoring in biology, chemistry-biochemistry, computer science, and mathematics can join Advancing Science and Technology in Eastern Oregon (ASTEO) and live in a STEM community in the campus residence halls.

ASTEO Scholars participate in hands-on learning beginning their first year of study, attend regular activities with STEM faculty, become eligible for summer internships, and sometimes qualify for paid positions as an ASTEO Ambassador for EOU.

EOU RESEARCH: Undergraduate students regularly get to work alongside EOU's skilled professors across disciplines. They compete in the international math-modeling competition (at which EOU usually finishes in the top five worldwide); create new software for senior computer science projects; and engage with aspiring scientists through school outreach programs.

Original research appears regularly in the award-winning Eastern Oregon Science Journal—the first student-published, undergraduate scientific research journal in the state.

"As a manager in the healthcare industry, I use the analytical, personal, and communication skills I learned at EOU on a daily basis. I am a proud graduate and can confidently say this program has made me a better leader in my field." – *Emily Higgins*

STUDENT PROFILE

2,587 undergraduate students

65% of undergrad students are full-time

60% female – 40% male

32% of students are from out of state

68% freshman retention rate

FACULTY PROFILE

17 to 1 student/faculty ratio

ADMISSIONS

Selectivity: 98%

SAT Ranges: E 470-572.5, M 470-560

ACT Ranges: C 18-23, M 17-23, E 15-22

TUITION & COST

Tuition (in-state): $5,010

Tuition (out-of-state): $13,440

Fees: $429

Room: $5,800

Board: $4,050

GEORGE FOX UNIVERSITY

NEWBERG, OREGON

GEORGE FOX
UNIVERSITY

Located in Newberg, OR, George Fox offers bachelor's degrees in more than 40 majors, degree-completion programs for working adults, five seminary degrees, and 12 master's and doctoral degrees. Undergraduates think with clarity, act with integrity, and serve with passion. The university's vision is to become one of the most innovative and engaging universities in the western United States known for both academic excellence and its connection of Jesus Christ's message to opportunities for the future.

SERVING CHRIST, SERVING THE COMMUNITY: George Fox takes seriously the Christ's challenge for people to be agents of love and reconciliation in the world. The school hosts spring, winter, and May service trips that allow students to serve in diverse, cross-cultural settings that range from Los Angeles to Swaziland. Some programs, such as engineering and nursing, integrate service into the curriculum.

FELLOWSHIP: At George Fox, faith is a verb. The university wants to help students pursue their passions and calling. As their relationships with God grow deep and wide, so too do their desires to engage the world and do the work of Jesus. Through chapel, small-group study, service trips, and everyday living on campus, students have the opportunity to make their spiritual journeys ones of great adventure.

ALUMNI FOR EVERY SKILL: George Fox University graduates don't simply receive "book knowledge." They aren't simply prepared for a career. They graduate with an education that empowers them spiritually, academically, and professionally. They reimagine the world.

A computer programmer in China, a Peace Corps volunteer in Bolivia, and a film editor in Los Angeles are just a few of the people who credit George Fox University as the place that helped them discover and prepare for their calling. Notable alumni include former president Herbert Hoover, best-selling Christian book author Richard Foster, and Oregon Court of Appeals judge Darleen Ortega.

www.georgefox.edu
(503) 554-2240
admissions@
georgefox.edu

STUDENT PROFILE
2,698 undergraduate students

92% of undergrad students are full-time

57% female – 43% male

45% of students are from out of state

83% freshman retention rate

FACULTY PROFILE
14 to 1 student/faculty ratio

ADMISSIONS
Selectivity: 82%

SAT Ranges: E 530-650, M 520-620

ACT Ranges: C 21-27, M 20-27, E 20-28

TUITION & COST
Tuition: $34,500

Fees: $516

Room: $6,300

Board: $4,586

PACIFIC UNIVERSITY

FOREST GROVE, OREGON

www.pacificu.edu
(503) 352-6151

With programs designed for the individual, Pacific offers an excellent education at a great value. Pacific University places a high value on the importance of integrating a liberal arts philosophy and curriculum with professional education. Graduates gain a solid academic background and build practical skills in over 50 majors. Because of the practical knowledge already gained in the course of the undergraduate experience, Pacific students are truly prepared for exceptional careers or graduate schools.

SUMMER RESEARCH: Students have the opportunity to apply to spend a 10-week summer session collaborating on research with a faculty member. They even receive a stipend for their work along with new skills and experiences.

While students may only work on the project for a short period of time, they sometimes incorporate this collaborative work into their own studies or senior capstone projects.

PATHWAYS: The Pathways program is designed to help students figure out who they want to be and where they want to go. Students get the chance to explore different careers and courses through 1-credit courses and get high-quality practicing in interviewing and résumé building.

OUTDOOR RECREATION: The Outdoor Recreation program is offered to students starting as soon as they send in a deposit. The program is designed so students can explore the community and surrounding area with their peers, faculty, and staff. Some activities include hiking, biking, and kayaking.

CAREER SERVICES: Students are first introduced to Career Services and their career advisor during the summer before their first year. While the office has a primarily "you come to us" system, Pacific already has programs in place and integrate career and academic advisors to ensure all students are on the right path to the career they desire.

The Career Services office offers access to Handshake, résumé writing, interview prep, internship searching, and job searching.

STUDENT PROFILE

1,876 undergraduate students

97% of undergrad students are full-time

60% female – 40% male

62% of students are from out of state

79% freshman retention rate

FACULTY PROFILE

10 to 1 student/faculty ratio

ADMISSIONS

Selectivity: 84%

SAT Ranges: E 540-630, M 530-630

ACT Ranges: C 22-27, M 21-27, E 21-27

TUITION & COST

Tuition: $41,624

Fees: $970

Room: $6,710

Board: $5,452

PORTLAND STATE UNIVERSITY

PORTLAND, OREGON

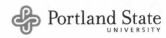

Portland State University is a public research university whose mission is rooted in sustainable living, accessibility, and community engagement. Its location within the city inspires students to solve problems and promote prosperity within rapidly changing, urban environments.

THE CENTER OF THE CITY: Portland State is a vibrant campus located within an equally vibrant city. With some 50 academic buildings, the campus boundaries dovetail almost seamlessly with the rest of downtown.

Portland's bus and light rail lines, as well as its ubiquitous bike paths, give students easy access to the campus and to the surrounding city, which is a magnet for foodies, book store lovers, and microbrew enthusiasts. PSU's Urban Plaza, occupied by the College of Urban and Public Affairs and the Academic and Student Recreation Center, is Portland's busiest transit hub.

A PRACTICAL URBAN FOCUS: Engaged professors provide rigorous instruction and personalized academic support at PSU's University Honors College, the only urban-focused honors college in the United States.

Guided by PSU's motto "Let knowledge serve the city," faculty scholarship and research addresses some of society's most pressing challenges. Student learning converges with real opportunities created through faculty-facilitated community collaborations.

UNIVERSITY STUDIES PROGRAM: The foundation of Portland State's undergraduate student experience is the four-year, award-winning University Studies Program. Started in 1994, the program has revolutionized general education at PSU, providing students with interdisciplinary, connected learning experiences that lay the groundwork for lifelong learning.

The program also provides opportunities for student engagement and co-creation in the classroom through its peer mentoring program. In a nutshell, it teaches students how to learn. University Studies brings relevance and meaning to a student's general education.

www.pdx.edu
(503) 725-3511
admissions@pdx.edu

STUDENT PROFILE

18,571 undergraduate students

75% of undergrad students are full-time

54% female – 46% male

16% of students are from out of state

74% freshman retention rate

FACULTY PROFILE

20 to 1 student/faculty ratio

ADMISSIONS

Selectivity: 90%

SAT Ranges: E 510-630, M 500-600

ACT Ranges: C 18-25, M 17-25, E 18-25

TUITION & COST

Tuition (in-state): $8,078

Tuition (out-of-state): $26,910

Fees: $1,500

Room: $9,765

Board: $3,846

UNIVERSITY OF PORTLAND

PORTLAND, OREGON

A Tradition of Extraordinary Teaching, A History of Extraordinary Students. University of Portland's education is guided by knowledge that is imparted by award-winning professors, enhanced by real-world experiences, and underscored by the values the University has embraced since its founding in 1901. University of Portland has a commitment to service and the unwavering belief that the mind is little without the heart.

TEACHING THE MIND, EMPOWERING THE HEART: The faculty at the University of Portland live and breathe what they teach. They are active, passionate scholars who are highly respected in their fields. Relatively small classes help professors discover the strengths and needs of their students. One faculty member notes, *"Activity, creativity, discovery—those are the habits of mind I am trying to teach my students."*

University of Portland faculty members are recognized for their willingness to meet one-on-one with students outside class hours. They are also more than willing to support their students on service days and during other university activities.

LIVING TOGETHER AS A FAMILY: As a way of supporting living-and-learning communities, the university offers special-interest housing for groups of eight to sixteen students. Some houses, such as the social justice house, are available each year. Others are individually established so that a group of students with a particular interest can live together for a single year.

EVENTS FOR ALL: A steady assortment of interesting guest speakers, fiction and poetry readings, dialogues on faith and justice, theatrical offerings, and other activities fill the campus calendar. Throughout the school year, students actively cheer for their competitive Division I athletic teams.

Students also enjoy the Outdoor Pursuits Program to take advantage of the campus' location, which is in close proximity to the mountains. They go on skiing and snowboarding trips and take to the Oregon coast for beach adventures.

---

www.up.edu
(503) 943-7147
admissions@up.edu

STUDENT PROFILE

3,883 undergraduate students

98% of undergrad students are full-time

60% female – 40% male

75% of students are from out of state

88% freshman retention rate

FACULTY PROFILE

12 to 1 student/faculty ratio

ADMISSIONS

Selectivity: 70%

SAT Ranges: E 580-660, M 560-660

ACT Ranges: C 23-29, M 23-30, E 23-28

TUITION & COST

Tuition: $43,686

Fees: $340

Room & Board: $12,658

WARNER PACIFIC UNIVERSITY

PORTLAND, OREGON

WARNER PACIFIC
UNIVERSITY

Warner Pacific's Christ-centered, liberal arts approach invites students to seek answers to difficult questions and challenges students to expand their comfort zone in order to explore the ways in which they understand society, community, and faith.

MURDOCK SCHOLARS: Warner Pacific Murdock Scholars are young scientists who spend ten weeks during the summer between their junior and senior years working full-time on a scientific project under the direction of an established scientist at Oregon Health and Sciences University.

During their senior year, the scholars continue to work part-time with their mentors to complete their research projects, write their scientific theses, and present their research at local conferences.

The program brings the brightest science majors from local, private institutions of higher education to work in the nationally recognized laboratories of the OHSU Heart Research Center and the Knight Cancer Institute.

MUSIC BUSINESS/ENTREPRENEURSHIP: The Music Business/ Entrepreneurship degree prepares students for careers in business that are related to the music industry, such as retail, recording and production, publishing, and instruction. The beautiful campus recording studio provides a valuable resource for those wishing to develop their skills in production and sound engineering.

SOCIAL ENTREPRENEURSHIP: The first of its kind in Oregon, the Social Entrepreneurship major at Warner Pacific equips students with the expertise needed to create innovative business ventures that address society's most pressing challenges.

During the senior year, in conjunction with their internship, Social Entrepreneurship majors identify a need within the community and then create a small entrepreneurial business to meet that need.

www.warnerpacific.edu
(800) 804-1510
admissions@
warnerpacific.edu

STUDENT PROFILE

400 undergraduate students

99% of undergrad students are full-time

60% female — 40% male

62% freshman retention rate

FACULTY PROFILE

9 to 1 student/faculty ratio

ADMISSIONS

Selectivity: 95%

TUITION & COST

Tuition (in-state): $23,840

Tuition (out-of-state): $23,840

Fees: $660

Room: $3,830

Board: $5,430

WILLAMETTE UNIVERSITY

SALEM, OREGON

WILLAMETTE
THE FIRST UNIVERSITY IN THE WEST

www.willamette.edu
(503) 370-6303
bearcat@willamette.edu

A *Premier Liberal Arts University in the Northwest*. Whether they are pursuing innovative research, interning with a business or nonprofit, working one-on-one with a professor, studying abroad, or leading a campus organization, Willamette University students hone their creativity, global perspectives, and critical thinking for a lifetime of success. Willamette's rich curriculum and collaborative learning environment allow students to explore a wide variety of subjects that are critical to helping them navigate the world. Students research side-by-side with professors and improve their communities through service.

JOINT DEGREES: In addition to nearly 50 undergraduate academic programs, Willamette students may also choose a joint degree program, pairing their liberal arts education with a master's degree so that they may stand out from the competition and get a jumpstart on their career.

Willamette offers three joint degrees, including a bachelor of arts/master of business administration (BA/MBA), a BA/master of arts in teaching (BA/MAT) and a BA/juris doctor (BA/JD).

INTERNSHIPS: Politics, biology, economics, and psychology are among our top majors, but our students nevertheless explore a wide spectrum of interests.

A majority of students investigate their academic interests and career possibilities through one or more internships—from the Oregon State Capitol across the street to Intel and the Art Institute of Chicago—as they gain work experience to enhance their job and grad school applications.

STUDENT INITIATIVES: Willamette students are always looking for new ways to make their mark on the world, frequently launching new endeavors both on campus and in the community while learning valuable skills of teamwork and productivity. The Bistro coffee shop on campus, the Wulapalooza art and music festival, and Zena Farm are just a few examples of student-created initiatives.

STUDENT PROFILE

1,948 undergraduate students

98% of undergrad students are full-time

57% female – 43% male

72% of students are from out of state

86% freshman retention rate

FACULTY PROFILE

11 to 1 student/faculty ratio

ADMISSIONS

Selectivity: 89%

TUITION & COST

Tuition: $47,840

Fees: $318

Room: $6,160

Board: $5,920

CABRINI UNIVERSITY

RADNOR, PENNSYLVANIA

Cabrini University is a non-profit, co-educational school that offers more than 40 majors, six master's degrees, and two doctoral degrees. From their first semester, students learn how to advocate for social change and explore where they stand in the fight for human rights and dignity.

JUSTICE MATTERS CORE CURRICULUM: Each student begins the Cabrini University experience with the Justice Matters core curriculum, which builds writing and analytical skills with a focus on issues of human rights, inclusivity, and other social issues.

Engagements with the Common Good (ECG) classes sit at the heart of the curriculum, leading students on a journey of self-discovery and greater awareness of the world.

SPECIALTY CENTERS: Cabrini's academic centers provide students with more opportunities to meet industry experts, connect with communities, and learn from faculty and staff outside the classroom.

In 2017, four new centers were launched to become "think tanks" for the university's faculty and the broader community. The Center for Urban Education, Equity, and Improvement; The Center for Immigration; The Center for Children of Trauma and Domestic Violence Education; and the Center for Global Learning are great sources of social advocacy-related information for both the Cabrini community and the country at large.

"At Cabrini, I was able to flourish tremendously with my grades, because for once, I was able to take classes that were very meaningful to me... I owe it to this wonderful school for showing me my true identity and allowing me to do what the university really strives for: to live with purpose."

– Eric Stone ('19)

www.cabrini.edu
(800) 848-1003
admit@cabrini.edu

STUDENT PROFILE

1,557 undergraduate students

95% of undergrad students are full-time

62% female – 38% male

71% freshman retention rate

FACULTY PROFILE

11 to 1 student/faculty ratio

ADMISSIONS

Selectivity: 72%

SAT Ranges: E 500-590, M 490-580

ACT Ranges: C 18-22

TUITION & COST

Tuition: $31,875

Fees: $990

Room: $7,560

Board: $5,030

CALIFORNIA UNIVERSITY OF PENNSYLVANIA

CALIFORNIA, PENNSYLVANIA

CALIFORNIA UNIVERSITY OF PENNSYLVANIA

California University of Pennsylvania (Cal U) was founded in 1852 to prepare teachers for Pennsylvania's classrooms. Today, Cal U has grown to a mid-size public university that offers over 100 undergraduate and more than 95 graduate programs of study in education, human services, the liberal arts, business, science, and technology.

REAL-WORLD EXPERIENCE: Cal U students have translated their passion and knowledge into amazing internship experiences throughout the United States—and in other countries, too. Some internships have taken them outdoors to work on stream restoration projects or to lead off-road driving experiences and geocaching quests. Others have taken them into courtrooms or legislative offices.

Some internships have involved sharing a love of art or science with younger generations through educational programming at museums, and still others have given students an insider's view of corporations and sports franchises.

SUPPORT FOR FIRST-YEAR STUDENTS: The transition to college is exciting, but also a bit daunting. It takes time to learn the ropes. Cal U makes it easier with such benefits as the First-Year Seminar course as well as the Peer Mentoring Program, which matches participating first-year students with upperclassmen to help them stay afloat and thrive. Peer mentors are assigned to first-year "protégés" based on similarities—they usually have the same major and may have other interests in common or come from the same place.

"Places that I go, they always say, 'Oh, Cal U has the best— you're always so much more professional than other schools, and you're already so much more prepared, and we love Cal U graduates, and we just want them.'"

– Rachel Wilkinson, Early Childhood Education Major

www.calu.edu
(724) 938-4404

STUDENT PROFILE
5,065 undergraduate students

83% of undergrad students are full-time

54% female – 46% male

7% of students are from out of state

71% freshman retention rate

FACULTY PROFILE
18 to 1 student/faculty ratio

ADMISSIONS
Selectivity: 97%

SAT Ranges: E 450-560, M 450-540

ACT Ranges: C 17-23, M 16-22, E 15-22

TUITION & COST
Tuition (in-state): $7,716

Tuition (out-of-state): $11,574

Fees: $3,392

Room: $6,592

Board: $3,594

CARLOW UNIVERSITY

PITTSBURGH, PENNSYLVANIA

Carlow emphasizes a well-rounded liberal arts education with a solid foundation in ethics and social justice. Its students carry with them the values that have defined Carlow University for nearly a hundred years. They go on to do good—and do well—in their chosen professions. According to a recent career outcomes report, 94 percent of Carlow alumni were employed or continuing their studies at Carlow or other universities within six months of graduation.

HISTORY OF ACTION: Carlow's students and faculty have been at the forefront of such issues as environmental protection, women's empowerment and education, and racial equality, having participated in different activist events like the Civil Rights marches in Selma.

With the 2017 launch of the Social Justice Institutes, Carlow addresses the epidemic of gun violence with a scholarship available to eligible students affected by what the American Medical Association calls "a public health crisis."

PITTSBURGH: Carlow has one of the safest campuses in one of the safest cities in the country, situated in the heart of the Eds, Meds, and Tech section of Oakland in Pittsburgh, PA. Its proximity to world-renowned hospitals and laboratories offer unique access to students interested in pursuing science or health care degrees.

UNDERGRADUATE RESEARCH: Thanks to the size of Carlow University, undergraduate research has always been an important dimension of its biology and chemistry programs. Together, students and faculty pursue meaningful research projects that can lead to publications in journals and presentations at professional conferences.

For example, Dr. Sandi DiMola's public policy courses connect research with real community need by partnering with YWCA of Greater Pittsburgh, designing training modules to encourage women to take on appointed roles as board and commission members.

www.carlow.edu
(412) 578-6059
admissions@carlow.edu

STUDENT PROFILE

1,365 undergraduate students

79% of undergrad students are full-time

84% female – 16% male

6% of students are from out of state

78% freshman retention rate

FACULTY PROFILE

12 to 1 student/faculty ratio

ADMISSIONS

Selectivity: 92%

SAT Ranges: E 460-520, M 440-520

ACT Ranges: C 20-24, M 17-23, E 19-25

TUITION & COST

Tuition: $27,950

Fees: $646

Room: $5,680

Board: $5,428

CEDAR CREST COLLEGE

ALLENTOWN, PENNSYLVANIA

Cedar Crest College

www.cedarcrest.edu
(800) 360-1222
admissions@
cedarcrest.edu

The foundation of the Cedar Crest College education is a grounding in the liberal arts and a dedication to academic excellence. As a college primarily for women, Cedar Crest integrates women's leadership into all aspects of academic and student life. These efforts go beyond an emphasis on leadership positions to include academic coursework, independent and collaborative thinking, alumnae and peer mentoring, student activities and events, and experiential opportunities.

EXPERIENCE: Students learn through experience in every major. From internships to service projects, Cedar Crest students graduate with skills that employers find valuable as well as the wherewithal to contribute immediately to their career fields and communities.

In 2017, the college launched the Student Employment Center, which guarantees on-campus employment for anyone interested. The position usually aligns with the student's intended major and career goals.

EXPOSURE: It's said that success is "all about who you know," but Cedar Crest College knows that it's far more than that. Highly credentialed faculty members develop close-knit relationships with their students as they help to build a solid platform for a successful career.

Students are also connected to professionals through their professors' networks, getting to know industry experts on first-name bases. Not only are they acquainted with experts, but they are friends and colleagues with them. This ultimately provides in-depth exposure to opportunities that perfectly communicate the value of a Cedar Crest education.

EXEMPLIFY: Not only does the College provide students with an outstanding education grounded in the liberal arts, but it also ensures that they graduate in four years through its Four-Year Guarantee program. Students can also save both time and money through a dual degree program, which allows students to pursue both their bachelor's and master's degrees simultaneously.

STUDENT PROFILE

1,433 undergraduate students

65% of undergrad students are full-time

88% female — 12% male

82% freshman retention rate

FACULTY PROFILE

10 to 1 student/faculty ratio

ADMISSIONS

Selectivity: 63%

SAT Ranges: E 480-600, M 460-570

ACT Ranges: C 19-26, M 17-25, E 18-24

TUITION & COST

Tuition: $37,492

Fees: $600

Room: $5,262

Board: $5,946

CHATHAM UNIVERSITY

PITTSBURGH, PENNSYLVANIA

Founded in 1869, Chatham University is a fully coed institution with over 60 undergraduate and graduate programs in four areas of excellence: sustainability; health & wellness; business & communications; and the arts & sciences. Chatham is recognized as a leader in the field of sustainability, having been mentioned as one of the places "contributing to Pittsburgh's transformation into a destination for green living."

BACHELOR OF SUSTAINABILITY: In 2010, Chatham established the Falk School of Sustainability & Environment in order to produce leaders in the ever-developing field of environmental studies.

Its unique sustainability program for undergraduates allows students to pursue such important concentrations as sustainable technology, natural resource management, sustainable business & management, and sustainable policy & communications.

SELF-DESIGNED MAJOR: Understanding that some topics cannot be explored fully through a single lens of thought, Chatham allows students to design their own major through an interdisciplinary combination of courses.

The self-designed major allows students to delve deeply into topics that may not be common but are nevertheless vital and best understood through a complex combination of lessons.

"When I was applying for internships my first year, Career Development helped me tailor my résumé to art galleries. Then, when I was applying to marketing internships, it was also international, so they worked with me to tailor it to what Europeans want to see in a student résumé. And it worked—this summer, I'm doing a marketing internship in Dublin." *- Kelly O'Donnell '19*

chatham UNIVERSITY

www.chatham.edu
(800) 837-1290
chathamadmissions@
chatham.edu

STUDENT PROFILE

1,006 undergraduate students

99% of undergrad students are full-time

70% female — 30% male

21% of students are from out of state

79% freshman retention rate

FACULTY PROFILE

10 to 1 student/faculty ratio

ADMISSIONS

Selectivity: 55%

SAT Ranges: E 530-630, M 510-620

ACT Ranges: C 21-26, M 18-26, E 20-26

TUITION & COST

Tuition: $36,276

Fees: $1,335

Room: $6,240

Board: $5,850

CHESTNUT HILL COLLEGE

PHILADELPHIA, PENNSYLVANIA

CHESTNUT HILL COLLEGE

Chestnut Hill College is proud to serve as a launchpad for students to develop personally, professionally, and spiritually. As an inclusive Catholic institution, CHC provides a well-rounded curriculum that challenges and inspires all students to become their best possible selves so they can lead meaningful, successful lives. Engagement with the both the local and the global community comes naturally with a CHC education, as courses and extracurriculars emphasize service work and assisting those who are in need.

URBAN PLUNGE: One noted service-learning program is known as the Urban Plunge, an immersive opportunity in which students can spend their summer or winter break providing aid to underrepresented communities in the cities of Kensington, Philadelphia, and Camden, New Jersey.

Meanwhile, students can discover something new about the causes of urban poverty and the various factors that make it one of today's most important problems in desperate need of a solution. This experience allows students to confront their own prejudices, meet and bond with new friends, and impart life-changing assistance to those who need it most.

NEW PROGRAMS: Chestnut Hill College continuously updates its curriculum to match the needs of an ever-evolving world. Within the past year, CHC has added new majors that align with the requirements of today's marketplace, such as cybersecurity, law and legal studies, exercise science, and forensic sciences, all of which were designed to help students find successful careers in today's most in-demand fields.

UNDECLARED UNDERGRADS: Students who have yet to declare a major are sure to find themselves and their vocation with the help of CHC's Academic Discovery Program (ADP). Alongside an invested student success advisor, students receive one-on-one guidance and support as they search for a foundation on which they can build their lives.

No matter how much exploring they do, they are always met with a helping hand, as their advisors work to ensure their class schedules remain efficient and enable them to graduate on time.

www.chc.edu
(215) 248-7001
chcapply@chc.edu

STUDENT PROFILE

1,245 undergraduate students

81% of undergrad students are full-time

61% female – 39% male

21% of students are from out of state

71% freshman retention rate

FACULTY PROFILE

10 to 1 student/faculty ratio

ADMISSIONS

Selectivity: 96%

SAT Ranges: E 470-570, M 470-550

ACT Ranges: C 16-20

TUITION & COST

Tuition: $36,950

Fees: $250

Room & Board: $11,000

DREXEL UNIVERSITY

PHILADELPHIA, PENNSYLVANIA

As one of the largest private schools in the U.S., Drexel is constantly making strides in both the realms of research and personal achievements. Students are exposed to new technologies, taught to be strong leaders, and prepared to make positive changes within the global community.

STAR SCHOLARS: STAR, which stands for Students Tackling Advanced Research, is open to first-year students the summer after their freshman year. STAR allows students to collaborate with faculty on research projects—a valuable experience most often given to master's students.

Those who participate are awarded a $4,000 dollar stipend and on-campus housing all summer long as they work a total of 400 hours before their next semester starts. There are many benefits to participation, including one-on-one interaction with faculty and experience with research processes.

LEARNING COMMUNITIES: The Engineering Learning Community (ELC) is a residential option open to students accepted into the Engineering program. Students live together on the same floor and take classes as a group, promoting academic success and support among peers.

Extracurricular activities and networking events are planned throughout the year, giving members plenty of options to build their skillset and discover their interests.

COMMUNITY-BASED LEARNING: Drexel works with the Lindy Center for Civic Engagement to establish community-based learning courses (CBL) that bring service to the forefront of education.

"Side-by-side" is a very special part of Drexel's educational experience that engages both Drexel students and local community members. Drexel students take courses with local students who are underprivileged and underrepresented, often starting great conversations about access and diversity.

www.drexel.edu
(215) 895-2400
enroll@drexel.edu

STUDENT PROFILE

15,534 undergraduate students

87% of undergrad students are full-time

48% female – 52% male

49% of students are from out of state

89% freshman retention rate

FACULTY PROFILE

11 to 1 student/faculty ratio

ADMISSIONS

Selectivity: 79%

SAT Ranges: E 580-670, M 580-690

ACT Ranges: C 24-30, M 24-29, E 23-31

TUITION & COST

Tuition: $49,632

Fees: $2,370

Room: $8,682

Board: $5,208

DUQUESNE UNIVERSITY

PITTSBURGH, PENNSYLVANIA

Duquesne University is a private Catholic institution in the center of Pittsburgh, Pennsylvania, a vibrant and safe city that is home to a welcoming environment and plenty of professional opportunities. The University Core Curriculum incorporates the liberal arts into each students' development in order to expand their self-understanding and knowledge of the world. Students are exposed to a wide range of experiences and opportunities with regional corporations, high-tech businesses, health systems, and nonprofits that recognize the quality of a Duquesne degree.

PITTSBURGH: Duquesne University is located in the heart of Pittsburgh—one of the most livable cities in America. The lively city offers a wide range of interactive, "instagrammable" activities, including green spaces, galleries, concerts, breweries, and music venues. Home to businesses that seek an educated workforce, Pittsburgh offers endless opportunities for networking.

COMMUNITY ENGAGEMENT: The Office of Community Engagement motivates students to become active members of service by connecting resources across five areas of impact: Growth and Innovation, Health and Wellness, Education, Individual Empowerment, and Volunteerism. Students can support their community through a wide range of opportunities, such as identifying and responding to social and environmental issues, providing services to veterans, and responding to natural disasters.

STUDY ABROAD: Global opportunities are plentiful, and students may take semester-long or short-term trips, earn an Intercultural Engagement Certificate/Minor, and even partake in an international internship. And these unique experiences are not limited only to current students; alumni can work with the University to travel as well!

"As a student athlete, my professors and I work together to make sure I am on top of my coursework. They are always willing to make time for students." *- Joshua Gills, Business Finance*

---

www.duq.edu
(412) 396-6000

STUDENT PROFILE
5,942 undergraduate students

98% of undergrad students are full-time

64% female – 36% male

31% of students are from out of state

86% freshman retention rate

FACULTY PROFILE
13 to 1 student/faculty ratio

ADMISSIONS
Selectivity: 72%

SAT Ranges: E 570-640, M 550-630

ACT Ranges: C 24-29, M 23-27, E 24-30

TUITION & COST
Tuition: $36,394

Room: $6,658

Board: $5,456

ELIZABETHTOWN COLLEGE

ELIZABETHTOWN, PENNSYLVANIA

Elizabethtown College

The Elizabethtown College educational experience blends a high standard of scholarship with a relationship-centered learning community that prepares its students for purposeful lives. These ideals are blended in the College's five unique Signature Learning Experiences: supervised research; community-based learning; cross-cultural experiences; internships, field experiences or practicums; and capstone experiences. The Signature Learning Experiences challenge students to think beyond the classroom, traveling across borders and going behind the scenes.

MOMENTUM: Elizabethtown College offers the Momentum experience to first-generation college students whose families are unfamiliar with the transition to college. Momentum students arrive on campus a week prior to fall orientation, easing into the college lifestyle with plenty of time to adjust. Throughout this early week, the students attend workshops and go on field trips to build camaraderie with their new peers as well while priming themselves for academic and personal development.

LIVING-LEARNING COMMUNITIES: The College offers Living-Learning Communities (LLCs), which mix the curricular, co-curricular, and residential components of a student's college life. The LLCs focus on academics and activities related to specific courses, programs of study, or themes.

Past LLCs have centered on eating disorder awareness, service and mentorship through jazz, developing activities for older citizens, simple living, and hunger and homelessness awareness

SCHOOL LOCATION: Elizabethtown College, located on the East Coast in Elizabethtown, Pennsylvania, is a short drive from Hershey, Lancaster, and the Pennsylvania state capital of Harrisburg.

Daytrippers can enjoy the vibrant offerings of Baltimore, Philadelphia, Pittsburgh, and New York City, or they may go on outdoor adventures along the Susquehanna River, Appalachian Trail, Poconos, Chesapeake Bay, and Delaware Water Gap.

www.etown.edu
(717) 361-1400
admissons@etown.edu

STUDENT PROFILE

1,602 undergraduate students

99% of undergrad students are full-time

61% female – 39% male

32% of students are from out of state

89% freshman retention rate

FACULTY PROFILE

11 to 1 student/faculty ratio

ADMISSIONS

Selectivity: 76%

SAT Ranges: E 540-640, M 530-650

ACT Ranges: C 21-28, M 20-27, E 21-28

TUITION & COST

Tuition: $32,000

Room & Board: $11,710

GENEVA COLLEGE

BEAVER FALLS, PENNSYLVANIA

Geneva College is a Christ-centered academic community that provides a comprehensive education to equip students for faithful and fruitful service to God and neighbor. Geneva offers over 80 traditional undergraduate majors and programs, including nursing, management, marketing, and cybersecurity, an array of fully online bachelor's programs designed to be attainable for busy adults, and five high-demand graduate degrees in both classroom and online formats.

TECHNOLOGY DEVELOPMENT: The Pinkerton Center for Technology Development (PCTD) offers Geneva's engineering and technical resources to local companies through a project-based learning environment. Engineering students also obtain hands-on experience by participating in national contests such as the SAE Baja, Steel Bridge Building, and Solar Splash Boating Competitions.

HONORS PROGRAMS: The Geneva College Honors Programs provide opportunities for students to challenge themselves by digging deeper into the college experience. Students explore what it means to be a Christian scholar, all while discovering the lordship of Christ in every aspect of academic life.

First-Year Honors students receive a $2,000 Travel & Research Honorarium that may be used for such specific purposes as off-campus study, academic research, and conference attendance.

"The virtue of my Geneva experience... is that my eyes are not set on what they once were. I cringe to be cliché, but the Christ who was crucified for me, rose for me, has shifted my vantage point from self-righteous career orientation to a radical knowledge of my inadequacy (and how little it matters)." *– Matthew Lines, senior*

GENEVA COLLEGE

www.geneva.edu
(800) 847-8255
admissions@geneva.edu

STUDENT PROFILE

1,331 undergraduate students

94% of undergrad students are full-time

49% female – 51% male

27% of students are from out of state

80% freshman retention rate

FACULTY PROFILE

12 to 1 student/faculty ratio

ADMISSIONS

Selectivity: 69%

SAT Ranges: E 460-600, M 490-610

ACT Ranges: C 20-26, M 18-26, E 19-26

TUITION & COST

Tuition: $26,730

Fees: $500

Room & Board: $10,170

LA ROCHE UNIVERSITY

PITTSBURGH, PENNSYLVANIA

LA ROCHE UNIVERSITY

With more than 50 undergraduate majors, La Roche offers competitive programs in high-demand and creative industries, with particular strengths in business, criminal justice, design, education, psychology, and health and medical sciences. The residential university provides a vibrant campus community for more than 1,400 men and women who enjoy over 30 student organizations and an exciting NCAA Div. III athletics program. La Roche welcomes students of all religions, nationalities, and backgrounds, including students from 16 states, two territories, and 37 countries.

TRAVEL INCLUDED IN TUITION: La Roche's Study Abroad + Study USA program, included in the cost of tuition, allows students to travel the U.S. or study abroad. The program covers the cost of travel, lodging, and most meals. From Alaska and California to Cuba, Europe, and South America, students have experienced new places and other cultures at no additional cost.

Another unique study abroad initiative is the Semester in Rome program, offered for students who want a traditional study abroad experience. Students can spend a semester abroad at the same cost of regular tuition, room, and board.

THE LA ROCHE EXPERIENCE: One highlight of the College's core curriculum is The La Roche Experience, which introduces students to the principles of peace and justice, giving them the skills and perspective to make a positive impact in today's society.

Coursework includes service learning, value-based simulations, spiritual self-exploration, reflective journal exercises, and college-wide seminars that focus on global issues.

"The name of La Roche got my foot in the door. Even more fortunately, the education and training I received got me the position." - Erin May '03

www.laroche.edu
(800) 838-4572
admissions@laroche.edu

STUDENT PROFILE

1,315 undergraduate students

88% of undergrad students are full-time

54% female – 46% male

10% of students are from out of state

68% freshman retention rate

FACULTY PROFILE

12 to 1 student/faculty ratio

ADMISSIONS

Selectivity: 97%

SAT Ranges: E 480-590, M 470-550

ACT Ranges: C 18-23, M 16-23, E 16-24

TUITION & COST

Tuition: $22,714

Fees: $425

Room: $7,316

Board: $4,240

LAFAYETTE COLLEGE

EASTON, PENNSYLVANIA

Lafayette wants its students to be in a constant state of learning–a process that involves participation in class, engagement in subject matters, and challenging one's surroundings. The student that takes control of their educational experience has the freedom to explore their potential, while learning to adapt to the changing needs of society. And that makes for one marketable–and remarkable–individual.

THE COLLEGE WRITING PROGRAM (CWP): The College Writing Program has been a part of Lafayette's curriculum since 1987. The program incorporates writing into several different courses across all disciplines. CWP is meant to increase students' understanding and practice with the writing process.

The ability to communicate through writing is an incredibly useful tool, and Lafayette works hard to ensure that each graduate has had the proper training. Select undergraduates can even train as writing associates and, once trained, act as tutors to their peers.

ACTIVITIES: The campus community at Lafayette is an exciting combination of Art, athletics, and various clubs and organizations. Students have access to more than 250 clubs with many diverse interests as well as more than 20 NCAA Division I athletic programs.

GIVING STUDENTS THE RIGHT TOOLS: Lafayette students humbly demonstrate their intellectual capabilities in an ever-changing and demanding society. Such skills include: innovation, critical thinking, problem solving skills, communication skills, and applied knowledge.

Lafayette students are well-equipped to succeed after graduation. Most have had hands-on experience in their area of study through internships or field experience. Many go on to graduate school at some of the nation's top institutions. For those who decide to enter right into a career, start an internship, or volunteer, Lafayette's post-graduate success rate is 95% after just six months.

LAFAYETTE COLLEGE

www.lafayette.edu
(610) 330-5100
admissions@lafayette.edu

STUDENT PROFILE

2,594 undergraduate students

98% of undergrad students are full-time

52% female – 48% male

74% of students are from out of state

95% freshman retention rate

FACULTY PROFILE

10 to 1 student/faculty ratio

ADMISSIONS

Selectivity: 31%

SAT Ranges: E 630-710, M 630-730

ACT Ranges: C 28-31, M 27-32, E 28-33

TUITION & COST

Tuition: $50,400

Fees: $1,200

Room: $9,300

Board: $5,740

LYCOMING COLLEGE

WILLIAMSPORT, PENNSYLVANIA

Lycoming College is a private, residential, four-year liberal arts and sciences college in Williamsport, PA, that takes an innovative, high-impact learning and high-reward career-advising approach to education. With a close-knit student population, Lycoming facilitates engaging classroom discussions and hands-on experiences, giving students the individual attention they need to pursue careers of significance and lives of meaning.

WARRIOR COFFEE: The Warrior Coffee Program is a truly unique interdisciplinary and global experience, funded in part by every delicious cup of coffee served on campus. Through research, and a trip to the Dominican Republic, Lycoming students learn how mutually beneficial partnerships can produce excellent coffee, all while advancing responsible agriculture and providing sustainable incomes for the farmers of El Naranjito and Peralta.

The sales of Warrior Coffee altogether fund quality-of-life projects for these regions while subsidizing the cost of travel for Lycoming students.

BIOLOGY FIELD STATION: The College recently established a biology field station set alongside the nearby Loyalsock Creek. This space provides a living laboratory for students studying aquatic biology, ecology, plant science, vertebrate and invertebrate zoology, and environmental biology. The College's Clean Water Institute also utilizes the space to conduct water quality testing and assess wetlands.

"My time at Lycoming has been filled with so many experiences that have bolstered my love of learning both in and out of the classroom. I have been blessed to have professors who use real-world examples to enforce theoretical concepts and to have experienced hands-on learning in the majority of my classes." *– Rebecca Forbes '19, Economics & Spanish double major with a minor in business administration*

LYCOMING COLLEGE

www.lycoming.edu
(570) 321-4026
admissions@lycoming.edu

STUDENT PROFILE

1,131 undergraduate students

100% of undergrad students are full-time

53% female – 47% male

41% of students are from out of state

75% freshman retention rate

FACULTY PROFILE

12 to 1 student/faculty ratio

ADMISSIONS

Selectivity: 66%

SAT Ranges: E 510-600, M 500-600

ACT Ranges: C 19-24, M 17-24, E 18-25

TUITION & COST

Tuition: $40,896

Room: $6,634

Board: $6,374

MANSFIELD UNIVERSITY OF PENNSYLVANIA

MANSFIELD, PENNSYLVANIA

At Mansfield University, students are afforded incredible opportunities from the moment they first enroll at MU right up to the time they graduate. A Mansfield University experience develops the student holistically by combining rigorous academics with a broad range of extracurricular opportunities at an affordable cost. Student success is the primary focus of the Mansfield faculty and staff, all of whom strive to develop and maintain a premier learning environment with premier opportunities for the entire student body.

IMPACT MENTORING: The IMPACT Mentoring Program is an initiative headed by the Office of Retention to address the common challenges that face first-year students.

This program has helped students—freshmen and upperclassmen alike—overcome such challenges as finding friends, selecting courses, and interacting with professors. It is with the guidance of such dedicated staff that Mansfield students truly feel at home.

THE MANSFIELD NEIGHBORHOOD: Nestled in beautiful north central Pennsylvania, Mansfield University is in the middle of somewhere special. The University is located near thousands of acres of state land, lakes, and spectacular mountain views, including the nearby Pine Creek Gorge—Pennsylvania's "Grand Canyon."

INTERNATIONAL EXCHANGE: Students who participate in international exchange and study abroad gain valuable skills in cross-cultural communication and education.

Currently, the University has exchange agreements with 150 institutions across the world through a membership with the International Student Exchange Programs (ISEP), including partnerships in such countries as Australia, Canada, France Germany, and Spain.

www.mansfield.edu
(800) 577-6826
admissions@
mansfield.edu

STUDENT PROFILE

1,552 undergraduate students

93% of undergrad students are full-time

61% female – 39% male

17% of students are from out of state

71% freshman retention rate

FACULTY PROFILE

14 to 1 student/faculty ratio

ADMISSIONS

Selectivity: 92%

SAT Ranges: E 480-580, M 470-550

TUITION & COST

Fees: $2,880

Room: $8,468

Board: $3,460

MERCYHURST UNIVERSITY

ERIE, PENNSYLVANIA

Mercyhurst University, founded in 1926 by the Sisters of Mercy, is a fully accredited, four-year, Catholic comprehensive institution for men and women in Erie, Pennsylvania. The university offers more than 60 undergraduate majors, nine graduate programs, and a variety of post-baccalaureate and advanced certificates. Its motto—*Carpe Diem*, Latin for "Seize the Day"—is at the heart of everything it does. At Mercyhurst, students find a community that celebrates experiences both inside and outside the classroom, experiences that challenge them to write more, practice harder, dig deeper, and see the world from an unconventional perspective.

ON-TIME GRADUATION: Graduating on time is the best way to avoid any unnecessary tuition costs in one's college education, so Mercyhurst makes earning a degree within four years a priority. In fact, the university's four-year graduation rate is the highest in Erie County and one of the highest in the region.

Mercyhurst's 15-to-Finish program encourages students to take 15 credits every semester, helping them make wise decisions with their academic advisors as they schedule their courses.

REACH CURRICULUM: The REACH Curriculum acts as a foundational core that supplements every major. Adopted in 2016, the interdisciplinary REACH curriculum includes a specialized introductory course for freshmen (iMU 101), a senior capstone experience, and a unique service-learning and civic engagement component.

STUDY ABROAD: In the recent past, 75% of students have taken a single intensive course or study abroad through Mercyhurst's flexible scheduling.

Among the most popular study abroad programs are the Faculty-Student Academic Travel (FSAT) opportunities, which have taken students and professors to study narrative and film in Spain; aquatic ecology in Belize; video storytelling in Peru; and dance appreciation in France and Israel.

www.mercyhurst.edu
(814) 824-2202
admissions@
mercyhurst.edu

STUDENT PROFILE
2,750 undergraduate students

54% female – 46% male

78% freshman retention rate

FACULTY PROFILE
14 to 1 student/faculty ratio

TUITION & COST
Tuition: $35,400

Fees: $2,670

Room: $6,420

Board: $6,460

MESSIAH COLLEGE

MECHANICSBURG, PENNSYLVANIA

Messiah College is nationally recognized for bringing together top-tier academics and Christian faith. The College's motto, "Christ Preeminent," shapes every experience: Lifelong friendships. Support from faculty mentors. Outstanding preparation for life and career. Championship athletics. Celebrated arts programs. Transformational service and ministry. Eye-opening study abroad. At Messiah, one's life, faith, world, and possibilities open up. Students come to see anew.

CALLED FOR COMMUNITY: In the "Created and Called for Community" course, students consider a central question: "What is my vocation as a faithful steward of God's creation?"

They seek answers by engaging biblical themes of creation, forgiveness, compassion, peacemaking, and reconciliation. Using the lens of Messiah's distinctive foundational values, students develop the ability to be theologically reflective and cultivate their intellect and character in preparation for lives of leadership.

RESEARCH: Research experiences, which are often connected to local and global clients, are embedded throughout the undergraduate curriculum in science, engineering, and health. For example, the engineering curriculum is crafted around an innovative 'integrated projects curriculum' in which all students work on projects meet the needs of real-world nonprofits.

"I wanted a school that would prepare me personally, spiritually, and professionally... I can say in full confidence that Messiah has exceeded my expectations in each of the areas. Messiah has specifically taught me how to reconcile my faith with my career path and has empowered me to serve and lead as a Christian in the areas of accounting and finance." – *Regan Hershey '18*

www.messiah.edu
(800) 233-4220
admissions@messiah.edu

STUDENT PROFILE

2,734 undergraduate students

95% of undergrad students are full-time

61% female — 39% male

38% of students are from out of state

87% freshman retention rate

FACULTY PROFILE

12 to 1 student/faculty ratio

ADMISSIONS

Selectivity: 79%

SAT Ranges: E 550-650, M 530-660

ACT Ranges: C 23-29, M 22-28, E 22-30

TUITION & COST

Tuition: $35,280

Fees: $840

Room: $5,630

Board: $4,950

MILLERSVILLE UNIVERSITY OF PENNSYLVANIA

MILLERSVILLE, PENNSYLVANIA

Millersville University

Millersville has focused its each of its program initiatives to enhance student learning and engagement. A Millersville education is about providing students with the tools to lead—lead themselves, their families, and their communities. Millersville students are highly engaged individuals who are actively involved in their educational journey. It all comes down to commitment. As a college student, one can't sit by and watch their four years pass by; rather, they have to be part of their own journey by challenging themselves to reach their highest potential.

CLUBS WITHIN MAJORS: Students have the option to get involved in departmental honors programs and societies or academic clubs within their majors. Just one example would be the Collegiate Entrepreneurs' Organization, a group within the Business major. Other academic clubs include Association of Technology, Management and Applied Engineering, French Circle, Economics Society, and Social Work Organization.

Beyond academics, students can join groups like the Creative Writers Guild or the Jewelry and Metal Arts Guild. There are also several organizations dedicated to music performance and appreciation.

GLOBAL STUDENTS: Millersville provides its students with global studies opportunities in the form of study abroad, international internships, student teaching abroad, research collaboration, and professional training. Through many partnerships, students are afforded the ability to study around the globe in places like Australia and China.

The Office of Global Education & Partnerships works with students and parents to ensure that each effort to study or work abroad is met with the most sincere and valued assistance. Millersville recognizes study abroad, in any capacity, as an integral part of a college experience.

www.millersville.edu
(717) 871-4625
admissions@
millersville.edu

STUDENT PROFILE

6,758 undergraduate students

84% of undergrad students are full-time

57% female – 43% male

10% of students are from out of state

77% freshman retention rate

FACULTY PROFILE

19 to 1 student/faculty ratio

ADMISSIONS

Selectivity: 79%

SAT Ranges: E 490-590, M 480-570

TUITION & COST

Tuition (in-state): $9,270

Tuition (out-of-state): $18,730

Fees: $2,588

Room: $8,440

Board: $5,000

MOUNT ALOYSIUS COLLEGE

CRESSON, PENNSYLVANIA

Mount Aloysius College

Established in 1853, Mount Aloysius is a liberal arts and science-based institution with a commitment to career-directed study. Rooted in Catholic tradition, Mount Aloysius is one of the nation's 17 Mercy sponsored colleges. MAC began as an Academy but has since evolved into a comprehensive college that provides both undergraduate and graduate educations.

A WELL-ESTABLISHED FOUNDATION: MAC continually researches employment trends and market demands, adding or changing programs to address the world's emerging needs. It all begins with the core curriculum, which helps students become analytical and reflective of their work within the context of the larger world beyond MAC's borders. It's a "classic" college curriculum reinvented for today's career-centric students.

MOUNT MERCY: The spirit of service is alive at Mount Aloysius, and students are consistently sharing their time and talents to the world. Many student organizations use the Mercy heritage as a stepping stone to help others. In the past, students have traveled to Honduras to build an orphanage and volunteered at a school for deaf children in Jamaica.

They have also collected food donations for regional food banks, involved themselves in Earth Day, practiced the UN Day of Peace, and contributed to Coaches vs. Cancer.

"The small class sizes here really helped me a ton because it gave me that sense of a one-on-one learning experience. Mount Aloysius has definitely evolved since I graduated. The campus is continuing to grow with new buildings and additional resources to make this place even greater."

– Patrick McKee, Sustainability Program Manager in the Office of Environmental Policy, University of Connecticut, MAC Class of 2011

www.mtaloy.edu
(814) 886-6383
admissions@mtaloy.edu

STUDENT PROFILE

1,379 undergraduate students

81% of undergrad students are full-time

71% female – 29% male

6% of students are from out of state

FACULTY PROFILE

12 to 1 student/faculty ratio

TUITION & COST

Tuition: $24,690

Fees: $1,240

Room: $5,356

Board: $4,820

ROSEMONT COLLEGE

BRYN MAWR, PENNSYLVANIA

Rosemont doesn't just train students for the workplace; it cultivates their cultural, religious, and artistic sensibilities in order to improve the quality of their lives. Students develop a sense of social responsibility, strong intellectual and practical skills that span all areas of study, and a demonstrated ability to apply everything they've learned in real-world settings. Here, the power of small leads to big opportunities

THE ROSEMONT DIFFERENCE: At the beginning of their first year, each Rosemont student participates in a special program to evaluate their individual academic skills, personality traits, and learning styles. Their findings are then reviewed and applied to a personalized learning plan that gives them a better understanding of their abilities.

This plan serves as a touchstone to chart academic growth and progress, helping foster success both at Rosemont and beyond.

LEARNING WITHOUT LIMITS: With a diverse student body composed of 53% minority students, Rosemont encourages a community that embraces diversity, change, and inclusion.

The College's core values are trust in and reverence for the dignity of each person; diversity in human culture and experience; and persistence and courage in promoting justice with compassion

EXPLORATIVE PROFESSORS: With small classes, Rosemont professors often teach "on location." Their classrooms can span across a plethora of cultural and educational sites in Philadelphia or even in a foreign country, studying everything from policy to languages.

THE POWER OF SMALL: The student body is comprised of more than 400 undergraduate students, with a student-to-faculty ratio of 10:1 and an average class size of 12. This allows for more personal classroom attention. Approximately 75 percent of full-time faculty members hold a Ph.D. or the highest degree in their field.

ROSEMONT COLLEGE
the POWER of small

www.rosemont.edu
(610) 526-2966
**gpsadmissions@
rosemont.edu**

STUDENT PROFILE
635 undergraduate students

87% of undergrad students are full-time

71% female – 29% male

22% of students are from out of state

71% freshman retention rate

FACULTY PROFILE
11 to 1 student/faculty ratio

ADMISSIONS
Selectivity: 86%

SAT Ranges: E 460-580, M 450-560

ACT Ranges: C 16-21, M 17-21, E 16-20

TUITION & COST
Tuition: $18,900

Fees: $1,000

Room & Board: $12,438

SAINT FRANCIS UNIVERSITY

LORETTO, PENNSYLVANIA

Saint Francis University offers academic study within the Franciscan tradition of using one's talents to serve others. The more than 60 offerings include highly targeted, career-focused majors grounded in the liberal arts tradition of inquiry and self-discovery. Highly regarded programs in health science, education, business, and science attract a diverse student body to the beautiful campus setting.

WHAT MAKES SFU DIFFERENT: Simulation labs, Esports, SCUBA diving, Aviation, experiential learning, two public museums, Canine Learning and Behavior class, and a snow tubing park are some of the opportunities unique to Saint Francis University. Students enhance their academic and campus experiences with programs that fit their personalities.

COMMUNITY ENRICHMENT SERIES: The University sponsors a wide range of cultural events that are integrated into the curriculum as "CES" credits. By attending lectures, concerts, theatrical performances, or other select events on campus, students can receive community enrichment credits toward the completion of their degree. For example, students can earn CES credits attending an American Sign Language / English theatre performance or by visiting the Southern Alleghenies Museum of Art located right on campus.

GREAT OUTDOORS: High in the Laurel Highlands of Pennsylvania, students find that ecreational activities abound for all four seasons both on campus and at nearby state and national parks. Many academic programs take advantage of the natural setting to promote environmental advocacy and conduct research.

"As an undergrad, these courses inspired in me a true heart of service and taught me how to be empathetic in patient interactions. These are skills I could not have gleaned from a medical textbook and continue to shape not only the care provider, but also the person I am today." – *Lisa B.*

www.francis.edu
(814) 472-3100
admissions@francis.edu

STUDENT PROFILE

2,102 undergraduate students

71% of undergrad students are full-time

65% female – 35% male

26% of students are from out of state

87% freshman retention rate

FACULTY PROFILE

14 to 1 student/faculty ratio

ADMISSIONS

Selectivity: 74%

SAT Ranges: E 520-630, M 520-620

ACT Ranges: C 19-26, M 19-26, E 20-26

TUITION & COST

Tuition: $36,970

Fees: $1,200

Room: $6,148

Board: $6,200

SAINT JOSEPH'S UNIVERSITY

PHILADELPHIA, PENNSYLVANIA

Saint Joseph's University is a nationally recognized, Catholic, Jesuit university that has advanced the professional and personal ambitions of men and women by providing a rigorous education. The university recognizes that experiential learning opportunities lead to more successful undergraduate careers and thus provides students with resources to get involved. In fact, the university works so hard that 95% of students graduate with at least one experiential learning experience, whether that be through study abroad, service-learning, or internships.

SUMMER AND WINTER STUDY ABROAD: While study abroad is an incredible experience, not every student can commit to an entire semester. For those students, there are short-term study abroad programs held in the winter and summer. Short-term programs are led by Saint Joseph's faculty and last about a month.

During the summer and winter abroad excursions, students have the opportunity to immerse themselves in new culture, all while learning from experienced faculty. Some previous short-term programs have included China, Greece, Chile, and Rome.

PHILADELPHIA: While there is an endless number of on-campus activities, there are also great opportunities available through the city of Philadelphia. Philly is the fifth largest city in the U.S., which means it has a ton to offer.

Students are invited to explore the city and take advantage of all the cultural attractions, recreational activities, restaurant scene, and shopping. On top of that, Philadelphia offers incredible access to internships, jobs, and networking.

COMMUNITY SERVICE: Saint Joseph's considers community service both a personal mission and an integral part of the undergraduate experience. Students can get involved through Alternative Spring Break, service-learning courses, and weekly volunteer opportunities.

www.sju.edu
(610) 660-1300
admit@sju.edu

STUDENT PROFILE

5,144 undergraduate students

87% of undergrad students are full-time

54% female – 46% male

54% of students are from out of state

91% freshman retention rate

FACULTY PROFILE

11 to 1 student/faculty ratio

ADMISSIONS

Selectivity: 77%

SAT Ranges: E 560-640, M 550-650

ACT Ranges: C 23-28, M 23-30, E 22-27

TUITION & COST

Tuition: $43,700

Fees: $180

Room: $9,424

Board: $5,416

SETON HILL UNIVERSITY

GREENSBURG, PENNSYLVANIA

As a Catholic institution, Seton Hill opens its doors to students of all faiths, creating a warm environment for those with a passion to make a difference in the world. It's in the everyday teachings and caring community that the University is living out its mission in the tradition of Saint Elizabeth Ann Seton, who said to her own students, *"I would wish to fit you for that world in which you are destined to live."*

CONTEMPORARY EDUCATION: Every student is given the tools to succeed—literally—as Seton Hill was the first university in the world to provide an iPad to every full-time student.

Along with new technologies, the University is also a spearheading force in academic development; new majors are introduced every year! Recent additions to Seton Hill's repertoire include data analytics, cybersecurity, global studies, educational studies, healthcare administration, innovative instruction, and special education with specialization in autism.

CAREER SERVICES FROM DAY ONE: In addition to its "Fit for the World program" (which provides a structured program for career exploration that is linked to a current student's academic progress), Seton Hill's Career and Professional Development Center also offers a full range of career services and support for all students and alumni.

The Center makes use of a variety of apps and online services, including video interview prep and career search services. Students also have access to e-portfolios and podcasts that supply comprehensive employer information.

HILLTOP COMMUNITY: Seton Hill's 200-acre, hilltop campus is located in the scenic Laurel Highlands of Greensburg, PA, just 35 miles from Pittsburgh. Nearby, there are plenty of places to shop, eat, golf, ski, hike, and more.

The downtown campus is vibrant with a Performing Arts Center, a Visual Arts Center, and a train station that connects students to such cities as New York City and Philadelphia.

www.setonhill.edu
(724) 838-4281
admit@setonhill.edu

STUDENT PROFILE
1,660 undergraduate students

95% of undergrad students are full-time

64% female – 36% male

23% of students are from out of state

82% freshman retention rate

FACULTY PROFILE
14 to 1 student/faculty ratio

ADMISSIONS
Selectivity: 72%

SAT Ranges: E 510-630, M 510-610

ACT Ranges: C 21-27

TUITION & COST
Tuition: $36,306

Fees: $550

Room: $6,700

Board: $5,512

SHIPPENSBURG UNIVERSITY

SHIPPENSBURG, PENNSYLVANIA

Fully engaged in their education, Shippensburg University students are empowered to create a future that is uniquely their own. They thrive off a selection of more than 100 nationally and internationally accredited programs, study abroad opportunities, and one of only five Peace Corps Preparation programs in the state. At Ship, faculty know their students by name and are committed to taking them beyond the classroom with hands-on experience, service-learning, field work, research, and much more.

RAIDERS CONNECT 365: The Raiders Connect 365 mentorship program connects students with an alum or Ship employee to establish a positive mentor relationship. Guided by caring and friendly professionals, students are educated, advised, and inspired to excel.

SHIP RESEARCH: In all disciplines, students are encouraged to dive into what interests them most and conduct original, inspiring research. The university offers support to ensure that curious minds are enabled to discover unknown phenomena, develop theories, and construct original work.

In the Summer Undergraduate Research Experience (SURE), for instance, can conduct research alongside faculty members, all while receiving compensation for their time. Student researchers are also recognized at the Minds@Work research conference at which they present their scholarly and creative works to the campus community and the general public alike.

"My internship with IBM was one of the most valuable experiences in college. It helped me to see how I could apply information learned in the classroom to real business-world situations. The opportunity to interact with different departments enabled me to determine what areas I would like to pursue before actually committing to a full-time position." *- Julie M. Zeiters*

www.ship.edu
(717) 477-1231
admiss@ship.edu

STUDENT PROFILE

5,357 undergraduate students

93% of undergrad students are full-time

51% female – 49% male

7% of students are from out of state

72% freshman retention rate

FACULTY PROFILE

18 to 1 student/faculty ratio

ADMISSIONS

Selectivity: 88%

SAT Ranges: E 490-590, M 480-580

ACT Ranges: C 17-23

TUITION & COST

Tuition (in-state): $9,570

Tuition (out-of-state): $17,362

Fees: $3,148

Room: $8,038

Board: $4,230

SLIPPERY ROCK UNIVERSITY

SLIPPERY ROCK, PENNSYLVANIA

Founded in 1889, Slippery Rock University is a Carnegie Master-L, four-year, public, coeducational, comprehensive University offering a broad array of undergraduate and graduate programs to more than 8,800 students. The University, a member of Pennsylvania's State System of Higher Education, provides students with a superior learning experience that intentionally combines academic instruction with applied learning opportunities that will help them succeed in an increasingly complex world.

SRU RESEARCH: At SRU, the spirit of discovery and the challenge of tackling real problems underpin the undergraduate research experience.

For example, a group of social work majors conducted animal-assisted intervention at local prisons, helping inmates deal with mental afflictions and prevent recidivism. And two chemistry majors are attempting to find ways to isolate amino acids to prevent the forming of amyloids, which are proteins that, when folded on the human brain, lead to Alzheimer's disease.

Slippery Rock University professors help students find their passions and challenge and work with them to put those passions into action.

STUDENT LEADERSHIP: Through SRU's Office for Student Engagement and Leadership and Office for Community-Engaged Learning, students participate in programs that give them the chance to make a difference in the lives of people both at home and around the world, practicing academic skills and earning certifications for their competence in leadership.

KALEIDOSCOPE: For two weeks each spring, the entire northwest region of Pennsylvania is alive with the sights and sounds of SRU's annual Kaleidoscope Arts Festival.

The festival is sponsored by the College of Liberal Arts and features student work, guest artists, community events, and more. The community-campus celebration brings free and low-cost arts to an underserved region.

www.sru.edu
(724) 738-2015
asktherock@sru.edu

STUDENT PROFILE

7,457 undergraduate students

94% of undergrad students are full-time

56% female – 44% male

9% of students are from out of state

81% freshman retention rate

FACULTY PROFILE

22 to 1 student/faculty ratio

ADMISSIONS

Selectivity: 73%

SAT Ranges: E 510-590, M 500-580

ACT Ranges: C 19-25, M 18-25, E 19-24

TUITION & COST

Tuition (in-state): $7,718

Tuition (out-of-state): $11,576

Fees: $2,780

Room: $6,880

Board: $3,650

SUSQUEHANNA UNIVERSITY

SELINSGROVE, PENNSYLVANIA

Susquehanna University educates enterprising, independent thinkers—about 2,300 students from 29 states and 25 countries. Students graduate with the broad-based academic foundation and essential 21st-century job skills—critical thinking, writing, teamwork, and communication—that employers and graduate schools seek. Challenging academics, plus internships and research opportunities, result in 96% of new alumni employed or pursuing an advanced degree within months of graduation.

GO PROGRAM: Susquehanna is one of only a handful of universities to require a domestic or overseas study-away experience. The GO experience allows students to become more culturally aware and better prepared to be leaders in a diverse, dynamic, and interdependent world.

As a result, Susquehanna students see firsthand how different social and cultural forces shape the world—and discover how to make a difference.

FUTURE BUSINESS LEADERS: Business students get hands-on learning in the state-of-the-art student investment center, a functioning trading room with Bloomberg Terminals, and place trades on Bloomberg's electronic trading platform. Students even get to manage a real investment portfolio with funds allocated by the Student Government Association.

EMERGING MEDIA: Communications majors help run WQSU-FM, one of the most powerful college radio stations in Pennsylvania, broadcasting on 12,000 watts. They enjoy access to superb production facilities and equipment, including an audio, video, and graphics lab; multi-camera television studio with green screen; and professional-quality audio and video field equipment.

NATURAL AND ENVIRONMENTAL SCIENCES: The nearby Susquehanna River provides unparalleled access to field research, as do the state-of-the-art LEED Silver-certified Natural Sciences Center, a Center for Environmental Education and Research, and a 400-acre Ecology Laboratory. The school's Freshwater Research Initiative further explores the ecological issues impacting the Susquehanna River and its tributaries.

www.susqu.edu
(570) 372-4260
suadmiss@susqu.edu

STUDENT PROFILE

2,214 undergraduate students

100% of undergrad students are full-time

55% female — 45% male

25% of students are from out of state

84% freshman retention rate

FACULTY PROFILE

12 to 1 student/faculty ratio

ADMISSIONS

Selectivity: 72%

SAT Ranges: E 558-640, M 540-620

TUITION & COST

Tuition: $48,560

Fees: $620

Room: $6,900

Board: $6,240

THE UNIVERSITY OF SCRANTON

SCRANTON, PENNSYLVANIA

Situated in the heart of Scranton, PA, the University of Scranton employs a strong Jesuit educational tradition based on the principle that students must be prepared to lead in their faith as well as their academic careers. These roots give students the chance to change world for the better.

UNDERGRADUATE RESEARCH: Throughout the school year, students can work closely with professors on research projects. And during the summer months, they might be selected for a Summer Research Fellowship, which awards stipends to top achievers. Scranton is proud of its student researchers; every year, the Office of Research and Sponsored Programs displays students' work at the Annual Celebration of Student Scholars and takes steps to help get their research recognized nationally.

GET OUT OF "THE OFFICE": The university is located in Scranton, Pennsylvania, known as the "Electric City." Just moments from the Pocono Mountains and two hours from NYC and Philadelphia, Scranton has outlets for all interests. Scranton's local theatre, minor league sports, and a historic downtown district welcome all who are interested. Anyone can get out and explore what the city has to offer… or they can just stay in "The Office."

WEAVING A T.A.P.E.S.T.R.Y.: Students in the Kanuska College of Professional Development go a step beyond their curriculum in the T.A.P.E.S.T.R.Y. Program, a four-year series of co-curricular events that help Scranton students become leaders in their workplace and beyond. Following in the Jesuit tradition, T.A.P.E.S.T.R.Y. engages students in major-specific activities designed to prepare them for what's next—with their "head, heart, and hands."

"I traveled to Haiti as part of Scranton's International Service Program (ISP) ... We spent 10 days in Haiti, building houses and reaching out to a special-needs orphanage. It was an eye-opening experience to be immersed in the culture of a developing nation." – *Maggie Parks, Marketing, '16*

www.scranton.edu
1 (888) SCRANTON
admissions@scranton.edu

STUDENT PROFILE
3,810 undergraduate students

95% of undergrad students are full-time

58% female – 42% male

62% of students are from out of state

87% freshman retention rate

FACULTY PROFILE
12 to 1 student/faculty ratio

ADMISSIONS
Selectivity: 75%

SAT Ranges: E 550-640, M 530-640

ACT Ranges: C 23-28

TUITION & COST
Tuition: $42,910

Fees: $400

Room: $8,562

Board: $6,056

UNIVERSITY OF PITTSBURGH AT BRADFORD

BRADFORD, PENNSYLVANIA

University of Pittsburgh
Bradford

www.upb.pitt.edu
(800) 872-1787
admissions@upb.pitt.edu

The University of Pittsburgh at Bradford is a supportive, friendly institution for students who want to earn a world-renowned degree in a personalized environment. Since Pitt-Bradford is a regional campus of the University of Pittsburgh, students receive the University of Pittsburgh degree, which is recognized and respected all over the world.

GROUNDBREAKING FACILITIES: There are several exciting areas on campus at which students can get cutting-edge experience. Students who major in computer information systems and technology work on projects in their own dedicated labs, including a new virtual reality lab.

Additionally, criminal justice majors investigate simulated crime scenes in the Crime Scene Investigation (CSI) House, nursing students practice their techniques on computerized mannequins, and psychology students practice and observe counseling in the psychology lab suite.

REAL-WORLD LEARNING: Many professors take advantage of the university's location to lead exciting, hands-on projects for their students. For example, some students are collaborating with the U.S. Forest Service to perform an environmental assessment in the forest, the first step before mountain biking trails are created on the federal lands.

"My professors went above and beyond to share real-life experiences and helpful insight that I'll keep with me throughout my law enforcement career... You are not just a number, which makes life on campus very personable."

– Clayton Johnson, Criminal Justice Major '16,

U.S. Secret Service Uniformed Division Officer assigned to The White House

STUDENT PROFILE

1,281 undergraduate students

94% of undergrad students are full-time

56% female – 44% male

24% of students are from out of state

69% freshman retention rate

FACULTY PROFILE

15 to 1 student/faculty ratio

ADMISSIONS

Selectivity: 54%

SAT Ranges: E 490-580, M 490-580

ACT Ranges: C 20-25, M 18-25, E 17-25

TUITION & COST

Tuition (in-state): $12,940

Tuition (out-of-state): $24,184

Fees: $960

Room: $5,656

Board: $3,676

UNIVERSITY OF PITTSBURGH AT JOHNSTOWN

JOHNSTOWN, PENNSYLVANIA

University of Pittsburgh
Johnstown

The first regional campus of the University of Pittsburgh system—and one of the first regional campuses of a leading university in the United States—University of Pittsburgh at Johnstown supports inquisitive minds across 70 programs of study. Pitt-Johnstown is proud to employ a curriculum that is up to date with the world's demands. This kind of responsive educational framework creates leaders who are prepared for careers in nursing, engineering, the humanities, and more.

FACILITIES FOR EXCELLENCE: Pitt-Johnstown maintains more than one million square-feet of facility space with the resources needed to support all areas of study. For example, the Nursing and Health Sciences Building is equipped with state-of-the-art nursing simulation equipment, all of which run on sustainable/green energy. New technology has also helped give rise to the University's new, ABET-accredited programs in computer science and chemical, civil, computer, electrical, and mechanical engineering.

PARTNERS IN RESEARCH: Even in the lush landscape of the Laurel Highlands, Pitt-Johnstown acts as a beacon of cutting-edge inquiry with such events as The Symposium for the Promotion of Academic and Creative Inquiry, in which students from all disciplines showcase their innovative work. From health and engineering to literature and the arts, Mountain Cats are sinking their teeth into groundbreaking work.

"The growth in facilities, programs, and community involvement at Pitt-Johnstown has been phenomenal and continually evolving. However, more important is the institution's product: a quality education producing graduates...ready to contribute to and advance our area."

— *Robert Layo, President & CEO*

Greater Johnstown-Cambria County Chamber of Commerce

www.upj.pitt.edu
(814) 269-7050
upjadmit@pitt.edu

STUDENT PROFILE

2,598 undergraduate students

98% of undergrad students are full-time

44% female – 56% male

3% of students are from out of state

72% freshman retention rate

FACULTY PROFILE

17 to 1 student/faculty ratio

ADMISSIONS

Selectivity: 65%

SAT Ranges: E 510-600, M 510-600

ACT Ranges: C 21-26, M 20-26, E 19-24

TUITION & COST

Tuition (in-state): $13,198

Tuition (out-of-state): $24,666

Fees: $958

Room: $6,040

Board: $4,020

VILLANOVA UNIVERSITY

VILLANOVA, PENNSYLVANIA

VILLANOVA
UNIVERSITY

www1.villanova.edu
(610) 519-4000
gotovu@villanova.edu

Villanova University was founded in 1842 by the Order of St. Augustine. To this day, Villanova's Augustinian Catholic intellectual tradition is the cornerstone of an academic community in which students learn to think critically, act compassionately, and succeed while serving others. There are more than 10,000 undergraduate, graduate, and law students in the University's six colleges.

RESEARCH AS A FRESHMAN: The Match Research Program gives bright, highly motivated freshmen the opportunity to participate in research during their spring semester. Selected students work as assistants to faculty who are conducting research, working 10 hours a week for 10 weeks while earning a stipend of $1000.

LEVEL: LEVEL is a unique campus initiative aimed at closing the gap between the abled and disabled. With inclusivity being the focal point of its mission, Villanova strives to bring light to a situation that is often misunderstood.

People with disabilities are often regarded in a negative way and are thus given less opportunity to succeed in life. LEVEL works very hard to disband these myths while providing access to the disabled community.

FALVEY SCHOLARS: Undergraduate research is alive and well at Villanova. For many years now, the university has excelled at research, with many works going on to be published or presented.

The Falvey Scholars program awards this kind of superior work in undergraduate research. Each year, a group of students is nominated for their exceptional work. A committee then selects the recipients from the group of nominated students.

Awards are given in five areas—Arts, Sciences, Engineering, Nursing, and Business. Selected students are given the opportunity to share their findings with the campus community.

STUDENT PROFILE

6,950 undergraduate students

94% of undergrad students are full-time

53% female – 47% male

79% of students are from out of state

95% freshman retention rate

FACULTY PROFILE

11 to 1 student/faculty ratio

ADMISSIONS

Selectivity: 36%

SAT Ranges: E 620-710, M 630-730

ACT Ranges: C 30-33, M 28-33, E 30-35

TUITION & COST

Tuition: $50,554

Fees: $730

Room: $7,217

Board: $6,330

WAYNESBURG UNIVERSITY

WAYNESBURG, PENNSYLVANIA

Waynesburg offers more than 70 major concentrations and five integrated bachelors-to-masters programs in athletic training, business, counseling, criminal investigation and education. The University's top academic programs include business, communication, criminal justice, education, forensic science, and nursing. What makes Waynesburg truly special, though, is that its academics are not just about class. They're the foundation for a culture of growth, championed through academic excellence and personalized guidance that nurtures mind, spirit, and future.

WAYNESBURG AND BEYOND: Waynesburg University offers a unique International Studies minor option, employing many opportunities for students to gain a global education. One such example is the Vira I. Heinz Program for Women in Global Leadership, which provides scholarships to female students who have never left the United States to study abroad for a summer.

FIAT LUX: Every Waynesburg University freshman is enrolled in WBE 108 – *Fiat Lux*, named for the University's motto (Latin for "Let there be Light" from Genesis 1:3). This introductory course serves to familiarize new students with Waynesburg's mission of faith, learning, and service.

STOVER SCHOLARS: The Stover Scholar Program invites applicants from outstanding students who would like to understand—and ultimately influence—the way the United States Constitution shapes American life today.

Stover scholars are engaged in their community through Boys/Girls State, Model U.N., electoral campaigns, student government, debate teams, church-related programs, school newspapers, and civic organizations.

"My time at Waynesburg University taught me a lot about myself. It taught me to believe in myself, and it showed me the strength I didn't know I had."

– Amanda Lucas, 2019 valedictorian and education graduate

www.waynesburg.edu
(800) 225-7393
admissions@
waynesburg.edu

STUDENT PROFILE
1,376 undergraduate students

97% of undergrad students are full-time

59% female – 41% male

76% freshman retention rate

FACULTY PROFILE
13 to 1 student/faculty ratio

ADMISSIONS
Selectivity: 95%

SAT Ranges: E 495-580, M 475-580

ACT Ranges: C 18-24, M 17-24, E 17-23

TUITION & COST
Tuition: $23,160

Fees: $850

Room: $4,970

Board: $4,850

WEST CHESTER UNIVERSITY

WEST CHESTER, PENNSYLVANIA

Located just 25 miles from Philadelphia, West Chester University of Pennsylvania is a public, regional, comprehensive institution committed to providing high-quality undergraduate education as well as a vibrant on-campus community. Students who can demonstrate experience as leaders show that they are capable handling advanced roles in challenging situations and, considering that leadership is a powerful skill, West Chester provides its students numerous opportunities to gain experience.

CO-CURRICULAR PORTFOLIO: The Co-Curricular Portfolio is WCUPA's way to make a meaningful record of a student's involvement outside of the classroom. The point of the portfolio is to demonstrate that students have impactful experiences outside of their schoolwork.

Résumés can only fit so much information, and so extracurricular experiences must often be excluded or abbreviated. The portfolio allows students to showcase their experiences in clubs, sports, service, leadership, and more. This detailed scope says much more about students' overall abilities and skillsets.

WOMEN LEADING UP: Women Leading Up is both a celebration and exploration of female leadership. Members of this community learn from great women leaders in the Philadelphia area and study what it takes to make a great female leader. Influential speakers come to share their wealth of knowledge, and all discussions are followed by group collaboration.

PRE-MAJOR ADVISING: Deciding a major isn't always easy, and many students may even need a guiding hand to see all their possible choices. Faculty members are happy to act as pre-major advisors in order to help their students select the appropriate major for them.

Undecided students are given a wealth of resources in order to let them explore their choices before coming to a conclusion. Through pre-major advising, students can discover passions they never knew they had.

www.wcupa.edu
(610) 436-3411
ugadmiss@wcupa.edu

STUDENT PROFILE

14,451 undergraduate students

90% of undergrad students are full-time

59% female – 41% male

13% of students are from out of state

85% freshman retention rate

FACULTY PROFILE

19 to 1 student/faculty ratio

ADMISSIONS

Selectivity: 69%

SAT Ranges: E 530-610, M 510-600

ACT Ranges: C 21-26, M 19-26, E 21-26

TUITION & COST

Tuition (in-state): $7,492

Tuition (out-of-state): $18,730

Fees: $2,619

Room: $5,408

Board: $3,652

WILSON COLLEGE

CHAMBERSBURG, PENNSYLVANIA

www.wilson.edu
(717) 264-4141
admissions@wilson.edu

Wilson has many opportunities for every student to grow in a thriving community. Wilson College strives to *"empower students through an engaged, collaborative, liberal arts education that combines the skills and focused study needed for success in work and life. [It is] a close, supportive community that develops the mind and character of all students, preparing them to meet the challenges of a global society."*

ADVENTURES ABROAD: Students at Wilson College have a wide variety of multidisciplinary opportunities to engage in a dynamic learning experience that speaks to their individual passions.

Whether they travel and learn abroad as part of the College's Global Studies Program, earn course credit and life experience through an off-campus internship, or complete a Capstone research project as a senior, students are sure to find a unique environment that meets their learning needs and life goals. Options span cultures and environments, taking students to places like Washington, D.C., London, France, Chile, Korea, South Africa, Thailand, and more.

ROWLAND LEAP: Wilson College invites new students kick off their college careers with an exciting challenge and welcoming community experience. In place of the typical First-Year Seminar, Rowland LEAP incorporates adventurous trips and service into an academically rigorous program.

Students who are up for a challenge will "leap from high school to college" with daily excursions, leadership-building opportunities, and helpful workshops that teach them to succeed in college-level coursework.

"...the Wilson experience is about more than academics—it's about finding your place. That's where LEAP comes in... to help you successfully transition to college life: learning, exploring, achieving, and participating." *— Wilson College*

STUDENT PROFILE

832 undergraduate students

78% of undergrad students are full-time

82% female — 18% male

23% of students are from out of state

76% freshman retention rate

FACULTY PROFILE

12 to 1 student/faculty ratio

ADMISSIONS

Selectivity: 92%

SAT Ranges: E 490-570, M 460-560

ACT Ranges: C 17-23, M 18-20, E 15-23

TUITION & COST

Tuition: $24,450

Fees: $850

Room: $5,500

Board: $6,094

YORK COLLEGE OF PENNSYLVANIA

YORK, PENNSYLVANIA

YORK COLLEGE
OF PENNSYLVANIA

Students come to York College of Pennsylvania because they want to take action. They want internships and paid cooperative learning. They want to conduct research with faculty and meet with their professors one-on-one. They want to get engaged right away, joining the school's award-winning radio station or entering in the Elevator Pitch Competition. And they want to pay half of what other top private colleges are asking without sacrificing a solid education. From day one, York College does all that and more.

FROM DAY ONE: Students find that it doesn't take long to get hands on at York College, where "From Day One" is both a motto and the school's approach to learning. Students get instruction from their professors 100% of the time, and they don't have to wait long to start using state-of-the-art equipment in the labs or to get involved in such department activities as an on-campus radio show and the YCP Hacks coding and creation event.

READY AND ABLE: Career readiness is a priority at York College. Students can conduct research alongside their professors and present their findings at national conferences. They can also participate in group projects and plan such student-run events as the popular Spartapalooza.

Further professional development comes naturally with all of York's access to internships. In fact, engineering students are required to take paid cooperative learning assignments, and many other programs require capstones. These all give students the ability to display tangible proof of their acquired skills to potential employers.

"From day one, I hoped that YCP would set my career in motion, and it has far surpassed by expectations, as I not only have started my career, but my dreams have expanded to places I never even considered."

– Kara Oldenburg-Gonzales '18, Fine Arts

www.ycp.edu
(717) 849-1600
admissions@ycp.edu

STUDENT PROFILE
4,079 undergraduate students

93% of undergrad students are full-time

54% female – 46% male

40% of students are from out of state

81% freshman retention rate

FACULTY PROFILE
15 to 1 student/faculty ratio

ADMISSIONS
Selectivity: 70%

SAT Ranges: E 500-590, M 500-600

ACT Ranges: C 20-25, M 18-26, E 19-24

TUITION & COST
Tuition: $18,180

Fees: $1,920

Room: $6,330

Board: $4,870

PROVIDENCE COLLEGE

PROVIDENCE, RHODE ISLAND

PROVIDENCE
COLLEGE

www.providence.edu
(401) 865-2535
pcadmiss@providence.edu

"Transform Yourself. Transform Society." That's the invitation and the promise Providence College offers to more than 4,000 undergraduate students each year, challenging them to engage in a life-changing educational experience. A Catholic, liberal arts college—the only one in the United States to be administered by the Dominican Friars—Providence has earned a national reputation for providing a distinctive education in a stimulating intellectual, spiritual, and social environment.

THE CIV: The Development of Western Civilization Program, or Civ, is the cornerstone of the Providence College core curriculum. Western Civilization covers the areas of history, philosophy, literature, theology, and the fine arts from ancient Mesopotamia to modern times.

D.C. SEMESTER: The Washington, D.C., Semester Program combines academic study and experiential learning in a full-semester program spent at American University in Washington, D.C. In any one of a dozen areas of study, the program consists of a two-course seminar that features academic professors and professional policy makers; a one-course research project served by the excellent libraries of Washington, D.C.; and practical work experience in a one-course, two-day-per-week internship.

Internships range from positions at the Office of the Vice President of the United States to apprenticeships under the director of the National Smithsonian Museums Network.

PROVIDENCE, RHODE ISLAND: Providence College's 105-acre campus is located within two miles of the heart of Rhode Island's capital city. The intimacy of the campus—with everything and everyone just a short walk away—enables students to enjoy a private, tranquil oasis with a vibrant city just minutes away.

Providence has been nationally recognized for its urban renaissance. One of America's first cities, it is rich in history, culture, and tradition.

STUDENT PROFILE

4,079 undergraduate students

94% of undergrad students are full-time

55% female – 45% male

90% of students are from out of state

92% freshman retention rate

FACULTY PROFILE

12 to 1 student/faculty ratio

ADMISSIONS

Selectivity: 52%

SAT Ranges: E 580-660, M 580-670

ACT Ranges: C 26-30, M 24-29, E 25-32

TUITION & COST

Tuition: $47,870

Fees: $894

Room: $8,210

Board: $6,030

THE UNIVERSITY OF RHODE ISLAND

KINGSTON, RHODE ISLAND

THE
UNIVERSITY
OF RHODE ISLAND

The University of Rhode Island is the flagship university of a small state that thinks big. With a diverse community and small class sizes, students feel welcome in an environment designed for personalized education.

A GRAND CHALLENGE: As part of the general education requirements, all students take a "Grand Challenge" course that examines a global problem through an interdisciplinary lens. These classes are designed for students to think big and find innovative solutions to the world's biggest issues. Through the Grand Challenge, Rhode Island students become informed citizens with the ability to understand a subject from multiple perspectives.

THE CAPSTONE EXPERIENCE: URI's capstone project, which serves as the culmination of a student's coursework and experiences in college, can take the form of an internship, a thesis, a design project, and more. One example of a URI capstone experience is the ELECOMP Capstone for Electrical Engineering and Computer Engineering students. Participants learn more about their subject, themselves, and the professional world as they work together to solve real problems at real businesses.

UCAS: URI's University College of Academic Success (UCAS) aims to help each student have a successful undergraduate experience. The Early Alert system ensures that no student is overlooked or left unsupported. With connections to counselors, academic advisers, students, and faculty and staff, students who are struggling can find help when they might otherwise be afraid to ask for it. Rhode Island students have a proactive support network to draw from.

> "More than anything, UCAS is dedicated to being a warm and welcoming place for all students. Our mission is to welcome, challenge, support, and care about students."
>
> – Jayne Richmond, Dean

www.uri.edu
(401)874-7000
admission@uri.edu

STUDENT PROFILE
15,107 undergraduate students

84% of undergrad students are full-time

56% female – 44% male

56% of students are from out of state

85% freshman retention rate

FACULTY PROFILE
17 to 1 student/faculty ratio

ADMISSIONS
Selectivity: 70%

SAT Ranges: E 530-620, M 520-610

ACT Ranges: C 22-27, M 21-27, E 22-27

TUITION & COST
Tuition (in-state): $12,002

Tuition (out-of-state): $28,252

Fees: $1,790

Room: $7,952

Board: $4,500

COASTAL CAROLINA UNIVERSITY

CONWAY, SOUTH CAROLINA

www.coastal.edu
(843) 349-2170
admissions@coastal.edu

Coastal Carolina University is a dynamic, public institution located near the resort area of Myrtle Beach. It offers 73 areas of study toward the baccalaureate degree, 25 master's degree programs, two specialist degrees, and two doctorate programs. One of the University's most outstanding assets is Waties Island, a 1,105-acre tract including part of a pristine barrier island, which provides a superb natural laboratory for marine science research.

ACADEMIC DEGREES: Marine science, communication, management, exercise and sport science, and communication are the most popular majors at CCU, which also offers unique degree programs in theatre and intelligence and national security studies. Marine science has been one of the most popular majors for the past decade; its distinguished faculty provides students with remarkable research opportunities.

Studies conducted by the University's Burroughs & Chapin Center for Marine and Wetland Studies play a vital role in shaping public policy relating to coastal resource management issues, not only along the South Carolina coast, but along other U.S. shorelines as well.

INTEGRATED ENGAGEMENT: A central focus of CCU's mission is to prepare students both to excel in the classroom and to succeed in life. In order to achieve this goal more effectively, the University has created Experienced@ Coastal, an integrated approach to student engagement.

This initiative brings experiential learning to the center of the educational culture by building on a strong tradition of active learning through undergraduate research, internships, international experiences, and community engagement.

"CCU has opened my life to new and challenging first-hand experiences that I wouldn't receive personally from any other institution of this caliber." - *Abby Barnes, marketing major*

STUDENT PROFILE

9,747 undergraduate students

91% of undergrad students are full-time

53% female – 47% male

55% of students are from out of state

69% freshman retention rate

FACULTY PROFILE

17 to 1 student/faculty ratio

ADMISSIONS

Selectivity: 61%

SAT Ranges: E 460-540, M 470-550

ACT Ranges: C 20-25, M 18-24, E 19-24

TUITION & COST

Tuition (in-state): $10,696

Tuition (out-of-state): $24,940

Fees: $180

Room: $5,440

Board: $3,450

COLLEGE OF CHARLESTON

CHARLESTON, SOUTH CAROLINA

The College of Charleston is a public liberal arts and sciences university located in the heart of historic Charleston, South Carolina. Founded in 1770, its mission remains to provide an undergraduate education that is both of superior quality and at an affordable price. CofC offers more than forty majors; the school's most popular majors are business and economics, education, and arts. The College also boasts a strong program in biochemistry and a well-regarded Honors College that draws 6.5 percent of College of Charleston's students.

HOLY CITY HISTORY: The College of Charleston's fifty-two-acre campus, outlined by herringbone-patterned brick sidewalks, is located in historic Charleston, also known as the Holy City. Its history is truly part of the fabric of American history, as three of its founders were signers of the Declaration of Independence.

In addition to its historic significance and beauty, CofC's hometown is an important seaport and has a population of about one hundred thousand.

HIGDON LEADERSHIP: The Higdon Student Leadership Center provides programs to create opportunities for student involvement and learning through individual and group leadership activities.

One such program, Leadership College of Charleston, gives thirty junior and senior student leaders, selected through a competitive application and interview process, the opportunity to meet monthly with each other and network with local and state leaders. Connected with real professionals, these students are able to dig in and discuss issues facing them as future leaders of society, communities, and corporations.

COMMITMENT TO SERVICE: CofC students explore the world beyond Charleston, participating in such service projects as helping the homeless in Chicago, doing environmental work in Seattle, and working with schools in the Dominican Republic.

www.cofc.edu
(843) 953-5670
admissions@cofc.edu

STUDENT PROFILE

9,895 undergraduate students

92% of undergrad students are full-time

63% female – 37% male

43% of students are from out of state

78% freshman retention rate

FACULTY PROFILE

15 to 1 student/faculty ratio

ADMISSIONS

Selectivity: 80%

SAT Ranges: E 550-630, M 520-600

ACT Ranges: C 22-27, M 20-26, E 22-28

TUITION & COST

Tuition (in-state): $12,352

Tuition (out-of-state): $30,740

Fees: $070

Room: $7,828

Board: $4,220

FURMAN UNIVERSITY

GREENVILLE, SOUTH CAROLINA

Furman is a liberal arts institution that places a dedicated focus on student-faculty interactions. The University recognizes the immense value of these interactions as a system of intellectual give and take. Students are taught to think critically, communicate effectively, and engage in higher-level conceptualization. While Furman is known for its top-notch academics, the University also has an exciting community life. Students have access to over 150 clubs and organizations, the interests of which span from Greek life to film clubs.

ACADEMIC ADVISING: Academic advising is taken seriously at Furman, putting students in close contact with all they need to succeed. Each student is assigned an advisor who provides academic and career counseling.

The goal of this advising is to help students discover their intellectual and personal talents so that they may understand how their interests fit within their field and the workforce at large.

STRONG ROOTS: A liberal arts degree is incredibly useful in today's global society. Furman provides its students with a well-rounded educational experience—one that transcends disciplines and departments.

Ultimately, students still commit themselves to a specific area of study, but they are also equipped with a wide range of skills. They are given responsibility over their educations and are encouraged to take advantage of all the academic and personal resources that Furman has to offer.

CAREER SERVICES: Furman provides services to help students prepare for their first interview, write a great résumé, and choose a career path.

The student success rate at Furman is very high thanks to these services and the dedication of both the faculty and the students themselves. Within six months of graduation, in fact, 97% of graduates find employment.

www.furman.edu
(864) 294-2034
admissions@furman.edu

STUDENT PROFILE

2,734 undergraduate students

97% of undergrad students are full-time

59% female – 41% male

71% of students are from out of state

93% freshman retention rate

FACULTY PROFILE

10 to 1 student/faculty ratio

ADMISSIONS

Selectivity: 61%

SAT Ranges: E 600-690, M 590-690

ACT Ranges: C 26-31, M 25-29, E 26-34

TUITION & COST

Tuition: $47,968

Fees: $380

Room: $6,540

Board: $5,618

PRESBYTERIAN COLLEGE

CLINTON, SOUTH CAROLINA

Four years at Presbyterian College are transformative. Blue Hose leave the College's oak-lined plazas with confidence because they remember. They remember the lessons learned at Neville Hall. They remember the leadership opportunities the Honor Council and Greek life provided. They remember the advice their favorite professor gave to them at the end of their sophomore year. It's these formative experiences that enable them to be different, to stand out from the crowd. The data speaks for itself: 95% of graduates are employed or in graduate school within six months of graduation.

THINK OUTSIDE OF THE BOX: Some popular majors at PC include business administration, pre-med, history, and music. Many history majors are pre-law, and many intern in the local area with circuit court judges.

Students are encouraged to get creative with their academic interests no matter their field of study. This often leads to academic pairings that many may consider unconventional, but at PC, that's the norm.

100% INVOLVED: At Presbyterian College, there is a belief that learning can and should take place outside of the four walls of the classroom. This is why 100% of PC students participate in study abroad, research, or internships during their time as an undergraduate student.

In the last year, PC students have traveled to the Galapagos Islands to study the local wildlife, researched and designed prosthetic limbs, and interned at the Greenville Zoo.

STUDENT/FACULTY INTERACTION: Professors have noted that they chose to teach at PC because of the high amount of contact they're able to have with their students. This is one of the reasons why the College maintains an average class size of 15 students.

Of the professors at PC, 95 percent hold terminal degrees in their field, and six noted professors have received the CASE Professor of the Year award—more than any other school in South Carolina.

www.presby.edu
(800) 476-7272
admissions@presby.edu

STUDENT PROFILE

1,016 undergraduate students

96% of undergrad students are full-time

51% female — 49% male

34% of students are from out of state

82% freshman retention rate

FACULTY PROFILE

12 to 1 student/faculty ratio

ADMISSIONS

Selectivity: 63%

SAT Ranges: E 510-620, M 510-630

ACT Ranges: C 21-27

TUITION & COST

Tuition: $34,982

Fees: $2,860

Room: $4,992

Board: $5,306

THE CITADEL

CHARLESTON, SOUTH CAROLINA

Coming from 45 states and 12 countries, 2,300 undergraduates make up the South Carolina Corps of Cadets. Throughout their undergraduate education, these students encounter The Citadel's core values of honor, duty, and respect. And while The Citadel provides a military education, only about one-third of students continue on to U.S. military service. The college's institution-wide focus on leadership allows students to graduate with the skills they need to be leaders in whatever industries they pursue.

SUCCEED: The Citadel supports the student experience with its four institutional pillars: academics, military, fitness, and character. And through the SUCCEED fellowship, students find that their character develops naturally through meaningful service.

The SUCCEED as Leaders (Summer Undergraduate Community-based Civic Engagement Experience for Development as Leaders) program takes Citadel out to serve individuals with disabilities. Trusted scholars and leaders alike, students are trusted to engage in every stage that helps these community partners function, engaging not only in service itself but also data processing and training within the organizations.

NATIONAL CENTER OF ACADEMIC EXCELLENCE: With 23 majors across a range of disciplines, The Citadel has something to offer for every student. One of the most up-and-coming majors, for example, is cybersecurity. The National Security Administration has designated The Citadel as a National Center of Academic Excellence in Cyber Defense Education.

> "The Citadel develops the person and the professional... Because of the leadership focus at The Citadel, there are amazing networking opportunities with alumni and influential leaders in the military and many industries."
>
> – Dillon Graham, Regimental Commander, Class of 2018

www.citadel.edu
(843) 953-5230
admissions@citadel.edu

STUDENT PROFILE

2,814 undergraduate students

91% of undergrad students are full-time

10% female – 90% male

32% of students are from out of state

84% freshman retention rate

FACULTY PROFILE

12 to 1 student/faculty ratio

ADMISSIONS

Selectivity: 81%

SAT Ranges: E 520-610, M 510-610

ACT Ranges: C 20-25, M 19-25, E 20-25

TUITION & COST

Tuition (in-state): $14,448

Tuition (out-of-state): $37,650

Room & Board: $7,700

UNIVERSITY OF SOUTH CAROLINA AIKEN

AIKEN, SOUTH CAROLINA

UNIVERSITY OF
SOUTH CAROLINA
AIKEN

www.usca.edu
(803) 641-3366
admit@usca.edu

Operating with a dedication to active learning, the University of South Carolina Aiken inspires students through collaborative scholarship between themselves and their professors, groundbreaking research, creative activities, and meaningful service. Its expansive offering of 50+ programs span the arts, sciences, and such professional fields as business, education, and nursing.

USCA ICE: USC Aiken's Inter-Curricular Enrichment (ICE) initiative ensures that every student is exposed to diverse curricular enrichment opportunities. This program expands students' perspectives, promoting lifelong learning through such events as film presentations, guest lectures, musical recitals, and other performances.

These engaging activities provide insight and challenge students to stretch the limits of their cultural and intellectual perceptions.

LEARNING COMMUNITIES: Students are able to join a learning community to form strong bonds with a group of peers who enroll in the same classes that are linked by a common theme. Additionally, they get the privilege to participate in a variety of out-of-class activities connected to their group's focus, the topic of which can include leadership, science, globalization, culture, and more.

AIKEN: USC Aiken is located 55 miles west of Columbia, SC, and 15 miles east of Augusta, GA. The university is located in the beautiful city of Aiken, which is known historically as a wintering playground for some of the country's most affluent families.

The area is noted for its rich equestrian culture of thoroughbred horses, steeplechase races, and polo matches. Just a few miles from the Augusta National Golf club and the Masters Tournament, the area is also known for its excellent golf courses and vibrant arts and cultural community.

STUDENT PROFILE

3,354 undergraduate students

81% of undergrad students are full-time

64% female – 36% male

8% of students are from out of state

68% freshman retention rate

FACULTY PROFILE

14 to 1 student/faculty ratio

ADMISSIONS

Selectivity: 53%

SAT Ranges: E 470-570, M 450-550

ACT Ranges: C 18-23, M 17-23, E 16-23

TUITION & COST

Tuition (in-state): $10,164

Tuition (out-of-state): $20,364

Fees: $338

Room: $4,942

Board: $2,650

UNIVERSITY OF SOUTH CAROLINA UPSTATE

SPARTANBURG, SOUTH CAROLINA

The University of South Carolina Upstate offers more than 40 bachelor's degree programs in the liberal arts and sciences, business administration, nursing, and teacher education, as well as master's degrees in education, informatics, and nursing. It also offers a growing number of courses through distance-learning education. The USC Upstate student body is diverse, representing over 45 states and countries and enriching the campus with a world of perspectives.

THE STRATEGIC PLAN: *Up. Together*: The Strategic Plan for USC Upstate 2018-2023 ensures that student success is the top priority. The university is dedicated to creating transformative opportunities for students by providing a rigorous, career-relevant education; enhancing the quality of life in Upstate, South Carolina; and being the university of choice for faculty, staff, students, and the community.

BUSINESS INCUBATOR: The George Dean Johnson, Jr. College of Business and Economics houses a startup incubator that helps students launch their own businesses, standing as a launchpad for new companies that have earned more than $85 million in collective revenue.

Opened in 2010, this 60,000 square-foot building houses smart classrooms with the latest technology, three art galleries, and a state-of-the-art stock trading lab at which students make real-time transactions based on current stock market activity.

TV PRODUCTION STUDIO: Students in the communication program have a unique opportunity to learn the ins and outs of TV production in a real production studio right on campus.

Operated by South Carolina Educational Television, the production facility serves as a living laboratory where students gain hands-on training with the same modern equipment and technology they'll find in the real world.

UPST☀TE
University of South Carolina Upstate

www.uscupstate.edu
(864) 503-5246
admissions@uscupstate.edu

STUDENT PROFILE
5,775 undergraduate students

79% of undergrad students are full-time

65% female — 35% male

5% of students are from out of state

68% freshman retention rate

FACULTY PROFILE
15 to 1 student/faculty ratio

ADMISSIONS
Selectivity: 58%

SAT Ranges: E 470-560, M 450-540

ACT Ranges: C 17-22, M 16-22, E 15-22

TUITION & COST
Tuition (in-state): $11,040

Tuition (out-of-state): $22,368

Fees: $480

Room: $5,110

Board: $3,224

BELMONT UNIVERSITY

NASHVILLE, TENNESSEE

From here to anywhere: Belmont University encourages its students to succeed both inside and outside the classroom. With a liberal arts and sciences focus and a mission based upon Christian ideals, Belmont develops well-rounded individuals who make significant contributions both domestically and abroad. Over 95 diverse and challenging majors encompass not only the arts and sciences, but pre-professional areas as well.

AMAZING PROGRAMS: Belmont's liberal arts base offers intensive studies in all the liberal arts and humanities in addition to highly regarded professional and pre-professional programs in accounting, nursing, pre-law, and more.

Belmont may be well known for its music résumé; it was named one of the best music business programs in the country by *Rolling Stone* and *Time*. And it leads the way further with pioneering interdisciplinary majors like music therapy, public health, global leadership studies, and experiential design.

GPS: All students have access to the GPS (Growth & Purpose for Students) program, which offers academic coaching, preparation, planning, and support. GPS staff coach students through discerning his or her unique path along with career goals and to aid in identifying the best opportunities and resources available through an educational journey at Belmont.

PRIME LOCATION: Belmont students are just miles from downtown, which means that they benefit greatly from being part of a larger community. Belmont benefits from Nashville's thriving business community, which provides abundant internship opportunities in a variety of fields, including entertainment, healthcare, and business, among many others.

"I love being a student in the College of Sciences & Mathematics because it is such an intentional community. Our professors know us by name and they really care about us and are always there whenever we have questions or concerns." – *Samantha Chu, Biology Major*

www.belmont.edu
(615) 460-6000
admissions@belmont.edu

STUDENT PROFILE

6,620 undergraduate students

96% of undergrad students are full-time

65% female – 35% male

69% of students are from out of state

82% freshman retention rate

FACULTY PROFILE

13 to 1 student/faculty ratio

ADMISSIONS

Selectivity: 82%

SAT Ranges: E 580-660, M 540-640

ACT Ranges: C 24-29, M 22-27, E 24-33

TUITION & COST

Tuition: $34,000

Fees: $1,650

Room: $6,860

Board: $5,660

CARSON-NEWMAN UNIVERSITY

JEFFERSON CITY, TENNESSEE

CARSON-NEWMAN
A CHRISTIAN UNIVERSITY

Carson-Newman University students experience what higher education can be at this nationally recognized university, founded in 1851. This liberal arts-based institution integrates faith and learning in a nurturing and rigorous teaching environment where students come first. C-N offers the resources necessary for the enrichment of each student's education, from quality faculty and academic programs to state-of-the-art technology and facilities. Every day, students prepare to compete on the world stage.

JEFFERSON CITY: Carson-Newman offers a spectacular location in one of America's most scenic regions. Set in the foothills of the Great Smoky Mountains and between two lakes, students can enjoy both the bustling city life of Knoxville and hiking and rafting less than 30 minutes from campus.

THE FILM PROGRAM: Carson-Newman's film program offers students the opportunity to earn college credit while participating in internships with regional filmmakers. Through a partnership program with the Los Angeles Film Studies Center, accepted students also have an opportunity to live in L.A. and to work and study with Hollywood filmmakers.

SPOTS AND SERVICE: Student volunteers are committed to building and sustaining a caring community through integration of academic excellence and community engagement. The Appalachian Center, for example, serves the physical needs of rural Appalachia, and the Samaritan House provides housing for the homeless.

"Had I gone to the school I thought was for me, I would not be a nurse. I needed the individual attention and encouragement... I also know that I would not be where I am now in my faith journey; therefore, I am forever grateful to the staff and faculty at Carson-Newman."

— Mary Armstrong, Class of 2012

www.cn.edu
(865) 471-3223
admitme@cn.edu

STUDENT PROFILE

1,812 undergraduate students

96% of undergrad students are full-time

58% female – 42% male

21% of students are from out of state

70% freshman retention rate

FACULTY PROFILE

13 to 1 student/faculty ratio

ADMISSIONS

Selectivity: 63%

SAT Ranges: E 400-560, M 440-560

ACT Ranges: C 20-26, M 18-25, E 20-26

TUITION & COST

Tuition: $25,200

Fees: $1,160

Room: $3,930

Board: $4,500

CHRISTIAN BROTHERS UNIVERSITY

MEMPHIS, TENNESSEE

www.cbu.edu
(901) 321-3205
admissions@cbu.edu

As a Catholic university committed to preparing students of all faiths and backgrounds, CBU provides challenging educational opportunities in the arts, business, engineering, the sciences, and education. CBU's commitment to the Lasallian ideals of faith, service, and community is reflected in an often-repeated phrase on campus, *"Enter to Learn, Leave to Serve."*

STRONG COMMUNITY: At CBU, learning transcends the classroom and the lab. Making people feel welcome and at home on campus is one of CBU's five core values, which means that CBU is a community where people care about and treat each other with respect in the classroom, on the playing field, and everywhere they are living, learning, and working together every day.

As a CBU Buccaneer, part of the college experience is pursuing individual interests within a thriving campus life community. Whether they participate in a student organization, compete in intramural sports, attend campus ministries, serve with volunteer efforts, or utilize other campus resources, CBU helps every student find their interests, their passion, their story.

AWARD-WINNING: CBU students regularly put their skills to the test through upper-level research projects. For example, engineering students annually build off-road cars to race over the harshest elements of rough terrain as well as compete in self-constructed moon buggies and mini-bajas. Science majors publish their research papers in peer-reviewed journals, and liberal arts and social science majors regularly present at prestigious conferences.

STUDENT PROFILE

1,791 undergraduate students

80% of undergrad students are full-time

52% female – 48% male

26% of students are from out of state

80% freshman retention rate

FACULTY PROFILE

13 to 1 student/faculty ratio

ADMISSIONS

Selectivity: 53%

ACT Ranges: C 21-27, M 20-26, E 22-28

TUITION & COST

Tuition: $31,000

Fees: $870

Room & Board: $8,754

"Honestly, the teachers at CBU are simply amazing. I think that what gives CBU its value is that it's a place where you can get as much or as little as you're willing to put into it. It's a place where, if you put in the work, you can achieve anything you want." *- Gabriela Morales Medina, Class of 2019*

KING UNIVERSITY

BRISTOL, TENNESSEE

There are a few givens of college life. Students will study. They will learn. They will play. They will meet people who can change their lives. At King University, they will also grow—as students, certainly, but perhaps more importantly, as people. A great education prepares students for a successful future. Many colleges promise just that, alone. The difference lies in how one gets from point A to point Z. At King University, students' journeys are filled with new experiences to challenge (and even change) the way they view themselves and the world. They go beyond the usual and learn in an environment that encourages exploration.

THE ARTS: Creative talents are supported through majors in music, music education, digital media art and design (photography, videography, graphic design), and theatre.

Participants might get the chance to perform at Carnegie Hall; travel to Scotland, England, or even Greece for performances; or head down to the "World's Fastest Half Mile" to take photos of NASCAR legends at Bristol Motor Speedway.

EMBRACE THE CHALLENGE: Students are guaranteed to participate in stimulating classes led by people who will fully engage their minds.

Examples of research opportunities have included a study of the solar orbits of asteroids and star clusters as well as frontline research on the effect of pesticides on human biology.

INSTITUTE FOR FAITH AND CULTURE: Through its thought-provoking lecture series, the King University Institute for Faith and Culture aims to address issues of faith engaging culture not only for the King community but for audiences throughout the region as well.

The Institute offers opportunities for focused consideration and reflection. One notable highlight of the lecture series is a moving and enlightening lecture from a survivor of the Holocaust.

www.king.edu
(423) 652-4861
admissions@king.edu

STUDENT PROFILE

1,799 undergraduate students

89% of undergrad students are full-time

61% female – 39% male

54% of students are from out of state

70% freshman retention rate

FACULTY PROFILE

13 to 1 student/faculty ratio

ADMISSIONS

Selectivity: 51%

SAT Ranges: E 470-562, M 482-591

ACT Ranges: C 18-26, M 19-26, E 17-25

TUITION & COST

Tuition: $27,024

Fees: $1,548

Room: $4,230

Board: $4,194

LIPSCOMB UNIVERSITY

NASHVILLE, TENNESSEE

Lipscomb University is a 125-year-old private coeducational institution in Nashville, TN. Its primary mission is to integrate Christian faith and practice with academic achievement, which the entire campus community carries out not only in the classroom but also through numerous services to the church and surrounding neighborhood. The university numbers about 2,900 undergraduate students and 1,600 graduate students in more than 145 areas of study. Located in one of America's newest "It" cities, Lipscomb draws on Nashville's multifaceted corporate and creative community to deepen its students' educational experience.

AN INNOVATIVE EDUCATION: Majors like Sustainability, Law Justice and Society, Entrepreneurship, Missions, Animation, and Art Therapy offer students the opportunity to receive training in cutting-edge fields that are rarely addressed by other institutions.

The same commitment to innovation and academic leadership permeates all of Lipscomb's programs; from Nursing to Engineering, and Business to Education, Lipscomb students consider the future of their field and effectively synthesize the overwhelming amount of information that defines our time.

SALT: Lipscomb integrates "Service and Learning Together," hence the name of its institution-wide program, SALT. All students participate in at least two SALT courses or experiences, exposing them to the wonders that come with applying their knowledge to the aid of others.

NASHVILLE: Lipscomb's great location just minutes from downtown Nashville affords students easy access to a tremendous number of educational, professional, cultural, and entertainment opportunities. Additionally, university provides all of its students with a free, year-round Nashville Metro bus pass to ensure that they can take advantage of all the city has to offer.

A major metropolitan area of more than one million, Nashville is still one of the friendliest places in the country.

www.lipscomb.edu
1 (877) 58-BISON
admissions@lipscomb.edu

STUDENT PROFILE

2,986 undergraduate students

89% of undergrad students are full-time

62% female – 38% male

39% of students are from out of state

85% freshman retention rate

FACULTY PROFILE

12 to 1 student/faculty ratio

ADMISSIONS

Selectivity: 61%

SAT Ranges: E 500-638, M 490-630

ACT Ranges: C 22-28, M 22-27, E 23-31

TUITION & COST

Tuition: $27,472

Fees: $2,284

Room: $6,500

Board: $5,040

MARYVILLE COLLEGE

MARYVILLE, TENNESSEE

maryvillecollege.edu
(865) 981-8092
admissions@
maryvillecollege.edu

Maryville is one of the oldest colleges in the United States and is known for its academic rigor across nearly 60 pre-professional programs of study. Ideally located between the Great Smoky Mountains National Park and Knoxville, Maryville offers quick access to both exciting outdoor activities as well as the vibrant Knoxville culture and resources. Maryville's core curriculum is non-traditional in all the best ways, taking an interesting and explorative spin on the classroom, laboratory, and studio environments.

THE SENIOR STUDY: Since 1947, the Senior Study has been a distinctive part of every Maryville student's experience. In this two-semester, faculty-supervised undergraduate research project, students choose a topic related to their major and explore their career goals and passions. Completed studies take many forms (traditional research, original compositions, field work, etc.) and are impressive additions to résumés and graduate school applications. Studies that are deemed "exemplary" by the Maryville College faculty are added to the College library's permanent collection.

MOUNTAIN CHALLENGE: Located on the Maryville campus, Mountain Challenge, LLC, is an outdoor adventure and team-building program that strives "to provide high-quality, safe outdoor experiences designed to change the world for the better, one person at a time." Mountain Challenge activities are incorporated into Orientation classes and, year-round, students can sign up for off-campus trips to canoe, hike, raft, bike, rock-climb, and cave.

THEMED LIVING COMMUNITIES: Launched in the fall of 2018, themed living aims to build communities of like-minded students within the residence halls. Currently, programming is focused on three themes: Fit. Green. Happy.®, community engagement, and scholar-athlete.

The College's wellness residence, Gibson Hall, adopted Fit. Green. Happy.® in partnership with Mountain Challenge. The community engagement theme helps members get involved with the local community through service. The scholar-athlete community in Gamble Hall is dedicated to helping athletes balance the demands of athletics and academics.

STUDENT PROFILE
1,181 undergraduate students

98% of undergrad students are full-time

54% female – 46% male

72% freshman retention rate

FACULTY PROFILE
13 to 1 student/faculty ratio

ADMISSIONS
Selectivity: 49%

SAT Ranges: E 460-580, M 470-570

ACT Ranges: C 20-27, M 18-25, E 19-28

TUITION & COST
Tuition: $33,402

Fees: $794

Room: $5,562

Board: $5,582

MIDDLE TENNESEE STATE UNIVERSITY

MURFREESBORO, TENNESSEE

Founded in 1911, Middle Tennessee State University is a Carnegie Research Doctoral University that offers more than 140 degree programs within eight undergraduate colleges. Middle Tennessee State University is committed to cultivating an environment that fosters academic excellence and student success. Everything the University does is an embodiment of the community values of honesty and integrity; respect for diversity; engagement in the community; and committing to reason—not violence—in its motto, "*I am True Blue.*"

RESEARCH AND PUBLIC SERVICE: MTSU's academic centers improve the academic experience for students on campus while also providing tremendous benefits to the local and state government, various businesses, and more. The extensive and cutting-edge research performed right on campus add to the worldwide discussion of a variety of intellectual feats.

Just a few of MTSU's centers include include the Albert Gore Research Center, the Business and Economic Research Center, the Center for Chinese Music and Culture, the Center for Energy Efficiency, the Center for Environmental Education, and many more.

LEADERSHIP AND COMMUNITY: The Center for Student Involvement and Leadership oversees all student activities, including student government, Greek life, student organizations, service-learning, and more. It operates to support students as they explore opportunities beyond their studies; well-rounded lifestyles are crucial to becoming citizen-leaders at MTSU, in Tennessee, and beyond.

The Student Organizations and Service Office further implements such involved initiatives as the Bridge Leadership Summit, Leader Lessons, Alternative Breaks, Habitat Blitz Build, and more to broaden students' possibilities and access.

MIDDLE TENNESSEE STATE UNIVERSITY

www.mtsu.edu
(615) 898-2233
admissions@mtsu.edu

STUDENT PROFILE
19,523 undergraduate students

81% of undergrad students are full-time

54% female – 46% male

9% of students are from out of state

76% freshman retention rate

FACULTY PROFILE
18 to 1 student/faculty ratio

ADMISSIONS
Selectivity: 59%

SAT Ranges: E 520-620, M 470-590

ACT Ranges: C 20-25, M 18-25, E 19-26

TUITION & COST
Tuition (in-state): $6,840

Tuition (out-of-state): $24,576

Fees: $1,772

Room: $5,304

Board: $3,850

RHODES COLLEGE

MURFREESBORO, TENNESSEE

www.rhodes.edu
(901) 843-3700
adminfo@rhodes.edu

Real Experience. Real Success. The Rhodes Reality. Rhodes isn't just about learning: it's about learning to live, about putting ideas and ideals into practice, about making it real. Students looking for a classical liberal arts education with a practical edge should consider the Rhodes reality: a beautiful campus, challenging academics, caring faculty, personal development, and all the opportunities of a culturally rich and vibrant city.

REAL RESEARCH: Flexible independent study is encouraged at Rhodes. Choices include self-designed interdisciplinary majors, individualized study options, directed inquiry projects, the tutorial plan, and study abroad.

State-of-the-art technology is everywhere on the wireless campus at Rhodes. "Smart" classrooms, located throughout the campus, offer the latest computer tech and video displays. The college's science facilities have been recently updated to offer students top-of-the-line technology and instruments.

A ROARING CITY: There's more to Memphis than Graceland and Elvis Presley. From blues on Beale Street to stadium sports, Memphis offers a rich mix of entertainment options. Memphis, the 18th largest city in the United States, is renowned for its great food, outstanding museums, and rich Southern heritage.

The campus, which spans across 100 acres in midtown Memphis, is right across from Overton Park, which contains the Memphis Zoo, the Brooks Museum, and the Memphis College of Art.

THE HONOR CODE: The Honor Code, a century-old tradition, makes a huge difference in the Rhodes community. Upon enrolling at Rhodes, students pledge not to lie, cheat, or steal. Honesty is a given, integrity matters, and values are put into practice every day.

Faculty members feel free to leave the classroom during tests, students trust each other, and individuals live in harmony with the community. The Honor Code makes Rhodes an easy place to live and a great place to learn.

STUDENT PROFILE
1,988 undergraduate students

100% of undergrad students are full-time

56% female – 44% male

91% freshman retention rate

FACULTY PROFILE
10 to 1 student/faculty ratio

ADMISSIONS
Selectivity: 51%

SAT Ranges: E 620-720, M 600-690

ACT Ranges: C 27-32, M 25-30, E 27-34

TUITION & COST
Tuition: $46,194

Fees: $310

Room & Board: $11,290

ABILENE CHRISTIAN UNIVERSITY

ABILENE, TEXAS

ABILENE CHRISTIAN UNIVERSITY

The ACU experience—whether on the Abilene campus, in Study Abroad programs, at education centers, or through an ACU virtual community—helps students develop intellect, grow closer to God, prepare for a meaningful career, and address global challenges with a Christian worldview. Because ACU professors know their students well and often serve as mentors, they are able to provide excellent references to medical schools, law schools, graduate programs, and future employers.

INNOVATIVE STUDY: At ACU, students experience rare opportunities to prepare for their future careers. In the physics program, undergraduate students regularly participate with faculty members at national nuclear physics laboratories and make national and international presentations. Journalism students produce a twice-weekly newspaper, *The Optimist,* that has received All-American honors every year since 1975.

ACU is committed to making learning accessible, far reaching, and unhindered. It happened to be first university to give iPhones and iPod touches to freshmen, and it continues to be a world leader in the study of mobile-learning technology for use in higher education.

ACU ACTIVITIES: As a residential campus, ACU is alive with activities, from concerts and weeknight devotionals to poetry readings. Many students participate in intramural sports, men's and women's social clubs, Spring Break mission campaigns, and the annual Sing Song performance event. More than 100 campus organizations give students many venues for involvement and leadership.

IN DEMAND: Each year, some of the nation's top businesses come to campus to interview ACU students due to their fantastic reputation of success.

Outstanding faculty, great facilities, and successful post-graduate jobs are all the result of ACU's uncommon commitment to teaching and learning. ACU prepares its graduates for Christian service and leadership throughout the world.

www.acu.edu
(800) 460-6228
info@admissions.acu.edu

STUDENT PROFILE

3,666 undergraduate students

96% of undergrad students are full-time

58% female — 42% male

8% of students are from out of state

77% freshman retention rate

FACULTY PROFILE

14 to 1 student/faculty ratio

ADMISSIONS

Selectivity: 58%

SAT Ranges: E 510-620, M 515-600

ACT Ranges: C 21-26, M 20-26, E 20-26

TUITION & COST

Tuition: $33,280

Fees: $50

Room: $5,186

Board: $5,192

ANGELO STATE UNIVERSITY

SAN ANGELO, TEXAS

www.angelo.edu
(325) 942-2041
admissions@angelo.edu

Angelo State University, a member of the Texas Tech University System, is a vibrant "Ram Fam" community of 10,000 students. ASU offers over 100 majors and concentrations through six colleges as well as an unparalleled Honors Program and Center for International Studies, giving students opportunities to expand their education through research and study abroad.

HEALTH AND HUMAN SERVICES: Opened in January 2018, ASU's Health and Human Services Building features expanded labs for several departments as well as state-of-the-art technology, including six simulation labs for practical use by nursing, physical therapy, and health science students.

MIR CENTER: ASU's Management, Instruction, and Research Center includes a 6,000-acre working ranch on which agriculture and animal science students experience all aspects of the agriculture industry. Its building houses the USDA-inspected Food Safety and Product Development Lab, Mayer-Rousselot Agricultural Education and Training Center, and ASU Meat Market, where student-produced meat products are sold to the public.

ONE OF A KIND: The ASU Modular Theatre allows production groups to completely transform the look and feel of the stage. Theatre students host several productions here every year, including three dinner theatre shows.

Additional distinctive resources include the Biology Department Greenhouse, ROTC Flight Simulator, Entertainment Computing Lab, dedicated psychology and sociology labs, and a high-tech Scanning Electron Microscope.

> "The focus is on you as a student. It's not going to be, 'the faculty is worried about their research.' It's going to be, 'how can I prepare this student, not only to become successful, but to ready them for the workplace and work on a team to come up with the best solution possible for whatever project they're working on?'" – *Deyton Riddle, '18, civil engineering*

STUDENT PROFILE

6,036 undergraduate students

90% of undergrad students are full-time

55% female – 45% male

32% of students are from out of state

67% freshman retention rate

FACULTY PROFILE

20 to 1 student/faculty ratio

ADMISSIONS

Selectivity: 73%

SAT Ranges: E 480-580, M 470-560

ACT Ranges: C 18-24, M 17-24, E 16-23

TUITION & COST

Tuition (in-state): $5,415

Tuition (out-of-state) $18,075

Fees: $3,306

Room & Board: $9,130

DALLAS BAPTIST UNIVERSITY

DALLAS, TEXAS

Founded in 1898, Dallas Baptist University provides world-class, Christ-centered higher education to more than 5,000 students. Service-learning is integrated into each degree plan, and a culture of mentoring pervades the campus. Dallas Baptist University is a Christian liberal arts university that seeks to develop servant leaders who have the ability to integrate faith and learning through their respective callings.

POLITICS, PHILOSOPHY, AND ECONOMICS: Introduced in Fall 2017, DBU offers a new undergraduate major called Politics, Philosophy, and Economics. The PPE degree has attracted students who would go on to become leaders and influencers in business, government, journalism, foreign service, diplomacy, law, consultancy, and the list goes on.

PAIDEIA COLLEGE SOCIETY: The Paideia College Society challenges students to carry out their various callings in both public and private life with Christ-like knowledge, virtue, and wisdom. This group hosts a weekly symposium at which intellectuals present papers and give presentations with a view to serve as a catalyst for cultural transformation.

DALLAS, TX: DBU is located in the southwestern sector of Dallas, situated on 292 picturesque acres overlooking Mountain Creek Lake. Strategically positioned in the thriving Dallas-Fort Worth Metroplex, the University is 13 miles from downtown Dallas and 29 miles from downtown Fort Worth. Dallas provides an ideal climate for graduates to find valuable internships.

COLLABORATIVE ASSIGNMENTS: The College of Business provides an excellent example of the kind of innovative Collaborative Assignments offered across all of DBU's programming.

The Strategic Management 4320 course affords students the opportunity to analyze a business in the DFW area and write descriptive assessments of the company in the areas of industry, value chain, generic strategy, integration, and execution.

www.dbu.edu
(214) 333-5360
admiss@dbu.edu

STUDENT PROFILE

3,161 undergraduate students

77% of undergrad students are full-time

59% female – 41% male

70% freshman retention rate

FACULTY PROFILE

13 to 1 student/faculty ratio

ADMISSIONS

Selectivity: 39%

SAT Ranges: E 560-640, M 530-610

ACT Ranges: C 19-24

TUITION & COST

Tuition: $26,580

Fees: $900

Room: $3,790

Board: $3,950

HARDIN-SIMMONS UNIVERSITY

ABILENE, TEXAS

www.hsutx.edu
1 (877) GO-HSUTX

Hardin-Simmons is a private, co-educational university located in Abilene, TX, and is affiliated with the Baptist General Convention of Texas. Academic excellence continues as a priority at Hardin-Simmons University— as it has for more than a century—and small classes taught by experienced scholars give the opportunity for interactive learning. The institution's commitment to excellence is best illustrated through the lives of graduates who traditionally have excelled in any career they have chosen.

PHYSICIAN ASSISTANT PROGRAM: Hardin-Simmons University has one of the newest Physician's Assistant programs in the state. Students in this program are prepared to enter the medical field as exceptional medical professionals who are ready to work in any context.

HSU students have a particularly unique experience, as the University maintains a close connection with the Hendrick Medical Center and surrounding rural communities.

A DYNAMIC PLACE TO BE: Blend an old West town and a modern, medium-sized city, then throw in a good dose of hospitality as well as a large helping of recreation, and one has Abilene, Texas.

As a leading education center, HSU is often described as "an oasis" with lush grounds, a duck-filled pond, and stately, red brick buildings. HSU is a place of higher learning that warmly opens its doors to students seeking a Christian, liberal arts education within a supportive and spiritual community.

MAJORS: HSU offers more than fifty majors through its Colleges of Liberal Arts and Business as well as its Schools of Education, Music, Nursing, Theology, and Sciences and Mathematics.

The foundational curriculum involves students in a broad range of inquiry-related general studies alongside whatever requirements are included with a student's chosen major. Small classes taught by experienced scholars ensure interactive learning.

STUDENT PROFILE

1,721 undergraduate students

94% of undergrad students are full-time

54% female – 46% male

3% of students are from out of state

68% freshman retention rate

FACULTY PROFILE

12 to 1 student/faculty ratio

ADMISSIONS

Selectivity: 84%

SAT Ranges: E 500-590, M 500-580

ACT Ranges: C 18-24, M 17-24, E 16-25

TUITION & COST

Tuition: $28,390

Fees: $1,750

Room: $4,470

Board: $5,380

LUBBOCK CHRISTIAN UNIVERSITY

LUBBOCK, TEXAS

LUBBOCK CHRISTIAN UNIVERSITY

www.lcu.edu
(806) 720-7151
admissions@lcu.edu

Lubbock Christian University is committed to educating leaders whose lives will have a lasting effect on their family, church, community, and job. At LCU, everything is based on faith. A student's character is what forms a foundation for success, so LCU endeavors to prepare them to thrive in all aspects of their lives—from spiritual formation and intellectual growth to personal stewardship and leadership development. Lubbock Christian University promotes unique educational opportunities with a strategic focus on student success.

LCU HONORS COLLEGE: The University Honors College offers challenging and provocative courses, colloquia and seminars, occasions for cultural enrichment, and assistance for semester internships and study abroad opportunities.

One such internship opportunity, the LCU Washington Program, provides qualified students with a semester-long internship in the nation's capital. Students complete a full-time, entry-level professional internship in their chosen career field, and they participate in various professional development and academic learning experiences.

CORE IN SPAIN: In the fall of 2016, LCU launched its 14-week Semester in Spain program, which brings students and faculty to the beautiful city of Avila in the heart of the Spanish countryside. Students take 15 hours of University Core-type credits with LCU professors in the medieval walled city, allowing immersion in another culture alongside LCU faculty.

SIDE-BY-SIDE RESEARCH: The Undergraduate Research Program involves every participant in a working relationship with a Faculty Mentor.

Not only may students reach out to faculty guidance themselves, but some professors even seek out students to join them in preparation for such events as the National Conference for Undergraduate Research or the annual Scholar's Colloquium.

STUDENT PROFILE

1,439 undergraduate students

88% of undergrad students are full-time

60% female — 40% male

10% of students are from out of state

69% freshman retention rate

FACULTY PROFILE

13 to 1 student/faculty ratio

ADMISSIONS

Selectivity: 90%

SAT Ranges: E 480-620, M 475-590

ACT Ranges: C 18-25, M 17-25, E 16-24

TUITION & COST

Tuition: $22,440

Room & Board: $7,700

MCMURRY UNIVERSITY

ABILENE, TEXAS

McMurry University is guided by core values of faith, personal relationships, excellence, and service, all of which support students to become well-rounded, global leaders. Students are fully engaged in their coursework, going above and beyond through research and personal relationships with faculty and staff. This individualized approach to learning provides each student with a support network that ensures success in both their coursework and their extracurriculars.

SERVANT LEADERSHIP: Servant leadership is central to McMurry—in amd out of the classroom. Offered as both a course as well as an entire minor, the Servant Leadership discipline allows students to grow as leaders and contribute to both academic and co-curricular transcripts, which document the good each has done for their community.

GLOBAL LEARNING: Students looking to take an independent trip abroad can head to Harlaxton College in London, McMurry's international "anchor" institution. Here, they can take a full course load while still having the ability to travel across Europe on the weekends. Those at Harlaxton travel, on average, to nine countries in their time abroad, all in addition to their already immersive experience of living in the United Kingdom.

RESEARCH: While many institutions focus on graduate student research, McMurry is fully dedicated to offering robust research opportunities for undergraduates. Through research teams comprised of students and faculty, McMurry has contributed to the body of research across multiple fields. For example, the biology department has an extended breast cancer research team that has allowed students to get hands-on experience, present at conferences, and more.

But research isn't limited to presentations, reports, or papers; business students take an in-depth look at international markets by managing a real investment portfolio from McMurry's endowment. This kind of hands-on experience is a modern form of research that ensures students get an accurate look at the world in which they will work.

www.mcm.edu
(325) 793-4700
admissions@mcm.edu

STUDENT PROFILE

1,080 undergraduate students

92% undergrad students are full-time

50% female – 50% male

3% of students are from out of state

62% freshman retention rate

FACULTY PROFILE

11 to 1 student/faculty ratio

ADMISSIONS

Selectivity: 41%

SAT Ranges: E 480-580, M 470-570

ACT Ranges: C 18-23, M 17-23, E 16-22

TUITION & COST

Tuition: $27,834

Fees: $90

Room: $4,286

Board: $4,534

SCHREINER UNIVERSITY

KERRVILLE, TEXAS

Schreiner University is a private, Presbyterian university that offers a personalized, integrated, and holistic educational experience among the open lands of the Texas Hill Country. Named after Captain Charles Schreiner, the university strives to epitomize its founder's grit, tenacity, and courage through thoughtful, individualized instruction. Students graduate with the skills and abilities needed to excel in their specific area of study while knowing how to navigate an increasingly diverse, complex world.

COMMUNICATION DESIGN: Schreiner's Communication Design program takes a comprehensive look at the arts in a real-world career environment. Compelling aesthetics are crucial for the success of a company within a saturated market. Developing both their strategy and artistry, students learn the practical application of their passions, whether they lie in illustration, web design, animation, or any kind of visual medium.

As with Schreiner's other hands-on programs, the Communication Design major comes with plenty of opportunities to intern, practice, and travel while learning to apply their studies to a career path.

ONGOING DEVELOPMENT: Established in 2012 through a U.S. Department of Education Title V grant, the Center for Teaching and Learning (CTL) enables faculty to explore new models of teaching and access helpful resources. It's through the CTL that Schreiner helps its professors develop their coursework and provide the best classroom experience possible. This commitment to engaging work ensures that students are given the chance to enjoy up-to-date, innovative classes.

SCHREINER GROW: The Schreiner GROW (Guided Reflection on Work) program was created to help students draw a clear connection between their learning and their experiences. Students learn how to reflect in a productive way that supports their success, translating their knowledge to actionable skills. It's not always obvious how to apply class work to the real world, but Schreiner GROW makes it easy to reflect, assess, and apply what they've learned for their future success.

Schreiner University
FIND YOUR WAY HERE

www.schreiner.edu
(830) 792-7217
admissions@schreiner.edu

STUDENT PROFILE

1,249 undergraduate students

91% of undergrad students are full-time

58% female – 42% male

1% of students are from out of state

71% freshman retention rate

FACULTY PROFILE

13 to 1 student/faculty ratio

ADMISSIONS

Selectivity: 92%

SAT Ranges: E 480-580, M 480-560

ACT Ranges: C 19-24, M 16-23, E 17-23

TUITION & COST

Tuition: $24,990

Fees: $1,910

Room: $4,980

Board: $5,172

SOUTHERN METHODIST UNIVERSITY

DALLAS, TEXAS

SMU provides a great education for future professionals interested in more than just their professions. It combines an expansive curriculum to ensure that students can immerse themselves in their particular interests while still benefiting from exposure to different academic disciplines. SMU is large enough to offer almost unlimited opportunities and small enough for students to truly take advantage of them.

SMU SCHOLARS: The University provides several opportunities for undergraduates to conduct research, and the Richter Fellowship goes even further to award grant money in support of the costs incurred while researching international or multicultural topics, often in a foreign country.

Students studying biomedicine can take advantage of summer research opportunities through the Biomedical Researchers in Training Experience Scholars Program. SMU psychology majors start researching and conducting experiments as early as their sophomore year.

A THRIVING NEIGHBORHOOD: In addition to all the exciting activities on campus, there's also a lot to do in both the neighborhood across the street and within the city (accessible by a nearby light-rail system!).

Some of the best shopping, art. and cultural activities in the world can be found in Dallas; SMU's Meadows Museum houses one of the finest and most comprehensive collections of Spanish art outside of Spain.

HEGI CENTER: Whether students are planning to attend graduate school or join the workforce, the SMU Hegi Family Career Development Center is prepared to help with academic guidance, seminars on résumé building, and mock interviews.

The career center also has a job and internship placement program and is proud to say that there are more internships available to SMU students than there are students to fill them.

www.smu.edu
(214) 768-2058
ugadmission@smu.edu

STUDENT PROFILE
6,452 undergraduate students

97% of undergrad students are full-time

50% female – 50% male

57% of students are from out of state

91% freshman retention rate

FACULTY PROFILE
11 to 1 student/faculty ratio

ADMISSIONS
Selectivity: 49%

SAT Ranges: E 630-710, M 640-730

ACT Ranges: C 28-32, M 27-31, E 28-34

TUITION & COST
Tuition: $46,594

Fees: $5,904

Room: $10,665

Board: $5,845

ST. EDWARD'S UNIVERSITY

AUSTIN, TEXAS

Established in 1885 and located in the heart of Austin, Texas, St. Edward's is a private, liberal arts-based Catholic university rooted in the Holy Cross tradition. With over 90 academic programs, St. Edward's continues its founding tradition of academic excellence and educating the whole person.

AUSTIN: St. Edward's is located in Austin, TX, a quickly growing metropolis. Because the University is so close to the city, students have access to amazing professional opportunities as well as endless recreational activities.

Austin is known for its live music, outdoor activities, and tech industry. There are plenty of attractions, including Austin City Limits, South by Southwest, and Fun Fun Fun Fest.

LIVING-LEARNING COMMUNITIES: Living-Learning Communities (LLCs) bring together students from different backgrounds who share common interests or academic goals. These students have the unique opportunity to live and learn among similarly minded peers 24 hours a day. This structure allows students to collaborate both in and out of the classroom, thus enhancing the educational experience through the participation in special events, discussions, and service projects.

Examples of St. Edward's University's LLCs include Active Living, Honors, Leadership, Natural Sciences, and "Wicked Problems," a community dedicated to approaching complex social issues.

HONORS PROGRAM: The Honors program brings together academically gifted students from all majors and schools. Alongside faculty, these students create an intellectually stimulating community that promotes both academic and personal growth.

Most of the Honors seminars are taught in a team-teaching style, boosted by professors who teach from different disciplines. Their work culminates in an Honors Senior Thesis, which stands as a reflection of each student's passions and academic capabilities.

www.stedwards.edu
(512) 448-8500
seu.admit@stedwards.edu

STUDENT PROFILE

3,941 undergraduate students

90% of undergrad students are full-time

61% female – 39% male

12% of students are from out of state

80% freshman retention rate

FACULTY PROFILE

13 to 1 student/faculty ratio

ADMISSIONS

Selectivity: 84%

SAT Ranges: E 550-640, M 530-610

ACT Ranges: C 22-28, M 21-26, E 22-28

TUITION & COST

Tuition: $42,550

Fees: $750

Room: $7,600

Board: $5,340

ST. MARY'S UNIVERSITY

SAN ANTONIO, TEXAS

ST. MARY'S UNIVERSITY

St. Mary's University, founded by Marianist brothers in 1852, is the first higher education institution established in San Antonio. It offers a strong educational experience—integrating liberal arts, professional preparation, and ethical commitment. St. Mary's students receive the value of quality programs, holistic learning, and community support, helping graduates discover what they love to do and how to apply their knowledge in meaningful ways.

UNIQUE EXCELLENCE: St. Mary's is a Hispanic-serving Institution, committed to fostering the academic success of students, particularly those interested in STEM fields. In 2015, St. Mary's received Fair Trade University certification the only fair-trade-designated university in Texas—to promote businesses that respect human and environmental factors that go into creating consumer products.

St. Mary's is also home to several communities of Marianists—religious brothers and priests whose faith tradition traces back to Blessed William Joseph Chaminade, the founder of the Society of Mary. Marianists are still very much involved in educating and socializing with students on campus.

SPEAKERS AND SEMINARS: The Cimadevilla Memorial Seminar Series invites health care professionals to provide their expertise on a weekly basis. Additionally, the Lin Great Speakers Series, Catholic Intellectual Tradition Lecture Series, Escobedo Saint John's Bible Lecture Series, and Conference on Justice and Social Concerns invite thought leaders to discuss religious freedom, bioethics, the arts in faith, Bible illuminations, and more.

COMMUNITY-BASED RESEARCH: Community-based research is a striking way in which students can serve while discovering something new.

As researchers, students explore real-world scenarios and needs within the university community, developing management tools to help deal with existing challenges. These projects are often focused in the Greehey School of Business and the School of Science Engineering and Technology.

www.stmarytx.edu
(210) 436-3126
uadm@stmarytx.edu

STUDENT PROFILE

2,354 undergraduate students

96% of undergrad students are full-time

55% female – 45% male

8% of students are from out of state

75% freshman retention rate

FACULTY PROFILE

11 to 1 student/faculty ratio

ADMISSIONS

Selectivity: 75%

SAT Ranges: E 530-630, M 620-610

ACT Ranges: C 21-27, M 19-26, E 20-26

TUITION & COST

Tuition: $31,170

Fees: $970

Room: $6,860

Board: $3,860

TEXAS CHRISTIAN UNIVERSITY

FORT WORTH, TEXAS

With nearly 8,900 undergraduates from across the country and around the world, Texas Christian University offers many benefits of large universities, including rigorous academic programs, over 100 undergraduate majors, excellent high-tech facilities, professors who are leaders in their fields, and Division I athletics. Grounded in the liberal arts, Texas Christian University (TCU) can help individuals realize their creative potential, assuring that graduates are well prepared for professional careers.

ALUMNI NETWORK: Not only can TCU students use Career Services for guidance into the real world, but they can also keep in touch with a helpful network of fellow Frogs. Alumni can be found around the world as leaders of companies, cities, and even countries.

This network gives TCU students easy access to internships, graduate school connections, or mentorships in future careers. With over 75,000 members and around 20 alumni chapters nationwide, one can find a Frog wherever they go.

A MAJOR FOR EVERYONE: TCU is home to seven colleges and schools that all work together to provide an outstanding education to all students. Whichever one (or two or three) of over 100 majors one chooses, they have the opportunity to sample a wide range of disciplines through TCU's extensive core curriculum.

NEW FACILITIES: In the last decade, TCU has invested over $500 million in top-of-the-line facilities and in upgrading residence halls, classrooms, and laboratories.

Recent facilities include the Campus Commons, four new, state-of-the-art dormitories, and a new academic building that houses the Honors College. All these fantastic new facilities surround a green space amphitheater in which students can mix and mingle. High-tech classrooms and wireless networking throughout campus provide easy, secure access to information technology resources.

www.tcu.edu
(817) 257-7490
frogmail@tcu.edu

STUDENT PROFILE

9,011 undergraduate students

97% of undergrad students are full-time

59% female — 41% male

53% of students are from out of state

91% freshman retention rate

FACULTY PROFILE

13 to 1 student/faculty ratio

ADMISSIONS

Selectivity: 41%

SAT Ranges: E 570-660, M 560-670

ACT Ranges: C 25-30, M 25-29, E 26-33

TUITION & COST

Tuition: $44,670

Fees: $90

Room: $7,520

Board: $4,840

THE UNIVERSITY OF TEXAS AT DALLAS

RICHARDSON, TEXAS

The University of Texas at Dallas is a collaborative institution with a strong emphasis on research. The University offers a wide range of programs, affording students several opportunities to find their niche. UT Dallas is quickly progressing and turning out students who are well equipped to succeed.

CURRICULAR PRACTICAL TRAINING: UT Dallas recognizes co-ops and Curricular Practical Training (CPT) as existing under the umbrella, "Internship." In all cases, students apply what they have learned in the classroom to real-world experience.

Students can also engage in job shadowing through externships. Externships and job shadowing allow participants to gain industry knowledge without a long-term commitment. Some of the activities one might experience during an externship include tours of facilities, staff meetings, and observations of customer/client interactions.

INTERNATIONAL EXCHANGE: UT Dallas has several partnerships with international institutions that allow UT Dallas students to swap places with a student from a different part of the world. Participants develop cross-cultural communication skills and learn to become independent thinkers in a foreign environment.

Some of international schools at which students may study include Dublin City University in Ireland; City University of Honk Kong; Universidad de Lima in Peru; University of Sheffield in the United Kingdom; and O.P. Jindal Global University in India.

On top of study abroad, UT Dallas offers opportunities in international internship, independent study, and academic research. Students interested in pursuing an internship are placed in positions that are directly related to their field of study, independent study has students take control of their abroad experience by pursuing academic work outside of class, and approved research abroad is funded by UT Dallas itself!

www.utdallas.edu
(972) 883-2270
interest@utdallas.edu

STUDENT PROFILE
18,470 undergraduate students

83% of undergrad students are full-time

43% female – 57% male

5% of students are from out of state

88% freshman retention rate

FACULTY PROFILE
24 to 1 student/faculty ratio

ADMISSIONS
Selectivity: 76%

SAT Ranges: E 600-700, M 620-730

ACT Ranges: C 26-32, M 26-32, E 25-34

TUITION & COST
Tuition (in-state): $11,528

Tuition (out-of-state): $29,656

Room: $7,224

Board: $3,888

THE UNIVERSITY OF TEXAS AT SAN ANTONIO

RICHARDSON, TEXAS

The University of Texas at San Antonio™

www.utsa.edu
(210) 458-4011

Located in one of the most vibrant, fastest-growing cities in the country, UTSA actively embraces multicultural traditions while serving as a center for intellectual and creative resources. And with 60 undergraduate areas of study and over 360 student organizations, students can practice what they love to do both inside and outside of the classroom. The UTSA community is full of social interaction, cultural engagement, and service to the community, all of which shape roadrunners into well-rounded, active citizens. UTSA's top-tier education goes beyond the workplace—it sets students on the path toward becoming who they're meant to be.

UNDERGRADUATE RESEARCH: UTSA plays a distinctive role among research universities due to its devotion to undergraduate research. With a strong belief that students at all levels of learning can benefit from academic research opportunities, UTSA focuses on complementing their classroom-based instruction with real-life research experiences.

The university offers first-class laboratories, 23 research centers and industry-sponsored institutes, and faculty with recognized expertise in a wide range of fields. Students can gain hands-on experiences in research from long-term, multi-million dollar projects to modest, short-term explorations.

STUDENT LEADERSHIP CENTER: The Student Leadership Center serves as a centralized resource to help students commit to a life of community engagement and active citizenship. It provides opportunities and resources that encourage students to participate in initiatives that promote positive change to both the UTSA campus as well as the greater San Antonio community.

ROWDY CORPS: Rowdy Corps is a community-based work-study program that connects UTSA students with local nonprofits or public agencies under the common goal to make a positive impact in the broader San Antonio community. Students receive career-focused trainings, attend networking events, and engage in learning projects.

STUDENT PROFILE
26,444 undergraduate students

81% of undergrad students are full-time

50% female – 50% male

2% of students are from out of state

74% freshman retention rate

FACULTY PROFILE
25 to 1 student/faculty ratio

ADMISSIONS
Selectivity: 79%

SAT Ranges: E 520-610, M 510-600

ACT Ranges: C 20-25, M 18-25, E 18-24

TUITION & COST
Tuition (in-state): $5,308

Tuition (out-of-state): $16,507

Fees: $2,661

Room: $4,890

Board: $3,684

TRINITY UNIVERSITY

SAN ANTONIO, TEXAS

new.trinity.edu
(210) 999-7207
admissions@trinity.edu

Noted for its superior academic quality, outstanding faculty, and exceptional academic resources, Trinity is committed to the intellectual, civic, and professional preparation of its students. Because Trinity is so close to the downtown area of San Antonio (the seventh largest city in the U.S.), students are given amazing access to the city's many attractions. San Antonio has museums, theme parks, the Alamo, 4 professional sports teams, The River Walk, and so much more!

SUSTAINABILITY: Trinity is highly dedicated to practices and lifestyles that promote sustainability. This dedication can be seen, not only in volunteer and service efforts, but in the curriculum as well. Ultimately, Trinity wants to reduce its global footprint and promote the benefits of sustainable practices.

Trinity's Environmental Studies program includes variety of courses in the sciences, arts, humanities, and social sciences. On top of coursework, students are also involved in service initiatives, field work, and internships that deal with the environment.

CO-CURRICULAR SERVICE: As part of Trinity's commitment to smart environmental practices, the university offers outlets for students to get their hands dirty working outdoors, in a local garden, or on some other environmentally-focused project.

The university is also very active with Earth Week, during which earth-themed events take over the campus and coursework reflects the issues that face sustainability and the environment.

THE PLUNGE: The Plunge is a four-day excursion that takes place before new student orientation. The trip is sponsored by Trinity's Chapel Fellowships and involves a mixture of mission work, reflection, and worship.

The Plunge is a great way for new students to meet and connect with future peers and upperclassmen. After the trip has ended, students can choose to remain involved with the Chapel Fellowships, which are Christian faith groups that meet weekly on campus.

STUDENT PROFILE

2,395 undergraduate students

98% of undergrad students are full-time

53% female – 47% male

89% freshman retention rate

FACULTY PROFILE

9 to 1 student/faculty ratio

ADMISSIONS

Selectivity: 38%

SAT Ranges: E 620-710, M 610-700

ACT Ranges: C 27-32, M 26-30, E 27-34

TUITION & COST

Tuition: $40,728

Fees: $616

Room: $8,478

Board: $4,658

UNIVERSITY OF HOUSTON

HOUSTON, TEXAS

The University of Houston is a tier-one research university with a sprawling campus that offers students over 100 cutting-edge programs, award-winning faculty, and innovative research centers. UH prides itself on student success and regularly engages students with the Houston community through outreach projects, internships, industry partnerships, and alumni leadership. Cougar-driven projects cultivate excellence, address community challenges, and place students on a lifelong path of civic engagement.

UNDERGRADUATE RESEARCH: At the University of Houston, undergraduate research is highly valued and encouraged. The Houston Early Research Experience (HERE), for example, is a two-week workshop that orients rising sophomores and juniors to the fundamentals of academic research, encouraging all to take part. Likewise, the Summer Undergraduate Research Fellowship (SURF) program then gives sophomores, juniors, and seniors the opportunity to participate in a full-time, 10-week research experience over the summer. It doesn't stop there; research is an everyday privilege across the entire UH community.

FIRST LECTURE: Every year, UH College of Education Dean Bob McPherson treats students, faculty, staff, and guests to an inspiring and memorable first lecture to kick off the academic year. One recent example includes that of speaker and performer Stephanie Rice. A UH graduate herself, Stephanie spoke about her time as a contestant on NBC's *The Voice* as well as her personal story of resilience and LGBTQ+ advocacy.

ARTS: The arts are celebrated on UH's campus, and students can appreciate contemporary art from emerging and underrepresented artists at the Blaffer Art Museum or explore the nuances of performing, visual, and literary arts at the Cynthia Woods Mitchell Center of the Arts. UH also hosts numerous concerts, lectures, and comedy at the Cullen Performance Hall.

HOUSTON: As the fourth most populous city in the nation, Houston is a diverse hub of arts, culture, sports, cuisine, and more. Life on and around campus is loaded with chances to make connections and discover new interests.

UNIVERSITY of HOUSTON

www.uh.edu
(713) 743-2255

STUDENT PROFILE
37,215 undergraduate students

73% of undergrad students are full-time

50% female – 50% male

2% of students are from out of state

85% freshman retention rate

FACULTY PROFILE
22 to 1 student/faculty ratio

ADMISSIONS
Selectivity: 61%

SAT Ranges: E 560-640, M 550-640

ACT Ranges: C 23-27, M 22-27, E 21-27

TUITION & COST
Tuition (in-state): $8,724

Tuition (out-of-state): $21,084

Fees: $982

Room: $6,204

Board: $3,780

UNIVERSITY OF MARY HARDIN–BAYLOR

BELTON, TEXAS

UNIVERSITY OF MARY HARDIN-BAYLOR

The University of Mary Hardin-Baylor is dedicated to the proposition that an educated person is one who not only has mastered a chosen field of study but also has gained an understanding and appreciation for the intellectual and cultural traditions of a diverse world. Through traditional liberal arts programs and professional programs, the university seeks to develop graduates of strong Christian character and integrity. UMHB strives to inspire a lifelong love for learning so that graduates may face challenges successfully in an ever-changing world.

DEEP IN THE HEART: UMHB is located in the "heart of Texas," only 55 miles from the state capital of Austin and 135 miles from the Dallas-Fort Worth metroplex on Interstate 35. With a population of 20,128, Belton offers the charm of a college town with the amenities of larger cities just minutes away in Temple and Killeen.

CAMPUS TRADITIONS: Founded in 1845, UMHB is the oldest continually operating university in Texas, so it comes as no surprise that the campus has many unique traditions. Like knights of old, first-year students are "dubbed" with a real sword, making them "Crusaders for Life."

For over a century students have shown off their talents to vie for top honors at Stunt Night. And Easter Pageant, Homecoming, Charter Day, and the Midnight March connect today's students with generations past, fostering friendships and meaningful network connections.

ARTISTIC CORE: Fine arts experiences give students the chance to experience a wide variety of artistic works by attending campus programs related to art or music.

Recognizing that no education is complete without a familiarity and understanding of the arts, the core curriculum has all undergraduates attend at least one fine arts program each semester.

www.umhb.edu
(254) 295-4520
admission@umhb.edu

STUDENT PROFILE

3,333 undergraduate students

91% of undergrad students are full-time

64% female – 36% male

4% of students are from out of state

73% freshman retention rate

FACULTY PROFILE

18 to 1 student/faculty ratio

ADMISSIONS

Selectivity: 79%

SAT Ranges: E 510-610, M 510-590

ACT Ranges: C 19-25, M 18-25, E 18-25

TUITION & COST

Tuition: $25,350

Fees: $2,250

Room & Board: $7,894

UNIVERSITY OF THE INCARNATE WORD

SAN ANTONIO, TEXAS

University of the Incarnate Word was established by three determined Catholic women who were committed to the service of others in the name of God—a tradition that lives on in the students, faculty, and staff at Incarnate Word. The spirit of Christian service manifests in the university through teaching, scholarship, research, and artistic expression by promoting academic excellence within the context of faith in Jesus Christ, the Incarnate Word of God. Through a comprehensive liberal arts education, students are educated wholly and are prompted to develop values of lifelong learning.

SAN ANTONIO: The University of the Incarnate Word has been seated in the front row to witness San Antonio's fast-paced, inspiring evolution over the years. Today, the city has grown to be the second largest in Texas with the fastest-growing economy in the nation. Students learn and grow a city known for its unparalleled diversity, cultural richness, and economic prosperity.

SERVICE-LEARNING: Students are encouraged to further exemplify Incarnate Word's values by participating in service-learning opportunities. Rooted in the value of service to others, these opportunities allow students to learn while giving back to the surrounding community. One example of perspective-enhancing service includes the Honors Program's social justice trips to McAllen and El Paso, which steep students in the issues at the U.S.-Mexico border.

TRiO: The Student Support Services at UIW is a federally funded TRiO program, which provides academic support and leadership development at no cost to students. The program gives particularly helpful service to first-generation or low-income students as they work toward graduation.

STUDENT ORGANIZATIONS: Incarnate Word is made unique by the contributions of each student. Their individuality is reflected in the many student organizations that make campus a fun and inspiring place to be. Students can make friends in academic, honorary, professional, special interest, or university-sponsored organizations.

UNIVERSITY OF THE INCARNATE WORD

www.uiw.edu
(210) 829-6005
admission@uiwtx.edu

STUDENT PROFILE

5,312 undergraduate students

76% of undergrad students are full-time

60% female — 40% male

6% of students are from out of state

74% freshman retention rate

FACULTY PROFILE

11 to 1 student/faculty ratio

ADMISSIONS

Selectivity: 88%

SAT Ranges: E 480-580, M 470-560

ACT Ranges: C 17-22, M 16-22, E 15-22

TUITION & COST

Tuition: $29,900

Fees: $2,676

Room: $7,520

Board: $5,304

SOUTHERN UTAH UNIVERSITY

CEDAR CITY, UTAH

Southern Utah University provides a personalized, career-ready experience that prepares students to be successful upon graduation. The valuable educational opportunities ensure students enter the job market with a competitive advantage. Students come first at SUU, where small, personalized classes are the norm. Its more than 144 undergraduate and 18 graduate & certificate programs make SUU an incredible place to grow.

AVIATION: SUU's Professional Pilot Aviation Program offers rotor- and fixed-wing pilot training in a partnership with SkyWest Airlines. This partnership creates industry-leading career options for prospective pilots.

UNIVERSITY OF THE PARKS: With adventure around every corner, SUU's 100-acre, eco-friendly campus stands within a five-hour drive of 20 national parks, monuments, and recreation areas. SUU is a tree-lined campus surrounded by mountains, lakes, and trails.

SCIENCE AND ENGINEERING: The College of Science and Engineering is a customized and stimulating science learning environment. With resources like the Utah STEM Action Center and the Intercollegiate Rocketry Club, students may supplement in-class education with extracurricular learning projects.

INTERNSHIPS: SUU believes in working with the community to prepare students for a successful career. For example, SUU's Intergovernmental Internship Cooperative partners with 19 federal and state land agencies and the Paiute Tribe with 250-300 internships in regional and public lands.

> "I love the hard-working students who are curious about the world around them and want to learn and serve. I love the small classes and the opportunities to get to know my students. I love that we have a beautiful campus where we are surrounded by amazing, world-class arts and theatre."
>
> – *Professor Liz Olson, Anthropology*

SUU
SOUTHERN UTAH UNIVERSITY

www.suu.edu
(435) 586-7740
adminfo@suu.edu

STUDENT PROFILE
9,271 undergraduate students

73% of undergrad students are full-time

58% female – 42% male

18% of students are from out of state

73% freshman retention rate

FACULTY PROFILE
19 to 1 student/faculty ratio

ADMISSIONS
Selectivity: 79%

SAT Ranges: E 510-640, M 500-610

ACT Ranges: C 21-27, M 19-26, E 20-28

TUITION & COST
Tuition (in-state): $6,006

Tuition (out-of-state): $19,822

Fees: $764

Room: $3,325

Board: $4,024

WESTMINSTER COLLEGE

WESTMINSTER COLLEGE OF UTAH

SALT LAKE CITY, UTAH

At Westminster, education is not just about landing a first job; it's also about paving a path to a meaningful life. Westminster challenges its students to see the world through others' eyes in celebration of the diversity of thought. Students experience the liberal arts blended with professional programs. Westminster College of Utah provides transformational learning experiences for students in a truly student-centered environment that empowers and inspires students to live meaningful lives.

NOT SO GENERAL GEN ED: WCore is Westminster's liberal education program. Students have exciting choices for their Gen Ed, including "Counting Votes," a look at U.S. voting methodology that puts mathematics to use in new ways; or "Bust that Psych Myth," which exposes such legends as the power of hypnosis.

WCore gives students the opportunity to explore new subjects and ideas through unique courses. WCore courses offer small-group settings, all of which focus on synthesis, communication, and disciplinary research.

MAY TERM: May Term is a month of offbeat and inspiring classes, laid-back trips around Utah, and international adventures. After a year of hitting the books, May Term takes students outside of the classroom and outside of their comfort zones.

Students travel as close as Utah's national parks or as far away as Thailand or the Netherlands. May Term study experiences cover a range of topics, including cats, pop culture, and deconstructing capitalism.

"Everyone at Westminster is here for you in case you fall, but they won't hold your hand. So, every failure is yours to learn from, and every accomplishment is yours to carry forward." – *Elaine Sheehan, '18*

westminstercollege.edu
(801) 832-2200
admission@
westminstercollege.edu

STUDENT PROFILE

1,946 undergraduate students

95% of undergrad students are full-time

60% female – 40% male

36% of students are from out of state

82% freshman retention rate

FACULTY PROFILE

8 to 1 student/faculty ratio

ADMISSIONS

Selectivity: 93%

SAT Ranges: E 540-638, M 540-620

ACT Ranges: C 21-27, M 19-26, E 20-28

TUITION & COST

Tuition: $33,480

Fees: $520

Room: $5,526

Board: $3,998

CASTLETON UNIVERSITY

CASTLETON, VERMONT

Castleton University offers more than 75 diverse and challenging programs of study for undergraduate and graduate students, 29 varsity sports, and over 40 clubs and organizations. It is Vermont's first institution of higher education and the 18th-oldest institution of higher education in the United States. The University has invested nearly $85 million into the campus' 21 buildings in the past ten years, including spaces such as the Castleton Pavilion, an open-air timber and stone structure, the University's 12 residence halls, and 2 LEED Gold-certified buildings.

EXTENDED LEARNING: For those looking to continue their education, Castleton offers several dual-degree options through a 4+1 format in various disciplines. This process allows students to earn both a bachelor's and master's degree in only 5 years.

CASTLETON IN THE COMMUNITY: In recent years. Castleton has committed to investing in the Rutland Region, including the addition of the Spartan Arena in 2009, the Castleton Downtown Gallery in 2011, and the Castleton Polling Institute and Center for Entrepreneurial Programs. Each location provides unique learning opportunities for its students, all while providing valued services for the surrounding region.

DEDICATED FACULTY: Students' lives are greatly enriched by the outstanding work and scholarship by their professors, 94% of whom hold the highest degree in their field.

CASTLETON POLLING INSTITUTE: Tying together the skills of teaching, researching, and public service, the Castleton Polling Institute serves as a place at which students can learn and take part in the science and art of polling and survey research methodology.

Students work with governments, businesses, media, and nonprofits to help collect and analyze data that contribute to their work. The institute has been featured nationally and frequently provides survey research for both public and private entities.

www.castleton.edu
(800) 639-8521
info@castleton.edu

STUDENT PROFILE

1,855 undergraduate students

86% of undergrad students are full-time

53% female – 47% male

70% freshman retention rate

FACULTY PROFILE

15 to 1 student/faculty ratio

ADMISSIONS

Selectivity: 82%

SAT Ranges: E 470-570, M 450-560

ACT Ranges: C 17-23, M 16-22, E 15-22

TUITION & COST

Tuition (in-state): $10,872

Tuition (out-of-state): $26,424

Fees: $1,098

Room: $6,128

Board: $4,162

CHAMPLAIN COLLEGE

BURLINGTON, VERMONT

CHAMPLAIN
COLLEGE

champlain.edu
(800) 570-5858
admission@champlain.edu

At Champlain, students are invited to pursue their passions, showcase their individuality, and forge their ideal future through 30 career-focused majors, 33minors, and 40 specializations. The College endeavors to be a leader in educating students to become skilled practitioners, effective professionals, and engaged global citizens. Furthermore, its agile and entrepreneurial approach to higher education blends technology, leadership, market savvy, innovation, and fiscal responsibility with a commitment to liberal learning, community involvement, and "the human touch."

INSIGHT PROGRAM: Champlain's distinctive InSight Program equips students with the career readiness and personal financial skills to ensure their successful transition from college to career.

The four-year, curriculum-embedded program works alongside students' major and the Core curriculum in order to enable career-building opportunities early on, taking advantage of cutting-edge recruiting technologies to fast-track and target their job search. Plus, students also learn how to manage their finances and pay back any student loans after graduation.

UPSIDE-DOWN CURRICULUM: The Upside-Down Curriculum is a unique educational approach that allows students to take essential courses and begin experiencing their major starting in their first semester. Not only does its format allow students to get into internships earlier, but it also allows students to have four full years to develop their field-specific skills.

"I was drawn to Champlain originally for its tight-knit community and rigorous academics. As a Filmmaking major, it was important to me to be able to expand my skills within my craft from day one. Being on a film set as a first-year student definitely sets my experience apart."

– *Montserrat, Filmmaking major*

STUDENT PROFILE

2,107 undergraduate students

97% of undergrad students are full-time

38% female – 62% male

79% of students are from out of state

78% freshman retention rate

FACULTY PROFILE

12 to 1 student/faculty ratio

ADMISSIONS

Selectivity: 75%

SAT Ranges: E 560-650, M 530-630

ACT Ranges: C 22-28, M 20-27, E 21-28

TUITION & COST

Tuition: $41,728

Fees: $100

Room: $9,856

Board: $5,910

THE UNIVERSITY OF VERMONT

BURLINGTON, VERMONT

The University of Vermont provides a mixture of big-school opportunities and small-school benefits. Students enjoy collaborating with their professors while growing into successful leaders of tomorrow.

FIGS: First-year interest groups, or FIGs, allow students to live among peers who share similar interests and academic schedules. A FIG takes the learning experience outside of the classroom and integrates it into residence life, allowing students to get the most out of their majors from the very beginning of their college lives.

For example, UVM offers BioFIG for first-year biology, biological science, zoology, and plant biology students. BioFIG allows students to take classes with one another and participate in a weekly seminar, which is incredibly important for developing peer collaboration and supplementary course discussion.

CUPS: The Office of Community-University Partnerships & Service-Learning (CUPS) is responsible for community-based learning initiatives. Students are given the chance to integrate academic theories into real-world situations, allowing for higher-level conceptualization and application of subject matter. There are plenty of different options available. UVM supports direct and indirect service, consulting, and community-based research.

With 91 service learning courses offered at UVM, so there are plenty of ways to get involved. The university collaborates with 200 community partners, 90% of which have reported high levels of satisfaction with UVM's service.

Examples of courses available include Sustainable Development in Small Island States; Critical Perspectives on Service Learning and Communication; Intro to Early Childhood Education; Sustainable Food Purchasing; and Community and International Economy Transformation. Students can also join the Dewey House for Community Engagement, a residential community that allows students to live and serve together.

 The University of Vermont

www.uvm.edu
(802) 656-3370
admissions@uvm.edu

STUDENT PROFILE

11,339 undergraduate students

92% of undergrad students are full-time

58% female – 42% male

62% of students are from out of state

86% freshman retention rate

FACULTY PROFILE

16 to 1 student/faculty ratio

ADMISSIONS

Selectivity: 67%

SAT Ranges: E 600-680, M 580-670

ACT Ranges: C 25-30, M 25-29, E 25-32

TUITION & COST

Tuition (in-state): $15,504

Tuition (out-of-state): $39,120

Fees: $2,236

Room: $7,900

Board: $4,122

AVERETT UNIVERSITY

DANVILLE, VIRGINIA

Since 1859, Averett University has grown and developed into a dynamic institution that serves students of all ages, offering more than 30 undergraduate majors, minors, and special programs, along with five graduate programs with a number of concentrations. Dedicated to preparing students to serve and lead as catalysts for positive change, the University's historic main campus is embedded in the heart of Southern Virginia with regional campuses throughout Virginia and online. Averett enrolls a diverse student body and boasts an alumni network that spans the globe.

HEALTH SCIENCES INITIATIVE: Averett has significantly expanded in the health sciences, establishing its Health Sciences Innovative Practice Center to provide current and future nurses some of the most sophisticated simulation technology opportunities in America. By practicing in this interactive learning environment, its nursing students gain critical experiential knowledge that will help them improve the quality of healthcare and help save lives.

Students interested in related fields can explore Averett's Department of Biological Sciences, where students often move onto medical, dental, or veterinary school upon graduation, and those who dream of a career in sports medicine and athletic training can learn from highly sought professors.

TECHNOLOGY IN THE CLASSROOM: Averett knows that learning technology plays an important role for students in other majors too! A full-motion flight simulator allows Aeronautics students to gain experience in conditions and locales they might not experience in thousands of hours of real flying.

LEADERS ON CAMPUS: Averett University's educational philosophy is simple yet powerfully important: prepare Averett students for a lifetime of success. Averett students take an active role in shaping not only their own college experience, but also the future of the University. Student representatives on Averett boards and committees have an equal voice in matters of programs, issues, and policy. In this way and others, Averett develops students into thoughtful leaders for the future.

www.averett.edu
1 (800) AVERETT
admit@averett.edu

STUDENT PROFILE

927 undergraduate students

96% of undergrad students are full-time

45% female – 55% male

44% of students are from out of state

62% freshman retention rate

FACULTY PROFILE

14 to 1 student/faculty ratio

ADMISSIONS

Selectivity: 61%

SAT Ranges: E 420-523, M 410-510

ACT Ranges: C 17-22, M 17-20, E 16-21

TUITION & COST

Tuition: $33,350

Room: $6,184

Board: $3,500

COLLEGE OF WILLIAM & MARY

WILLIAMSBURG, VIRGINIA

William & Mary, the second oldest college in the nation, continues to attract attention for its ongoing history of excellence in research and a talented student body. Students at the College of William & Mary are well-rounded individuals who are altogether committed to both academic achievement and service to others.

FIRST YEAR EXPERIENCE INITIATIVES: The First Year Experience (FYE) at William & Mary is made up of four components called "Essential Initiatives:" Making a Tribe Choice, Community Values and Responsibilities, Tribe Unity, and Healthful Relationships.

Each of the Essential Initiatives is considered an integral part of both the FYE and the undergraduate experience as a whole.

COLLEGE PARTNERSHIP FOR KIDS: College Partnership for Kids (CPK) is a volunteer effort that connects W&M students to local public schools. CPK allows W&M to work with local students, both one-on-one and in a group, to help improve confidence and self-esteem among the children.

PROJECT PHOENIX: Project Phoenix, also known as ProPho is a tutoring and mentoring service that enables W&M students to work with students in the Berkeley and Toano middle schools.

Volunteers work Tuesdays and Wednesdays to help the local middle schoolers as well as organize mentoring activities that take place on select Saturdays. The activities generally focus on one of five areas—community engagement, career exploration, culture education, health/fitness, and life skills.

LOCAL INTERNSHIP PROGRAM: Local internships allow students to gain hands on experience while still attending school. Students involved in this program typically work 7-10 hours a week. William & Mary has developed internships with several different organizations in the Williamsburg area and across disciplines.

www.wm.edu
(757) 221-4223
admission@wm.edu

STUDENT PROFILE

6,285 undergraduate students

99% of undergrad students are full-time

58% female – 42% male

29% of students are from out of state

95% freshman retention rate

FACULTY PROFILE

11 to 1 student/faculty ratio

ADMISSIONS

Selectivity: 36%

SAT Ranges: E 660-740, M 640-740

ACT Ranges: C 29-33, M 27-32, E 30-35

TUITION & COST

Tuition (in-state): $16,370

Tuition (out-of-state): $37,425

Fees: $5,674

Room: $7,183

Board: $4,616

EMORY & HENRY COLLEGE

EMORY, VIRGINIA

Emory & Henry College embraces the ampersand as a symbol of the kind of "connected learning" that happens both on and off campus. A real education is about tying all of one's college experiences together, so E&H students make connections across disciplines, between the curricular and co-curricular, to personal experiences and interests, and with the larger world. Student-centered programs include the liberal arts core academic curriculum focused on developing students for careers and citizenry with skills in technology, language, math, communication, critical thinking, and ethics.

SERVICE: For all students, Emory & Henry seeks daily to fulfill its mission of joining education with service to the local community, the region, and the world. Through the Appalachian Center for Civic Life, the College practices a place-based model of education and service to develop global citizens.

CIVIC INNOVATION: Situated at the intersection of academic knowledge, vocational exploration, and a commitment to the common good, the one-of-a-kind Civic Innovation degree provides an understanding of the interdisciplinary nature of public life and various issues, including the interplay of the natural environment, the built environment, and human culture and history. in places and the role of that in developing innovative solutions to civic issues and problems.

As a central part of the curriculum in Civic Innovation, students are actively solving community-identified problems to contribute to an innovative body of just practices for the better of the world and those who inhabit it.

> "While other similarly sized institutions have fallen by the wayside and ceased to exist, Emory & Henry continues to blaze the trail towards new frontiers. It makes me so proud to be a part of the Emory & Henry family because I sincerely believe the best is yet to come."
>
> *– Virginia House Delegate Israel O'Quinn ('02)*

www.ehc.edu
(800) 848-5493
admission@ehc.edu

STUDENT PROFILE

1,000 undergraduate students

97% undergrad students are full-time

51% female — 49% male

42% of students are from out of state

76% freshman retention rate

FACULTY PROFILE

11 to 1 student/faculty ratio

ADMISSIONS

Selectivity: 72%

SAT Ranges: E 498-590, M 490-580

ACT Ranges: C 19-25, M 18-25, E 18-27

TUITION & COST

Tuition: $33,500

Fees: $200

Room: $6,000

Board: $5,450

JAMES MADISON UNIVERSITY

HARRISONBURG, VIRGINIA

James Madison University invites students to come forth, learn great things, and brighten the future. With plenty of global study and civic engagement opportunities, students have plenty of room to grow and succeed.

INFORMATION LITERACY: James Madison recognizes the importance of effective communication and information literacy, especially with the ever-growing influx of skepticism in the public sphere.

All students are required to take and pass the MREST information literacy test within their first year at JMU. James Madison insists that all students pass before their sophomore year, as information literacy skills are necessary for navigating the undergraduate experience.

THE HUMAN COMMUNITY: Every student, no matter their major or professional program, is participates in the Human Community. James Madison's Human Community examines the foundations of a college education and seeks to prepare students for academic and personal success.

The program is broken into five separate clusters, each with its own focus. Students build a repertoire of marketable skills through an exploration of Critical Thinking, the Arts and Humanities, Scientific Investigation, Social Processes, and Individuality within Community.

RESIDENTIAL LEARNING COMMUNITIES: Residential Learning Communities (RLCs) allow students the unique opportunity to live and take classes with a small group of peers who share similar interests. There are several benefits to participation, including increased interaction with faculty, additional academic support, and a community of peers who share common goals.

James Madison offers several different community options. Just a few of the residential learning communities in which students have been involved include Arts, The Honors Living and Learning Center, the SEEDs of Science, and the Psychology Living Community.

JAMES MADISON
UNIVERSITY.

www.jmu.edu
(540) 568-5681
admissions@jmu.edu

STUDENT PROFILE

19,975 undergraduate students

95% of undergrad students are full-time

59% female – 41% male

90% freshman retention rate

FACULTY PROFILE

16 to 1 student/faculty ratio

ADMISSIONS

Selectivity: 75%

SAT Ranges: E 560-640, M 540-620

ACT Ranges: C 23-28

TUITION & COST

Tuition (in-state): $6,250

Tuition (out-of-state): $22,064

Fees: $4,580

Room: $4,998

Board: $5,114

MARY BALDWIN UNIVERSITY

STAUNTON, VIRGINIA

MARY BALDWIN UNIVERSITY

At Mary Baldwin University, students find the skills and the inspiration to become the architects of their lives. Mary Baldwin students experience the proven advantages of a close-knit women's college combined with the opportunities and access of a multifaceted, coed university, preparing them to lead both on the job and around the world.

ANNUAL THEME: Each year, a theme is chosen to unite the Mary Baldwin community around a central idea that fosters civic engagement. The theme gives definition to the academic year and provides a way to link together the work of students, faculty, and staff from all disciplines. Past years' themes have included Courage, Place, Power, Heart, and Identity. Students in all programs are encouraged and inspired to write an essay or design a creative piece that addresses the theme and its relation to civic engagement in a global context.

VWIL: The Virginia Women's Institute for Leadership is a one-of-a-kind program at MBU. Through rigorous academics, physical training, military leadership training, and broad-based leadership development, VWIL students become part of the corps of cadets, the only all-female cadet corps in the nation. Women in the program earn a minor in leadership studies.

RESEARCH: From field to studio, from library to laboratory, from far-away places to right next door, Mary Baldwin students know there are multiple ways to search for answers. Whether investigating medieval frescos in an Italian cathedral or collecting feather and blood samples from songbirds to quantify differences in parasite loads, excellence in research is their goal.

> "I would never have been appointed by the president to work in the West Wing of the White House at age of 23 if it had not been for Mary Baldwin. My political science professors were always challenging me to do better, while still praising me for the accomplishments I had achieved."
>
> – *MBU Alumna*

www.marybaldwin.edu
(800) 468-2262
admit@marybaldwin.edu

STUDENT PROFILE

1,243 undergraduate students

76% of undergrad students are full-time

88% female – 12% male

27% of students are from out of state

75% freshman retention rate

FACULTY PROFILE

10 to 1 student/faculty ratio

ADMISSIONS

SAT Ranges: E 490-590, M 460-540

ACT Ranges: C 18-24, M 17-23, E 17-25

TUITION & COST

Tuition: $30,690

Fees: $395

Room & Board: $9,730

OLD DOMINION UNIVERSITY

NORFOLK, VIRGINIA

Old Dominion University is Virginia's entrepreneurial-minded doctoral research university, an educational powerhouse boasting seven colleges, with 75 undergraduate programs plus 100 online programs in virtually every field. Old Dominion University is known for an award-winning faculty and an ever-evolving campus footprint. Its determined entrepreneurial approach to problem-solving drives cutting-edge research and eminent scholarship.

CAREER DEVELOPMENT: Career Development Services is structured with a centralized administration and decentralized delivery. Each college within ODU has a career services specialist assigned to work with all students as early as their freshman year. Career specialists in each college post and market internship positions, facilitate student registration, and work with employers to develop internship-serving relationships.

LEADERS: LeADERS is a signature ODU undergraduate program through which students gain practical skills and prepare a professional portfolio to demonstrate their real-world experiences.

Students can earn a Bronze, Silver, or Gold medal to wear at graduation by participating in LeADERS' multi-dimensional academic experience with emphasis on Leadership, Academic Internships, Diversity, Entrepreneurship, Research, and Service-Learning.

LeADERS gives students a competitive edge in their chosen career with enriching learning experiences, whether they be creating green spaces, conducting behavioral analysis, or establishing a new business. Students may also participate in co-curricular leadership training to strengthen their professionalism and soft skills.

"Creating my ePortfolio helped me to pull together all my experiences at ODU. I'm confident and ready to start applying for jobs." – *Glen, 2017*

OLD DOMINION
UNIVERSITY

www.odu.edu
(757) 683-3685
admissions@odu.edu

STUDENT PROFILE

19,194 undergraduate students

78% of undergrad students are full-time

56% female – 44% male

8% of students are from out of state

79% freshman retention rate

FACULTY PROFILE

17 to 1 student/faculty ratio

ADMISSIONS

Selectivity: 87%

SAT Ranges: E 500-610, M 490-590

ACT Ranges: C 18-24, M 17-25, E 17-24

TUITION & COST

Tuition (in-state): $10,872

Tuition (out-of-state): $29,772

Fees: $312

Room: $7,248

Board: $5,090

RADFORD UNIVERSITY

RADFORD, VIRGINIA

RADFORD UNIVERSITY

Founded in 1910, Radford University is a comprehensive, mid-sized university located in the heart of Virginia's New River Valley. Radford University's Honors Academy, LEAD Scholars Program, Service-Learning, Scholar-Citizen Initiative, and International Education provide further opportunities for motivated students to lead and explore. All faculty are committed to engaging their students—both inside and outside the classroom—exposing them to "doing" their disciplines, showing them the world, and assisting in their growth to becoming engaged citizens.

SELU: The SELU Conservancy is located along the Little River, just minutes from campus. It is primarily used as an outdoor classroom and research site. The Barn houses a science lab for field work on the lower level, and the attached silo is home to the observatory. The Farm at SELU is a 1930s homestead replica used for teaching and community outreach. Similarly, the SELU Teams Course is used for education and outreach.

RARE: The Radford Amazonian Research Expedition (RARE) project aligns with the university's commitment to providing undergraduates of all majors unique opportunities to explore the world and their place in it. As participants in RARE, students enjoy an experience that is equal parts education and exploration, encountering rare and endangered species, visiting local markets, and seeing the impact of deforestation first hand.

SCHOLAR-CITIZEN INITIATIVE: The Radford University Scholar-Citizen Initiative (SCI) offers students from all majors the opportunity to apply academic skills and disciplinary knowledge to the challenges facing local, national, and global communities. The diversity of experiences in which students can immerse themselves provides them with career skills—like problem-solving, adaptability, and interpersonal communication—that are useful in every work environment.

SCI experiences prepare students for their lives after college by integrating classroom and co-curricular activities. Students put their intellectual skills to work for the public good while emphasizing collaborative problem-solving, intercultural awareness, and self-reflection.

www.radford.edu
(540) 831-5371
admissions@radford.edu

STUDENT PROFILE

7,880 undergraduate students

96% of undergrad students are full-time

57% female — 43% male

6% of students are from out of state

71% freshman retention rate

FACULTY PROFILE

16 to 1 student/faculty ratio

ADMISSIONS

Selectivity: 75%

SAT Ranges: E 480-580, M 460-550

ACT Ranges: C 17-23, M 16-22, E 16-23

TUITION & COST

Tuition (in-state): $7,922

Tuition (out-of-state): $19,557

Fees: $3,288

Room: $5,281

Board: $4,114

SWEET BRIAR COLLEGE

SWEET BRIAR, VIRGINIA

Established in 1901, Sweet Briar College is a private liberal arts and sciences college for women of consequence. The College's unique community fosters strength and resilience in every student by surrounding her with excellent faculty and staff who challenge her to bring her best self forward—and to own it with confidence, courage, and grit. The intensive residential liberal arts environment produces graduates who are agile, creative, and unafraid of life's twists and turns. Students have a rallying cry: *"There's nothing that you cannot do."* Sweet Briar women prove it every day.

WOMEN'S LEADERSHIP: Traditional "gen ed" courses are replaced by Sweet Briar's unique core curriculum, which focuses on women's leadership in the 21st century. In addition to critical thinking and effective communication, Sweet Briar students learn design thinking, marketing, and financial literacy.

These skills take effect right away; Sweet Briar women are constantly establishing their own initiatives to help others, using the expertise they learn to make an enormous impact. Student-run charitable events benefit nonprofits in the area, all while offering students the opportunity to get hands-on experience in marketing, event-planning, and business management.

IMMEDIATE SUCCESS: Nearly 80% of students (and 100% of engineering majors) complete at least one internship while at Sweet Briar, and many times, these internships turn into post-graduate jobs. Overall, about 90% of students are employed or in graduate school six months after graduation.

"At GLAD Manufacturing, I work on real machines, learn software, and take courses such as pneumatics and programmable logic controllers. Because Sweet Briar's program is so broad, I've been able to work with any type of engineer..." – *Victoria Lawson '20, engineering major*

www.sbc.edu
(434) 381-6142
admissions@sbc.edu

STUDENT PROFILE

365 undergraduate students

98% of undergrad students are full-time

98% female – 2% male

50% of students are from out of state

50% freshman retention rate

FACULTY PROFILE

5 to 1 student/faculty ratio

ADMISSIONS

Selectivity: 93%

SAT Ranges: E 460-620, M 420-560

ACT Ranges: C 18-27, M 17-26, E 16-28

TUITION & COST

Tuition: $21,420

Fees: $600

Room & Board: $13,200

THE UNIVERSITY OF VIRGINIA'S COLLEGE AT WISE

WISE, VIRGINIA

www.uvawise.edu
(276) 328-0102
info@uvawise.edu

The University of Virginia's College at Wise is one of the top public liberal arts colleges in the nation. A division of the University of Virginia, UVa-Wise is home to innovative majors like Virginia's only undergraduate degree program in software engineering. UVa-Wise is a member of the Council for Public Liberal Arts (COPLAC). The College offers accredited programs in nursing, education, computer science, management information systems, and software engineering.

PROFESSIONAL OPPORTUNITIES: UVa-Wise is the only school in Virginia with an undergraduate software engineering major, welcoming such companies as Norththrop Grumman and CGI to work closely with students and faculty. Through partnerships with these companies, students have a wide variety of opportunities for internships and future employment.

Sykes, Inc. has partnered with UVa-Wise's Department of Business and Economics to offer students another unique opportunity for student internships with its international technical support sector.

LIFE OUTSIDE THE CLASSROOM: Southwest Virginia is home to the State Theater of Virginia and great local music, but it's the natural beauty that truly defines the area. Students can enjoy the outdoors by bicycling, hiking, fishing, skiing, and horseback riding.

WISE RESEARCH: Undergraduate research opportunities are abundant at UVa-Wise. Students work in the laboratory and field with their professors, making excellent discoveries through engaging projects.

Student research at UVa-Wise has been published in *The New York Times* and presented at national conferences. Other opportunities for research include Healthy Appalachia, a unique partnership between the University of Virginia and UVa-Wise, which works to improve the quality of life and health care in southwest Virginia.

STUDENT PROFILE

1,187 undergraduate students

95% of undergrad students are full-time

51% female – 49% male

6% of students are from out of state

70% freshman retention rate

FACULTY PROFILE

11 to 1 student/faculty ratio

ADMISSIONS

Selectivity: 77%

SAT Ranges: E 490-580, M 460-550

ACT Ranges: C 18-25, M 17-24, E 17-25

TUITION & COST

Tuition (in-state): $5,527

Tuition (out-of-state): $23,262

Fees: $4,725

Room: $6,388

Board: $4,363

UNIVERSITY OF MARY WASHINGTON

FREDRICKSBURG, VIRGINIA

www.umw.edu
(800) 468-5614
admit@umw.edu

The University of Mary Washington is a coeducational public university with three colleges—arts and sciences, business, and education—all of which feature small, highly interactive classes taught by accessible professors. UMW produces critical thinkers and lifelong learners who communicate effectively and engage meaningfully. Located midway between two capitals—Washington, D.C., and Richmond, VA—UMW students are surrounded by opportunities for internships, research, recreation, and service-learning.

SERVICE: Community involvement is a hallmark of a UMW education. Whether they build houses, live on $2 a day, or clean up the surrounding neighborhood, students are imbued with a service mentality. And it starts at the top: in his recent Strategic Vision for UMW, President Troy Paino argued passionately about the institution's ability to "provide an increasingly diverse population with the opportunity to improve their lives, their communities, and the world around them" and to equip students to "address society's demands, to challenge injustices, and to embrace the world's possibilities."

EXPERIENTIAL LEARNING: All UMW students fulfill an experiential learning requirement, which can take the form of an internship, individualized learning experience, or research project. Some majors, like psychology, even support an experiential project with a community-engagement-focused capstone. Many science students complete a research project alongside faculty, while others conduct independent research or create original work.

> "The research experience at UMW was critical in my being a competitive applicant for graduate school. Now that I am a psychologist I realize how much I took that experience for granted. Without [it]...I would have no idea how to get published or give a professional presentation."

– *Dixie Turner, Class of 2006*

STUDENT PROFILE
4,398 undergraduate students

89% of undergrad students are full-time

64% female – 36% male

10% of students are from out of state

84% freshman retention rate

FACULTY PROFILE
14 to 1 student/faculty ratio

ADMISSIONS
Selectivity: 73%

SAT Ranges: E 550-650, M 530-610

ACT Ranges: C 22-27, M 21-28, E 19-26

TUITION & COST
Tuition (in-state): $6,032

Tuition (out-of-state): $21,278

Fees: $6,096

Room: $6,210

Board: $4,006

UNIVERSITY OF RICHMOND

RICHMOND, VIRGINIA

Students enrolled at the University of Richmond quickly become engaged and active members of their campus community. They benefit from close collaboration with faculty, and they have access to several learning opportunities and extracurricular activities that expose them to the potential of their individual skills and talents.

THE RICHMOND GUARANTEE: The Richmond Guarantee says *"Every undergraduate student will receive up to $4,000 for a summer internship or faculty-mentored research."* University of Richmond extends an amazing opportunity for each and every student to gain hands-on experience before they graduate.

This is a testament to the university's commitment to graduate intelligent, experienced individuals with valuable skill sets. Students need only find a program that suits their academic needs, and University of Richmond will help fund their effort.

SPIDER CONNECT: Spider Connect, the online recruiting database, is a great resource for students looking to secure either a full-time position or internship. Students can utilize Spider Connect to search for and apply to jobs.

Student recruitment also happens on campus. Every year, a handful of employers conducts interviews in the Careers Services office, and students of all majors are invited to participate.

THE TOCQUEVILLE SEMINARS: The Tocqueville Seminars examine U.S. history and culture from an international viewpoint. Inspired by the work of Alexis de Tocqueville, students engage in topics like global exchanges of peoples, cultures and economic power, and ethnic and religious violence.

Some examples of the courses include "Seeing America through French Eyes;" "Documenting the Iraq war;" "Global Hip Hop;" "Transatlantic Abolitionism;" and "America in India, India in America."

---

www.richmond.edu
(800) 700-1662
admission@richmond.edu

STUDENT PROFILE

3,265 undergraduate students

93% of undergrad students are full-time

54% female — 46% male

93% freshman retention rate

FACULTY PROFILE

8 to 1 student/faculty ratio

ADMISSIONS

Selectivity: 33%

SAT Ranges: E 630-710, M 640-750

ACT Ranges: C 29-32

TUITION & COST

Tuition: $50,910

Room: $5,440

Board: $6,380

VIRGINIA WESLEYAN UNIVERSITY

VIRGINIA BEACH, VIRGINIA

An inclusive community dedicated to scholarship and service grounded in the liberal arts and sciences, Virginia Wesleyan University inspires students to develop relationships, learn new skills, cultivate new ways of looking at the world, and stretch and excel in new ways. The University annually enrolls approximately 1,600 students in undergraduate, graduate, and online programs, all of which inspire students to build meaningful lives through engagement in Coastal Virginia's dynamic metropolitan region, the nation, and the world.

THE EXTRA MILE: Students are exposed to a myriad of internship, study-away, and undergraduate research experiences through The Lighthouse: Center for Exploration and Discovery. The Lighthouse assists students in gaining experiences that pave the way for success.

From meeting the Maori in New Zealand, visiting film studios in Hollywood, and conducting biology experiments in Belize, to experiencing theatre in New York, studying ecotourism in Maui, and serving in Ghana, students have opportunities to expand their learning around the world.

LIBERAL ARTS EDUCATION: As a liberal arts institution, Virginia Wesleyan embraces the values inherent in a liberal education—an education dedicated to open-minded, disciplined reflection. Classes are small, and students develop intellectual confidence as well as respect for others, humility in the face of complexity, and openness to a better argument.

VWU ACTIVITIES: Students at Virginia Wesleyan discover just how rich and valuable the campus experience can be. There are many student clubs and organizations available to engage interests and ignite passions—everything from *The Marlin Chronicle* student newspaper and Habitat for Humanity to the Virginia Wesleyan Choirs and Marlins Vote.

There's something for everyone; the Wesleyan Activities Council, a student programming board, brings a steady stream of musicians, comedians, speakers, and other entertainment to campus to keep students' days full of opportunities.

www.vwu.edu
(757) 455-3208
enrollment@vwu.edu

STUDENT PROFILE
1,302 undergraduate students

96% of undergrad students are full-time

59% female – 41% male

24% of students are from out of state

62% freshman retention rate

FACULTY PROFILE
12 to 1 student/faculty ratio

ADMISSIONS
Selectivity: 70%

SAT Ranges: E 500-610, M 480-570

ACT Ranges: C 21-25, M 16-25, E 20-24

TUITION & COST
Tuition: $36,010

Fees: $650

Room & Board: $9,998

EASTERN WASHINGTON UNIVERSITY

CHENEY, WASHINGTON

Eastern Washington University (EWU) is located in Cheney, Washington, a short drive to downtown Spokane, the state's second-largest city. The neighborhood provides shopping, concerts, cultural events, and an abundance of outdoor activities throughout the year. EWU is a diverse, friendly, and student-centric university that offers more than 137 areas of study, including 9 master's degrees, 39 graduate programs, and an applied doctorate.

INQUIRY AND CREATIVE EXPRESSION: EWU hosts the Annual Research and Creative Works Symposium at which more than 500 students present, show, act, sing, or display the results of their experiments, dramatic creations, and/or field research. Additionally, the University sends more students to the National Conference on Undergraduate Research than any other school in the Northwest.

EWU also offers the McNair Scholars program, which provides qualifying, high-achieving, and PhD-focused undergraduates with research and scholarly opportunities.

PHYSICAL THERAPY: EWU has launched a partnership with St. Luke's Rehabilitation Institute to provide an outpatient clinic with physical and occupational therapy services, giving students experience in a clinical setting and a chance to impact the community.

ONE-OF-A-KIND TECH PROGRAMS: Students at EWU can now earn a BS in data analytics, which is integrated with the Microsoft Professional Preparation program. EWU is the only university in the nation to have Microsoft's program integrated within a degree.

What's more, the University also has the only industrial robotics and automation program in a three-state area, where students get hands-on training with 10 industrial robots.

www.ewu.edu
(509) 359-2397
admissions@ewu.edu

STUDENT PROFILE
10,379 undergraduate students

90% of undergrad students are full-time

53% female – 47% male

5% of students are from out of state

74% freshman retention rate

FACULTY PROFILE
21 to 1 student/faculty ratio

ADMISSIONS
Selectivity: 63%

SAT Ranges: E 440-550, M 430-530

ACT Ranges: C 17-23, M 16-23, E 15-22

TUITION & COST
Tuition (in-state): $6,522

Tuition (out-of-state): $24,018

Fees: $939

Room: $7,260

Board: $5,448

GONZAGA UNIVERSITY

SPOKANE, WASHINGTON

At Gonzaga University, students discover a stunning array of opportunities to develop the knowledge, skills, experience, and character that lead to a fulfilling life of purpose and principle.

HOGAN ENTREPRENEURIAL LEADERSHIP PROGRAM: Students in any major who are interested in business can take advantage of Gonzaga's innovative Hogan Entrepreneurial Leadership Program. The program, which includes intensive seminars, lectures, site visits, internships, projects, and mentoring, immerses students in the challenges of starting a new venture in the public or private sector.

Students in the program receive a $500-per-year scholarship as well as other benefits like the opportunity to participate in a special summer program and funding for a business plan. Participants graduate with an Entrepreneurial Leadership Concentration alongside their regular major.

ETHICS: Ethics play a prominent part in a Gonzaga education thanks in part to the Gonzaga Institute of Ethics. Established in 2000, the Institute of Ethics has brought excellent resources to not only the Gonzaga University community, but also businesses, schools, non-profit organizations, professional groups, and government agencies in the Spokane area and beyond.

SCHOLARLY COMPETITION: Gonzaga students aren't shy about putting what they have learned to the test in competition. For example, a group of mechanical engineering students, in partnership with Professor Max Capobianchi, entered and won a hydropower engineering efficiency competition.

Each member of the team won a scholarship from the American Society of Mechanical Engineering. Gonzaga engineering students have also won awards at the international Student Safety Engineering Design Contest for six straight years.

www.gonzaga.edu
(800) 322-2584
admissions@gonzaga.edu

STUDENT PROFILE
5,192 undergraduate students

98% of undergrad students are full-time

52% female – 48% male

53% of students are from out of state

94% freshman retention rate

FACULTY PROFILE
12 to 1 student/faculty ratio

ADMISSIONS
Selectivity: 65%

SAT Ranges: E 590-670, M 590-680

ACT Ranges: C 26-30, M 25-29, E 25-32

TUITION & COST
Tuition: $40,540

Fees: $790

Room: $5,900

Board: $5,650

NORTHWEST UNIVERSITY

KIRKLAND, WASHINGTON

Northwest University (NU) is located near Seattle, Washington, a region that offers a thriving economy, technological innovation, and natural beauty. Established in 1934, NU a regionally accredited, Christian institution awarding associate, bachelor's, master's, and doctoral degrees. As a liberal arts college, NU meets the needs of an ever-changing society and offers multiple ways for students to achieve their academic goals—including online courses that can be taken anywhere, anytime.

CHRIST-CENTERED UNIVERSITY EXPERIENCE: NU began as a Bible College in 1934. While it has grown into a liberal arts university offering over 70 majors and programs, it has not wavered from its Christian roots.

Students are encouraged to grow in their faith via Chapel, small groups, mission trips, and the support of its Christian community. Professors are hired not only for their academic prowess, but also for their love of students and God. NU provides a rigorous education where faith and academics intersect.

LOCATED IN A THRIVING ECONOMY: Northwest University is located in the Pacific Northwest, home to Microsoft, Amazon, Boeing, Starbucks, and other successful companies. Students at NU are able to spend their 4 years not only developing relevant job skills, but also building their career network in a region that is booming.

BUILDING A SUPPORTIVE COMMUNITY: The Student Development Department has a mission to provide an engaged, collaborative environment in which students participate in, take ownership of, and apply their learning to God's call in their life.

The Student Development staff work together with faculty in the unified purpose of enabling Northwest students to integrate their faith, learning, and living. From classroom to chapel, and from student center to residence hall room, Northwest University is committed to maturing and developing the whole human being.

www.northwest.edu
(425) 889-5231
admissions@
northwestu.edu

STUDENT PROFILE

950 undergraduate students

98% of undergrad students are full-time

64% female — 36% male

80% freshman retention rate

FACULTY PROFILE

8 to 1 student/faculty ratio

ADMISSIONS

Selectivity: 97%

SAT Ranges: E 510-630, M 500-600

ACT Ranges: C 19-26, M 18-26, E 18-27

TUITION & COST

Tuition: $29,900

Fees: $420

Room & Board: $8,400

SEATTLE PACIFIC UNIVERSITY

SEATTLE, WASHINGTON

www.spu.edu
(206) 281-2021
admissions@spu.edu

As its mission states: *"Seattle Pacific University is a Christian university fully committed to engaging the culture and changing the world by graduating people of competence and character, becoming people of wisdom, and modeling grace-filled community."* In support of this dedication, SPU has created a plan to grow on the basis of four core themes: Academic excellence and relevance; Transformative and holistic student experience; and Vital Christian identity and purpose. As the University thrives, so too will the talented students who join its community.

SPU SCHOLARSHIP: SPU's General Education program is made up of two parts—Common Curriculum and Exploratory Curriculum—to prepare every student for excellence.

The Common Curriculum challenges students to reflect on the importance and impact of Christian living and ask big questions about Christian faith in today's complex society.

It's through the Exploratory Curriculum that they are then able to dive deeply into intricate topics. These advanced courses approach a variety of viewpoints through a variety of disciplines, challenging students to think outside of their specific major and ultimately develop a well-rounded way of thinking.

SERVICE WITH SPU: At Seattle Pacific, students are inspired to bring their Christian values and scholarly minds out into the community around them, all while earning credit. For example, many faculty in the School of Business, Government, and Economics structure their courses in a way that incorporates service to local businesses, churches, nonprofits, and more.

> "It's a calling. By God's grace I've been invited to serve in this richly rewarding work that weaves together my business experience, theological studies, and pastoral ministry."

– Bruce Baker, Assistant Professor of Business Ethics

STUDENT PROFILE

2,900 undergraduate students

96% of undergrad students are full-time

67% female – 33% male

37% of students are from out of state

79% freshman retention rate

FACULTY PROFILE

13 to 1 student/faculty ratio

ADMISSIONS

Selectivity: 91%

ACT Ranges: C 21-27, M 20-26, E 21-29

TUITION & COST

Tuition: $40,464

Fees: $429

Room: $6,093

Board: $5,139

SEATTLE UNIVERSITY

SEATTLE, WASHINGTON

Founded in 1891, Seattle U offers a full range of undergraduate and graduate programs on its 55-acre, carbon-neutral campus, set in the heart of a city of commerce, community, global engagement, and forward-thinking industries. The university has long-standing partnerships with many of the world's most innovative businesses, medical centers, and nonprofits, including the Bill and Melinda Gates Foundation, Boeing, Microsoft, Costco, Amazon, Starbucks, Fred Hutchinson Cancer Research Center, and PATH.

EMERALD CITY: Cultures, corporate headquarters, and cutting-edge technology co-mingle in Seattle. Many important lessons in life are learned in Seattle's dozens of coffeehouses—or while scoping out the Cascade or Olympic Mountains from a ferry, the city skyline from atop the Space Needle, or the Puget Sound waterfront from a giant Ferris wheel.

Seattle University is only a short walk or a quick bus ride from downtown. The campus is eco-friendly, pesticide-free, and ultimately committed to environmental leadership, energy conservation, recycling, and composting.

AREAS OF STUDY: New programs develop each year, such as the Bachelor of Business Administration in Business and Law, which allows students to begin Seattle U School of Law courses as an undergraduate, effectively saving on a year of undergraduate tuition.

Additionally, the Bachelor of Science in Marine and Conservation Biology allows students to study marine environments while researching successful conservation efforts.

CORE: At the center of Seattle U's Jesuit academic experience is the Core Curriculum. The Core's emphasis on rigorous, engaging courses develops students into critical thinkers able to tackle any challenge they encounter.

Some Core classes students take include What does "America" Mean Now?; Rhetoric of Sustainable Food; God, Money and Politics; The Genetics of Disease; Literary Bad Boys; and more.

www.seattleu.edu
(206) 220-8040
admissions@seattleu.edu

STUDENT PROFILE
4,751 undergraduate students

95% of undergrad students are full-time

61% female – 39% male

59% of students are from out of state

85% freshman retention rate

FACULTY PROFILE
11 to 1 student/faculty ratio

ADMISSIONS
Selectivity: 76%

SAT Ranges: E 570-660, M 560-660

ACT Ranges: C 24-30, M 23-28, E 24-32

TUITION & COST
Tuition: $45,765

Fees: $825

Room: $8,481

Board: $4,050

WESTERN WASHINGTON UNIVERSITY

BELLINGHAM, WASHINGTON

Western Washington University is a public, four-year university located in Bellingham, Washington. Western is known for having the best of both worlds: the faculty access and student focus of a smaller institution in addition to the resources, choices, and diversity found at larger research universities.

CAMPUS 2 COMPASS: Campus 2 Compass is a mentoring program that connects Western Washington students to local schools. The initiative addresses the needs of underrepresented and underprivileged students with the intent of pushing them toward opportunities in higher education.

WWU students provide various services to the local schools, including one-on-one mentoring, group discussion, and teacher support. WWU also works with students during recess, after school, during lunch, and any time in between. The ultimate goal of the program is to ignite educational goals and show how they can be attained.

MARINE SCIENCE SCHOLARS PROGRAM: The Marine Science Scholars Program (MSSP) is a unique, 2-year program designed to engage students with the sciences and prepare them for fruitful careers.

Participants are given incredible benefits like exclusive internship opportunities, research experiences, and side-by-side working with marine scientists from the Shannon Pointe Marine Center.

GUR STRANDS: GUR Strands are highly involved learning communities that span over the course of a year and link 2-3 Gen Ed courses together, providing beneficial context to each course's perspective.

Through a structured strain of classes, freshmen can build upon what they learn and greatly enhance their educational experience. GUR Strands take an interconnected approach to academics, enabling students to draw from what they have learned and link it to new ideas.

www.wwu.edu
(360) 650-3440
admissions@wwu.edu

STUDENT PROFILE

14,968 undergraduate students

92% of undergrad students are full-time

56% female – 44% male

16% of students are from out of state

81% freshman retention rate

FACULTY PROFILE

18 to 1 student/faculty ratio

ADMISSIONS

Selectivity: 85%

SAT Ranges: E 550-650, M 530-630

ACT Ranges: C 22-28, M 20-27, E 22-29

TUITION & COST

Tuition (in-state): $6,879

Tuition (out-of-state): $21,391

Fees: $1,304

Room: $7,187

Board: $3,784

DAVIS & ELKINS COLLEGE

ELKINS, WEST VIRGINIA

avis & Elkins College is an energized and beautiful place—a place that prepares and inspires students for success and for thoughtful engagement in the world. Just hours from Pittsburgh and Washington, D.C., D&E is home to a vibrant arts community as well as a leader in entrepreneurship, sustainable studies, health care, education, the sciences, and much, much more. Safe and supportive, stimulating and friendly, it's a small school where big things happen.

MODELS FOR SUCCESS: Davis & Elkins College alumni provide models for success in nearly every field. From science to art, medicine, business, and professional sports, D&E alumni are recognized for their achievement on a national and worldwide scale.

These role models truly remain a valued part of the College family. Through special events, internships, and the Office of Career Services, students are given the opportunity to network with and learn from D&E alumni.

SUSTAINABILITY: Davis & Elkins College is a leader in sustainability studies, offering West Virginia's first Bachelor of Arts program in the field. D&E students have encouraged recycling in the city of Elkins, helped the College reduce energy consumption with three different solar panel projects, developed several community gardens, and consulted on the construction of a LEED-certified housing project.

"I'm a LIFE volunteer (in the Peace Corps), which means we Link Income, Food Security, and the Environment... My environmental science and sustainability education from D&E... gave me the confidence to pursue sharing my education with others for the preservation of world's natural systems." – *Brittany Bolinger, sustainability studies*

www.dewv.edu
(304) 637-1230
admission@dewv.edu

STUDENT PROFILE

805 undergraduate students

96% of undergrad students are full-time

59% female — 41% male

33% of students are from out of state

66% freshman retention rate

FACULTY PROFILE

13 to 1 student/faculty ratio

ADMISSIONS

Selectivity: 50%

SAT Ranges: E 420-530, M 440-530

ACT Ranges: C 17-23, M 16-22, E 16-23

TUITION & COST

Tuition: $28,000

Fees: $842

Room & Board: $9,250

CARDINAL STRITCH UNIVERSITY

MILWAUKEE, WISCONSIN

CARDINAL STRITCH
UNIVERSITY

www.stritch.edu
(414) 410-4000
admissions@stritch.edu

Cardinal Stritch University began as a teaching institution for the Sisters of St. Francis of Assisi in 1937. Since then, it has developed over 60 undergraduate and graduate programs to provide a phenomenal education to a variety of students with a wide range of academic interests. Stritch majors provide a comprehensive education in the arts, science, business, education, and nursing in addition to many liberal arts programs.

CAREER EDUCATION: The Experiential Learning and Career Education office at Cardinal Stritch University helps give students the ability to put their skills into action. The office's faulty provide one-on-one career counseling and organize outreach activities to guide students toward their professional callings.

Additionally, the Stritch Briefcase online tool is full of resources to connect students, alumni, and prestigious employers with one another. With Stritch's solid career-development strategy, students are one large step closer to living out their potential.

MISSION-DRIVEN LEADERS: The Mission-Driven Leaders Speaker Series invite Stritch alumni to share their groundbreaking work as postgraduates. Mission-Driven Leaders are recognized for incorporating their ethical values into their careers, enlivening their businesses with their faith. Stritch students have the chance to see where their education may take them one day when they see how engaged alumni are serving local and global communities alike.

"During my senior year of high school, I had decided that I wasn't going to pursue a post-secondary degree, but after hearing about Stritch and its amazing programs and community, I changed my mind immediately—it really is a testament of the institution."

– Uriel Robles, B.A. Broad Field Social Studies, B.A. Secondary Education, '19

STUDENT PROFILE

891 undergraduate students

56% of undergrad students are full-time

68% female – 32% male

13% of students are from out of state

77% freshman retention rate

FACULTY PROFILE

10 to 1 student/faculty ratio

ADMISSIONS

Selectivity: 47%

SAT Ranges: E 443-568, M 463-595

ACT Ranges: C 18-23, M 17-23, E 17-23

TUITION & COST

Tuition: $14,999

Room & Board: $4,312

CONCORDIA UNIVERSITY WISCONSIN

MEQUON, WISCONSIN

In the midst of today's rapidly changing academic landscape, Concordia University Wisconsin has embarked on a mission that prepares all of its students to stand apart from the crowd. Undergraduates are encouraged to venture outside their comfort zones and "*live a life uncommon*," sharing their God-given gifts and talents in service to others. The university's central purpose continues to be delivering a distinctive, Christian higher education experience and preparing graduates for successful careers.

CAMPUS ACTIVITIES: While academics are a key component to CUW careers, student involvement helps shape students in other ways. Across the campus is a strong vibe of campus community and support. The Concordia Cares club, for example, is active across campus, hosting self-defense classes, bringing in guest speakers, and raising awareness for Title IX.

CU Launch, a new program for the entrepreneurial-minded student, functions as a mini "Shark Tank" club for all students, not just business majors.

INTERDISCIPLINARY COURSEWORK: Throughout their academic career at CUW, students will experience some coursework outside of their designated discipline so that they may excel as well-rounded scholars. For their freshman seminar, students are assigned common read that they learn to apply to a number of different program areas.

But it doesn't stop there; within each designated are intentional interdisciplinary courses that require problem solving across different industries. For example, a nursing student might need to address a situation in the healthcare system with skills and ideas taken from business or the arts.

"We are gifted by grace and prepared for a purpose. It is part of what makes Concordia University uncommon."

– President Dr. Patrick T. Ferry

---

www.cuw.edu
(262) 243-5700
admissions@cuw.edu

STUDENT PROFILE

3,273 undergraduate students

73% of undergrad students are full-time

64% female — 36% male

28% of students are from out of state

76% freshman retention rate

FACULTY PROFILE

12 to 1 student/faculty ratio

ADMISSIONS

Selectivity: 65%

ACT Ranges: C 20-26, M 19-26, E 20-26

TUITION & COST

Tuition: $30,060

Fees: $292

Room: $8,390

Board: $2,780

MARQUETTE UNIVERSITY

MILWAUKEE, WISCONSIN

MARQUETTE
UNIVERSITY

B*e the Difference.* Marquette's challenging curriculum and commitment to excellence in all things helps produce some of the most talented and successful graduates in the nation. But that's just the beginning; Marquette works to develop in its students an intellectual curiosity that not only asks questions, but also demands right action. And this aligns with the university's belief that the mind is nothing without the heart.

MARQUETTE CARES: Each year, Marquette students perform more than one hundred thousand hours of community service in such programs as Big Brothers/Big Sisters, Habitat for Humanity, and the Senior Citizens' Prom. Advertising and public relations students help create information campaigns for nonprofit organizations, and accounting students offer volunteer tax-preparation services.

The university also offers a service-learning program in South Africa, which enables students to give voice to disadvantaged people. Nursing students take part in Marquette's HIV/AIDS program in Africa.

LES ASPIN CENTER: Marquette's Les Aspin Center for Government began as a single student internship and has since grown into one of the nation's leading congressional internship programs. Sitting in the shadow of the Capitol Building in Washington, D.C., the Aspin Center provides living and classroom space for students interested in government. Students meet and discuss issues with officials from the Pentagon, the Department of State, and the Central Intelligence Agency.

RESIDENCE LIFE: As it has expanded through the years, Marquette has absorbed several nearby buildings—a hospital, the downtown Milwaukee YMCA, and several hotels—and converted them into attractive residence halls.

About 94 percent of students choose to live on campus or adjacent to it. Themed housing options include floors dedicated to engineering, nursing, leadership, and honors scholarship.

---

www.marquette.edu
(414) 288-7302
admissions@marqette.edu

STUDENT PROFILE

8,200 undergraduate students

98% of undergrad students are full-time

54% female – 46% male

69% of students are from out of state

87% freshman retention rate

FACULTY PROFILE

14 to 1 student/faculty ratio

ADMISSIONS

Selectivity: 82%

SAT Ranges: E 580-660, M 570-660

ACT Ranges: C 24-30, M 24-28, E 24-31

TUITION & COST

Tuition: $43,350

Fees: $586

Room: $8,660

Board: $4,540

NORTHLAND COLLEGE

ASHLAND, WISCONSIN

Located on the shore of Lake Superior, amid the Apostle Islands National Lakeshore, Chequamegon-Nicolet National Forest, three tribal communities, a vibrant farming community, and a post-industrial small city, Northland researchers and students have access to an unparalleled living laboratory. The College takes advantage of its unique location with a focus on place-based learning, continually renewing its educational programs to address the challenges of modern times while still maintaining the fundamentals of the liberal arts.

LEARNING CENTERS: In the last decade, Northland has developed one of the first sustainable community development undergraduate programs in the country; created the Center for Rural Communities with a polling laboratory; launched the Indigenous Cultures Center, the Center for Freshwater Innovation, the Food Center; and reimagined a 40-year-old Environmental Institute.

These learning centers altogether enhance the student experience by enabling them to explore, understand, and advocate for effective solutions to complex climate and social justice problems.

ECOLEAGUE: Northland is a founding member of the EcoLeague, a consortium of six colleges and universities that share missions based on environmental responsibility and social change. The EcoLeague gives students the opportunity to spend a semester at a different school so they can experience a diverse range of terrains, cultures, and ways of thinking.

"We work really hard to help students transfer the learning experience they have here to any community, any environment, anywhere in the globe they might want to work. That's an incredibly important part of experiential education." *– Stacy Craig, alumna and coordinator of applied learning*

NORTHLAND COLLEGE

www.northland.edu
(715) 682-1224
admit@northland.edu

STUDENT PROFILE

602 undergraduate students

99% of undergrad students are full-time

53% female – 47% male

50% of students are from out of state

72% freshman retention rate

FACULTY PROFILE

11 to 1 student/faculty ratio

ADMISSIONS

Selectivity: 61%

ACT Ranges: C 20-26, M 19-25, E 20-26

TUITION & COST

Tuition: $33,640

Fees: $1,517

Room: $4,069

Board: $4,817

ST. NORBERT COLLEGE

DE PERE, WISCONSIN

www.snc.edu
(920) 403-3005
admit@snc.edu

A *Degree of Difference.* Producing graduates with the requisite skills to succeed, lead, and serve in the world, St. Norbert College provides students with a classic liberal arts education, teaching them to think critically, write clearly, and communicate effectively. Situated on a residential campus along the banks of the Fox River, St. Norbert College offers an active, stimulating community environment that encourages students to learn and grow throughout their lives.

LEARNING IN COMMUNITY: SNC ensures that all of its graduates acquire a broad-based liberal arts education. All students at St. Norbert take a core curriculum that emphasizes critical-thinking and problem-solving skills.

The most popular majors are biology/pre-med, teacher education, business administration, communication, history, and English. All programs at St. Norbert are designed to be completed in four years, rather than the five or more years that are now typical of many colleges and universities.

SNC ALUMNI: St. Norbert students have achieved notable success in many different fields, with teaching being a particularly strong area. Just a couple of examples of outstanding alumni include the late Robert John Cornell, a former member of the U.S. House of Representatives from Wisconsin, and twelve generals in the military, who graduated from St. Norbert's military science program.

Overall, St. Norbert graduates enjoy a 96% placement rate for those seeking full-time employment or admission to graduate school.

> "It seems I am always on the move during the school year, there is never really a regular day... My campus involvement has taught me so much. I have learned to become a better leader and worker, and have gained knowledge of what it takes to be successful in the world." *– Gavin Sorenson '20*

STUDENT PROFILE

2,067 undergraduate students

98% of undergrad students are full-time

57% female – 43% male

22% of students are from out of state

83% freshman retention rate

FACULTY PROFILE

13 to 1 student/faculty ratio

ADMISSIONS

Selectivity: 79%

SAT Ranges: E 570-630, M 540-600

ACT Ranges: C 22-27, M 21-26, E 21-27

TUITION & COST

Tuition: $35,878

Fees: $715

Room: $5,077

Board: $4,390

UNIVERSITY OF WISCONSIN–LA CROSSE

LA CROSSE, WISCONSIN

www.uwlax.edu
(608) 785-8939
admissions@uwlax.edu

UW-La Crosse is a public institution within the University of Wisconsin system. The University is hailed as a leading Midwest institution with vast opportunities in research and personal development.

EAGLE APPRENTICES: The Eagle Apprentices program selects 25 incoming freshmen to work with a faculty member on a research project. If chosen, they work side-by-side with faculty as they pursue a project within their area of study. Students put in 2-3 hours a week for an entire semester. What's more, the program includes a stipend of $1,000, which increases to $2,000 if apprentices return for a second year!

THE FIRST-YEAR SEMINAR: The first-year seminar (FYS) focuses on one central question: "*What does it mean to be an educated person?*" Students will contemplate this question both as individuals as well as part of a group.

The purpose of the FYS is to push students to consider how they learn and what it takes to be successful. In the seminar, students build upon their critical thinking and writing skills while collaborating with peers and faculty.

GLOBAL VILLAGE: The Global Village is a themed residence community that brings together international and domestic students to foster the exchange of ideas, culture, and interests. Students from diverse backgrounds learn from one another as they pursue topics of world affairs, foreign language, and culture. The Global Village is perfect for students who want to expand their knowledge of global citizenship and acceptance.

RECREATION: The Outdoor Recreation Living and Learning Community is great for students who love to be outdoors! Students participate in outdoor activities, challenges, and extracurriculars that always keep them on their toes. Participants in this living-learning community also take an Environmental Studies course to expand upon the activities they experience outside of the classroom.

STUDENT PROFILE

9,705 undergraduate students

94% of undergrad students are full-time

56% female – 44% male

17% of students are from out of state

83% freshman retention rate

FACULTY PROFILE

19 to 1 student/faculty ratio

ADMISSIONS

Selectivity: 73%

ACT Ranges: C 22-26, M 22-27, E 21-26

TUITION & COST

Tuition (in-state): $7,585

Tuition (out-of-state): $16,254

Fees: $1,511

Room: $3,750

Board: $2,456

UNIVERSITY OF WISCONSIN–PARKSIDE

KENOSHA, WISCONSIN

A proud member of the renowned University of Wisconsin System, UW-Parkside provides students a truly unparalleled educational value. Its highly respected academic reputation, along with its location on the Milwaukee-Chicago corridor, provides students with access to the region's top employers. UW-Parkside supports student success by designing custom-tailored degree programs that meet both the needs of today's demanding job market as well as students' unique curiosities.

APP FACTORY: The UW-Parkside App Factory is a creative group that develops mobile apps for community clients throughout southeastern Wisconsin. The App Factory provides the opportunity to design and prototype mobile-app services that tackle modern challenges. Students and faculty from such disciplines as Computer Science, Business, Art, and more collaborate to develop apps in a start-up, entrepreneurial environment.

UW-PARKSIDE DIVERSITY: UW-Parkside is the most diverse campus in the University of Wisconsin System, having created an educational environment that reflects the communities in which graduates will pursue professional careers or advanced study.

All UW-Parkside students must complete an ethnic diversity requirement, which can be fulfilled through a variety of programs, including academic minors in Asian Studies; Ethnic Studies; Global Management; International Studies; Women's, Gender, and Sexuality Studies; and World Politics.

"Our advisors in the College of Business, Economics, and Computing will actually send out applications from Fortune 500 companies in the area... [C]ompanies want our students to come and work for them as interns. We're very much in demand." *- Haley Willis, marketing major*

UNIVERSITY OF WISCONSIN PARKSIDE

www.uwp.edu
(262) 595-2355
admissions@uwp.edu

STUDENT PROFILE

3,998 undergraduate students

80% of undergrad students are full-time

53% female – 47% male

18% of students are from out of state

70% freshman retention rate

FACULTY PROFILE

19 to 1 student/faculty ratio

ADMISSIONS

Selectivity: 87%

SAT Ranges: E 470-570, M 480-568

ACT Ranges: C 18-23, M 16-23, E 17-23

TUITION & COST

Tuition (in-state): $6,298

Tuition (out-of-state): $14,287

Fees: $1,351

Room: $4,494

Board: $3,532

UNIVERSITY OF WISCONSIN– STOUT

MENOMONIE, WISCONSIN

www.uwstout.edu
(715) 232-1232
admissions@uwstout.edu

The University of Wisconsin–Stout, Wisconsin's Polytechnic University, combines applied learning with a liberal arts education, preparing students for successful and demanding careers in their respective industries. Ninety-seven percent of the university's undergraduate students are employed or pursuing graduate degrees within six months of graduation.

ACTIVE CAMPUS CULTURE: UW–Stout is a leader in sustainability and promotes a holistic wellness culture, featuring a tobacco-free campus, excellent recreational facilities, and a commitment to fostering an ethical and diverse campus environment.

Students enjoy a rich campus life with 150+ student organizations. The "Pick One" program encourages students to pick an experience in which to immerse themselves so that they may get involved actively on campus and advance both academically and socially.

POLYTECHNIC APPROACH: UW–Stout's polytechnic designation and approach to comprehensive education immerses students in career-focused opportunities that earn them real-world experiences. And, with twice as many labs as classrooms, there are multiple opportunities to participate in applied research.

AN EFFICIENT EDUCATION: UW–Stout's academic programs are led by field leaders who infuse their expertise and connections into curriculum. They also rally their networks to help fuel the largest two college career conferences in the Midwest.

UW–Stout is committed to keeping college affordable for students, offering three- and four-year graduation guarantees, a streamlined and efficiently structured curriculum, fully equipped residence hall rooms, cost-effective textbook rentals, and laptops and software.

STUDENT PROFILE

7,413 undergraduate students

83% of undergrad students are full-time

43% female – 57% male

34% of students are from out of state

70% freshman retention rate

FACULTY PROFILE

19 to 1 student/faculty ratio

ADMISSIONS

Selectivity: 92%

ACT Ranges: C 20-25, M 18-26, E 18-24

TUITION & COST

Tuition (in-state): $7,014

Tuition (out-of-state): $14,981

Fees: $2,443

Room: $4,280

Board: $2,644

UNIVERSITY OF WISCONSIN–WHITEWATER

WHITEWATER, WISCONSIN

**UNIVERSITY OF WISCONSIN
WHITEWATER**

Founded in 1868, UW–Whitewater is a premier four-year public university located in southeastern Wisconsin. The most popular undergraduate majors include accounting, marketing, biology, finance, education, psychology, social work, and communication. New and trending majors include criminology, computer science, sports management, occupational and environmental safety and health, and media arts and game development.

CAMPUS DIVERSITY: Numerous UW–Whitewater student organizations provide opportunities for diverse intellectual, cultural, creative, and service opportunities related to diversity. Its Diversity Leadership Certificate is designed to assist students across disciplines to engage in conversations around issues of race, gender, class, ethnicity, sexuality, and ability.

UW–Whitewater also has a mission to serve students with disabilities. More than 1,000 students annually use the Center for Students with Disabilities' services to ensure academic success and stay on track to degree completion.

TIES TO THE COMMUNITY: The relationship between the university and the surrounding community is strong. Student organizations and the Greek community regularly participate in service-learning events downtown and within the area schools. A strong relationship with Downtown Whitewater and the Whitewater Area Chamber of Commerce facilitate internship opportunities, as does the Innovation Center at the Whitewater University Technology Park, a university-city collaboration.

RESEARCH: Every year, undergraduates present their research in various disciplines at state and national conferences. Student researchers are even regularly included as co-authors with faculty in scholarly journals. Within the Undergraduate Research Program, the Group Grant Program supports student teams in their scholarly and creative activities. Collaborative work is also embedded in a curriculum that crosses departments and disciplines and, in some cases, even global boundaries.

**www.uww.edu
(262) 472-1440
uwwadmit@uww.edu**

STUDENT PROFILE

10,170 undergraduate students

92% of undergrad students are full-time

49% female – 51% male

17% of students are from out of state

82% freshman retention rate

FACULTY PROFILE

20 to 1 student/faculty ratio

ADMISSIONS

Selectivity: 87%

ACT Ranges: C 20-25, M 18-25, E 18-24

TUITION & COST

Tuition (in-state): $7,692

Tuition (out-of-state): $16,265

Room: $4,172

Board: $2,520

VITERBO UNIVERSITY

LA CROSSE, WISCONSIN

VITERBO
UNIVERSITY

Viterbo students are known by name and build strong connections with faculty both in and outside of the classroom. Most programs feature internships, study abroad, service, and field research opportunities that enhance the classroom experience. The university's beautiful campus and vibrant community are located in La Crosse—a city nestled between scenic bluffs and the Mississippi River and named the top college town in Wisconsin.

UNIQUE SEMINAR COURSES: Knowledge should be acquired with purpose and meaning. Viterbo's unique core curriculum allows students to select seminar courses that align with their interests and are infused with Viterbo's mission: Franciscan Values and Traditions, Living in a Diverse World, Serving the Common Good, and The Ethical Life.

THE ARTS: Viterbo is the region's home to the fine and performing arts. The university features an outstanding and diverse lineup of fine arts events each year, from world-renowned concert pianists to amazing singers and incredible musicians at the Viterbo University Fine Arts Center.

HANDS-ON: A Viterbo education means much more than traditional books, classrooms, and computer labs. Viterbo offers hands-on learning. Just a few of the options available for students include spending the night outside in February—a simple but profound gesture—to raise awareness about people experiencing homelessness; harvesting organic vegetables at the local community garden; and gaining nursing experience assisting the people who are utilizing the services of the Salvation Army.

Viterbo students have also collaborated with area schools to introduce philosophical problems and lead respectful and meaningful discussions.

IDENTITIES PROJECT: The Identities Project is a cross-campus collaboration with the Diversity Committee, Breaking Barriers Diversity Club, and other campus entities that provides opportunities for the community to explore facets of identity through intentionally-reflective civil dialogues, lectures, documentaries with discussions, and other programs.

"www.viterbo.edu
(608) 796-3010
admission@viterbo.edu

STUDENT PROFILE

1,709 undergraduate students

82% of undergrad students are full-time

74% female – 26% male

38% of students are from out of state

77% freshman retention rate

FACULTY PROFILE

11 to 1 student/faculty ratio

ADMISSIONS

Selectivity: 76%

SAT Ranges: E 520-660, M 520-740

ACT Ranges: C 21-26, M 21-26, E 20-25

TUITION & COST

Tuition: $27,960

Fees: $690

Room: $4,125

Board: $5,170

WISCONSIN LUTHERAN COLLEGE

MILWAUKEE, WISCONSIN

Wisconsin Lutheran College, a Christian college in Milwaukee, provides quality teaching, scholarship, and opportunities for service that are rooted in Holy Scripture. Communities, workplaces, families, and churches desperately need moral and ethical Christian leaders. Preparing students to be these leaders in the world is a key component of WLC's mission; it's why the college exists. The Certificate for Christian Leadership program, offered to undergraduate students through the college's Center for Christian Leadership, further intentionalizes the college's mission. At WLC, students can work side-by-side with professors doing groundbreaking heart disease research, teach in local schools, and travel to Zambia for a nursing clinical.

WINNING TEAM: One organization on campus combines research and teaching to compete annually at an international event. During the 2018 International Genetically Engineered Machine (iGEM) competition, WLC's team of student researchers earned a medal for the sixth consecutive year, competing against 300 teams from schools around the world. Their project involved developing an efficient kit that tests water for *E. coli* contamination.

GENERAL EDUCATION: The new General Education curriculum is a complement, not an addendum, to students' majors. It lays the groundwork for collegiate scholarship through personal opportunities and experiences outside students' desired professional sectors. As part of the curriculum, students achieve six Essential Learning Outcomes: creative thinking, critical thinking, effective communication, ethical reasoning, inquiry and analysis, and intercultural knowledge and competence.

"WLC provided me with soft, technical, and emotional intelligence skills and also sowed the seed for my leadership skills... Now, when faced with ethical considerations that lie in the gray area, because of my solid WLC preparation, it is possible to remove the ambiguity and make the right choice." *- Stella, WLC Class of 1993, Solutions Engineer*

---

www.wlc.edu
(414) 443-8811
admissions@wlc.edu

STUDENT PROFILE

1,037 undergraduate students

92% of undergrad students are full-time

55% female – 45% male

27% of students are from out of state

79% freshman retention rate

FACULTY PROFILE

11 to 1 student/faculty ratio

ADMISSIONS

Selectivity: 80%

SAT Ranges: E 503-600, M 513-598

ACT Ranges: C 20-26, M 19-26, E 20-26

TUITION & COST

Tuition: $30,406

Fees: $444

Room & Board: $10,496

ABOUT THE AUTHORS

WES CREEL

Founder

Having helped his four daughters find their dream schools, Wes knows firsthand what parents go through during the complicated and intimidating college search process. He founded Colleges of Distinction in 2001 to help high school students and parents navigate the college admissions landscape. The first in his family to attend college, Wes was interested in helping other aspiring college grads.

Wes would later help launch the Center for Student Opportunity (CSO) in 2005, a national nonprofit organization based in Bethesda, Md., that works to empower first-generation college students throughout their college careers. The CSO develops and provides tools and resources to help first-generation college students and their supporters — parents, counselors, and mentors — on the road to and through college.

Wes grew up in Texas and New York. He attended the Virginia Military Institute on an Army ROTC scholarship and received his bachelor's degree in history from Syracuse University. While working on a Ph.D. in American Civilization at the University of Texas, he was bitten by the entrepreneurial bug. He founded his first company in 1978, and for 10 years served as President and CEO of Creel Morrell, a marketing communications firm headquartered in Houston. In the 1980s, Creel Morrell became an industry leader and was on Inc. Magazine's list of the 500 fastest-growing companies in America for three straight years.

Wes' interests include running (including the Boston Marathon — six times!) and following the sports teams of Syracuse University and Texas Christian University (his fourth daughter is a recent grad). He also contributes to the CollegesofDistinction.com resource section and is loving his newfound status as grandfather to his three granddaughters.

TYSON SCHRITTER

Chief Operating Officer

In 2009, Tyson joined the Colleges of Distinction team as editor of its website and Guidebook. Now editor and operating partner, Tyson is also in charge of marketing and media relations. In addition, he is a critical member of the Colleges of Distinction qualification team. A graduate of the University of Idaho in Moscow, Idaho, Tyson received a bachelor's degree in Political Science.

As a member of the Colleges of Distinction qualification team, Tyson has been visiting college campuses and interviewing college staff across the country for the past seven years. He brings those years of experience to helping students find a college or university that is the right fit for them and that helps them learn, grow, and succeed.

NATHAN WILGEROTH

Associate Director of Outreach & Senior Editor

Editor-in-Chief

Nathan joined Colleges of Distinction as an intern in the summer of 2016, just before finishing up his senior year at Boston University. He has since taken on the role of Associate Director of Outreach & Senior Editor, working directly with schools to develop their CoD image and highlight the practices that make them unique. Beyond member relations, Nathan oversees profile and content creation for both Colleges of Distinction and its sister initiative, Abound.

Nathan's education as an English and sociology student taught him to value not only the nuance and complexity of societal issues, but also the power of art and communication to effect positive change. He has loved his growing involvement with Colleges of Distinction, getting to know hundreds of institutions that recognize the importance of a holistic, interdisciplinary perspective.

ANA-MARCELA LOPEZ

Outreach Associate & Assistant Editor

Ana-Marcela recently joined the team as Outreach Associate & Assistant Editor. She values the pursuit of knowledge and is excited to use her research and writing skills to help others fuel their intellectual curiosity.

Ana-Marcela is a native Austinite and she earned her Bachelor's in English Literature from St. Edward's University. Her favorite author is Gabriel Garcia Marquez. Ana-Marcela spends her free time hiking the greenbelt, cruising the aisles of half price books, or cuddling her cats.

WHAT'S NEXT FOR COLLEGES OF DISTINCTION?

Our team is always working to find ways that schools are paving the way for student success. Later this year, we will undergo a rigorous vetting process to award the Colleges of Distinction that are giving extra support and attention to student populations whose needs are just as diverse as they are. Visit **CollegesOfDistinction.com** for more advice, more details about the schools in our cohort, and more updates about our up-and-coming initiatives!

Follow Us:

facebook.com/**CollegesOfDistinction** | twitter.com/**CoDSchoolSearch** | instagram.com/**CollegesOfDistinction**

Head over to CollegesofDistinction.com to learn even more about the schools in this book! We also have a treasure trove of advice about admissions, financial aid, and getting prepared for your college journey!

And don't forget to connect with us on social media!

Twitter: @CoDSchoolSearch

Instagram: @collegesofdistinction

Facebook: @CollegesofDistinction

COLLEGES
OF
DISTINCTION

Made in the USA
Middletown, DE
06 December 2019